INTEGRATIVE THEOLOGY

Volume 2

INTEGRATIVE THEOLOGY

Volume 2

Our Primary Need: Christ's Atoning Provisions

GORDON R. LEWIS
BRUCE A. DEMAREST

ZONDERVAN ACADEMIC

ZONDERVAN ACADEMIC

Integrative Theology, Volume 2

Published by Zondervan, 3950 Sparks Drive SE, Suite 101, Grand Rapids, MI 49546, USA. Zondervan is a registered trademark of The Zondervan Corporation, L.L.C., a wholly owned subsidiary of HarperCollins Christian Publishing, Inc.

Requests for information should be addressed to customercare@harpercollins.com.

Zondervan titles may be purchased in bulk for educational, business, fundraising, or sales promotional use. For information, please email SpecialMarkets@Zondervan.com.

This edition: ISBN 978-0-310-52108-2

The Library of Congress cataloged the previous edition as follows:

Demarest, Bruce A. Integrative Theology
Vol. 1-3 by Gordon R. Lewis and Bruce A. Demarest
Includes bibliographical references and index.
Content: v. 1 Knowing ultimate reality. The living God—v. 2. Our primary need. Christ's atoning provisions.—v. 3. Spirit given life
1. Theology, Doctrinal. 2. Theology—Methodology. I. Lewis, Gordon Russell, 1926—.
II. Title.
BT75.2.D37 1987 230
ISBN: 0-310-39230-6 (v. 1)
ISBN: 0-310-39240-3 (v. 2)
ISBN: 0-310-59830-3 (v. 3)

HarperCollins Publishers, Macken House, 39/40 Mayor Street Upper, Dublin 1, D01 C9W8, Ireland (https://www.harpercollins.com)

Cover Design: Tammy Johnson

Printed in the United States of America

---

26 27 28 29 30 31 32 33 34 /TRM/ 16 15 14 13 12 11 10 9 8 7 6

VOLUME II

Preface

As we come to the last decade of the twentieth century, and influences shaping history in the twentieth century are in place, the need for understanding global humnanity's most basic predicament has never been greater.

A particular diagnosis of humanity's deepest need is developed in chapters 1–4. It turns on one's view of humanity's origination in the world (chap. 1), human activity in relation to God's activity providentially (chap. 2), the ontic nature of human beings (chap. 3), and a realistic assessment of our accountability and moral condition (chap. 4). Progress toward just and lasting peaceful relationships personally and socially, as well as locally and globally, can be made by candidly acknowledging our most basic moral affliction and deepest spiritual need. The relativistic doctoring of symptoms by naturalists and pantheists who deny a revealed, realistic diagnosis will continue to be a help superficially and temporarily. But humanity's deepest needs are not to attain harmony with nature's laws, or union with its inner energy, or self-justification. Given our moral perversity, we desperately need a supernatural re-creation, a supernaturally provided just basis for amnesty from all our insolence, and an authentic reconciliation to the living God, one another, and the earth's limited resources.

Following the diagnostic bad news concerning the human condition (chaps. 1–4), we consider the prescriptive good news (chaps. 5–8). The Holy One from above has come. The eternal Son or Word of God who became flesh was supernaturally conceived by the virgin Mary (chap. 5). As the God-man, Jesus is the one Mediator who can alleviate not only mere symptoms of our human plight but also their deepest cause (chap. 6). More than a marvelous example, Jesus of Nazareth gave up his life once-for-all as a sacrifice to reverse all the tragic results of sin in human existence (chap. 7). Jesus Christ no longer hangs on the cross or lies in the grave. The risen One lives and rules today far above all other powers (chap. 8). Never was there greater need for grasping the uniqueness of this spriritual Master of masters than in our pluralistic times. The unparalleled provisions of Jesus Christ's atonement and resurrection ought to be heralded to the ends of the earth. For apart from this Prince of Peace the finest of human efforts will produce no lasting or just peace personally or socially.

For the sake of a fallen world in urgent need of guidance from divine revelation we offer this volume with the prayer that through those who proclaim its message God will graciously bring many to the abundant salvation Christ came to give. May the Lord of all be pleased to convict many of their addictive worship of drugs, alcohol, spouse, child, academic achievement, or financial success. Author of all life, turn back the counterproductive forces of evil and death. Help, we pray, those honest enough to admit that they are not all they should be to abandon superficial antidotes offered in countless "new" spiritual, social, or political movements. May many persons who know they are not all they ought to be find help toward a lifelong commitment to the supernatural Christ, who alone can justly forgive, powerfully redeem, and effectively reconcile to both God the Father and other people.

It has been rewarding to hear encouraging words from professors, pastors, youth leaders, and lay readers who have used volume 1 of *Integrative Theology*. Their anticipation of this second volume has been encouraging. We have considered carefully, not only the many positive comments about volume 1 but also proposals for strengthening the approach. Several of those constructive suggestions have significantly helped enrich the present volume, and for them we are grateful.

Readers unacquainted with volume 1 are urged to read especially its first chapter in order to understand the verificational method of reasoning we use. After defining the problem, we present alternative answers from the earliest days of Christianity to the present, survey the extensive biblical evidence relevant to the topic from Genesis to Revelation, formulate a systematic answer inclusive of the strengths of various positions, interact with the views with which we do not find reason to agree, and exhibit some of the enriching relevance of our conclusion for a Christian's life and ministry.

Although our approach has appeared to some to evince a negative attitude toward contemporary theology, what we oppose is the reductive exclusivism of relational, functional, existentialist, and naturalistic systems of thought. We often agree with what these theologies affirm but differ with what they deny of the logical, ontological, and supernatural assumptions and implications of the biblical content. The method here adopted is open to all kinds of human experience interpreted with the discernment provided by the primary scriptural sources. Our criteria of truth and method require us to employ not only logical and factual data but also existential data from ethical, axiological, psychological, and spiritual aspects. This internal experience is emphasized in the concluding section of each chapter—Relevance for Life and Ministry. The Systematic Formulation and Apologetic Interaction sections present and defend positions in a manner consistent with their personal and relational significance. For example, in volume 1 our doctrine of divine revelation was both propositional and relational, and our doctrine of God stressed both ontological and relational categories. It is the less comprehensive and less integrative approaches that are categorically more negative. Because of the contemporary impact of these anti-integrational approaches we have felt it necessary to respond to their negations of essential elements of a biblically based theology at some length.

Those who allege that we choose only passages in harmony with our conclusions fail to realize that we have not assumed the thing to be proved in a vacuum but have been genuinely involved in the research method and have chosen evidence, as in any investigation, in terms of its relevance. Since the Biblical Teaching sections are far more comprehensive in amassing the relevant biblical data than most theologies, the dangers of selective attention in the use of the evidence have been to that extent reduced. Although in some doctrines these sections approach the ideal of including every explicit text relevant to the chapter's basic issue, we do not claim to have exhausted the biblical evidence for any doctrine. Readers are encouraged to incorporate any additional biblical evidence that is relevant. We maintain only that the passages included are indeed relevant and do require assessment in coming to doctrinal conclusion on the issue of a given chapter. To counter the presented biblical evidence effectively one needs to demonstrate its irrelevance to the issue or its misinterpretation exegetically in its biblical and thological contexts.

We are indebted to too many people for us to mention all of them (such as the authors cited in the end notes), but we appreciate especially the discussions we have had with Denver Seminary colleagues on particular issues and the important contributions of instructor Charles Moore on the entire manuscript. Dr. James Beck made helpful suggestions for the chapters on humanness and sin, and Dan Davis did the same for the chapter on creation. Efficient assistance with computer difficulties and revising the manuscript in final form was always available from Denver Seminary's Director of Word Processing, Kris Smith. The faithful editorial work of Gerard Terpstra at the Zondervan Corporation has improved the volume. For the limitations that remain, however, the authors acknowledge responsibility.

Abbreviations

AB — *The Anchor Bible*, ed. W. F. Albright and D. N. Freedman
BAGD — *A Greek-English Lexicon of the New Testament*, ed. William F. Arndt and F. Wilbur Gingrich; rev. by F. Wilbur Gingrich and Frederick W. Danker. (Chicago: University of Chicago Press, 1979)
BDT — *Beacon Dictionary of Theology*, ed. Richard S. Taylor. (Kansas City, Mo.: Beacon Hill, 1984)
CD — *Church Dogmatics*, ed. G. W. Bromiley and T. F. Torrance.
CGTC — *The Cambridge Greek Testament Commentary*, ed. C. F. D. Moule
CR — *Corpus Reformatum* (Berlin et al.: C. A. Schwetschke, 101 vols., 1834–1956)
EBC — *The Expositor's Bible Commentary*, ed. Frank E. Gaebelein (Grand Rapids: Zondervan, 1976–).
EDT — *Evangelical Dictionary of Theology*, ed. Walter A. Elwell. (Grand Rapids: Baker, 1984)
EP — *Encyclopedia of Philosophy*, ed.Paul Williams. 8 vols. (New York: Macmillan, 1967)
HNTC — *Harper's New Testament Commentary*, ed. Henry Chadwick
ICC — *The International Critical Commentary*, ed. J. A. Emerton and C. E. B. Cranfield
ISBERev — *The International Standard Bible Encyclopedia*, revised, ed. Geoffrey W. Bromiley, 4 vols. (Grand Rapids: Eerdmans, 1979–88)
LCC — *Library of Christian Classics*, ed. J. A. Baillie, John T. McNeill, and Henry P. Van Dusen. 26 vols. (Philaldelphia: Westminster, 1953–69)
LKGNT — *A Linguistic Key to the Greek New Testament*, ed. Fritz Rienecker and Cleon Rogers (Grand Rapids: Zondervan, 1982).
LW — *Luther's Works*, ed. J. Pelikan and H. T. Lehman. 55 vols. (St. Louis: Concordia, and Philadelphia: Fortress, 1955–76)
NBCRev — *The New Bible Commentary: Revised*, ed. D. Guthrie and J. A. Motyer (London: Inter-Varsity, 1970)
NBD — *New Bible Dictionary*, ed. J. D. Douglas. Revised by N. Hillyer (Wheaton, Ill., Tyndale House, 1982)

NCBC	*The New Century Bible Commentary,* ed. R. E. Clements and M. Black
NCE	*New Catholic Encyclopedia,* ed. F. J. Corley. 15 vols. (San Francisco: McGraw-Hill, 1967)
NDT	*New Dictionary of Theology,* ed. Sinclair B. Ferguson, David F. Wright, and J. I. Packer. (Downers Grove, Ill.: InterVarsity)
NICNT	*The New International Commentary on the New Testament,* ed. Ned B. Stonehouse and F. F. Bruce
NICOT	*The New International Commentary on the Old Testament,* ed. R. K. Harrison
NIDNTT	*The New International Dictionary of New Testament Thcology,* ed. Colin Brown. 3 vols. (Grand Rapids: Zondervan, 1975–78)
NLBC	*The New Layman's Bible Commentary,* ed. G. C. D. Howley, F. F. Bruce, and H. L. Ellison (Grand Rapids: Zondervan, 1979)
NIGTC	*New International Greek Testament Commentary,* ed. I. Howard Marshall and W. Ward Gasque
OTL	*The Old Testament Library,* ed. G. Ernest Wright, John Bright, James Barr, and Peter Ackroyd
SCG	Thomas Aquinas, *Summa Contra Gentiles.* 4 vols. in 5 (Notre Dame: Notre Dame University Press, 1975)
ST	Thomas Aquinas, *Summa Theologica.* 22 vols. (London: Burns, Oates and Washbourne, 1927–35)
TDNT	*Theological Dictionary of the New Testament,* ed. G. Kittel and G. Friederich. 9 vols. (Grand Rapids: Eerdmans, 1965)
TDNTAbr	*Theological Dictionary of the New Testament,* abridged by G. W. Bromiley (Grand Rapids: Eerdmans, 1965)
TDOT	*Theological Dictionary of the Old Testament,* ed. G. Johannes Botterweck and H. Ringgren. 6 vols. (Grand Rapids: Eerdmans, 1977)
TI	Karl Rahner, *Theological Investigations.* 21 vols. (New York, Seabury: 1947–88)
TNTC	*Tyndale New Testament Commentaries,* ed. R. V. G. Tasker
TOTC	*Tyndale Old Testament Commentaries,* ed. D. J. Wiseman
TWOT	*Theological Wordbook of the Old Testament,* ed. R. Laird Harris; Gleason L. Archer, Jr.; and Bruce K. Waltke. 2 vols. (Chicago: Moody, 1980)
WA	*D. Martin Luthers Werke: Kritische Gesamptausgabe* (Weimar, 1883–)
WBC	*Word Biblical Commentary,* ed. David A. Hubbard and Glenn W. Barker
ZPEB	*Zondervan Pictorial Encyclopedia of the Bible,* ed. Merrill Tenney. 5 vols. (Grand Rapids: Zondervan, 1975–76)

PART ONE

OUR PRIMARY NEED

CHAPTER 1

THE ORIGIN OF THE WORLD AND HUMANITY

The Origin of the World and Humanity

THE PROBLEM: HOW DID THE UNIVERSE, PERSONS, AND ALL LIVING FORMS AS WE NOW KNOW THEM COME INTO EXISTENCE?

This chapter considers the first of the outward operations of the triune God (creation, providence, preservation), in distinction from the inner operations considered in volume 1, chapter 7 (eternal generation of the Son and eternal procession of the Spirit). The Judeo-Christian doctrine of creation affirms the relation between the God who is and everything finite in the universe. The doctrine of creation informs us that the world is neither divine (thus avoiding idolatry) nor illusory (avoiding despair) and that people are neither demigods (negating idolatry) nor meaningless accidents (negating nihilism). The insight of Aquinas is profoundly true that one's view of the origin of creation greatly influences one's understanding of God (vol. 1, chaps. 5–7), for an inevitable correlation exists between how one pictures the universe and how one views God. Likewise one's concept of creation significantly influences one's understanding of the human person (vol. 2, chap., 3) and the meaning of life. Questions such as who men and women are, why they are here, and where they are going all rest on the larger issues of the nature and meaning of the world. Similarly, one's view of creation significantly shapes one's attitude toward the environment and the larger issue of the utilization of earth's natural resources.

A host of questions and problems surround the origin of the universe and all living forms. Was the universe specifically created by the living God, or is it an emanation from the being of God? Did all things come into existence by a cosmic accident or by some sort of natural process? If God created the universe, as Jews and Christians claim, did he create all things in six solar days or over a long period of time, or possibly from eternity past? Are the theories of naturalistic evolution and theistic evolution supported by scientific facts and consistent with a biblical view of God and persons? Furthermore, how should Christians respond to numerous scientific findings that the universe and lower forms of life are very old? What do the data of general and special revelation indicate concerning the antiquity of the universe and human beings? Can the Genesis creation accounts be responsibly interpreted in a way that agrees with the findings of modern astronomy, geology, and paleontology? The present chapter, then, explores a problem of universal interest: how the universe, persons, and all other living forms came into existence.

ALTERNATIVE PROPOSALS IN THE CHURCH

The following is a summary of the principal ways in which the origin of the world and humanity has been understood by authorities within the church throughout history.

Pantheistic Emanationism

As affirmed by Neoplatonists, philosophical pantheists, Hegelian idealists, and certain Christian mystics, pantheistic emanationism claims that all things flow from God, the first principle of being. Thus the world is said to emerge eternally from the being of God, much as light flows from the sun. Plotinus, the founder of Neoplatonism, held that the world is the result of an eternal chain of emergences from the One or the Absolute and thus is a phenomenal manifestation of God.

One of the profoundest thinkers of the Middle Ages, John Scotus Erigena, sought to reconcile Neoplatonist emanationism with the Christian doctrine of creation. Persuaded that God's essence and operations are one, Erigena insisted that all things emanate from or flow out of God, the first principle of being. The biblical statement that God created all things *ex nihilo* means that he created the same out of himself. Thus in what was patently a pantheistic schema, Erigena held that the universe is a "theophany" or a manifestation of God. In the end all animate and inanimate things will return to the original unity of being from whence they have come. A similar theory of emanation was advanced by Meister Eckhart, sometimes called a mystical Erigena. As ideas flow from the mind, so the visible world represents the temporal unfolding of the eternal world of ideas. God, according to Eckhart, is the fountain from which the spiritual and material universe flows and to which it returns.

Eternal Creationism

So-called eternal creationists, who assume that God and the exercise of his perfections are inseparable, postulate that God's eternal existence has always been accompanied by a universe in some stage of being. In the early church Origen was the chief proponent of this theory of eternal creation. Persuaded that God could not be omnipotent or loving apart from the active exercise of his power and love, Origen concluded that God created a plurality of worlds that eternally succeed one another. "Not for the first time did God begin to work when He made this visible world; but as, after its destruction, there will be another world, so also we believe that others existed before the present world came into being."[1] Origen viewed the Genesis days as a literary form to describe the instantaneous creation of all things in logical fashion for human minds.

From a different perspective, F. D. E. Schleiermacher judged that the postulate of a beginning to God's creative activity would implicate him in change and make him a temporal being. Thus, according to the Romantic theologian, the traditional doctrine of creation means only that the world is absolutely dependent on God, a dependence that in reality cannot be restricted to an event in time. In the end, Schleiermacher reinterpreted the doctrine of creation in virtually a pantheistic sense to connote the totality of causality in nature.

William Newton Clarke, who prefers to speak of God as "the Source" rather than "Creator" in the traditional fiat sense, believes that from eternity God has always been accompanied by a universe dependent on himself. Thus God "always has about him a universe, or a sum or organized being, into which always flows the fulness of his energy and love. The divine will is eternally productive, and God has never been without a creation, and will never be alone."[2]

Rejecting the notion of God as autonomous controlling Power, process theology affirms that God and the world exist only in relation to each other. God needs the world to be God, and the world needs God to be the world. Process theologians hold to be an inexplicable mystery how all reality, including God, had its beginning. Whiteheadians insist that in the interactive process of physical prehensions it is just as true to affirm that the world creates God as to affirm that God creates the world.

The View of Augustine

This renowned church father and theologian interpreted the Genesis days allegorically and held that the "days" are not units of time but six states of cognition by the angels in heaven as they beheld God's formative activity. Augustine believed that simultaneous with the inception of time the triune God in goodness created all things out of nothing. Augustine in fact postulated two main stages in creation. First, God in the beginning instantaneously created "the heavens" (the angelic world) and "the earth" (the material universe) in an unformed state (Gen. 1:2), having impregnated all living forms with seminal reason or the seedlike principles from which the myriad forms of life would later develop. Thus "as mothers are pregnant with young, so the world itself is pregnant with the causes of things or things that are born."[3] Second, in the six days described in Genesis 1 God gradually brought to formation all living species out of the seminal forms embedded in the unformed matter. Augustine asserted that the Mosaic record that describes the full development of the original formless creation is not to be taken literally. Hence the Genesis "days" are not units of time (for there were "days" before the appearance of the sun), but rather ineffable, God-delimited "days." The Genesis "days," which "are beyond the experience and knowledge of earth-bound men,"[4] may, after the allegory is set aside, translate into the boundaries of great formative epochs.

The Fathers' primitive understanding of the universe should be noted. All believed in a flat earth located at the center of the solar system. Many fathers, such as Lactantius and Augustine, rejected the notion that the other side of the globe was inhabited with Adamic people. "Is there anyone so senseless as to believe that there are men whose footsteps are higher than their heads? Or that the crops and trees grow downwards? Or that the rain, and snow, and hail fall upwards to the earth?" The philosophers falsely "thought that the world is round like a ball, and they fancied that the heaven revolves in accordance with the motion of the heavenly bodies."[5] Such beliefs remained unchallenged until the rise of modern science.

Theistic Evolution

Theistic evolutionists, both Protestant and Roman Catholic, hold that God supernaturally created the world and the beginnings of life, but ordained organic evolution as the mechanism for producing the myriads of living forms. Many hold that at a certain point in the evolutionary process God endowed an ape with a soul to produce Adam in the divine *imago*. Proponents of the view interpret the Genesis creation account more figuratively, some denying the historicity of Adam and the Fall. The latter interpret the story of Eve's creation from Adam's rib as a symbolic representation of the unity of male and female before God.

According to A. H. Strong, Genesis 1 and 2 describe both an original creation and a subsequent development that arose from energy latent within all living forms. "If science should render it certain that all the present species of living creatures were derived by natural descent from a few original germs, and that these germs were themselves an evolution of inorganic forces and materials, we should not therefore regard the Mosaic account as proven untrue."[6] Not a few British and European evangelical scholars subscribe to theistic evolution. James Orr notes that the theory of evolution has been fairly well established by the scientific community. Thus he upholds creation from within living forms and postulates a sudden genetic mutation to account for Adam. "That species should have arisen by a method of derivation from some primaeval germ (or germs) rather than by unrelated creations, is not only not inconceivable, but may even commend itself as a higher and more worthy conception of the divine working than the older hypothesis."[7] Orr, however, retains belief in the original sin and guilt of the human race.

Richard Bube and some colleagues of the American Scientific Affiliation synthesize biblical faith and evolutionary mechanisms. Bube rejects philosophical evolution (the world-view dominated by indeterminism and chance) with its denial of divine creation, the fall of the race, and humanity's need for spiritual recreation through Christ. But Bube regards the general theory of evolution well attested scientifically and the probable means God used to produce all living forms, including Adam. Bube asserts that God brought lower forms of life into being by a process of physical interaction, and he brought man and the human soul into being by a process of biological interaction. The characteristics commonly associated with spirit arose from the natural interaction of man's bodily parts. Claims Bube: "It does not matter at all whether God created man in a process of evolutionary development or whether God created man in an act of divine fiat. The only significant thing for him to know is that God *did* create him."[8] Bube designates his synthesis of biblical creation and evolutionary process as "biblical evolutionism."[9]

Teilhard de Chardin developed a unique theory of theistic evolution. Instead of a punctiliar creation in the past, God has been creating since the beginning of time through a continuous transformation from within the universe. The mechanism of creation is a special kind of evolution. It is not, however, an evolution characterized by random selection, but a unidirectional development that moves inexorably toward a predetermined goal (orthogenesis). Teilhard's "cosmic law of complexity consciousness" postulates that through time matter tends to become increasingly complex and to take on consciousness. Thus an evolutionary development proceeds from the geosphere (inorganic matter), to the biosphere (simple forms of life), to the noosphere (intelligent man), to the christosphere (Superconsciousness), to a final convergence in the Omega-Point, which represents the parousia of Christ. Teilhard concludes that Christ is the initiator, the energizer, and the final end of the cosmic evolutionary process.

The Dutch *New Catechism,* an influential authority among European Catholics, also advances an evolutionary vision of the universe. In the incalculably distant past from inorganic matter simple forms of life appeared, which in turn gave rise to the more advanced species of animals. Humans, in fact, evolved from the beasts. "Primitive man on the steppes and in the forests and in the caves had still to grow into a humane being. He had to leave the beast behind him."[10] The *New Catechism,* identifies evolution as the mechanism God employed to create the vast universe. In a similar vein, Hans Küng believes that some thirteen billion years ago the universe came into existence through a gigantic cosmic explosion or "big bang" (Gen. 1:3, "Let there be light"). Moreover, he believes that science has satisfactorily shown that the cosmos as a whole and the human being in his bodily nature has developed naturally, i.e., by an evolutionary process. Science, however, cannot answer the questions, "What existed before the fireball?" and "What is the meaning of the world process?" According to Küng, faith discerns from Scripture that God is the creator and conserver of the evolutionary structure. Thus the Lord is the "primal ground, primal support and primal meaning of everything, a creator, ruler and finisher of the evolutionary process."[11]

Neoorthodox and Theistic Existentialist View

Persuaded that the biblical world view is mythological, most neoorthodox and theistic existentialists regard the Genesis account as "myth" and "saga." Adam was not a historical person, and Genesis provides no scientific data. Scholars in the tradition subject the Genesis text to radical reinterpretation along Christological and existential lines.

Karl Barth's understanding of creation is governed by the ideas of covenant and Christology. The two Genesis accounts view creation from different perspectives and thus richly complement one another. The first account (Gen. 1:1–2:4a) expounds creation as the external basis of the covenant. That is, creation is the work of the triune God in fulfillment of the election of grace. Its purpose was to make possible the history of the covenant, whose beginning, center, and consummation is Jesus Christ. Barth's supralapsarian scheme of decrees is thus evident. "Creation is the external . . . basis of the covenant. It can be said that it makes it technically possible; that it prepares and establishes the sphere in which the institution and history of the covenant take place."[12] Since creation includes the beginning of time, Barth argues that God's creative activity eludes all historical description and thus must be expressed in the form of "saga." Neither fairy tale nor myth, saga for Barth is a poetic account of a prehistorical reality enacted *in* time and space. Hence the Genesis accounts impart no scientific or cosmological information. Barth believes that the world was not created in six days and that Adam was not an historical person. Rather, Barth interprets the creation saga typologically in terms of the history of salvation. Thus the separation of light from darkness, dry land from the seas, and day from night uphold the relationship between God's grace and his wrath. Moreover, the second creation account (Gen. 2:4b–25) affirms "the covenant as the internal basis of Creation."[13] By this Barth means that the covenant of redemption is the meaning, presupposition, and inner basis of creation.

Likewise holding that the Genesis account of creation is irreconcilable with modern science, Brunner argues that Genesis is purified ancient world-myth—a concept different from Barth's notion of saga. Thus there was no historical Adam and no historical Fall. The creation narratives, he argues, must be interpreted Christologically and existentially. Through the Genesis record God encounters me as the sovereign Creator of all things. In my own existential response I discover myself as a creature and a sinner. Faith thus posits a beginning of all things by the power of the eternal God. Science, however, suggests that the world attained its present form by the process of "creative evolution." The latter expression, borrowed from Henri Bergson, affirms the sudden appearance in the evolutionary continuum of new forms of life that cannot be explained by natural factors. Brunner believes that the Christian must acknowledge the reality of both creation and evolution. "Evolution is the mechanism of creation; creation is the spiritual source and the Final Cause of evolution."[14]

Even more radically, Bultmann claims that the Genesis story was borrowed from early Babylonian and Canaanite creation myths. That the Genesis account is nonhistorical is no loss, for only those theological statements are valid that deal with the existential relation between God and the person. For Bultmann, the Genesis record focuses on the existential situation of persons rather than on the origin of the universe. "The Old Testament doctrine of creation expresses a sense of the present situation of man. He is hedged in by the incomprehensible power of Almighty God. The real purpose of the creation story is to indicate what God is doing all the time."[15]

Creation in Six Twenty-Four-Hour Days

Many older authorities (early Fathers, Reformers, and orthodox theologians) and a few recent conservatives (F. Pieper, H. C. Leupold, and L. Berkhof) argue that God created *ex nihilo* the primal energy from which he fashioned the present universe and earth in six twenty-four-hour days in the recent past. Adherents of the "Flood Geology" movement add that God created all things with the appearance of age in six solar days, and that all fossil remains, strata formations, and coal beds are due to the universal Noachian Flood.

Theophilus was the first church father to indicate that the creation days were literal twenty-four hour days. From a study of the Old Testament genealogies he concluded that from the creation of the world to his own time 5,698 years had passed. Theophilus calculated that God created the universe about the year 5,529 B.C. Julius Africanus claimed that the period from Adam to Jesus occupied 5,531 years, whereas for Clement of Alexandria the figure was 5,590 years. It did not occur to the Fathers that the Genesis genealogical lists might be selective rather than exhaustive. Barnabas and Irenaeus likewise held to solar days and believed on the basis of 2 Peter 3:8 that each of the six days of creation further pointed to a millennium of world history.[16] Thus the consensus of the early Fathers was that God created the earth approximately five and one-half millennia B.C., many believing that Christ would consummate history six thousand years later about A.D. 500.

Luther likewise upheld a strictly literal interpretation of the Genesis creation accounts. God created the world in six twenty-four-days about four thousand years before Christ in the spring of the year. Calvin similarly claimed that God created heaven and earth in a confused state (Gen. 1:1) some six thousand years before his time. During the six solar days that followed, God arranged the earth into its present habitable form, utilizing second causes, and he supernaturally created animal and human life. Most post-Reformation Lutheran and Reformed divines made the same distinction between God's primary creation of the formless mass of the universe and his secondary creation, which involved the shaping of the undisposed materials to form the world as we know it.

Thus up to the year 1750 a general consensus existed among Protestants that God created the universe *ex nihilo* in six solar days some six millennia ago. The Westminster Confession affirms: "It pleased God the Father, Son, and Holy Ghost, for the manifestation of the glory of his eternal power, wisdom, and goodness, in the beginning, to create or make of nothing the world and all things therein, whether visible or invisible, in the space of six days, and all very good" (art. IV.1). Some orthodox theologians chose to be more specific. Archbishop Ussher, working with the Genesis genealogical registers, concluded that there were 4,036 years from the creation of the world to Christ, and so identified the year of creation as 4,004 B.C. John Lightfoot, the Cambridge biblical scholar, declared that creation took place during the week of October 18–24, 4,004 B.C., and that God created Adam on October 23 at 9 A.M., fourth-fifth meridian time![17]

Proponents of "flood geology" or "catastrophism" claim that God created all things with a superficial appearance of age in six twenty-four-hour days only a few thousand years ago. The theory asserts that the only adequate explanation for all strata formation, fossil remains, volcanic activity, and mountain formation is a universal Noachian Flood of one year's duration. Proponents insist that catastrophism represents the theistic outlook, whereas uniformitarianism (the idea that "the present is the key to the past") is a fundamentally atheistic vision. The findings of astronomy and geology that point to an old solar system and earth are rejected as enhancing the evolutionary hypothesis. Contrary to the judgment of Warfield and other conservatives, flood geology regards issues such as the late date of Adam and Eve and the absence of any developmental mechanisms as essential to theological orthodoxy.[18]

Gap or Reconstructionist Theory

The eighteenth and nineteenth centuries produced considerable evidence from the fields of geology, astronomy, and paleontology to suggest that the earth was of great antiquity. Some Evangelical authorities such as Chalmers, Delitzsch, and the *Scofield Reference Bible* made room for an old earth by positing the Gap-Reconstructionist theory. According to this view, Genesis 1:1 describes the original creation of a perfect universe that allegedly was inhabited by a race of pre-Adamic or Old Stone Age people. Due to the rebellion of Lucifer and the sin of these pre-Adamites, God reduced the original creation to a state of ruin (Gen. 1:2; cf. Isa. 24:1; 45:18; Jer. 4:23–26). Proponents of the theory translate Genesis 1:2 as follows: "But the earth became without form and empty." Then after millions of years, about 4,000 B.C., God undertook the reconstruction of the sin-cursed earth in six twenty-four-hour days (Gen. 1:3–2:7) and created Adam as a New Stone Age man. The theory accounts for the long periods of time required by geology in the creation, destruction, and re-creation of the planet. Adherents of the theory maintain that *bārā'* in Genesis 1:1 (the orignal creation) is a strong verb meaning to "create," whereas *'āśāh* in Genesis 1:7, 16, 25, 26, 31; 2:2 (the reconstruction) is a weaker verb signifying to "remake." Advocates also claim that the verb *mālē'* in Genesis 1:28 ("fill the earth") really means to "fill up again." The Gap theory became popular in conservative circles through the influence of the *Scofield Reference Bible* (1909).[19]

Revelation-Day Theory

A few conservatives, such as J. H. Kurtz, P. J. Wiseman, and James M. Houston, uphold the Revelation-Day theory, which postulates that creation was revealed to Moses, not performed, in six consecutive days. Proponents of the theory view the Genesis days as vehicles of revelation or days in the life of Moses, rather than periods of actual creative activity. The purpose of Genesis 1 and 2, it is claimed, is not to teach science, but to communicate the great fact that God is Creator of all and to evoke from the reader praise and adoration to God for all his works. Wiseman, indeed, argues that the Hebrew *ʿāśāh* (to "make"), widely used in Genesis 1 and 2, more properly means to "show." James M. Houston comments as follows: "What then was God doing in these six days? He was speaking to man, revealing what He said to bring creation into being. . . . A statement of command to all creation, it is also a statement of revelation to man."[20]

The Framework Hypothesis

Nicholas Ridderbos, Meredith Kline, and Ronald Youngblood interpret Genesis 1 in terms of the "framework hypothesis." According to this theory, Moses carefully crafted a literary framework in which the work of creation was distributed over six "days." Proponents maintain (1) that the "days" are not time periods but literary devices to teach the theological truth that God is Creator of all and (2) that the arrangement is not chronological, but topical. Accordingly, a horizontal parallelism is pointed up, in which the work of day one parallels that of day four, the work of day two parallels that of day five, and so on. Youngblood, in addition, notes that there exists a vertical parallelism structured by the phrase "formless and empty" (Gen. 1:2). "As it turns out, the phrase itself is the key that unlocks the literary structure of Genesis 1: The acts of separating and gathering on days 1–3 give form to the formless, and the acts of making and filling on days 4–6 give assurance that the heavens and the earth will never again be 'empty.' "[21] Ridderbos sums up as follows:

> In Genesis 1 the inspired author offers us a story of creation. It is not his intent, however, to present an exact report of what happened at creation. By speaking of the eightfold work of God he impresses the reader with the fact that all that exists has been created by God. This eightfold work he places in a framework: he distributes it over six days, to which he adds a seventh day as the day of rest.[22]

Advocates of the framework hypothesis emphasize that since the theory eliminates time sequences in Genesis, no conflict exists between the biblical record and the events proposed by modern science.

Various Day-Age Proposals

Many orthodox authorities (e.g., C. Hodge, W. G. T. Shedd, J. Miley, F. Godet, B. Ramm) seek to harmonize Genesis and science by upholding variants of the Day-Age theory, which postulates that God created heaven and earth in six epochs of indefinite duration. Others, such as J. O. Buswell, argue that the "days" are overlapping eras, thus maximizing the agreement between Scripture and recent scientific findings.

Proponents of the theory appeal to the following considerations: (1) The Hebrew word *yôm* in Scripture frequently connotes an extended period of time (Gen. 2:4; Joel 1:15; Zech. 12:3); (2) "evening" and "morning" sometimes are used figuratively in Scripture (Ps. 90:5–6); (3) the sun did not function as a measure of time before the fourth day (Gen. 1:14–18); (4) expressions such as "let the land produce vegetation" (Gen. 1:11) suggest a period of considerable length of time for their accomplishment; (5) the events of the sixth day would have required more than twenty-four hours (Gen. 1:24–31; 2:4–23); (6) the seventh day, the Sabbath of the Lord, continues to the consummation of the age; and (7) the Old Testament genealogies, used by some to uphold a recent creation, are selective rather than exhaustive.

Shedd's explication of the theory is typical of older interpretations. Genesis 1:1 provides a comprehensive statement of God's *ex nihilo* creation of the spiritual ("the heavens") and the material ("the earth") worlds. Genesis 1:2 describes the chaotic nature of the newly created earth. A vast period of time intervened between the original creation and the series of divine acts described in the six epochs (Gen. 1:3–31). According to Shedd, the first, second, and fourth days describe how God, working through natural laws of which he is the author, brought about the gradual penetration of light, the formation of the earth's crust, the ocean beds, and finally the full clearing of the atmosphere so that sun, moon, and stars might shine forth undiffused. Days three, five, and six describe God's special creation of vegetation, fish, birds, reptiles, animals, and finally man himself. Like Hodge and others, Shedd believes that minerals, vegetation, and animals may be very old; human life, however, goes back no more than six to eight thousand years.

Bernard Ramm affirms that Scripture tells the *Who* of creation, whereas astronomy and geology tell the *how* and the *when*. Ramm's theory of "progressive creationism" (creation in stages) mediates between what he calls the "arbitrariness" of fiat (instantaneous) creation and the "uniformitarianism" of theistic evolution. "Progressive creation is the means whereby God as world ground and the Spirit of God as World Entelechy bring to pass the divine will in nature."[23] Thus Genesis 1:1 relates the *ex nihilo* creation of the universe, Genesis 1:2 refers to the chaotic condition of the earth awaiting formation. The remainder of the chapter describes God's several acts of fiat creation to produce the root-species and the Spirit's working through natural means to effect development within physical nature and within the living "kinds." Ramm's alternative to theistic and naturalistic evolution upholds both instantaneous creative acts and lengthy processes of development. "The laws of Nature, under the direction of the Holy Spirit, actualize over a period of time and through process, the plan of God."[24] According to Ramm, science confirms that the universe is four to five billion years old and that humans are of great antiquity.

Robert C. Newman and Herman J. Eckelmann, Jr., two biblical scholars and scientists who believe that Scripture and responsible science can be harmonized, offer a variant of the Day-Age theory. Their Modified Intermittent-Day theory maintains that each of the six creative epochs was preceded by a twenty-four-hour solar day. The universe began fifteen to twenty billion years ago when God-created matter and energy, concentrated in a hot mass, expanded explosively and subsequently condensed. Genesis 1:1 relates that God created the materials that would make up the heavens and the earth. The following verses describe God's activity in forming this gaseous material into the myriads of heavenly bodies and living forms. The "days" of Genesis 1 are ordinary solar days, but not consecutive. Each twenty-four-hour day introduces a new creative epoch that overlaps the preceding ones. But since God created the universe during the epochs, what is the significance of the introductory days? The authors claim:

> God highlights these seven days, among the many actually occurring during creation, in order to set up an ordinance by which man is to commemorate creation. The six days of work remind him that he was created by God, and the seventh day of rest looks forward to God's rest, when redeemed man will rejoice with all creation in the new heavens and new earth.[25]

Additional helpful studies on creation include works by Arthur C. Custance,[26] Norman L. Geisler,[27] and Davis A. Young.[28]

BIBLICAL TEACHING

We now proceed to the primary biblical data to determine which hypothesis concerning the origin of the world and humanity best accords with the teachings of Scripture.

Pentateuch

"In the beginning God created [bārā'] the heavens and the earth" (Gen.1:1). The opening verse of the Bible immediately confronts the reader with the timeless and transcendent God who is there. Indeed, some thirty-five times in the creation narrative (Gen. 1:1–2:3) the name *'ᵉlōhîm* comes to the fore. These majestic opening words of the Bible indicate that God is the transcendent source of all existence. Before any other reality came to be, *'ᵉlōhîm* was present in his timeless eternity. Moreover, the universe as we know it was not always there. Genesis 1 describes the cosmos as created and temporal, not uncreated and eternal. The first seven words of the Hebrew Bible further suggest that the creation event was a free act of a sovereign will. God brought the universe into existence not of necessity, but by his own free determination.

Scholars have debated whether the first word of Genesis, *bᵉrē'šît,* should be taken in the construct or in the absolute state. If the former, the text would read: "When God began to create the heavens and the earth—the earth being formless and empty, and darkness being over the surface of the deep, and the Spirit of God hovering over the waters—God said, 'Let there be light.' " On this showing, the earth was empty and waste before God began to create. Creation then would describe God's transformation of preexistent matter into an organized universe. The fact that the absolute form reflects the common Hebrew usage and that all ancient versions (e.g., LXX, Vulgate) translate *bᵉrē'šît* as absolute suggest that Genesis 1:1 is best rendered by the familiar independent sentence: "In the beginning God created the heavens and the earth."

Although some authorities view Genesis 1:1 as a caption to the creation account that follows, it is preferable to regard this first sentence of the Bible as a comprehensive statement affirming God's creation of the energy-matter that would constitute the universe. "In the beginning," denotes the moment when, by a spoken word, God brought the universe from nonexistence to existence. With Augustine and against Cullmann, the text suggests that time and space began at the moment of God's creative act. Since the Hebrews had no word for universe, the phrase "the heavens and the earth" (cf. Gen. 2:1, 4) conveyed the intended meaning. Several factors point to God's creation of the universe out of nothing (*ex nihilo*): (1) The phrase "In the beginning," (2) the absence of any preexistent material that God might have used, (3) repeated references to the divine fiat as causative (Gen. 1:3, 6, 9), and (4) the testimony of later biblical writers. Thus, as opposed to God's subsequent creative activity that employed existing materials, Genesis 1:1 clearly depicts an immediate and instantaneous creation of the material and immaterial realms.

Attention turns in Genesis 1:2 from the initial creative act to the condition of the earth: "Now the earth was formless and empty . . ." *Hāyᵉtāh,* the third-person feminine singular of the verb "to be," should be translated "was" rather than the "became" that Gap theorists prefer. After relating the initial creative act, the text describes the gas cloud that was proto-earth as "formless and empty." The first noun, *tōhû,* denotes an amorphous, trackless waste (cf. Deut. 32:10; Job 6:18), whereas the second noun, *bōhû,* connotes an expanse of desolate, uninhabited emptiness (cf. Isa. 34:11; Jer. 4:23). The following phrase, "darkness was over the surface of the deep [*tᵉhôm*]," indicates the absence of light amidst the primal gaseous material. The phrase, "and the Spirit of God was hovering over the the waters [*mayim*]," denotes the role of the Holy Spirit in creation. The Spirit brooded (cf. Deut. 32:11) over the watery chaos preparing the world for God's further creative activity.

Genesis 1:3–13 records a series of creative fiats whereby in three "days" or stages God progressively formed the dark nebula into the vast cosmos. God's first word, "Let there be light" may refer to the massive primal explosion ("big bang") that God effected by the contraction of the created gas cloud. In this first "day" God also separated the light from the darkness, although the heavenly bodies were not yet visible. This division of light from darkness may have been caused by the gradual clearing of the atmosphere as the material produced by the "big bang" slowly cooled. Verse 5 indicates that the first creative day was bounded by "evening" and "morning," the beginning and ending of the period. The fact that sun, moon, and stars were not "made" until the fourth day (Gen. 1:14–19) suggests that the "first day" probably was not twenty-four hours long.

In a second "day" or stage (Gen. 1:6–8) God continued to form the now-solid earth by effecting through his spoken word the separation of the waters of the atmosphere above from the waters of the earth's surface. Thus "God made [*'āśāh*] the expanse [*rāqîa'*] and separated the water under the expanse from the water above it" (v. 7). The common creation word *'āśāh* is a broad term meaning to "form" or to "fashion." This creative activity was followed by a second day, "evening" and "morning" referring to the boundaries of this indeterminate period.

The creative process of forming the earth continued for a third "day" or stage (Gen. 1:9–13), when by God's spoken word (fiat) the waters that covered the surface of the earth separated to form land and seas. With the forming of the shapeless earth now complete, God pronounced the result "good" (*ṭôb*), or suited for the purpose for which it had been prepared. Verse 12 relates that God commenced the process of filling the earth with living things. The text states that God caused the land to sprout with seed-bearing plants and fruit-bearing trees "according to their kinds." The sense of the text is not that the *élan* of plant production resided in the earth, but that plant and vegetable life sprang forth from the soil by the power of God. Thus the filling of the earth began by a secondary divine creation using existent materials. Some interpreters explain the appearance of vegetation before the full appearance of the sun by the fact that several forms of plant-life grow well in diffused light. The time required for the land to produce vegetation and the fact that the sun and moon were not yet "made" suggests that the "third day" of creation was more than twenty-four hours long.

In a fourth "day" or stage (Gen. 1:14–19), once again by his spoken word, God "made" (*'āśāh*) the sun, moon, and stars. But if, as we believe to be the case, the heavenly bodies were formed by the congealing of the material produced by the supernaturally produced big-bang, the fourth day likely describes God's work of unveiling the luminaries that were created aeons earlier. Indeed, the verb *wayya'aś* in verse 16 is better translated "had made" rather than the simple past tense. Whereas pagans deify and fear the heavenly bodies, Scripture teaches that God created the luminaries to serve several beneficient purposes: (1) to divide day and night (v. 14), (2) to distinguish seasons of the year (v. 14), and (3) to provide energy for the entire earth (v. 15). The text states that this "fourth day" or epoch was bounded by "evening" and "morning."

In a fifth "day" or stage (Gen. 1:20–23) God by divine fiat continued filling the earth by creating (*bārā'*, the second use of this verb) sea creatures, reptiles, and birds "according to their kinds." The creative utterance "Let the water teem with living creatures" (v. 20) suggests that God's creation of these living forms was mediate and may have involved a lengthy process, albeit not by evolutionary mechanisms. The "fifth day" of unspecified length was bounded by "evening" and "morning."

In a sixth "day" or stage (Gen. 1:24–31) God continued the work of filling the earth by making (*'āśāh*) domesticated animals, small creatures, and game, all "according to their kinds." Although the biological equivalent of the "kind" (*mîn*) is not identified, it is evident that development of plants and animals within well-defined limits did occur, perhaps by natural selection or some other God-ordained force. The expression "Let the land produce living creatures" (v. 24) once again points to a mediate creation effected over time. The climax of God's work over the six days was his special creation of male and female as image-bearers. "So God created [*bārā'*] man in his own image, in the image of God he created [*bārā'*] him" (v. 27). God's resolve "Let us make man" (v. 26), contrasts with his action vis-à-vis lower forms of life (viz., "Let the land produce"; "Let the water teem", vv. 11, 20) and indicates an instantaneous creation of a fully developed Adam (cf. v. 28). God's command to Adam and Eve to "fill [*mālē'*] the earth" (v. 28) does not imply replenishment, as advocates of the Gap or Reconstruction theory suggest.

The events of the sixth day were far-ranging indeed. The creation of the animals (Gen. 1:24–25), the creation of Adam (1:26–27), the planting of the garden (2:8–14), Adam's naming of the animals (2:19–20), the sleep of Adam, and the creation of Eve (2:21–23) likely were not accomplished in a single twenty-four day.[29] At the end of the six stages of forming and filling the earth, Genesis 1:31 states that "God saw all that he had made [*'āśāh*], and it was very good." God judged the individual aspects of the creation to be "good," and the whole "very good." Angelic beings must be included in the "all" that God created prior to the sixth day (cf. 2:1). Although the Mosaic record is silent on the subject, angels may have been included in the primal creation "in the beginning" (Gen. 1:1). Like the other creative epochs, the "sixth day" was bounded by "evening" and "morning."

On a seventh day (Gen. 2:2–3) God finished his work of forming and filling the earth and so "rested [*šābat*] from all his work." The divine rest involved a cessation of creative activity, not complete inactivity, for God continues his work of preservation, providence, and spiritual recreation, and one day he will fashion the universe anew. The absence of any reference to "evening" and "morning" suggests that the sabbath of God continues to the present. God's sabbath (v. 2) represents the basis and pattern for the human day of rest (v. 3). As God rested one day out of seven, so persons made in his image are enjoined to do the same.

The meaning of "day" (*yôm*) in Genesis 1 and 2 requires comment. The identical application of "evening" and "morning" to each of the six days may suggest that they were all of equal length. Yet the first three days existed before the sun, moon, and stars were "made." Moreover, as we have seen, "day" in Scripture frequently connotes a long period of time (Gen. 2:4; Job 20:28; Amos 9:11; 2 Thess. 2:3). Psalm 90:4 and 2 Peter 3:8 indicate that from God's perspective a thousand years are as one day. In addition, *yôm* in its nearly 1,300 occurrences in the Old Testament is variously translated by the AV as time, year, age, life, space, weather, etc. Carl Henry observes that "the term day in Genesis has no consistent chronological value."[30] A further consideration is that the words "evening" and "morning" often signify longer periods of time (Ps. 90:5–6; Jer. 6:4). Furthermore, Scripture seems to indicate that the seventh day continues through the present age (Heb. 4:1–11). Ultimately, responsible geology must determine the length of the Genesis days, even as science centuries earlier settled the issue of the rotation of the earth about the sun. Derek Kidner judges on the basis of empirical evidence that "a scientific account would have to speak of ages, not days."[31] Since Scripture elsewhere teaches that God *made* the universe in six days (Exod. 20:11; 31:17), it is probable that the "days" represent the creative epochs.[32]

Contrary to some critical theories, Genesis 2 is not a contradictory account of creation. Genesis 1 describes the creation of the universe chronologically and culminates in the making of man and woman in the divine *imago*. The second chapter, however, differs from the first in emphasis and order. Anticipating the account of the Fall in chapter 3, it begins with man, sets man at the center of things, and relates all else to the man and woman. Genesis 2:4a—"This is the account [*tôlᵉdôt*] . . ."—suggests that what follows in the text is a recitation of the history of the habitable world, beginning with the first man.[33] The shift from the divine name *'ᵉlōhîm* ("God") in Genesis 1 to *yahweh 'ᵉlōhîm* ("Lord God"), which occurs twenty times in Genesis 2–3, underscores God's role as the Creator who will manifest himself in the sphere of human history as Redeemer.

Genesis 2:7, which gives a fresh slant on Adam's origin, relates that "the Lord God formed [*yāṣar*] the man [*hā'ādām*] from the dust of the ground [*'ᵃdāmāh*] . . ." The description of the forming conveys the work of a craftsman, and the play on the Hebrew words for "man" and "ground" indicates that Adam's origin is earthly; God created him from the substances found in the earth's crust. The verse continues that the Lord God "breathed into his nostrils the breath of life," which means that Adam's material body received life-breath by a direct creative act of God. The final phrase of the verse, "and man became a living being [*nepeš hayyāh*]," affirms simply that Adam became a living creature, even as the lower life forms by God's power had become living creatures (Gen. 1:21, 24; cf. 9:16). Adam, of course, differed from the lower animals by virtue of his creation in the divine *imago*. Although the process of Adam's formation is not specified, the language conveys the idea of a special creation from inorganic matter, rather than a development from some extant organic form. The creation of vegetation (v. 9) after the creation of Adam (v. 7), and the forming of the animals (v. 19) after Adam, indicates that the Genesis 2 account is structured topically rather than chronologically.

According to Genesis 2:21–22, "the LORD God made [lit. "built," *bānāh*] a woman from the rib he had taken out of the man." This enigmatic act implies the ontological equality of the male and the female, as well as their intrinsic unity. The fact that God fashioned Eve from Adam's side appears to be a fatal blow to the theistic evolutionist claim that humanity was genetically derived from a nonhuman ancestor.

Genesis 5:1–2 represents a recapitulation of God's creation of humanity as male and female: "When God created [*bārā'*] man, he made [*'āśāh*] him in the likeness of God. He created [*bārā'*] them male and female and blessed them. And when they were created [*bārā'*], he called them 'man.'" This verse indicates that *bārā'* is occasionally juxtaposed with the verb *'āśāh* (cf. Gen. 2:4). But whereas *'āśāh* connotes the idea of shaping (Gen. 1:7, 16, 31; 2:18), and *yāsar* fashioning (2:7–8, 19) in the creative process, *bārā'* indicates God's supernatural initiation of something new—primal energy and matter (1:1), sea creatures, reptiles, and birds (v. 21), and man as male and female (1:27; 5:1–2).

Genesis 4:17–24 records the development of Cainite culture, with nomads building cities (v. 17), the domestication of cattle (v. 20), the development of music and art (v. 21), and the forging of implements of bronze and iron (v. 22). Most authorities locate this stage in the development of civilization toward the beginning of the neolithic or New Stone Age some eight to ten thousand years B.C. Inasmuch as this activity appears to be the work of the near descendants of Adam, it would seem that Adam should be dated close to that time. Most physical anthropologists, however, claim that humans have been on earth for a million years or more. Appeal is made, for example, to the Neanderthal cave man in Europe 50,000–100,000 years ago, to Florisbad man in Africa some 80,000 years ago, and to Cro-Magnon man in Europe some 20,000–35,000 years ago. The most reasonable solution seems to be that these creatures were pre-Adamic anthropoids, highly developed apes, who nevertheless were not created in the image of God and thus had no covenant relation with him.

The ten-member genealogy of Genesis 5:3–32, which traces the line from Adam to Noah, was used by older scholars to date creation some four millennia B.C. It is now universally recognized that the listing is selective rather than exhaustive; not every link in the family chain is given. The purpose of the listing is more theological than exhaustively chronological; it affirms the continuance of Adam's line to the time of the Flood. The genealogy of Genesis 11:10–26, which traces the line from Shem to Abram, is likewise selective in composition.

Whereas in Genesis 1 God brought order out of chaos, in Genesis 6–9 God's judgment on unrepentant human wickedness rendered the created order a watery chaos. In the greatest judgment since the Fall, God brought a great flood upon the earth for more than a year. The face value of the language of the biblical text concerning the Flood suggests a deluge of universal extent. Thus God said, "I am going to bring floodwaters on the earth to destroy all life under the heavens, every creature that has the breath of life in it" (Gen. 6:17; cf. 7:4). Moreover, "all the high mountains under the entire heavens were covered" (Gen. 7:19; cf. 8:9). Certain scholars, however, argue that in Scripture "all" frequently signifies the whole of a part and not all possible parts (e.g., Gen. 41:54–57; Deut. 2:25;

Dan. 2:37–38) and that "the heavens" (*haššāmayim,* Gen. 6:17; 7:19) can denote only the region of the sky visible to the observer (1 Kings 18:45). Thus some maintain that Moses' language could be understood phenomenologically from the limited standpoint of his personal experience. "The Flood covered a vast area, the 'whole world' of man's early history as recounted in Genesis 2ff."[34] But if Moses described a limited flood by virtue of his restricted knowledge of the earth, his account of creation would suffer the same limitation, which cannot be. R. K. Harrison concludes, "While some arguments may suggest a limited flood, the fact that the mountains were submerged implies a more extended one (Gen. 7:19–20). Genesis thus supports arguments for both a local and a universal deluge, with traditional biblical teaching favoring the latter and regarding the flood as a punishment for unrepented wickedness (Gen. 6:5)."[35]

The sequential events of the Genesis creation week serve as a paradigm for the biblical doctrine of the sabbath rest. The fourth commandment states that since God created the universe in six days and rested (lit. "relaxed") on the seventh, humankind in God's plan should rest one day in seven (Exod. 20:11). By following this prescription, persons would realize maximal physical, emotional, and spiritual renewal. The language of Exodus 31:17 is highly anthropomorphic: "In six days the LORD made the heavens and the earth, and on the seventh day he abstained [*šābat*] from work and rested [*nāpaš,* lit., 'caught his breath']." In Exodus 23:10–11 and Leviticus 25:4–7 the creation sequence provides the basis for causing the land to lie fallow for one year after six years of cultivation. Thus the most that the Genesis creation-rest teaching establishes is the ratio of six units of labor to one unit of rest. Hence no proof for a literal twenty-four-hour day derives from the sabbath-day injunction. "While God's seventh-day rest sanctions the sabbath day, Genesis hardly limits God's rest to a twenty-four-hour period."[36]

Poetry and Wisdom

In its hymnbook Israel repeatedly confessed a fundamental datum of its faith, namely, that the Lord is "the Maker [*'ōśēh*] of heaven and earth" (Pss. 115:15; 121:2; 124:8). A frequent refrain in the Psalms is the impotence of the pagan idols and the power of the Lord who created all things (96:5). Joyfully Israel lifted its heart heavenward and acknowledged, "You founded [*yāsad*] the world and all that is in it" (89:11; cf. 24:2; 119:90). The psalmist was careful to affirm that Yahweh is prior to and above the natural order: "Before the mountains were born or you brought forth the earth and the world, from everlasting to everlasting you are God" (90:2). The universe is not eternal, but had a discrete beginning in time (102:25). Neither is the universe an emanation from the being of God, for by a free act of the will God spoke and the cosmos came into being (148:5–6).

In Job 38, one of the great creation pericopae of the Old Testament, the Lord revealed himself to Job as the Creator of earth's vast structure (Job 38:4–7). As the Lord was founding the earth, "all the angels shouted for joy" (v. 7)—a statement that suggests that God created the angels prior to the material universe. Job continues by saying that the seas are a creation of God, called forth and controlled by him (vv. 8–11). Thus in Job, "the world is described as a vast edifice whose designer and maker is God"[37]

Many creation texts in this portion of the Old Testament prove to be poetic reflections on the Genesis creation narrative. Thus the statement that the universe was created by the Spirit of

God (Pss. 33:6; 104:30) corresponds to the teaching of Genesis 1:1–2. The Spirit's work of implanting in persons the breath of life (Job 33:4) reflects the language of Genesis 2:7. The statement of Psalm 33:9, "He spoke and it came to be," corresponds to the reiterated phrase "And God said . . . And it was so" of Genesis 1:6–7, 9, 11, 14–15, 24, 29–30. Moreover, the poetic image of dry land rising out of the waters (Ps. 24:2) is an allusion to Genesis 1:9–10. The discussion in Psalm 74:16–17 of the division of land and sea, the establishment of sun and moon, and the delineation of the seasons corresponds to the events of days three and four in Genesis 1. Finally, one discovers in Psalm 104 a striking correspondence to what God wrought in the six creative days of Genesis 1.

The Old Testament closely links God's creative and redemptive activities (e.g., Ps. 74:12–17). Psalm 33 relates that the God who fashioned the universe (vv. 6–9) is the same God who directs the course of saving history (vv. 10–12). Psalm 124:8 makes the point concisely: "Our help is in the name of the LORD, the Maker of heaven and earth" (cf. 121:2; 146:5–6).

Job 28:25–27 and Psalm 104:24 affirm that God's creative activity was conceived and executed in wisdom. Proverbs 3:19 makes the same point: "By wisdom [*ḥokmāh*] the LORD laid the earth's foundations, by understanding [*tᵉbûnāh*] he set the heavens in place." The most complete explication of wisdom's role in creation, however, is poetically set forth in Proverbs 8:22–31. There wisdom, inseparable from God, was with God eternally (vv. 22–26). The text depicts wisdom as God's creative agent in the forming of the universe (vv. 27–31). On balance, this text presents a personification of wisdom—an attribute of God—for the sake of poetic vividness. The author's point is that if God made nothing apart from wisdom, neither should believers act apart from divine wisdom. The apostle Paul clearly saw that the sum of God's wisdom was revealed in Christ (Col. 2:3); hence he denoted the latter "the wisdom of God" (1 Cor. 1:24; cf. v. 30).

The Psalms also state the purpose for which God created the vast universe. A subsidiary goal was the welfare of the persons God would create to inhabit his world (Ps. 115:16). The primary purpose of creation, however, was the display of God's glory, or the aggregate of the divine perfections (8:1; 19:1). The cosmos is not something to be worshiped (as if it were God), but a richly adorned created entity that would lead the beholder to the living God himself.

The Prophetic Literature

The Old Testament prophets accepted the Genesis creation doctrine and repeatedly appealed to it as proof that Yahweh is the Sovereign of the universe and the Lord of history. Compared with impotent idols, the Creator is a God of incomparable power and knowledge: "God made [*'āśāh*] the earth by his power; he founded the world by his wisdom and stretched out the heavens by his understanding" (Jer. 10:12; 51:15). Hezekiah's prayer indicates that since the Lord Almighty is Creator of all, he possesses absolute dominion and authority (Isa. 37:16). Jonah's creedal confession, "I worship the LORD, the God of heaven, who made [*'āśāh*] the sea and the land" (Jonah 1:9), implies that the world is under God's control and fulfills his purposes, as the remainder of the book plainly demonstrates. Amos declares that the sovereign, all-powerful Creator will punish Israel with captivity for their sins (Amos 4:12–13; 5:8–9), and Jeremiah states that the Creator will do the same to Judah (Jer. 27:5).

On the other hand, Isaiah declares

that the Creator God will comfort and strengthen his chosen people (Isa. 40:25–31). The God of Isaiah's message of grace and hope in chapters 40–66 is none other than "the Creator [*bôrē'*] of the ends of the earth" (Isa. 40:28). The Lord who fashioned the earth and the heavens (Isa. 44:24; 48:13) will bring his people back from captivity (Isa. 43:5–7; cf. 44:2–3). Moreover, the Lord "who stretches out the heavens, who lays the foundation of the earth, and who forms the spirit of man within him" (Zech. 12:1), as the Sovereign of history, will overthrow the enemies of Jerusalem.

In another sublime description of the omnipotent Creator, Isaiah affirms that he who created the heavens, earth, and persons (Isa. 42:5) is also the architect of human redemption (e.g., vv. 6–7). So close is the link between the two, that God's "former" work of creation springs forth to his "new" work of salvation (v. 9). And toward the end of the prophecy, in language reminiscent of Genesis 1:1, God declares that his work of creation and redemption will consummate in a newly fashioned order of righteousness and peace: "Behold, I will create [*bārā'*] new heavens and a new earth. . . . I will create [*bārā'*] Jerusalem to be a delight and its people a joy" (Isa. 65:17–18).

Gap theorists maintain that Jeremiah 4:23–26 supports the notion of a great primal cataclysm that devastated the earth. Careful examination of the context suggests that these verses point to the future and describe the desolation God would inflict on Judah at the hand of the Babylonians for their national apostasy. So destructive would be God's judgment that Jeremiah found it useful to describe it in the language of Genesis 1:2. Similarly Isaiah 24:1 refers to the final worldwide eschatological judgment. Isaiah 45:18, also cited in favor of the Gap theory, more accurately states that God created the ordered universe for a purposeful end, namely, to provide a suitable habitation for human beings.

Synpotic Gospels

Jesus clearly endorsed the validity of the Old Testament creation doctrine. Thus in the Olivet Discourse the Lord reflected Genesis 1 language when he spoke of a coming distress "unequaled from the beginning, when God created the world" (Mark 13:19). The Greek verb for "create," *ktizō*, always has God for its subject and corresponds to the Hebrew *bārā'*. Jesus furthermore grounded monogamy and the permanence of marriage in the Genesis creation ordinance. In Matthew 19:4 (cf. Mark 10:6) the phrase "at the beginning" echoes Genesis 1:1, and the clause "the Creator [*ho ktisas*] made [*epoiēsen*] them male and female" recalls Genesis 1:27. The verb *poieō*, "to make," corresponds to the Hebrew creation verb *'āśāh*. Furthermore, Matthew 19:5 (cf. Mark 10:7–8) is a direct quotation of Genesis 2:24. Finally, the saying of Jesus, "The Sabbath was made [*egeneto*] for man" (Mark 2:27) corroborates God's hallowing of one day in seven as a time of rest and worship (cf. Gen. 2:3).

Primitive Christianity/Acts

The prayers and speeches of the early Christians reflect the Old Testament outlook on creation. The prayer of thanksgiving uttered after the release of Peter and John from prison conveys the common conviction of the church at Jerusalem: "Sovereign Lord, . . . you made [*poieō*] the heaven and the earth and the sea, and everything in them" (Acts 4:24). Stephen's speech to the Sanhedrin, quoting Isaiah 66:2, affirms that the hand of the Lord made all that is (Acts 7:50). Paul and Barnabas, in their announcement of the Good News to Gentiles at Lystra, began with the fundamental truth of religion, namely, that "the living God . . . made heaven and earth and sea and everything in them" (Acts 14:15).

Preaching to Athenians steeped in Stoic ideas, Paul began with the assertion, drawn from the Old Testament (Exod. 20:11; Neh. 9:6), that God is Creator and Lord of all (Acts 17:24). The apostle continued by claiming that God did not create out of necessity, as if he had need to complete himself in some way. Far from being a contingent being, God "himself gives all men life and breath and everything else" (v. 25; cf. Isa. 42:5). Finally, Paul acknowledged the familiar Old Testament truth that God made the entire human family from the first man Adam (v. 26).

Pauline Literature

Paul accepts as indisputable the fact of creation (*ktisis*) by the omnipotent God (Rom. 1:20). According to the apostle, God "created [*ktizō*] all things" (Eph.3:9) and he "gives life [*zōogoneō*] to everything" (1 Tim. 6:13). The apostle's saying, "from him [*ex autou*] and through him [*di autou*] and to him [*eis auton*] are all things" (Rom. 11:36; cf. Eph. 4:6), indicates that the Godhead is the source, the agent, and the end or goal of all reality. Paul insists that God's creation was wrought "in conformity with the purpose of his will" (Eph. 1:11) and infers, against incipient forms of Gnosticism that regarded matter as evil, that "everything God created [*ktizō*] is good" (1 Tim. 4:4). The latter pronouncent recalls God's words of approval in Genesis 1: "it was good" and "it was very good.'

Paul further specifies that the cosmic Christ is the Lord of creation (Col. 1:16). The clause *en autō ektisthē ta panta* ("in him all things were created") may indicate that Christ is the sphere in which the work of creation took place. He is the *raison d'etre* for the world of visible objects and the realm of invisible spirits. The phrase "all things were created by him [*di autou*] and for him [*eis auton*]" in this verse identifies the cosmic Christ as the agent and the goal of creation. He is both the *archē* and the *telos* of the vast universe. "From start to finish the created order is bound up with the person of Christ."[38] The apostle combines the roles of Father and Son in the creation drama in 1 Corinthians 8:6: "There is but one God, the Father, from whom [*ex hou*] all things came and for whom we live; and there is but one Lord, Jesus Christ, through whom (*di hou*) all things came and through whom we live." All things thus originate from the Father through the agency of the Son. The phrases "for whom we live" and "through whom we live" attest that the Creator of the physical order is also the Recreator of the new spiritual order. This relationship is further taught in 2 Corinthians 4:6, where the spiritual light that dispels the darkness of sin is the correlate of the physical light that illumined the darkness of the primal chaos (cf. Gen. 1:3). In 2 Corinthians 5:17 Paul establishes the same relationship between the original physical creation and the new spiritual recreation.

Paul bases his teaching concerning the role of women in the church on transcultural principles deduced from the order of creation. A woman should pray with head veiled, thus acknowledging submission to her husband, (1) because "woman came from man" (1 Cor. 11:8, 12; cf. Gen. 2:22–23) and (2) because "woman [was created] for man" (v. 9; cf. Gen. 2:18). Paul's bottom line, however, is that "everything comes from God" (*panta ek tou theou*, 1 Cor. 11:12). Moreover, in 1 Timothy 2:12–14 Paul forbids a woman to teach or wield authority over a male elder or bishop in the church, because (1) "Adam was formed [aorist of *plassō*, to "form," "create"] first, then Eve" (cf. Gen. 2:7, 22) and (2) the woman succumbed to Satan's deception (cf. Gen. 3:6). Concerning the relation between male and female in the church, Guthrie concludes: "The priority of man's creation places him in a position of superiority over woman, the assumption being that the original creation, with the Creator's own imprimatur upon it, must set a precedent for determining the true order of the sexes."[39]

Johannine Literature

The beginning of John's Gospel affirms the central role of the Logos in creation. John 1:3 states that "through him [*di autou*, i.e., the Logos] all things were made [*ginomai*]." The "all things" of creation include the stars, quasars, asteriods, angels, earth, persons, animals, and vegetation. The aorist of *ginomai* signifies that all these entities "became" or "came into existence." The phrase *di autou* and its location in the sentence stress the agency of the Logos in the creative event. The second half of the sentence emphatically excludes all creative agencies other than the Christ. John, in effect, affirms that "everything that has reached existence must have passed through the will of the Logos."[40]

In the Apocalypse the twenty-four elders ascribe glory and honor to God, offering his creative wisdom as their rationale: "For you created [*ktizō*] all things, and by your will they were created [*ktizō*] and have their being" (Rev. 4:11). Here the cause of all that exists is the sovereign will of the all-powerful God. John cites God's creation of heaven and earth and all that is in them (Rev. 10:6; 14:7) as the rationale for the awesome end-time events of redemption and judgment. The Creator, as Ruler over all, is fully capable of achieving his eschatological purposes.

In fulfillment of the prophecies of Isaiah 65:17 and 66:22, Revelation 21 correlates God's primal creation with the coming new creation. God's promise "I am making everything new" (v. 5) embodies the promise of a new order in which "the first heaven and the first earth" will give way to "a new heaven and a new earth" (v. 1). In the coming renovation God will reshape the present fallen universe in such a manner as to provide the optimal dwelling place for the redeemed in the eternal state of blessedness.

Other New Testament Writings

The writer of Hebrews had a lively recognition of God as Creator. Hebrews 3:4 states that "God is the builder of everything," the verb *kataskeuazō*, to "construct," to "furnish," connoting here both God's original fashioning and his subsequent furnishing of the universe. Agreeable with Romans 11:36, Hebrews 2:10 indicates that everything exists "for" God and "through" God; that is, God is the ultimate goal or purpose of life, and he is the agent or instrument of the world's creation. Hebrews 11:3 is an important text on the subject: "By faith we understand that the universe was formed at God's command, so that what is seen was not made out of what was visible." It is significant that Hebrews' catalogue of faith (Heb. 11:3–38) begins with the foundational truth that the universe exists by God's creative fiat (*rhēma*). The faith that holds fast to changless verities posits God as the one efficient cause of the universe. The latter half of the verse denies that the universe came into being from any extant material. Hence, against prevailing Greek views, verse 3 upholds the fact of creation out of nothing (*ex nihilo*). Hebrews 3:7–4:11 finds in God's rest (*katapausis*) on the seventh day (cf. Gen. 2:2) an anticipation of the spiritual rest (*sabba-*

tismos) the believer realizes in Christ. Here again we discover the close link that exists between God's works of creation and redemption.

Analagous to John 1:3 and Colossians 1:16, Hebrews identifies Christ as the preexistent agent of creation. Thus the Son is the one "through [*dia*] whom he [i.e., God] made the universe" (Heb. 1:2). The early Christians clearly were convinced that Jesus of Nazareth who lived among them created the universe in its vast array. Thus in Hebrews 1:10, Psalm 102:25 (originally directed to God) is applied to the Son: "In the beginning, O Lord, you laid the foundations [*themelioō*] of the earth, and the heavens are the work of your hands." Similar to Revelation 21:1–5, but without the apocalyptic imagery, 2 Peter 3:13 correlates God's primal creation with the coming new creation: "We are looking forward to a new heaven and a new earth." At the end of the present age God's creative power will transform this sin-cursed world into a new order in which righteousness and peace will prevail.

SYSTEMATIC FORMULATION

We now seek to test the historical views above by the primary biblical data, consider the debated issues, and develop a coherent doctrine of origins. Does Scripture teach an original creative act? Did a series of creative acts follow? If so, are they given in chronological order? What, then, is the length of time between them?

God's Immediate Creation of Matter-Energy

Although often the Scriptures speak of "God" as the Creator, the three triune Persons contributed to creation in distinctive and harmonious ways. In accord with the Father's plan, the Logos spoke the original finite energy (raw material) into existence (John 1:3), formed everything that was made (v. 3) and gave it life (v. 4). At the same time the Spirit "was hovering over" the original creation, bringing to fulfillment the Father's purposes in the world (Gen. 1:2).

Careful thought about the beginning of the triune God's creative activity distinguishes between the original supernatural creation out of nothing (immediate creation) and the successive supernatural creative acts forming particular kinds of things out of "raw materials" (*mediate creation*). By immediate creation we mean God's extraordinary action in the past that brought into existence out of nothing the basic raw materials of the universe—its underlying matter-energy.

In 1769 before the rise of modern science John Gill's *Body of Divinity* distinguished the mediate creations of Adam out of dust and of Eve out of Adam from the earlier immediate creation out of nothing.[41] The source of the distinction was Scripture, not scientific theory. "In the beginning God created the heavens and the earth" (Gen.1:1). Other translations put it this way: "When God began to create" the earth was formless and empty, implying the preexistence of the unformed earth (RSV note). However, as found in the Biblical Teaching section above, the Bible's first statement is not a dependent clause, but an independent clause, as the most natural and obvious interpretation of the grammar as understood throughout both Jewish and Christian traditions.[42] The Father created *ex nihilo* the basic "raw materials" (at present called energy-matter) out of which things in the universe are made.

Several lines of evidence support a supernatural understanding of God's creative acts rather than a nonmiraculous providential direction of alleged evolutionary processes:

1. In Genesis 1:1 creation *ex nihilo*

best fits the meaning of the Hebrew term for create, *bārā'*. It differs from *yāṣar* "to fashion" in that the latter primarily emphasizes the shaping of an object while *bārā'* emphasizes the initiation of the object."[43] The word is used in the Hebrew Qal stem only of God's supernatural activity "initiating something new" (Isa. 41:20; 48:6–7), and "bringing into existence" (Isa. 43:1; Ezek. 21:30; 28:13, 15). "The limitation of this word to divine activity indicates that the area of meaning delineated by the root falls outside the sphere of human ability."[44] Although "out of nothing" is not necessarily inherent in the meaning of the word, it "never occurs with the object of the material, and since the primary emphasis of the word is on the newness of the created object, the word lends itself well to the concept of creation *ex nihilo*."[45] Where something previously created is used, as in dust for man, the term indicates God's supernatural or miraculous use of dust in producing a living being from inanimate materials.

2. The case for creation of the "raw materials," or "the substance of the universe"[46] *ex nihilo* rests with even greater weight on the fact that *everything other than God was created by God*. The creation of the heaven and earth was the actual beginning of all things. The existence of any primeval material is precluded by the object created: "the heavens and the earth," the most all-inclusive terms available to the Hebrew writer. The earth being "formless and empty" (Gen. 1:2) is the result of God's original creative act.[47] The "universe was formed" at God's command (Heb. 11:3). The Greek term for universe "includes in it all that exists under the conditions of time and space together with those conditions of time and space themselves."[48] The verb "was formed" means was "made to be and to be what we find them."[49] All the necessary ingredients and the designs of things in the cosmos owe their existence to Almighty God.

3. Everything other than God, furthermore, had a *beginning* in the finite past, for nothing but God is eternal. Because everything other than God had a beginning in the finite past, so also did the earth's energy. "The statement 'In the beginning God created the heavens and the earth' (Gen. 1:1) is not a mere heading, nor a summary of the history of the creation, but a declaration of the primeval act of God by which the universe was called into being."[50] The eternal God existed, furthermore, when the mountains, the earth, and the world did not (Ps. 90:2).

4. That which came to be, arose *out of God* by God's will expressed in God's Word. "For from [*ex*] him and through him and to him are all things" (Rom. 11:36). In fact, "everything comes from [*ek*] God" (1 Cor. 11:12). In the biblical context all things come from God, not by a necessary pantheistic process of emanation, but *by a free act of God's will expressed in his Word*, in other words, by divine *fiat*. "By the word of the LORD were the heavens made, their starry host by the breath of his mouth. . . . For he spoke, and it came to be; he commanded, and it stood firm" (Ps. 33:6, 9; cf. 148:5). Creation by divine command (fiat) is not arbitrary. God acts in accord with his nature. The decision and command to create is a sovereign act in accord with God's wise, loving, and just purpose.

Creation out of God by his authoritative order ought not be confused with an automatic emanation from God's being. "Speaking is the revelation of thought; the creation, the realization of the thoughts of God, a freely accomplished act of the absolute Spirit, and not an emanation of creatures from the divine essence."[51] So "Through him [the Word who was with God and was God] all things were made; without him nothing was made that has been made"

(John 1:3). Because the Christian believes the Scriptures for good and sufficient reasons, faith is not wishful thinking. "By faith we understand that the universe was formed at God's command, so that what is seen was not made out of what was visible" (Heb. 11:3).

The world's energy was no imperfect thing at the time of creation, even though as yet the world was formless and uninhabited, for it fulfilled the Father's plan at that point. Eventually God's purpose did include inhabitants (cf. Isa. 24:1; 34:11; 45:18; Jer. 23–26). But no evidence of a "catastrophe" or divine judgment on an alleged pre-Adamic race can be found; the command to Adam and Eve was not to "replenish" the earth (AV), but to "be fruitful and increase in number; *fill* the earth and subdue it" (Gen. 1:28). The hypothesis that the formless state of the earth is the result of judgment on fallen angels who were cast out of heaven to earth, is logically possible, but not as probable because this idea is not explicitly in the text. So belief in a catastrophe ought not be made a test of belief in the Bible.

How long the earth "was formless and uninhabited" we have no way of telling. The Bible has not told us. And we do not have adequate evidence to insist on the hypothesis of a recent creation. It is possible that the earth was "formless and uninhabited" for a very long time. However great the age of energy or matter in the universe, many of those years may be included while the earth was in this unformed and uninhabited state.

The Subsequent Series of Creative Acts (Mediate Creation)

By God's *mediate creation* we mean that series of extraordinary events in the past by which God brought into existence out of the precreated raw materials (at present understood as energy-matter), light, atmosphere, water, dry land, vegetation, animals, and humanity.

Deists and theistic evolutionists may admit that Genesis informs about a single supernatural creative act but deny that it also teaches a subsequent series of creative acts during six periods of time called "days." Theistic evolutionists think that everything evolved from lower forms of life, including human beings, without any miraculous activity. But God "spoke" six different times, and several different kinds of things came to be: light (Gen. 1:3), space (v. 6), water and dry land (v. 9), vegetation (v. 11), the light of day versus the night and the seasons (v. 14), fish and birds (v. 20), land animals (v. 24), and man: male and female (vv. 26–27).

In the light of the informative purpose throughout the Book of Genesis, we take not only the original creative act cognitively, but also understand the six subsequent creative acts cognitively. Alleged contradictions between the Genesis 1–2:3 and Genesis 2:4–25 accounts do not preclude their informative purpose. The second account does not attempt another complete order of events. Since its purpose is not chronological, it cannot be regarded to be in conflict with Genesis 1 on that basis. Genesis 2 zooms in on the man and woman to set the background for the drama of sin's origin (chapter 3). Although the biblical and Babylonian accounts of origins are often alleged to have been derived from one another or a common Babylonian source, the evidence is insufficient to sustain that theory. Both allude in general to sunlight, vegetation, animals, and man, but do not have enough detailed similarities to require the derivation of one from the other, or from a third common source.

We interpret Genesis 1 and 2 not only as evocative and devotional but also as cognitive or informative for several reasons:

1. The purpose of Genesis 1 is to provide an account of the origin of each of the kinds of things in the world in order that people might worship and serve, not the gods of the sun, the moon, and the rain, but the Lord of all. The feeling of dependence evoked is drawn from the Creator's production of all the kinds of things made, not just of a part of nature.

2. Although the events take place before human written history, the passage is not an imaginary human saga about the past, but a divine revelation of a series of divine acts.

3. The writer's informative purpose in Genesis 2:4–25 is indicated by the use of the same phrase "this is the written account of" that introduces cognitive histories of subsequent lives. Just as there is an informative "written account of" the lives of Jacob (37:2); Esau (36:9); Edom (36:1); Isaac (25:19); Ishmael (25:12); Terah and Abraham (11:27); Shem (11:10); Shem, Ham, and Japheth (10:1); Noah (6:9); and Adam's line (5:1), so there is an informative "[written] account of the heavens and earth when they were created" (2:4).

4. One of the author's major informative purposes was to set the actual cultural stage and introduce the lead characters for the following informative account of the origin of sin among humans in (Genesis 3).

5. The literary genre of Genesis 1–3 as Old Testment scholar Alan A. MacRae has shown, is *not* that of Hebrew poetry.[52] There are poetical accounts of creation in the Bible, such as Psalm 104, but they contrast remarkably with the first chapter of Genesis. Informative accounts may include figures of speech and symbols, but the general frame of reference in context is literal narrative.

6. If the passage were not informative, what nonliteral purpose could there be, for example, in the paragraph of detailed description of four rivers watering the garden (Gen. 2:10–14)? That passage takes pains to locate the Garden of Eden in relation to four rivers, two of which remain with the same names to this day. Only irresponsible allegorization could lead the Jewish writer Philo to claim that the four rivers represent the four major virtues of Plato's ethics!

7. Furthermore, how can the genealogy in Genesis be taken noncognitively? The people mentioned toward the end of the genealogy are literal individuals with literal descendants. At what point early in the genealogy did a figurative father beget a literal son?

8. The Lord Jesus Christ and his apostles who wrote the New Testament by the Spirit's inspiration understood the early chapters of Genesis to be informative. Jesus said, "At the beginning the Creator 'made them male and female' " (Matt. 19:4); he also stated, "As it was in the days of Noah, so it will be at the coming of the Son of Man" (24:37). Jesus spoke of the blood shed from the beginning of the world, the blood of Abel (Luke 11:51), and of the similarity between the days of Lot in Sodom and the days before Jesus' return (17:28–30). Paul taught that Adam was the first man (1 Cor. 15:45) and that Adam was formed first, then Eve (1 Tim. 2:13–14). No stronger case can be made for a cognitive approach to the early chapters of Genesis for those who consider Christ their example and who bow to him as Lord than that from Christ's informative interpretation of the Old Testament accounts. People who deny what Jesus taught of earthly things will not long find viable the spiritual or existential values Christ drew from the Old Testament.

9. In general, biblical values, in contrast to Hindu-Buddhist values, are inseparably grounded in actual facts that take place in the flesh. The theolog-

ical meaning of Christ's incarnation, for example, evaporates if the eternal Logos (John 1:1) did not become flesh (v. 14) cognitively or factually (1 John 4:1–3).

Given a basically informative purpose, then, a normal interpretation of Genesis 1 and 2 is that, in addition to the immediate, creative act, (1) there was *a series of creative acts* on each of the six days (length undetermined as yet). (2) God created each of the living "kinds" (Genesis 1:11–12, 21, 24–25). As a word study shows, the Hebrew word for kind (*min*) designates classifiable biological beings that are capable of reproducing. "Kind" is used in describing the animals that went into Noah's ark (Gen. 6:20; 7:14), of ravens (Lev. 11:15), hawks (v. 16), herons (v. 19), locusts, catydids, crickets, grasshoppers (v. 22), and lizards (v. 29; cf. Deut. 14:13–18). (3) Living animals will reproduce "each according to its kind" (Gen. 1:24). This allows for development of varieties within the kinds, but not evolution beyond the limits of the kinds. Since the Scriptures do not define the limits of the kinds of animals other than by reproductive capability (1:11, 24), we may leave it to the actual (not imagined or constructed) empirical data to determine where the limits are.

Given a series of at least six creative acts on an informative interpretation of Genesis, the processional or developmental is not ruled out within the kinds, for several ictic (sudden or abrupt) events occurred. The great gaps in the fossil evidence and any evidence of developments (within the kinds) are not a problem. "The Christian is not embarrassed by evidence of hiatus nor evidence of link."[53]

The Order of the Series of Creative Acts

Are the days in Genesis 1 numbered so that we may understand the order of creative acts and of the appearance of things in the universe? Not according to the pictorial-day interpretation, which takes them as days of revealing activity to the writer of Genesis. The chronological element is said to designate the order in which God revealed the topics to the writer, not necessarily the order in which they came into existence. On such a revelation-day hypothesis, no problems can arise between observational knowledge of the order of origins and scripturally derived knowledge, because the Bible has nothing to say about the order in which things were created.

Although the revelation-day or pictorial-day theory alleviates all apparent difficulties with related observed data, it does not fit well with the text of Genesis. The purpose of the early chapters is to convey information about the origin, not of Genesis, but of the things in the world. The six days refer not to God's revelatory acts, but to his creative acts. The phrases "And God said . . . and it was" apply to creations, not revelations (Pss. 33:6, 9; 148:5). The subsequent summary statement reads, "For in six days the LORD *made* the heavens and the earth, the sea, and all that is in them, but he rested on the seventh day" (Exod. 20:11). Although occasionally the verb "made" means "show" (44 times, according to Wiseman), in the overwhelming majority of instances (2,240 in *Young's Complete Concordance*) it means to "do, execute, perform, work."

> The seven days' works are not so many prophetic-historical tableux, which were spread before the mental eye of the seer, whether of the historian or the first man. The account before us does not contain the slightest marks of a vision, is no picture of creation, in which every line betrays the pencil of the painter rather than the pen of a historian, but is obviously a historical narrative, which we could no more transform into a vision

than the account of paradise or of the fall.[54]

From considerations like these the most probable interpretation is that the six days of Genesis 1 refer to a series of creative acts occurring in the order of their numbering from one through six. Genesis 1 does teach a chronological order of origins. Therefore we may look for a general correlation of the data from nature as to when the designated aspects came into existence.

1. First, then, the Logos of God made *light* (Gen. 1:3). Although the earth's solar system was not arranged as at present until the fourth "day," God created light on the first day. The light of the first day may have come from the energy-matter of the immediate creation (Gen. 1:1). Light, heat, and electricity are different forms of energy. May it not be that God's first mediate creative command produced a big bang that would illuminate the world? Is it possible that God then invested the universe with its basic amount of energy (according to the first law of thermodynamics) and regulated the law of entropy (according to the second law of thermodynamics) governing the usefulness of energy in its forms of light, heat, and electricity? In view of the universality of energy and its relation to light this interpretation may be worth pursuing.[55]

Robert C. Newman and Herman J. Ecklemann, Jr., *Genesis One and the Origin of the Earth,* suggest that as a result of this creative act of God "the contracting gas cloud [of the original creation Gen. 1:1–2], having become dark within, eventually heats up to the point that it begins to glow" (1:3). Assuming a uniform speed of light since the first day of creation, Newman and Ecklemann seek to determine the age of our galaxy, sun, and universe. From the expansion of the observable universe since the big bang and the structure of the stars, they conclude that our galaxy is 15 billion to 20 billion years old; the sun, 5 to 10 billion years old; and the earth's solar system, about 5 billion years old. If this was not the case, then God must have created the light speeding to the earth as if from distant stars when actually it was not![56]

The phrase with each of the days—"there was evening and there was morning" (v. 5) refers to the beginning and ending of the period in which God supernaturally formed light and the time that elapsed until God's next creative act. Although in our culture we think of the day beginning with the morning, in the Hebrew culture a day began with the evening at 6:00 P.M. The first day started in darkness and ended with light, and so the analogy to the literal Hebrew days was easily drawn. As the phrase "evening and morning" occurs repeatedly, it emphasizes how each stage of God's work progressed from the beginning chaos to the order intended.

2. God then made the "expanse" of the sky, the earth's *atmosphere and space* (vv. 6–8). Just as God divided the darkness from the light, he divided the atmospheric heavens from the earth. A perfectly uniform mass would have been meaningless and boring. God's creative informing of the earth involved "pounding" or "stretching" the moisture out to separate the clouds from the ocean by something very thin. The earth's atomosphere is unique as far as human exploration has penetrated. It provides a great life-support system, supplying water, oxygen, and carbon dioxide. The atmosphere shields life on earth from the ultraviolet rays of the sun and other rays, and moderates the earth's temperatures. "Who has measured the waters in the hollow of his hand, or with the breadth of his hand has marked off the heavens?" (Isa. 40:12).[57]

3. At the Creator's command the

waters were gathered into *seas,* an occurrence that divided them from the *dry land* and made possible the *kinds of vegetation* (Gen. 1:9–13). The continents were once submerged and rose from the oceans. The division of land from water on earth did not occur by chance, blind geologic forces, or fallen angels. By this act God wisely prepared the globe for the coming human population. The land produced vegetation: seed-bearing plants and trees according to their kinds. The Bible does not ask us to believe that the incredibly complicated chemical substances that make up a tiny seed happened by chance. The highly complex structures of living plants, including trees, grains and vegetables, are not said here to have come from nothing but from the earth. The fact that the command of God is involved most probably means that the essential elements were supernaturally brought together by the intelligence of the Creator to produce living vegetation.

4. God ordered the earth's solar system uniformly to give *light and regulate time on earth.* Because there had been light since the first day, most probably on the fourth day God ordered the solar system as it is now. The sun may have been created on the first day, and on the fourth day God placed it at the right distance away healthfully to provide for light on earth and, with the moon, to mark seasons, days, nights, and years (vv. 15–19; cf. Ps. 104:19). From the perspective of relativity, one can choose either the earth or the sun as the primary reference point. The Creator has established not only the distance of the sun from the earth, but also the speed of the earth in orbit around it, etc. Here is the beginning of *time* as the marking of successions of events on earth by literal days, nights, months, seasons, and years. In a biblical context, in contrast to a Greek philosophical context, furthermore, time is not some alien thing limiting the eternal God, but a manifestation of his free will in fulfillment of his creation purposes. On the fourth day God provided for a linear view of history and meaningful evaluation of human achievements in time. God's work on the fourth day also makes emphatic that the sun and moon are not gods as has been thought in Babylonia, Assyria, Egypt, and elsewhere; they are but parts of the craftsmanship of the one Lord of all. They are part of God's plan to provide for life and supremely human life on one planet!

5. God "created" (the second use of *bārā'*) living and moving things (v. 21), specifically, the *kinds of fish* in the seas and the *kinds of birds* in the air (vv. 20–23). The creation of self-moving living creatures required a specific command and *ex nihilo* act of God. He created the seas and the air, not purposelessly on the previous days, but to be inhabited, to sustain the life of great varieties of small and large living things. God's temporal purposes are rich and even humorous, as evidenced in aquariums and museums. Stewards of God's world will give account for treatment of these species and their habitats. Any receptive reader of Genesis 1 will refuse to worship and serve any fish or bird or any artistic likeness of it because he will recognize the Creator, who is God over all.

6. God made the *kinds of animals* (vv. 24–25), and finally, God "created" (the third use of *bārā'*) *humans* the one and only *self-moving kind in the divine image.* To humans God delegated authority to rule over the animals and the earth (vv. 26–27). Although the Hebrew for "Adam" may mean mankind universally, at the beginning mankind included one particular man. God made Adam out of the dust (2:7)—that is, in the context, nonliving matter, the ground to which the body returns at death (3:19). It is unlikely that Adam's

body was formed out of lower forms of animal life (as some theistic evolutionists suppose). To interpret the "dust" as a reference to similar chemical elements in the human body and dust introduces into the Bible's language scientific technicalities anachronistically. The point is that from the dust that was not alive God created a living man (2:7). The fact that Adam was "the first man" is foundational to progressive revelation as finally expressed in Paul's theology (1 Cor. 15:45). The first man Adam, heads the fallen race; the second man Christ, heads God's redeemed people (Rom. 5:12–19). The literal facts need emphasis here because the same interpretive assumptions that lead to denying a literal Adam have led consistent interpreters to deny a literal Christ. And to deny that the Christ came in literal flesh is a tragic error (1 John 4:1–3).

Although God created Adam first and Eve second, both the female and male were distinctly created by God; this is indicated by the third and fourth uses of *bārā'* (1:27). Both female and male were created in God's image (v. 27). Because they are made in God's image, human males and females are a unique "kind" distinct from the animals and ought never to be bestialized figuratively or literally. Furthermore, as if to answer theistic evolutionists who would have the woman as well as the man evolving from lower forms of animal life, the author repeats, "Male and female he created them" (v. 27). Clearly none of the female animals could serve as a companion for Adam nor as a mate for reproduction of humans. The animals were of different "kinds" and were to be ruled by man. In order to provide "a helper suitable for him" God created a woman, not by evolution from animals, but out of Adam (2:18, 20). That God made them male and female "at the beginning" is taught by no less than the Lord Jesus Christ, the supreme source of divine revelation (Matt. 19:4). This interpretation of the male and female in God's image is supported by the Logos and the inspired New Testament report of his words. In the context of progressive biblical revelation, then, it seems improbable that any hermeneutical device could successfully suggest that the account of God's creation of woman from man (2:23) teaches that Eve's body evolved (according to the theory of theistic evolutionists) from lower forms of animal life. Eve, no less than Adam, was created by God and created in the divine image, and so she is of no less inherent dignity and value than he.

The Length of Time Between the Creative Acts

What is at issue here is important. The question is not how long it took God supernaturally to speak things into existence. Whether God's supernatural creative acts are separated by twelve hours, twenty-four hours, or many thousands of years does not make them less miraculous. Creation did not need to take the omnipotent Creator six literal days. Any view that posits more than one divine creative act in a series in time is a progressive-creation view. A biblically based view of progressive creations with long periods intervening between, therefore, is by no means to be confused with views that may deny an actual series of supernatural creative acts (as in theistic evolution). The only issue at this point is the length of time between the supernatural creative acts.

At first reading the creation account seems to indicate that these six days of creative activity were twenty-four hours each. "Day" is usually literal, and elsewhere always so with a numeral. And the Sabbath command based on the six days of creation and one of rest seems to imply literal days (Exod. 20:11). Certainly God could have created all kinds of things in one week of seven twenty-four-hour days, or of twelve-hour days, or of one-second days. But the question is not in what time God *could* create the world, but in what time periods God in fact *did* create all the basic kinds of things in existence.

Further examination of Scripture indicates that the term "day" does not always designate twenty-four hours. The Hebrew term for "day" (*yôm*) can denote (1) the period of light in contrast to the period of darkness, (2) a period of twenty-four hours, (3) a point of time, (4) a year, or (5) a long "time." "Day" meant a month (Gen. 29:14), seven sabbaths of years (Lev. 25:8), "a long time" (forty years) in the desert (Josh. 24:7), and another "long time" when Israel was without the true God (2 Chron. 15:3).

In the context of Genesis 1 the solar system was not arranged to regulate days and nights until the fourth day, and then the "day" was not twenty-four hours, but the period of light in contrast to the darkness of the night (Gen. 1:18). This most literal use of "day" for, say, twelve hours of light as distinct from the period of darkness lacked a literal referent before the fourth creative period. Other indications in the Genesis account also suggest a period of time involved between the successive creative acts. "Let the land produce vegetation" (v. 11) and "let the water teem with living creatures" (v. 20). A period of time longer than twenty-four hours is also indicated between the creation of Adam and of Eve. Both male and female were created on the sixth "day" (v. 27). But before Eve was created, Adam's initial excitement with his new vocation of caring for the garden subsided long enough for him to become lonely (2:15, 18). And enough time then had to pass for all the kinds of animals and birds God created to pass before him for classifying and naming (2:19–20). Only after Adam had completed the encyclopedic task of naming the animals was Eve created (2:21–23).[58]

Although references to the "evening" and the "morning" on each of the creation days (Gen. 1) has seemed to many to indicate twenty-four-hour days, the literal meaning is not invariable even after the fourth day. Sometimes the beginning of the day is evening (Est. 4:16; Dan. 8:14) and sometimes morning (Deut. 28:66–67). And clearly figurative uses for longer periods of time do, in fact, occur. The brevity of human life is like that of grass, for "in the morning it springs up new, by evening it is dry and withered" (Ps. 90:5–6). As the original *Scofield Bible* note on Genesis 1:5 explained, "The use of 'evening' and 'morning' may be held to limit 'day' to the solar day; but the frequent parabolic use of natural phenomena may warrant the conclusion that each creative 'day' was a period of time marked off by a beginning and ending."

To hold that the "days" of creation are not literal, however, is not to say that they are merely literary devices for something other than periods of time. Although biblical usage of the term shows that a "day" may refer to an indefinite period of time, word studies do not reflect figurative uses of non-chronological sorts. The most probable conclusion is that the six consecutive creative acts were separated by long periods of time.

The cognitive and chronological purposes in Genesis 1 do not necessarily exclude other purposes such as providing a pattern to facilitate memorization. As J. Oliver Buswell, Jr., suggests, the parallel pattern of Genesis 1 (in contrast to the account in chapter 2), though not poetic, may serve a *mnemonic* purpose. As in some other passages of Scripture (e.g. Jesus' genealogy in Matthew 1 and Psalm 119), the items are arranged both in chronological sequence and "in convenient symmetrical patterns for memorizing."[59]

We may conclude with Edward J. Young that Genesis 1 is trustworthy history "intentionally patterned, chronological, of indeterminable length," showing "step by step how God changed the uninhabitable and unformed earth of verse two into the well-ordered world of verse thirty-two."[60]

Recent Creation and Flood Geology

Advocates of a recent creation observe that the most common use of "day" in the Old Testament is for a twenty-four-hour period, especially when numbered. When evening and morning are mentioned, literal days are most often in view. The Sabbath commandment seemingly refers to six literal days of work and one of rest. On such biblical arguments as these, many argue for twenty-four-hour days or one literal week of creation. Usually to this is added a case for a recent date of the creation of the universe and mankind from genealogies. Although this view opposes progressive creations separated by longer periods of time, the interpretive hypothesis involves a kind of progressive creation. The omnipotent God could have created everything in one day. Clearly he did not choose to do that. Rather he chose to produce the world in a series of creative acts. But the recent creationist view regards the possible figurative use of "day" for longer periods of time as less probable than that the progressive acts of creation marked off from each other by twenty-four-hour days.

For the public-school context the recent-creation view is called "scientific creationism." A textbook by that title seeks to deal "with all the important aspects of the creation-evolution question from a strictly scientific point of view, attempting to evaluate the physical evidence from the relevant scientific fields without reference to the Bible or other religious literature."[61]

The recent-creation hypothesis involves not only creation but also the curse and the Flood (both of which are biblically derived, are they not?). This threefold hypothesis seeks to explain indications of the permanence of all things, the Fall, and uniformity following the Flood. Morris explains these three worldwide events: (1) a period of six twenty-four-hour days of God's creation and the formation of all things, the completion and permanence of which are now manifest in the law of conservation of energy; (2) the rebellion of humans and the resultant curse of God on all mankind's dominion, formalized now in the law of increasing entropy; and (3) the world-destroying flood in the days of Noah, leaving the new world largely under the domain of natural uniformity. The main key to true interpretation of the physical data of the world is found in a recognition of the effects of creation, the curse, and the flood.[62]

Although by a strict scientific method one may observe some of the relevant data, one cannot observe the connection between evidence of a wise plan and great power and six twenty-four-hour days of creation apart from the scriptural teaching. Neither can anyone by a strict scientific method verify the moral connection of entropy with God's curse on human sin. Nor can an observed uniformity be connected with the Flood by a strict scientific observation. The judgments of the Flood and the curse are parts of the hypothesis supplied by biblical revelation. Other elements of the hypothesis also are revealed: an absolutely moral, all-wise, all-powerful, and triune God. Even the case for creation by the God of theism depends on some method of reasoning beyond the strictly observed data and scientific method. Scientists as such cannot observe, repeat, or control the actual acts of creation or of judgment by the invisible God.

The doctrine of creation cannot be reduced to the physical evidence for it, nor even to the minimal elements of a doctrine of God in a theism apart from special revelation. A fully Christian doctrine of origins integrates careful interpretation of all the relevant Scriptures, a historical survey of the doctrine in the church, a systematic formulation of the Scripture's teaching, an interaction with alternative views, and an application to life and ministry. So although the scientific creationist doctrine may provide some interesting data from science, it cannot, by its own limitations, provide an alternative full-orbed *theological* position for consideration.

As appealing as recent creationism may be to people giving priority to literal biblical interpretation, several additional difficulties with it need to be noted:

1. It tends to make an inferred recent date of the earth's origin a test of faith and fellowship, though the Bible teaches no explicit date of the origin of the earth.

2. Those who make the inference that Scripture teaches a recent date of creation unwisely assume that the genealogies provide a sufficient basis for computing an approximate date of the origin of mankind. But the gaps in a comparative study of them shows that they were not intended to be complete. Benjamin Warfield wrote, "In a word, the scriptural data leave us wholly without guidance in estimating the time which elapsed between the creation of the world and the deluge, and between the deluge and the call of Abraham."[63]

3. Recent-creationists infer literal twenty-four-hour days before the fourth day when literal days were not possible. This inference overlooks the probability of longer periods, at least for the first three days and for the state of emptiness (Gen. 1:2). Only after God appointed the sun to mark days and nights could there have been literal days. By assuming literal days before literal days were possible recent-creationists assume the point to be established. They fallaciously reason in a circle.

4. Granting that Adam and Eve were created mature, they may have appeared to be something like twenty-one or thirty years old rather than one-day-old infants. But it is hardly justifiable to take this highly probable conclusion and extrapolate it into a warrant for compressing billions of years into six thousand.[64]

5. Recent-creationist attempts to undermine the results of the several scientific methods of dating are insufficient to discount these methods entirely. The data for scientific dating are drawn from many different sources and show a significant degree of agreement.[65] Even granting a large margin of error—something comparable to a ratio of one day to thirty years of age for humans, the evidence for the age of God's world is difficult to harmonize with their interpretation of God's Word. For the recent-creationist hypothesis to fit all of the relevant data coherently, a vast amount of experimental data will be needed to overthrow data to the contrary.

6. With all the work that has been done by the Creation Research Society, this organization has yet to make a sufficiently conclusive case for the hypothesis that the Flood of Noah's day was the efficient cause of the bulk of the fossils and geological formations everywhere around the world. "The vast majority of professionally engaged geologists, both Christian and non-Christian, reject the arguments for flood geology as indefensible science."[66] Although according to the biblical account, the Flood seems repeatedly and

emphatically to have been universal, scientific creationists face a stupendous task if they are adequately to support the hypothesis that the one flood accounts for all the observable geological evidence by observable evidence from all areas universally.

Common Ground Among Creationists

Regardless of their intramural differences on the dating of the origin of the world and humans, all progressive creationists have much in common and should stand together where possible. Consider some of the crucial points on which creationists from several perspectives might constructively agree: (1) The cognitive significance of the early chapters of Genesis in providing an account of origins. (2) An original immediate, supernatural creation of matter-energy out of nothing. (3) An undeterminable length of time in which the earth was formless and empty. (4) A series of subsequent creative acts producing distinct kinds of things that can reproduce themselves (progressive creations, whatever the time between). (5) Development of varieties within kinds (microevolution). As Henry Morris says, "There is certainly room for variations within each kind."[67] (6) The improbability of the philosophical hypothesis of universal evolution (macroevolution). It has not been adequately confirmed and is not scientific fact. (7) The providential uniformity of nature's laws, but not in such a manner as to forbid miracles and catastrophic judgments. (8) Some truth in the view that catastrophic judgments like those following both the Fall and the unbridled immorality at the time of Noah have made some differences in the earth and the remains of human history.

Creationists should avoid making guesses on the date of the origin of the earth or of humankind a test of orthodoxy. Since the Scriptures do not explicitly teach dates for the origin of the earth or mankind, interpreters of Scripture should not make explicit dates normative. Differences on the length of the creation "days" should not become tests for dividing personal, church, or other Christian fellowships. Specifically, since "day" is used literally in Scripture, those who hold a day-age interpretation should respect those who consider the day to have been one of twenty-four hours. Similarly, since Scripture uses "day" and "evening" and "morning" figuratively and because "days" prior to the fourth could not have a literal meaning, people holding to a twenty-four-hour day ought to respect those who take it as a longer time.

APOLOGETIC INTERACTION

Relating Interpretations of God's Word and God's World

In volume 1 we found good reason for holding that what the Bible teaches God teaches, and so scriptural teaching is the final court of appeal in matters of Christian faith and practice. God also revealed some truth about himself in the things he made (Rom. 1:20). Hence *Integrative Theology* seeks to relate the truth of God's special revelation to truth of God's universal revelation. Where there appears to be contradiction between the truth of God's Word and the facts of God's world we give priority to the teaching of the inspired Scriptures. However, our initial impression of biblical teaching may not be adequately informed, as the interpretations of some church fathers show. Conflicts alleged between scientific understandings of nature and theological understandings of Scripture may be traced to misinterpretations of either nature or Scripture or both.

Students of theology need to distinguish the Scriptures as originally given (by the inspired writers) from the Scriptures as they are presently read (interpreted by readers of varying competence thousands of years later). From the hard data of scientific observation we may realize that the Bible does not teach that the earth is the center of the universe, nor that it has four corners, nor that the sun rises and sets. Theologians have been known to be wrong in their interpretations of Scripture! And all the conflicting views on creation cannot correctly match the biblical authors' intentions. That is why critical thinking in theology involves the rethinking of interpretative hypotheses, reexamining the biblical and scientific data and accepting the account that is most coherent. While doing so, we must keep in mind that the Bible was written for people generally in lay (newspaper) language, not in the technical scientific jargon of contributors to professional journals. But remember that what the Bible teaches about origins in common language is not false, but true.

Students of science must also distinguish the given data of nature from the interpretations taken from it. From reexaminations of the data, scientific theories also have been discovered to be untrue or in need of revision. Scientists have learned that the atom is complex and divisible, not uncuttable as formerly thought. Scientists differ regarding the age of human life on earth and of the age of the earth and the solar system. Scientific views that prevail today may in the future be regarded improbable. Hence we must avoid undue dogmatism concerning scientific evidence. However, revolutions in scientific paradigms, reported by Thomas S. Kuhn,[68] do not justify a total renunciation of a cognitive use of scientific evidence in favor of a sheer pragmatic use as in Gordon Clark's *Philosophy of Science and Belief in God*.[69] The reason why some theories work is that they have a relationship to reality. Open-minded scholars in science as well as theology are always humble before new evidence and are willing to revise their prior theories in the light of more coherent explanations.

Genuine scientific advances begin with the premise that there is order or regularity throughout the universe and that critically evaluated human observations of it can be meaningful. Even though a round coin looks to be of a different shape by an observer directly above it and by an observer in some other place in the room, the relative perspectives occur in actuality and can be checked from other standpoints. Relative perspectives on a coin do not make the existence of the coin less conclusive. Naturalistic scientists merely assume an ordered world and the ability of the human mind to make sense of it. In a Christian world view those are not *ad hoc* assumptions or matters such as those of Kant's practical reason having no theoretical justification. The intelligent Creator has made humans in his image to know, love, and serve him and to rule in the world as accountable stewards. Hence we have good reason for believing that the categories of our minds are like those of the Creator's mind and world. So we have solid reasons for faith in an ordered world and in our observations of it and the reliability of our limited and correctable knowledge that is critically tested and confirmed.

By similar testing and confirmation we have identified divine revelation in Christ and the inspired Writings. When our interpretations of them, limited and correctable as they may be, have been carefully subjected to criteria of truth, we have a solid base for faith. The dangers of misinterpretation are less for the linguistic revelation than for the revelation in nature and historical events. In both fields we have the same criteria of truth, but in investigations of Scripture we have in addition a host of hermeneutical checks and balances. So if irresolvable contradictions arise, we give precedence to critical interpretations of the written Word above our critical understandings of the changing consensus in physics, geology, biology, and astronomy.

Common Ground Among Evolutionists and Creationists

Both nontheistic evolutionists and theistic creationists, because of their basic humanness, can communicate ethically with one another about both their similarities and their differences. They have several beliefs in common: (1) The universe as we know it is not eternal; it had a beginning in the finite past, and it did not originate in 4004 B.C. (2) On the one hand, development (evolution) within the "kinds" of living organisms has occurred. On the other hand, great gaps in the evidence for transitional varieties of life remain (sometimes labeled sudden "emergences" of new species or "quantum leaps" in evolution or new creations of God). (3) Humanity is the highest form of life on earth, and some the earliest fossil finds are fully human. (4) People properly classify kinds of existing beings. (5) Both the evolutionist and the creationist comprehensive explanations of the origins of existing things do not fully explain the nature of those things.

The two accounts of origins also have important differences. Where they differ, we must ask, Does a nontheistic evolutionary theory or does a doctrine of progressive creation provide the more probable interpretation?

Ultimate Origins

Nontheistic scientists and theists differ in their approach to the question of the ultimate origin of anything at all, such as matter-energy. A pure empiricist does not even address questions beyond observation and repetition. Scientists *as scientists* properly avoid even suggesting answers to ultimate questions. Becoming philosophers or theologians, however, scientists may propose theories of ultimate sources. No scientific observer was present at the beginning, and the big bang cannot be repeated under controlled conditions according to a strict scientific method. Scientists playing unscientific roles may speculate about primeval gases or energy. But these had a beginning in the finite past and require more ultimate explanations. Ultimately naturalists have to come up with such entities out of nothing without a creator. In contrast, in apologetics and theology there are good reasons for belief in the eternal God's intelligent purpose and great power to create energy and the entire universe.

Naturalistic speculations about ultimate origins do well to avoid fantasies about ultimate origins like the contradictory nonsense of American philosopher Charles Sanders Pierce:

> In the beginning—infinitely remote—there was a chaos of unpersonalized feeling, which being without connection or regularity would properly be without existence. This feeling sporting here and there in pure arbitrariness, would have started the germ of a generalizing tendency. Its other sportings would be evanescent, but this would have a growing virtue. Thus the tendency to habit would be started; and from this with the other principles of evolution, all the regularities of the universe would be evolved.[70]

The imagination may suggest hypotheses to be tested, but it is no substitute for the verifiable and verified proposals of philosophers, scientists, and theologians. A growing agreement has developed between science and theology, at least on the fact of a beginning of the universe in the finite past. Aristotle's notion that the cosmos is ungenerated and indestructible is not commonly received. And the more recent "steady state" theory has been losing ground. Most astronomers now hold that the universe had an instant of origin in a fireball explosion 15 or 20 billion years ago. The "shrapnel" from that big bang is still flying outward from the focus of the blast. One of those fragment clusters is the galaxy we call the Milky Way. One of its billions of stars is the earth's sun with its tiny orbiting planets. And one of these planets is the earth. Empirical scientists assume that every consequent has antecedents, but they fail to propose a cause of the big bang that began the universe or the orderly way in which the "fallout" fell into place. "Adopting, therefore, the big bang scenario, it would seem that we have little choice but to assume that the universe went bang in a remarkably orderly way, even though an accidental creation would, with a probability that is virtual certainty, produce a totally disordered universe."[71]

The faith and assumptions of the scientists, Robert Jastrow explains, indicate that the scientists cannot bear the thought of a natural phenomenon that cannot be explained. Their religious faith in natural causation, Jastrow argues, is violated by three lines of evidence supporting a beginning: the outward motions of the galaxies, the laws of thermodynamics, and the life story of the stars. Unable to discover with unlimited time and money the cause of the origin of the universe, the scientist as such ought to lose confidence in the exclusiveness of his method and naturalistic presuppositons.

> For the scientist who has lived by his faith in the power of reason, the story ends like a bad dream. He has scaled the mountains of ignorance; he is about to conquer the highest peak; as he pulls himself over the final rock, he is greeted by a band of theologians who have been sitting there for centuries.[72]

The explanation of ultimate origins that makes the most sense is creation by an intelligent, powerful God who has life in himself.

The Origin of Life

The theistic and nontheistic hypotheses radically differ also in their accounts of the origin of life. Today many scientists think that living organisms emerged gradually from nonliving material even though all indications are that life always arises from other life. So noncreationists sometimes suggest that life arose by a kind of spontaneous generation; theists, however, propose creation by an intelligent transcendent Being.

To decide between the two hypotheses, we need to understand something of the complexity of the simplest biological life. Biomolecules contain proteins that consist of chains of amino acids linked together in a certain way. Amino acids are compounds of nitrogen, hydrogen, carbon, and oxygen that combine in various ways to form the proteins making up living matter. Eight or ten amino acids are regarded as the building blocks of the proteins that make up the bulk of the cells of the human body. To achieve the proper orderings of the amino acids, enzymes speed up the chemical reactions that make life possible for biopolymers. A typical enzyme has a chain of some two hundred links with about twenty possibilities for each link. Hence the numbers of useless arrangements for one enzyme is enormous, more than the number of atoms in all the galaxies visible in the largest telescopes. This correlation exists for one enzyme, and there are upwards of two thousand of them, mainly serving different purposes.[73] So how did the complex situation of life get to where we find it to be? A biologist faces the problem of accounting for life with a vast amount of information in a very intricate formula (involving many steps with precise timing).

The theory of spontaneous generation without intelligent planning and direction lacks evidence in its support and so is highly improbable. A theory of gradual change from simple enzymes to complex ones exacerbates the problem. The time involved in gradual change can work against life, rather than contributing to it. The vast majority of mutations are harmful to the species, not helpful to it. Hence Sir Fred Hoyle found it to be "apparent that the facts point overwhelmingly against life being of terrestrial origin."[74] Hoyle then explored an interstellar source of life, but observed, "Try as I would, I couldn't convince myself that even the whole universe would be sufficient to find life by random processes—by what are called the blind forces of nature. The thought occurred to me one day that the human chemical industry doesn't take a chance on its products by throwing chemicals at random into a stewpot. To suggest to the research department at Du Pont that it should proceed in such a fashion would be thought ridiculous."[75]

What is the simplest explanatory theory to account for the origin of life on earth? "By far the simplest way to arrive at the correct sequences of amino acids in the enzyme would be by thought, not by random processes. . . . Rather than accept the fantastically small probability of life having arisen through the blind forces of nature, it seemed better to suppose that the origin of life was a deliberate intellectual act." Hoyle concludes:

> A common sense interpretation of the facts suggests that a superintellect has monkeyed with physics, as well as with chemistry and biology, and that there are no blind forces worth speaking about in nature. the numbers one calculates from the facts seem to me so overwhelming as to put this conclusion almost beyond question.[76]

Further complicating the problems for theories of the spontaneous generation of life is entropy. Entropy expresses in a word the result of the second law of thermodynamics. The first law of thermodynamics asserts that the total energy of the universe (as a closed system) is constant, neither increasing nor decreasing with time. The second law asserts that any process decreases the amount of energy available for work. Although on earth there may be a local replacement of useful energy, it is always at the expense of an overall decrease of useful energy in the universe. The energy for useful work in the universe, including our earth, is being depleted. If energy is not fed into the universe from beyond it, the processes in the system will eventually terminate and all life on earth will be snuffed out. Nontheists assume that the universe is a closed system into which no energy is introduced by God; therefore, on their view all life will eventually suffer a cold death. Ecologists warn that humanity faces a steady decrease in energy available for conversion into work. Even recycling increases entropy. Even though it retards the loss rate, it uses more available energy in the overall environment than it replaces.

The second law of thermodynamics becomes severely problematic for any view that suggests that life arose spontaneously through the random interaction of natural forces. A mere appeal to *open* system thermodynamics on earth does little good. "What must be done is to advance a workable model of *how* the available energy can be coupled to do the required work."[77] After an examination of scientific theories, these scientists conclude, "The primary difficulty was not lack of suitable energy sources. Rather it was both a lack of sufficient energy mobilizing means to harness the energy to the specific task of building biopolymers and a lack of means to generate the proper sequence of, say, amino acids in a polypeptide to get biological function."[78] They add, "There is no hint in our experience of any mechanistic means of supplying the necessary configurational entropy work. Enzymes and human intelligence, however, do it routinely."[79] Again, "Many facts have come to light in the past three decades of experimental inquiry into life's beginning. With each passing year the criticism has gotten stronger. The advance of science itself is what is challenging the notion that life arose on earth by spontaneous (in a thermodynamic sense) chemical reactions."[80]

> Over the years a slowly emerging line or boundary has appeared which shows observationally the limits of what can be expected from matter and energy left to themselves, and what can be accomplished only through what Michael Polanyi has called "a profoundly informative intervention." When it is acknowledged that most so-called prebiotic simulation experiments actually owe their success to the crucial but *illegitimate* role of the investigator, a new and fresh phase of the experimental approach to life's origin can then be entered.[81]

These scientists conclude that "the undirected flow of energy through a primordial atmosphere and ocean is at present a woefully inadequate explanation for the incredible complexity associated with even simple living systems, and is probably wrong."[82]

Another way of understanding the difficulty atheists face is to recall that although living things today reduce the entropy of the earth's ecosystem, this does not violate the second law, because it is at the expense of an overall increase in the entropy of the universe. Living things are able to continue to process available energy and increase entropy, however, only because incredibly complex (low entropy) structures already exist that permit them to do so. An irresolvable problem faces nontheists—how to account for an initial reduction in entropy when life with its increased complexity first appeared supposedly by pure chance. As Harold F. Blum asks, "How, when no life existed, did substances come into being which today, are absolutely essential to living systems, yet which can only be formed by those systems?"[83]

Could life have formed by chance, given the addition of aeons of time? Given sufficient time, it may be argued, even wildly improbable events become virtual certainties. Tossing a coin ten times may not produce five heads in a row. But tossing the coin a hundred million times dramatically increases the probability of five heads in a row. The analogy does not fit, however, because, unlike a coin toss, the chemical reactions necessary to form a living creature are reversible. The addition of great ages of time simply increases the probability that any complex organic molecule will be destroyed. In other words, if one tosses a series of five heads, the noted outcome is irreversible. Molecular chains such as proteins, however, are relatively fragile. Without some sort of protection over a period of time they are far more likely to spontaneously disintegrate than to form. Time is the enemy, not the friend, of spontaneous abiogenesis (the origin of life from nonlife).

Despite facile appeals to "mutation steps," the problems facing the critic of creation who believes that life arose rapidly or through a series of spontaneous steps from nonliving compounds are extremely serious. Robert Jastrow has put the issue succinctly:

> Perhaps the appearance of life on earth is a miracle. Scientists are reluctant to accept that view, but their choices are

> limited; either life was created on the earth by the will of a being outside the grasp of scientific understanding, or it evolved on our planet spontaneously through chemical reactions occurring in nonliving matter lying on the surface of the planet.[84]

Since none of us was there to observe the first living organism, both views involve faith in what was unseen. One can believe in spontaneous generation despite well-established natural laws that render it so highly improbable as to be unthinkable, or one can believe the well-attested revelation of the Lord of all.

The authors of *Fundamentals of Classical Thermodynamics,* Gordon J. Van Wylen and Richard E. Sonntag, cautiously raise questions about the beginning and the end of the natural world as we know it, and whether it is a closed system to which the second law of thermodynamics applies as a whole. They acknowledge that "it is impossible to give conclusive answers to these questions on the basis of the second law of thermodynamics alone." They themselves, however, see the second law of thermodynamics as "man's description of the prior and continuing work of a Creator, who also holds the answer to the future destiny of man and the universe."[85]

Another who looks at the implications of entropy for our past and future with less caution is Jeremy Rifkin. He said,

> It's strange indeed that we in the modern world are willing to see the history of the universe as beginning with a perfect state and moving toward decay and chaos and yet continue to cling to the notion that earthly history follows the exact opposite course, i.e., that it is moving from a state of chaos to a "progressively" more ordered world.[86]

Although Rifkin takes notice of a Christian world view,[87] he hopes to escape the ultimate randomness of entropy by resorting to a God *within* the cosmos experienced in a collective consciousness[88] or Buddhist enlightenment.[89] He fails to see that even such a monistic reality must incorporate entropy. The more plausible account lies in a God *beyond* the cosmos with its entropy, in the transcendent Creator of all. The transcendence of the particular by union with universal energy does not escape the dismal end of entropy. For that, one needs communion with the eternal Lord over all.

Distinguishing Species

Theists and nontheists may also differ on the real divisions between species. The distinguishing line can be drawn in a way harmonious with either an evolutionary or a creation doctrine. In classifying living beings, evolutionists often emphasize similarities and magnify incidental or accidental differences in proposing a million or a million-and-half species in order to "find" intermediate forms. If, however, by "species" we mean organisms with the same essential qualities, in spite of numerous accidental variations, there could not be intermediate forms.[90]

For the crucial example, shall we classify human beings as different from animals essentially or only accidentally? Do people differ from animals only in degree or also in kind? The issue turns out to be as much a matter of principles of classification as it does of observation. Definition of the human species is as much philosophy or theology as science. And the classification may depend on a prior assumption that all reality is ultimately nonpersonal. Only the mind of humans, however, can even frame the question of an impersonal or personal Source. Only humans are responsible morally. So humans are essentially unique. The hypothesis of an ultimately impersonal universe inadequate to account for: (1) the unique personhood of the evolutionists themselves, (2) their nonnegotiable ideal of intellectual honesty, (3) their universal and necessary disapproval of injustice, and (4) their wise hesitancy to approve an ethic of the survival of the fittest in human conduct. The value of human personal existence in accord with moral norms is more adequately explained by theism.

Fossil Groupings and Gaps

Of the two hypotheses, creation and evolution, which accounts most coherently for the fossil groupings and gaps? The fossilized remains of former life indicate that all of the major groups of animals originated simultaneously, they were similar to animals of the present day, and they have maintained their relations with each other back to the time when the first evidences of life appeared. There is not the slightest evidence that any of the major phyla or groups arose from any other.[91]

A nontheistic evolutionary philosophy that believes that all living things, including humans, are derived from nonorganic energy-matter through gradual, minor changes fails to fit the facts. Seven major evolutionary assumptions, G. A. Kerkut has shown, have insufficient or no evidence supporting them: (1) Something (energy-matter) came from nothing at all. (2) Nonliving things gave rise to living things. (3) Spontaneous generation occurred only once. (4) Single-celled organisms (protozoa) developed gradually into many-celled organisms (metazoa). (5) Viruses, bacteria, plants, animals, and minerals are all interrelated. (6) The various vertebrates are interrelated. (7) Invertebrates gradually produced vertebrates. (8) Fish, amphibia, reptiles, birds, mammals, and mankind are all interrelated.[92] But humans, most evolutionists agree, are on one diverging branch from that of the apes, both being developed from an undiscovered allegedly common ancestor. Writing in an international science series of volumes, Kerkut found that these seven beliefs are unsupported by actual empirical evidence and are projected on extremely limited data of a circumstantial sort. More popularly, Luther D. Sunderland points up the lack of transitional forms in the macroevolutionary scheme from fish to amphibian, amphibian to reptile, reptile to bird, reptile to mammal.[93]

At each of these gaps a theistic view of origins derived from the data of special revelation provides a coherent account. (1) Something (finite energy-matter) comes from nothing (*ex nihilo*) by the power of an eternal God in accord with his intelligent plan. (2) Life is given to the kinds of organisms by the eternal Creator, who has life in himself. The kinds of living things need be created only once, for they can reproduce. (3) So God created single-cell and many-celled organisms, the basic kinds of viruses, bacteria, plants, animals—invertebrate and vertebrate. (4) and he created man—male and female. Thus God created the kinds of fish, amphibia, animals, and humans.

Sudden Novelties

Where the model of nontheistic evolution has traditionally pictured a gradual progressive process over a long period of time, a theistic model includes *both gradual development* within the limits of the kinds *and sudden creative novelty*. If questions remain about differences developing (evolving under God's providence) within the created "kinds," consider the many varieties of human beings, yet all one species (*homo sapiens*) from one set of original parents (Acts 17:26).

Even where the case for biological evolution is the strongest, in hypothesizing that all life on earth is based on essentially the same genetic code and that given the right combination of environmental influences the varieties of life will inevitably arise, it *lacks sufficient time* for the development of all the varieties of life forms that exist.

According to Darwin's gradualistic model, "it may metaphorically be said that natural selection is daily and hourly scrutinizing, throughout the world, the slightest variations; rejecting those that are bad, preserving and adding up all that are good; silently and insensibly working, *whenever and wherever opportunity offers,* at the improvement of each organic being in relation to its organic and inorganic conditions of life."[94] So gradual is this process that Darwin admits that it is unobservable. He continues by saying, "We see nothing of these slow changes in progress, until the hand of time has marked the lapse of ages, and then so imperfect is our view into long-past geological ages, that we see only that the forms of life are now different from what they formerly were."[95]

However, the fossil evidence has failed to show essential changes in the species. The earliest remains of living creatures continue to turn up with the same characteristics as they have today. Embarrassed by the quality of the fossil record in his day Darwin said, it "displayed discrete species that showed virtually no change in shape between their first and last appearances." The earliest finds fall into existing groups today. A. H. Clark has suggested that from the single cell all of the major phyla developed simultaneously and at once in every possible direction![96] Although geologists should find an abundance of missing links shunted aside by natural selection, these have not appeared. There are embarrassingly few fossil fragments, and huge gaps still exist in the fossil record. The human fossil record is the sketchiest of all.

A Punctuated Process?

In 1954 Ernst Mayr suggested that the sudden appearance of evolutionary novelties in the fossil evidence might reflect the actual pattern of evolution rather than the extreme imperfection of the record. This has led to a radically different *punctuational model* of evolution, which holds that the "budding" of one species from another may involve sudden, rather than gradual, change. Some such "speciation events," not all, accomplish major changes, and they account for most evolution in the history of life.[97]

After documenting several examples of fixed species, Stanley presents "a message to geneticists:"

> The abundant evidence that species of animals and plants have remained stable in form while groups to which they belong have experienced substantial evolutionary change can be translated into the simple language of population genetics. It is now apparent that barring its extinction, a typical established species of mammals, marine invertebrates, land plants, or insects has undergone little measurable change in form during at least one hundred thousand generations, and often a million or 10 million generations.[98]

Why has an average species undergone little evolution in the course of millions of generations? Why are well-established species resistant to change? And why, in the past forty thousand years or more in Europe has human anatomy undergone extremely little change? Darwin's gradual model of evolution provides neither the time nor the mechanism to answer this question. Others describe the phenomenon within a large evolutionary framework, but fail to answer these questions.

Spokespeople for the punctuational

model propose "evolution by sudden changes," "catastrophic selection," or "quantum speciation events."[99] We may be excused for thinking that a figurative use of "budding" and a tautologous assertion that "evolution" (essential change) is brought to pass by "sudden change" cover an astounding ignorance of any satisfactory explanatory hypothesis. It used to be popular to charge theists with believing without evidence in the "God of the gaps" in scientific knowledge. Now scientists without evidence seem to be defending an "evolution of the gaps!" Stanley continues to believe in evolution, but not a gradual evolution. A theory that essential changes occur through inexplicable, sudden catastropic phenomena remains the same as naturalistic evolutionary theories only in denying the explanatory power of God's creative plan and power. After long years of research, unbridgeable gaps remain in the scientific picture.

Robert Jastrow explained,

> Theologians generally are delighted with the proof that the Universe had a beginning, but astonomers are curiously upset. Their reactions provide an interesting demonstration of the response of the scientific mind—supposedly a very objective mind—when evidence uncovered by science itself leads to a conflict with the articles of faith in our profession. It turns out that the scientist behaves the way the rest of us do when our beliefs are in conflict with the evidence. We become irritated, we pretend the conflict does not exist, or we paper it over with meaningless phrases."[100]

Henri Bergson concluded that a gradual accumulation of acquired characteristics fails to explain the sudden appearance of multicellular animals or organisms like a vertebrate eye, for which any survival or adaptation required the functional whole at once, not individual parts over a long period of time. To account for the sudden novelties in nature, Bergson turned to metaphysics. He claimed to be intuitively aware of a vital impetus (*elan vital*) pushing him on in his own development as a person with a continued identity in time. Bergson extrapolated from his interpretation of his intuitions to "an original impetus of life that pervades the whole evolutionary process." Accordingly, Bergson viewed the evolutionary process creatively rather than mechanistically.[101] However, unless the "Vital Force" has foreknowledge of alternative directions and wisdom to choose the best ends in accord with what is just and loving, there is no reason to imagine that its direction is commendable. Bergson made recalcitrant matter the source of evil that resisted the "Life Force" at every turn. He envisioned the Life Force constantly striving to transcend the physical limitations of the stage it has reached. Like the Gnostic and Hindu traditions, Bergsonian endless, impersonal, emergent evolution contradicts the data of divine revelation concerning God, matter, humanity, morality, and spirituality.

The Future of Evolution?

Even with the paucity of evidence for an all-encompassing physical evolution, some now hope for an *evolution of human consciousness*. After seven years of traveling to lecture on the implications of the new physics, Fritjof Capra reports, that the nineteen sixties and seventies have generated a whole series of social movements that all seem to go in the same direction. The rising concern with ecology, the strong interest in mysticism, the growing feminist awareness, and the rediscovery of holistic approaches to health and healing are all manifestations of the same evolutionary trend.[102]

Note the leap from physical data alleged to support biological evolution to an evolution of thought spiritually (involving mystical experience) and morally (involving feminist awareness). If a biological evolution were supported with high probability, that would not justify a moral or spiritual evolution. Studying the relation of consciousness to physics and biology, David Bohm suggested a model of all reality from a physical hologram. Each of the parts of a hologram in some sense contains the whole, the whole being enfolded in each of its parts.[103] Fallaciously, then, Fritjof Capra and others reason from that physical analogy to the pantheism of the Vedas: "I am That, you are That, and all this is That." Analogies may illustrate points otherwise confirmed, but analogies of themselves prove nothing. Physical holograms confirm nothing about the relationship of the creation to the Creator morally or spiritually.

Evolutionary theories in the New Age movements of eastern, occult, and new-consciousness contexts, abandon the classical ideal of scientific objectivity[104] and create their own world. Allegedly New Age scientists become increasingly conscious of their alleged inner divine energy while experiencing the dance of Shiva. Those who have difficulty making the transition from the former biological evolution to the evolution of the One Consciousness can be helped along the way as Carlos Castenada and Capra himself were, by "power plants."[105] Mystical experiences themselves, whether induced by mantras or drugs, are often thought to prove an evolutionary spiritualism involving pantheism and reincarnation. By definition mystical experiences are noncognitive. So the reincarnationist interpretations given them afterward are mere hypotheses subject to critical investigation. As pantheistic interpretations of human experience, they do not fit the facts as well as classical Christian theism.

From the dubious quantum leap from the new physics to mysticism comes "a radical reformulation of the most fundamental aspects of reality . . . that seemed to turn common sense on its head and find closer accord with mysticism than materialism."[106] Undermining objective truth, the relativism of Hindu and Buddhist doctrines of maya undercut scientific as well as specially revealed theological truths. The radical distinction between Creator and creature is erased encouraging selfishly inclined sinners to fall victim to narcissistic self-deification. And this "blasphemy" of these humans visualizing themselves as gods is uttered in the name of evolution to a "higher" state of consciousness!

Concluding the apologetic section, we propose that the most coherent and probable explanation of origins is a biblically based progressive series of supernatural creative acts. Since the dates of the origin of neither the earth nor humanity are conclusively settled by Scripture or science, the dates ought not be the prime emphasis. A series of creations coherently accounts for the ultimate origin of anything at all, the beginning of life, the distinctiveness and persistence of the "kinds" of beings, the continuities and novelties in the fossil evidence, and above all for the uniqueness of human beings.

RELEVANCE FOR LIFE AND MINISTRY

Bow to the Sovereign Creator

"To know the Creator," Emil Brunner explained, "means to become conscious, first and foremost, that God is sovereign Lord. Because he is absolute Lord he [Christ] is 'above' all and 'before' all. The One who originates all things and is himself originated by none; he is the one who determines all things and is determined by none." Brunner added, "Schleiermacher's phrase 'absolute dependence' is right, indeed it is excellent. . . . The idea of creation means that I, together with the whole of nature to which I belong, am absolutely dependent upon God, while he, on the other hand, is dependent neither upon me nor upon it."[107]

As dependents we bow before God in humility. "What do you have that you did not receive? And if you did receive it, why do you boast as though you did not?" (1 Cor. 4:7). We have not created even those unique abilities wherein we differ from others. Whether we are like Paul, Peter, or Apollos, we ought not take pride in one against another (1 Cor. 4:6). We all need each other's fellowship and gifts. "Every good and perfect gift is from above" (James 1:17). Humbly bow before the source of all being ontologically. "Praise God from whom all blessings flow, praise him all creatures here below."

Because God first loved you, bow before the Creator in love. The world of men and women has derived ultimately from God's *agapē* (love). God did not have to create anything. As Emil Brunner said, "God created the world because he willed to communicate himself . . . as the loving God he willed to give himself to others. . . . The love of God is the *causa finalis* of the creation."[108] How, then, should humans respond? Our Creator desires nothing from us more than our love (Matt. 22:35–38). It is the first and greatest commandment. What is your ultimate love, care, or concern? We ought not seek first our pleasure, money, or success. God made us to love him, and our hearts are restless until they find their highest fulfillment in him.

Those who love the Creator ought also love all he created in his image. Although all things were made by God, only humans were made in the divine likeness. By creation all people are "children" of God, and God is the ultimate Father of the being of all persons (Acts 17:28–29). Even though God is not the moral and spiritual Father of all (John 8:44), every human being created and sustained by God deserves to be treated with respect, justice, consideration, and love. The second greatest commandment from the Creator is to love our neighbors as ourselves (Matt. 22:39). This text allows no exception for those of different racial or social backgrounds. Indeed, as Creator God is the Father of all, and all humans are children of God (Acts 17:28–29). "So in everything, do to others what you would have them do to you, for this sums up the Law and the Prophets" (Matt. 7:12). In all human relationships creationists seek to exhibit their love for God's image-bearers by keeping that golden rule.

Refuse to Deify Nature

Although creationists love every good gift the Creator has made, they will not bow to nature as God. Pantheism and panentheism tend to idolize the world by including it within the deity. Christian theists disallow worship of any part of the universe or even the whole of it as God. We ought to value creation highly as a great achievement of the most creative Being who is. But the powers of the earth's processes and energy, whether physical or psychic, are not to be deified. Theists avoid worshiping and serving the creature rather than the Creator. The godly in Scripture never blur the line between Creator and creature. To make "mother nature" or the whole of creation our ultimate concern insults the Creator.

The prophets exposed the futility of those who were more terrified by the signs in the sky, such as astrological configurations (Jer. 10:2), than by God's Word. The endless counsel of the magicians, sorcerers, and astrologers month after month, Isaiah observed, "has only worn you out" (Isa. 47:12–

13). The prophet added that they cannot save anyone from what is coming, they are "like stubble; the fire will burn them up. They cannot even save themselves from the power of the flame. . . . Each of them goes on in his error; there is not one that can save you" (vv. 14–15). Jeremiah displayed the absurdity of worshiping our own artistic works: The idol-makers select a tree, cut it down, and shape it with a chisel. They adorn it with silver and gold, and fasten it with hammer and nails so that it will not totter. "Like a scarecrow in a melon patch, their idols cannot speak; they must be carried because they cannot walk. Do not fear them; they can do no harm nor can they do any good" (Jer. 10:3–5). In dramatic contrast the living God wisely and lovingly chooses his people, calls them out of the world, warns them of future danger, and acts in their behalf. People trusting the Creator who knows the future, hears, speaks, and acts need not fear (Isa. 44:6–10).

The creationists' ultimate concern goes beyond harmony with nature to harmony with its transcendent Creator. As appreciative as we are of a homemade pie, we do not thank the pie, we thank its maker! While seeking God's kingdom in nature, we do not confuse God with the power exhibited in the ocean, the mountains, the atom, or space. By a sound doctrine of God we must always direct our adoration beyond the things that are made to their Creator. We give our ultimate honor to the Lord of all. We ascribe the glory, not to the universe, but to its great Architect and Builder. We bow to the Ruler of all by actively aligning ourselves with his providential and redemptive purposes. From this point of view we can understand what the world is by Creation and the Fall and how God's purpose is finally revealed and recovered in Jesus Christ.[109]

Use Physical Things for Good, not Evil

At Creation God pronounced all things "good," including the bodies of both the male and the female (Gen. 1:31). Neither the matter-energy nor the desires of our bodies are inherently evil. Our bodies (*sōmata*) are not the fundamental source of our problems. With all the frustrations of our finitude, our deepest need is not to be free from our physical, spatial, temporal, and energy limitations. We need not engage in bodily aceticism or self-flaggelation. Neither need we be asexual. Our bodily abilities are like instruments that God's fallen image-bearers can use either for the ends of pride, greed, and lust or to please our Creator, who has our best interests at heart. Our perverse desires and wills spring from our depraved hearts. Our fallen nature (*sarx,* flesh) initiates unjust and immoral uses of our bodies. Although everything God created is good in itself, fallen people can use their bodies for evil as well as good.

We can use every material thing we possess also either to please or displease God. How can we use our material acquisitions in a way that will please the Creator? The general pattern comes out in the three conditions Paul taught Timothy (1 Tim. 4:4–5): "Everything God created is good, and nothing is to be rejected, if (1) it is received with thanksgiving, because (2) it is consecrated by the word of God and (3) prayer" [parentheses mine]. Accept with thanksgiving everything you have: your food, clothing, dishes, furniture, books, magazines, television, sports equipment, and means of transportation. Determine to use all for purposes consistent with God's Word and set apart all you have to glorify God by a prayer of dedication.

Singles may choose to give up a spouse for the sake of God's kingdom (Matt. 19:12; 1 Cor. 7:25–38). But those who receive divine revelation do not *command* abstinence from sexual intercourse. The sexual union of husband and wife is neither morally evil nor shameful, but a beautiful portrayal of divine love when expressing the partners' mutual faith, love, and covenanted commitments to each other. Hence arguments for the celibacy of spiritual leaders fail whether in Hinduism or Buddhism or Roman Catholicism. People can marry to the glory of the Creator.

Some first-century people also imagined that the more spiritual ought to be vegetarians. Although created by God, animals are not God and are not made in the image of God. So it is not morally wrong to kill them for food. "Everything that lives and moves [animals and birds] will be food for you. Just as I gave you the green plants, I now give you everything" (Gen. 9:3). The sixth commandment (not to kill) does not forbid hunting animals or fighting justifiable wars through which God providentially brought deserved judgment on morally corrupt nations. This commandment is more accurately translated in the *New International Version*, "You shall not murder" (Exod. 20:13). The intentional taking of human life is immoral because "in the image of God has God made man" (Gen. 9:6).

Although creationists have liberty to eat meat, there may be occasions when they do not. People are not to eat meat that has its lifeblood still in it (Gen. 9:4). For good reasons in their situation Hebrews had dietary laws also forbidding eating meat designated "unclean" (Lev. 11; cf. Acts 10:9–16). In New Testament times, however, Christians are not to reject anything as common that God made (Acts 11:9), nor should they waste it. Although creationists are free to eat meat, Jesus taught that food was not the most important thing in life (Matt. 6:25). Paul sharply rebuked lazy gluttons (Titus 1:12–13). A "companion of gluttons disgraces his father" (Prov. 28:7; 23:20–21). Like any other material thing, meat may be taken if received with thanksgiving, eaten moderately according to God's Word, and dedicated to purposes honoring to God. But if eating meat would cause a brother to stumble, creationists willingly give up their right to eat meat (Rom. 14:13–21; 1 Cor. 8:8–13). In India and some other countries Christians give up their right to eat meat because their Hindu relatives think they became Christians in order to become meat-eaters.

Avoid Addictions

Although some have imagined that Christians are commanded totally to abstain from wine and other "strong drinks" made from fruit or grain, wine as a creation of God is no more inherently evil than meat. Creationists have liberty to drink wine so long as it is used for good ends (1 Tim. 4:4–5). The psalmist praised God for providing wine that "gladdens the heart of man" (Ps. 104:15). For that reason wine was often used at celebrations. At the wedding in Cana Jesus turned water into wine (John 2:1–11). The Lord frequented dinners where wine was served, and this led to allegations that he was a glutton and a drunkard (Matt. 11:19). The situation of these dinners and the possibility of drunkenness makes a translation of unfermented "grape juice" improbable. Even so by eating and drinking with tax collectors and sinners Jesus did not become a glutton or a drunkard. The research of Anderson Spickard, M.D., indicates that "Nations and communities that drink only at the dinner table and do not tolerate public drunkenness do not have high rates of alcoholism."[110]

People in Old Testament times took wine beneficially also as a depressant or narcotic to alleviate pain (Prov. 31:6). In the first century wine mixed with myrrh served as an anesthetic.[111] People offered this to Jesus on the cross to ease the pain (Matt. 27:34). Paul encouraged Timothy to "use a little wine" for medicinal purposes (1 Tim. 5:23). A "little wine" may be taken, like other addictive substances, when medically advisable. Creationists should consider alcoholic drinks like other material things. Whether Christians eat or drink, they do it to the glory of God (1 Cor. 10:31).

Although alcoholic drinks in moderation can serve good purposes, "alcohol abuse" expresses voluntary disregard for God's precepts. Voluntary drunkenness violates emphatic biblical teaching (Luke 21:34; 1 Cor. 5:11; Gal. 5:21; Eph. 5:18). It reflects disrespect for the wisdom of God's commands and, like all flagrant disobedience, separates us from God's fellowship. Doubtless the Bible forbids drunkenness also because alcohol harms the abusers' minds and bodies, damages their home lives, and interferes with their jobs. For our good God disallows drunkenness. But God forgives the sin of drunkenness as he forgives disobedience to any other biblical commands when we call it the sin it is against God, others, and ourselves, repent of it, and turn from it.

Persistent alcohol abuse can develop with little if any notice into an involuntary addiction or "alcoholism," a disease that can be fatal. The disease of alcoholism affects the whole person, the outer and inner person. Hence alcoholism should be treated holistically both as a physical and psychological disease and as a spiritual problem. At least in its initial stages it is a sin against one's Creator, oneself, and one's neighbors. Alcoholics need medical and psychological help; they also need unconditional *agapē* and forgiveness. Divine enabling through providentially provided alcohol treatment centers and programs like Alcoholics Anonymous have set alcoholics free. Churches ought to be aware of these resources in their communities, help people involved in alcohol abuse to acknowledge their need, and refer them for specialized treatment.

Quite inconsistently contemporary American society accepts drunkenness at parties, but condemns driving under the influence of alcohol. This hypocritical approach to drunkenness in America has led to alcoholism for one out of every ten drinkers or ten million people.[112] "Alcohol abuse is involved in most murders, most assaults, most child abuse cases, most traffic fatalities, and most fire and drowning accidents. It is also a primary factor in the development of alcohol addiction. For both reasons we do ourselves and our society a great disservice when we laugh at drunkenness or treat it lightly."[113] Rather than get involved in the debauchery of drunkenness contemporary Christians drink of the Spirit's fullness (Eph. 5:18). Christians have a source of inner peace and lasting joy far more effective than wine.

Total abstinence from alcoholic beverages is not necessary to Christian faith and life, but Anderson Spickard, M.D., suggests reasons why all Christians and especially elders, teachers, and counselors, should give serious consideration to total abstinence: (1) If indications of addiction appear in the family history, we are wise to abstain. (2) Most of the drinkers who become alcoholics drift into the disease unconsciously; so an ounce of prevention is worth a ton of cure. (3) Drinking has a deleterious effect on the part of the brain that controls judgment and inhibits evil. In view of the temptations we face in our constant warfare with evil, the risk of lowering our ability to resist enticements to sin may be greater than we want to take.[114] The slowing effect of even two or three alcoholic drinks on mental judgment and reaction time may seriously affect the safety of autmobile drivers. So in cultures with much traffic Christians may choose to give up their right to drink to reduce the risk of maiming and killing their "neighbors." "Wine is a mocker and beer a brawler; whoever is led astray by them is not wise" (Prov. 20:1).

Overseers, elders, deacons and their wives must be "temperate, self-controlled, . . . not given to drunkenness [or] indulging in much wine" (1 Tim. 3:2–3, 8, 11). Christian leaders may choose to give up their right to temperate drinking for total abstinence because of the force of their example. Out of consideration for the special needs of alcoholics among their children, relatives, church members, and friends, they may refrain. Some leaders choose to abstain because they know that one in ten drinkers cannot take even one drink without renewing the agony of their addiction. "It is better not to eat meat or drink wine or to do anything else that will cause your brother to fall" (Rom. 14:21).

The differences between Christian nondrinkers and moderate drinkers ought not destroy personal fellowship nor split churches. On the one hand, total abstainers ought not condemn others who can drink a little wine with self-control (Col. 2:16) and not cause alcoholics to stumble. On the other hand, Christians who drink moderately ought not feel uncomfortable around Christians who choose to say, "No thank you." Both moderate drinkers and abstainers need to emphasize together that "the kingdom of God is not a matter of eating and drinking, but of righteousness, peace and joy in the Holy Spirit" (Rom. 14:17).

The Bible does not provide explicit teaching on abuse of other substances, but the principles given for alcoholic drinks may be applied. The use of any unprescribed substances that shatter one's Spirit-enabled self-control and produce addiction, altered states of consciousness, drowsiness, sleep, or less pain should be evaluated by the same principles as alcohol.

Conserve Earth's Limited Resources

The Creator delegated to his image-bearers responsibility for ruling the world. All humans will give account to God for carrying out this creation mandate well. The Creator produced the limited resources of our planet for the benefit of all human beings, including coming generations. So those who love God and their neighbors should live by a responsible conservationist ethic. As Francis Schaeffer said in *Pollution and the Death of Man:* "When people take advantage of their special relationship by taking over God's creation as their own, using it for their own ends rather than God's glory, they have broken covenant and are rebelling against God."[115]

The stewardship doctrine provides an answer to the ultimate question, "Why should I take responsibility of caring for and preserving the natural order?" That answer is "Because it is God's order." It is not for mere pragmatic reasons. If I love God, I will love what he has made. The almighty God created nature's resources and the covenant-making God entrusted human beings with the responsibility of overseeing their use.

"It comes down to a question of serving God," Jeremy Rifkin said, "or rejecting Him."[116] In a posttheistic age we must ask to which God he refers. Although Rifkin takes note of the Christian God as being distinct from the world, he does not see the blatant contradiction in founding his own future on a monistic view. If all is God, then entropy diminishes the usefulness of divine energy! So although Rifkin's pantheistic God transcends Rifkin, it is not transcendent enough or personal enough. Rifkin hopes to escape the physical plane altogether in a "collective consciousness" or Buddhist "enlightenment." But the sense of total responsibility of mankind that Rifkin seeks will not be achieved apart from the accountability of everyone to the transcendent, personal Creator.

The ultimate practical goal of Christian creationists is not, as for adherents of monistic religions, harmony with nature. Our goal is harmony not only with nature but beyond that with nature's Creator. Everything in nature has importance and worth because it was made by God for a just and loving purpose. Everything is teleologically related to the Logos. And to its Creator we shall give account of our stewardship. So Christian theists will not treat nature as if it were nothing, or illusory. Neither will they waste or pollute its resources for their own selfish gain. The responsibility of ruling over the animals and earth (Gen. 1:26, 28) is not license to waste them. Creationists will not avoidably waste gasoline or any other resource, nor will they pollute the environment; they will use created resources altruistically as good stewards.

Because we are accountable to the Creator for our dominion over nature's energy resources, we ought not ignore creation's finite limitations. Energy resources had a beginning and will have an end. Finite energy is subject to entropy. We ought not rationalize unlimited wealth for selfish reasons. Stewards dare not rationalize irresponsible individualism, unaccountable enterprise, or unlimited exploitation of limited resources. This "unaccountable theology" must be replaced by a concept of human dominion in the earth as stewards accountable to God. Energy users who are aware of the fact that they are accountable to the Lord of all and considerate of their own descendants, as well as the needy around the world, will not waste or pollute the planet's limited life-support system.

Enjoy Working Six Days a Week

Christians enjoy each day of life on earth, whether they are working or retired. Like the psalmist, they say, "This is the day the LORD has made; let us rejoice and be glad in it" (Ps. 118:24). Rather than putting their hope in riches, they "put their hope in God, who richly provides us with everything for our enjoyment" (1 Tim. 6:17).

The Creator ordained that we work: "Six days you shall labor and do all your work" (Exod. 20:8). The ultimate stimulus for the work ethic comes from God's example in creation: "For in six days the LORD made the heavens and the earth, the sea, and all that is in them" (v. 11). God created humans to share not only his fellowship, but also his work. As a general rule, when health and opportunites make it possible, we work six days a week. Theists know that they are not gods, angels, or animals, but God's image-bearers made to commune with God and work for God. More important than what we do for a livelihood is whom we live for. Whatever Christians do, they work at it ultimately for the glory of God (1 Cor. 10:31).

What is work? Negatively, work is neither an evil nor a punishment for the Fall. Affirmatively, work is the use of God-given abilities and the expenditure of God-given energy as a means to achieve good ends. We misunderstand work if we think it is an end in itself, like play. Before the Fall God gave Adam work to perform for the good of creation (Gen. 2:15). Since the Fall work may be more irksome, but it still benefits others and provides purpose and fulfillment. In losing ourselves in service for others we find ourselves. By way of *definition,* work is the expenditure of mental and physical energy to the best of our trained abilities in making quality products or doing needed services that we "may have something to share with those in need" (Eph. 4:28).

The primary goal of work is not to make money for selfish purposes but to provide the best possible service or product. It is the quality of our products and services that merits pay, not the time we put in. In order to produce a more beneficial service or product one may need to get more education or training. In education also it is the quality of the papers turned in, not the time spent on them that merits the grades. Efficiency and excellence in learning to serve well reflects faithfulness as stewards. The level of productivity in what may seem to be small things in school or in an internship may indicate whether we are ready for greater responsibilities.

No business or nation owes money to capable people who refuse to produce a needed service or a quality product when opportunity is available. If our training or work seems meaningless, we may need to realign our values. We may lack respect for ourselves as image-bearers of God and disregard our own need for fulfillment through using our gifts in servant ministries. Or we may have insufficient concern for others and for helping meet their needs well. Or we may lack love for God and a desire to serve God's righteous causes in the world. A Christian's daily work is primarily rendered to the Lord and not humans (Eph. 6:7), and it is to be done with integrity (Col. 3:22–24). People who have not become self-starters in producing quality work in their Christian churches and schools are not likely to produce self-disciplined work in Christian service.

The lowliest task on earth can be viewed as a service for others when we love God who gave us gifts for our work and when we love others for whom and with whom we work. No amount of success, fame, and private accumulation of goods will save us from the essential emptiness of selfishness. We live life with others and essentially for others' safety, health, clothing, housing, education, protection, justice, and education. And in so doing we find ourselves fulfilled. With servants' hearts like our Lord's, we live not to be served in high positions but to serve in humility (Mark 10:43–45). Our Lord did not try to get away with as little work as possible but lived as a carpenter until the beginning of his ministry (Mark 6:3).

Paul had a small business, buying skins from hunters, making tents of the skins, and selling quality merchandise in the market to people in need. The apostle worked night and day, laboring and toiling. He teaches that Christians should do something useful with their hands to (1) avoid dependence on others (1 Thess. 2:9–12; 2 Thess. 3:8), (2) provide for their own family's needs (1 Thess. 4:11, 12), and (3) to share with the needy (Eph. 4:28). As Wesley put it, "Earn all you can, save all you can, and give all you can."

God's creation mandates provide a healthy context for using our natural abilities in earning a livelihood, but Christians do not live to work. Above earning a living, Christians live to fellowship with their Redeemer and extend his church. Christians will not let earning a temporal living take the place of their redemptive vocations. God "calls" his people to repentance and faith for fellowship and service in his redemptive program. Jesus worked as a carpenter but had a redemptive calling to perform. Paul made tents but that was not what he lived for. The apostle lived to take the gospel to the Gentiles. Mechanics, secretaries, and physicians may have gifts of evangelism, teaching, administration, helping, and giving—gifts that can well be used in the church. The Christian's highest spiritual fulfillment is not met in creation work, however successful and valuable, but in their work for the redemptive kingdom. For some this means a change of creation work, but for most it may not. But God has called and endowed all members of Christ's body with gifts to help take the gospel to the whole world.[117] That meets humanity's deepest need.

Employers, in addition to meeting the requirements of other workers, ought to treat workers as they would be treated, without threats and without favoritism, knowing that they face the judgment of God (Eph. 6:9). Overseers should provide for their workers what is right and fair, for they also have a Master in heaven (Col. 4:1). If certain economic structures are inherently unfair and oppressive, they ought to be changed. The laborers whose excellent work produces greater profits for a multinational corporation, for example, should participate in profit-sharing, even though they may live in other countries. Owners and board members ought not let covetousness and greed lead them to exploit their employees. Laborers are worthy of their wages in every situation, and certainly in Christian churches, schools, or mission boards (1 Tim. 5:18).

How should Christians work? "Whatever you do, work at it with all your heart, as working for the Lord and not for men" (Col. 3:23; Eph. 6:7–8). The ultimate Owner of the universe is distinct from it, and so no private ownership of land and resources is ever ultimate, but a temporary stewardship under the Creator. God lends us some property and its resources temporarily for use in efficient service of others. God asks us not only to work, but to work energetically, giving a full day's work for a full day's pay. So God's stewards may pray: "Creator and Lord of all, thank you for my life and for trusting me temporarily with the abilities, material resources, and opportunities I have. Sharpen my discernment so that I can see ways to conserve and invest them that will help expand your rule throughout the world. May your will be done in my work on earth as it is in heaven."

Set Apart One Day in Seven

The Creator knows that those who work six days need rest! Rest from the usual work, however, need not mean total inactivity. God, who is spirit, neither slumbers nor sleeps and was not exhausted after six periods of creation so that he would have needed literal rest (John 5:17). Although God ceased creating, he remained active in sustaining the world and redeeming the lost. Analogously, one day a week we need a change. We need to devote a day a week for special personal and communal fellowship with God. Goethe well expressed the attitude of non-Christians: "Bitter week, happy festival." In contrast, Christians say, "Refreshing Sunday, fulfilling week!" Christian creationists live all week in the joy of the first day with God. That day brings not only devotion to God but also personal renewal spiritually, mentally, and physically. And it provides opportunity for fellowship with other Christians and for helping people in need.

"The Sabbath," as Jesus explained, "was made for man, not man for the Sabbath" (Mark 2:27). Since the sabbath rest was planned to meet our need for enrichment, workaholics who do not sanctify one day in seven miss its blessings. Those who overwork seven days a week may identify too much with their work and fail to realize the importance of who and what they are as persons. Workahololics devalue the importance of fellowship with their Creator and his people. God himself "blessed the Sabbath day and made it holy" (Exod. 20:11). "The sabbath is holy—not in a magical sense, but as set apart to the covenant God who is the Lord of time."[118]

The practice of keeping the Sabbath as rooted in Creation is beneficial for all, not just Israelites seeking to keep Moses' law. The Mosaic stipulations for the Sabbath were fading away in the first century (2 Cor. 3:7–11) but the principle remains. Although the New Testament repeats all other nine commandments, it does not repeat the one on the Sabbath. So some Christians think there is no longer any need to observe the Sabbath, even in principle. Other Christians believe that the fourth commandment remains inviolable and that we ought to worship on the seventh day of the week (which starts at 6:00 Friday evening).

Most Christians think that the principle of the Sabbath is now fittingly fulfilled on the first day of the week when our Redeemer victoriously fulfilled all the Old Testament ceremonies and rose from the dead. Strangely the Jewish writers of the New Testament ingrained in centuries of traditional seventh-day worship, emphasized a new time of celebration—the first day of the week. Jesus rose from the dead on the first day (John 20:1) and appeared to the disciples on that day (v. 19). One week later he appeared to the eleven disciples (v. 26). The promised coming of the Holy Spirit occurred on Sunday (Lev. 23:16). On that day Peter preached Christ's death and resurrection, and three thousand people received the gospel, were baptized, and were added to the church (Acts 2). At Troas the Christians assembled for worship on the first day of the week (20:6–7). The Corinthians brought their offerings on the first day of the week, (presumably when they met for worship) (1 Cor. 16:2). Since the Jewish Sabbath commemorated not only Creation but also the deliverance from Egypt (Deut. 5:15), it is fitting that the Christian Sabbath commemorate the deliverance Christ provided on the cross and by his triumphant resurrection. We rest from our own works on the first day in order that Christ's Spirit may do his renewing work in us. Hence the first day of the week is fittingly called "the Lord's Day" (Rev. 1:10).

Those who need to work only five days a week could conceivably celebrate two days a week! Saturdays could be set apart in special gratitude for the blessings of work and of rest. Sundays could be set aside to honor the risen Christ and his gracious provision of eternal spiritual rest. Doubtless most people will still need to combine the two purposes on Sundays. Whatever time we regard holy we must remember that Jesus did not conform to the heartless Pharisaic notions of the Sabbath that reduced it to little more than an external show. On Sabbath days Jesus healed the man with the shriveled hand (Mark 3:1–6), a woman crippled for eighteen years (Luke 13:10–17), a man suffering from dropsy (14:1–6), an invalid for thirty-eight years at the pool of Bethesda (John 5:1–18), and the man born blind (9:1–16). Healings and other acts like these not only countered Pharisaic Sabbath traditions but also exhibited Jesus' messianic consciousness. By these acts Jesus disclosed his awareness of the fact that "the Son of Man is Lord even of the Sabbath" (Mark 2:28). So Christian theists avoid judging Sabbath keeping by legalistic taboos on that day. Paul also emphasized that externals should not become a matter of judgment of one Christian by another (Rom. 13:8–10; 14:4–6, 10, 12–13; Gal. 4:9–10; Col. 2:13–17).

Only people with authentic faith in the Creator and Redeemer can keep the Lord's Day holy in motive as well as act. Believers' primary motivations in keeping Sunday different should be to (1) love their Lord who enables them to work and plans for their rest, (2) worship in spirit and truth together with others in the church, (3) give proportionately as God has prospered them

(1 Cor. 16:1–2), (4) help others who are in need, and (5) anticipate eternal rest from all their work in the world of space and time (Heb. 4:3–11).

Cooperate With Other Creationists

Creationists of the world unite! You have nothing to lose but taxation for public education without representation! In pluralistic societies one would expect public education to represent the major pluralistic worldviews. Public education would present the three major philosophical traditions—naturalism, pantheism, and theism, not just naturalism or naturalism and an exploding pantheism. The first amendment to the Constitution of the United States, for example, while prohibiting the establishment of one denomination as the state religion, guarantess freedom of religion. In schools valuing academic freedom, furthermore, the worldview of theism has as much right to representation in the textbooks and classrooms as the worldviews of naturalism and pantheism. Hence there should be freedom to teach a theistic philosophy of life, not only in courses in science, but also in courses in history, sociology, psychology, philosophy, etc. Teachers who are theists in America should not be intimidated by misinterpretations of the first amendment to the United States Constitution. It does not erect a wall between public education and religion nor limit public education in a pluralistic society to secular or pantheistic views of life. The amendment wisely forbids an established state religion while guaranteeing freedom of religion. Surely that means freedom for theists as teachers or students in public education.

Quite apart from differences on the length of the days (Gen. 1), creationists together should present a theistic-creationist point of view in free societies, not on sheer authority, whether scientific or religious, but because Creation provides a coherent account of more of the data concerning origins with fewer difficulties than naturalistic or pantheistic evolutions. In short, teachers can indicate that the theistic-creationist hypothesis makes more sense. Theism does not ask students to believe in an unfounded chance or accident in the beginning. Theism justifies the scientists' belief in an ordered world and in the ability of the human mind to know it. Science originated and thrives among theists. Science will not survive as well among naturalists without normative values such as intellectual honesty, nor among pantheistic occultists depending on the deceptions of channeling and uncritical visualizations of their own imagined quantum leaps into godhood. For the sake of freedom in education and benefits to the scientific endeavor in pluralistic societies, teachers ought to present theism at least as one of three major worldviews with which all students should have reliable knowledge.

REVIEW QUESTIONS

To Help Relate and Apply Each Section in This Chapter

1. *Briefly state the classical problem* this chapter addresses and indicate reasons why genuine inquiry into it is important for your worldview and your existence personally and socially.

2. *Objectively summarize the influential answers* given to this problem in history as hypotheses to be tested. Be able to compare and contrast their real similarities and differences (not merely verbal similarities or differences).

3. *Highlight the primary biblical evidence* on which to decide among views—evidence found in the relevant teachings of the major divisions of Scripture—and decide for yourself which historical hypothesis (or synthesis of historical views) provides the

most consistent and adequate account of the primary biblical data.

4. *Formulate in your own words your doctrinal conviction* in a logically consistent and adequate way, organizing your conclusions in ways you can explain clearly, support biblically, and communicate effectively to your spouse, children, friends, Bible class, or congregation.

5. *Defend your view* as you would to adherents of the alternative views, showing that the other views are logically less consistent and factually faced with more difficulties than your view in accounting for the givens, not only of special revelation but also of human experience in general.

6. *Explore the differences the viability of your conviction can make in your life.* Then test your understanding of the viability of your view by asking, "Can I live by it authentically (unhypocritically) in relation to God and to others in my family, church, vocation, neighborhood, city, nation, and world?"

MINISTRY PROJECTS

To Help Communicate This Doctrine in Christian Service

1. *Memorize one major verse or passage* that in its context teaches the heart of this doctrine and may serve as a text from which to preach, teach, or lead small-group studies on the topic. The memorized passages from each chapter will build a body of content useful also for meditation and reference in informal discussions.

2. *Formulate the major idea of the doctrine in one sentence* based on the passage memorized. This idea should be useful as the major thesis of either a lesson for a class (junior high to adult) or a message for a church service.

3. *State the specific purpose or goal of your doctrinal lesson or message.* Your purpose should be more than informative. It should show why Christians need to accept this truth and live by it (unhypocritically). For teaching purposes, list indicators that would show to what extent class members have grasped the truth presented.

4. *Outline your message or lesson in complete sentences.* Indicate how you would support the truth of the doctrine's central ideas and its relevance to life and service. Incorporate elements from this chapter's historical, biblical, systematic, apologetic, and practical sections selected according to the value they have for your audience.

5. *List applications of the doctrine* for communicating the difference this conviction makes in life (for sermons, lessons, small-group Bible studies, or family devotional Bible studies). Applications should make clear what the doctrine is, why one needs to know it, and how it will make differences in thinking. Then show how the difference in thought will lead to differences in values, priorities, attitudes, speech, and personal action. Consider also the doctrine's possible significance for family, church, neighborhood, city, regional, and national actions.

6. *Start a file and begin collecting illustrations* of this doctrine's central idea, the points in your outline, and your application.

7. *Write out your doctrinal statement on this subject in one paragraph* (half a page or less). To work toward a comprehensive doctrinal statement, collect your formulations based on a study of each chapter of *Integrative Theology.* As your statement of Christian doctrine grows, you will find it personally strengthening and useful when you are asked your beliefs and when you apply for service with churches, mission boards, and other Christian organizations. Any who seek ordination to Christian ministry will need a doctrinal statement that covers the broad scope of theology.

CHAPTER 2

EXISTENCE UNDER PROVIDENTIAL DIRECTION

Existence Under Providential Direction

THE PROBLEM: TO WHAT EXTENT AND BY WHAT MEANS DOES THE ALL-WISE, ALL-LOVING, AND ALL-POWERFUL GOD GOVERN THE UNIVERSE, HISTORY, AND PERSONS TO HIS PREDETERMINED END?

In chapter 8 of volume 1 we saw that in eternity past the sovereign God devised a wise plan, both directive and permissive, for all times. Chapter 9 of volume 1 explored how God began to implement that plan by creating the cosmos, persons, and all living forms. The present chapter considers the next step in the execution of the divine plan, namely, how God sustains and guides all that he has brought into existence. A moment's reflection suggests that creation, preservation, and providence are inextricably linked, since it is unlikely, if not impossible, that a wise, loving, and omnipotent God (see vol. 1, chaps. 5 and 6) would create a vast universe without upholding it in existence and guiding it to a suitable end.

Problems arise when we relate the doctrine of providence to the actual world in which we live. Consider, first, the relation of providence to the laws of nature. Scientists inform us that the Sahara Desert creeps southward several miles each year, destroying valuable farm and grazing land, thereby displacing thousands of already impoverished African villagers. Furthermore, how does the doctrine of providence relate to powerful typhoons that seasonally wreak destruction on many poor people in Sri Lanka and Bangladesh? How does it relate to famines that tragically cut short the lives of thousands in Ethiopia? or to severe droughts that impoverish peoples in various parts of the world?

Reflect for a moment on the relation of the doctrine of providence to humanly caused evil. Is it reasonable to believe that God rules the world, given Hitler's barbarous annihilation of six million or so Jews during World War II? Can one adhere to providence in the face of the extensive human suffering inflicted by the cultural revolution in China, or by Idi Amin in devastated Uganda, or by "Papa Doc" Duvalier in poverty-ridden Haiti? How does providence relate to the present AIDS epidemic? Medical authorities, for example, predict that the entire population of several African countries will be carriers of the AIDS virus before the end of the century. In the face of such widespread human suffering, can we believe that a good and powerful God controls the world? Or is the tragedy-ridden human story merely "a tale told by an idiot, full of sound and fury, signifying nothing"?

Does the Judeo-Christian hypothesis of divine providence allow room for human freedom and meaningful involvement in the affairs of history? To what extent does God accomplish his purposes through the will and efforts of human beings such as we? How does God operate in relation to the evil intentions and acts of persons? The doctrine of providence raises the question as to whether both good and evil historical events are efficiently ordered by the sovereign God, or whether morally evil acts are merely permitted. Does God effectively limit or restrain the malicious designs of evil persons? Does God redirect the nefarious deeds of wicked persons to worthy ends unimagined by the perpetrators? In our study of providence it will be important to consider distinguishing between God's unconditional (decretive) and conditional (permissive) wills, as discussed in chapter 8 of volume 1.

Moreover, is God's governance of history accomplished solely by secondary causes (i.e., by the laws of nature and the free acts of persons), or are there grounds for believing that God can and does work through exceptional events in nature and history known as miracles? Is there sound basis for believing that God may employ immaterial angelic beings to accomplish his providential purposes? Furthermore, is belief in supernatural spiritual powers such as Satan and demons tenable in the modern world? If so, how does their activity cohere with God's providential rule of history? Finally, what effect does prayer to God have in the events of everyday life? Can people in an advanced scientific age sustain the belief that prayer effects objective changes in nature and human history?

ALTERNATIVE INTERPRETATIONS IN THE CHURCH

The data of Scripture and human experience are extensive, and the issues associated with the doctrine of divine providence are complex. Consequently a number of hypotheses have been advanced on the subject of divine providence in the history of the Christian church.

Supralapsarian Calvinist Perspectives

Consistent with their understanding of the divine decrees, supralapsarians emphasize God's absolute sovereignty and effectual working over the whole range of human (and nonhuman) activity. Authorities view the government of persons and history, not in terms of God's permissive will, but as a function of his effectual will. Supralapsarians throughout history underscore the fact that the control of the world and the outcome of history are in the hands of God, not finite persons. Theologians in the tradition are reluctant to explain the occurrence of evil in terms of bare permission. The fact that God actively governs the world and that persons nevertheless act freely and responsibly generally is viewed as a mystery incomprehensible to finite human minds.

Luther's high view of divine causality led him to conclude that God's providential operations embrace all occurrences, both good and evil. Luther understood God's word in Isaiah 45:7, "I form the light and create darkness," to mean, "I hold good fortune and misfortune in my hand."[1] In this regard Luther viewed the immediate agent of an act as the disguise under which God both works and hides himself. Thus Luther refers to "God's mask, under which he conceals himself and so marvelously exercises dominion and introduces disorder into the world."[2] In spite of the fact that Satan and sinners are impelled by God's power, Luther stopped short of affirming that God works sin. He viewed the seeming contradiction between God's efficient governance of all things and his holiness as a mystery hidden to human reason.

Zwingli staunchly maintained that God is absolute controlling providence. His God is the efficient cause of all occurrences: "all things are so done and disposed by the providence of God that nothing takes place without His will and command."[3] So absolute is the divine providence that second causes, including the agency of finite persons, is denied. Since God's providence excludes human service, Zwingli avers, persons are no more than tools in the hands of the divine Majesty. "By the providence of God, therefore, are taken away together free will and merit; for if it disposes all things, what part have we that permits us to think anything done of ourselves?"[4] This deterministic view of providence appears to make God the efficient cause of evil. Zwingli, however, denied that God is morally responsible for sinful acts, for the reason that the Sovereign transcends all temporal laws.

Closer to Luther than to Zwingli, Calvin repeatedly insists that the sovereign God actively governs all things in accordance with his secret purpose. "Governing heaven and earth by his providence, God so regulates all things that nothing takes place without his deliberation."[5] Again, "God by the bridle of his providence turns every event whatever way he wills."[6] Calvin believes that in addition to effecting the good, God also governs the plans and intentions of evildoers. Thus "Satan and all the impious are so under God's hand and power that he directs their malice to whatever end seems good to him."[7] In one section of the *Institutes* (I.18.2) Calvin explains how God inspires and even impells evildoers. He suggests that God works inwardly in the impious to bend their minds and to harden their wills such that they act perversely. On the basis of Proverbs 21:1 and other texts, he concludes that "Satan performs his part by God's impulsion."[8] Calvin dismisses the thesis of permissive providence as a clever subterfuge. Yet Calvin (unlike Zwingli) insists that God's active governance does not nullify human agency and responsibility, for God uses intermediate causes to achieve his ends. Does the scheme of government thus proposed implicate God in sin? On the basis of the divine incomprehensibility, whereby God's ways transcend the capacity of finite minds, and on the basis of the divine holiness, whereby God remains undefiled, Calvin responds with a firm no!

The supralapsarian position on miracles, angels, and prayer is similar to that of moderately Reformed authorities discussed below.

The Arminian View

The distinctive hypothesis of the Arminian tradition is the so-called moral view of providence. Most Arminian theologians hold to (1) God's conservation of the universe by the laws of nature, (2) his preservation of the animate realm by his power, and (3) his moral government of persons. We focus on the third tenet of the Arminian view, as follows: Emphasizing the maintenance of human initiative and freedom, the Arminians argue that God's providential working is not causative but is chiefly moral. Authorities in this tradition view divine providence neither in terms of an absolute decree nor in terms of a coercive power. Rather, they believe that God exercises providential control over the world by setting before free and responsible persons moral and religious precepts that ought to be obeyed. God permits but does not cause the manifold evils in the world; he limits their effects and rules over all in love.

Jacob Arminius understood providence in the sense that God "preserves, regulates, governs and directs all things, and that nothing in the world happens fortuitously or by chance."[9] Yet Arminius quickly follows with the distinctive that would characterize the tradition that bears his name: "I place in subjection to Divine Providence both the *free will* and even *the actions of the rational creature*."[10] That is, whereas God wills and performs morally good actions, he preserves human freedom by freely permitting persons to oppose his will and perpetrate evil. Reformed contemporaries of Arminius claimed that the latter seriously limited divine providence by shifting control of history from the sovereign God to autonomous persons.

John Wesley believed that God sustains the cosmos in its existence and operations. But in the human realm providence consists of God's work of overruling human disobedience so as to achieve his saving plan for the world. Wesley wrote:

> In the natural world all things roll on in an even, uninterrupted course. But it is far otherwise in the moral world. Here evil men and evil spirits continually oppose the divine will and create numberless irregularities. Here, therefore, is full scope for the exercise of all the riches both of the wisdom and knowledge of God, in counteracting all the wickedness and folly of men and all the subtlety of Satan, to carry on his own glorious design—the salvation of lost mankind.[11]

Charles Finney likewise maintains that in the human order God's providential operations represent a moral influence exerted over free and responsible agents. Finney explicates his theory of moral government as follows: It is "the government of free will by motives as distinguished from the government of substance by force. . . . It is a government exercised in accordance with the law of liberty, as opposed to the law of necessity. It is the administration of moral as opposed to physical law."[12] God guides the course of human affairs primarily by extending to persons the promise of rewards and the threat of punishment.

Recent Arminian writers reflect a similar emphasis. God's conservation of the physical universe and his preservation of all living forms in existence is properly effectual. Yet in respect of persons "a change in the activity of divine providence is noted. Here God's relationship is not causative, as in conservation and preservation. Rather, God's providential care and government is moral. Providence is exerted in the form of motive rather than compulsion."[13]

The Arminian tradition interprets miracles, angels, and prayer in much the same way as moderately Reformed authorities discussed below.

The Deistic Position

Deists in seventeenth- and eighteenth-century England, assuming the radical transcendence of God and the unity of nature, posited a First Cause who created the universe and who instituted universal laws by which the cosmos functions. From the beginning the Creator caused the universe to operate as a well-ordered machine, thereby eliminating the need for direct supernatural intervention in its affairs. The deists thus viewed preservation negatively as God's refusal to destroy the work of his hands, and they viewed providence positively as God's general oversight of the properties and laws by which the universe functions.

Thomas Chubb, in *A Short Dissertation on Providence* (London, 1738), advanced many reasons why God does not intervene in the world in works of special providence. Voltaire, the French deist, upheld a general providence (God's oversight of the laws by which the universe functions), but dismissed as absurd the notion of special providence (God's watchful care of individual lives). Thomas Paine, who conceived of God as "the great mechanic of the creation,"[14] had in mind divine providence when he wrote of that "system of principles as fixed and unalterable as those by which the universe is regulated and governed."[15] Since the deists viewed the universe as a vast machine, they had no cogent rationale for life's evils and disasters. Their best explanation for evil was superstition, ignorance, and the alleged sinister influence exerted by the clergy.

Given their fundamental presuppositions, the deists refused to countenance the possibility of miracles. The biblical accounts of miracles—including the incarnation and the resurrection of Christ—were variously described as "absurdities," "impossibilities," and "lying wonders." Thomas Paine wrote, "We have never seen in our time nature go out of her course."[16] The most the deists would affirm is that the remarkable orderliness of the universe, with its inviolable laws, is the most profound "miracle." The world view of the deists also precluded the efficacy of prayer. Finite creatures cannot alter the functioning of a universe that operates on the basis of fixed laws and properties.

The Classical Liberal View

Traditional liberalism, guided by the Enlightenment theme of inevitable progress, interpreted providence as the purposive force that has guided human history from crude beginnings to present heights of social cooperation, political freedom, and economic prosperity. Liberal thinkers, many of whom worked on the fringes of pantheism, denied that God actively directs particular occurrences in history. Rather, the active force or soul of the universe effects progress by means of the laws of nature, emergent evolution, and the moral achievements of persons. Liberal thinkers supplanted the direct governance of a personal God by the forces of material causality and free human actions.

Schleiermacher firmly denied any special divine governance of nature or history. The term *providence,* which the Romantic theologian used sparingly, refers to the forces of nature that the Most High has set in motion and to the free acts of responsible persons. Following Kant and Hegel, Schleiermacher upheld the notion of a relentless cosmic progress.

W. A. Brown concurs with the definition of providence as the uniform evolutionary advance within nature and history:

> Instead of confining God's activity to a series of isolated interpositions . . . , we think of him as ever at work, forming, training and perfecting the moral personalities whom he has designed for union with himself. In the gradual development which science recognizes, from the lower forms to the higher, from the more simple to the more complex, we see the slow unfolding of God's providential plan.[17]

From a similar perspective Gordon Kaufman defines providence as "the ordering of all finite being in terms of processes of development in history."[18] The Harvard theologian insists that via evolution and the flow of history the world is moving toward its final goal. In Kaufman's mind the distinction between general and special providence is unfounded. All events are explicable in terms of the ordinary operations of nature and history.

As we saw in chapter 8 of volume 1, process theology denies that God is the controlling Power that guides history to a predetermined end. Rather, by providing each entity with its initial aim, God lures or persuades entities to new opportunities and satisfactions. Indeed, with respect to his consequent nature, God is said to be part of the process itself. In sum, according to process thought, God does not order the world; he experiences or feels it.

Liberalism's quasi-pantheistic and evolutionary worldview allows no room for miracles as instruments of providence. Schleiermacher defined a miracle as any religiously significant event. Thus for the truly religious person every event is a miracle. According to Harnack, the biblical picture of miracles derived from a prescientific view of the world. Said the Ritschlian liberal, "Miracles, it is true, do not happen; but of the marvelous and the inexplicable there is no lack."[19] Modern liberalism retains the notion of miracle as any event that bears religious import.

The liberal tradition likewise dismisses angels as products of the imagination of primitive people or as poetic personifications of the powers of nature. Belief in Satan and demons as personal malignant powers is rejected as antithetic to the tradition's vision of cosmic progress. Said DeWolf, "We would best regard the belief in demons reflected in the New Testament as belonging merely to the pseudoscience of the first century."[20] Untrained in medical science, the biblical writers falsely ascribed to demons what modern enlightened people understand as diseases of the mind and nervous system.

From the perspective of its evolutionary worldview, liberalism denies that prayer effects objective change in the world. Theological liberals uniformly view prayer as the soul's personal communion with God. The chief effect of prayer is to alter the disposition and attitudes of the one who prays.

The View of Theistic Existentialists and Some Neoorthodox

As a result of the traumas of the twentieth century, existentially orientated theologians argue that no purpose or meaning can be found in nature or history. Because history is soiled with brutality and death, many thinkers limit divine providence to the hearts of believers. This means that the present rule of God is spiritual and subjective only. God's governmental dealings with the unbelieving world will be manifest only in the eschaton. Such considerations lead one authority to conclude that "Providence is the forgotten stepchild of contemporary theology."[21]

Russian theologian Nicolas Berdyaev denies that God governs the course of nature and history, given the stark reality of cruelty, barbarism, and suffering in the world. History, that narrative forged by human freedom, is a horrible tragedy and a horrendous failure. Simply put, "God does not govern this world, the world of objectivity which is under the power of its own Prince."[22] Berdyaev makes his point more fully:

> This world into which we are thrown is not God's world and in it the divine order and divine harmony cannot hold sway. God's world only breaks through into this world, the light of it shines through only in that which really exists, in living beings and their existence. . . . There is nothing of God in the dull and prosaic normality of the objective world order.[23]

The rule of God will be manifest in the historical sphere only in the age to come, when God will have the final word.

Given his emphasis on the existential summons of God to personal decision, Bultmann denies as an abstraction the doctrine that God directs the course of history: "The New Testament has no knowledge of . . . the *concept of providence*."[24] History, the continuum of the consciously willed actions of persons, possesses no meaning whatsoever. Only the particular moment has meaning, when the individual encounters God in an act of personal decision.

Brunner argues that the dual realities of the divine government of the world and human responsibility for evil deeds represent an insoluble paradox, which the thesis of permission cannot resolve. For Brunner the problems of providence and theodicy are solved, not philosophically or even theologically, but existentially. Before the cross of Christ the believer stands in the abyss, feels his own guilt and sin, and knows that God acts with justice and compassion. Thus in regard to the problem of theodicy, "the real solution lies in the acknowledgment of guilt and in the hope of redemption."[25]

Existentialists join with liberals in rejecting miracles as a negation of the uniformity of nature. Any alleged intrusion of God into the cause-effect nexus is dismissed as mythological. Bultmann argues that the real miracle (*Wunder*) is that God meets a person in grace in his concrete existence. For John Macquarrie miracle is a perfectly natural event that excites awe in a person. Existentially interpreted, miracle is "an event that opens up Being and becomes a vehicle for Being's revelation of grace or judgment."[26] Angels and demons likewise belong to a prescientific understanding of the universe. Comments Bultmann, "Now that the forces and laws of nature have been discovered, we can no longer believe in spirits, whether good or evil."[27] After being demythologized, angels depict those powers that stimulate persons to rise above earthly existence to a realm of spiritual power, and demons highlight the suprahuman and sometimes systemic character of evil in the world.

Existentialists likewise reject as mythological the view of prayer as human conversation with God. Prayer is said to be an expression of a person's finitude and frail dependence on the ground of Being. According to Bultmann, by prayer to God the believer certifies his eschatological existence. On the other hand, theistic existentialists view intercessory prayer as an expression of a person's freedom and openness to others. Heinrich Ott, Barth's successor at Basel, insists that the traditional view of prayer as verbal petition and intercession is unrealistic. Rather, prayer is a dialogical "I-Thou" relation with God that embraces the believer's total existence. "The one who prays opens himself for God, he bears himself up toward God and exposes his whole life before him." Adds Ott, "He does this . . . in that he casts his future into God."[28]

Liberation Theology

Proponents of the theology of liberation minimize God's providential working in history and stress rather the revolutionary struggles of the poor and oppressed to transform history. Gutierrez believes, not that God actively guides history, but that he is revealed in history amid human efforts (violent if necessary) to forge a just society. For the Peruvian theologian, man rather than God is the artisan of human destiny.

The "messianic humanism" proposed by Rubem Alves envisages the formation of a pact between God and persons, and in this pact both parties, as co-creators, jointly build a new society. According to Alves, God alone cannot guide the course of history, for his being, yet incomplete, requires human activity to be fully constituted. "In the context of the politics of human liberation man encounters a God who remains open, who has not yet arrived, and who is determined and helped by human activity. God needs man for the creation of his future."[29].

Advocates of a black theology of

liberation see God as more actively involved in providential activity. Albert Cleage believes that through Christ, the Black Messiah, God works in history to liberate blacks from oppression and to build a Black Nation.[30] God's operations in history are consistently for blacks and against whites. James Cone has a similar vision of the divine providence: "God is at work in the black community vindicating black people against white oppression."[31]

The various forms of political theology are generally skeptical of angels and miracles. The miracles alleged in the Bible involve no supernatural interruption of the natural order. Liberation theologians instead view miracles as momentous events, namely, as signs of liberation or the arrival of the kingdom of God. Moreover, political theologians generally hold that the traditional view of prayer as petition to God to change conditions represents an evasion of personal responsibility and a substitute for action. Thus they view prayer as a reflective exercise that sharpens conscience and so prepares a person to participate in the struggle for the political liberation of the oppressed.

Moderately Reformed Position

Many Fathers, medieval authorities, Reformers, and evangelicals maintain that God works providentially through the laws of nature, miracles, the free actions of persons, and supremely through the life, death, and resurrection of Jesus Christ. God effects some of his providential ends unconditionally, according to his decretive will, and others conditionally, according to his preceptive and permissive wills. Although God in part works permissively, he nevertheless retains control of all things by limiting (setting bounds to) evil acts and by redirecting their effects to worthy ends unintended by the doer.

The church fathers upheld God's providential governance of the cosmos and all living things through the Word, while insisting that God is in no way responsible for evil. They commonly called God's providential ordering of the whole his "economy" (*oikonomia*). Clement of Alexandria delineates the scope of God's "economy" as follows:

> Providence begins by ordering the world and the heavens, the course of the sun's orbit and the movements of the other heavenly bodies, all for the sake of man. Then it concerns itself with man himself. . . . And because it considers this as its most important work, it guides man's soul on the right path by the virtues of prudence and temperance, and equips his body with beauty and harmony. Finally, into the actions of mankind it infuses uprightness and some of its own good order.[32]

God never causes suffering and evil, although he permits such for the sake of the larger good: "We must not think that God actively produces afflictions; but we must be persuaded that he does not prevent those that cause them, but overrules for good the crimes of His enemies."[33] Athanasius emphasizes that God governs the universe through the agency of the Logos. At Christ's bidding the heavens revolve, the sun shines, the birds fly, plants grow, and persons live and die.

Against the contrary doctrines of fate and chance, Augustine maintained that God sovereignly governs the entire creation by a twofold providence. The "natural" working of providence refers to God's hidden governance of the material world according to an established order, whereas the "voluntary" working of providence pertains to his control and direction of the decisions and actions of free agents.[34] Seeking to defend the reality of second causes and to avoid the idea that God is responsible for evil, Augustine judged that God's providence embraces both his divine command and the acts of human beings.

That is, "Whatever is done in the world is done partly by divine agency and partly by our will."[35] Evil, defined as privation of the good and rebellion of the will, is permitted by God and wisely employed to serve his purposes. Thus "even what is done in opposition to his will does not defeat his will. For it would not be done did he not permit it. . . . Nor would a good Being permit evil to be done but that in his omnipotence he can turn evil into good."[36] Augustine went on to say that God employs wicked spirits and persons in his service to judge evildoers and to purify the righteous. Since the sovereign God turns evil to salutary ends, Augustine argued that specific evil deeds may be judged good when viewed in the light of the whole.

Several Reformed confessions explicate this understanding of divine providence. The Belgic Confession reads as follows:

> We believe that the same good God, after he had created all things, did not forsake them or give them up to fortune or chance, but that he rules and governs them according to his holy will, so that nothing happens in this world without his appointment; nevertheless God neither is the Author of nor can be charged with the sins that are committed. . . . This doctrine affords us unspeakable consolation, since we are . . . persuaded that he so restrains the devil and all our enemies that without his will and permission they cannot hurt us (art. XIII).

According to the Heidelberg Catechism:

> Providence is the almighty and ever-present power of God by which he upholds, as with his hand, heaven and earth and all creatures, and so rules them that leaf and blade, rain and drought, fruitful and lean years, food and drink, health and sickness, prosperity and poverty—all things, in fact, come to us not by chance but from his fatherly hand (Lord's Day 10, Q. 27).

More recently, Carl Henry maintained that God is "providential Orderer of the world, the supreme Ruler who constantly disposes nature and the history of man in a rational, purposive plan."[37] Providence is purposive in that God actively directs all things toward the realization of his eternal plan in Jesus Christ. It is furthermore all-encompassing, embracing the powers of nature, the pattern of history, evil deeds of persons (without ascribing evil to God), miraculous redemptive events, and chiefly the incarnation, death, and resurrection of Jesus Christ, who will return to lead history to its final destiny. Divine providence, moreover, is specific, in that God works out his purposes in the minutiae of life. The chief focus of providence is the believer, for whose ultimate good God lovingly rules and overrules in human affairs.

Orthodox Christian authorities maintain that miracles are not violations of nature but are purposeful exceptions to the customary way in which God works. God usually operates through the known laws of nature. But to achieve his redemptive purposes, the Almighty occasionally overrules the usual processes to produce unexpected results. Augustine affirmed that miracles cannot be contrary to nature, for God's will defines the nature of every creature. The Westminster Confession states, "God, in his ordinary providence, makes use of means, yet he is free to work without, above, and against them, at his pleasure (ch. V.3). Ramm adds, "With providence working with the theistic view of nature, a normal, natural, credible doorway was left open for God to answer prayer, work the miraculous, and even send his Son into the world with all the attendant supernatural activity the incarnation and resurrection involved."[38]

Most Christian theologians view angels as created spiritual intelligences, organized in various ranks and assisting in the providential ordering of history. According to Augustine, "God the Creator rules over all creation by means of holy spirits, his heavenly and earthly ministers."[39] Although some Fathers and medieval authorities speculated excessively about angels, most orthodox scholars view these holy ones as guiding the affairs of the nations, protecting believers, and punishing the enemies of God. On the other hand, they regard Satan as an archangel who pridefully rebelled aginst God, and they view demons as lesser angels who were carried away by Satan's apostasy. Satan and the demons oppose God and his will, oppress the people of God, incite sinners to evil, and cause mental and physical disorders. Observed Augustine, "The devil fell by pride from the beginning of time and never lived in peace and blessedness with the holy angels, but apostasized from his Creator at the very outset of his creation."[40] Some recent evangelicals, such as Yoder and Stringfellow, point out Satan's role in the formation of structural evil in the political, social, and economic realms.

Theologians in the tradition likewise view prayer as an instrument of divine providence. Understood as communion, petition, and intercession, prayer has both a subjective and an objective efficacy. As an act of worship, prayer produces godly attitudes and dispositions in the one who prays. "Prayer clears and cleanses our heart, and makes it more capable of receiving the divine gifts which are spiritually infused into us."[41] On the other hand, prayer causes things to occur in the objective world that otherwise would not have come to pass. This is generally explained in the sense that God from eternity past ordained not only the ends, but also the means for the realization of his purposes. Henry observes that prayer, as a crucial element in the realization of God's providential purposes, "has more than a subjective value; it not only 'changes us' but it 'changes things.'"[42]

Additional information on this unit can be found in helpful studies by C. S. Lewis,[43] G. C. Berkouwer,[44] and Colin Brown.[45]

BIBLICAL TEACHING

To determine which historical proposal is closest to the teaching of Scripture, we proceed with a study of the relevant biblical materials on the subject of providence and the means God employs to achieve his purposes in history, namely, miracles, angels, and prayer.

Pentateuch

The doctrine of providence takes its name from a phrase in the text of Genesis 22:8. When Isaac on Mount Moriah asked Abraham where the lamb was for the burnt offering, Abraham responded, "God himself will provide the lamb for the burnt offering, my son." The Hebrew phrase is *'ᵉlōhîm yir'eh-lô*, and that of the Latin Vulgate is *Deus providebit*. The Hebrew verb *rā'āh*, to "see," here bears the extended meaning to "provide." When Abraham had thus demonstrated faith and obedience, God directed the patriarch to a ram caught by its horns in a thicket (v. 13). At the end of this remarkable episode, "Abraham called that place The LORD Will Provide" (v. 14). In the words of one scholar, "God saw! God provided! God's divine provision took care of everything."[46]

At the most basic level God accomplishes his purposes through the observable operations of nature. Thus God said after the Flood: "As long as the earth endures, seedtime and harvest, cold and heat, summer and winter, day and night will never cease" (Gen. 8:22).

More specially, divine providence

expresses itself in God's care and protection of his own people. Recalling their experiences in the wilderness, Moses reminded Israel, "The LORD your God carried you, as a father carries his son, all the way you went until you reached this place" (Deut. 1:31; cf. 7:18). The peace, protection, and safety God provides for the righteous is beautifully affirmed in Deuteronomy 33:12, 25–28. God, moreover, promises to provide his obedient people with material prosperity in the form of rain and bountiful harvests (Lev. 26: 3–4) and with victory over their enemies (vv. 6–9). Although Israel had to contend against its foes, success in battle was clearly a provision of the Lord (Deut. 3:2–3).

God's providential dealings with his people include not only blessing but also discipline (Deut. 4:36; 8:5). If Israel failed to submit to God's discipline and persisted in evildoing, the Lord would send as a negative providence disease, poor harvests, famine, plagues, war, and exile among the nations (Lev. 26:23–39; Deut. 28:15–68). In the case of persistent disobedience, God would permit unfriendly nations to punish Israel with military defeats (Num. 14:43).

God providentially directs not only the great but also the small issues of life, such as the time and circumstances of a person's death. In his sovereignty God caused Moses to die on Mount Nebo without entering the Promised Land (Deut. 32:49–52; Num. 27:12–14). Likewise God prevented Aaron from entering Canaan by terminating his life also (Num. 20:22–26).

The Pentateuch attests several ways by which God exercises control over evil acts. First by a restraining kind of providence God prevents sin that otherwise would occur. When Abimilech tried to add Sarah to his harem, believing she was unmarried, God told the Philistine king not to "touch her" but to return her to her husband (Gen. 20:1–7). Since God's plan for Sarah was that she should bear a son by Abraham (Gen. 17:16–21), the Lord kept Abimelech from thwarting his plan and also from sinning (Gen. 20:6). In similar fashion God warned Laban not to harm his son-in-law Jacob in any way (Gen. 31:24), thus preventing the shedding of innocent blood.

A redirecting kind of providence, whereby the Lord channels evil acts to worthy ends unimagined by the perpetrator, occurs in the account of Judah's lust with Tamar his daughter-in-law, whom he thought to be a harlot (Gen. 38). In the plan of God, Perez, the illegitimate son of Judah and Tamar, occupies a place in the family line of the Messiah (Matt. 1:2–3; Luke 3:33).

The familiar story of Joseph provides the clearest account in the Old Testament of a redirecting providence. Joseph was thrown into a cistern by his brothers, rescued by Midianite traders, sold as a slave in Egypt, and made Pharaoh's prime minister. God informed Joseph in a dream that seven years of famine were coming and told him to set aside ample food stores for the lean times. Joseph's prudent planning saved his family from starvation when they journeyed to Egypt to buy food. In an emotional confrontation, when Joseph's brothers expressed their shame for mistreating him, Joseph reassured them three times that God had sent him to Egypt to provide for the chosen people (Gen. 45:5–8). " 'Not you . . . but God' (v. 8) expresses the fact of Providence in a typically sweeping biblical idiom."[47] Joseph's testimony, "You intended to harm me, but God intended it for good to accomplish what is now being done, the saving of many lives" (Gen. 50:20), confirms that the God who controls history redirected the brothers' evil act to a salutary end. Thus divine providence overrules and transforms the worst forms of human malice.

Exodus 1–2 relates the beautiful story of how God overruled the evil intentions of a pharaoh to spare the life of the infant Moses, who later would become the liberator of Israel from Egypt. "God's providence used natural factors: motherly love, sisterly love, a woman's pity, Israelite acumen, Egyptian culture. . . . It was precisely the commandment to throw the boys into the Nile that brought Moses to the Egyptian court."[48]

In the Old Testament, miracles—viewed as exceptional events in nature or history—contributed to the deliverance and preservation of Israel as a special people. The focal miracle of the Old Testament was the deliverance of Israel through the Sea of Reeds (Exod. 14). When Moses stretched out his right hand, the Lord drove back the sea with a strong east wind (v. 21). In his song of thanksgiving to the Lord, Moses interpreted the wind as "the blast" of Yahweh's nostrils (Exod. 15:8, 10). With Israel safely through the sea, Moses again stretched out his hand in obedience to God's command, whereupon the waters flowed back on the pursuing Egyptians destroying every last warrior. Repeatedly throughout Israel's history God led his people by miraculous events. Yet without doubt, "the miracle at the Red Sea is the paradigm of God's acting."[49]

Angels, who constitute a mighty army of spiritual beings (Deut. 33:2), are represented in Scripture as special agents by which God executes his providential purposes. Thus an angel led Israel in their flight from Egypt and protected the people against Pharaoh's pursuing army (Exod. 14:19; cf. Num. 20:16). Moreover, God used angels to guide Israel into the Promised Land and to destroy their enemies (Exod. 23:20, 23). Scripture also depicts a malignant spiritual power named Satan (*śāṭan*, "adversary"), who actively opposes God's purposes. Genesis 3:1–5 describes Satan's instigation of the fall of the first pair into sin. Satan, who indwelt a serpent, cast God in the role of a deceiver who sought to inhibit Adam and Eve's happiness (v. 5). "With one stroke Satan reinterpreted God as a devil, a liar possessed by jealous pride, and the way of the curse as the way to blessing."[50] Genesis 3:15 anticipates not only the struggle between Christ and Satan that would culminate in the victory of the cross, but also the agelong enmity that would exist between the people of God and the forces of Satan. Scripture, furthermore, recognizes malignant spiritual powers, or demons, who assist Satan in opposing God's providential activity. Thus in Deuteronomy 18:10–14 Moses warns against using occult powers to predict the future and communicate with the deceased. Yet in spite of God's manifold goodness, Israel abandoned God, worshiped alien gods, and sacrificed to demons (*šēdîm*; Deut. 32:17). The latter text suggests that pagan sacrifice actually represents sacrifice to demonic powers.

Scripture represents prayer as a purposeful instrument of God's providence. For example, in Genesis 24 Abraham sent his servant Eliezer to secure a wife for Isaac from among Abraham's kinfolk. Eliezer prayed earnestly that God would grant him success in the mission (vv. 12–14). Yet, according to verse 15, God answered Eliezer's prayer even before he had finished praying. As a result, the line that would lead to the Messiah was established. On the other hand, Abraham's intercession for Sodom, although uttered with persistence and compassion, yielded no tangible result (Gen. 18:22–33).

Historical Books

In his prayer celebrating the building of the temple, Ezra said of God, "You give life to everything" (Neh. 9:6). By these words Ezra acknowledged that the creator God sustains all things in existence by his power. Likewise Hannah in her prayer confessed that God guides in all the circumstances of life (1 Sam. 2:6–10).

The historical books affirm that God actively guided the affairs of the nation Israel. The Lord raised up David to be a shepherd and ruler of his people (2 Sam. 5:2; 12:7–8) and chose Solomon to succeed him as king (1 Kings 3:7; 1 Chron. 22:10). God not only selected kings, but he also rejected kings, as in the case of the wicked Saul (1 Sam. 16:1). The Scriptures relate that because of persistent idolatry, the Lord delivered the northern kingdom into the hands of Assyria (2 Kings 17:18–20). Sennacherib, in fact, was God's chosen instrument to punish Israel (2 Kings 19:25). Likewise, God delivered Judah and Jerusalem into the hands of Nebuchadnezzar, king of Babylon, who burned the temple and deported the remaining Jews to Babylon (2 Kings 24:2–3, 20; 2 Chron. 36:17–20).

In 539 B.C. the Persians conquered the Babylonian Empire. One of the first public acts of Cyrus was to issue a decree allowing the Jews to return to Jerusalem and rebuild the temple (Ezra 1:1–4). The decree of Cyrus likely was a matter of personal political expediency, for the Persian king cultivated the loyalty of subjugated peoples by granting them a measure of self-determination and by respecting their religious traditions.[51] Nevertheless, the sovereign God providentially used Cyrus' political maneuvering in a way that perpetuated the life and worship of the Jewish nation.

The providence of God is the principal theme of at least two books of the Old Testament. The Book of Ruth relates God's providential workings in the lives of ordinary people. Following the death of her husband, Ruth the Moabitess accompanied her widowed mother-in-law Naomi to Bethlehem. A poor woman, Ruth "happened" to be gleaning in a field belonging to Boaz, the kinsman of Naomi's late husband. After Ruth's nearest kinsman refused to redeem her (i.e., buy back her deceased husband's land and marry her, Ruth 4:3–6), Boaz himself purchased the property and took Ruth as his wife. Through this marriage to Boaz, Ruth entered the family of David and Jesus Christ, who centuries later was born in the same town of Bethlehem (Ruth 4:18–20; Matt. 1:1, 5).[52]

The Book of Esther tells the story of a plot to exterminate the Jews in the reign of Xerxes and of God's working to preserve his chosen people. When queen Vashti was deposed because she refused to be displayed at the king's lavish party, Esther, a Jewess, was chosen out of many aspirants to be the new queen. Meanwhile Haman, Xerxes' self-seeking prime minister, conceived a plot to kill Mordecai (Esther's cousin) and all the Jews who remained behind in Persia. One night when the king could not sleep, he read of Mordecai's role in foiling an asassination plot against himself. Ironically, through an astonished Haman, the king elevated Mordecai to a position of honor in his palace. Later, when Haman appeared to molest Esther, the king ordered Haman hung on the gallows that he, Haman, had prepared for Mordecai. Meanwhile Mordecai had urged Esther to intercede before the king on behalf of the Jews. The heart of his argument is the famous line: "And who knows but that you have come to royal position for such a time as this?" (Est. 4:14). Esther prevailed in her plea, and the king issued a second decree permitting the Jews to defend themselves against attack. Mordecai's rise to power within Xerxes' administration spared the Jews from any further persecution (9:1–4; 10:3). Clearly the Book of Esther attests God's overruling in the affairs of men and nations and his unfailing care for his people. The fact that God's name is not mentioned in the book serves to underscore God's providential working behind the scenes.[53]

Through miracles God furthered his plan for the chosen people. When Joshua made a late-night attack on the Amorites, God caused the sun to stand still (Josh. 10:12–14), thereby allowing Israel to complete the battle under cover of semi-darkness. The reduction of light may have been due to an eclipse of the sun or the result of a severe hailstorm (v. 11). Whatever the cause,[54] the point is that God miraculously lengthened the darkness to enable Israel to gain a military victory. The miracle God wrought in connection with Elijah's contest with 450 priests of Baal on Mount Carmel (1 Kings 18:17–40) demonstrated that God is the true God and that Baal is helpless. After Elijah prayed to the Lord fervently (vv. 36–37), fire fell from heaven and burned both the sacrifice and the stones of the altar.

Wisdom and Poetry

Scripture affirms that created entities are not self-sustaining, but are held in existence by the active power of God. Thus Job says of the Lord: "In his hand is the life (*nepeš*) of every creature and the breath (*rûaḥ*) of all mankind" (Job 12:10; cf. Ps. 36:6). "If [God] withdrew his spirit and breath, all mankind would perish together" (Job 34:14–15).

Job believed that God exercises providential control over the affairs of nations: "He makes nations great, and destroys them; he enlarges nations and disperses them" (Job 12:23). When the psalmist says, "The kings of the earth belong to God" (Ps. 47:9), he means that the world's rulers wittingly or unwittingly serve God's purposes and further his ends.

A prominent theme in Job and the Psalms is God's wise governance of the inanimate and lower animate realms. According to Job 38, God controls all the operations of the natural world, namely, the earth and the sea (vv. 4–8), the daily rising of the sun (vv. 12–15), the underworld (vv. 16–18), hail and snow (vv. 22–23), storms (vv. 24–30), the stars (vv. 31–33), and clouds and lightning (vv. 34–38). The phenomena of nature are not fortuitous nor are they products of a blind force (popularly called "mother nature"), for the psalmist confesses that "lightning and hail, snow and clouds, stormy winds . . . do his bidding" (Ps. 148:8; cf. Job 37:5–13). Psalm 65:9–11 asserts that the fructification of the soil, the provision of early and latter rains, and bounteous harvests all attest God's providential supply. Psalm 104 teaches not only God's governance of the physical world (vv. 3–13), but also the marvelous way he provides for and orders the vegetable (vv. 14–17) and animal (vv. 17–22) worlds. The Lord gives food to every creature (Ps. 136:25; cf. 147:9).

The Psalms repeatedly attest God's encircling providential care for the righteous (Ps. 5:12). The Lord protects his people from danger, sustains them in time of want, delivers them from their enemies, and destroys their foes (Pss. 34:17, 19; 37:17, 28). Entire Psalms (e.g., Pss. 91, 121) praise God for his providential care in times of trouble or need. The wicked, however, are the objects of God's providential judgment (Ps. 11:6; 75:8).

In relation to evil, the psalmist acknowledges God's restraining providence when he prays that God would spare him from the bondage of "willful sins" (Ps. 19:13). Permissive providence is evident in God's determination to remove the hedge of protection around Job and allow Satan to ravage his property (Job 1:10–12). Limiting providence occurs in God's refusal to allow Satan to touch Job's person. Similarly, in Job's second test God permitted Satan to afflict Job himself short of taking his life (Job 2:6). The story of Job indicates that God establishes specific boundaries for suffering and evil in the world. God's permission of affliction for the accomplishment of spiritual goals is also evident in Psalm 119:67, 71, 75.

A redirecting kind of providence, by which God turns human sin to serve his ends, is indicated in the words of Psalm 76:10: "Surely the wrath of men shall praise thee; the residue of wrath thou wilt gird upon thee" (RSV). God takes the evil that opposes him and marvously redirects it to serve his purposes. The saying "The king's heart is in the hand of the LORD (Prov. 21:1) similarly affirms that God ultimately accomplishes his purposes in the lives of rulers (cf. Prov. 16:9; 19:21).

The Psalms indicate that the universe is populated with myriads of angels organized in the form of an "assembly" (*qāhāl*) or a "council" (*sôd*) (Ps. 89:5, 7). The cherubim appear to be a high order of angels who guard the throne of God (Pss. 18:10; 80:1), whereas the greater number of angels are lesser messengers dedicated to doing God's will (Ps. 103:20). A primary function of the common angels is to minister to the needs of the saints (Pss. 34:7; 91:11–12). Prayer in the Psalms is also seen to be a potent instrument of providence. God answers the petitions of his people with "awesome deeds of righteousness" (Ps. 65:2, 5) that inspire terror in the unsaved (Pss. 46:2; 76:7). In response to believing prayer he delivers the righteous from all their troubles (Pss. 34:17; 91:15).

Prophetic Literature

Divine providence is seen in God's selection and empowering of Jeremiah to serve as his prophet to the nations (Jer. 1:5–10). God promised his servants in the course of their ministry that he would providentially guide (Isa. 42:16; Jer. 10:23), succor (Isa. 40:11), and save them (63:9). God's providential protection is vividly seen in his preservation of Shadrach, Meshach, and Abednego in the fiery furnace, where not a hair of their head nor a thread of their clothes was singed by the intense heat (Dan. 3:19–27).

The prophecy of Jonah dramatically portrays God's providential working to extend his grace to the nations. The Lord's response to Jonah's disobedient flight from duty was to cause a violent storm to erupt at sea, thus prompting the mariners to throw Jonah overboard. In a further display of his control of the natural world, God miraculously "provided [piel of *mānāh*] a great fish to swallow Jonah" (Jonah 1:17). When Jonah prayed in desperation from within the fish, God answered by causing the sea creature to vomit the prophet onto the shore (2:1–10). The outcome of these dealings was the wholesale repentance of the Ninevites in response to Jonah's message. Finally, when Jonah wallowed in self-pity, God "provided" (piel of *mānāh*] a gourd, a worm, and a hot wind (4:6–8) to teach the prophet how great was his love for the pagan city.

Prominent in the prophetic books is God's control over the destiny of rulers and nations. Daniel acknowledges that "the Most High is sovereign over the kingdoms of men and he gives them to anyone he wishes" (Dan. 4:17, 25, 32; cf. 5:21). The metalic image of Nebuchadnezzar's dream (2:32–45)—interpreted as the succession of Babylonian, Medo-Persian, Greek, and Roman empires that would ultimately be crushed by the kingdom of the Messiah—further affirms God's providential direction of human history.

Isaiah prophesied that God would

send Assyria "the rod of [his] anger" (Isa. 10:5) to conquer the northern kingdom and lead them into captivity (cf. 7:20). The prophet describes the conquest of the chosen people by pagan forces as "his [i.e., God's] work" (Isa. 10:12). Moreover, God gave Egypt and its wealth to Nebuchadnezzar as a reward for the Babylonian's service to him (Ezek. 29:18–20). God later would raise up the Babylonians to punish Judah with captivity (Hab. 1:6; Isa. 39:6–7; cf. Lam. 3:37–38). In due course God stirred up the Medo-Persian Empire under Cyrus to vanquish the mighty Babylonian kingdom (Isa. 13:17). Finally, God called Cyrus "in righteousness to his service" (Isa. 41:2), designated this unbelieving ruler as his "shepherd" (Isa. 44:28), and so used him to restore the Jews to the land and to rebuild the temple (Isa. 45:1–7). Clearly the prophets depict God as actively guiding the affairs of the nations for the realization of his general and redemptive purposes.

Synoptic Gospels

Jesus affirmed God's general providence by saying that the "Father in heaven . . . causes his sun to rise on the evil and the good, and sends rain on the righteous and the unrighteous" (Matt. 5:45). Since God is Father of all by virtue of creation, he sends undeserved blessings to all humankind through the ordinary processes of nature. Jesus also upheld God's special providence in Matthew 6:25–34. As the disciple seeks God's kingdom and righteousness, he need not be anxious about material needs. Arguing from the lesser to the greater, Jesus reasoned that since God manifestly feeds the birds and adorns the flowers, so he will feed, clothe, and provide his servants with every material necessity. God's loving concern extends even to trivial matters: the Father who watches the common sparrow fall to the ground has numbered the hairs on the head of his people (Matt. 10:29–30).

The Gospels represent angels as personal, immaterial, and asexual beings that exist in great numbers (Matt. 22:30; 26:53; Luke 2:13). "Holy angels" (Mark 8:38; Luke 9:26)—those beings that retained their spiritual integrity—frequently are depicted as agents of divine providence. Thus God sent the angel Gabriel to inform Mary that she would conceive by the Holy Ghost and give birth to the Son of God (Luke 1:26–38). An angel of the Lord communicated the same message to Joseph in a dream (Matt. 1:20–21) and later commanded Joseph to flee to Egypt with his family (Matt. 2:13). During Jesus' earthly ministry, angels comforted the Lord following his temptations by the devil (Matt. 4:11) and strengthened him during his agony in Gethsemane (Luke 22:43). Jesus taught that every childlike believer has at least one ministering angel with direct access to the Father in heaven (Matt. 18:10). At the end of the age, the angels who accompany Christ at his second coming will gather up the elect (Matt. 24:31) and execute judgment upon the wicked (Matt. 13:41, 49).

The Gospels identify demons as angels who were carried away by Lucifer in his rebellion against God (Matt. 25:41). Demons frequently possess unbelievers (e.g., Mark 1:23–24; 5:2–5; 7:25–26), causing manifold physical and psychological disorders (Matt. 9:32; 12:22; 17:15). By his divine power and authority, Jesus exorcised demons from the possessed (Matt. 8:16, 32; 12:22; Luke 4:36), as did the disciples acting in his name (Luke 10:17).

The Gospels say much about prayer as an instrument of providence. By means of three imperatives—"ask . . . seek . . . knock"—Jesus enjoined believers to pray. He also taught that God delights to give good gifts to his children in response to their prayers (Matt.

7:7–11). God performs the seemingly impossible in response to prayer offered in unwavering faith (Matt. 21:22). The model prayer Jesus taught his disciples (Matt. 6:9–13) petitions God to bring to fruition his kingdom purposes and providentially to supply the physical, moral, and spiritual needs of his children.

Primitive Christianity/Acts

Paul proclaimed to pagan Athenians (Acts 17:28) what their own poets had discovered to be true from general revelation, namely, that all living things owe their existence to God's sustaining power: "in him we live [*zōmen*] and move [*kinoumetha*] and have our being [*esmen*]." God's general providence is seen in the wise ordering of the universe, by which he causes the seasons, rainfall, growth of crops, and food to nourish the body (Acts 14:17). Likewise, God guides the course of history, having established political boundaries and assigned the epochs in which the individual nations flourish (Acts. 17:26).

God's special providence, directed to the outworking of his redemptive purpose, is evident in the phenomena of Pentecost (Acts 2:1–41). When the disciples were gathered in the upper room, God sent a powerful visitation of the Spirit in the form of a violent wind and tongues of fire (vv. 1–4). When the disciples mingled among the multitudes assembled for the feast, the people were amazed to hear them speaking in their own languages (vv. 5–12). The upshot of it all was that in response to Peter's preaching, three thousand persons were converted and the church came into being (v. 41). The special providence that leads to Christ is seen in Philip's encounter with the Ethiopian eunuch (Acts 8:26–39). It seemed strange that an angel of the Lord directed Philip to a hot desert road. Yet enroute Philip encountered an Ethopian official who was puzzled about the meaning of the fifty-third chapter of Isaiah. Philip interpreted this prophetic text and led the Ethiopian to Christ. Clearly Philip was God's man in God's place at God's time.

In relation to evil, Paul attests God's permissive providence in Acts 14:16: "In the past, he let [*eiasen*] all nations go their own way" (cf. Acts 17:30: "In the past God overlooked such ignorance"). What Paul declared at Lystra was that in former days, before the coming of special revelation in Christ, God in seeming complacency left the pagan world to itself. But now that Christ has come, he calls the unbelieving world into judgment through the One whom he raised from the dead (17:31). Peter attests a kind of redirecting providence in Acts 2:23–24; 3:13–15; 4:27–28. Filled with malice, the Jews, assisted by the Romans, killed the Lord's Christ. But the sovereign God redirected the evil he permitted by making atonement for the sins of the world and openly displayed the triumph by raising Jesus from the dead.

Angelic ministers of providence are prominent in the Book of Acts. In Acts 10 an angel in a vision to Cornelius ordered him to send for Peter (vv. 3–6). On the following day God supernaturally informed Peter not to judge unclean what God had made clean (vv. 9–16). Led to Cornelius by messengers, Peter preached Christ and saw that the Holy Spirit fell on all who heard the gospel (vv. 44–48). Through this course of events God opened the church to Gentile believers. Angels abetted the advance of the gospel when through miraculous occurrences they delivered Christian preachers from jail (Acts 5:18–24; 12:5–11). Prayer not only led to the miraculous release of Paul and Silas from prison but also resulted in the conversion of the Philippian jailor and his household (Acts 16:25–34).

Pauline Literature

In Colossians 1:16–17 Paul maintains that Christ is the cosmic agent of creation and preservation. The origination of the universe and its maintenance in existence are related but distinct works. The apostle's words, "in him all things hold together [*synistēmi*]," affirms that the power of Christ renders the universe a cosmos rather than a chaos. Romans 11:36 juxtaposes God's preservation and his providence: "For from him [*ex autou*] and through him [*di autou*] and to him [*eis auton*] are all things." Or as the NEB expresses it: God is "Source, Guide and Goal of all that is." Murray correctly comments that God "is the agent through whom all things subsist and are directed to their proper end."[55] Ephesians 4:6 makes the same point.

Paul affirms God's special providence in relation to believers in Galatians 1:15–16. God set Paul apart from his birth, revealed his Son to him in the Damascus experience, and made Paul the greatest missionary in the church. From a broader perspective, God causes all of life's circumstances to fall out for the ultimate good of the saint who loves him (Rom. 8:28). Things do not cooperate fortuitously, for the subject of *panta synergei eis agathon* is "he" (i.e., God), which some manuscripts rendered explicit by inserting the nominative phrase *ho theos*.[56] In Philippians 4:19 Paul encourages believers by saying, "God will meet [*plērōsai,* to "fill up"] all your needs according to his glorious riches in Christ Jesus."

In relation to evil, God's limiting providence is affirmed in 1 Corinthians 10:13. God mitigates the intensity of trials and provides a way of escape so that believers will be able to stand and not fall. Second Thessalonians 2:6–7 teaches that the anarchy to be unleashed by the man of lawlessness presently is restrained by what he describes as *to katechon* (v. 6) and *ho katechōn* (v. 7). Who or what is "the restrainer" that holds the mystery of lawlessness in check? The interpretation that best explains the neuter and masculine genders posits "the restrainer" as God-instituted government (neut.), which in Paul's day was personified by the Roman emperor (masc.). "Paul viewed established government as imposing a salutary restraint on evil (Rom. 13:3–4), and in his mission field established government was effectively the Roman Empire personally embodied in the emperor."[57]

Permissive providence is clearly seen in Romans 1:24, 26, 28. There Paul affirms of those who rejected the rudimentary knowledge of God afforded by general revelation that "God gave them over" (*paradidōmi,* to "deliver over") to the lusts of their sinful natures. In the words of C. S. Lewis, the unsaved "enjoy forever the horrible freedom they have demanded, and are therefore self-enslaved."[58] A further example of permissive providence is seen in the Corinthian church's handing over an immoral brother to Satan's influence (1 Cor. 5:5). Similarly God allowed Paul to be imprisoned in Rome for preaching the gospel (Phil. 1:12–14). Because of Paul's chains, the palace guard and other officials heard about Christ, and the Christians were encouraged to preach Christ more courageously.

Paul depicts Satan as "the ruler of the kingdom of the air" (Eph. 2:2), who holds sway over "the dominion of darkness" (Col. 1:13). In the battle between the two kingdoms, believers contend "against the rulers, against the authorities, against the powers of this dark world and against the spiritual forces of evil in the heavenly realms" (Eph. 6:12). In the last days demonic activity will increase, and many people will follow these "deceiving spirits" and deny the truth (1 Tim. 4:1). Yet Paul teaches that God's kingdom will prevail over that of the ursurper. On the cross Christ scored a victory over Satan and his legion (Col. 2:15) in anticipation of his final triumph over every alien power (Phil. 2:10–11; Eph. 1:20–21).

Johannine Writings

Jesus upheld divine preservation when he affirmed, "My Father is always at his work [*ergazomai*] to this very day . . ." (John 5:17). God's seventh-day rest is not one of inactivity, for he actively sustains the world he created and also redeems his people through mighty acts in history. See also Revelation 4:11.

God's providential activity consists in upholding believers in the faith. Jesus acknowledged before the Father: "While I was with them, I protected them [*tēreō*] and kept them safe [*phylassō*] by that name you gave me" (John 17:12). God occasionally permits affliction to strike so that through his supply of the person's need his own excelling glory might be displayed (John 9:1–34).

The course of end-time events outlined in the Apocalypse confirms God's providential control of history. "The Lion of the tribe of Judah" who opens the seven seals to the scroll will set in motion the awesome complex of eschatological events (Rev. 5:1–8:1). This symbolism of the Lion connotes that the Christ who triumphed on the cross (Rev. 5:5) is "lord of history and master of the world's destiny."[59] Seven angels will sound seven trumpets that announce the unleashing of a series of natural disasters and demonic assaults on the human race (Rev. 8:2–11:19). After that seven angels will pour out on the sinful world system seven bowls containing yet more intense plagues from the angry God (Rev. 15:1–16:21). The fall of Babylon, "the great prostitute," anticipates the collapse of the God-rejecting, self-exalting nations of the world (Rev. 17:1–19:5). Finally Satan—that liar and murderer who caused the Fall (John 8:44; 1 John 3:8) and who subsequently "leads the whole world astray" (Rev. 12:9)—will be seized by an angel, bound, and cast into the abyss for a thousand years (Rev. 20:1–3). After a final brief rebellion in which he deceives the nations (vv. 8–9), Satan will be thrown into the lake of fire to be tormented forever (v. 10). Thus God's victory and his purpose for humanity will be complete.

Other New Testament Writings

Hebrews 1:3 affirms God's preservation of the universe through the agency of his Son by the phrase, "sustaining [*pherōn*] all things by his powerful word [*rhēma*]." Through his creative word Christ called the universe into existence, and through his sustaining word he maintains it in its course. Christ "upholds the universe not like Atlas supporting a dead weight on his shoulders, but as One who carries all things forward on their appointed course."[60]

God's permissive providence is seen in the disciplinary sufferings he allows his children to experience, according to Hebrews 12:5–11. This text affirms that as God used suffering to make the author of our salvation "perfect" (Heb. 2:10), so he uses hardships and persecution to lead his blood-bought children to the goal of personal holiness (Heb. 12:10–11). In a similar vein, James teaches that Christians should rejoice in the trials (*peirasmoi*) of life, for such God-permitted testings produce perseverance that leads to spiritual maturity (James 1:2–4).

Scripture affirms that angels are intelligent (1 Peter 1:12) and powerful (2 Peter 2:11) "ministering spirits [*leitourgika pneumata*] sent to serve those who will inherit salvation" (Heb. 1:14).

According to this general statement, angelic agents of providence minister to the spiritual and physical needs of believers in Christ. The General Epistles attest the fall of certain angels who, overcome with pride and not content with their God-given "positions of authority" (*archē*), rebelled against God (2 Peter 2:4; Jude 6). The Lord has consigned these malignant spirits to pits of darkness to await the day of judgment. Although *de jure* a defeated foe, Satan and his forces *de facto* oppress the saints by stalking and seeking to overwhelm them as an animal hunts down its prey (1 Peter 5:8). When overcome by trials or misfortunes or when sick, believers are to petition the God who is able to effect objective changes in their circumstances (James 5:13–18).

SYSTEMATIC FORMULATION

God's acts of creation called something into existence out of nothing and formed things into the basic "kinds." God's acts of providence enable creation to continue (in spite of sin and its consequences) and fulfill both God's uniform and special, redemptive purposes. As Charles Hatfield succinctly explained, "God not only made the world, but He manages the world and guides it productively toward worthy goals."[61] By providence we refer to God's continuous use of his great power to achieve his wise, just, and loving values in nature and history. Everything that exists in nature and takes place in history fulfills some aspect of God's wise purposes envisioned in holy love. Temporary appearances notwithstanding, evil does not have the last word in either the objective or humanly subjective worlds. Everything is ultimately relatable to God's presence and purposes in providential activity.

We noted previously five of God's revealed purposes for history, the first two being realized in God's universal rule, the last three in his redemptive rule: (1) to create self-determining beings in his image to function in the world according to uniform physical and moral laws; (2) to permit the Fall, unfaithfulness to him and his laws with the physical, moral, and spiritual consequences; (3) to send his Son to provide atonement as a just basis for universal and redemptive grace; (4) to send the Holy Spirit to call out from the kingdom of evil a people to bless the whole world not only individually, but also in their families, nations, and churches; and (5) to unite the whole of heaven and earth under Christ's kingdom (I:314–17).

To achieve these ends for his glory, we saw that God planned to use unconditional strategies apart from human agents and conditional strategies with human agents (1:317–19). In this chapter we investigate God's deployment of these strategies. To achieve the ends of the unconditional decretive will God, according to his miraculous strategy, acts either apart from any second causes or uses human agency or nature's laws in extraordinary (miraculous) ways. Thus God accompishes his unconditional ends supernaturally. Ordinarily, however, God achieves his preceptive and permissive wills through human means according to a conditional (providential) strategy. God makes known his moral requirements in the heart or in the written law (the requirements of the Ten Commandments). People may either believe and obey them or disbelieve and disobey them. When people believe and obey his revealed desires, God's preceptive will is done and he is pleased. When people disbelieve and disobey them, God's preceptive will is not done and he is displeased. In either case God achieves his preceptive ends conditionally through people. In this chapter's biblical section we found numerous illustrations of God's conditional will at work in history. Scripture repeatedly attests the fact that God not only permits evil, while sovereignly restraining or limiting it, but also redirects it, overcoming evil for goods not otherwise obtainable. We now attempt to understand more specifically God's providential working in relation to nature, time, persons, free will, and moral evil.

God Rules Universally in Space

The cosmos is not a supreme, self-existent expanse. God is the only eternal, self-existent being. He created and sustains the vast extent of the universe. And God providentially rules in space through natural laws. The laws of nature depend on the Creator's freely chosen purposes and freely exercised power to carry them out in the ways planned. What, then, is God's continuous relation to space? How is the ordinary activity of the living God related to the regular functions of the cosmos?

Creation's space and laws are not absolute or ultimate, but they depend on God. Scientifically described laws do not determine final purposes. They are means or instruments created and sustained to accomplish God's usual purposes. Nature's laws may limit human freedom, but they do not limit God's freedom. God freely made these laws what they are to accomplish his universal objectives through ordered processes and relationships. Because he is omnipresent, God is not removed from nature's laws as deists think. Because he is transcendent and changeless, God's being is not continuous with the temporal, changing being of nature as pantheists and panentheists think. The transcendent Creator remains the Lord of space and everything extended in space.

The naturalistic worldview dominant in much Western education has influenced many to imagine that the so-called laws of nature are *ultimate explanations* of natural phenomena. To respect the observations of science it is not necessary to add to one's worldview naturalistic presuppositions as did Bultmann. Naturalists simply *assume* the regularity of natural laws. Nontheists have no adequate basis, however, for their faith that the law of gravity will hold tomorrow. The observations of regularity that have been made as science has developed do not guarantee anything about the future. A turkey with naturalistic assumptions could readily assume that because every morning the farmer comes with water and feed he will do so tomorrow. Tomorrow the farmer may have a different purpose, however, such as the celebration of a holiday like Thanksgiving, and come with an axe! Mere descriptions of past regularities, important as they are, provide no guarantee of future regularities.

Theists, in contrast, have a reason for believing that nature's regularities will be the same tomorrow. The uniformity of nature depends on the sustaining power of the God who faithfully keeps his Word. God promised Noah that as long as the earth remains, he will not again destroy "all living creatures" by a flood (Gen. 8:21). "As long as the earth endures, seedtime and harvest, cold and heat, summer and winter, day and night will never cease" (8:22). Indeed we are dependent on God, "for in him we live and move and have our being" (Acts 17:28).

As the final cause of everything, God has chosen to accomplish some of his goals through both (1) material causes informed by the Logos (John 1:1–3) and (2) personal agents as efficient causes (on personal and impersonal causes, see 1:310). Natural regularities being sustained by God are not unnecessary, insignificant, nor alien to God. Rather, they are given eternal significance in God's plan. For example, God has designed physical organisms like human bodies so that, given normal circumstances, they heal themselves. Hence natural healings are ultimately divine healings through the secondary causes.

The "laws" of nature are not autonomous powers, but statistical probabilities based on our observations of the way God ordinarily chooses to accomplish his purposes through real, but dependent material entities. Some of God's purposes are achieved on earth through impersonal causes within the range of possibilities provided by the regular patterns of nature that God created and sustains. Within that range of possibilities, God also achieves his purposes through personal causes, the often unpredictable individual choices that actually do take place.

We find ourselves a long way from Eden in a world affected by humanity's sin. Since the Fall God's ways of accomplishing his purposes through nature differ. Natural evils have resulted from moral evil (Rom. 8:20). Some sinners, through what insurance people call "acts of God," justly receive some of the deserved consequences of their rebellion against God here and now, while others will receive most of the consequences after this life. For God's moral and spiritual children by faith, natural evils may also serve purposes of chastening, education, and discipline.

Unquestionably, natural evils such as hurricanes, earthquakes, and floods seem cruel, especially when they take lives. No one who dies, however, dies unjustly, for all have sinned and deserve to die physically at some time. By touching a high voltage wire an electrician can be electrocuted, and so equally can a young athlete. At a small lake at a church camp two boys broke through thin ice and drowned. So did their leader who tried to save them! The population of Pompeii was destroyed by burning volcanic ash and lava and superheated air. Natural laws are no respecters of persons. When we hear of events like these, we think that there must be a better way to run the universe. Imagine, however, how impossible life would be if nature did not function according to regular laws! Imagine, if you can, what it would be like trying to live in a world where people could be electrocuted without notice by wood or plastic, suffocated by warm air, or burned by cold water! Without the order of nature, life would not only be worse, it would be impossible! Wisely God has chosen to sustain an ordered world. With the decision to sustain an ordered world came the consequences for all who break either natural or moral laws without respect of persons.

In *Why Bad Things Happen to Good People* Rabbi Harold S. Kushner finds it impossible to attribute nature's laws to divine providence. Unfortunately he fails to take into account God's permissive will and attributes suffering to other sources like the laws of nature, "which God did not cause and cannot stop."[62] This may seem to make his child's illness easier to accept, but Kushner's God is too small. The hypothesis of a limited God does not fit the abundant data of Scripture that attributes natural laws and conditions to divine creation and providence. Our comfort may be short-lived if our God is too small to be the final cause of all things and to work through nature's regularities for wise, just, and good ends. Although God is the final cause of everything, he is not the efficient or blameworthy cause of moral evil (I:310).

Living by God's providence in a universe ordered, rather than chaotic, our building codes, driving patterns, and health guidelines need to be in harmony with nature. Confucianism and many "back to nature" movements have a part of the truth. Harmony with natural law contributes to a healthy life.

To be in harmony with nature, however, is not necessarily to be in moral and spiritual harmony with the transcendent Lord of all. God is distinct from nature and his redemptive purposes are not discovered in nature (chap. 2, vol. 1). Harmony with nature's laws may reflect harmony with God's physical purposes, though not necessarily from motives of honoring the Lord of all. Neither does harmony with God's physical purposes alone necessarily indicate harmony with God's moral rule nor with his gracious redemptive purposes for the unjust. The Christian cannot ultimately divorce any level of creation from the purposes of God. Everything in the world of space is intended to promote communion with the Lord who is present in all of nature and support his values.

God Rules Universally Through Time

Every event in time as well as everything in space speaks of the transcendent Lord of providence. Before creation apparently there was no time, other than its potential in the changeless God's plans for creation. But with creation came the changing world with its succession of events. The earth had a beginning, is dependent, and is passing away. In a biblical view, however, temporal history is neither unreal nor cyclical. On the fourth "day" of creation God appointed the sun and moon for measuring the successions of events on earth by days and nights, weeks, months, seasons, and years. Providentially God sustains the earth in its orbit around the sun for the marking out of time sequences. The Bible does not explicitly emphasize scientific time relative to the speed of light, but majors on historical time and its significance for personal decision making.

God is not limited by time, but knows and understands and sustains the temporal sequence as we experience it. The Creator provided for temporal reality by creating accountable people who, like him, have ability to transcend the present moment. We are not limited to the present moment but can remember the past and anticipate the future. So we can be conscious of meaningful successions of events in our lives. Hence humans have unique biographies, and societies have unique histories. In the temporal arena humans have unrepeatable opportunities to know love and obey the creator and the redeemer. Within the historical matrix every thought, word, and deed is known by the Lord of all. However insignificant one's life may seem, each day has significance in the light of eternity. For each opportunity we will give account to our all-knowing Judge.

God knows and sustains all that transpires in time, both history's long ages, and history's major turning points. The scriptural "age" (*aiōn*) refers to the Lord's managing of the great epochs of history. The aeons are not authorities in their own right (as in Gnosticism) nor emanations or delegates of God (as in pantheism). Within God's long-range purposes for the ages of human history, however, are some definite temporal turning points especially appropriate for a given undertaking. The prime turning point (*kairos*) for all time came at Christ's first advent.

After the creation of the first Adam, history's greatest turning point occurred at the second Adam's first advent. The end of the present age will occur at Christ's return in power and glory. The infinite qualitative disjunction between God and humans assumed by Kierkegaard, Barth, Brunner, Bultmann, and many biblical theologians tends to undermine universal providence by limiting divine acts to vertical, internal experiences. Cullmann's corrective in *Christ and Time* correctly puts the incarnate Christ at the center of God's continuous work horizontally in history. But Cullmann's mythological treatment of the beginning and end of history raises the possibility that all biblical events, including Christ's incarnation, may be reduced to myth.[63] The Lord of time created the first Adam and providentially guides historical opportunities from his day to this, and from this day to the end.

The great biblical themes of self-determination, responsibility, and decision, of unbelief or belief, and final judgment can best be appreciated in this concept of time as humans experience it. Persons in historical time inescapably face responsibility for moral conduct *now*. In the present moment we live life and make decisions and commitments. We cannot alter our past. No amount of regret will change the opportunities that parents or children, church officers or church members have lost. Historians cannot experiment with their material. But the most distinctive characteristic of the future is the variety of its possibilities. To humans the future seems pregnant with possibilities of all sorts. As gamblers, with their limited purviews testify, until a thing has happened, almost anything can happen and does!

To human consciousness everything in the future appears to be open and alterable. Only those events that God achieves unconditionally are not. In the ordinary conditional strategy, although God is the final cause of everything, God does not unconditionally determine the future nor become the efficient cause of ordinary human conduct. Neither preoccupation with divine foreknowledge nor the probabilities of scientific time and relativity can eliminate the existential givenness of the present moment and our consciousness of the radical distinction between the past and the future.[64] As we make choices in the openness of our futures, we do so under the knowledge of the all-seeing God and under his wise, holy, and loving influences. But in these decisions we are the responsible agents. How the great Sustainer, Teacher, and Guide is able to bring together unique convergences of real human choices in history to realize his purposes needs further consideration.

God's Universal Rule and Human Wills

Granting that God uses nature's regular operations and the unique convergences of factors at the great moments of history to accomplish his ends, it may seem more problematic for him to work ordinarily with human persons who have "free wills." In theism, in contrast to pantheism, however, God is not the only real agent. God initially gave his image-bearers the ability to examine alternatives, to choose among ends, and to do what they desired, whether moral or immoral. No human beings lack some knowledge of God's desire for communion with them (Acts 17:27) and of God's moral requirements (Rom. 2:14–15; see chap. 2, vol. 1). Some have Moses' law in addition and some have the example of Christ's fellowship with the Father and his fulfillment of God's moral demands.

It seems paradoxical or contradictory to many that, given God's moral suasion, people determine their own choices and actions and at the same time do God's will. The frequent tendency of people who lack a method of theological decision-making is to pronounce biblical emphases on divine sovereignty and human responsibility an irreconcilable antinomy, a paradox, or a mystery. In the final analysis no finite, fallen mind fully comprehends either the divine or human wills separately, let alone in relationship. But the limited information God has disclosed does make sense. An integrative approach to understanding providence seeks to display the coherence and viability of revealed truth about the activity of both the divine and the human persons in history.

In the light of the biblical evidence we cannot deny the reality of either the divine or the human factors. It does not follow that if God directs, then we have no part in a matter, or if we decide, God has nothing to do with it. It was not the case that if the Father willed the cross Jesus did not, or vice versa. Not just one will, but many wills may contribute influentially to significant personal, family, church, and national events. In any event in a personal biography or a church's history many human wills may have suggested possibilities, methods, ethical principles, and consequences of certain decisions. As other persons may influence our decisions and actions, so God's influence can be noted in a biography or any complex historical event. We will never understand divine providence in human decision-making if unrealistically we assume a single cause for each event. And it is not enough to recognize many finite factors as antecedents if God is ignored or excluded.

Seeking to be fair to all strands of evidence, we incorporate the data concerning both the divine and the human factors in history. But the cases for both are not equally strong and they are not equally ultimate. Hence in the ordinary usage of the word, people should not call them "antinomies."[65] Appeals to antinomies since Kant admit that our reasoning has come to an irrecoverable stalemate with equally good (or bad) arguments on both sides. If such an eventuality appears, however, we ought not attribute our logical difficulties taken from Scripture by our interpretive processes to God's teaching as actually given in Scripture.

Neither is it prudent to attribute to the Scriptures our psychological "tensions" about God's personal relationship to persons. No unhealthy tensions divided God's mind as the Holy Spirit inscripturated the Word! In Holy Writ human agency is not presented as an embarrassment to its creator's or sustainer's providential purposes. And it does not help to add that here we face an irresolvable "mystery." In the tragic poets *mystērion* meant "that which must not or cannot be said" and in Plato "the very negation of speech."[66] But in the New Testament it "betrays no relation to the mystery cults."[67] "Mystery in the New Testament does not deal with the unknowable, but with what is imparted by revelation."[68] The content of biblical mysteries when finally revealed, may not be understood fully, but it can be understood in part. Unlike the Buddhist koans, biblical mysteries when revealed do make sense.

With exceptional insight at this point G. C. Berkouwer explained,

> Hesitation where Paul was bold has caused the Church often to make only a problem of God's rule and man's responsibility. She thus undermines either the Providence of God or human responsibility. *They do not exist in the Scriptures as something problematic.* They both reveal the greatness of Divine activity, in that it does not exclude human activity and responsibility but embraces them and in them manifests God on the way to the accomplishment of His purposes.[69]

God created and providentially preserves humans with wills. Through their decisions he achieves his chosen *ends* in history with pleasure when they follow his precepts and with displeasure when they disobey. God made and sustains self-determining persons, not to ignore them or obliterate them, but that they might share his fellowship, values, and work. Persons with minds, emotions, and wills are a real, highly valued part of God's grand design for lived history.

What does it mean for humans to have "free will"? Two major historic definitions have been given. Free will has been defined as (1) the power of contrary or alternative choice and (2) the power of self-determination and action according to one's nature and apart from coercion. Whether one or the other of both of these major meanings is appropriate depends on the conditions of the era under consideration and the substantial differences made by the Fall, regeneration, and glorification. Hence we must consider the meaning of freedom in four distinct situations.

Before the Fall Adam and Eve experienced freedom not only as the power of responsible self-determination but also as the power of contrary choice. Adam and Eve and the angels could have chosen and determined either to love and obey God or not. But they refused God's ethical persuasion, disobeyed God's command, and so separated themselves from God's fellowship.

Since the Fall the unregenerate freely determine themselves in accord with their depraved natures. Fallen human freedom is the power of responsible self-determination, but it fails to receive redemptive truth, choosing rather motives and acts in accord with a fallen nature. By nature apart from the assistance of divine grace depraved people do not in heart and mind fully accept God's counsel, obey God's laws, believe the gospel, trust Christ, and dominantly seek to please the Lord. When the unregenerate choose objectively good acts, they do so from motives other than the honoring of God and the building of his kingdom. Hence their best acts in actuality come short of the ideal.

At present the regenerate, in addition to the old fleshly nature, have a new spiritual nature. The one self must decide between these two conflicting inclinations or motivations to evil and good. The basic power of self-determination must decide whether to yield to temptation and commit sin or not to yield to temptation and not to commit sin. Hence the regenerate now have the power of contrary choice. For their acts to be worthy in God's sight they must not only have objective morality but also worthy motives. So they need to decide and act in the energy of the Holy Spirit, not the flesh.

In the eternal state the believer's freedom will be self-determination in accord with a fully sanctified nature like Christ's. Then Christians will consistently determine every thought, word, and action wisely, justly, and lovingly. In the new heavens and the new earth, thank the Lord, there will no longer be the freedom of contrary choice, or freedom to obey and to disobey God. In a fully sanctified freedom our self-determination will decide and act consistently in accord with a Christlike nature from motives that please God. That is a freedom like that of God, who cannot deny himself. God does not have the power of contrary moral choice or of sin. Making choices consistent with nature confirmed in righteousness will be our highest freedom!

Unfortunately many discussions of free will fail to consider these temporal differences as Augustine did.[70] This neglect makes untenable generalizations like the claim that freedom always and essentially involves contrary choice. We prefer the simplest possible hypothesis to account for the givens, but when the givens differ at different times we must avoid oversimplification. Oversimplified hypotheses do not fit as many facts as a comprehensive one that accounts for the real volitional differences before and after the Fall, before and after regeneration, and before and after glorification.

God Uses Ethical Persuasion

God used the lure of love and ethical persuasion with Adam and Eve before the Fall, warning them of the consequences of disobedience to a simple command. As necessary and valuable as ethical persuasion was, it did not prove effective for our original parents even in their unfallen state and environment. After the Fall, loving moral suasion has become even less effective because the dominant desires of the unregenerate prevent them from knowing, loving, and serving God with pure motives and with all their capacities. In the regenerate the old nature remains, rendering less than effective the mere knowing of what we ought to be and do. Even for its limited values, however, with either the regenerate or unregenerate God may work indirectly through human teachers and leaders to introduce or stimulate thoughts, feelings, and volitions. The Holy Spirit's presentation of rules, reasons, and consequences of decisions for our consideration finds biblical support.

How do the best parents and teachers work with maturing children and students? They do not make decisions for others who are past childhood, but they treat them as adults. Parents and teachers provide the opportunity for young people to decide, indicating the basic rules or methods of making good decisions in view of sound reasons. They also use ethical persuasion, pointing out the consequences of alternative courses of actions. No analogies are perfect, but another may help.

Think of the God of providence as greater than those who excel in the management of persons in large businesses. People are the manager's most important asset. Managers get things done through people. Good managers treat people with dignity and respect as adults, as partners.[71] The worth that God places on people is higher than the value an excellent manager places on his colaborers.

Managers get things done through people who share similar values. People with shared values are one of God's most important assets in the world. God, like the leader of a business, is primarily an expert in the promotion and protection of values.[72] God who is the source and support of all values affirmed the value of people in creating them uniquely in his image and sustaining a life support system on planet earth for them. Above all else God values the love of people. God shares his wise, holy, and loving purposes and methods with people. Not mechanistically, but as a wise manager God works with people. Productivity in corporations dedicated to excellence comes through people. A manager is value-driven and so leads, organizes, evaluates, and exercises quality control. Similarly the divine manager of human history does all of these par excellence. In managing people in the world God promotes and protects values as he leads, organizes, evaluates, and exercises quality control in history. His actions, like ours, express his priorities.[73]

The quality control of God's enterprise in history called for people who shared his values. At the heart of any successful enterprise are the shared values of the people in it. Unfortunately, left to mere ethical persuasion, no depraved sinners came to live authentically by God's values! The good that the unregenerate do would be far worse if it were not for God's inner and outer persuasion to do good. But the liberal emphasis on ethical persuasion as God's only means of working with people is insufficiently realistic concerning the debilitating effects of habitual pride, selfishness, greed, lust, and hatred.

God Governs Through Families

God works not only with individuals but also with social groups. Providentially God promotes good and restrains evil through primary social institutions such as families and nations. The Lord of all established *the family* to provide for stable, structured personal relationships. In the providence of God, a male and female leave their fathers and mothers and become one flesh (Gen. 2:24). The mutual commitment of spouses is designed for lasting and healthful relations between persons in spirit and body. Jesus reinforced the creation ordinance by adding, "Therefore what God has joined together, let man not separate" (Matt. 19:4–6). Marriage is not mandatory. Jesus himself remained unmarried, and Paul recognized the validity of celibacy (1 Cor. 7:1). Generally, however, "since there is so much immorality, each man should have his own wife, and each woman her own husband" (v. 2). The wife's and the husband's bodies belong not only to themselves, but also to each other (v. 4). The author of Hebrews taught that "marriage should be honored by all, and the marriage bed kept pure, for God will judge the adulterer and all the sexually immoral" (13:4). The marriage ceremony expresses publicly and legally the spouses' mutual respect, trust, and lifelong commitment.

In God's providence faithful *marital relationships* promote several great values. Faithful, loving husbands and wives enjoy lifelong loving companionship and mutual helpfulness in their work as stewards of the earth. Marital fidelity promotes personal security, family stability, and community solidarity. The moral problem of adultery involves not only consequences of the physical act itself but the breaking of freely assumed vows and the flouting of self-determined commitments (even if in some cultures these only amount to accepting one's parents' prearranged marriage). The heinousness of breaking faith with one's spouse is analogous to the evil of God's people breaking faith with their Lord (Mal. 2:11–14). Hence the prophet Malachi exhorts, "So guard yourself in your spirit, and do not break faith with the wife of your youth. 'I hate divorce,' says the LORD God of Israel" (vv. 15–16). Nevetheless God permitted divorce where it was justified (Matt. 19:8–9), but he did so with displeasure. Breaking faith with your spouse leaves scars, not only on spouses and children, but also on other family members.

No matter how attractively adultery may be portrayed in literature, movies, and television, it compromises the integrity of the persons involved, breaks moral commitments, degrades the significance of sexual relationships, and hurts all involved, especially the children. Christian theists, in accord with God's providential order, must decisively choose between mere recreational views of sex that reduce persons to objects (as in lust-inducing pornography) and an understanding of sex as a beautiful gift of God to be enjoyed in the marital commitment for nurturing spouses in an enduring, intimate relationship. As God's gift, sexual intimacy expresses the spouses' *agapē* love for each other and so symbolizes God's faithful *agapē* for his people. Although marriage is not a sacrament that conveys saving grace, it is a beautiful sign of common grace, pointing to the greatness of God's steadfast love. For Christians the self-giving love of husbands for wives also portrays Christ's love for the church in giving himself up for her (Eph. 5:25).

Faithful marital relationships generally tend to produce children, and the *parent-child relationship* is crucial in God's management of the world for the upbringing of the coming generation. God gives parents not only the privileges and joys of parenthood but also its responsibilities. Some of these responsibilities are the following:

1. Parents respect their children's inalienable rights and value children highly, for they also bear the image of the Creator. The "qualities of the child as image-bearer of God—intrinsic significance, possession of gifts and capa-

bilities, and heavenly foundation for identity—speak eloquently to parents. They declare that the child has the right to be respected; they assert the child's unique individuality and worth; and they trace our children's origin to God."[74] For such reasons believers in creation and providence consecrate their children to the Lord of all (Luke 2:23).

2. In divine providence parents ought to exhibit God's love for them in parental *love* (Eph. 5:1). With unconditional love parents will provide for their imperfect children's need for acceptance and for necessities, such as food and clothing. Even non-Chistian parents give their children good gifts (Luke 11:11–13). "After all, children should not have to save up for their parents, but parents for their children" (2 Cor. 12:14). "If anyone does not provide for his relatives, and especially for his immediate family, he has denied the faith and is worse than an unbeliever" (1 Tim. 5:8).

3. Loving parents also are responsible to *teach* their children what they need to know spiritually. Parents may be helped in this responsibility by church teachers, youth leaders, and ministers, but parents who delegate the entire task to others will be dissappointed. It is their joy to teach their own children about the truths of divine revelation. Children coming to an age of accountability for their actions need to learn the lessons of universal revelation first. They need to realize that they depend on God and are accountable to God. They need to know that there is a real, objective difference between right and wrong (in the mind of God) and that they have the potential for doing both great good and great evil. Parents need to teach their children honestly to admit it when they have distorted the truth, coveted the gifts and possessions of others and dishonored their Sustainer. One of the best ways to do this is for parents to exhibit confession of the wrongs they have done to their children and seek their forgiveness as well as God's. After children can appreciate their own moral and spiritual sinfulness before God they can helpfully grasp the redemptive significance of God's mighty acts like the deliverance of his people from Egypt (Exod. 12:26–27; Deut. 4:9) and Christ's bearing of their penalty for them. God's great commandments (Deut. 5:6–21) are to be taught morning, noon, and night (Deut. 6:4–6; 11:18–19).

4. Loving parents know that they will need to *discipline* their children to avoid hurting themselves and others. Fathers ought not exasperate or embitter their children, but lovingly and justly bring them up "in the training and instruction of the Lord" (Eph. 6:4; Col. 3:21). Parents ought to discipline the children they love for their good, following God's example (Heb. 12:5–11). In our times it is not easy to know how to do this, but several methods of helping your child develop more acceptable behavior patterns with suggestions for applying them have been developed.[75] In spite of the home-shattering moral, economic, and educational pressures of recent years, the faithful, loving husband-wife and parent-child relationships serve as God's established means for providentially accomplishing in the home the ends of peace with justice. Then as children mature and leave home, they should carry these values with them.

As members of families we may be implicated in the moral choices of the solidarity of the family. Collectively we often enjoy the blessings of a family that made wise and good choices. Unfortunately we may also experience the effects of unwise and morally unjust choices of our families. In addition to individual guilt, collective guilt and its temporal consequences for the family members may be experienced for up to three or four generations (Exod. 20:5; 34:7).

God Governs Through Nations

As the descendants of fallen families encountered each other, there arose the need for an additional institution to arbitrate disputes between families, to restrain and punish evil, and to reward the good. The descendants of Noah were fruitful and multiplied, and their family's descendants developed into nations (Gen. 10:1–32). To scatter the nations over the earth geographically God used linguistic differentiations at the tower of Babel (Gen. 11:5–9).

A nation is a people, race, or tribe usually having the same descent and history, occupying the same country, united under the same government, and usually speaking the same language. "Nation" may also be used in Scripture to refer to heathen nations or Gentiles in contrast to the Jewish nation with the gracious advantage of the oracles of God. Members of the Jewish nation in addition to all the commonalities for other nations uniquely received the blessings of a divine covenant with Abraham (Gen. 12:2–3; 15:9–21; 17:1–16). Although nations that cursed Israel would be cursed, through Israel "all people on earth will be blessed" (Gen. 12:3). God, in his providence among all the nations, ultimately desired that people seek him, reach out for him, and find him (Acts 17:27). Even though they would not, Israel's descendant, Christ, would finally bring blessing to the whole world.

God authorized national governments to protect a nation's citizens, promote justice, and restrain evil by wise legislation and equitable judicial decisions (Rom. 13:1–5). In God's general purposes for humanity he rules all the nations, permitting the evils that ensue, and using one nation to judge another for its evil. For example, God promised the land of Canaan to Abraham many years before Joshua led the Israelites into that land. "In the fourth generation your descendants will come back here, for the sin of the Amorites has not yet reached its full measure" (Gen. 15:16). Not until the corruption of that Canaanite nation was so pervasive that its people deserved death, did God allow their destruction by Israelite armies under Joshua. In New Testament times Paul observed that "from one man he made every nation of men, that they should inhabit the whole earth; and he determined the times set for them and the exact places where they should live" (Acts 17:26).

In the outworking of his providential justice God is no respecter of nations. God warned Israel that if they did the same evils as the Canaanites, they would receive the same penalties. "If you ever forget the LORD your God and follow other gods and worship and bow down to them, I testify against you today that you will surely be destroyed. Like the nations the LORD destroyed before you, so you will be destroyed for not obeying the LORD your God" (Deut. 8:19–20). Eventually both Israel and Judah suffered the agonies of captivity as the divided groups at different times were providentially dispersed.

In the order of justice God does not show favoritism for persons' positions in nations—whether dictators, prime ministers, presidents, legislators, judges, law-enforcement people, or mere citizens. All are accountable before divinely revealed moral norms for the good of themselves and those they influence. As a result of their involvement in any nation, however initially blessed, citizens, like those in Canaan and Israel, may incur a measure of collective guilt and so collectively suffer deserved punishment. If there were ten righteous people in the midst of the wicked of Sodom God would have preserved the city (Gen. 18:20–32).

Thankfully with Abraham we have good reason to believe that the judge of all the earth does right (v. 28).

God Permits but Redirects Moral Evil

God abhors responsible rebellion against his physical, moral, and spiritual laws by individuals, parents, and civil leaders. Nevertheless the longsuffering Lord of history permits moral evil. Admittedly a concept of God's permissive will construed to imply that human freedom is on a par with divine sovereignty, or as an ultimate threat to God's sovereign purposes, fails to account for the Scriptures on the ultimacy of the divine nature and rule. If the concept of God's permissive will is sovereignly granted by God and is "within his ruling for human freedom and responsibility," as Berkouwer has said, "then the line of Biblical thinking has not been wholly abandoned. For this freedom, this creaturely freedom, receives a place *in* God's rule of the world."[76] As enterprising as God's enemies may be, they are unable to undermine his divine supremacy. They owe their very ability to act against God to God and their uses of that ability to God's permissive will.

How, then, does God relate to the moral evil permitted to self-determining parents and children, rulers, and citizens? As the scriptural section shows, God sometimes restrains or limits sin, sometimes judges sinners for what they are in history, and sometimes redirects and overrules evil for values otherwise unobtainable. In the final judgment God will correct any injustices not adequately vindicated in history.

Even when God permits moral evil, however, he does not initiate it. God is not the efficient or blameworthy cause of rebellion against himself. He is the final cause, for without him no one would exist to disbelieve and disobey his holy and loving desires for them. Although Satan owes his existence to the Creator, the determination to rebel against his source is wholly his own. The will of the creature is the final explanation of the rebellion. The creature was not influenced by the Creator to rebel but, if anything, to know, love, and obey. The creature chose to question God's Word, love himself more than God, and go his own way.

An objective difference between good and evil exists (Isa. 5:20; Amos 5:14–15). Evil is not relative, nor is it illusory. It is not eternal but began with the rebellion. It is not traced ultimately to matter, nor to the body or its reproductive organs (1 Tim. 4:1–5). Sin originated with the misuse of the creature's will (Rom. 5:12–18; 2 Cor. 11:3). God is not the author or blameworthy cause of evil. No more ultimate blameworthy cause can be found than the self-determination of angels and humans. God has not only permitted moral evil but has also done some highly significant things about it. Sometimes he judges it in history, sometimes in the future life. The culmination of history will see a major battle with the demonic powers of the world.

Initially the supralapsarian strategy of the execution of God's purpose (vol. 1, chap. 8) seems best to exalt God's sovereignty. However, we have found extensive evidence that God does not relate in the same way to the evil events in the world as to the good. To assign evil to the God's sovereign initiation contradicts the fact that God is so pure as not even to tempt people to evil (James 1:13–14). In contrast an Arminian strategy leaves God no more involved in the redemptive acts of people in history than in the evil acts. In this scheme, after restoring ability to believe and obey to sinners, God appears as a spectator who observes people trying to exercise their evil-oriented wills toward the good. He simply foreknows what people will do, whether they believe or disbelieve, obey or disobey.

An Augustinian or sublapsarian Calvinistic hypothesis provides a more adequate account of the biblical data. It is the outworking of the sublapsarian (or infralapsarian) doctrine of God's purposes that sees the divine initiative active in the production of good and simply foreknowing and permitting the creature's sinful acts. God may actively answer intercessory prayer in accord with his holy and loving purposes in ordinary or extraordinary ways. God may test his people and actively judge moral evil with natural evils, but he does not literally initiate moral evil or sinful rebellion against himself.

The primary purposes of God's universal rule are to preserve and govern human life and activity in a fallen world subject to self-destruction and acts of demonic terrorism, as in the life of Joseph. Because depraved and condemned sinners deserve the benefits of neither the universal nor the redemptive kingdoms, both kingdoms are a result of unmerited favor. The benefits of both realms can ultimately be traced to God's mercy and grace. And the primary end of preservation is to allow for the outworking of the redemptive goals. So in a sense both common and special grace rest ultimately on the salvific purposes in Jesus Christ.

God's Rule Under Attack by the Satanic Kingdom

A kingdom of deception and destruction fights against God's kingdom of light (Col. 1:12–13). The kingdom of darkness (metaphysically, intellectually, morally, and spiritually) is headed by the Devil, who among the created angels initiated and headed up the insurrection of creatures against the Creator's sovereignty. Unable to create, he enviously seeks to destroy. Unable ultimately to rule all things, this jealous creature rebels in every way possible, especially by deceiving humans.

The deceived followers of Satan are not thankful to God, do not glorify God, and exchange his glory for images of birds and beasts and reptiles. Followers of the evil kingdom may degrade their bodies in sexual impurity. They exchange the truth of God for the lies of the great Deceiver (Rom. 1:21–27). Their depraved minds become filled with every kind of wickedness, evil, greed, envy, murder, strife, deceit, and malice. They become gossips, slanderers, God-haters, insolent, arrogant, and boastful. They invent ways of doing evil, disobey their parents, and are senseless, faithless, heartless, and ruthless (vv. 28–31). In ways like these the ruler of darkness instigates acts of terrorism against the kingdom of light.

Given the evils of history, including the holocaust, it seems increasingly difficult for naturalistic theologians to account for humanity's inhumanity to mankind apart from the reality of Satan. Two Sunday school youths allegedly argued about the reality of the Devil. One believed in a personal devil. The other sought to demythologize the biblical teaching. He said to the other, "The Devil isn't another personal being. The Devil is like Santa Claus, he turns out to be your father!" Unfortunately, the distinct reality of Satan cannot be so lightly dismissed. Jesus recognized the reality of Satan and cast out demons. Paul made it clear that "our struggle is not against flesh and blood, but against the rulers, against the authorities, against the powers of this dark world and against the spiritual forces of evil in the heavenly realms" (Eph. 6:12). Hence a realistic view of history must reckon not only with humanity's inhumanities, but also behind the scenes with evil principalities and powers.

As the spiritual conflict of the ages continues, Christian leaders not only in animistic cultures but also in all others do well to discern direct as well as indirect demonic terrorism. People who deny the reality of the demonic labor under the false assumption that all that is supernatural is of God. Unfortunately, as the scriptural writers knew, this is not true. Not all that is supernatural is of God! False Christs and false prophets will appear and perform great signs and miracles to deceive even the elect—if that were possible (Matt. 24:24). God's people "do not believe every spirit, but test the spirits to see whether they are from God" (1 John 4:1). Not everyone may have a special gift of discernment any more than the gift of evangelism. But just as every Christian needs to evangelize, every Christian needs to distinguish the supernatural that is demonic and far from divine.[77] Christians need not live in fearfulness, however, for the power of Christ's name is greater than any other name in heaven or earth.

In the great conflict with Satan, God is still supreme. The Lord Jesus Christ heads God's government of all things in heaven and earth, visible and invisible, whether thrones or powers or rulers or authorities (Col. 1:16). In Him "all things hold together" (v. 17). The Lord of creation and preservation, Jesus Christ also governs history. The Christ who is preeminent in creation and providence is also supreme in the redemptive kingdom. "For he has rescued us from the dominion of darkness and brought us into the kingdom of the Son he loves, in whom we have redemption, the forgiveness of sins" (vv. 13–14).

Christ's Redemptive Rule Through Believers

God is now retrieving from the fallen world a people to share his fellowship, values, and work. To provide the just basis for this the Son of God became incarnate, suffered, died, and rose. The Savior is the Logos by whom all things were created (John 1:1–3) and hold together (Col. 1:17). So the Lord heads all things in heaven and earth, visible and invisible, whether thrones or powers or rulers or authorities (1:16; 2:10). He reconciles all in the church as well as the world, making peace through the blood of his cross (1:20). It is Christ who has "disarmed" the demonic powers and authorities, making "a public spectacle of them . . . by the cross" (2:15). Jesus Christ came supremely to bear the just wrath of the Creator on the destroyer of his magnificent work. Allowing the evil designs of Satan, Jews, and Roman Gentiles against Jesus Christ, the heavenly Father overruled their betrayal, false accusations, mistrials, scourging, and crucifixion to satisfy justice while providing for their reconciliation, redemption, and forgiveness.

In the future God will bring Satan's acts of terrorism to an abrupt end, judge the unrepentant, and establish a reign of justice and love. In eternity the joys of sharing divine knowledge, love, and service will outweigh comparisons with the suffering of the present evil world. At present God works with people not only by providential ethical persuasion but also by miraculously regenerating their hearts. Shared values are central to God's creative purposes. Unlike some human managers, God did not just fire the whole human race for having rejected his values. God anticipated and planned for the first people who rebelled against justice, love, and wisdom. Anticipating the need of sinners from before the foundation of the world, God showed how adroit he could be in responding to the change in them. While remaining just, God devised a constructive response to the change, a liberating plan that is just, loving, and wise. So now at the heart of God's activity in the world are not only creative values but also redemptive covenants and mighty renewing acts. God's regenerative activities do more than satisfy legal justice, they restore the sinners' lost ability to see, desire, and follow spiritual values.

The companies that excel in business are "brilliant on the basics." In those companies "tools didn't substitute for thinking. Intellect didn't overpower wisdom. Analysis didn't impede action."[78] Divine providence is also "brilliant on the basics." In an increasingly complex world, God highly regards all people, but works redemptively with those who by his enabling now share his values. God, as well as others, may influence us, but tools do not substitute for thinking. God restores our lost abilities to know, love, and serve him. But knowledge needs to be used wisely. Unethical modes of coercion are as unworthy of God as they are of cultic programers or anticult deprogramers.

In thinking of the Holy Spirit's work with believers, we must avoid impersonal and mechanical analogies. How does one person influence another? Think of the best pastors you have ever known. If the best pastors can achieve certain worthy, prechosen goals without reducing regenerate people to robots, cannot God do so? If the best pastors may have goals for their churches and work toward them in, with, and through thinking, decisive people, cannot God? If effective orators, apologists, and counselors can be ethically persuasive, so can God. "It is no more subversive of human free agency for God to influence effectively a man's volitions and secure a certain course of action than it is for one ethical person effectively to influence another."[79] As Charles Hodge has pointed out, "It is in vain to profess to hold the common doctrines of Theism, and yet assert that God cannot control rational creatures without turning them into machines."[80]

Christ's Redemptive Rule Attested by Miracles

In removing the tragic effects of sin and defeating demonic hordes God may choose to act in supernatural or miraculous ways. A miracle, or a supernatural act, (1) is an extraordinary phenomenon transcending natural law, a "mighty act," so extraordinary that it (2) elicits awe as a "wonder" and (3) serves as a "sign" indicating that either God or Satan are acting in extraordinary ways for either good or evil purposes.

Too many definitions of miracle attribute all supernatural events to God. We must challenge that very influential and disastrous presupposition. Many assume that if a person seems to be supernaturally healed the healing must be a miracle of God, and the healer is therefore confirmed as a servant of God. Because such mighty acts may be performed by false christs, false prophets, and false apostles, the occurrence of a miracle does not guarantee that every wonder worker is of God (Matt. 24:24; 1 John 4:1–3; Rev. 13:13). Only if a miracle worker's character and his concepts of God, Christ, and salvation are sound is he to be regarded truly of God. We need to be alert to counterfeit miracles (2 Thess. 3:9).[81]

Although God ordinarily achieves his purposes through real secondary agents (providentially), at times of crisis the redemptive rescue operation has called for his extraordinary, once-for-all direct acts (miracles). Divine miracles occurred in clusters at Creation; the Flood, supporting the integrity of Noah; the Exodus, supporting the leadership of Moses; the Baal crisis, supporting the ministries of prophets Elijah and Elisha; the Incarnation, attesting the claims of Jesus of Nazareth to be the Messiah; and the beginning of the Christian church, attesting the claims of the apostles in the hostile environment of the Romans and many Jews, such as the Pharisees and Sadducees.

When God performs "miracles," natural laws are not obliterated or even temporarily suspended. Neither does the God who acts unusually "intervene" in an otherwise independent and alien cosmos. Rather, while sustaining the world's regularities, God may perform "mighty acts" to correct irregularities resulting from sin. Miracles may take place in two ways. First, God may achieve his startling ends independently of second causes. When a leper cried out for help, Jesus simply touched him and said, "Be clean," and the leper was healed (Matt. 8:2–3). On other occasions God uses secondary causes in an extraordinary way. Jesus asked the man who had been blind from birth and on whose eyes Jesus had placed mud mixed with saliva to wash in the Pool of Siloam (John 9:6–7). Such mighty acts evoked "wonder" and provided a "sign" confirming his special messianic claims.

Miracles in Scripture are closely related to God's redemptive program. By his mighty acts God may either (1) overcome counterproductive forces of evil, as in preserving the line of the coming Messiah; (2) supernaturally authenticate the claims of the incarnate Messiah; (3) confirm the teaching of his spokesmen, prophets, and apostles; and (4) build the church in a hostile environment (Acts). God can, of course, perform miracles for other reasons at other times, but he has chosen primarily to do so for these reasons. We ought not look for miracles constantly. If they happened every day, we could not recognize them. Only against the background of natural law can we recognize extraordinary mighty acts. The constant desire for miracles may reflect disregard for God's wisdom in providence or a failure to share God's ordinary values.

Take physical healing as an example. God customarily heals through ordinary providential means over a period of time. In contrast to providential healings, miraculous healings are complete and quick and not only help the person healed but also strengthen God's redemptive program at the time. The majority of biblical miracles occurred during times of crisis in the battle with the kingdom of darkness. Clusters of miracles happened as Moses led God's people out of Egyptian slavery, as Elijah and Elisha defeated the prophets of Baal, as Christ became incarnate and provided atonement for the sin of the world, and as the apostles planted the church.

God's Redemptive Rule Advanced by Prayer

God has chosen to work powerfully and effectively in the world for good through the prayers of righteous people (James 5:16). Prayer involves far more than petition. Persons relate to God in different ways. We may contemplate his purposes and the blessings of universal grace and of special grace. In prayer we respond in awe to his mighty redemptive acts. Included in the prayer life may be elements of faith, worship, confession, adoration, praise, thanksgiving, and dedicated action.

Christian prayer also may include requests ideally offered in faith and motivated by love for God and others. Intercessory prayer is not a means of compelling an unwilling God to do our bidding. It is not magic that compels impersonal powers to do what we want when we want it. In prayer we express our desires to God as requests to a person. Requests to persons do not have predictable responses. The responses of persons to requests are not automatic. God may give us what we ask, or grant us something better. But he may also keep us waiting or in wisdom respond negatively.

What then is the connection between asking and receiving? C. S. Lewis has suggested some helpful illustrations. Ask a neighbor to feed the cat, an employer to give you a raise, or a woman to marry you. "Your neighbor may be a humane person who would not have let your cat starve even if you had forgotten to make arrangements. Your employer is never so likely to grant your request for a raise as when he is aware that you could get better money from a rival firm, and he is quite possibly intending to secure you by a raise in any case. As for the lady who consents to marry you—are you sure she had not decided to do so already? Your proposal, you know, might have been the result, not the cause, of her decision. A certain important conversation might never have taken place unless she had intended that it should." So it is that as we come to know more of God and his purposes we have greater confidence that his nature and purposes are such as to grant our requests.[82]

In summary, the God of providence ordinarily achieves his decretive or permissive purposes for the world by governing space, time, laws of nature, and human decisions through ethical persuasion via families, nations, and churches, as well as intercessory prayer. But when God's rule is under direct demonic attack, God may act in extraordinary (supernatural, or miraculous) ways to serve his redemptive program.

APOLOGETIC INTERACTION

Wolfhart Pannenberg, like many other recent theologians, has despaired of defending the classical doctrine of providence for this scientific generation. According to Pannenberg, "the idea of a divine providence that not only conserves the world but also guides the course of history is admittedly so problematic to the modern mind that any return to it, at least in its traditional form, can hardly be expected."[83] It is important to examine some of the perspectives that seem to make divine guidance of nature and history unreasonable to our contemporaries.

Not Merely a Mechanistic (Clockwork) World

Science seems to support a world that runs on its own like a self-winding watch. Naturalists hypothesize that the universe is "self-existent, self-explanatory, self-operating and self-directing . . . the world process is purposeless, deterministic, and only incidentally productive of human life . . . and human values, compulsions, activities, and restraints can be justified . . . without recourse to supernatural sanctions."[84] For religious naturalists values are just another dimension of nature and a by-product of a system of physical laws closed to any supernatural influence. Human actions are determined by impersonal factors in all decision making. Not only divine but also distinctively human "interventions" become problematic. In a mechanistic universe persons are reduced to unaccountable, impersonal cogs.

God's providential activity is not to be left to the unexplained gaps in scientific descriptions; it underlies everything observed by scientists and underlies the scientists themselves. Artists are not one more object in a scene to be painted. Persons are self-conscious, creative, self-determining, morally accountable agents. Naturalistic scientists have overlooked important elements of the evidence—the scientists themselves and the absolutes that make their lives and work meaningful! In short we must reject a reductive naturalistic hypothesis as anthropogically depersonalizing and ethically demoralizing. Intellectual honesty is nonnegotiable in any situation if scientific conclusions are to be trusted. Since persons with inherent value and nonnegotiable values are part of reality, scientific persons (*sic*!) have not "proved" that "the cosmos is all that is, or ever was, or ever will be."[85]

The naturalists' explanations are fallaciously reductive. They insist that humans and values are "nothing but" by-products of physical processes. Have they forgotten how difficult it is to confirm universal negative propositions? And dogmatic naturalists overlook the fact that scientific conclusions are tentative and probable because the scientific method has self-imposed limits and is always open to new evidence. The scientific method tests hypotheses by observed evidence and at best arrives at highly probable conclusions in circumscribed areas. So the very general "laws of nature" need not be regarded as all that is or as alternatives to divine activity. Rather, scientific laws are "our codification of that activity in its usual manifestations."[86]

We do not adequately portray the values of a scientific text if we ignore its author. We have missed something in literature if we reduce a poem to electrical processes in a poet's brain. If we try to reduce the just causes of oppressed minorities to cranial secretions, have we not overlooked the value of persons, the importance of justice, and accountability for human conduct? By adding literary, ethical, and spiritual values persons do not destroy scientific description but complement it. The complexity of human experience does not support a reductive idealism any more than it supports a reductive materialism. Both scientific and providential explanations include what is confirmed by observation and by analysis of personal and ethical significance.

The naturalists' addition of the hypothesis of *blind fate* does not supply a more coherent account of human experience. The hypothesis that the operative forces of the universe are merely mechanistic does not fit the biblical data on God's nature and providential activity nor the broad teleological accomplishments of history, particularly in Israel. Disraeli was asked to explain in a word why he believed in God. He replied, "The Jew." Jesus' detailed fulfillment of predictions hundreds of years in advance reflects an intelligence at work to accomplish overarching purposes in the flux of human history.

Again, a *mere chance* cannot coherently account for events apart from the sustaining and governing activity of God. Chance must not be considered a distinct agent that causes these unique events. To attribute a human decision and action to chance means that given a set of causative influences, the operations of history are incalculable to human forecasters. The scriptural data allow for no ungoverned or irresponsible factors. Even the casting of lots is under the supervision of the Lord of all (Prov. 16:33). Within the possibilities and probabilities of creation's natural laws, "histories" and biographies with their unique sequences of events that actually occurred are not fortuitous. So far as the laws of nature and logical possibilities are concerned, the universe *could* have had many histories other than the one it had.[87] But the particular events that happened only once as distinct from repeated events may be said to involve "chance" and "accident" but can be traced to volitional decisions for which persons are responsible. And persons are instruments or means of accomplishing God's purposes.

Indeterminacies in history may also be attributed to *accidents*. Accidents are those "situations in which two or more chains of events that have no causal connection with each other coincide in such a way as to decide the course of events."[88] From that perspective, the history of the planet could have been quite different had it not been for Eve and Adam's disobedience, Cain's killing of Abel, the deliverance of Noah, the scattering of people by diverse languages at Babel, Moses' courage to lead the people out of Egypt, Paul's journey to Rome, and the Allies' victory over Hitler. But other logical possibilities do not rule out empirical decision making on the basis of divinely revealed principles or the overruling of human decisions by providence. Putting our confidence in divine providence, we do not take an uncertain leap into the dark but trust in the all-knowing One for whom not even the humanly unpredictable, exceptional, once-for-all events in history are surprises.

Deists deny divine providence and miracles even though they affirm the reality of a Creator. The divine source of persons and values makes no difference in ongoing historical events. The deists' God is like a business person who started a company and left it to run on its own. Like the naturalists, deists reduce the cosmos to a closed system of observable effects determined by observable causes, and no miracles are possible. Having regarded God an alien to their scientific world, many recent thinkers faced an insuperable problem of how God could act in the world except by "intervention." God has become a stranger to his own world! When God acts in extraordinary ways in creation, he is not "intervening" in someone else's world, but engaging in a redemptive operation in his creation.

Not Merely a Subjective Response to a Meaningless World

Existentialists and many biblical theologians assume such a closed naturalistic system of natural law and so their view of providence asserted nothing about the activity of a transcendent God in an objective world. For existentialists, belief in God's providence simply reflects the subjective attitudes of people toward the conundrum of the cosmos. Bultmann naïvely accepted the world picture of nontheistic scientists, and regarded a biblical view of creation and providence to be crude and prescientific.[89] For Paul Tillich providence "is not a theory about some activities of God: it is the religious symbol of the courage of confidence with respect to fate and death. For the courage of confidence says 'in spite of' even to death."[90] In effect existentialists say that even though there is no objective basis for belief in divine providence, they will heroically cultivate an inner faith, hope, and love as if there were.

Talk of faith and courage seems hypocritical if the Lord of all does not transcend nature and have qualities distinct from those of the cosmos (vol. 1, chaps. 5–6). God is self-existent and eternal; the universe is dependent, having a beginning in the finite past. And to say that nature is self-directed attributes intelligence to the nonintelligent. Apart from a transcendent God, the impersonal physical world has no mind or will and hence no wisely chosen "direction." Any lasting meaning of historical existence has lost its foundation if the case for an objectively real God and accountability are not accepted.

Talk of divine sovereignty and lordship is empty also if God exists but does not have a relationship to our environment as well as to our hearts. God's redemptive rule is now primarily in the hearts of believers, but God's providential rule is over all of nature. The failure to distinguish between the universal and the redemptive rules may be at the base of the existentialist difficulty. To regard nature as objectively meaningless and yet talk about the mighty acts of the Lord of history (as in some biblical theology) creates an artificial bifurcation. Langdon Gilkey has said, "Contemporary views are left with an action that is a mere inward influence which leads man, as in existentialism, to make decisions in an alien, meaningless world, and to have 'faith' in a God who is sovereign only elsewhere."[91]

The data noted in the scriptural section showed that divine providence cannot be relegated to the hearts of believing people. The doctrine affirms the activity of God in the objective world and the events of history. For example, providence was not just an internal belief in the mind of Joseph; he believed it internally because God actually redirected the the betrayal of his brothers and the Egyptian government by leading a Jew to become prime minister! God also permitted the famine that brought Joseph's jealous brothers and grieving parents to him for food. An informed view of providence must fit the multitudes of instances like this in the biblical section above. God achieves his purposes objectively through the laws of nature and specific historical events beyond individual control, as well as the inner attitudes of human beings. In respect to evil, God's will is accomplished permissively; in respect to good, God's will is accomplished through his revealed precepts, ordinary guidance, and miraculous acts.

Not Occult Manipulation

Divine providence is not to be confused with "The Age of Aquarius." The amazing thing is not that people at times find belief in God's righteous providence difficult to understand and accept but that they find it possible to believe almost everything else! Although alleged to have "come of age," people now spend millions of dollars on horoscopes with their astrological generalities. However, to turn to the counsel of astrologers is to turn one's back on a biblically based divine guidance through responsible decision and action. For many people the astrologer has replaced the pastor or counselor.

The hypothesis that our characters and destinies are in some mysterious way determined by the positions of the stars at our births lacks both clear meaning and adequate support. Consider the following points:

1. In reality it is impossible for people to know what their astrological sign is. The "sign" for a given birth date in the Eastern lunar calendar differs from that in the Western solar calendar.

2. The meanings of astrological "signs" are derived from meaningless ancient, primitive traditions. Leo, for example, derived its name from the coincidence of lions arriving at the riverside and the position of the visible stars in the sky. Astrological meanings must be read into the sky; they are not read in it.

3. In the ancient world about nine thousand stars were visible to the naked eye. If the visible stars had some hidden influence, what about the power of millions of other stars recently discovered with the help of telescopes?

4. The advice of the horoscopes is often so general as to be applicable in some sense to anyone. What one horoscope predicted of then Republican President Nixon anyone could have "predicted": in August and September of that year Nixon would experience Democratic opposition!

5. Astrological predictions that become more specific, often err, as newspaper articles point out annually.

6. If that is not enough, read the advice of different astrologers for the same sign on the same day. They may contradict each other.[92]

7. People who cannot accept responsibility for their conduct may wish to blame it on alleged cosmic influences or vibrations. As responsible agents, how-

ever, Christians accept responsibility for their choices and actions.

8. We challenge astrologers to come with a message to save people destined for divine judgment as did the prophets of old. Like stubble, the astrologers are unable to save themselves or others from the flames (Isa. 47:13–15). Fearing the signs in the sky, in Jeremiah's view, is a worthless heathen custom (Jer. 10:1–3). The only dependable revealer of mysteries, Daniel showed, is God who worked through accredited prophets (Dan. 2:27–28). With mediumistic channelers, astrological diviners must be called "to the law and to the testimony! If they do not speak according to this word, they have no light of dawn" (Isa. 8:20). Confidence in astrologers discloses a lack of confidence in God's inspired prophets and apostles or a lack of courage to take responsibility for one's own decisions in accord with biblical principles.

9. What about the Magi seeing the star over Bethlehem at the time of Christ and thinking that it signified the birth of a ruler of the Jews (Matt. 2)? An isolated event like this is no endorsement of astrology. It may have been a nova; a comet; a conjunction of planets such as Jupiter, Mars, and Saturn; or a supernatural light in the sky. At Jesus' death the sun was darkened and at his second coming there will be signs in the sun, moon, and stars (Luke 21:25). Why should there not have been a supernatural sign in the heavens at his first coming?[93]

Also, belief in divine providence ought not be confused with belief in *magic*. Magicians seem to have the ultimate powers of the universe at their disposal. However, in the world of entertainment magicians may be simply sleight-of-hand artists. Some magicians practice a deceptive "con game" in which they merely seem to use hypnosis, extrasensory perception, telepathy, clairvoyance, and precognition. Acceptance of the supernatural by the undiscerning creates a power base and wealth. People who trust in magic imagine that the forces of the universe orbit around their desires or prayers. The ends served by magical manipulation of hidden knowledge and power are at best temporary and limited, and at worst, fraudulent or demonic. To the extent that people rely on the secrets of occultists, they do not rely on public revelations from God. Magicians seek to manipulate the "principalities and powers" of the cosmos for their own ends rather than trusting the wisdom of God. Here is another major difference between the people of God and the people of the world. By this you can discern who are of God and who are not. The people of God use the world to honor God's wise and good purposes; the people of the world use hidden powers to serve their own often unwise and evil ends.

Scripture attributes any supernatural occult powers ultimately to Satan, but theists need to be careful not to consider more to be supernatural than in fact is. Much entertainment that takes place in the name of magic is nothing more than a con game. The remarkable phenomena are achieved by sleight of hand or illusions. They are pseudo-occult happenings. "Pseudo-occult phenomena are events which appear to be caused by secretive, supernatural powers and yet are brought about by physical or psychological means."[94]

Christians need to develop discernment in spying out activities primarily stimulated by channelers of the satanic hosts. Before concluding that any person or event is demonized, however, we must examine, test, try, prove, and eliminate naturalistic fraud. The magicians of Egypt were able to duplicate some of the plagues that came upon them by divine judgment at the time of the Exodus. But others were beyond their powers, and these magicians could not save the Egyptians from punishment.

Satan's unholy angels or demons are engaged in a centuries-long warfare with God and the holy angels. And Christians specifically may be targets of demonic schemes (Eph. 6:11–12). Hence Christians need to arm themselves with truth, righteousness, the gospel of peace, faith, salvation, and the Word of God (vv. 13–17). Christians also need to pray in the spirit in all situations and keep on praying for all the saints (v. 18).[95]

Problems in Relating Prayer to Providence

A spiritual life will be permeated with prayer to God rather than manipulations of hidden cosmic vibrations or the powers of dead spiritual masters. But if God has planned everything and is working in everything that comes to pass, why do Christians need to pray? For one thing, God wants our fellowship. Prayer is more than making requests, it includes loving personal response to the Lord of all in faith, worship, confession, adoration, praise, thanksgiving, and dedicated action. But God also wants us to express our requests to him. God asked us to bring to him our petitions for our own needs and intercessions for those of our friends and our enemies. Jesus prayed for all his followers and those who through them will believe. Jesus taught us to pray for the fulfillment of the Father's will on earth, for the establishment of his kingdom, the supply of necessary food, the forgiveness of sins, deliverance from temptations, and the final triumph of his kingdom over evil.

Since God plans and governs all things, why do we have to present our requests? We pray because God asks us to, and God asks us to pray because he chose to accomplish certain things through the intercession of his people. Prayer is not magic, so we should not expect to compel greater powers to do our bidding and have invariable "success." Prayer is not just using impersonal spiritual laws or powers of the righteous kingdom as we will. Rather, prayer with all the variables of our personal desires, loyalties, understandings, and purposes asks God to do as he wills in accord with his wisdom, justice, and love.

Several fallacies or misconceptions often contribute to unnecessary difficulties about the role of petition in providence. The *predestination fallacy* reasons that prayer is pointless because God has predestined all things. This overlooks God's two distinguishable strategies, the conditional and the unconditional. Although prayer will not change those events that God predestined to be accomplished by his own power unconditonally, many aspects of our lives are not unconditionally determined. Most are envisioned in God's conditional strategy. "*If* my people . . . will humble themselves and pray and seek my face and turn from their wicked ways, *then* will I hear from heaven and will forgive their sin and heal their land" (2 Chron. 7:14). In accord with God's conditional strategy, he forgives and revives only in answer to prayer. Although prayer that asks God to act contrary to his nature or unconditional purposes is of no avail, our petitions in other matters have great and eternal significance.

Others struggle in thought about prayer because of the *foreknowledge fallacy*. Since God foreknows our needs, does that not render our requests meaningless? A medical doctor's foreknowledge of requests from patients recovering from heart surgery does not make them meaningless. Rather, a wise physician prepares to answer those needs in advance of the requests. Analogously God's foreknowledge of our requests from the beginning of history does not make them pointless. Rather, God has wisely built the answers to our prayers into the structure of the universe and developments in history. From the beginning he planned the world for significant personal relationships with his people and so for significant communion in prayer. Having been away from home for a long time, our foreknowledge of a coming reunion with a spouse and children does not lessen the warmth of the embraces when one finally arrives. Anticipation actually enhances the joy! Similarly God's anticipation of those times in history when we finally express our love does not detract from them. We ought, then, to overcome the foreknowledge roadblock to prayer that imagines that if some eventuality is foreknown it is in vain to pray.

The *single-cause fallacy* attributes historical events in our lives either to God or to humans, but not to both. It assumes that if God does something, then human agency has no part, or if we do something, it is not of God or an answer to prayer. Most significant events in our lives are the product of complex antecedents, not a single factor. We need to understand that among the many contributing factors to events in our lives in the course of history is "presenting our requests to God" (Phil. 4:6). Intercessory prayer can serve as one factor in receiving certain blessings without being the sole and sufficient condition of some of God's good gifts. Disciplined memorization of Scripture and meditation upon it may be important also.

The *punctiliar fallacy* in thinking about prayer imagines that if God answers, his answer will be identifiable at a single, dramatic point in time. Immature as we are, we want what we want when we want it. Some answers to prayer may indeed be complete and sudden. But other answers to prayer may develop gradually over a long period of time. We have become so used to instant coffee and tea that we imagine we can receive instant spirituality. Prayers for Christlike maturity will not be answered instantly. We do well to avoid imagining that if our prayer is not answered instantaneously it is not answered.

The *sufficient-cause fallacy* in thinking about prayer assumes that if intercession is important it must be the sole and sufficient cause of the result requested. Many necessary conditions of results are not sufficient causes of effects. A light bulb is a necessary condition of artificial illumination in a room, but it is not the sufficient cause. It must be connected to a properly wired light fixture. And the wiring in the building must be connected to the generating source of the public service company. In addition the utility bills must be paid! Prayer is one of many necessary factors in God's providential interweaving of many factors contributing to states of affairs. Intercession may be a necessary condition of certain things happening, even though it may not be a sufficient condition in and of itself. The Scriptures mention several associated factors: praying in the Holy Spirit (Eph. 6:18), according to God's revealed will (1 John 5:14), in faith (James 1:5–7) while remaining in Christ, with Christ's words remaining in us (John 15:7), and in Jesus' name (John 14:13–14; 16:24) or as he would pray for the sake of his kingdom. Hence in our thinking about prayer and providence in general we need to avoid thinking of praying as a sufficient cause of divine acts but still realize that it is a necessary factor among many in divine providence.

God has chosen not only the ends of the redemptive rule but also the strategies, using human means for their accomplishment. God chose to accomplish many of the ends of redemption through the prayers of his people. *Any view of God's predestination or provi-*

dence that keeps people from praying indicates something out of line with the Bible's teaching.

RELEVANCE FOR LIFE AND MINISTRY

Since God is working out all things in the universe according to a wise, holy, and loving plan, events do not happen to us without a reason in God's design or permission. However absurd and pointless things may seem on the surface, everything is related teleologically. Human minds have been created in God's image to know reality and assess it responsibly. Hence some knowledge is possible from nature and history about the universe and about God from universal and special revelation. From these sources we grow in appreciating many values. We list a few of them here.

A Sense of Reality and Adventure in Life

For Christian theists life is no mere illusion or dream. Theists have a sense of the reality of both physical and spiritual realms. God has endowed us with real capacities and has sustained their real, not merely apparent, efficiency as second causes. So healthy Christian theists are not autistic; they are not removed from intellectual reality, emotional reality, or volitional reality. Rather, they have a sense of knowing reality (in part) by a conceptual revelation. Theists respond emotionally to the reality they face in God's providence with gratitude and praise. They need not seek to escape reality, but, as God's stewards, they make decisions and accept responsibility for their attitudes, words, and actions.

When former secular scientist William G. Pollard became a Christian, he found that, "Life in a world which is consciously apprehended as the expression of the will of its Creator is not a sequence of baleful incidents thwarting human purposes, but a meaningful and joyous adventure."[96]

Humility to Accept What Is Not Within Our Power

Being limited creatures in a huge universe, we know that there are factors beyond our control. God works through an ordered cosmos. The laws of nuclear energy are not going to bend to our personal wishes. God's laws of justice and morality are not respecters of persons. And neither are the laws of meaningful thought (logic). Being fallen creatures and facing the ravages of selfishness, injustice, political power, arrogance, and sensuality, we know that some evils are beyond our power to prevent and correct.

> There are innumerable aspects of the world and the shaping of history about which, in the nature of things, we can do nothing. True humility is simply the recognition and acceptance of this primary reality of our finite status in creation. But secular man does not dare admit to any such predicament. How can he? In a world without God there is nothing short of an act of defeat, a giving up of struggle. He can see in it nothing beyond an unnecessary self-imposed resignation, a forfeiture of man's right to use and change the world as he thinks best, and an attitude of submission which sits back and merely lets things happen.[97]

Knowing that God accomplishes many of his purposes independently of us, and some through us, we may appropriately pray the serenity prayer:

> God give me the serenity
> to accept the things I cannot change,
> the courage to change the things I can,
> and the wisdom to know the one from the other.

Commitment to Improve What We Can

The Christian doctrine of providence does not produce a Stoic resignation nor a fatalistic submission to the status quo. In our finite, fallen world many things need to be changed. What God has put within our power to change for the better, Christians dedicate themselves to improve. Far from passivity, the ideal of theists, as J. I. Packer said in *Knowing God,* is an "active yieldedness." God has chosen to accomplish many things through peoples' decisions, determinations, and actions. In areas such as health care, family fulfillment, education, the nation, transportation, communication, and safety theists may be in the forefront of invention and creative contribution.

Stewardship of Health

Given God's use of orderly patterns as means to accomplish his ends in history, people who want health will not neglect needed nourishment, rest, and exercise. Except in extraordinary cases connected with his redemptive program, God grants healthy eyes, teeth, and lungs to those who take care of them. When Christians claim to be too busy in God's service to take care of themselves, they suffer the consequences.

Notwithstanding the best of diets, rest, and exercise, we sometimes face illness and accident. In cases of injury and disease believers in divine providence strongly favor medicine, physicians, nurses, and paramedics. The prescribed medicines and certified persons that are available for healing are there in the providence of God. Understanding God's guidance in the development of every good thing, including medicine, Christians do not refuse the medical provisions God has made possible in preventive and corrective ways. Total dependence on miraculous healings may express faith in God's supernatural power, but it may also express a tragic failure to understand and accept God's ordinary ways of working with mature people through medical means that are available providentially.

Christian theists eat and drink and do whatever they do to the glory of God (1 Cor. 10:31). We recognize that God created a multitude of foods with a rich variety of tastes for our good. So for balanced nutrition we eat a variety of vegetables, legumes, fruits, nuts, and meats. God has shown kindness by giving rain from heaven and crops in their seasons (Acts 14:17). We feed and care for our own bodies (Eph. 5:29). Deceiving spirits forbid people to marry and command them to abstain from certain foods that God created to be received with thanksgiving (1 Tim. 4:1–3). Anorexia is not the spiritual ideal, even in the name of spiritual discipline. Scripture recommends temporary fasting but not starvation.

Given the continued influence of our depraved natures, we often find that the good that we would do (in diet and exercise) we do not in fact do. And what we would not do, on holidays and under all kinds of imagined and real pressures, we end up doing (Rom. 7:15, 20). "Now if I do what I do not want to do, . . . it is sin" (v. 20). The inclination to sin wages war against the law of the mind, making us prisoners (v. 23). But God has provided an antidote for slavery to self-destructive, sinful behavior. God forgives our guilt and empowers us to counteract and overcome temptations of all sorts. In place of a lack of self-control, the Spirit enables believers to develop self-control (Gal. 5:22–23).

Overcoming the world by faith in Christ (1 John 5:4–5) and by quoting Scripture (1 John 3:6), Donna Platt found her life changed from the inside out. What she needed, she said, was not another diet plan, but power to do the good she knew. Committing herself to eat to honor God and consciously depending on Christ living in her, she changed from a dress size of 22 to size 10. When she realized that Christ lived in her she said no to compulsive eating and junk food. She realized she could do nothing without Christ (John 15:5) but that she could do everything through him who gives strength (Phil. 4:13). "Most important," wrote Donna, "keep an awareness of Christ's presence with you continually."[98]

Fidelity to the Family

The providentially authorized institution of the *family* survived throughout biblical history across varied cultures to the present day. In spite of contemporary attacks on it, the family structure ought to be sustained. Through years of loving relationships, instruction, and discipline a family becomes a unified whole composed of members who function in structured interrelationships. Family members become interrelated not only genetically and legally but also by a sense of oneness morally and spiritually. In God's providential strategy faithfulness to spouse and children supports several values: overcoming loneliness, avoding promiscuity, populating the earth, and educating and disciplining children.

As important and valuable as the family with its ethical persuasion is, however, since the Fall the best of filial relationships come short of the divine ideal. The family of dependent, fallen members ought not usurp the prerogatives of God. Allegiance to the family can be required only under God. If and when family members, however well-meaning they may be, would coerce a Christian to break God's precepts, believers ought to follow the higher authority. Parents should not usurp the place of God in the lives of children nor should children occupy the place of God in the lives of parents. The highest value and ultimate concern of all family members should be to please God. When we put God's kingdom and his righteousness first, however, he often grants us the blessings of food and clothing (Matt. 6:33), and we may add rewarding family relationships.

Some ask, "Is AIDS a special judgment of God upon sinful individuals or a natural consequence of certain behavior?" When the first-century media reported that Pilate took the lives of some people from Galilee, Jesus replied, "Do you think that these Galileans were worse sinners than all the other Galileans because they suffered this way? I tell you, no! But unless you repent, you too will all perish" (Luke 13:1–3). Jesus then recalled eighteen who died when the tower in Siloam fell on them; he said, "Do you think they were more guilty than all the others living in Jerusalem? I tell you, no! But unless you repent, you too will all perish" (vv. 4–5). So to ask if God particularly judges homosexuals is like asking if Legionnaire's disease is a special judgment on the American Legion. Sexually transmitted diseases may be natural consequences of certain kinds of human conduct rather than special judgments of God on individuals. Disease, accidents, earthquakes, and war—all can be used by God to bring any or all of us as sinners to repentance. Just as we would relate to alcoholics with compassionate treatment of support groups for psychological, physical, and spiritual needs, so we ought to minister to people with AIDS. If, however, entire communities should rebel against God's institution of the family, the possibility of divine judgment may have a precedent in the judgment that occurred long ago at Sodom and Gomorrah (Gen. 19:24–29).

Those who would seek leadership in the church should begin with their own homes. Before they attempt to lead the church, there should be sufficient evidence of their marital fidelity and ability to lead their own children in worthy directions (1 Tim. 3:5; Titus 1:6). Presumably a reasonably demonstrated ability to bring up one's own children to live morally while serving God and others constitutes a necessary qualification also for leadership in church. We might infer that those who would seek to promote a just and lasting peace throughout the world should begin in their own families.

Patriotism Under God

Knowing that God has providentially worked with nations to promote justice, theists obey the laws of their *nation,* pay their taxes, and actively participate in its drama. Theists are generally loyal to their governments. "Everyone must submit himself to the governing authorities, for there is no authority except that which God has established" (Rom. 13:1). This passage does not teach that God is responsible for misuses of governmental authority, but that God is the final cause of all governmental authority as a providential means of restraining evil and promoting justice. With Paul we "urge, then, first of all, that requests, prayers, intercession and thanksgiving be made for everyone—for kings and all those in authority, that we may live peaceful lives in all godliness and holiness" (1 Tim. 2:1–2).

We seek to be worthy citizens of our temporal nations because we are involved in a higher spiritual kingdom or "holy nation" (1 Peter 2:9). Christians seek first the kingdom of God and his righteousness. But God's righteousness requires justice for all, especially the unfortunate. God is a jealous God, and we dare not value our national leaders idolatrously. Thoughtful theists evaluate their governments, opposing them whenever they demand allegiance due only to God or take over the role of the church. Revelation 13 stands in stark contrast to Romans 13. God's people cannot support the government of a leader who demands worship. No government should take the place of God in the obedience of its citizens. Christ and the apostles generally obeyed the Roman government even though that government was far from ideal. However, when the government forbade preaching the gospel, they chose to obey God rather than men (Acts 4:17–20). Christians ought not subscribe to slogans like "My country, right or wrong" if by that they mean they are willing to condone what is wrong, but as far as possible they should support only what is right. And theists will not submit to governmental leaders who abandon their God-given responsibilities to preserve life and to maintain order and justice.[99]

In the light of Revelation 13 Christian theists ought to look even more critically on movements toward a world government. New Age politics alleges that the primary source of evil in the world is found in the conflicts of the different governments. We are told that we will never have peace until we escape the prison of nationalism. Nationalism allegedly encourages national chauvinism and leads inevitably to war. So New Age hope lies in giving up our national citizenships for global citizenship with a planetary consciousness. That hope lies not in divine regeneration but in transformation by world citizenship under a world tribunal and law enforcement agency.[100] However, Jesus explained that evil arises from within people (Mark 7:20–23), and so power would very likely corrupt the hearts of leaders in a global government. New Age meditation techniques are not adequate to change human nature. The diversity of governments has its disadvantages, but may provide more checks and balances on people in power than could be possible in a global government. Not until the Prince of Peace himself returns to reign in righteousness will nationalism be dissolved and a lasting planetary guidance system be established with justice for all.

Encouragement to Pray

The doctrine of providence stimulates prayer as Christians understand that the transcendent Lord of all accomplishes many ends through praying people and has answered many prayers providentially in the past. Some people think that prayer makes a difference only in the minds of those who pray. Indeed it does that. Petitioners themselves receive freedom from anguish and fear (Ps. 118:5–6), strength of soul (138:3), guidance and satisfaction (Isa. 58:9–11), wisdom and understanding (Dan. 9:20–27), deliverance from harm (Joel 2:32), reward (Matt. 6:6), good gifts (Luke 11:13), fullness of joy (John 16:23–24), peace (Phil. 4:6–7), and freedom from anxiety (1 Peter 5:7).

Can prayer make a substantial difference also in the lives of others? Moses cried, " 'In accordance with your great love, forgive the sin of these people . . .' The LORD replied, 'I have forgiven them as you asked' " (Num. 14:19–20). Although the responsible adults did not enter the Promised Land, the children did, and Israel was not put aside for another nation. The apostle Paul believed prayer could result in greater wisdom and power (Eph. 1:15–19), strength in the inner person, knowledge of the love of Christ, and filling with the fullness of God (3:16–19). To another church Paul wrote that prayer could contribute discernment, approval of what is excellent, filling with the fruits of righteousness (Phil. 1:9–11), knowledge of God's will, spiritual understanding, a life pleasing to God, fruitfulness, endurance, patience, and joy (Col. 1:9–12). Paul considered prayer effective in others for love for one another, holiness before God (1 Thess. 3:10–13), worthiness of God's call, and fulfillment of every good resolve (2 Thess. 1:11, 12; see also Philem. 6; Heb. 13:20–21).

Some have held that prayer can change people, but not things. Prayer also changes things, such as conditions in nature and the human body. Elijah prayed for the cessation of rain, and it did not rain for three and a half years. Again he prayed, and the heavens gave rain (1 Kings 17:1; 18:41–45; James 5:15–16). From the belly of the great fish Jonah prayed and was delivered (Jonah 2:7–10). The prayer of faith may heal the sick (James 5:17–18). Jesus prayed for daily bread (Matt. 6:11), and Paul for the sound and blameless keeping of body as well as soul and spirit (1 Thess. 5:23). Indeed in God's providence, "the prayer of a righteous man is powerful and effective" (James 5:16).[101]

Appreciation for Every Good Thing

"Every good and perfect gift is from above, coming down from the Father" (James 1:17). Whether coming directly from God's activity or indirectly through his creature's human instrumentality, everything is ultimately from God. Since God's creation reflects his broad interests in the kinds of experience he has made possible, Christians develop broad interests, especially those who would lead others. This important quality is often overlooked by pulpit committees. An elder is not only one who is not overbearing, quick-tempered, drunk, violent, or dishonest, but he is also one who is hospitable and who "loves what is good" (Titus 1:8). Lovers of goodness revere all that comes from God, as appreciated in varied fields of music, art, business, sports, science, psychology, philosophy, and theology. The "world" is theirs so long as their interests in everything are dedicated to God's kingdom (1 Cor. 3:22).

Christians, then, thank God from whom all blessings flow! Anyone with a theistic understanding of whatever comes to pass has the basis for living doxologically! We are not ungrateful for life itself and the lives of our loved ones. Our dependent lives come from the eternal One who has life in himself.[102]

We may gratefully meditate, for example, on the blessings of our God-given five senses, or as many as we have. To the sighted vision brings the great variety of sights enjoyed during a walk along a seashore or mountain trails. We praise not only the artists but the ultimate source of aesthetic values when we see the exceptional beauty of the sculptures in Athens, the Louvre in Paris, the Sistine Chapel ceiling in Rome, and the cathedrals of Florence. Although *The David* of Michelangelo is one of the greatest of sculptures, it does not think or create. It remains motionless. With all the regard Christian theists have for Michelangelo's art, they have far more for the Creator of Michelangelo, who thought and moved!

Christians also thank God for the blessing of hearing, as some of us did at the dedication of a beautiful new electronic organ at Denver Seminary. Thank the Lord of providence for its capacity and the skill of a world-class organist who dedicated it with classics from Bach! But most of all, thank the Lord of all for the sense of hearing and for the gift of music with its varieties and enriching affects on our lives.

Theists also thank God for the sense of taste. What a great variety of tastes in foods await hungry people. Before or after a delicious meal it is appropriate that we thank the skillful and dedicated cook. Gratitude is in order also for the Sustainer of the unbelievably complex life-support system that makes the growth of foods possible. To his creative and providential work we owe the joys of eating and the opportunities for fellowship and respite from work it provides. So theists appropriately express their gratitude at meals and other times of regular worship, adoration, and praise.

Theists also express gratitude for the sense of smell. Recall a walk through a rose garden or a pine forest. Remember coming home after a busy day and walking in the door to smell a delicious meal cooking! Perfumes enrich many experiences in life. And what would life be without the sense of touch? We would greatly miss the warmth of friendships communicating common interests in a meaningful handshake or embrace. What joy the embrace of a baby brings to its parents and grandparents! Theists thank God for the feeling of relaxation after a vacation. Consider even the smoothness of a sanded piece of fine furniture. Summing up, theists thank God for the combination of delights through all the senses—as for example in the consummation of a married couple's mutual expression of their faithful love!

Patience in Adversity

We may suffer in many ways in a temporally limited and fallen world full of conflict with the powers of evil. Those who love God, his moral values, and his redemptive program will gladly suffer when necessary to serve his holy and loving purposes. At any cost they will seek first his kingdom among their physical and spiritual relatives and neighbors. If they suffer the loss of health, they may struggle initially, but they will learn to trust the Lord of all for sufficient grace each day. And although struggling with acceptance at the loss of a loved one, theists eventually discover sufficient grace to say with Job, "The LORD gave and the LORD has taken away; may the name of the Lord be praised" (Job 1:21).

Faith in Uncertainty

Having good and sufficient evidence for believing that the ultimate power with which we have to do is sovereign, wise, holy, and good, and has a reason for all that he does and allows, we trust God even in those baffling times when we cannot appreciate what has happened.

Those who are called by God can be confident that God is working in all the circumstances of their lives. "And we know that in all things God works for the good of those who love him, who have been called according to his purpose" (Rom. 8:28). God works all things together not so much for our ease as for our education, not so much for our comfort as for our discipline, not so much for our pleasure as for our chastening. Through suffering we ought to develop patience. In God's providence all things, however initially shocking, paradoxical, or disturbing, are teleologically related. God has a wise, just, and loving purpose in either his permissive, perceptive, or unconditional purposes and strategies. Knowing God, knowing his purposes and strategies, and knowing his power to bring them to pass in history in the way he has chosen, theists trust God even when in agony they cannot fathom what that purpose can be.

Hope for the Future

We cannot now understand why God has permitted the kingdom of darkness to do battle so long and inflict such anguish on so many lives in so many ways. In times of potential nuclear bribery and massive destruction, none of us knows what the future may hold. But theists do know who holds the future. And they know that the Lord of all is wise, just, and loving. Prophecy assures us that when Christ returns, there will be humans on earth. Although the spiritual battle of the two kingdoms will intensify, theists know that the ultimate future will be one of which they can approve. For they know that God's great power can bring his wise philosophy of history to a victorious conclusion. Knowing God's wisdom, power, and love, we find sufficient courage in our present time of need. With Job we can say, "Though he slay me, yet will I hope in him" (Job 13:15). Death itself cannot separate us from the love of God (Rom. 8:38–39). Even though we walk through the valley of the shadow of death, we will fear no evil (Ps. 23:4).

REVIEW QUESTIONS

To Help Relate and Apply Each Section in This Chapter

1. *Briefly state the classical problem* this chapter addresses and indicate reasons why genuine inquiry into it is important for your worldview and your existence personally and socially.

2. *Objectively summarize the influential answers* given to this problem in history as hypotheses to be tested. Be able to compare and contrast their real similarities and differences (not merely verbal similarities or differences).

3. *Highlight the primary biblical evidence* on which to decide among views—evidence found in the relevant teachings of the major divisions of Scripture—and decide for yourself which historical hypothesis (or synthesis of historical views) provides the most consistent and adequate account of the primary biblical data.

4. *Formulate in your own words your doctrinal conviction* in a logically consistent and adequate way, organizing your conclusions in ways you can ex-

plain clearly, support biblically, and communicate effectively to your spouse, children, friends, Bible class, or congregation.

5. *Defend your view* as you would to adherents of the alternative views, showing that the other views are logically less consistent and factually faced with more difficulties than your view in accounting for the givens, not only of special revelation but also of human experience in general.

6. *Explore the differences the viability of your conviction can make in your life.* Then test your understanding of the viability of your view by asking, "Can I live by it authentically (unhypocritically) in relation to God and to others in my family, church, vocation, neighborhood, city, nation, and world?"

MINISTRY PROJECTS

To Help Communicate This Doctrine in Christian Service

1. *Memorize one major verse or passage* that in its context teaches the heart of this doctrine and may serve as a text from which to preach, teach, or lead small-group studies on the topic. The memorized passages from each chapter will build a body of content useful also for meditation and reference in informal discussions.

2. *Formulate the major idea of the doctrine in one sentence* based on the passage memorized. This idea should be useful as the major thesis of either a lesson for a class (junior high to adult) or a message for a church service.

3. *State the specific purpose or goal of your doctrinal lesson or message.* Your purpose should be more than informative. It should show why Christians need to accept this truth and live by it (unhypocritically). For teaching purposes, list indicators that would show to what extent class members have grasped the truth presented.

4. *Outline your message or lesson in complete sentences.* Indicate how you would support the truth of the doctrine's central ideas and its relevance to life and service. Incorporate elements from this chapter's historical, biblical, systematic, apologetic, and practical sections selected according to the value they have for your audience.

5. *List applications of the doctrine* for communicating the difference this conviction makes in life (for sermons, lessons, small-group Bible studies, or family devotional Bible studies). Applications should make clear what the doctrine is, why one needs to know it, and how it will make differences in thinking. Then show how the difference in thought will lead to differences in values, priorities, attitudes, speech, and personal action. Consider also the doctrine's possible significance for family, church, neighborhood, city, regional, and national actions.

6. *Start a file and begin collecting illustrations* of this doctrine's central idea, the points in your outline, and your application.

7. *Write out your own doctrinal statement on this subject in one paragraph* (in half a page or less). To work toward a comprehensive doctrinal statement, collect your formulations based on a study of each chapter of *Integrative Theology*. As your own statement of Christian doctrine grows, you will find it personally strengthening and useful when you are called on for your beliefs in general and when you apply for service with churches, mission boards, and other Christian organizations. Any who seek ordination to Christian ministry will need a comprehensive doctrinal statement that covers the broad scope of theology.

CHAPTER 3

HUMAN BEINGS IN GOD'S IMAGE

Human Beings in God's Image

THE PROBLEM: HOW SHALL WE VIEW THE NATURE OF PERSONS IN TERMS OF THEIR INTRINSIC BEING AND CAPACITIES?

Having considered in chapters 1 and 2 God's creation and providential control of the cosmos and humanity, we now investigate the nature of the highest expression of God's handiwork—namely, persons as male and female. This is a central question for faith, since Scripture tells the inspired story of how the triune God once created and now relates to human persons.[1] To understand aright the drama of Scripture we need to understand the nature of persons as God created them.

God endowed the human race, as the pinnacle of his creative activity, with special dignity and honor. Because God constituted human persons as he did, Augustine acknowledged that "a weeping man is better than a happy worm."[2] Yet history and experience tragically confirm that persons are an enigma to themselves and others. Their behavior and actions span the spectrum between brilliance and decadence. Pascal pointed out this antithesis between the person's greatness and his meanness or wretchedness: "What sort of freak then is man! How novel, how monstrous, how chaotic, how paradoxical, how prodigious! Judge of all things, feeble earthworm, repository of truth, sink of doubt and error and refuse of the universe!"[3] Calvin, however, rescues us from despair on the subject when he insists that the human person does have meaning and dignity, but only in the light of the prior reality of God. Christians, then, can make sense of what human persons are from the reliable data of God's revelation.

Many modern authorities deny that Scripture discusses the ontological structure of persons and claim that traditional statements about persons' being and nature represent the fruit of Greek rationalism. Some contemporary thinkers insist that in lieu of the being and nature of persons we must speak only of their existential situation, i.e., of their self-understanding, decisions, and guilt. Traditionally, however, Christians have affirmed that the Bible levies no embargo against viewing the person ontologically. The axiological worth of man depends on man's ontological nature. Believing that God has answered the question posed by the psalmist, "What is man?" (Ps. 8:4; cf. Job 7:17), we follow Christian history in exploring several issues concerning persons as they came from the creative hand of God. The most important matter in Christian anthropology concerns the meaning of the proposition that God created the human person in his own image and likeness (Gen. 1:26–27). Modern non-Christian opinion regards the person as an advanced animal. What is it, we ask, that distinguishes the human person from the lower animals? Moreover, must we think of the person as an undifferentiable whole, as much contemporary thought suggests, or can we identify material and immaterial aspects of man? Does Scripture indicate that the person ontologically is monistic, dichotomous, or trichotomous? If we find that the person possesses a separate reality called the soul, the question arises as to how the soul came into existence. Since Scripture identifies the human person as an image-bearer of God (cf. vol. 1, chaps. 5–6), our task in this chapter is to examine the nature of the person metaphysically, intellectually, ethically, emotionally, volitionally, and relationally.

One's understanding of humanness ontologically has a direct bearing on many crucial issues in the contemporary world. For example, when does human life begin to exist? Whether or not the fetus is a person, or when it becomes human, lies at the heart of the abortion controversy. Remarkable advances in medical technology raise urgent ethical questions. Among these is, when and under what conditions ought the life of an ill or aged person be terminated? In the realm of Christian outreach and mission, should the church focus strictly on the spiritual side of the person, i.e., the immortal soul? Or ought the church minister to both the person's spiritual and material needs?

ALTERNATIVE INTERPRETATIONS IN THE CHURCH

One is not surprised that the nature of God has been subjected to a variety of interpretations. It is equally true that the nature of the human person, the image-bearer of God, has been widely debated throughout the history of the church. To these alternative interpretations of what it means to be human we now turn.

Early Church View Emphasizing Rationality

Many early Fathers, influenced in part by Greek philosophy, defined the *imago Dei* chiefly in terms of the natural faculties of reason and free will. Justin Martyr wrote: "When he [God] created man, he endued him with the sense of understanding, of choosing the truth, and of doing right."[4] Athenagoras identified the distinctive of the human person as follows: ". . . whose nature involves the possession of mind and who partakes of rational judgment."[5]

Irenaeus, the first Father to discuss the *imago* systematically, posited a distinction between "image" and "likeness" (Gen. 1:26). He defined the former as the endowments of a rational mind and a free will[6] retained after the Fall, and the latter as the gratuitous life of the Spirit lost at Eden but restored by grace. By so arguing, Irenaeus laid the foundation for the medieval differentiation between the person's natural endowments and the superadded gift of righteousness. By implication, Irenaeus held that the unsaved person ontologically is dichotomous (consisting of body and soul), but that the believer quickened by the indwelling Spirit becomes trichotomous (consisting of body, soul, and spirit). He wrote, "The perfect man consists in the union of the soul receiving the spirit of the Father, and the admixture of that fleshly nature which was moulded after the image of God."[7] Clement of Alexandria similarly distinguished between "image" and "likeness," defining the former as the powers of reason and free will and the latter as moral excellence that may grow or diminish.[8]

Gregory of Nyssa likewise located the *imago* chiefly in the intellect. "The form of man was framed to serve as an instrument for the use of reason."[9] Similarly, "the soul finds its perfection in that which is intellectual and rational."[10] John of Damascus claimed that the image consists of the person's "reasoning and thinking soul," or his "mind and free will."[11]

Gordon Clark, a modern Idealist, also identifies the image of God as reason. Appealing to such Scriptures as Job 32:8; Isaiah 33:6; John 1:9 (where *phōs* is "the light of logic");[12] and Colossians 3:10, Clark interprets the *imago* as "knowledge," or "the innate equipment for learning."[13] Clark argues that fellowship with God, right moral conduct, personal responsibility, and having dominion over the animals all require thinking and understanding. Thus Clark concludes that "the distinction between truth and falsehood . . . is the basic element in the image of God."[14]

As for the dichotomy-trichotomy issue, most Western theologians, such as Ambrose, Jerome, and Augustine, favored a twofold division of human nature. Athenagoras claimed that the person is a unity consisting of body and soul: "The whole nature of man in general is composed of an immortal soul and a body which was fitted to it in the creation."[15] Leading Greek Fathers, including Clement, Origen, and Gregory of Nyssa, followed Plato in upholding trichotomy. The person consists of an immortal spirit, a rational soul, and a material body. The theory of trichotomy lost favor following the Council of Constantinople's condemnation of Apollinarius (A.D. 381), who had constructed a heretical Christology on the basis of a trichotomous nature of man.

The Fathers discussed at length the question of the genesis of the human soul. Guided by the preexistence philosophy of Plato, Origen held that God created all human souls, or rational natures, before the formation of Adam. After sinning in the heavenly realm, these souls sought redemption and so united with physical bodies by ordinary generation.[16] Scotus Erigena adopted this theory of the soul's preexistence in the ninth century. Creationism, the Aristotelian theory that God brought the soul of each person into existence simultaneous with the body, was held by most authorities in the East and by a few in the West (e.g., Hilary, Ambrose, Jerome). Hilary wrote, "Every soul is the direct work of God."[17] Traducianism, the view that both body and soul are begotten by natural generation, gained wide acceptance in the West through the writings of Tertullian. The latter claimed that by the joining of two seeds, one soulish and one physical, the entire human race propagated naturally.[18] Tertullian insisted that the embryo or fetus is a genuine human being. In his essay *On the Soul* he vividly describes the procedure physicians used to do an abortion. Tertullian denotes abortion "murder within the womb" and calls the aborting physician a child-killer. He observes that all the doctors "were convinced that a living thing had been conceived" and "that they all felt pity for the poor child who must be killed in the womb."[19]

The Traditional Roman Catholic View

Medieval Catholic theologians enlarged on Irenaeus' distinction between "image" and "likeness" to create a distinctive anthropology. They identified the "image" as the natural powers of reason and free will and the "likeness" as the added endowment of righteousness (*donum superadditum*). Catholic authorities claim that the Fall left the original natural endowment untarnished but destroyed the supernatural endowment. Constituted in God's image, the sinner retains considerable intellectual power and is capable of choosing freely and of actualizing the good. Fashioned in God's likeness, the person is given the resources to curb fleshly desires and to merit eternal life. This common distinction between "image" and "likeness," or between natural and supernatural endowments, undergirds the Roman nature-grace distinction and provides the basis for a far-ranging natural theology. In the light of these considerations, Catholics conclude that by the exercise of their intellect persons can learn much about God and moral duty, short of heavenly blessedness.

Peter Lombard endorsed this position by saying, "Man is made . . . to the *image* according to memory, intelligence, and love and to the *likeness* according to innocence and justice which are naturally in the rational mind. Or, *image* may be considered in the cognition of truth, and *likeness* may be considered in the love of virtue."[20] The Franciscan Bonaventure argues similarly. Insofar as the person is a likeness to God, he "is related to God as to a gift infused into it." Thus "every creature which knows God is an image, and every creature in which God dwells is a likeness."[21]

Thomas Aquinas likewise posits a distinction between "image" and "likeness," the latter signifying "a certain perfection of the image."[22] The image, according to Aquinas, consists chiefly in the person's intellectual nature. Inherent in the rational mind is not only the capacity for virtue, but also the aptitude for understanding and loving God. Aquinas boldly states that all persons by nature love God more fully than they love themselves.[23] Such powers common to humanity cannot be forfeited. Furthermore, the "likeness" represents a "supernatural endowment of grace," the content of which is actual love for and obedience to God.[24] This grace was lost at the Fall, but when restored by baptism, it enables the person to love and serve God meritoriously. Aquinas clearly consolidated a two-tiered theology of the natural and the supernatural.

The *New Catholic Encyclopedia* articulates this same position:

> Man, in the whole of his being, was created; his soul by immediate (first) creation; his body in a manner that has not been precisely revealed, i.e., the possibility of evolution is not excluded. In addition, man received supernatural gifts of grace and virtue that made him a partaker of the nature of God (2 Peter 1:4) and other prerogatives and powers transcending ordinary human nature.[25]

Most Catholic theologians uphold the Western twofold material-immaterial division of human nature. Following Augustine, Anselm argued that the real person is not a bodiless soul but is a composite being that includes a corporeal as well as a spiritual-rational-volitional affective nature. Guided by Aristotle rather than Plato, Aquinas judged that the human person is a complex union of body and soul, the soul uniting to the body as its "form." As for the origin of the soul, traditional Catholicism upholds creationism. Anselm, Lombard, and Aquinas, the encyclical *Humani Generis,* and other Catholic authorities affirm that God creates each individual soul at its infusion into the human body.

The Lutheran Postulate of Righteousness and Holiness

Whereas the Reformers as a whole repudiated the Roman distinction between image and likeness with its sub-biblical implications, the Lutheran wing of the Reformation claimed that the *imago* consists chiefly of moral likeness to God. Commenting on Genesis 1:26, Luther rejects both Augustine's thesis that the image resides in the triad of memory, intellect, and will and the dualistic medieval schema involving natural and supernatural endowments. Luther believed that such theories painted too optimistic a picture of humanity under sin. Moreover, "if these powers are the image of God, it will follow that Satan was created according to the image of God, since he surely has these natural endowments, such as memory and a very superior intellect and a most determined will, to a far higher degree than we have them."[26] Troubled by the semi-Pelagianism of the Roman definition—whereby the person works for salvation by his natural powers—Luther insists that the *imago* consists of the righteousness, holiness, and wisdom God gave to Adam, but which subsequently were lost at the Fall. Comments Luther, "My understanding of the image of God is this: that Adam . . . not only knew God and believed that He was good, but that he also lived a life that was wholly godly; that is, he was without the fear of death or of any other danger, and was content with God's favor."[27] The wisdom, moral uprightness, freedom of will, and fitness for eternity (the content of the *imago*), forfeited by sin, is restored to the believer in this life by the Gospel (1 Cor. 15:48; Eph. 4:21–24).

Melanchthon agrees that the *imago* consists of the wisdom and righteousness with which Adam was originally endowed: "Through the Holy Spirit God kindled in Adam and Eve the wonderful light of wisdom, through which they knew God, number, order, virtue, and vice, and their hearts and members were pure and in true order, and obedient to the light in the understanding, and their hearts glowed with love and joy to God."[28]

The Lutheran doctrinal standards concur that the *imago* resides in Adam's original righteousness and capacity to know God. Thus the Formula of Concord states: "Man was created of God in the beginning pure and holy and free from sin."[29] The Lutheran dogmatician Quenstedt typically defines the *imago* as "an entire conformity with the wisdom, justice, immortality, and majesty of God, which was divinely concreated in the first man, in order that he might perfectly know, love, and glorify God, his Creator."[30]

Lutheran anthropology largely upholds an essential dichotomy. The doctrines of creation, redemption, and the resurrection of the dead confirm that within the unity of the person one may posit material (i.e., body) and immaterial (i.e., soul/spirit) realities.[31] Luther, however, appears to have favored an essential dichotomy and a functional trichotomy. He observed that analogous to the temple with its Holy of Holies, Holy Place, and outer court, we may speak functionally of the human person's spirit (the faculty for comprehending God), soul (the instrument of reason and the emotions), and the body (the material vessel that houses the immaterial self).[32] On the other hand, Delitzsch and a few Lutheran contemporaries argued for an essential trichotomy. Concerning the origin of the soul, Luther and his followers favored traducianism. They claim that it is most consistent with original sin and that it avoids implicating God in the creation of a sinful soul. Quenstedt, for example, teaches, "The soul of the first man was immediately created by God; but the soul of Eve was produced by propagation, and the souls of the rest of men . . . are propagated, *per traducem,* by their parents."[33]

The Functional View of Pelagians, Socinians, and Others

Pelagians in the patristic era, Socinians at the time of the Reformation, rationalistic Arminians in the seventeenth century, and certain mediating theologians in recent times interpret the *imago* functionally as the person's exercise of dominion over the earth. The argument proceeds by declaring that as God reigns over the universe as Lord, so the human person as image-bearer rules the earth in God's stead. Pelagius identified the *imago* as the endowment of reason whereby the person knows God, of free will whereby he chooses to do the good, and of power to rule the lower creation. Pelagius also placed emphasis on the person acting responsibly to fulfill his God-given tasks. The Socinians denied that original righteousness was lost in Eden, and defined the *imago* as the person's exercise of dominion over the earth. According to the *Racovian Catechism,* the image of God "properly imports the authority of man, and his dominion over all inferior creatures, which result from the reason and judgment communicated to him."[34] The rationalistic Arminians, or Remonstrants, in Holland held a similar view.

According to Gerhard von Rad, the *imago* has nothing to do with the being of a person: "The divine likeness is not to be found in the personality of man, in his free Ego, in his dignity or in his free use of moral capacity, etc."[35] Rather, the Old Testament focuses on the task or mission of the person. Von Rad notes that in the ancient world a king set up images of himself throughout the empire in order to establish his claim to dominion. The author of Genesis appropriated this ancient sense of *ṣelem* to indicate that "man is placed upon earth in God's image as God's sovereign emblem. He is really only God's representative, summoned to maintain and enforce God's claim to dominion over the earth. The decisive thing about man's similarity to God, therefore, is his function in the nonhuman world."[36] D. J. A. Clines, who follows von Rad, begins with the common non-evangelical judgment that the person is not a composite of various parts, but is a psychosomatic unity. Thus the whole person, not merely some higher reality, is the image of God. Clines interprets the *imago* in terms of man's functioning as God's representative or vizier over the lower creation: "The image is to be understood not so much ontologically as existentially: it comes to expression not in the nature of man so much as in his activity and function. This function is to represent God's lordship to the lower orders of creation."[37]

Leonard Verduin, the Calvinist scholar, argues that God created the human person in his image to exercise sovereignty and to subdue the rest of creation. Man is the divinely appointed "dominion-haver" and "conquerer" of the created order. Concerning God's creation of the person as *imago,* "the idea of dominion-having stands out as the central feature. That man is a creature meant for dominion-having and that as such he is in the image of his Maker—this is the burden of the creation account given in the book of Genesis."[38]

The Relational View of Neoorthodox and Theistic Existentialists

Neoorthodox authorities generally follow the existentialist indifference to questions pertaining to human nature and focus rather on the the person's relation to God and others. Thus Dietrich Bonhoeffer claims that the *imago* pertains not to an *analogia entis* (analogy of being) but to an *analogia relationis* (analogy of relation). The likeness between Creator and creature resides chiefly in the experience of being free for the other. God, as the prototype, is free for man. Correspondingly, the human person enjoys a threefold freedom that constitutes him the image of God. (1) The person, by means of the Word of God, is free to worship the Creator. (2) The person is free to relate to his fellow creatures. In this regard Bonhoeffer sees the male-female relation as paradigmatic. "Man is free for man, *Male and female he created them*. Man is not alone, he is in duality, and it is in this dependence on the other that his creatureliness consists."[39] And (3) the person enjoys freedom vis-à-vis the lower creation. The person is not enslaved to the cosmos, but is free to rule over it as lord. Bonhoeffer concludes thus: "Man's being-free-for God and the other person and his being-free-from the creature in his dominion over it is the image of God in the first man."[40]

Karl Barth's mature thinking on the *imago,* stimulated by Bonhoeffer's seminal ideas, appears in volume 3 of his *Church Dogmatics*. The key to understanding the being of God and thus the being of man is the plural pronoun in Genesis 1:26—"Let *us* make man . . . ." Barth observes that God is not a solitary being; rather, he exists in unbroken face-to-face relationship. That is, within the triune God there exists a profound "differentiation and relation between the 'I' and the 'Thou.' "[41] On the human side of the analogy, in what proves to be a relation of nature, Barth finds that "the coexistence and cooperation in God himself is repeated in the relation of man to man."[42] Since the Genesis statement of the person's creation in God's image is immediately followed by the reference to man as "male and female" (Gen. 1:27; 5:1–2), Barth judges that the differentiation and relationship of male and female is the great paradigm of the relation between the person and God and between the person and his fellow. Thus fundamentally Barth defines the *imago* in terms of the polarity of the sexes, i.e., as the "juxtaposition and conjunction of man and man which is that of male and female."[43] But this "I-Thou" relation between the sexes can be extended to the person's "I-Thou" confrontation with his fellow human being. In each case, Barth claims, a face-to-face relationship constitutes human personhood.

Barth continues that man as *imago* is capable of personal relations with God. In what proves to be a relation of grace, Barth views the person as a being whom God addresses as "Thou" and who can answer as "I." The exact nature of man's relation with God is seen in terms of the incarnate Christ's relation to God. But Jesus of Nazareth, the true Man, is the Elected One. Consequently, Barth argues, the image defined in terms of the person's relation to God consists in his eternal election or in his being God's covenant partner—i.e., in hearing the Word of God and in obedient service to God. For the person to forsake this relationship and persist in godlessness would be to forfeit his humanity. But the divine will to save ensures that ultimately this will not occur. Barth's explication of the *imago* thus relates to his doctrine of universalism: "To be a man is to be in the sphere where the first and merciful will of God toward his creatures, his will to save and keep them from the power of nothingness, is revealed in action."[44] We conclude that for Barth persons are image-bearers of God because they are capable of sustaining a broad range of "I-Thou" relationships.

Brunner likewise argues that the ontological definition of the *imago* must be replaced by a relational one. Thus it is necessary "to interpret the *imago Dei* as *relation* and not as *substance,* as something which is part of man's nature."[45] Brunner argues that as in all theological statements, so here we must begin with Jesus Christ, namely, with the Logos of John's Gospel. Thus Brunner states that human personality is constituted by an "I-Thou" relation to the Logos of God, even in those who do not explicitly acknowledge Christ. In the Bible, Brunner continues, the rubric "image of God" is used in two senses. The first relation, the *formal image,* is that which distinguishes the person from the animal. By virtue of his relation to the Light—i.e., the Logos—the person is endowed with understanding, freedom, self-determination, and moral responsibility. Uniquely the person is an "I" that can respond to and glorify God, the supreme "Thou." As Brunner expresses it:

> The heart of the creaturely existence of man is freedom, selfhood, to be an "I," a person. Only an "I" can answer a "Thou," only a Self which is self-determining can freely answer God . . . . Thus the formal aspect of man's nature, as a being "made in the image of God," denotes his being as Subject, or his freedom; it is this which differentiates his specifically *human* quality; it is this which is given to him.[46]

The foregoing relation, which establishes a point of contact between God and the human person, is universal and cannot be forfeited.

The second relation, the *material image,* exists where the preceding is actualized in faith, i.e., where the person concretely trusts, loves, and glorifies God. In Brunner's language, the material aspect of the *imago* "is identical with 'being-in-the-Word' of God;" it is "existence in Jesus Christ, the Word made flesh."[47] This relationship was lost at the Fall and can be restored only through a saving experience with Christ. This second aspect of the *imago* is peculiar to the believer; the sinner has no share in the material image.

According to existentialist philosophy, thinking that deals abstractly with the person or objectifies him truly depersonalizes him. Rather, this school focuses on the person as a conscious self in the concrete situations of life. John Macquarrie, a Scottish existentialist theologian, insists that one cannot talk of a substantial self or an implanted soul that at death separates from the body. Christian anthropology deals rather with the authentic self that is actualized in community through an open-ended process of decision and commitment. Thus "the self is not given ready-made but has to be made in the course of existence . . . . What is given at the outset is not a fixed entity but a potentiality for becoming a self."[48] Macquarrie regards the *imago* as a function of existence rather than essence. "We must think of the *imago Dei* more in terms of a potentiality for being that is given to man with his very being, than in terms of a fixed 'endowment' or 'nature.' Man is a creature, but as the creature that 'exists,' he has an openness into which he can move outward and upward."[49] A constellation of factors constitute authentic selfhood. These include, in addition to openness to others, self-giving love and the capacity for letting others be. In the Christian life, however, the person "gains his true being, and the intention of the Creator is realized."[50]

Most neoorthodox, theistic existentialists, and so-called "biblical theologians" view the person as a psychosomatic unity. Biblical words such as "spirit," "soul," "heart," "flesh," and "body" are nontechnical terms, each of which is said to connote the whole person. Edmond Jacob, writing in Kittel's *Wordbook,* claims that Greek speculation significantly influenced the traditional Christian formulations. Consequently, "older distinctions between dichotomy and trichotomy must be abandoned so far as Old Testament anthropology is concerned. Israelite anthropology is monistic. Man is always seen in his totality, which is quickened by a unitary life."[51] In teaching that the whole person is annihilated by death just as he is restored to life by the Resurrection, Cullmann upholds the radical unity of the person. "The Jewish and Christian interpretation of creation excludes the whole Greek dualism between body and soul."[52] J. A. T. Robinson, similarly concerned with the whole person in relation to God, affirms that the Hebrew mind knew nothing of the Greek antithesis between a mortal body and an immortal soul. The biblical terms *sarx, sōma, pneuma,* and *psychē* fail to support a dichotomy or trichotomy of distinctive elements. "The parts of the body are thought of, not primarily from the point of view of their difference from, and interrelation with, other parts, but as signifying or stressing different aspects of the whole man in relation to God."[53] G. C. Berkouwer, Dale Moody, and Richard H. Bube likewise uphold monism and refuse to posit any essential differentiation in the human person.

The View of Augustine and Some Reformed and Evangelical Authorities

Augustine viewed the human person as a unity of soul and body, where the soul is "the whole life of the body."[54] Thus "man is a noble being created to the image and likeness of God, not insofar as he is housed in a mortal body, but in that he is superior to brute beasts because of the gift of a rational soul."[55] Statements such as this lead some to conclude that Augustine posits a rationalistic view of the *imago*. But Augustine's holistic interpretation makes the person's intellectual and rational capacities inseparable from one's desires and will. The person metaphysically is a soul (*anima*) in a body. The one person thinks, feels, and wills. Augustine insists that these three capacities of the human soul cannot be divorced from one another, just as the three persons of the Trinity cannot be separated.[56] Thus the mind does not function apart from the feelings, nor the will apart from the mind, etc. The soul's thinking capacities consist of *intellectus,* the intuitive cognizance that knows changeless wisdom (*sapientia*), and *ratio,* the rational cognizance that knows facts (*scientia*). Love, which Augustine views as the "weight" of the soul,[57] consists, positively, of desire for God above the creation, and, negatively, as sinful lust (*libido*) for the creation rather than the Creator. Finally, the will refers to the self-moving or self-determining power of the soul. The exercise of the will produces the emotions, such as joy, fear, and sadness. As created, the human will was free to choose between good and evil. How the will is exercised determines the person's ethical condition.

As the preceding suggests, Augustine viewed the human person holistically as an essential dichotomy. Each human "unites in one person a rational soul and a body."[58] He affirmed that the soul is superior to the body in that the former gives life to the latter. Without the soul the body would cease to exist. Augustine appears, however, to make a subtle distinction between a higher set of capacities independent of the body (*spiritus*) and a lower set of capacities related to the body (*animus*). "The entire nature of man is certainly spirit (*spiritus*), soul (*anima*), and body (*corpus*)."[59] While not dogmatic on the issue of the soul's origin, Augustine appears to favor the traducian hypothesis. This view is preferable because Augustine judges it more consistent with the Bible's teaching on original sin.

John Calvin claims that "the likeness of God extends to the whole excellence by which man's nature towers over all the kinds of living creatures."[60] The proper seat of the image, however, is the soul, although Calvin grants that the image shines forth in the person's corporeal being. "The primary seat of the divine image is in the mind and heart, or in the soul and its powers, yet there is no part of man, not even the body itself, in which some sparks do not glow."[61] The integrity of soul that constitutes the *imago* includes both natural and supernatural endowments. What these consisted of prior to their corruption in Eden is seen in the restoration of the image effected by Christ's redemption. Exegeting 2 Corinthians 3:18; Ephesians 4:24; and Colossians 3:10, Calvin identifies the natural gifts included in the *imago* as "perfect intelligence," "right judgment," free-will, sound affections, and properly ordered emotions.[62] Calvin emphasizes not only the possession of these faculties, but also their proper use vis-à-vis God and the neighbor. From these same Pauline texts Calvin identifies the supernatural gifts that form the *imago* as "faith," "love of God," "righteousness," and "zeal for holiness."[63] Not content with the functional definition of dominion over the creation, Calvin prefers a comprehensive definition of the *imago* that does justice to persons as God intended them to be and to live. Thus Calvin concludes, "God's image was visible in the light of the mind, in the uprightness of the heart, and in the soundness of all the parts."[64]

The Reformed Confessions reaffirm Calvin's explication. The Belgic Confession states that God formed man "after his own image and likeness, good, righteous, and holy, capable in all things to will agreeably to the will of God" (art. XIV). According to the Heidelberg Catechism, "God created man good, and after his image—that is, in righteousness and true holiness; that he might rightly know God his Creator, heartily love him, and live with him in eternal blessedness, to praise and glorify him" (Lord's Day 3, q. 6). The Westminster Confession similarly affirms, "[God] created man, male and female, with reasonable and immortal souls, endued with knowledge, righteousness, and true holiness, after his own image, having the law of God written in their hearts, and power to fulfill it" (ch. IV.2).[65]

Reformed theologians generally preserved Calvin's formulation of natural and supernatural features that constitute the *imago,* some adding the notion of dominion over the lower creation. So John Wolleb writes, "The image of God consists partly of natural gifts—the simple, invisible substance of angels and of human souls, life, intellect, will, and immortality; and partly of supernatural ones—original blessedness, rectitude and majesty of intellect and will, and majesty and dominion over other creatures."[66]

Later Reformed theologians referred to the broader and narrower dimensions of the *imago,* the first retained in the sinner, and the second lost. Bavinck, for example, identifies three aspects of the broad sense of the *imago*: (1) Unlike the animals, humans possess a spiritual nature or immortal soul, by virtue of which we transcend the earth. (2) Persons are characterized by self-conscious existence that expresses itself in thinking, willing, and feeling (emotions). And (3) even the body is not excluded from expressing the image of God. "To the extent that the body serves as tool and instrument of the spirit, it exhibits a certain resemblance to, and gives us some notion of, the way in which God is busy in the world."[67] The narrower dimension of the *imago* includes knowledge of God, righteousness, and holiness, not as superadded gifts, but as intrinsic to humanity created by God. In order to escape dualism, Bavinck integrally relates the broader and the narrower dimensions of the *imago* in what he calls the "organic" view of the image.

Berkhof posits five aspects to the image of God in persons.[68] (1) The *spiritual image*: the person is a spiritual being, which means that one is endowed with the qualities of simplicity, spirituality, and immortality. (2) The *rational image*: the person is a rational and moral being, which means he has intellectual power, volitional freedom, and natural affections. (3) The *moral image*: the person was created in true knowledge, righteousness, and positive holiness. These qualities are being restored in the believer through the saving work of Christ. (4) The *corporeal image*: Scripture affirms that the whole person, not just the soul, was created in God's image. The body functions as the proper organ of the soul. And (5) the *functional image:* dominion over the lower creation forms part of the essence of the person.

Most Reformed theologians and many evangelicals favor dichotomy, although a few support the trichotomous theory. Calvin believed that a person consists of two parts, an immaterial soul or spirit and a material body. The soul, as an incorporeal substance distinct from the body, forms the nobler part of the person. It animates the body and blends its many members into a harmonious whole. The Reformed Confessions (i.e., Heidelberg, Second Helvetic) and post-Reformation theologians consistently viewed the person as an intimate union of soul and body. W. G. T. Shedd typically appeals to Genesis 2:7 to argue that God formed the person by infusing an immaterial rational spirit into a material body. L. Berkhof advances the theory of "realistic dualism," whereby soul and body mysteriously interact on each other in an organic union of life.[69] Strong favors the theory of essential dichotomy and functional trichotomy. Ontologically the person consists of an immaterial soul/spirit and a material body. But functionally *psychē* describes the person's immaterial part in its horizontal relations (i.e. those powers common with the animals), whereas *pneuma* describes the immaterial part in its Godward relations (i.e., its capacity to appropriate the Holy Spirit).[70] L. S. Chafer, *The Scofield Reference Bible* (1909), Watchman Nee, and other evangelical sources uphold trichotomy. *The Scofield Reference Bible* relates the *imago* to the person's triune structure as soul, spirit, and body.[71] Thus the spirit is the seat of God-consciousness (i.e., knowledge, morality), the soul the seat of self-consciousness (emotions, affections, desires), and the body is the seat of world-consciousness (the senses).

Most Reformed scholars follow Calvin in upholding the creationist theory of the soul's origin. Calvin views the notion that souls are passed on from parents to children as untenable.[72] John Wolleb states boldly, "The human soul is not reproduced by transmission of semen, but is put into the body as immediately created by God."[73] H. Heppe, the two Hodges, Kuyper, Bavinck, and L. Berkhof also uphold the creationist position. Other Reformed and evangelical scholars, such as Edwards, Hopkins, Shedd, Strong, Buswell, Thiessen, and G. Clark find the evidence for traducianism convincing. Shedd, whose treatment is most exhaustive, comments, "God created two human individuals, one male and the other female, and in them also created the specific psychico-physical nature from which all the subsequent individuals of the human family are procreated both psychically and physically."[74] Dabney suggests that the solution to this difficult problem may involve elements from both positions. Thus "it may be true that divine power (in bringing substance out of *nihil* into *esse*) and human causation may both act, in originating the being and properties of the infant's soul!"[75]

Other helpful evangelical discussions on the nature of the human person include works by J. Orr,[76] A. A. Hoekema,[77] and M. J. Erickson.[78]

BIBLICAL TEACHING

We now undertake a study of the relevant biblical materials to determine which of the several historical proposals concerning the nature of human persons is most accurate.

Pentateuch

The creation account addresses the nature of the human person with the brief but profound saying of God, " 'Let us make man in our image, in our likeness . . .' " (Gen. 1:26). The Hebrew word for "image," *ṣelem* (LXX, *eikōn*), means literally a statue or idol (Num. 33:52; Dan. 2:32) and metaphorically some kind of representation (Ps. 73:20). The word for "likeness," *d^emût* (LXX, *homoiōsis*), signifies a resemblance (Gen. 5:3; Ezek. 10:1, 22). Linguistic data and usage suggests that there is little difference in meaning between these two Hebrew words. Their equivalence is further established by the fact that (1) no conjunction "and" appears between the two words in the Hebrew text; (2) in Genesis 1:27 and 9:6, when the image is discussed, only *ṣelem* is used; and (3) in Genesis 5:1 only *d^emût* is used. Significantly the LXX of Genesis 5:1 translates *d^emût* by *eikōn* rather than the usual *homoiōsis*. In sum, then, "The words image and likeness reinforce one another: . . . Scripture does not use them as technically distinct expressions."[79] Since the two words connote the same thing, one is not justified in applying "image" and "likeness" to separate aspects of the person as does traditional Roman Catholic theology. Furthermore, the prefix *b^e*in *b^eṣalmēnû*, is likely a *bêt* of essence meaning "as," or "in the capacity of" (cf. Exod. 6:3)—hence God says, "Let us make man *as* our image" or "*to be* our image."[80] The point is that persons do not *have* the image; they *are* the unique representation of God (cf. 1 Cor. 11:7). The general statements concerning the *imago* in Genesis 1:26–27, 5:1, and 9:6 suggest that in the broadest sense (i.e., metaphysically, intellectually, morally, emotionally, volitionally, and relationally) persons closely resemble God their Maker.[81] Genesis 9:6 mandates death as the penalty for murder, given the special dignity of human persons as God's image-bearers.

Scripture depicts the person metaphysically as a complex material-immaterial unity. Genesis 2:7 describes the twofold action of God that corresponds to the human person's physical and spiritual aspects. Materially God formed Adam's body "from the dust of the ground" (*'āpār min-hā'^adāmāh*). Concerning the immaterial dimension, God "breathed into his nostrils the breath of life" (*nišmat hayyîm*; see Gen. 6:17 and 7:22 for animals endowed with the breath of life). As a result of this twofold creative activity, "man became a living being" (lit. a "living soul," *nepeš hayyāh*). Here *nepeš* is not a constituent part of the person, but the person or self in the totality of his being (applied to animals in the sense of living creatures, see Gen. 1:20, 30; 2:19; et al.). This complex unity breaks down at death when the breath of life departs the body (Gen. 35:18; 49:33), the latter returning to the ground whence it was formed (Gen. 3:19).[82] The divine command in Deuteronomy 6:5 hardly supports trichotomy: "Love the Lord your God with all your heart (*lēbāb*) and with all your soul (*nepeš*) and with all your strength (*m^e'ōd*)." Rather, in this text "heart" connotes the center of the person's inner being,[83] "soul," the whole self with its aggregate of thought, affections, emotions, and will,[84] and "strength" the idea of total commitment. Thus the verse brings together three quasi-synonyms for the purpose of enjoining total and unqualified love for God.

Of further relevance to the person metaphysically, Scripture provides some hints concerning the origin of the human soul. Genesis 1:28 indicates that God created both the male and the female as a body-soul unity and commanded them to propagate the species. Likewise Genesis 2:21–23 relates that Eve as a body-soul unity was produced from Adam, no mention being made of the creation of her soul. A further argument for traducianism is the fact that God completed his creativity on the sixth day and then rested (Gen. 2:2). Although God is now active in preservation and providence, "there is no hint that God ever created anything again."[85] Likewise Genesis 5:3 teaches that Adam (a body-soul unity) fathered a son "in his own likeness, in his own image." The language of Numbers 16:22 (cf. 27:16), describing *'ēl* as the "God of the spirits of all mankind," in context affirms only that God is the giver of all life, and thus he is able also to destroy life in judgment. Hence this verse does not address the issue of the soul's origin.

The early chapters of Genesis shed light also on the relational dimension of the *imago*. Immediately following the statement of man's creation as God's image the text adds: "male (*zākār*) and female (*nᵉqēbāh*) he created them" (Gen. 1:27). These two less commonly used words for the man and woman (cf. Gen. 5:2; Num. 5:3) stress the sexual distinction that underlies the male-female relation in marriage. This relational aspect is made clearer in Genesis 2:18, where God says, "It is not good for the man to be alone. I will make a helper suitable for him." Hence there is truth in the neoorthodox emphasis on the relational aspect of the *imago*. Scripturally the human person was not made for existence in isolation, but is most human in community with his mate, with other human beings, and with God. Kidner is right when he observes that the person "will not live until he loves, giving himself away to another on his own level."[86]

The creation of humanity as male and female (Gen. 1:27), the fact that man and woman were created to help each other (Gen. 2:18), and the fact that the woman (*'iššāh*) shares the same nature of the man (*'îš*) all argue for the ontological equality of the sexes. Yet the fact that the woman was created from the man (Gen. 2:21–23) suggests that fully consistent with this equality of personhood there nevertheless existed prior to the Fall a functional ordering of male and female within the marriage relation. The Lord's statement "He will rule over you" indicates the functional relation for unity in the family after the Fall. One authority comments, "Eve, standing for all wives, was given to understand that in the home the husband 'shall rule over thee.' Such leadership as is appropriate—and it varies greatly—for a man to give his family is meant."[87]

Given the juxtaposition of our being created as God's image and our investiture with dominion over the lower forms of life (Gen. 1:26, 28), the question arises whether dominion-having is an intrinsic part of the *imago*. In Genesis 1:26 the existence of a simple *wāw* ("and") between the statement of the person's creation as image and the command to exercise dominion suggests that the latter is a consequence of the former. God purposed that the human person, as the unique representation of God, should exercise stewardship over the lower forms of earthly life. That is, by virtue of his ontological status as God's image, the person is divinely entrusted with the special function of dominion-having.

Poetry and Wisdom

Psalm 8 vividly contrasts the greatness of God and the smallness of humans. Compared with the majesty of God and the magnitude of the universe, the human person appears highly insignificant (vv. 1–4). The rhetorical question, "What is man [*'enôš*]?" highlights the human person's frailty and mortality (cf. Pss. 39:4–6; 90:10). Nevertheless (according to a possible reading of v. 5), the person is clothed with dignity and honor by virtue of his creation in the divine *imago*. As a unique being constituted in the image of God, the human person exercises dominion over the lower creation (vv. 6–8; cf. Heb. 2:6–8). Therefore, the smaller man is in relation to the rest of the created universe, the greater he is because of his being a creature of God's special care and consideration. For this reason we can read the question of Psalm 8:4 as an exclamation: "What is man!" The sum of the matter is that "Psalm 8 gives no identification of *dominion* and image, even though the meaning of man's dominion and the special place which man occupies in the created world are strongly expressed."[88]

Metaphysically, the poetic literature confirms the body-soul/spirit unity of the person. When the psalmist exclaims to God, "My soul thirsts for you, my body longs for you" (Ps. 63:1), both *nepeš* and *bāśār* signify the whole person. Yet the phrase in Job 4:19 "how much more those who live in houses of clay" distinguishes between the immaterial and the material aspects of the person. A number of texts speak of the spirit (*nešāmāh* and *rûah*) from God that animates the physical body (Job 27:3; 32:8; 33:4; 34:14). Ecclesiastes 12:7 attests the twofold nature of the complex unity that is the person: "The dust returns to the ground it came from, and the spirit returns to God who gave it" (cf. 3:19–21). Here *rûaḥ*, as we have seen, denotes the principle of life and consciousness that quickens and controls the physical body (cf. Pss. 77:3; 143:7). With the words "You created my inmost being; you knit me together in my mother's womb" (Ps. 139:13; cf. Isa. 44:24), the psalmist confesses that God is Creator of both the psychological and the physical aspects of the person. Also from this text we may infer that the fetus is properly a living human being.

Ecclesiastes 7:29 affirms the human person's moral likeness to his Creator: "God made man upright, but men have gone in search of many schemes." This text teaches that the person was created neither sinful nor morally neutral, but in a condition of moral rectitude. The adjective "upright" (*yāšār*), predicated of God in Deuteronomy 32:4; Psalm 111:8, et al., here refers to "the state of the heart which is disposed to faithfulness or obedience."[89] Conscience, that faculty that attests a person's compliance or noncompliance with the implanted moral law, is described under the figure of a lamp in Proverbs 20:27: "The lamp of the LORD searches the spirit (*nešāmāh*) of a man; it searches out his innermost being."

The Prophets

Some scholars cite texts in the prophets to support the creationist hypothesis for the soul's origin. But Isaiah 42:5, far from teaching the specific doctrine of creationism, affirms that God's power, manifest in his creation of heaven, earth, and earth's human inhabitants, is capable of bringing salvation to the nations. Mention of God's endowment of persons with life is subordinate to the primary emphasis on his unlimited power. The same comment applies to Zechariah 12:1, where mention of the Lord as Creator of heaven, earth, and "the spirit of man within him," highlights the totality of God's sovereign power that is competent to direct history to its goal. The prophet's use of the verb *yāṣar* in relation to the soul, with its nuance of shaping or forming, might be seen as supporting the traducian position. But again, the issue of the soul's origin is nowhere in view. Isaiah 57:16, with its phrase "the breath of man that I have created," affirms only that God breathed into the person the life-force that animates his body (cf. Gen. 2:7).

Summary of Old Testament Terminology

A precis of the principal Old Testament anthropological terms follows. *Rûaḥ,* "spirit" (cf. *n^ešāmāh,* "breath") denotes the God-given breath of life that animates the body (Gen. 7:22; Job 12:10; Eccl. 12:7). The spirit is the center of rationality (Deut. 34:9), spiritual understanding (Job 20:3), the emotions (Ps. 77:3), volition (Dan. 5:20), jealousy (Num. 5:14, 30), etc. *Nepeš,* "soul," on the other hand, generally connotes the whole person or "I" (Gen. 36:6; Pss. 104:1; 119:175; of God, see Isa. 42:1). Thus Berkhof comments that in general "man *has* spirit, but *is* soul."[90] But in not a few texts *nepeš* signifies the immaterial principle of life that departs the body at death (Gen. 35:18; 1 Kings 17:21–22). As such the soul is the locus of the intellect (1 Sam. 2:35), the religious life (Pss. 42:1; 84:2), the emotions (Job 7:11; Ps. 6:3), the will (Gen. 23:8), and various drives and passions (Ps. 10:3; Prov. 21:10). In this sense, *nepeš* and *rûaḥ* overlap significantly (Job 7:11; Isa. 26:9; cf. Exod. 6:9 with Num. 21:4).

The heart, *lēb* or *lēbāb,* connotes the center of the inner life of the person (Exod. 7:3, 13; Ps. 9:1; Jer. 17:9). Scripture represents it as the locus of the intellect (Deut. 15:9), the emotions (Ps. 45:1; of God, see Gen. 6:6), and the will (Exod. 35:26). Thus frequently spirit, soul, and heart denote the same immaterial center of the person's being. As such, these three terms are differentiated not from one another but from the physical body. In sum, the Old Testament words describing the person are not technically precise by modern standards. Considerable flexibility in usage and overlapping of meanings occurs. The data indicates, however, that the Old Testament views the human person as a complex immaterial-material unity, where the link between soul/spirit and body is exceedingly intimate.

The Synoptic Gospels

The three Synoptic Gospels emphasize the fact that metaphysically the human person is dichotomous. In Matthew 6:25 Jesus exhorts the disciples not to be anxious about the needs of the "life" (*psychē*) and the "body" (*sōma*). Reflecting the general Jewish concept of *nepeš,* "*psychē* embraces the whole rational life of man for which he concerns himself and of which he takes constant care."[91] The immaterial life principle that is soul animates and directs the person's physical body. Jesus also upheld dichotomy when he said, "Do not be afraid of those who kill the body but cannot kill the soul [*psychē*]. Rather, be afraid of the One who can destroy both soul and body in hell" (Matt. 10:28; cf. Luke 12:5). Moreover, the Gospels indicate that shortly before Jesus died he cried out: "Father, into your hands I commit my spirit [*pneuma*]" (Luke 23:46; cf. Matt. 27:50). Here the word "spirit" bears the Hebrew meaning of the immaterial life-force that quickens the mortal body. The parable of the rich man and Lazarus (Luke 16:19–31) teaches the continued conscious existence of the immaterial self after the demise of the body. Quoting Deuteronomy 6:5, Jesus taught in Matthew 22:37 that the human person's highest duty is to "love the Lord your God with all your heart [*kardia*] and with all your soul [*psychē*] and with all your mind [*dianoia*]." Mark 12:30 and Luke 10:27 add a fourth word, "strength" (*ischys*). Each of these Greek words signify different aspects of the person's inner life—the aggregate of terms underscoring the totality of love due to God.

Primitive Christianity/Acts

Consistent with its evangelistic purpose, Acts says relatively little about the ontological nature of the person. Luke, however, attests dichotomy when he relates in Acts 7:59 that Stephen at his martyrdom prayed, "Lord Jesus, receive my spirit [*pneuma*]." At death the immaterial self separates from the body, leaving the latter lifeless and subject to decay. Likewise metaphysically, a statement of Paul at Athens would appear to support the traducian theory for the soul's origin: in Acts 17:26 Paul affirms of God: "From one man he made every nation of men, that they should inhabit the whole earth." The apostle here upholds the biological unity of the human family, of which Adam is the natural head. This suggests that both the material and the immaterial aspects of the human person are transmitted by procreation, since the solidarity of the race hardly pertains only to physical bodies. Acts furthermore reflects awareness of the nature of the person morally when it records Paul's claim to a good conscience (Acts 23:1; 24:16). The conscience (*syneidēsis,* "co-knowing") is the faculty of the soul that dialogues between the implanted moral law and the self, indicating compliance or noncompliance with God's unchanging standards. Paul's conscience did not condemn him, because of the rectitude of his life.

The Pauline Literature

Concerning the *imago* metaphysically, Paul consistently infers that human nature is dichotomous. The person is a complex unity consisting of "spirit" and "body" (Rom. 8:10; 1 Cor. 5:3, Col. 2:5), the "inner being" and the "body" (Rom. 7:22–23; cf. 8:23), and the inner and outer person (Rom. 2:28–29; 2 Cor. 4:16). Two principal Pauline doctrines, namely, the doctrine of redemption and the intermediate state, establish dichotomy. According to Romans 8:23, salvation in this life is applied to the inner or immaterial self, whereas in the life to come it will be applied to the outer self or the body. Philippians 1:22–24 attests Paul's longing to leave this earthly body (*sarx*) to be with Christ in the disembodied state.

Second Corinthians 5:1–10 warrants more extensive comment. Scholars such as J. A. T. Robinson interpret the text corporately as the body of Christ, the church.[92] But since believers already "have [been] . . . clothed with Christ" (Gal. 3:27), we judge that in this text Paul discusses the resurrection body of the believer. In verses 2–4 the apostle teaches that believers long to receive the resurrection body at the Parousia, rather than "to be unclothed" or "be found naked." The latter expressions signify the disembodied state of the soul at death. In what may be a veiled polemic against incipient Gnosticism, Paul states that the Christian hope includes being "clothed" (*ependysasthai,* v. 2) with a resurrection body suited for the life to come (cf. Phil. 3:21). Yet if the choice were between living or dying, Paul would elect the latter: "We . . . would prefer to be away from the body and at home with the Lord" (v. 8). In conclusion, "by his use of the word *gymnos* ['naked'] in 5:3 and by what he says in vv. 6–8, Paul shows that he was aware of the concepts both of a disembodied soul and the intermediate state."[93]

Does 1 Thessalonians 5:23 contradict the preceding? In the first half of the verse Paul prays for the sanctification of the whole person; and in the second half he repeats that concern in other words: "May your whole spirit, soul and body be kept blameless at the coming of our Lord Jesus Christ." That Paul emphasizes the whole person and not specific constituent parts is further indicated by the fact that the verb "kept" and the adjective "whole" are singular, even though they govern all three nouns. With F. F. Bruce we conclude, "It is precarious to try to construct a tripartite doctrine of human nature on the juxtaposition of the three nouns, *pneuma, psychē* and *sōma*."[94] Neither is trichotomy upheld in 1 Corinthians 2:14–3:4, where Paul distinguishes between the *psychikos anthrōpos* (2:14), *ho pneumatikos* (2:15; 3:1), and *ho sarkinos/ho sarkikos* (3:1, 3). Rather, the first expression ("the natural man," AV) denotes the person endowed with a human soul (Gen. 2:7) who lacks the Holy Spirit; the second ("the spiritual man," NIV) the Christian who lives in the realm of the Spirit; and the third pair of terms ("worldly," NIV; "carnal," AV) denote with slight shades of emphasis the believer who remains controlled by the flesh.

Paul sheds further light on the nature of the *imago* by pointing to the restoration through Christ of that which was tarnished by the Fall. Thus the apostle refers to the intellectual dimension of the *imago* when in Romans 12:2 he commands believers to "be transformed by the renewing of your mind [*nous*]." The *nous* that is being renewed by the Spirit is "mind, the thinking power, reason in its moral quality and activity."[95] Paul makes the same point in Colossians 3:10 when he commands: "Put on the new self, which is being renewed in knowledge [*epignōsis*] in the image of its Creator." The end of this process is the attainment of perfect knowledge in the age to come (1 Cor. 13:12): "Now I know in part; then I shall know fully *epiginōskō*)." Paul speaks of the renewal of the imago morally in Ephesians 4:22–24, where he urges the Ephesian Christians "to put on the new self, created to be like God in true righteousness and holiness [*en dikaiosynē kai hosiotēti tēs alētheias*]." Paul implies that originally the person possessed moral rectitude, but lost the same at the Fall. Nevertheless, by Holy Spirit sanctification, the primal purity and devotion to God is being restored in those who believe. As Berkouwer observes, "Grace brings about a historical transition from the old to the new man, to that man who is created after God's image in true righteousness and holiness."[96] The apostle further attests the moral dimension of the *imago* in Romans 2:14–15, where he claims that God has implanted the moral law on each person's heart so that even the pagan "by nature" (*physai*, i.e., instinctively) is guided by its precepts. In addition, the faculty of conscience communicates to the person not only a sense of moral oughtness or obligation, but also the extent to which one obeys the law of God.

For Paul the restoration of the *imago* means that the believer progressively becomes like Christ, who in a unique sense is the image *eikōn*) of God (2 Cor. 4:4; Col. 1:15; cf. Heb. 1:3, which uses the stronger word, *charaktēr*). The link between Christ and the renewed *imago* is that the Son, who shares God's very nature, is the head and prototype of the new humanity God is bringing into existence. The Christian's conformity to Christ is a process that begins in this life. So Paul affirms that "we, who with unveiled faces all reflect the Lord's glory, are being transformed into his likeness *eikōn*) with ever-increasing glory" (2 Cor. 3:18; cf.

Gal. 4:19). But complete moral conformity to Christ (Rom. 8:29) will be realized at the resurrection, when the believer will be clothed with a spiritual body. Thus, "just as we have borne the likeness [*eikōn*] of the earthly man, so shall we bear the likeness [*eikōn*] of the man from heaven" (1 Cor. 15:49).

Concerning the relation between the sexes, Paul in 1 Corinthians 11:11 argues for the full spiritual equality of male and female "in the Lord." The apostle makes this point of absolute spiritual equality most explicitly in Galatians 3:28: "There is neither . . . male nor female, for you are all one in Christ Jesus." Yet alongside this indisputable fact of spiritual equality, the apostle repeatedly affirms a functional ordering in the family and in the church for the sexes. Thus in 1 Corinthians 11:3 Paul teaches that God is the head (*kephalē*) of Christ, who is the head of the man, who is head of the woman. "Head" here signifies "a relationship of superior authority."[97] That "the woman is the glory of man" (v. 7) and that she was created for man (v. 9), appear not to be a local cultural perspective, given the apostle's appeal to the creation account of their respective origins: "for man did not come from woman, but woman from man" (v. 8). The notion of submission is made more explicit in Ephesians 5:22–24. Within the Christian society, Paul states generally that believers are to "submit to one another out of reverence for Christ," in the snse of mutual consideration and deference. He then proceeds to discuss specific examples of divinely ordained submission: wives to husbands, children to parents, and servants to masters. In particular, the wife's duty is to be subject (pass. of *hypotassō*) to her husband, "for the husband is the head of the wife as Christ is the head of the church" (v. 23). The passive of *hypotassō,* "be subject to," "be under the authority of," is used of the submission of the boy Jesus to his parents (Luke 2:51) and of the submission of citizens to the governing authority (Rom. 13:1). With respect to 1 Corinthians 11:3 and Ephesians 5:22–24, if Christ's submission to the Father's headship and the man's submission to Christ's headship are not culturally relative, neither is a wife's submission to her husband (cf. Col. 3:18; Titus 2:5; 1 Peter 3:1). Thus it appears true that "the subjection of wives to husbands . . . is according to a divinely willed order."[98]

Yet Paul lifts the male-female relation far beyond the standard of the pagan world with his insistence that, analogous to Christ's love for the church, the wife's submission to her husband must be matched by his love for her (Eph. 5:25, 28, 33). First Corinthians 14:34; 1 Timothy 2:12–14; and Titus 2:5 further attest the functional ordering of male and female. Foulkes sums up the matter as follows: "In the family, for its order and its unity, there must be leadership, and the responsibility of leadership is that of the husband and father, and his authority must be accepted."[99]

The Johannine Literature

Metaphysically, John differentiates between the material and immaterial aspects of the person. Thus in 3 John 2, the apostle prays that Gaius might prosper in health and in external circumstances, even as his soul (*psychē*) flourishes. Here again, *psychē* connotes the true immaterial self that departs the body at death. Revelation 6:9 speaks of the souls of the martyrs in heaven awaiting reunion with their bodies at the resurrection. Jesus' saying in John 3:6 tends to support the traducian proposal rather than the creationist: "Flesh gives birth to flesh [*sarx*], but the Spirit gives birth to spirit [*pneuma*]." *Sarx* here connotes not the material body, but the whole of human nature apart from God with its consciousness, determinations, and drives. As Plummer expresses it: "What man inherits from his parents is a body with animal life and passions; what he receives from above is a spiritual nature with heavenly capabilities and aspirations."[100]

The volitional aspect of the *imago* is indicated in John 7:17, where Jesus said that "if anyone chooses to do God's will [*ean tis thelē to thelēma autou poiein*], he will find out whether . . . I speak on my own." The Lord assumes that persons created by God are capable of making responsible decisions and commitments. The text further teaches that one attains authentic existence not merely by theoretical reflection or detached observation, but by concretely doing the truth. Responsible personhood, in other words, consists in authentic decision making. But John affirms that the full restoration of the image awaits the Parousia. Even though unaware of the full nature of this transformation, we who are believers have the confidence that "when he appears, we shall be like [*homoios*] him, for we shall see him as he is" (1 John 3:2). "It is enough for us to know that on the last day and through eternity we shall be both with Christ and like Christ."[101]

The descriptions of the operation of the Logos in John 1:4 ("that life was the light of men") and John 1:9 ("The true light that gives light to every man") impinge on the issue of the humanness ontologically. As indicated in volume 1, chapter 2, these two texts teach that the Logos is the personal power that sustains and energizes a person's intellectual, moral, emotional, volitional, and relational faculties. The Logos is the divine energy that enables people in a sinful order to function as the full-orbed beings God created them to be.[102]

Other New Testament Literature

In terms of the human person metaphysically, James concurs with the rest of Scripture by positing a material-immaterial dichotomy. Simply stated, "The body without the spirit is dead" (2:26). "The author likely refers to the concept rooted in the creation narrative of Genesis 2:7—the person is composed of body and breath (which could equally well be termed soul or spirit)."[103] Hebrews upholds dichotomy when it differentiates between a person's heart and his body (Heb. 10:22). Hebrews 4:12—"The word of God is living and active. . . . it penetrates even to dividing soul and spirit, joints and marrrow; it judges the thoughts and attitudes of the heart"—makes no metaphysical distinction between soul and spirit. Rather the text reflects a literary technique in which the author used four pairs of quasi-synonyms to stress the all-inclusive power of the Word in a person's life. "That the Word of God probes the inmost recesses of our spiritual being and brings the subconscious motives to light is what is meant."[104]

The argument of Hebrews 7:9–10 points in the direction of the traducian hypothesis for the soul's origin. Upholding the superiority of Christ's priesthood to that of the Levitical order, the author states that "when Melchizedek met Abraham, Levi was still in the body of his ancestor" (v. 10). That is, he viewed Levi as genetically present in his great-grandfather Abraham, as to both his material and his immaterial self. Hebrews 12:9 offers no proof for creationism. The plain contrast in the Greek between "the fathers of our flesh" (KJV) and "the Father of our spirits" (NIV) distinguishes between earthly fathers who discipline on the human level and God who exacts discipline at the spiritual level. "To try to trace metaphysical implications in the phrase is unwarranted."[105]

James points out the shameful inconsistency of using the tongue both to praise God and to curse man "made in

God's likeness" (*kath homoiōsin*, James 3:9). Quoting from the LXX of Genesis 1:26, James affirms that Christians should respect the intrinsic dignity of the person as the highest replication of God on earth. Jude is somewhat more specific as he contrasts the human person with "unreasoning animals" *al-oga zōa*) that operate "by instinct" (Jude 10; cf. 2 Peter 2:12). Jude assumes that the human person, as opposed to lower forms of life, is a rational being capable of weighing alternatives, choosing a plan, and acting responsibly. Concerning the male-female relation, Peter concurs with the Pauline explication. Thus Peter acknowledges the functional ordering between the sexes by observing that holy women of old "were submissive to their own husbands, like Sarah, who obeyed Abraham and called him her master" (1 Peter 3:5–6; cf. Gen. 18:12). Yet Peter was quick both to uphold the spiritual equality of the two sexes before God and to urge the husband to treat his wife, "as the weaker partner," with kindness and consideration (1 Peter 3:7).

Summary of New Testament Terminology

The New Testament anthropological terms follow the meanings of their Old Testament equivalents with some significant developments. Thus *psychē*, "soul," (1) in its broadest meaning connotes the entire person (Matt. 20:28; Acts 15:26; Rom. 2:9). More commonly, *psychē* (2) signifies the immaterial life-principle in the person and is frequently translated "life" (Matt. 10:28; Luke 14:26; James 1:21). This natural principle of life is the seat of the intellect, memory, emotions, and volition. And, given the new reality of the Holy Spirit, *psychē* (3) occasionally denotes that aspect of the immaterial self that relates to God and to spiritual concerns (Luke 1:46; Heb. 6:19; 1 Peter 2:25).

Pneuma, "spirit," (1) occasionally bears the common Old Testament meaning of the immaterial life-force that animates the physical body (Matt. 27:50; Acts 7:59; James 2:26). But with the advent of the Holy Spirit, *pneuma* (2) assumes the primary meaning of the immaterial self in relation to God and the spiritual realm. *Pneuma* is used in this extended sense in John 11:33; Acts 17:16; 1 John 4:2; et al., but it is most common in Paul (Rom. 8:16; 1 Cor. 14:14; Gal. 6:18). New Testament usage suggests that occasionally *psychē* approaches the meaning of the *pneuma*, i.e., the immaterial self in relation to God, so that here and there the two words are used interchangeably (Luke 1:46; cf. John 12:27 with 13:21; cf. Heb. 12:23 with Rev. 6:9). For Paul the *pneuma* of the believer returns to God at death (1 Cor. 5:5).

Kardia, "heart," corresponds to the Old Testament notion of the governing center of the person (Matt. 18:35; Rom. 6:17; Heb. 3:8). *Nous*, "mind," connotes the mind or the faculty of judgment (Rom. 1:28; 1 Tim. 6:5), particularly the power of spiritual understanding or discernment (Luke 24:45; 1 Cor. 14:14–15; Phil. 4:7).

SYSTEMATIC FORMULATION

We now organize the biblical data on humanness in the image of God (as we did the data concerning God) metaphysically, intellectually, morally, emotionally, volitionally, and relationally. In doing so we find sufficient reason to integrate what several of the alternative historical views of humanity affirm and differ with what they deny.

Human Beings Metaphysically

Intimidated by Kant's inability to know any reality in itself, many people have hesitated to speak of what persons *are*. Instead they speak only about what undefined "persons" *do*. The effect on psychology has been expressed in a semihumorous anecdote. Psychology began as the science (*logos*) of the soul (*psychē*). Then psychology lost its soul and became the science of mind. When psychology lost its mind, it became the science of human behavior! Theology followed a similar nonmetaphysical route.

From God's cognitive revelation, however, we discovered some truth, not only about what God does, but who God is. The Trinitarian distinctions are not merely in revelation to humans, but in God's being. God's great tri-personal essence and being make possible his great personal acts in history and relationships with humans. Similarly, given a cognitive revelation (which Kant in his metaphysical agnosticism did not utilize philosophically or theologically), we may discover some truths about humanness that make significant actions and personal relationships possible.

Humans are *real beings*. Critically interpreted Scriptures on creation, providence, and humanness, as well as the data of human experience in general, indicate that persons in their distinctness are neither ephemeral illusions (as Hinduism and Buddhism teach) nor mere bundles of impressions (as David Hume believed). Persons are substances because they are real subjects of change or subjects of predication characterized by existence as well as essence.[106] A person's essential attributes and capacities inhere in something. Linguistically, adjectives qualify nouns (substantives). Distinctively human qualities inhere in real individuals, entities who are self-conscious, active, and responsible causes of events.

What a person *is,* is not merely what a person *does*. What a person *does*, according to Christ, expresses what a person *is*. This point is explicit in moral contexts. Jesus said, "Make a tree good and its fruit will be good, or make a tree bad and its fruit will be bad, for a tree is recognized by its fruit" (Matt. 12:33). The moral condition of the heart determines the moral quality of a person's speech and actions. "For out of the overflow of the heart the mouth speaks. The good man brings good things out of the good stored up in him, and the evil man brings evil things out of the evil stored up in him" (vv. 34–35). Jesus did not say that we are what we do. Rather, our moral "fruit" discloses our moral character. To be responsible morally, we must be agents with the power of self-consciousness and self-determination. We must be ontologically real to remain accountable morally in this life and the next.

Humans are *distinct from the being of God*. People are not emanations from God's being, but creations of God's free will. God's being and energy are independent; ours are dependent. But to hold that we are dependent is not to hold that we are unreal or have no being as creatures. We are real creatures made like God. We are not gods ontologically. Our being is not continuous with God's being. To say that a person is *like* a tiger (in some respects) differs radically from saying that somehow a person *is* a tiger (in all essential respects). To blur the distinction between the Creator and human creatures is idolatrous and sinful (Rom. 1:25). Indeed, for mere humans to regard themselves as divine is blasphemous (John 10:33).

Humans are *distinct personal beings*. Each person is not a manifestation of one World Soul. There is more than one spirit or agent. Adam was one distinct, responsible person, and Eve was another. Cain and Abel, with all their similar heredity and environment, were distinct subjects of different kinds of moral actions and were accountable agents. Neither is a person an invention each of us is charged to create existentially without the help of God (Sartre). In their essence as human all persons share the same physical and spiritual qualities. But no persons are the same, for each has a unique, irrepeatable individuality, as existentialists insist. The truth in individualism, like all other truths, may be abused. It is abused when by it we rationalize loneliness and selfishness and use it to justify a neglect of relationships and responsitilities to others. To realize their fullest potential individual persons need relationships with others in society and most of all with the triune God. Without real individuals with whom to relate, however, relationships amount to empty abstractions. People are not mere relationships. Meaningful personal relationships are made possible by the existence of real human beings.

Each human is metaphysically *one being*. The oneness of a person is not like that of a mathematical abstraction, however. The oneness of an individual is like that of other existing beings, *a unity involving a multiplicity of factors*. A scriptural word study of "one" shows that husband and wife become one, a family is one, and a nation is one. Our study of the Trinity showed that God's oneness involves complexity in unity (1:270–72). Since the oneness of God's being involves the complexities of trinitarianism, it ought not be surprising that the wholeness or oneness of a human also involves complexity. That complexity may involve multiple personalities phenomenologically, or possession by other spirits, but metaphysically a person is an indivisible individual.

A person's complex oneness includes both an *outer material body* and an *inner immaterial spirit*. Paul distinguishes between the outward physical and inward spiritual aspects of a person (2 Cor. 4:16). The outward and inward aspects differ radically in this context, as radically as the momentary and seen differs from the eternal and the unseen (vv. 17–18). So in Paul's inspired teaching, the outward is a visible, temporal body; the inward is an invisible, everlasting spirit. Each has qualities not attributable to the other. The body has its publicly observable qualities, and a nonphysical spirit has its private, nonobservable qualities. Although they are related intimately in the present life, neither set of qualities can be reduced to the other. Each set of qualities must inhere in distinct kinds of substance.

The unity of the two physical and spiritual natures in humans is analogous in thought pattern to the oneness of two (divine and human) natures in Christ's person. The incarnate Christ has a human nature with its attributes and a divine nature with its attributes. Because of the unity of Christ's person he may be referred to either as God or as man. In the unity of the one person both natures are retained and neither is reduced to the other. So also, because of the unity of the two entities in us, the whole human person may be designated by either "body" or "spirit." The psalmist can say to God, "*I* seek you" emphasizing the oneness; he can also say, "*my soul* thirsts for you," or "*my body* longs for you" (Ps. 63:1).

Outwardly, humans exist in *visible physical bodies*. Although either body or soul may be used for the whole, the "body" does not refer exclusively to the whole person in relation to God. At birth Esau's "body" in itself was red and like a "hairy garment" (Gen. 25:25). The linen undergarments "as a covering for the body" of the priests reached from the waist to the thigh (Exod. 28:42). The psalmist spoke of the body in itself when he said, "My knees give way from fasting; my body is thin and gaunt" (Ps. 109:24). When John the Baptist was beheaded, his disciples "came and took his body and laid it in a tomb'' (Mark 6:29). When Judas died, his ''body burst open and all his intestines spilled out'' (Acts 1:18). Some passages speak of the body in itself. Paul could testify, ''I bear on my body the marks of Jesus'' (Gal. 6:17). ''Body'' often refers to the entity in itself, not to a nonentity's relation to God or alienation from God.

The body in itself is to be distinguished from the ''fleshly'' desires of fallen people. The body is not meant for sexual immorality (1 Cor. 6:13), and anyone who sins sexually sins against one's own body (v. 18). The body is intended to be the temple of the Holy Spirit (v. 19). God designed male and female anatomical differences for an intimate, faithful relationship of mutual love and trust as well as for reproduction. As created, the physical aspects of male and female were created ''very good'' (Gen. 1:31). But sinful uses of sex may need to be disciplined in order that the spirit may be saved on the day of the Lord (1 Cor. 5:5).

As important as the human body is scripturally, in itself it *does not mirror the image of God,* who is spirit. The human spirit, however, can manifest God's likeness through the instrumentality of the body. Attempts to find the divine likeness in the body fail for lack of clarity of content and they contradict the teachings that God is invisible and entirely unique and that we are not even to imagine a physical likeness to him. The second commandment forbids any idols or images replacing or representing God (Exod. 20:4). Neither male nor female bodies in themselves reflect God's being. ''God is spirit'' (John 4:24). Although the statues of Greek gods and goddesses portray some of the greatest attempts of gifted artists to visualize a god in human likeness, they are not like the God of the Bible. We ought not make God after our image. God, who is spirit, makes us in his image. Hence the likeness of God in humanity is to be sought, not in the outward, but in the inward self.

Inwardly a human is a *spirit in the image of God.* Like God's spirit, human spirits are *invisible, personal, indivisible, living, and active* (see 1:195–97). We differ from the divine being in that we are not self-existent, eternal, and immutable. Human spirits have a dependent existence, begin to exist in time, and, although changeless in essence, are not changeless in purpose and act. So God's attributes of aseity, eternity, and immutability as such are not communicable to humans. Like God as invisible, human spirits cannot be immediately verified by positivistic and empirical methods of knowing that begin with the physical senses exclusively. Since they are personal, human spirits think, feel, will, and relate to others. As indivisible, human spirits have an underlying metaphysical unity and a continuing identity. Because they are like God as living after their origin, human spirits are conscious and survive death and continue to exist endlessly. Since they are active as God is, human spirits initiate movement as subjects of action (not being passive objects of others' actions), and so are morally accountable agents. The biblical writers often figuratively call the spirit the *heart.* Colin Brown's word study concludes, ''The heart is the whole inner man, the center of the personality.''[107] Since the word ''center'' is figurative, for more precise purposes we ask the point and referent of the analogy. The primary nonfigurative biblical term for the ''center'' of the inner person is ''spirit.''

Inwardly a person may also be called a *soul* when the term does not refer merely to the life of the body. ''It is noteworthy that the term *spirit* is commonly applied to God, while the term *soul* is only rarely so used.''[108] It would be confusing to use the word *soul* to describe God, because in some contexts it may simply mean the organic life of the body, like that of the animals: a "living being" (Gen. 2:7). Or it may include that and the human spirit in reference to our having been created in the image of God. In many biblical texts *"soul" and "spirit" are often used interchangeably for the same functions.* Either "soul" or "spirit" may refer to the inner capacities such as thought, desire, or will. Some uses of "spirit" are listed first. The human spirit can be revived (Gen. 45:27), can be obedient or disobedient (Num. 14:24), may be stubborn and obstinate (Deut. 2:30), may be filled with wisdom (34:9), or it may be an evil attitude of distrust or bitterness (Judg. 9:23; 1 Sam. 30:6). Jonathan became one in spirit with David whom he loved as himself (1 Sam. 18:1). The spirit of king David longed to go to Absalom (2 Sam. 13:39), suffered anguish (Job 7:11), was broken (17:1), and crushed (Ps. 34:18). The human spirit gives understanding (Job 32:8) and compels one to speak (v. 18). Morally the human spirit may have no deceit (Ps. 32:2).

The "soul" functions intellectually, emotionally, and volitionally in the same way as the spirit. People love God with all their soul (Deut. 6:4–5). In bitterness of soul Hannah wept because of her barrenness (1 Sam. 1:10). Job also suffered from bitterness of soul (7:11). The perfect law of the Lord revives the soul (Ps. 19:7). The soul rejoices in the Lord (35:9). The soul thirsts for God (42:2). The soul finds rest in God alone (62:1). The soul may refuse to be comforted (77:2) or it may praise the Lord (146:1). The soul that sins will die (Ezek. 18:4, 20). The fruit of the body does not pay for the sin of the soul (Mic. 6:7). The body may be killed by humans, but the soul cannot be killed (Matt. 10:28). John prays that his friend's body may enjoy good health even as his soul was getting along well (3 John 2). A comparison of the uses of "spirit" and "soul" indicates that both may designate the inner person who thinks, emotes, wills, and relates.

People in most of the cultures of the world believe in the reality of the human spirit or soul from reflection upon their experience. Those who think about life merely from general revelation have pointed to distinctive human capabilities not meaningfully attributed to the body or to an empty human "wholeness." We are not mere objects, but *subjects who initiate action and agents accountable for it*. Grammatically sentences need subjects to initiate the action expressed by the verbs. Grammar indicates the fact that actions require subjects. Similarly distinctively human actions require subjects. Human acts are most coherently explained as the products of self-moving spirits. Far from being mere observers of life's drama from the balcony of a theater, we are creative actors on stage. We are self-starters, self-movers possessing the powers of self-determination. If we are living, personal spirits, like God metaphysically, we can understand why we are the unique subjects who, as existentialists insist, should act authentically or unhypocritically.

Humans also have a distinctive capacity of *self-transcendence*. The capabilities of "standing outside ourselves," "judging ourselves," and "controlling ourselves" indicate that in our spirits we are not limited to our bodies or to the present moment. Jesus said to a crowd, "Why don't you judge for yourselves what is right?" (Luke 12:57). Before partaking of the Lord's table a person "ought to examine" himself or herself (1 Cor. 11:28). Paul explained, "If we judged ourselves, we would not come under judgment" (1 Cor. 11:31). Prophets appealed to peoples' ability to transcend themselves. Rather than complain when we are punished for our sins, "Let us examine our ways and test them, and let us return to the

LORD" (Lam. 3:40). Isaiah warned, "Woe to those who call evil good and good evil" (Isa. 5:20). The wise control themselves. "Better . . . a man who controls his temper than one who takes a city" (Prov. 16:32; 25:28). Paul exhorted the elders from Miletus, "Keep watch over yourselves and all the flock of which the Holy Spirit has made you overseers" (Acts 20:28). In likening his life to that of a runner competing for a prize, Paul said, "I do not run like a man running aimlessly; I do not fight like a man beating the air. No, I beat my body and make it my slave" (1 Cor. 9:26–27). Because Paul was capable of self-transcendence, he—as distinct from his body—disciplined his body to achieve his chosen purposes.

As humans we are not prisoners of our bodies, nor of our own past habits or conditioning, for we have a reflexive ability to criticize ourselves and by God's universal or special grace to change some of our fundamental patterns of thought. Predicatability of human behavior has some limits. We can act differently, spontaneously. "We are *spirit* in so far as we can *change our minds,* in the strongest sense of that phrase."[109] We will trace the outworking of the view that we are self-transcendent subjects and accountable agents more fully when we discuss our capacities intellectually, morally, emotionally, volitionally, and relationally.

Once the human spirit exists, it has *a continuous, everlasting identity.* Our spirits have not always existed, for God alone is eternal or "immortal" in the past, as well as future (1 Tim. 6:16). But human spirits exist everlastingly, and that fact has several implications: (1) Personal identity persists throughout repeated complete changes of physical cells, including those of the brain, at least every seven years during this life. (2) Our spiritual being unites both the conscious and the unconscious aspects of our beings throughout our lives. (3) Death itself cannot separate a believer from the love of God that is in Christ Jesus our Lord (Rom. 8:38–39). Death is the humanly irrecoverable *separation of the spirit from the body* (James 2:26). The finality of death must be distinguished from the near-death experiences of people who have recovered with the help of God and modern medicine. The biblical figure of "sleep" refers to body sleep, not soul sleep. Death does not change the personal relationship of believers and unbelievers to God. Death changes only our relationship to the physical world. Jesus said to the dying thief who believed, "I tell you the truth, today you will be with me in paradise" (Luke 23:43). Furthermore, believers in Christ have already received eternal life in the sense of possessing unbroken fellowship with God the Father. Eternal life is a present reality (John 5:24; 1 John 5:13). If conscious fellowship with God were to cease between death and the resurrection, eternal life would not be eternal.

Additional implications of the everlastingness of the human spirit are these: (4) Personal identity continues in the intermediate state before the resurrection. Although God alone has life (John 5:26) or immortality in himself (1 Tim. 6:16), God has given both life and immortality to human beings. By God's works of creation and providence he has given all humans dependent, immortal souls. At Jesus' transfiguration to his state in glory Moses and Elijah appeared, talking with the Lord (Matt. 17:3). After death and before the resurrection believers are in Abraham's bosom ("gathered to their fathers" [2 Chron. 34:28] in paradise) and unbelievers are in torment (Luke 16:19–31).[110] To live is to be at home in the body, to die is "to be away from the body and at home with the Lord" (2 Cor. 5:8). This intermediate state is no limbo of flitting shades or shadows of the real person; it is a state that is "better by far" (Phil. 1:23). Until the resurrection of our bodies, we must consciously exist, for we are able to feel "naked" (2 Cor. 5:3) or "unclothed" (v. 4). (5) Personal identity continues after the resurrection of the body, not as in another "tent," but in an "eternal house in heaven" (v. 1). In that new body we in ourselves face final judgment, where each of us will give account of himself to God (Rom. 14:12; 2 Cor. 5:10). (6) Personal identity continues in the eternal states.

The matter-energy of the body cannot be reduced to the spirit and its energy, for each has a *mutually exclusive set of attributes*. The qualities of the matter-energy of the body include visibility, extension in space, build or figure, weight, color, measurable temperature, tangibility, and the predictable regularities. None of these serve as attributes of spirit. Jesus said that a spirit does *not* have flesh and bones (Luke 24:39). All *materialistic monisms,* on the one hand, make matter more than matter is. Biblical evidence does not support the hypothesis that a personal spirit is visibly extended in space with a figure or build, weight, a tenor voice, a certain skin color and texture, and a scent of cologne. The apparent physical manifestations of spirit in visions and temporary theophanies are irrelevant to spirit in itself. All *idealistic* monisms, on the other hand, make spirit more than spirit is. The body and the spirit have two mutually distinct and real sets of attributes, functions, and destinies after death; therefore metaphysical monisms and antimetaphysical holistic hypotheses oversimplify the data.

What then is the *relationship between the spirit and the body?* How such different entities as the body and soul can relate to one another is one of the most problematic issues for dualists or dichotomists.

1. The human spirit or inner self *abides in the body.* The physical organism is the spirit's temporary, fragile dwelling place. A person, who lives in "a jar of clay," receives his or her all-surpassing power from God (2 Cor. 4:7). "We [our spirits] who are alive are always being given over to death for Jesus' sake, so that his life may be revealed in our mortal body" (v. 11). We remain "in" the body so that in it we may visibly display the power and life of the Savior. "Though outwardly we are wasting away, yet inwardly we are being renewed day by day" (v. 16). Paul also speaks of the body as the spirit's "earthly tent" (2 Cor. 5:1, 4). A person dwelling in this "tent" is said to be "at home in the body" (v. 6). Although Paul would like to have gone to be with Christ, which is better by far, he said, "It is more necessary for you that I remain in the body" (Phil. 1:24). In this life Paul's spirit lived in and through his body. But he distinguished himself from his body and taught that he himself was separable from his body.

2. *The human spirit as an agent acts through its body as its instrument.* A moral person transcends the body's conditioning to distinguish right from wrong and do what is just. Persons (apparently addressable as moral agents distinct from their bodies) are exhorted not to let sin reign in their mortal bodies (Rom. 6:12). Paul asks Christians not to offer the parts of their bodies as "instruments" of wickedness, but as instruments of righteousness (v. 13). Thus spirits are agents who accountably use bodily capacities as means of accomplishing their good or evil purposes. Paul exhorts, "Offer your bodies as living sacrifices, holy and pleasing to God—this is your spiritual act of worship" (12:1). Having spoken of orgies, drunkenness, sexual immorality, and debauchery, Paul exhorts us not even to consider how to gratify the desires of the sinful nature in bodily acts (13:14). Again, because the body is the temple

of the Holy Spirit, Paul enjoins Christians at Corinth, "Honor God with your body" (1 Cor. 6:20). Like a professional athlete, Paul said, "I beat my body and make it my slave" (9:27). According to James, mature followers of Christ keep the "whole body in check" (James 3:2). The tongue needs special control. As small as it is, the tongue, like a spark, can set the whole course of one's life on fire, corrupting the whole person (vv. 5–6). Neither the tongue nor even the entire body is the whole self, but both are instruments the self as spirit uses for good or ill. In these and similar passages the inward spiritual self is addressed as distinct from the body as the agent responsible for controlling the body.

3. *The body also interacts on the spirit*. We daily experience the counterproductive influence of the body's fatigue on the accomplishment of inward purposes, and this calls for repeated refreshment breaks, exercise, and rest. The disciples had intended to watch and pray with Jesus in Gethsemane. Instead they fell asleep. That happened, Jesus explained, because though "the spirit is willing, . . . the body is weak" (Matt. 26:41). Paul's physical limitation kept him from becoming conceited (2 Cor. 12:7). Although the spirit has radically different qualities from those of the body, the condition of the body affects the spirit in different ways. The taking of drugs, for example, can affect the consciousness in varied ways as it functions through the brain and nervous system in this life. In at least the above three ways the spirit and body *interact* with each other in the unity of one person.

To sum up the doctrine of humanness ontologically, a person inwardly is like God, an invisible, personal, living, and active spirit, a conscious subject with a sense of presence and a continuing identity. A person outwardly is unlike God as an extended, visible, tangible physical organism. The whole person is a complex unity composed of two distinct entities, soul and body, intimately interacting with one another. Neither of them is the whole person, yet either part can stand figuratively for the whole person. While they are alive the two natures (physical and spiritual) are neither divided nor confused. A whole person has attributes of spirit and attributes of body. Although body and spirit are separate entities ontologically, in this life they are intricately united. For metaphysical purposes, then, we propose that a human being is composed of an *interacting dichotomy* of spirit and body.

The nature of humanness, as here outlined, is not to be confused with the views of Platonic or gnostic dualists. Just as there are different varieties of monism (materialistic, idealistic, pantheistic), there are different brands of dualism. In our interacting dichotomy the following facts should be noted: (1) Both body and spirit are equally real. The body is not less real than the spirit, nor is it a mere shadow of the more real world of invisible ideas. (2) Neither the human spirit nor matter existed eternally apart from divine creation. Both have a beginning and are dependent on God. (3) Self-transcendent human spirits are not "imprisoned" by bodies; rather, bodies are generally effective instruments of the spirit. (4) The body is not the blameworthy cause of human evil, the inner self is. (5) The existence of the naked spirit after death is an intermediate and incomplete state, not the eternal state. (6) In the eternal state humans are not immortal souls only, but spirits united with resurrected bodies. Granting these significant differences in content, most of the typical objections to the Greek philosophers' dualism do not apply to our interacting dichotomy.

The primary basis of our view is not the writings of Greek philosophers, but

Scripture (illustrated with everyday experience). No categories have been used for this concept of humans that have not already been used to fit the Scriptural teaching concerning God. Biblical thought need not be totally different from Greek thought. Some of the categories utilized in the koine Greek of the New Testament, of course, are common to the classical Greek of the ancient philosophers. Not everything the philosophers said was wrong! Surely God providentially prepared not only the Roman roads for the dispersing of the gospel, but also the Greek language for its preservation in the New Testament. But general similarities of thought and wording aside, the biblical view of humanness that is developed here differs from the Greek in six definitive ways.

Humans Intellectually

Consider now some of the capabilities of spiritual-physical persons as created. Those who abandon substantives also reject a faculty psychology, for they have nothing with which to possess or exercise abilities. Finding evidence for the reality of human spirits, we can speak meaningfully not only of their attributes but also of their abilities. Although we list the mental, emotional, and volitional capacities separately, all three are activities of every person. And they interrelate in all our conduct. We *will* to know and love. We *love* to know and will. And we *know* what we will and love. Together they make possible moral accountability and meaningful relationships. Even though intimately interrelated, they are not synonymous capacities, so we will consider each separately.

One of the distinctive abilities of the human spirit is a *capacity to know itself,* as we noted above. We can become healthfully *self-conscious.* Because we are spirits, our knowledge is not limited to the centimeters of our brains or even to ideas that begin with the data of the five senses. We are conscious of the reality of our own inner existence. Augustine reasoned, "I doubt, therefore I am" (*dubito ergo sum*). Paul said, "Who among men knows the thoughts of a man except the man's spirit within him?" (1 Cor. 2:11). Only a human spirit can know distinctively human thoughts. Like other gifts, our knowledge of ourselves as spirits needs to be developed. As self-transcending spirits we are morally responsible to know, examine, and judge ourselves. We can "search our hearts" (Ps. 4:4). "Examine yourselves to see whether you are in the faith; test yourselves" (2 Cor. 13:5). To the Galatians Paul wrote, "Each one should test his own actions" (6:4).

Human spirits also have an *ability to know their bodies and the physical world.* We can develop a healthy world consciousness through our five senses: sight, hearing, taste, touch, and smell. "Ears that hear and eyes that see—the LORD has made them both" (Prov. 20:12). God has not retracted the great cultural mandate to fill the world and subdue it (Gen. 1:28). Humans under God, Erich Sauer has written, are kings of the earth.[111] For that purpose God gave us reliable senses by which to know it. The general reliability of healthy senses in an ordered world has made possible truth about the temporal world whether expressed in everyday language or in scientific technicalities. The God who created the earth and mankind to know and rule it used similar categories in both, a point overlooked by Kant. With Augustine we may call all knowledge of temporal, changing things science (*scientia*). Although each of us may have a different perspective on other people and things, no one of us thereby exhausts the knowledge of reality. Other personal agents and things exist to be perceived and thought about. But different observers approach them with different preunderstandings, starting points, and emphases. The fact that tourists surrounding a statue each see it from a different angle, however, does not mean that no statue exists in reality.

We overcome our loneliness in the midst of our limited (I-that or I-it) experience of the impersonal world by becoming acquainted with *other persons*. Our knowledge of others' invisible spiritual presence is not immediate, however. It is mediated through observable signs, including the facial expressions, bodily gestures, words, and actions of these other persons. Hence personal knowledge requires faith in the genuineness of the signs. All personal knowledge involves belief in the credibility of the others' visual indicators such as treaties, contracts, and marriage licenses. The trustworthiness of others' signs in turn depends on the sincerity of their intention (not to deceive) and our ability critically to distinguish the authentic from the deceptive. After sifting out the con artists, how rich we are to have minds capable of authentic person-to-person relationships! From them we receive comfort, encouragement, stimulation, instruction, correction, and refreshment. Since all personal relationships involve discernment and trust, we should not be surprised that personal relationship with the living God (in the midst of countless idols) also requires careful discernment of visible signs and a reflective commitment to their invisible source.

We may also know *historical events*. Knowledge of the past is not immediate; it also must be mediated through extant evidences such as tombs and tools or credible written documents. Hence the importance of criteria and a method for determining genuine from spurious documents. Since the Bible mediates much information about history, our knowledge of scriptural history, like any history, involves faith. Any knowledge of the past is conditioned on belief in the reliability of the sources and of the historian who interprets them for us. Since much of the Bible records historical events, it is not surprising that we need to discriminate which are the genuinely prophetic and apostolic sources and then put faith in their inspired teaching.

As spirits in God's image, furthermore, we can transcend our consciousness of self, the world, and others and become *God-conscious*. The divine presence is not far from any one of us. All humans may have some consciousness of the higher being, however suppressed (I:75–76). To perceive God's redemptive presence we have good reason to trust the spoken, written, and acted signs of his authentic love. Through faith in these signs from God Christians can commune with God the Father, Christ, and the Holy Spirit! God said to Moses, "I will meet with you" over "the ark of the Testimony" (Exod. 25:22). Paul wrote, "[God] has called you into fellowship with his Son Jesus Christ our Lord" (1 Cor. 1:9). The believers at Corinth, Paul reported, enjoyed not only the grace of Christ and the love of God, but also "the fellowship of the Holy Spirit" (2 Cor. 13:14). John wrote his account of the first-century facts that he saw and heard, giving this as his purpose: "so that you also may have fellowship with us. And our fellowship is with the Father and with his Son, Jesus Christ" (1 John 1:3).

Persons as created in the divine image may also have immediate cognizance of *God's changeless moral principles*. Self-conscious, self-determining spirits clearly see God, and the requirements of his moral law are written on their hearts (Rom. 2:14–15). Although we are not able to invent eternal truths, we can mentally see some of them from God's universal revelation. In contrast to *scientia*, we may, with Augustine, call the immediate perception of moral norms "wisdom" (*sapientia*).[112] Two of the most prominent of these assert that we ought to love God with our whole being and our neighbor as ourselves. The Ten Commandments develop the details further as well as the exhortations of Christ to his disciples and of the apostles.

More is needed for knowledge of changeless intangibles than an intuitive capacity. The ability to see spiritual principles is closely related to our receptivity to them and our readiness to act upon them. Unfortunately these abilities and desires may be decimated by sinful desires. Nevertheless a general illumination enables all to know God's existence, power, and righteous demands. Given the capacity for *sapientia*, we can think about ultimate questions of individual morality and social ethics. Wisdom in harmony with God's mind is indispensable in the use of observed data for worthy ends. We need sapiential insights, for they provide logical principles and moral norms such as justice and love to help all in making wise choices in the use of scientific inventions. Human wisdom in applying moral principles to actual states of affairs has not kept up with the developments of human technology. In times of rapid change and culture shock we need leaders with well-founded moral guidelines and the experience to apply them to life situations.

Another distinctive function of the human spirit is its ability to know God's *freely chosen plans and purposes* when communicated in linguistic symbols. Through language, thoughtful spirits commune with spirits. The persons of the divine Trinity communicate with each other and with people created in their image. The first use of human language occurred when God gave Adam the cultural mandate to fill the earth, subdue it, and rule over it (Gen. 1:26–28). In order to do that, God created Adam with the senses to observe what is on earth and the rational capacity to judge what is true and distinguish what is false in matters of fact. We can also receive inner plans and purposes of others who speak. The human mind transcends sense data by envisioning objectives and communicating them through audible or visual *linguistic signs*. Although abstract thoughts are difficult to communicate effectively, one of the most distinctive human capacities is the ability to think of many similar things by the shorthand of general concepts.[113] Without the ability to abstract universals from particulars, our knowledge would be limited to each physical thing (one grain of sand after the other)! Like any other ability, the ability to abstract may be abused. Abstractions about human authenticity and morality may be confused with being authentic and moral as a particular person.

In the face of conflicting claims humans have the ability to *think critically*. We can distinguish objectively valid truth from erroneous rumors and counterfeit opinion. Three major methods of justifying our beliefs are used in pluralistic societies: (1) We may reason inductively from observed particulars to the probability of general conclusions. But often our experience is too limited and our time too short. Furthermore, empiricists may be insufficiently conscious of their own preunderstandings that make complete objectivity impossible. (2) Others emphasize reasoning deductively from universals to particular instances of them when we have evidence of their existence. If the universals are alleged to be self-attesting, they remain unjustified. (3) On a third method we propose hypotheses for verification and disverification. The verificational method most effectively follows the scriptural admonitions to examine, test, try, and prove. It is the most reliable method because it provides the most checks and balances on truth claims.[114]

Because we are, like God, transcendent spiritual beings, we have some ability and responsibility to work, think, speak, and write with *creativity*. We can compare and combine things differently, and imagine and propose new ways of doing things. We ought not think of ourselves as co-creators insofar as that involves a pantheistic or panentheistic equality with God. But God has given us the ability to conceive of alternative possibilities, select from among them, and move toward actualizing one or more of them. Any of these capacities can be misused and abused. We can worry unduly about the future and in the present frighten ourselves with imagined dangers. When humans wisely use these cognitive capacities, they produce cultures and subcultures with their distinctive types of art, music, architecture, horticulture, literature, religions, and mores.

The capacity for *rational intuition* may be a source of effable ideas, but it is not a reliable test of their truth. Although the intuitive capacity supplies sudden ideas sometimes accompanied by feelings of indubitable certainty, psychological certitude is not a guarantee of truth about reality. Intuitions sometimes contradict each other, fail to fit the relevant evidence, or prove to be impossible to embrace in life without hypocrisy. In those cases they turn out to be untrue. The psychological certitude that often accompanies intuitions ought not be confused with epistemological confirmation. So intuition is not a sufficient method of knowing by itself and does not take priority over other methods of justifying beliefs. Ideas suddenly "seen" to be true are to be regarded, like all otherwise derived ideas, as hypotheses to be either confirmed or disconfirmed by the same criteria of truth used throughout this text. Although not a reliable test of truth, intuition is one of several welcome sources of creative ideas to be tested.

Although Eastern mystics and Western devotional writers often say that the peak religious experience is an ineffable *mystical intuition,* God does not seek to erase the minds he created to make meaningful fellowship possible. If nothing can be known even in part about such alleged experiences, then they unsuccessfully claim to be ways of knowing. In Christian experience the ultimate goal is not mindless spirituality (Matt. 22:37; 1 Cor. 14:13–15), but a renewed mind (Rom. 12:2; Col. 3:10). Sound theological guidelines lead our nonrational desires away from unholy spirits and to experience with the God who is, hears, speaks, and acts in holy love.

Although self-conscious, world-conscious, and God-conscious, we cannot keep all that we have ever known before our conscious attention at any given time. Our spirits with their continuing identity store much of our knowledge (and associated emotions and motivations) in the *memory*. The retaining and influence of mental processes of which we are no longer aware seems to justify the widespread belief in the *unconscious*. Freud held that ideas and emotions of which we are now unaware, significantly influence our behavior. The recognition of the spirit's unconscious storage capacity need not lead to the conclusion, however, that human conduct is largely determined by unconscious factors.[115] Neither common human conduct need be attributed to a "collective unconscious" (Carl Jung). The common symbolism of people from diverse cultures can be attributed to the nature each person shares universally and to the similarity of natural laws. God will finally judge each individual, not an alleged collective unconsciousness.

In summary, humans intellectually are agents capable of knowing some truth about themselves and others, the cosmos, and God.

Humans Morally

As important as it is to have an adequate epistemology and ontology, the deepest problems of humans are neither physical nor metaphysical. The finite, limited, and conditioned nature of life in time and space prior to moral rebellion was "very good" (Gen. 1:31). It was not the corruptible body that made the soul sinful, Augustine said, but the sinful soul that made the flesh corruptible. Our most basic problems are ethical, and our moral condition affects our relationships with God and all others.

The ultimate human quest is not fulfilled merely in harmony with nature, but in harmony with the living God transcendent to the universe. Our greatest need is not for becoming as transcendent as God is, or attaining a divine level. What we *are* is not what we *ought to be*. We need to be forgiven and become holy as God is holy. In referring to God as personal, Christians (contrary to Hegel and Evelyn Underhill) are not just stating the truths of metaphysics in terms of personality: thus offering a third term, a "living mediator between the unknowable God, the unconditioned Absolute and the conditioned self."[116] The purpose of Christ was not to symbolize the fact that humans can come immediately into communion with God apart from a mediator. Christ came as actual mediator to provide the just basis on which the Father could remain morally just while justifying sinners and restoring them to fellowship.

Our ability to discern our own evil and feel guilt for it comes through our *conscience*. Our conscience may judge, not only ourselves but also our family, church, and society. More specifically it refers to a capacity for second-level awareness of right and wrong, an ability to judge conduct by moral standards, and to sense our obligation to follow just values personally and socially.[117] It is a court of appeal that cannot make moral laws, as God has done, but does deliver judgments on the cases before it.[118] A sensitive conscience can be poorly or well educated in God's revealed wisdom. Since the conscience can operate effectively only in relation to moral principles outside itself, a clear conscience is not a guarantee that we are right. We are commanded to have love "which comes from a pure heart and a good conscience . . ." (1 Tim. 1:5). But the reality is far from the ideal. The conscience is not the product of environment, habit, or education, but it may be influenced by all of these factors. The sin that affects every part of our nature can also scar the conscience. So Paul warned of being influenced by those whose consciences "have been seared as with a hot iron" (1 Tim. 4:2). Paul exhibited the transcendence of moral irresponsibility when he said to the Sanhedrin, "I have fulfilled my duty to God in all good conscience to this day" (Acts 23:1). Like Paul when he was on trial before Felix, we should strive always to keep our consciences clear before God and mankind (Acts 24:16). Even when we have a clear conscience to eat meat offered to idols, for example, we may choose not to eat it for the love of one whose conscience differs. Conscience serves as a red light coming on when a course of action is wrong and so serves only negatively; the positive influence on our moral judgment comes from Christ's loving fulfillment of the law.

To sum up, humans morally are agents capable of distinguishing God's normative counsel from the deceptive counsels of evil beings and from the ambiguous results of descriptive surveys of human conduct.

Humans Emotionally

Personal human spirits not only think and judge but also *experience and evoke feelings*. The inner human spirit, like the divine Spirit, has affections or feelings. God experiences righteous anger and pleasure. Human emotions cannot simply have resulted from the Fall. Undoubtedly Adam and Eve experienced emotions in their unashamed relationships with each other and with God, in the power to control the animals, and in the freedom to enjoy the fruit of every tree in the garden save one. Eve found the forbidden fruit also "pleasing to the eye" and "desirable" (Gen. 3:6). Since the Fall the Bible frequently describes the emotional states of people. "In fact, Scripture not only speaks about emotions, it also speaks to and through our emotions. The Bible itself is emotional literature, filled with emotional expression and designed not just to communicate with our rationality but also to stir us emotionally, thus affirming our emotionality."[119]

Humans evidently have the capacity for feelings of many sorts, closely associated with what they know, will, and do morally. Our good or evil conduct may include intense inner feelings that may produce tears or smiles. But we cannot reduce all the tensions and joys that we feel merely to smiles or tears, for these outward manifestations express deeper inner feelings. We are far from impassive. To list a few emotions, we may feel admiration, adoration, concern, empathy, love, elation, power, depression, distress, fear, anxiety, embarrassment, disgrace, scorn, neglect, shame, inadequacy, insecurity, inferiority, insignificance, anger, and hostility. When pleased, we may say, "Aha!" When displeased we may say, "O no, not again!" Strong feelings of enticement and attraction accompany temptation.

Our emotions, like our intellects and wills, can be used wisely or unwisely in conjunction with good or evil ends. The answer to wrong desires, however, is not desirelessness as in Buddhist prescriptions. Rather than to try unsuccessfully to suppress all desires, the Christian overcomes evil desires by cultivating worthy loves, esteeming values in harmony with God's nature and purposes above others. So, for example, Christians prize love, not mere sex.

We must get rid of our sinful rage and not let the sun go down on our selfish anger (Eph. 4:26, 31), for these grieve the Holy Spirit (v. 30). But Christ was righteously angry at stubborn hearts (Mark 3:5). "Jesus' anger in cleansing the temple was not merely the seamy side of his pity; it is the righteous reaction of his moral sense in the presence of evil."[120] Those who love human beings must hate all that wrongs them. How can we be both good and angry? At least three conditions must be met. (1) Righteous indignation is morally motivated. It boils over more at wrong done to others than to oneself. (2) Righteous anger is wisely focused and directed. It is not directed against persons but against evil deeds, situations, and institutions. (3) Justifiable anger is ethically implemented. It is followed by positive and constructive action to end the wrong that occasioned it.[121] "Anger, if consecrated to righteousness, may sometimes be an ethical duty," Carl Henry explained, "but it must appear in Christian experience against a background of God-tempered life, and not as a flareup of short temper which lives constantly near the borderline of sudden flight into rage."[122]

Is it possible to love people and hate their sin? Although our neighbor's sin stirs us to wrath, we can oppose it because we love our neighbor. C. S. Lewis thought this a silly hair-splitting distinction until he realized he had been regarding it crucial in regard to himself. "The very reason I hated things was that I loved the man. Just because I loved myself, I was sorry to find that I was the sort of man who did these things. Consequently, Christianity does not want us to reduce by one atom the hatred we feel for cruelty and treachery. We ought to hate them." Lewis then explained that Christianity wants us to hate them in the same way in which we hate such things in ourselves, being sorry that we should have them, and hoping, if it is in any way possible, that somehow, sometime, somewhere, we can be cured and made human again.[123]

In other words, as fallen persons in a fallen world we need to control our emotions by developing the virtue of patience, more aptly called *longsuffering*. Those who are slow to anger are patient with those who do evil to them, not condoning their sin, but hoping that mercy will lead them to repentance and reconciliation. The endurance of longsuffering provides emotional stability to endure in spite of unjust attacks on ourselves, our rights, and our possessions. Christians are longsuffering for several reasons: (1) God is longsuffering. (2) Christians are part of a community of concern and action, so the church will act in their behalf providentially. (3) When Jesus Christ returns, justice will triumph over the worst evils. So Christians do not take vengeance on others who have done wrong to them. They do not become judge, jury, and executioner all in one. Christians with Holy Spirit-aided control of their emotions do not render evil for evil, but forgive those who unjustly treat them and graciously return good for evil.

Our highest emotions will never be fulfilled by the finest people or things in this world, nor by the whole of the world (as pantheists imagine). Our emotional needs can be satisfied only by a personal relationship with God. God made us to share not only his world and the truth about it but also to have fellowship with him. With all of our emotional experiences with others, we are still restless until we find our rest in God—that is, until we experience a transcendent joy. C. S. Lewis felt an intense longing (*Sensucht*) for an Object that is never fully given and cannot be fully present in the subjective experience of persons in the space-time existence. His desire for the transcendent was not fulfilled by aesthetic experience, sexual experience, or pantheistic or occult religious experiences. No mere feeling appeases us. We desire not a state of ourselves, but Something Other and Outer. This longing for the transcendent is similar to the attraction of faraway places, mountains, fantasies, magic, and occultism. But C. S. Lewis confesses, "I have myself been deluded by every one of these false answers in turn, and have contemplated each of them earnestly enough to discover the cheat."[124]

Essentially humans are capable of loving God and the good and detesting evil.

Humans Volitionally

The capacity for human volition involves (1) a choice of an end and (2) an ability to move toward its fulfillment. Freedom of the will may mean both power to choose among options and ability to move toward realizing the one chosen. First, human freedom involves a *capacity of choice among ends*. We choose wisely when we select goals in accord with God's revealed values and purposes, for they are for our best. There may be several specific options that do not violate revealed moral guidelines, so we may have alternative choices that are moral. Freedom does not require ability to choose contrary to God's will. But we have that power also. When we choose courses of action inconsistent with God's universally or specially revealed will, we choose unwisely. At our disposal is an awesome potential for either good or evil.

Second, the human will also includes *a capacity for self-determination*. Having chosen an alternative, we are not free if we do not have ability to move toward that goal and do what we want to do. We are free volitionally when we have both freedom of alternative choices and ability to attain the selected end. Instead, we may frustrate ourselves by choosing objectives we are unable to attain. Because God is omnipotent, he can perform what he chooses in the way he chooses to do it. But often the things we decide to do, we cannot carry out (Rom. 7:18). Hence even when we are most sincere in seeking to fulfill a chosen course of action, we may find ourselves lacking in ability to complete it as planned. People are not only objects of investigation by others, but also active subjects who choose and perform actions. Since persons are causal agents, not all causes are impersonal factors. Persons may be efficient causal agents who determine and initiate actions. As subjects people decide on problems worth researching, initiate inquiries, decide on a reliable method of justifying beliefs, evaluate the work of others, and arrive at conclusions. When we are subjects who initiate action, we are accountable to God and others for those words or deeds. As dependent creatures of God, we are free, but without divine providence, of course, we could do nothing.

Persons are also like God in using their powers of self-determination with *creativity*. Like God, persons have a capacity for creative imagination, goal-setting, strategies, and actions. Artists, sculptors, architects, writers, and many others have enriched our lives by creatively developing fresh approaches. We may need courage to exercise our creative capacities to develop different strategies and methods for advancing God's universal and redemptive kingdoms. Like any other capacity, *imagination* can be either misused or properly used. Imagination is misused if we visualize ourselves as having infinite potential or as being wiser than God, independent of God, or equal with God. The most imaginative creations in literature have some relation to truth about reality. Constructively we can use imagination in several important coherent ways. It can propose new hypotheses for us to confirm or disconfirm, different ways of serving others on behalf of Christ, and stimulating plans for uses of leisure time that will refresh the human spirit. Beyond that, it may awaken and foster a degree of emotional sensitivity and personal engagement that is highly compatible with the life of faith, and in doing so it affirms the significance of spiritual values, personal commitment, beauty and love.[125] C. S. Lewis's fresh ways of formulating and communicating truth with feeling in his imaginative literary works is consistent with his more closely reasoned verificational approach to Christianity's truth. Persons think and write, mere minds do not.

The will also is a distinguishable capacity, but it does not choose and act with total independence of mind, emotions, desires, and relationships. Our choices and consequent actions are not made by a will sporting about in a vacuum. Persons, not mere wills, select among options and initiate actions. When choosing among ends and moving toward their realization, we may be attracted by the nonvolitional aspects of our natures, such as our *desires*. Free will gives to love its precious value, but right love gives will its freedom and fulfillment. Unfortunately, our wills may be moved also by evil desires to evil options. While we may be conscious of being free from external coercion, our wills may be influenced by unconscious habitual desires or moral natures. Hence even when most convinced that we are exercising our wills freely, we need to consider critically the hypothesis that our choices are influenced by our desires and basic moral nature.

Our wills, although free from external coercion, do not act independently of our *motives*. Motives are thoughts or feelings that influence us to choose certain ends and to act in certain ways. Our motivations may be either conscious or unconscious. Even though we may consciously choose to be intellectually honest, for example, we may be motivated to act in accord with a greater momentary desire to impress a friend or get some advantage for ourselves. Frequently, even when our primary motive is to give gratitude, obedience, and glory to God, there is not just a single motive, but our motives may be mixed. At the same time we may be seeking to fulfill biological needs, earn some recognition from peers or superiors, and serve some ideals. Then we may ask ourselves, "Which is our ultimate concern?" Singleness of purpose in life refers to everything that is done ultimately for the Lord.[126]

The freedom of our wills may be limited by the habitual moral inclinations of our *depraved natures*. Hence even when we are conscious of our freedom to choose and have the ability to do what we choose, we may be overwhelmed by our sinful desires. Fallen people have the power of self-determination, but their choices may be influenced not only by evil desires and motives, but also by good desires without the highest motivation. The best deeds of sinful people may not be done for the glory of God. "Free will," then, may be used in different ways. In reference to humans it cannot mean entirely what it means for God. For God, freedom means no external coercion and the ability to do anything he has chosen (in accord with his nature) in the strategy chosen. For human beings, free will may mean (1) no specific external coercion, (2) the ability to select among alternatives for morally mixed reasons, and (3) limited ability to move in the direction chosen. The ability to choose contrary to our own natures is not essential to human freedom any more than to divine freedom. What is essential to free will is the ability to choose and act according to the deepest desires or loves of one's moral nature.

Whatever the internal influences, when without external coercion, normal, mature persons act with premeditated intent; they are *responsible for their choices and their conduct*. Empirical scientists and behaviorists in psychology in their quest for impersonal antecedents may overlook a person's own choices and acts. History is not totally explained in terms of impersonal causes. To account for the history of a culture we must also recognize the reality and impact of personal causes (1:310–11). Brothers and sisters with similar heredity and environmental influences are personal spirits who may think, feel, will, and act very differently in their moral conduct. When two people have the same influences toward immoral conduct, one may participate with others in a life of crime, the second may choose to rebel against his environment and obey the laws. Regenerate persons become like God when they use their volitional abilities in harmony with God's nature and purposes.

Our most valuable freedom "is not the psychological freedom to do what we will, not the physical, social or political freedom which exempts us from illegitimate interference from others, not the Stoic freedom of following the law of nature nor the Kantian freedom of doing what we ought, but the Divine freedom described by Augustine of wanting to do what we ought because we love God and take delight in Him."[127]

Volitionally, humans are self-determining agents, responsible to decide and act wisely, lovingly, and virtuously.

Humans Relationally

Talk of relationships, contrary to neoorthodox theology, need not exclude information about the nature of personal agents capable of relating to one another. Significant relationships can develop only among real personal beings who initiate and sustain them. Relational categories are vitally important to Christian theology because the persons involved, being ontologically real, have inherent worth. No follower of Christ can fail to appreciate the supreme value of loving God with one's whole being because of who God is and one's neighbors as oneself because of who our neighbors are.

Real person-to-person relationships are possible because of the ontological reality of persons as spiritual and physical beings. Humans can relate to things and technology, but the most interesting, varied, and fulfilling relationships are with other persons. We relate to one another through physical "signs" or body language. Essential to lasting relationships is careful observation of physical signs and wise discernment of their significance. On the basis of the evidence seen we trust the others' invisible sincerity and faithfulness. Faithfulness results as both adhere to such moral conditions of meaningful relationships as those characterized by justice, love, and relatedness to reality and consistency.

Relationships should mutually enrich the participants rather than depersonalize one or more of them. The uniqueness of persons is a value that should not be destroyed by social relationships. Family solidarity in Judaism in biblical times was strong because individuals were strengthened by them, not reduced to impersonal cogs in a machine. National solidarity may seem strong also in countries under communism. But in the midst of the strongest collectives, persons remain distinguishable and accountable as individuals. Individuals will stand alone before the final Judge to account for their response to the pressures of their families, gangs, athletic teams, unions, tribes, and political or religious leaders.

In the West, insofar as there is deficient social regard and commitment under God to others in the family, the nation, and the church, people may suffer from an unhealthy individualism. In the East, insofar as there may be a lack of regard for the value of the individual, people may suffer from unhealthy collectivisms. In general the Bible recognizes the reality of accountable individuals in their common social loyalties and institutional commitments. Collectives should strengthen persons, and persons should strengthen collectives. In this reciprocal relationship, which is intended to benefit both, neither need destroy the other. We are not merely formed by these social relationships, we act and by acting help to form the character of these societies. Not only are we constituted by them, but we ourselves constitute them, modifying their quality for better or worse.[128]

The individual also is in a reciprocal relationship with the Lord of providence. In Scripture there is no such thing as an autonomous individual. Even the attempt to live as an atheist is regarded as utter folly (Ps. 14:1). In common grace the Creator-Sustainer provides the life support system on planet earth and gives life with all its opportunities. The grateful recipients in turn respond in love and service for their Source. Much more will be said about relationships in all the chapters to follow. Here we emphsize the truth actually communicated by trichotomists. Indeed humans have three levels of conscious relationships: to God, to others, and to the physical world.

To sum up, the whole person metaphysically is a complex agent, a unity of an inner (spiritual) and outer (physical) being with a multiplicity of capacities for developing excellence and ruling the world (Gen. 1:26, 28) intellectually, morally, emotionally, volitionally, and relationally. In other words, a human person is an accountable agent made up of an interacting dichotomy of spirit and body with a trichotomoy of three relationships—to the earth, others, and God. The truth in dichotomy is in two substances; the truth in trichotomy is in three major relationships. In Scripture the whole inner person relating to God is most frequently designated spirit. The whole inner person relating to oneself, others, and things is most frequently called soul. But the *one* inner person thinks, feels, wills, and relates, whether "vertically" or horizontally." Humans in themselves do have great (but not infinite) potential for sharing God's vital fellowship, relationships, and work. In the next chapter we investigate the effects of sin on the greatness of God's image-bearers.

APOLOGETIC INTERACTION

Persons Are Not Mere Bodies

We have concurred with materialists that the body is real but also deny that it is the ultimate reality. Even though our understanding of matter and atoms has changed as a result of nuclear studies, an element of truth remains in materialism. Solid material bodies are real. Unfortunately, however, materialism reduces all human spirituality and psychology to physics and its epiphenomenal by-products. The brain secretes thought, one says, as the liver secretes bile! Jacob Bronowski alleges that humans are "a part of nature, in the same sense that a stone is, or a cactus, or a camel."[129] Indeed our lives are dependent on the laws of creation, but such statements fail to reflect the uniqueness or value of the human spirit in the image of God. A Marxist dialectical materialism has an element of truth but oversimplifies the complexity of human existence and depersonalizes human agents. But as interacting dualist Karl Popper argues, inexplicably for materialists, matter somehow "transcends itself by producing mind, purpose, and a world of products from the human mind. One of the first products of human mind is human language."[130]

Behaviorism also denies that humans are constituted of two distinct interacting realities. According to behaviorists, all mental functions can be analyzed in terms of physical behavior.[131] The great riddle is how the physical universe created life, mind, and consciousness which illuminates the universe and itself becomes creative and self-transcendent! There is no evidence that atoms have conscious inner states. On a behaviorist hypothesis human conduct is not determined as much by the inner conscious agent as from without. Hence human behavior could theoretically be totally controlled by regulating the environment. Who then would decide which behaviorists will govern our environment and on what (nonphysical) principles shall that decision be made? In *The Abolition of Man* C. S. Lewis "insisted that man was not a thing, but an essence, a soul, and that it ill profits a man to gain the whole material world at the expense of the elementary self-knowledge that tells him that he is a soul qualitatively distinct from and superior to those things."[132]

Is the human spirit a mere emergent from bodily processes? Defending a theistic evolution, Richard H. Bube suggests not only that the body originated through an evolutionary process but also that the human spirit "results from the interaction between his bodily parts. . . . Just as flame bursts suddenly into being as a qualitatively new entity due to the interaction of wood and oxygen, so the spirit of man can be envisioned coming into being under the guidance of God." Again, "the spiritual nature of reality need not be imposed from the 'outside' upon the material, but may have its origin within material interactions in themselves."[133] Analogies, of course, do not prove anything, and Bube's analogy even fails to illustrate a sufficient qualitative difference, unless he regards the soul a physical epiphenomenon. Fire as qualitatively visible and tactual is not as different qualitatively as a personal, responsible agent.

The fact that persons may be *in some sense* identical with their bodies, C. Stephen Evans argues, is no more cause for alarm than the fact that a poem may be *in some sense* identical with a set of ink marks.[134] Several levels of description of poems may be distinguished: (1) a chemical description of the paper and ink, (2) a description of the poor or legible writing, (3) a description of the language used, (4) a description of the meanings of key words and of their sentences, and (5) a description of the entire poem in terms of its author's preplanned purpose and intended meaning, including the emotive impact and possible contribution of the poem to a new outlook and way of life. All these levels may be necessary for a comprehensive description of a poem. Similarly, for a comprehensive view of humans we need a description of the physical aspects of the body and its observable environment, but we also need descriptions of the person as a conscious, accountable agent.[135]

As materialism, behaviorism, and scientism have developed, many lament, wisdom seems not to be keeping pace. Both kinds of knowledge are important. As *homo sciens* we know *scientia:* matters of fact and quantity in the material world. As *homo sapiens* we should know *sapientia:* qualities of meaning, purpose, and value. "Enthusiasts of scientism fail to see that *scientia* is utterly dependent on *sapientia* for direction and meaning; their fervent attempts to pursue *scientia* in isolation from *sapientia* amount to a tragic rush into meaninglessness—the very antithesis of a genuine search for knowledge."[136] The exclusive use of *scientia* "is the great modern religion, our established church, with a whole panoply of priests, evangelists, saints, and bishops, and massive means of publicity and propaganda. It has the power, if it is allowed to grow uncontested in enough human minds, to bring about the end of *homo sapiens*. It may indeed prove to be the abolition of man."[137]

Scientific knowledge by perception involves more than perception itself. The mere presentation of publicly observable sense data to the mind does not constitute knowledge. Some animals perceive things we do not. Scientific conclusions involve interpretations of the data and judgments of the truth or falsity of allegations based on it. Judgments of truth or falsity involve the import of validity or invalidity, a factor quite distinct from the data received from the physical world. In making cognitive claims for their own views behaviorists or positivists either contradict themselves or lapse into absurdity. Do they really have minds or are they automata? "Philosophical behaviorists seem to be able to draw on unsuspected dialectical resources in meeting criticism. But in so doing they seem to purchase impregnability at the expense of those very features of the behaviorist outlook that attracted theorists to the position in the first place."[138]

The *human mind cannot be reduced to the physical brain*. The mind is more than an automatic telephone exchange or a computer. The brain cannot observe itself, but the mind is self-conscious (in varying degrees) and thinks about its own thinking. The brain occupies space, but the mind transcends space, imagining many other places in the world than one's skull. The brain is limited by time, but the mind can transcend the present to learn from the past and anticipate the future. We observe the brain as a physical thing; we conceive of the mind's meanings and values in nonphysical ways. The brain receives audio, visual, olfactory, and tactual signals, but the mind interprets the wave lengths or vibrations and makes assertions on the basis of this evidence that may be true or false, right or wrong. Awareness of ourselves is indispensable to our moral and spiritual accountability for our conduct in the use of our spiritual and physical capacities. We can overcome our perfectionism and pride and examine ourselves.[139]

Eccles dismisses the term "substance" because of atomic theory but nevertheless concludes that the mind is an independent "entity." The mind as an entity is actively engaged in reading out from the multitude of active centers in modules of liaison areas of the dominant cerebral hemisphere. The self-conscious mind selects from these centers in accord with its attention and its interests and integrates its selection to give the unity of conscious experience from moment to moment.[140] In memory the self-conscious mind commands, as it were, retrievals from the data of the storage banks in the cerebral cortex.[141] The dualist-interactionist hypothesis has the recommendation of its great explanatory power.[142] Our unity comes not from the neural system but from the self-conscious mind. Persons respond to the world of time and sense through the body and brain, and at the same time they respond to mental, aesthetic, and spiritual concepts, which are real, even though they are beyond the reach of the physical sciences. So the most probable explanation of human self-transcendence mentally, morally, teleologically, and in self-government is a spirit like God's that transcends matter and is moral, purposeful, and well controlled.[143]

Persons Are Not Mere Minds

In contrast to the reductive materialism stands reductive idealism. Both unwisely truncate reality to one kind of being. On the arguments above, idealists tend to regard only the inner soul or spirit real and the body unreal or illusory. Also in the reductive monism of multitudes in Vedanta Hinduism as well as its Bhakti tradition represented by Hare Krishna, the body is *maya*. The body is illusory also for many who see life from New Age pantheistic perspectives.

The idealist hypothesis, however, does not fit the fact that God created the earth and the first human body out of dust. The body cannot be reduced to nothing but idea or spirit any more adequately than the spirit can be reduced to nothing but matter. The complexity of human persons is no more adequately accounted for by the limited idealists' level of description than by that of the reductive materialist. Even in cultures where the body is regarded as illusory (*maya*), people are concerned about what they eat, get innoculations against hepatitis, and look both ways before crossing a busy street. Daily human experience indicates the reality of physical bodies beyond reasonable doubt. Bodies are fed, dressed, exercised, relieved, rested, weighed, medically examined, hospitalized, and buried.

Comprehensive scriptural descriptions of experience as well call for a recognition not only of humanity's inner spiritual reality, but also of our *outward reality as bodies.* One topical index of the Bible, besides giving ordinary references to the senses, lists passages on (are you ready for this?) manly beauty, female beauty, diminutive stature, giants, dexterity, appetites, the countenance, the hair, the beard, the forehead, stooping, prostration, sighing, tears, saliva, excretions, food, cooking, feasting, gluttony, fasting, famine, drink, sleep, the folly of anxiety about dress, the material, color, and seemliness of dress, ornaments, perfume, disguises, grief exhibited by dress, removal of dress, afflictions, sickness, weakness, restlessness, pain, consumption, fever, palsy, leprosy, cutaneous disorders, sores, boils, mutilation, wounds, lameness, sunstroke, blindness, pestilence, physicians, prescriptions, apothecaries, sickness caused by sin, recovery, old age, duties to the aged, death, preparing for death, instances of death, burying the dead, grief for the dead, corruption, nonburials, bodies devoured, and bodies burned! The Bible hardly minimizes the physical side of humanness! The resurrection body, furthermore, will be an even more marvelous reality.

Persons Are Not Mere Relationships, Functions, or Wholes

Relationships are connections between things, persons, or ideas. Unless we know something about the connected terms in themselves our knowledge of the alleged relationship may not hold in actuality. All relations are between terms or entities. What gives human and religious relationships great value is the nature of the persons involved in them. Given the reality of human spirits and their consequent inherent worth, personal relationships are of great value. The worth of personal relationships is enhanced, not displaced, when we recognize the inherent values and rights of persons. Knowing what was in humans, Jesus Christ said a person's soul is of greater value than the whole world. Why? Because persons have inalienable value.

Created persons always depend on God for life and breath and must always be seen in that dependent relationship. But who or what is the whole that always depends on God? G. C. Berkouwer claims that to speak of the mystery of persons *in themselves* at all is to speak abstractly.[144] In defining the ontological nature of humans as both spiritual and physical, however, we do not change their dependent status. We find some meaning to their continuous identity and responsibility under God. Berkouwer contradicts himself. On one hand he claims that he is not choosing relation over reality or the relational over the ontological, or choosing one horn of any such dilemma.[145] On the other hand Berkouwer says, "In Scripture we hear no ontological explanations, but rather religious affirmation."[146] The Scriptures cannot both include ontological truth in religious relationships and contain no such ontological truth. We agree that we never encounter in the Bible an "*independently existing* abstract, ontological, structural interest in man,"[147] but that does not mean that we never encounter ontological and structural implications concerning dependent humans. Initially Berkouwer allows the ontological in the relational, but does not supply the ontological with any content and later inconsistently excludes it from consideration.

Berkouwer claims "that Scripture never pictures man as a dualistic or pluralistic being, but that in all its varied expressions the whole man comes to the fore."[148] Such a claim in general fails to answer the question of what "the whole man" is composed and to fit the facts indicated in the scriptural section of this chapter. Specifically it overlooks Christ's clear distinction between the body and soul: "Do not be afraid of those who kill the body but cannot kill the soul" (Matt. 10:28). Correctly Berkouwer says that Paul's thought is far removed from gnostic dualism in which the soul is imprisoned in the body and longs for its escape,[149] but that does not exclude a dualism in which Paul is either at home in the body or at home with the Lord (2 Cor. 5:6, 8–9) and seeks in his soul (as distinguishable from his body) to exalt Christ in his body whether by life or by death (Phil. 1:20). Although Paul desired to depart (from his body) and be with Christ, he considered it more necessary to remain in the body for ministry at Philippi (vv, 23–24). Paul's distinctions between himself and his body are not adequately accounted for by the hypothesis of an undefined whole person or an unidentifiable whole mass of relationships.

Mistakenly Berkouwer says that in the Bible, not immortality, but mortality characterizes humans. He says, "The witness of the whole Bible is so clear on this point that no denial is possible"[150] However, his interpretation does not determine the limits of possibility because he has overlooked important evidence. Paul attributes mortality explicitly to the *body* (Rom. 6:12; 8:11; 2 Cor. 4:11). Concerning death Jesus and Paul teach body sleep, not soul sleep. Berkouwer acknowledges that a relation is always between two things and that his stress on relationalism does not dissolve reality.[151] But he has no distinguishable spirit to return to God when the body is buried and so he leaves the intermediate state an impossible muddle rather than a profound mystery. Although the body is in the grave, it is not a part of man but the "whole" that lives on![152] He finds no help for a solution in the Bible[153] but has no doubt that the church from the most ancient times was convinced of continued existence after death![154] The church's view of human nature allowed a meaningful assertion of life after death; Berkouwer's does not.

Berkouwer fails to see that a belief in the continued existence of the spirit need not entail the illicit connotations of Gnostic thought. Before accusing the whole historic Christian church of a Greek philosophical view of immortality, he should have paused to consider whether the view of immortality in Christendom entailed the notions of the body as the source of moral evil and as a prison of the soul, or the soul as complete before the resurrection. We cannot accept a merely functional hypothesis that fails to provide a coherent account of the biblical and experiential data above. The view of an interacting dichotomy provides the more coherent view of the whole person's constitution with fewer difficulties.

Persons Are Not Mere Fields of Energy

Some writers of the New Age movement reduce persons to small energy fields in the vast field of all energy. The psychological aspect, like our physical structure, may be "nothing more nor less than a configuration of energies."[155] W. Brugh Joy suspects that the *chakra* system interrelates the gross physical body and the subtle, etheric bodies, but he has only one basic energy operating in both bodily and spiritual systems called by various names such as chi, vital force, and prana.[156] Marilyn Ferguson claims to have discovered that the separate self is an illusion. The self is not an encapsulated individual. Instead Ferguson proposes that the self is "a field within larger fields."[157] She finds linkage with others "as if they were one self and merged with a another Self yet more universal and primary."[158] That transcendent universal self (indistinguishable from the Hindu Brahman) provides a new (to her in the West) view of the self as part of the whole of society and the world.

The hypothesis that reduces humanness to impersonal energy dehumanizes persons. Why not fold, mutilate, and spindle bits of energy that do not cooperate with the New Age world plan? Who makes the distinctions between cooperation and noncooperation if no individuals exist in reality? If there are no personal agents, who communicates with whom and who is responsible for moral conduct? And to what? To what field of energy shall we assign responsibility for the view that persons are nothing but their actions or relationships?

The hypothesis that personal agents are unreal fails to fit the facts of the great cast of characters in the jury system and the law courts. The hypothesis that we are mere *maya* cannot provide a coherent account of the scriptural data above. *Ex hypothesis* it does not leave responsible persons with whom to communicate.

Persons Are Not Mere Phenomena (Barth and Others)

Barth does not think of a person as a soul in a body. A person is a "bodily soul" or a "besouled body."[159] The spirit, according to Barth, is not something that the person *is,* in the sense that a person is both body and soul. Rather, a person *has* spirit, or, "spirit has him."[160] For Barth a person has "double determination"[161] toward creatures and toward God, but not two ontological natures. Descriptively this has value in terms of the relation between the body and the life or soul of the body in this life.[162] But it carries little explanatory power as to who we *are*. Just as some knowledge of God's "isness" ("I am who I am" [Exod. 3:14]) is basic to understanding divine acts in history, so some understanding of human "isness" is necessary to understanding our physical and nonphysical determinations.

Another phenomenological description of human experience portrays its twofold character psychosomatically. As Anthony Hoekema explains, "Man is *one* person who can, however, be looked at from *two* sides." Hoekema's work does not explain what it is that we have two sides of. He prefers to speak descriptively of a "psychosomatic unity."[163] Hoekema does not want to say what a person is ontologically. Hoekema's reference to the psychosomatic unity of a person also is useful descriptively for the present life but provides no account of what the *pneuma, psychē*, or *sōma* actually are. The uniting of the two unknown factors in the word "psychosomatic" seems to have no real referent. To call it the one human person is circular. Definitions do not repeat the word to be defined. To the extent that his work fails to define the mental and physical aspects in some meaningful and distinguishable manner his view fails to accommodate the biblical indications of their distinct attributes and separability as well as their interaction.

Arthur Koestler may be thought to have answered a dichotomous view of humanity in his *Ghost in the Machine.* Instead he has shown that neither "ghost" nor "machine" are appropriate concepts. Koestler proposes that humans are "a multileveled hierarchy." On the one hand he mentions levels of matter: macroscopic, molecular, atomic, and subatomic. On the other hand he distinguishes levels of consciousness: unconsciousness, dreamless sleep, dreaming, day-dreaming, drowsiness, epileptic automatisms, and so on, up to bright, wide-awake states with shifts of attention and control from rather mechanical to mindful behavior.[164] Koestler claims that one level emerges into the other but fails to confirm a continuity between the highest level of matter-energy and the lowest level of consciousness. He openly admits, "I am aware that in this chapter I have indulged in some momentous question-begging."[165]

None of the no-subject, no-agent, no-soul views of human functions and relationships provide adequate accounts of the data of human experience and Scripture to the extent that interacting dualism does. That a person is a spiritual agent (a spirit) accounts for his identity, continuity, self-transcendence, self-consciousness, purposive and moral responsibility for his behavior. In spite of modern opposition to the use of "substance," "entity," or "being," no better concept has been proposed for "what stands under." As complex as the levels of matter-energy may be, it is matter-energy that accounts for the unity of attributes and capacities in our bodies. And as multifaceted as spirit-energy may be, the soul unifies a person's nonphysical qualities and capacities. Together they compose the whole person. A person may be angry, brilliant, or hopeful, but he or she is more than a bundle of those qualities at any given time. The term *substance* expresses one's reluctance to say that one quality is sadness. We predicate the set of invisible qualities of the soul or spirit as subject and the set of visible qualities to the material body as home and instrument in this life.[166]

Because God created humans in his image ontologically an analogy of being holds between God and humans as well as an analogy of act. We agree with what Stuart Barton Babbage affirms—we are like God in acts and relationships. But we differ insofar as Babbage denies an analogy of being between God and his image-bearers.[167] The image of God in man includes more than relationships and acts. God made our dependent spirits like his infinite Spirit for his fellowship and service.

How Can Two Different Substances Interact?

Granting the holistic reality of soul and body, how can entities with such radically different qualities interact with each other? This has been the major concern of those who oppose an interacting dualism in humanity. Consider the following:

1. The fact is that the interaction of spirit and body takes place constantly. Daily the human soul interacts with the body and is morally accountable for its acts in this life and in the life to come. Every time we decide to go or stay, walk or run, drive through or stop, eat or fast, pray or exercise, the decision of the inner, invisible person moves the body. Even if there is no explanation of how the interaction takes place, the fact remains that interaction takes place constantly. For example, the inner person, while driving, decides to speed up and so moves the foot to the accelerator, and the car moves faster. Again, the inner self decides to stop and moves the foot to the brake, and the brake stops the car. Apparently the spirit is able by a kind of trigger action to release the energy stored up in the healthy body. As the conscious purpose releases the physical energy of the nervous system and the muscles, the foot moves from the accelerator to the brake. A spirit's conscious purpose in this change does not violate natural laws, but uses them. And the inner person of the driver is morally and legally accountable for avoidable accidents.

2. Believers in creation and providence have already accepted the interaction of spirit on the physical, just as God, who is a transcendent Spirit, created and providentially acts in, through and upon the material world.

The eternal spirit created matter and works in the physical world either through nature's laws or independently of them. Any who have followed the doctrines of divine creation and providence should not have any essential difficulty with the fact that a real spiritual being can act upon real physical beings. So, if our natural bias against being accountable for all our actions to the all-knowing Spirit can be overcome, we should be able to admit that a human spirit can act upon its human body.

3. Unfortunately, mechanical explanations are inappropriate to the actions of spirit, whether divine or human. If the "how" questions require complete mechanical answers, they are seldom provided by either Scripture, sociology, or psychology.

4. The problem should not be exaggerated, for as different as soul and body are, they have some things in common: (1) Both are *real entities,* real beings or substances created to interact in a world of both physical and spiritual realities. (2) Both substances have *distinct sets of qualities* attributed to them and sustained by them in divine providence without forming a hybrid. Because both body and spirit are realities in God's world, it need not be thought impossible that different kinds of real beings can make an impact on one another in a world created and sustained by God for that purpose.

The lack of a detailed explanation of *how* God acts in the physical world providentially does not diminish the conclusiveness of the evidence that the divine Spirit does in fact hold it all together. Analogously, if a lack of a full mechanical explanation of how the human spirit acts on the human body remains, it is a lesser difficulty than the problems faced by reductive monisms and all nonsubstantial skepticisms. Monistic hypotheses, whether materialistic or spiritistic, must reduce half of human experience to something it is not! Nonsubstantialist and nonagent views of humanity lose an adequate basis for continued identity in time and eternity, and for moral responsibility for all of our conduct. Wisdom chooses the hypothesis with the greatest coherence and the fewest difficulties—a holistic view of humanity involving an interacting dualism of soul and body.

Dichotomoy of Substances, Trichotomy of Conscious Relationships

Since the issue between monists and dichotomists is one of the number of substances making up a human being, one would expect trichotomists to propose that a human being is composed of three *substances.* Their diagrammatic illustrations often do suggest three spatially distinct entities. Some trichotomists visualize the spirit in a small circle encompassed by a larger circle of the soul within an even larger circle of the body. Others draw the circle of a person's being like a pie cut in three pieces. Each part or substance is said to have distinctive capacities, making possible distinct relationships and even fruitfulness and victory in the Christian life.

The trichotomists' definitions and explanations fail, however, to distinguish soul substance in itself from spirit substance in itself. Instead, trichotomists speak of the three capacities enabling humans respectively to have God-consciousness, self-consciousness, and world-consciousness.[168] Until this confusion of categories is clarified, progress in research or discussion will remain futile. If there is to be significant progress, both dichotomists and trichotomists must be addressing the same issue—the number of substances. Dichotomists believe as fully as trichotomists that humans can have relationships with God, humans, and the earth. If a trichotomy of relationships is the question, there remains no debate! Allegedly conflicting positions should not go on endlessly with confused categories. One theological problem should be considered settled!

The capacity of a person to understand God-consciousness and self-consciousness does not require two entities. A person has both awarenesses and world-consciousness through the physical nerves and the brain. One and the same person is conscious of God, of self, and of the physical world. In contrast, Watchman Nee's analysis has the spirit relating to God and the soul to self and others. The human spirit, according to Nee, has three main functions for relating to God: intuition, communion, and conscience.[169]

Nee maintains that by *intuition,* as the first function for relating to God, a human spirit allegedly directly knows God's mind and receives divine guidance. But the sudden intuitions of Christians sometimes conflict, let alone those of people in pantheistic religions. All intuitions must be tested by the teaching of Scripture interpreted with sound hermeneutical principles, sound criteria of truth, and a sound method of decision making. All of this requires the use of the mind, so it is hard to see how intuition is superior to the mental capacity alleged of the lower "soul." Second, the spirit at an assumed "deeper" level than thought, feeling, or will allegedly experiences *communion* with God. Significant personal communion with God, according to the greatest commandment, requires the fullest devotion of the whole person—mind, emotions, and will. Jesus did not demote these to a lower level and call for a noncognitive superspirituality. Some trichotomists mistakenly attribute evil, not to the "fleshly nature," but to the soul and the use of its capacities. Third, the *conscience* then reproves sin or approves righteousness. Again, how can conscience operate without mental distinctions between right and wrong, emotional regret for real guilt, and purposes of will to follow the Lord's revealed will? Dichotomists, as well as trichotomists, receive intuitions, have communion with God, and seek clear consciences, but they do not try to limit these capacities to different parts of a person. They are activities that, at least in their interpretation, involve other capacities and eventually the whole person.

Nee's trichotomist functions of the soul feature the *emotions,* the *mind,* and the *will.* Unworthy desires such as affections, desires, and feelings may enslave the believer. Influenced by these formidable enemies, most Christians are alleged to live "soulical" or unspiritual lives. The mind is the capacity for rational thought, and often is found in conflict with intuition. The will makes decisions for the whole person and in the spiritual life must be unshackled from the fleshly soul life so that it may freely cooperate with God. Nee's soul is alleged to be inferior to his spirit and so also is exegetical study of the Word inferior to intuitions. His mind primarily examines, explains, and develops the intuitive knowledge given by the Holy Spirit to his believing spirit.

The biblical evidence alleged for trichotomy does not attribute the intuitive and reasoning capacities to two distinctly different substances, but to the one inner person who dwells in the body. Relationships as well as substances can be distinguished by the figurative "sword," the teaching of God's Word (Heb. 4:12). The whole dichotomous person can be sanctified, including all three relationships (1 Thess. 5:23). From these two passages that mention spirit, soul, and body, we have no more basis for concluding three substances than we do four substances from the great commandment—to love God with heart, soul, mind, and strength (Mark 12:30).

The implications of three substances

lead to endless difficulties. If it is the soul that thinks, feels, and wills and the spirit that communes with God, is there no thought, feeling, or decision in communion with our Maker? If the spirit's intuitions do not involve intellectual concepts, they are contentless as well as without emotions or determinations of will. Intuitions granted some content are often wrong. The soul's mind then must distinguish which of the spirit's intuited truths are true and which are false! And whose conscience is it that is discerning right from wrong if not that of the person who thinks, feels, and wills? The conscience also is incapable of functioning independently of thinking, feeling, and willing. A person with all capacities functioning (conscience, communion and intuition, reason, emotion, and will) relates to God, others, and the physical world. Intuition is not an independent source of inerrant truth. Intuitions, if true, need to be confirmed by the reason's verificational process; and intuitions may in fact be disconfirmed or shown to be false.

Trichotomists appear to hold that a person is made up of a body and two kinds of nonphysical entities: one referred to as the spirit and the other as the soul. Although trichotomists think they oppose dichotomy, they have yet to distinguish the soul from the spirit as substances. The definitions trichotomists offer provide only functional or relational distinctions. Until trichotomists propose a substantial difference between soul and spirit, there is not a meaningful difference between trichotomists and dichotomists on the number of substances that make up a human person. At present the alleged debate between dichotomy and trichotomy, as far as entities are concerned, is merely verbal. If trichotomists were to succeed in distinguishing spirit and soul as substances, the view would then find difficulty fitting the scriptural instances displaying their interchangeability.

That persons have three primary relationships—to God, other humans, and the material world—dichotomists need not debate. On the interacting dichotomist view, the one inner person (spirit or soul) relates functionally through the brain and body to (1) God, (2) other humans, and (3) the physical world. Hence our view may be referred to as a dichotomy of substances and a trichotomy of functions. Although the three general relationships hold, more than three functions can be distinguished. The one immaterial person has the functions many trichotomists attribute to the soul, for the person thinks, feels, and wills. The same person has the functions trichotomists attribute to the spirit: intuiting possible truths, communion with God, and moral discernment and obligation (conscience). None of these functions that trichotomists attribute to the spirit would be possible without the use of the soul (intellect, emotion, and will). One and the same whole person with all his capacities either does or does not relate well to God, others, or the physical world.

The hypothesis of a trichotomy of substances raises serious difficulties for understanding all of Christian experience. In regard to creation: only a third of the person (the spirit) is created in the *imago Dei*. Only the spirit is affected by the Fall, regenerated, and sanctified. The battles in the Christian life may be considered a conflict of soul against spirit more than of two opposed desires, inclinations, or natures. Many great doctrines are altered if the implications of trichotomy are consistently developed. Since the evidence for trichotomy does not compare with the data against it, we find that God created the whole inner person in his image, the Fall affects all of a person's functions (in a holistic depravity), the Holy Spirit renews the entire inner believer and all the believer's inner functions in the image of his creator, and sanctification proceeds progressively for all functions.

How Human Spirits Originate

In the chapter on creation the evidence indicated that the spirits of Adam and Eve were specially created. How did the spirits of Cain and Abel originate? How and when do human spirits originate today? There is no biblical evidence to support the view that human spirits existed prior to conception and birth. Neither do we find adequate evidence to support the view that spirits are individually created at conception or birth. The passages teaching that spirits come from God can be interpreted providentially and ultimately rather than miraculously and proximately. "The spirit returns to God who gave it" (Eccl. 12:7; cf. Isa. 42:5; Zech. 12:1), and God is "the Father of our spirits" (Heb. 12:9). Every human being, like every other good gift, in the final analysis comes from the Father (James 1:17). But not every good thing comes from God by a miraculous creative act. Creationists raise the problem of how Christ could be without sin if souls are derived from parents along with bodies. The point is irrelevant to normal conceptions, however, because the conception of Jesus was miraculous. The conception of Jesus by a virgin involved both a biological miracle and a moral miracle so that Mary's sinful nature was not transmitted to Jesus, and he was holy (Luke 1:35).

The major problem with a creationist hypothesis is that for all normally born persons the Holy One allegedly directly creates their souls with sinful dispositions. Scriptural teaching traces sinfulness not to the body but to the inner soul or spirit (Jer. 17:9). The "flesh" refers in moral contexts only secondarily to the body as the instrument of the fallen spirit. Primarily the flesh is the sinful nature received at conception. Since throughout Scripture God is the source of good and not of moral rebellion against himself, it seems unthinkable that he, the Holy One, should specifically create each human soul with a bent toward disbelieving and disobeying him.

The traducian hypothesis attributes the origin of the soul as well as the body to one's parents. Whole spirit-body persons reproduce after their kind. The union of physical cells produces physical bodies and simultaneously the union of spirits produces the spirits of infants. This traducian view may startle at first, but those who have recognized the reality of spirit beings and know that God who is spirit created them in his image should not find the problems insuperable. A traducian hypothesis of the origin of the soul is in harmony with the psycho-physical interaction in all of human life on earth.

The major criticism that is made against traducianism is that it fails to explain *how* souls are propagated. Again, "how" questions are seldom answered. Some hints have been suggested from the development of multiple personalities. In *Three Faces of Eve,* according to authors Corbet Thigpen and Harvey Cleckley, one person was divided into three personalities with different mental characteristics. Working with the notion that personalities may be divisible, William T. Bruner develops a realistic position metaphysically. Bruner's theory asserts that when man was created, all humanity was generically present in one person. The whole human race had one body, one soul, one mind, one will, one consciousness, one personality. The race is propagated not only through a division of cells but also through a division of souls. Hence humans are dissociated selves or multiple personalities of the original pair.[170] Whether we can accept this explanation or have none at present, the difficulty of *how* souls originate is far less severe than the difficulty of tracing all sinful human natures to God.

Although there is not much explicit evidence on the origin of human souls in Scripture, traducianism is the more probable explanation, based on the following considerations:

1. The derivation of all persons from Adam and Eve accounts for the unity of the entire human population (Acts 17:26). The unity of human beings is not merely physical, but also moral and spiritual. Humanity is not a company of individually created spirits such as the angels are. The fact that human persons comprise a single race is crucial theologically as well as socially and politically (Rom. 5:12–14).

2. God is ultimately the "Father of our spirits" by establishing marriage, commanding Adam and Eve to populate the earth, and providentially sustaining mothers and infants through the birth process.

3. The hypothesis of unborn persons doing a deed when their fathers did that deed is not alien to Scripture. The family and national solidarity in Old Testament days is well known. Against that cultural background we can understand that "one might even say that Levi, who collects the tenth, paid the tenth through Abraham, because when Melchizedek met Abraham, Levi was still in the body of his ancestor" (Heb. 7:9–10). Analogously, when Adam sinned, the entire race was in his loins and from him receives sinful hearts.

4. Traducianism, furthermore, most coherently accounts for the Bible's teaching on the sinfulness of human nature from birth. Creationists have a more difficult time with the reality that what is born of flesh is flesh (John 3:6). Jesus explicitly attributes the fleshly nature of children to parents. The characteristics of the evil heart (Matt. 15:18–19) or sinful nature (Eph. 2:3) can hardly be the creation of a God who is of purer eyes than to look with favor upon sin (Hab. 1:13). Hereditary factors that pass along family and national characteristics from generation to generation are the highly probable sources of our bent toward evil.

5. A traducian view does not contradict divine justice in condemning all mankind for the one act of Adam (Rom. 5:16, 18). On this view Adam is not merely the legal or federal representative of the race as creationists maintain. God may have made a covenant of works with Adam as the legal head of the race, though biblical evidence for this is minimal. If we were not in some sense in Adam generically, physically, and spiritually, however, the covenant of works appears to be a legal fiction without basis in reality. From a traducian perspective (with or without a covenant of works) God can justly regard the race generically in Adam. So "in Adam all die" (1 Cor. 15:22), for in Adam all "sinned" (Rom. 5:12, Greek aorist tense). Hence a traducian view of the origin of the soul provides the more coherent position with the fewer difficulties. The difficulty of explaining how the soul originates is less than explaining how a holy God can create depraved souls.

RELEVANCE FOR LIFE AND MINISTRY

"The chief end of thought and action," said secular humanist Corliss Lamont, "is to further this-worldly human interests. . . . The watchword of Humanism is happiness for all humanity."[171] So that humans can be happy Lamont affirms the unity of the body and personality, holding that "the exterior of man reflects his essential being."[172] He reduces the soul to the brain to attain a monistic metaphysics and stimulate people in the direction of those human-centered ends and values that he thinks are supremely worthwhile, desirable, and for the common good.[173]

Happiness is also the by-product of Christian humanitarianism under God. The Christian's chief end is "to glorify God by enjoying him forever," as John Piper spells out in *Desiring God*.[174] The triune God enjoys himself, his creation, and especially his image-bearers, much as parents enjoy themselves, their work, and especially their children and grandchildren. Christ exhibited joy when he was united to a human spirit and body on earth. Consider the ways in which this Christian understanding of humanity can bring great significance and lasting joy to your life.

What is worthwhile, desirable, and for the common good of humans as spirits-in-bodies? Is an interacting dualism viable? Indeed it is. Viewing humans as spirits in the image of the divine Spirit provides for human values in a better way than agnostic, secular, pantheistic humanisms. Christians can live by this doctrine with authenticity while increasingly ruling the world as good stewards accountable to God.

Prize Persons for Their Intrinsic Value

Those who live by an interacting dualism *value humans highly for their inherent worth*. Because humans are real spiritual beings who will relate to God forever in loving fellowship or will be alienated from God, each person is of inestimable temporal and eternal value and significance. Persons have this inward worth inalienably as creatures of God made in the image of God. Their value goes far beyond that of their amazing bodies or that of being the highest animal on earth. Their value is not diminished when for some reason and for some time they are not useful to society in the form of their family, church, or nation. Every living human being is of instrinsic worth—poor or rich, female or male, educated or not, lighter or darker—because he or she is an endlessly existing active spiritual person like God.

Interacting dichotomists who live consistently with their view *treat humans as subjects, not objects*. Persons as spiritual beings are not things to be folded, mutilated, or spindled. As self-transcendent spirits humans are self-conscious and self-determining subjects and moral agents. Christians see in all other persons active beings who should be free from coercion to think, feel, will, and relate. Christians know that social regulations (like that of the Sabbath) are made for humans' health and well-being, not humans for social regulations of institutions (such as the Sabbath).

Interacting dichotomists appreciate also the inherent *dignity of human presence*. While walking in a park it is one thing for a person to pass bushes and squirrels; it is quite another to encounter persons. As souls, humans have inherent dignity and worth beyond the physical. Spirits in the presence of other spirits for any length of time (traveling on a bus or plane) find it difficult not to communicate. Paul could be "present . . . in spirit" though absent in the body (Col. 2:5; cf. 1 Cor. 5:3–4). Sometimes we sense the presence of others even before they come into sight or hearing. A sense of the presence of human spirits should not seem strange to those who have a sense of the presence of the divine Spirit. Even during tragedy the biblical writers did not yield to despair. They did not pronounce God dead but realized that they could not go anywhere to escape God's omnipresence (Ps. 139). Through universal revelation all people have some sense of the presence of God who is Spirit. Beyond that, Christians have a sense of the presence of the personal God as Redeemer. Followers of Christ sense the Holy Spirit witnessing with their spirits that they personally are children of God! Having consciousness of the divine Spirit, Christians may sense the presence of human spirits.

Respect Inalienable Human Rights

Along with the gift of existence as spirits God gave his image-bearers certain inalienable rights. Human rights have not been given by governments and ought not be taken by any national authority in any culture anywhere in the world. The rights of God's image-bearers ought not to be taken away by parents, educators, capitalists, communists, or charismatic religious leaders. The rights of human beings to fair treatment by other humans come from the Lord of justice and so are nonnegotiable; they are superior to any policy. No social goals of any collective can outwiegh the intrinsic authority of a human spirit's rights. God-given rights are universal and obligatory everywhere, always. No pragmatic ends justify violating the changless principles of just relationships to God and others.

In a fallen world God also graciously gave ten commandments to protect people from violations of their rights. Our rights to life and liberty while relating to God and others are supported by those ten basic responsibilities. They constitute a universal declaration of our most basic rights and freedoms. The first four responsibilities protect our rights in relation to God: (1) the right freely to value above all the Source who liberates us from enslavement to others (Exod. 20:1–3), (2) the right freely to worship the transcendent Lord of all (vv. 5–6), (3) the right and responsibility to bear God's name without hypocrisy (v. 7), and (4) the right to a day a week for rest and worship (vv. 8–11). The last six responsibilities protect human rights in relation to each other: (5) the right of parents freely to live long on the earth with the esteem of their children (v. 12), (6) the right of all to life without the threat of murder (v. 13), (7) the right of all to marital fidelity without suspicions of lust and adultery (v. 14), (8) the right of all to private ownership of property without threat of theft (v. 15), (9) the right of all to intellectually honest representation by others (v. 16), and (10) the right to a simple or different life-style free from coveting any person, animal, or thing belonging to neighbors.

We may not all agree on precisely how such just principles apply in any given situation, but do we not all agree that we ought to be treated justly? An equal right of all to justice is not relative to equal abilities. People with few talents have as much right to exist and freely pursue their goals as those with greater capacities. Life built on just normative commitments provides for meaningful human existence. In a sea of relativities all can cling to these lifesavers.

All people are entitled to the freedoms of religion, speech, and pursuit of goals while exercising these rights with responsibility to God and others. As moral agents we enjoy our freedom to swing our arms so long as we do not injure or offend others. All people deserve respect, whether they are female or male, students or teachers, rich or poor, owners or laborers, prisoners or free, church members or vocal atheists, secular humanists or New Age pantheists. Even in democracies with majority rule the inherent rights of minorities ought to be defended. To recognize these basic values as absolute rights is at the same time to admit that violations of them are absolute wrongs.

Similar human rights are spelled out in the American State Papers and the United States Bill of Rights. And on December 10, 1948, the United Nations adopted a Universal Declaration of Human Rights. Since that time all members of the United Nations recognize rights to life, liberty, security of person, equality before the law, and equal protection of the law without discrimination. These rights open the door to universal competition for benefits, entitling all to make the most of themselves, but not guaranteeing that any one person will make as much of himself or herself as others. Christians everywhere should respect pre-Christians' rights as they would have non-Christians respect theirs.

Develop a Healthy Self-Image and Sense of Reality

Our view of the worth of others may be low because of a low view of ourselves. Men and women who affirm the reality and dignity of God's image-bearers universally ought to see the implications of that truth for their own *self-image*. We ought to cease considering ourselves naked apes or meat machines. We are not mere victims of class interests, economic aggrandizement, genetic programming, cultural conditioning, or historical necessity. Like other persons, we ourselves have inestimable worth as self-transcendent subjects and moral agents. Our inherent value cannot be taken away by any mistake or failure. Because of what we *are* spiritually and physically, our lives are of greater value than any impersonal project in the whole world. People struggling to "find themselves" may be helped to realize who they are ontologically. One's sense of one's own identity and dignity begins with awareness of ourselves as real spirits who creatively initiate action as responsible moral agents.

An interacting dichotomy supplies a base for a healthy *sense of reality*. To strengthen this sense of our dichotomous reality in the image of God we may need to exercise all of our capacities. Intellectually, we need to accept ourselves as spiritual-physical beings. This may take time if we have been strongly influenced by naturalistic or pantheistic views. Morally, we may need to develop a sense of our reality as agents initiating great good or evil. This may be difficult if we viewed ourselves as victims of conditioning by others. Emotionally, we may need to joyfully accept ourselves for what we are in our essential spiritual-physical being with all of our distinctively human capabilities. What a privilege it is to be a person and not wallpaper! Volitionally, we may need to reaffirm our worth and dignity under God, make our own decisions, act upon them, and maturely accept our share of the responsibility for their consequences. Relationally, we will cultivate friendship with God and other humans. God and others can appreciate what it is like to be a self-critical spirit and understand our problems intellectually, morally, emotionally, volitionally, and relationally. Our highest joys in time and eternity result from fulfilling person-to-person experiences.

Apparently few people are totally satisfied with their bodies. Most of us feel some physical limitations in appearance or in coordination of athletic, musical, or artistic talents. If so, whether male or female, we may well meditate for twenty minutes on the fact that whatever the real or imagined defects may be, we can learn to be "at home" in our bodies. And we may improve our self-regard by strengthening our hearts through aerobic exercises and our basic muscle groups with guided weight lifting. Regular training programs for both purposes contribute to the effective use of our bodies as instruments of our spirits. Then we may feel well enough about ourselves to take up music, art, or theology!

One reason for a lack of self-esteem among women may stem from the dearth of recent preaching and teaching on the equality of women and men ontologically. Studies have indicated that in some churches women have suffered from a lack of self-esteem more than men. In view of that, although this entire chapter applies to women, an explicit application of an interacting dualism to their ontological status seems relevant. If women have unrealistic views of themselves, they may have concluded with most recent philosophy and theology that they cannot know anything about who they are in themselves (metaphysically). So they may have reduced their significance to that of fragile phenomena, pragmatic functions, or changing relationships. In such an intellectual climate it is little wonder that women have difficulty recognizing their identity and value. Since the evidence in this chapter indicates that women are real physical beings and more than that, real self-conscious, self-determining spiritual subjects and moral agents, they have solid reasons to respect themselves. One woman, whether single or married, young or old, educated or not, is of far more value than the whole nonhuman world. Women have inestimable intrinsic worth because they, not a whit less than men, are spirits made in the divine image for fellowship with God and service for God throughout time and eternity.

Tragically the metaphysical foundation of female dignity and inherent worth has been destroyed by the antimetaphysical spirit of the age. Ontologically a woman's human nature is not in any way inferior to a man's. Men ought to respect women because their essential human nature is as significant as theirs. Whatever differences remain functionally or relationally should in no way alter this basic reason for self-respect and self-esteem. By way of illustration, the distinct offices of Father, Son, and Holy Spirit are no basis for failing to esteem all three as equally divine in essence and being. (I:279). Analogously, since male and female are equally spiritual-physical beings, it follows that there ought be mutual respect. In the context of ontological equality, people need not be overly sensitive about the Bible's generic use of "man" for male and female in the image of God (Gen. 1:27).

Because we are spirits-in-bodies, both women and men may improve their self-esteem not alone by training their bodies, as indicated above, but also by a regular program for *training their spirits*. In order for the implications of an interacting dualism to become part of our consciousness we may need to meditate on its implications repeatedly, change inconsistent attitudes and habits, and act with new self-esteem and new respect for others. As important as is the disciplined training of our bodies, we should be even more concerned with training our spirits. Jesus, who sees the sparrow fall and counts the hairs of your head, said, "Don't be afraid; you are worth more than many sparrows" (Matt. 10:28–31). The human body is of great value for roughly seventy years, but Jesus viewed the soul as of far greater value. "What good will it be for a man if he gains the whole world, yet forfeits his own soul? Or what can a man give in exchange for his soul?" (Matt. 16:26). Our value does not consist in the amount of our earthly possessions (Luke 12:15). A person's worth is finally calculated by omniscience in heaven (Matt. 6:20, 25). So a development of the spiritual disciplines of Bible study, meditation, prayer, and fasting may be used by the Holy Spirit to strengthen our sense of well-being.

Overcome Fear of Death

Being told that they cannot know anything about their souls or spirits in themselves, people, fearing the unknown, fear death. Nonmetaphysical views of the inner person provide few answers; so people turn for information away from theologians and philosophers to mere descriptions of near-death experiences and to unreliable messages allegedly from the dead through mediums or channelers. Jesus emphatically distinguished the reality of the soul from that of the body and used his metaphysical dichotomy to help his disciples face persecution and death for his sake. Jesus said, "Brother will betray brother to death, and a father his child; children will rebel against parents and have them put to death" (Matt. 10:21). Then, "Do not be afraid of those who kill the body but cannot kill the soul" (v. 28). No terrorist on earth can kill your soul! We can know this about the soul in itself (apart from its relation to the body): it exists everlastingly. Hence Christian believers do not fear death as others do. Although Christians' bodies are buried, their spirits will go to be with Christ. That is great comfort also when the spirit departs from the body of a loved one.

Overcome Racial Prejudices

We must confess the sin of *racial discrimination* because all humans of whatever racial background are chidren of Adam and Eve, who are children of the Creator metaphysically. The Bible represents mankind as *one human race* derived from common original parents, not a company of individuals separately created like the angels. Adam and Eve were to be fruitful and multiply and fill the earth (Gen. 1:28), and Eve is "the mother of all the living" (3:20). "From one man he made every nation of men, that they should inhabit the whole earth" (Acts 17:26). All are one in Adam for moral and theological considerations (Rom. 5:12–18). "For as in Adam all die, so in Christ all will be made alive" (1 Cor. 15:22). Differences of pigmentation and culture should never be allowed to overshadow our basic human oneness. Red and yellow, black and white, all need to overcome biases and consciously emphasize equal human worth in the others.

Care About the Unborn

Abortion is not merely a private religious issue between individuals and God. It is also a universal human issue—among all human beings. Because a human soul has inherent value if it originates at conception, people ought not take the life of a growing human infant before birth. Admittedly the Bible does not explicitly teach that the soul originates at conception. So other suggestions have been made and may be regarded with some tolerance. Consider these alternative ideas for the time when life begins in the womb: (1) The soul originates with implantation in the uterus (starts the 7th or 8th day, completed by the 12th day), (2) when the blood system is formed (third week), (3) at quickening (motion felt at about four months), or (4) when the baby is able to survive outside the womb (six months).

The origin of the soul at conception seems more probable because we found that the whole child originates from the union of both parents. The entire RNA and DNA genetic potential is received at conception. And because the body and soul are inseparable throughout life, both most likely originate together. So from conception, a potential person, a human person in the most elementary form exists (Ps. 139:13–16). Hence from the moment of conception more than the mother's rights are involved. The rights of mother, father, and infant need to be respected. The general rule says no to aborting a life with inherent worth and human rights for the sake of convenience.

In rare exceptions in which the survival of the mother is endangered, however, she has the more fundamental claim. With limited wisdom, at times people fail to discover a good alternative action and resort to what seems the lesser of two evils (aborting the life of a child). In so doing, they sin, for even the lesser evil can never be called good. But those who minister to persons who have had abortions need to assure them that they have *not* committed the unforgiveable sin. God has forgiven premeditated murderers like Moses, David, and Paul. By the same divine mercy, people who have aborted unborn humans can be forgiven! God forgives their sin if they confess their sin for what it is (1 John 1:9).

Help Others

We may show our high regard for human life by helping those who are not able to improve their situations, such as *the hungry, orphans, widows, and prisoners*. Their inherent value as persons is not diminished by their circumstances. How can we do more, you say, than we are already doing? Whatever the limitations of the outer jar of clay, believers can receive the treasure of the all-surpassing power from God within (2 Cor. 4:6). Christians, like Paul, may be "hard pressed on every side, but not crushed; perplexed, but not in despair; persecuted, but not abandoned; struck down, but not destroyed" (v. 7). God has not promised believers perfect health and physical prowess in this life, and he did not answer Paul's prayers to remove his "thorn in the flesh." The Lord answered Paul's prayer in another way, saying, "My grace is sufficient for you, for my power is made perfect in weakness" (12:9).

Help *children and adolescents*. Infants and children are no less human just because they are young and economically unproductive. They should be wanted, loved, and cared for in spite of their apparent lack of utility! Infants and children are inwardly little people with inner spiritual natures of inestimable worth. The ugly reports of child abuse by Satanists and others may be in part attributed to the loss of a view of a child's inherent worth. There is also a failure to follow the example of Christ. Our Lord respected and loved children during his brief ministry on earth. And Jesus warned, "If anyone causes one of these little ones, who believe in me to sin, it would be better for him to have a large millstone hung around his neck and to be drowned in the depths of the sea" (Matt. 18:6).

Care for the *elderly*. The aged are no less human for outwardly "wasting away" (2 Cor. 4:16). Elderly persons should be wanted and loved because of their inherent worth, quite apart from what they can do for others. For their own self-esteem they should be aided in caring for themselves as long as possible. When they are unable to care for themselves, we should care for them as we would wish to be cared for when we are in a similar condition. Loving relationships should be sustained as normally as possible.

Care as well for the *sick and handicapped*. In his day Jesus cared about the lepers; we today must care about people with AIDS and other diseases. One who believed more in every human's right to life above the quality of life said, "The moral question for us is not whether the suffering and the dying are persons but whether *we* are the kind of persons who will care for them without doubting their worth."[175] In a fallen world people face debilitating injuries, allergies, and diseases. They remain persons with inherent worth and deserve our respect and esteem. They need to be treated, not as curiosities, but as persons.

Care for *your neighbors*. Who are our neighbors? They are those who have an urgent need like that of the man helped by the good Samaritan (Luke 10:25–37). Even though the Samaritan did not know that person before, he knew that he had not only a need but also great worth. Because a person in need is not a thing, we will do all in our power with our abilities and resources to help. We will treat our neighbors as we would be treated (Matt. 7:12). Care also for your *enemies*. Our political, social, ecclesiastical, and other opponents have inherent worth as persons. Because they are image-bearers of the Creator we should show them respect and love. Insofar as it is in their power to do so Christians will pray for those who oppose them because of their faith, and they will do so just as Christ prayed from the cross, "Father forgive them, for they do not know what they are doing" (Luke 23:34).

Secular and cosmic humanists talk about loving humanity in general, and they do many fine things. But Christ exhibited the greatest concern for human well-being, and his teaching remains unequalled. It is now crucial for Christian humanists to demonstrate their Master's superior values in every aspect of human existence.

Achieve Your Highest Human Potential

After a bad day at school a small boy in a televsion commercial reported, "My teacher says I am not living up to my full potentiality." Having pronounced the last word with difficulty, he complained, "I don't even know what 'full potentiality' means." Others have a similar problem. Is the highest human potential a fulfilling sex life (Freud)? fulfilling our social conditioning (Skinner)? freedom from nature's laws or anything outside ourselves? or transcendence of our humanness to become divine (like Maslow)? Have we unlimited potential (Fromm, May, Rogers)? In our development can we draw from the collective unconscious of all humans (Jung)? Have we infinite potential for spiritually evolving into gods (New Age writers)?

Participants in the most practical personal, business, and social programs for self-improvement need to know whether self-realization programs aim toward the goals of humanness as seen by naturalists, by pantheists, or by theists. People who understand that all humans are by nature an interacting dichotomy ought not give themselves to leaders or programs that either reduce them to mere animals or claim to help them realize their inner divinity. As creatures who bear the image of God we will seek to be the best we can be in reflecting God's communicable characteristics. We will be the best we can be both spiritually and physically. As spirits we will seek our highest potential, not through the guidance of channelers or magical coercion of occult powers, but through Holy Spirit-illumined guidance of Scripture and Holy Spirit-endued service. As real physical beings we will develop our aerobic capacity so that our hearts can achieve their fullest potential and regularly exercise each major muscle group in our bodies so that our physical instrument will serve its highest usefulness.

We have the privilege of relating in personal and fulfilling ways, not only to loved ones, friends, and associates each day, but to the Designer and Creator of the universe! Our highest potential goes beyond married love, parental love, and love of achievement, to love of God. Although our astounding relational potential can be used for evil, by grace we can creatively serve loved ones, friends, and associates each day, and in it all help establish the kingdom of the Most High. Our highest potential is not achieved in our excellent work in our homes, schools, or businesses as such, but in our labor for God's rulership in these relationships. So we keep ourselves in the best condition we can physically and spiritually to develop to the fullest our potential as stewards accountable above all to the Creator whose image we bear.

REVIEW QUESTIONS

To Help Relate and Apply Each Section in This Chapter

1. *Briefly state the classical problem* this chapter addresses and indicate reasons why genuine inquiry into it is important for your world view and your existence personally and socially.
2. *Objectively summarize the influential answers* given to this problem in history as hypotheses to be tested. Be able to compare and contrast their real similarities and differences (not merely verbal similarities or differences).
3. *Highlight the primary biblical evidence* on which to decide among views—evidence found in the relevant teachings of the major divisions of Scripture—and decide for yourself which historical hypothesis (or synthesis of historical views) provides the most consistent and adequate account of the primary biblical data.
4. *Formulate in your own words your doctrinal conviction* in a logically consistent and adequate way, organizing your conclusions in ways you can explain clearly, support biblically, and communicate effectively to your spouse, children, friends, Bible class, or congregation.
5. *Defend your view* as you would to adherents of the alternative views, showing that the other views are logically less consistent and factually faced with more difficulties than your view in accounting for the givens, not only of special revelation but also of human experience in general.
6. *Explore the differences the viability of your conviction can make in your life*. Then test your understanding of the viability of your view by asking, "Can I live by it authentically (unhypocritically) in relation to God and to others in my family, church, vocation, neighborhood, city, nation, and world?"

MINISTRY PROJECTS

To Help Communicate This Doctrine in Christian Service

1. *Memorize one major verse or passage* that in its context teaches the heart of this doctrine and may serve as a text from which to preach, teach, or lead small-group studies on the topic. The memorized passages from each chapter will build a body of content useful also for meditation and reference in informal discussions.
2. *Formulate the major idea of the doctrine in one sentence* based on the passage memorized. This idea should be useful as the major thesis of either a lesson for a class (junior high to adult) or a message for a church service.
3. *State the specific purpose or goal of your doctrinal lesson or message*. Your purpose should be more than informative. It should show why Christians need to accept this truth and live by it (unhypocritically). For teaching purposes, list indicators that would show to what extent class members have grasped the truth presented.
4. *Outline your message or lesson in complete sentences*. Indicate how you would support the truth of the doctrine's central ideas and its relevance to life and service. Incorporate elements from this chapter's historical, biblical, systematic, apologetic, and practical sections selected according to the value they have for your audience.
5. *List applications of the doctrine* for communicating the difference this conviction makes in life (for sermons, lessons, small-group Bible studies, or family devotional Bible studies). Applications should make clear what the doctrine is, why one needs to know it,

and how it will make changes in thinking. Then show how the change in thought will lead to differences in values, priorities, attitudes, speech, and personal action. Consider also the doctrine's possible significance for family, church, neighborhood, city, regional, and national actions.

6. *Start a file and begin collecting illustrations* of this doctrine's central idea, the points in your outline, and your application.

7. *Write out your own doctrinal statement on this subject in one paragraph* (in half a page or less). To work toward a comprehensive doctrinal statement, collect your formulations based on a study of each chapter of *Integrative Theology*. As your own statement of Christian doctrine grows, you will find it personally strengthening and useful when you are called on for your beliefs in general and when you apply for service with churches, mission boards, and other Christian organizations. Any who seek ordination to Christian ministry will need a comprehensive doctrinal statement that covers the broad scope of theology.

CHAPTER 4

GOD'S IMAGE-BEARERS IN REBELLION

God's Image-Bearers in Rebellion

THE PROBLEM: HOW DO WE ACCOUNT FOR THE IMPERFECTIONS AND FAILURES OF PERSONS CREATED IN GOD'S IMAGE TO BE THE NOBLEST BEINGS IN GOD'S WORLD?

One prominent European scholar affirms that "the church's anthropology revolves around the two concepts of 'the image of God' and 'original sin.' "[1] The previous chapter considered persons as God's image, the highest and noblest of living beings. It presented persons ontologically as created for fellowship with God and ordained to function as his vice-regents over the world and lower forms of life. The present chapter considers persons in rebellion against God and spoiled by sin. It draws out the implications of the fall of humans from their high estate and seeks to account for their conduct, which at times rivals that of the beasts. How one understands the problem considered this chapter will influence one's views of the purpose of Christ's coming to earth (vol. 1, chap., 5), the import of his death on the cross (vol. 2, chap., 7), and the meaning of salvation (vol. 3, chaps. 1–4).

Undeniably human persons are capable of extraordinary accomplishments. They can investigate the smallest particles of the atom and can propel themselves into space to search out the planets. Yet even the casual observer recognizes persons' capacity for horrible forms of brutality and inhumanity. Right-minded people are repulsed by the incidence of murder, rape, drug trafficking, highjackings, and white-collar crimes in our most enlightened societies. Human persons, as we know them, are an enigma of greatness and degradation bundled into single conscious beings.

How did humans become evil? Did their descent from grandeur begin with a Fall, a moral defection of the first man and woman? Can we point to the Fall as the greatest tragic episode in the history of the human race? We inquire further whether the historical reality of the Edenic drama, widely denied by critical scholars, can be factually sustained. Moreover, we must trace the consequences of what happened in Eden upon the mind, the will, and the emotions of Adam's descendants. To what extent has the Fall damaged human persons as image-bearers of God? Has the image of God in sinners been destroyed? Moreover, we must address the difficult question of how and to what extent Adam's sin has affected every individual born into the world. How could persons be held guilty for deeds perpetrated before they were born? Is it just of God to condemn all for the sins of one pair? Does the classical notion of imputed guilt and penalty negate *my* personal responsibility for crimes committed? How, then, should Christians view the relation between Adam's sin and the spiritual condition of the human race?

Next we explore the nature and effects of sin. Is the *fundamental* human problem childhood psychic traumas (Freudianism)? Or inequitable economic arrangements (Marxism)? Or the realities of anxiety and inauthentic existence (existentialism)? Or is the basic human problem what the church has called sin? Can the saying be sustained that "the heart of the human problem is the problem of the human heart"? The issue of sin is of the utmost importance, for the Bible suggests that all the physical diseases, mental disorders, and crimes, all the barbarism, brutality, and bureaucratic manipulation are the consequences of the malady called sin. Furthermore, we must as a matter of pastoral care for grieving parents address the question of the spiritual condition of infants. Are infants and small children afflicted with the scourge of sin and the guilt that arises from it? What should Christians believe concerning the standing of these little ones before God if they should die before an age of moral accountability?

ALTERNATIVE INTERPRETATIONS IN THE CHURCH

The leading answers to the problems concerning the Fall and sin will now be identified as hypotheses to be tested against the primary data of Scripture.

Pelagians, Socinians, Unitarians, and Modernists

Pelagius, Julian of Eclanum, Celestius, and others proceeded from the assumption that if persons are truly human they must possess the freedom to choose responsibly. Since persons are born into the world capable of willing and actualizing the good, it is perverse, these thinkers argued, to view men and women as fallen and depraved. Rather, the Pelagians insisted that each person who enters the world is by nature innocent and free from proclivity to evil. Pelagius acknowledged the rather obvious fact that persons do transgress God's law. He explained the fact of evil, however, not on the basis of imputation or inheritance but by the power of bad examples that persons tend to imitate. Some people, Pelagius argued, perfectly obey God and thus live sinless lives. Furthermore, the Pelagians rejected the idea that death represents God's punishment for original sin. On the contrary, they claimed that God created people mortal; they were destined to die irrespective of any sin committed. The church condemned Pelagianism at the Synod of Carthage (418) and again at the Council of Ephesus (431).

The sixteenth-century Socinian movement represented a revival of the old Pelagian heresy. Like their humanistic forebears, the Socinians denied original sin, the transmission of depravity and guilt to posterity, and the sentence of death as punishment for sin. "The fall of Adam, as it was but one act, could not have power to deprave his nature, much less that of his posterity."[2] Individuals sin through a combination of unfavorable circumstances and negative examples. Sin when committed does not eliminate free will or the person's ability to obey God, and certainly it does not vitiate the *imago*, which the Socinians defined functionally as the exercise of dominion over the world.

Unitarians such as William E. Channing and Henry Ware argued that the doctrines of original sin and total depravity are repugnant to the moral character of God. They judged it inconsistent with the divine goodness that a child should enter the world disposed to evil and subject to damnation. Said Ware, "Man is by nature . . . innocent and pure; free from all moral corruption. . . . He has natural affections, all of them originally good, but liable by a wrong direction to be the occasion of error and sin."[3] Channing, in fact, spoke of the "essential sameness" of human beings and God. Consequently, the person is not depraved, for he is intrinsically like God, even as Christ is like God.

Theological modernists likewise deny the fall of the race from a higher condition and uphold, rather, human ascent from an animal past to new heights of moral achievement. In the words of W. N. Clarke, "Humanity certainly is by nature a slowly rising race, with a native tendency to outgrow faults."[4] Liberals generally believe that persons were created as children of God, their potential for sonship needing only to be awakened. Thus the tradition consistently denies original sin, claiming that a sudden incursion of sin in the evolutionary ascent is psychologically impossible. According to W. A. Brown, "Sin is not a foreign intruder making its appearance in the universe suddenly at a moment of time, and bringing about an abrupt transformation in human nature as a whole."[5] Denying total depravity, he defined sin as sensuality, i.e., as the inevitable conflict between the person's residual animal impulses and the impulses of the spirit. Thus "sin is a necessary stage in the evolution of humanity—an essential element in God's training of mankind for higher things."[6] Brown argues that persons succumb to temptations and so sin as a result of parental influences and social environment.

Semi-Pelagians and Roman Catholic Theologians

Theologians such as John Cassian, Vincent of Lerins, and Faustus of Riez, reacting in the fifth and sixth centuries against the teachings of Augustine, affirmed that Adam's sin caused his posterity to be spiritually weak rather than radically fallen. The moral corruption transmitted to the human family is not total, does not constitute sin and guilt, and does not merit the wrath of God. As born into the world, persons remain capable of willing and performing the good. Each person, however, actualizes his weakened moral nature in the performance of specific sins and so becomes morally culpable before God. We may sum up as follows: according to the Pelagians, the person is spiritually well; according to the Semi-Pelagians, spiritually sick; and according to the Augustinian tradition, the unregenerate person is spiritually dead.

Medieval and modern Roman Catholic theology is predominantly Semi-Pelagian. As noted in the previous chapter, Catholic thought holds that to the person's more or less morally neutral human nature God subsequently added the gift of righteousness, which served as a check on sensuous impulses. At the Fall, the *donum superadditum* was lost, whereupon Adam reverted to his original condition, which involved conflict between flesh and spirit. Since Adam was the head of the race, his privation of righteousness and his tendency to concupiscence were passed on to the human family. Adam's posterity therefore suffers a spiritual deficiency, but not actual sin and guilt. Sin is not committed and legally reckoned until each individual willfully acts contrary to God's law. Thus Catholicism views sin not as a condition whose consequence is spiritual inability, but as a series of discrete acts that constitute the perpetrator sinful and guilty. Gregory the Great, the Franciscans, and Abelard adhered to these tenets.

The Council of Trent reiterated the judgment that as a result of sin Adam lost the superadded gift of righteousness. Moreover, by propagation, not merely by imitation, Adam's sin "injured" the entire human race, Mary excepted. It appears, however, that the Tridentine reference to racial "sin" does not connote sin in the strict sense of the word.[7] Thus, although Trent did not specify what Adam transmitted to his posterity, the best inference seems to be a nature devoid of righteousness, morally wounded, and inclined to sin. Trent clearly states that in spiritual matters free will was weakened but not lost. Thus "if anyone saith that, since Adam's sin, the free-will of man is lost and extinguished; . . . let him be anathema."[8] Trent commanded that infants be baptized for the remission of the contagion inherited from their parents.[9]

Not entirely consistent with Catholic formulations on sin and depravity, Pope Pius IX in 1854 promulgated the dogma of the immaculate conception of Mary. Many in the church argued that unless Mary was free from the pollution of sin, Christ would not have been born sinless.

McBrien acknowledges that "the doctrine of Original Sin does not play a very large part in contemporary Catholic theology."[10] Thus the Catholic manual of doctrine, *A New Catechism,* denies that the Fall was a historic event. The claim that "Adam is Man" means that Adam's experience in the scriptural myth portrays the experience of each person. Repeated mention of the sin of "one man" in Romans 5 is viewed as literary embellishment and not the true meaning of the text. *The New Catechism* rejects the notion that the race became depraved and guilty as a result of Adam's sin. Rather, with the loss of the supernatural gifts and the resultant exposure to concupiscence, each person freely violates God's law and so becomes corrupt. "Hence no one is condemned for original sin 'alone,' but only for the personal decisions by which he ratified original sin, so to speak, and stood over it."[11]

Piet Schoonenberg reinterprets the doctrine of hereditary sin from an evolutionary and existentialist perspective. The old view that sin passes down to the human race by propagation violates human responsibility. Schoonenberg argues that the genesis of sin resides not in Adam but in the world. That is, due to the collective pressure of the social situation and the power of negative examples, individuals transgress God's law and so incur condemnation. We must not "overlook the specific nature of original sin, which consists in this, that it comes to us from others, thus besetting our existence from the very start."[12] According to Schoonenberg, the sinner is afflicted not with total depravity, but with a wounded moral nature.

As suggested above, Catholicism emphasizes less the sinful nature or disposition than specific sins. It distinguishes between sins that are venial and those that are mortal. Venial sins are sins of lesser importance or sins of greater gravity done without full knowledge. Catholicism judges that venial sins hinder a person's access to God. They are said to be removed by prayer, fasting, and almsgiving. Mortal sins, on the other hand, are willful transgressions of a serious nature, such as apostasy, murder, or adultery, and they merit eternal punishment. Catholic theology maintains that mortal sins are forgiven only by the sacrament of penance, which involves confession, absolution by a priest, and satisfaction that might include the payment of indulgences.

Arminian Interpreters

Arminian theology focuses on the effects of the Fall on Adam's posterity and the mitigation of the consequences of it by prevenient grace. Two broad classes of opinion prevail. The first—espoused by Arminius, Wesley, and Wiley—holds that Adamic sin brought depravity, guilt, and punishment on the race as a whole. But through prevenient grace, which is said to flow universally and unconditionally from Christ's atonement, guilt and punishment are nullified and depravity is alleviated to such an extent that the sinner is able to cooperate with saving grace. The second class of Arminians—including the Remonstrants, Finney, and Miley—approximates the Semi-Pelagian position. According to this view, Adam's sin brought guilt and punishment on himself, but not on his posterity. The pollution inherited from Adam gives rise to specific sins, which God in turn reckons to each person as guilt and penalty. Once again, prevenient grace nullifies the effects of depravity, enabling the unregenerate person to cooperate with God.

According to John Wesley, God imputed to the human race Adam's sin and the depravity, guilt, and condemnation of it. Wesley believed that the polluted nature inherited from Adam ("We were all born with a sinful, devilish nature."[13]) is properly sin and that it renders the human family guilty before God. Said Wesley, "The sin of Adam, without the sins which we afterward committed, brought us death."[14] With great passion Wesley upheld "that entire depravity and corruption, which by nature spreads itself over the whole man, leaving no part uninfected."[15] Thus far Wesley was generally Augustinian. Believing, however, that a person is responsible only for deeds that he or she commits, Wesley insisted that inherited guilt and penalty are cancelled by "preventing grace," so that in reality each person born into the world is innocent until the perpetration of actual sins. Furthermore, Wesley claimed that the same prevenient grace alleviates inborn depravity. With the mind thus enlightened and the will freed, all persons are enabled to repent and exercise faith toward God.[16]

Wiley, who subscribes to both the natural and the federal headship of Adam, claims that Arminianism

> holds to the unity of the race in Adam, that "in Adam all have sinned," and that all men "are by nature the children of wrath." But over against this, it holds that in Christ, the second Man who is the Lord from heaven, the most gracious God has provided for all a remedy for that general evil which was derived to us from Adam, free and gratuitous in His beloved Son Jesus Christ.[17]

Wiley adds that on the basis of prevenient grace no person who enters the world is guilty of inbred sin. Each person, however, becomes guilty and subject to judgment when he follows his lower nature and commits actual sins. The *Beacon Dictionary of Theology* attempts to clarify the uncertainty surrounding the ascription of guilt with the following observation. "It is helpful to make a distinction between guilt as *culpability,* or personal blameworthiness; and guilt as *liability* for consequences. The former was Adam's guilt alone, the latter belongs potentially to the race, if the remedy in Christ is rejected."[18]

The position of these Arminians with regard to the spiritual condition of infants is as follows. Infants theoretically are afflicted with Adamic depravity, guilt, and punishment. But through the benefit of prevenient grace, guilt and punishment are removed such that no child of Adam is condemned eternally. "Where all were born sinful, they were also born in grace."[19] Each child at the age of moral accountability determines his or her destiny by a personal decision for or against Christ.

The second class of Arminians, introduced above, maintains that the only connection between Adam and his race is a polluted moral nature that predisposes each person to transgressions. This inherited condition involves neither sin, guilt, nor condemnation. Thus the Remonstrant theologians argued that prior to the actualization of the will the person is blameless before God. God reckons to each person sin and guilt only when he consciously actualizes his inborn propensities by specific transgressions.

John Miley, a Methodist theologian, affirms that by natural generation Adam transmitted to his posterity depravity—i.e., loss of original righteousness, corruption of the moral and sensuous nature, and a tendency toward evil. Miley emphasizes that, since it is a natural inheritance, depravity is not a penalty inflicted by God. Furthermore, humanity did not participate in Adam's *sin,* for native depravity is not a transgression of any law of God. Moreover, humanity did not inherit Adam's *guilt,* for a mere tendency toward evil is not blameworthy. And finally, humanity did not inherit Adam's *punishment,* for one cannot be justly condemned except for his own sin. In sum, "native depravity is a part of the Arminian system, and entirely consistent with its principles; native demerit is discordant and contradictory."[20] Miley concludes that in real life each person actualizes the tendencies of his corrupt nature and so sins, thereby incurring personal guilt and condemnation. In practice, however, prevenient grace mitigates the effects of depravity thus enabling the sinner to repent.

Charles Finney's position borders on Pelagianism. He vigorously denies that sin pertains to a person's moral state. More preposterous still, he believes, is the notion that one can inherit a sinful nature from his ancestors. "Man is not born sinful or virtuous, but innocent and acquires his sinful nature by his choices."[21] Finney judges that sin is wholly a willful violation of a known law of God. Furthermore, the supposition of inherited sin and guilt contravenes God's justice. "It is a monstrous and blasphemous dogma, that a holy God is angry with any creature for possessing a nature with which he was sent into being without his knowledge or consent."[22]

Neoorthodox Interpretation

Neoorthodoxy sought to uphold the seriousness of humanity's alienation from God, while rejecting aspects of the Fall and sin that classical theology judged important. Karl Barth denies the existence of Adam as a historical person and rejects the notion that there existed a morally upright couple in a pristine Garden environment. Barth views the Genesis account of the Fall not as history, but as a saga (a tale with symbolic features) that belongs to the realm of suprahistory (*Urgeschichte*). Sin originated in the Fall, but the when, where, and how of the event transcends human comprehension. According to Barth, the Fall of Adam describes an event that happens to everyone, so that each person "constantly reenacts the little scene in the garden of Eden."[23] Barth believes that the doctrine of hereditary sin (*Erbsunde*) is mistaken; we must not think of sin as a disease that passes from one person to another. Rather, "original sin" (*Ursunde*) is the radical, prideful departure of every person, and thus of the race, from the will of God. How does Barth interpret the relation between Adam, Christ, and humanity in Romans 5:12–21 and 1 Corinthians 15:22, 45? He begins, not with Adam, but with Christ and insists that as humanity is joined with Christ in redemption, so the race is linked with Adam in condemnation. In other words, Paul envisages Adam's act as the negative side of the work of Jesus Christ. Beyond that nothing can be affirmed.

By virtue of the universal Fall, God places all persons under the sentence of sin and guilt. Barth's description of the sinner's depraved moral condition is unequivocal. The person "is totally perverted and ruined by his sin and guilt."[24] He adds that "the realization of the total and radical corruption of human nature must not be weakened."[25] The will of the sinner is in bondage, and his mind is sinfully distorted. Yet contrary to his earlier stance in dialogue with Brunner,[26] Barth's mature view was that in spite of human degeneracy, the image of God has not been altogether effaced. Barth, however, concludes that this radical godlessness of the sinner is not final by virtue of election and status in the covenant of grace. Sin, in other words, is overcome in a world reconciled to Jesus Christ. "The sinful No of man has been matched and opposed and destroyed by the divine Yes spoken by Jesus Christ."[27]

Brunner's views about the Fall and sin are similar to those of Barth. The account of Adam and Eve, which Brunner calls a myth or parable, must be rejected on scientific grounds. The doctrine of sin must be developed "without this mythical idea of a Fall."[28] Since Adam means "man," what Genesis 3 relates about Adam and Eve describes the history of every person. That is, in one's determined quest for freedom, each person rebels against the authority of the Creator and sins in discrete acts. Like Barth, Brunner claims that the notion of inherited sin eliminates personal responsibility for one's actions. "The theory of Original Sin . . . is completely foreign to the thought of the Bible."[29] The New Testament teaches both that each person sins individually and that the race as a solidarity is under sin. How the sin of one person becomes the sin of the race Brunner believes is an impenetrable mystery. He hints, however, that the universality of sin results from the limitations imposed by human creatureliness; human persons as finite, contingent beings have an inherent tendency to defect from the sovereign God.[30] Since Brunner believes that sin is never a state but always a concrete act, he polemicizes against the notion of total depravity. "The expression 'the total depravity of man,' which in later Calvinism has become a slogan, is not biblical."[31] As for its effects, sin has damaged the formal image (natural likeness to God), but has destroyed altogether the material image (moral likeness to God).

Reinhold Niebuhr inveighs against modernists who fail to treat the story of Eden seriously and against so-called fundamentalists who interpret it literally. Although the Fall, as myth, belongs to the realm of suprahistory rather than history, it nevertheless enshrines important truths about the human condition. The Genesis 3 story, argues Niebuhr, conveys the fact that persons stand in the paradoxical relation of freedom and finitude. As spirit, persons transcend nature and so are free. But as creatures, they are part of nature's order and so are bound. As those both free and bound, persons inevitably experience anxiety (Matt. 6:31)—the internal precondition of sin. In this state of anxiety Satan tempts persons to deny their limitations through pride or to violate their freedom through sensuality. "When anxiety has conceived, it brings forth both pride and sensuality. Man falls into pride when he seeks to raise their contingent existence to unconditioned significance; he falls into sensuality when he seeks to escape from his unlimited possibilities of freedom . . . by losing himself in some natural vitality."[32]

Niebuhr, like Barth and Brunner, denies that original sin transmits to the race by generation. The myth of Adam proclaims the universal truth that every person inevitably falls into sin. "Original sin is not an inherited corruption, but it is an inevitable fact of human existence. . . . It is there in every moment of existence, but it has no history."[33] Moreover, the fact that each person sins inevitably and yet bears personal responsibility for his sins represents an insoluble paradox of the faith. Finally, Niebuhr claims that the assertion of total depravity is unduly pessimistic. If persons were totally corrupted, they could not be sinners at all. Thus sin has not destroyed essential human nature; the divine *imago* endures despite the reality of sin.

Liberation Theology

Included in this category are the so-called political theologians, third-world liberation theologians, and proponents of radical black and feminist theologies. The movement as a whole denies (1) that sin is individualistic, in the sense of personal enmity against God or violation of a divine law, and (2) that sin is an interior reality, such as a polluted moral nature. Rather, it argues that sin is a collective reality manifested in specific socio-political situations. In the words of Dorothy Sölle, a political theologian, "Sin is not to be understood in a special religious sense as the lack of love for God or as rebellion against a master, but it must be thought of in worldly and political categories."[34] James H. Cone, a leading proponent of black theology, makes the same point: "Sin is not primarily a religious impurity, but rather it is the social, political, and economic oppression of the poor. It is the denial of the humanity of the neighbor through unjust political and social arrangements."[35]

Liberationists claim that persons are naturally endowed with freedom, creativity, and the capacity to transform the world. Yet by virtue of political oppression, economic deprivation, social exploitation, and sexual domination, the person "falls," or is reduced to the status of a nonperson. As a result of these dehumanizing forces, the world becomes filled with poverty, hunger, illiteracy, and crime. Such a line of reasoning prompts liberation theologians to speak, not of a "state of sin" in the human heart, but of the "praxis of sin," that is, the practice of oppressive behavior that exploits and despoils the human race.

Liberation theologians extend the notion of sin to include the apathy of the despoiled toward oppression or active collaboration with the oppressor. The sinner is one who lacks the courage to oppose the exploiter. Thus, according to Cone, one sins when he attempts to love or even accept the agent of injustice. For many feminist theologians, sin represents the cowardly failure to affirm the female self. Evil is the false humility that passively resigns itself to masculine domination.

Many Fathers, Reformers, and Reformed Evangelicals

Authorities in this tradition maintain that God implemented his purpose for the race by an initial moral probation. Persons in a state of childlike innocence could become perfect only through a process of right moral decision making. Following a successful probation, Adam and Eve would have been confirmed in love for God and in holiness of life. Possessing the power both to persevere in holiness and to disobey God, they tragically chose the latter. This original sin of Adam and Eve brought on themselves and their posterity guilt, a depraved nature, and the sentence of condemnation. The tradition maintains that by virtue of total depravity, sinners apart from grace can do nothing to please God. Their sinful wills are unable to perform what God requires. Nevertheless, fallen persons are morally responsible for their sin-induced incapacity to fulfill God's law. Concerning the means whereby Adamic sin transmitted to the race, three main interpretations are proposed: (1) The natural headship or seminal view, holding to the traducian view of the soul's origin, maintains that the entire race was present in Adam in seed form and so participated in his original sin. (2) The representative headship or federal school, positing Adam as the covenant head of the race, maintains that God immediately imputed Adam's guilt, depravity, and punishment to the race he represented. (3) Others, like Berkouwer, Thiessen, and Ramm, insist that Scripture merely relates the fact of the Fall of humanity in Adam, not the how of it. As distinct from Arminianism, the broadly Reformed tradition insists that sin includes not only overt acts but also the underlying thought life and the evil disposition of the human heart.

Augustine made the doctrine of original sin the cornerstone of his theological system. Adam's self-determined sin of rebellion against God brought upon each person born into the world guilt, depravity, and liability to punishment. Augustine taught that the depravity of Adam and the entire human race is pervasive. In the first place, the intellect of the sinner is blind to *sapientia,* or the eternal, changeless truth about God. Augustine wrote that the mind "dulled by sins, blinded, enfeebled by infirmity" cannot of itself see God.[36] Only as the mind is illumined by the Logos in general grace can the sinner apprehend modest truths about God's character and moral demands. And only as the mind is illumined by the additional light of special grace by the same Logos can he attain saving wisdom. Second, Augustine believed that the will of the sinner is able only to oppose God and the purpose for which he or she was created. "The will is truly free only when it is not a slave to sin and vice. God created man with such a free will, but . . . that kind of freedom was lost by man's fall from freedom."[37] Whereas in Eden Adam was *posse non peccare et mori* (able not to sin and die), now as sinner man is *non posse non peccare et mori* (not able not to sin and die). Through the practice of sin, the person's God-given freedom has been turned into sinful necessity. Wrote Augustine, "A man's free-will, indeed, avails for nothing, except to sin, if he knows not the way of truth."[38] And third, concerning the emotions, Augustine held that in place of love for eternal things (the city of God), the sinner possesses a yearning or desire (*libido*) for fleeting, temporal things (the city of the world). Overcome by carnal lusts, the sinner experiences restlessness of soul rather than rest in God. Although sin erased the spiritual gifts of faith and holiness, it corrupted but did not destroy the natural capacities of the soul that constitute the *imago.* "God's image has not been so completely erased in the soul of man by the stain of earthly affections."[39]

Augustine believed that as the biological head of the race Adam transmitted original sin to his progeny by the process of natural generation. Since the race as a whole was in Adam seminally when he sinned, each member of it at birth receives the sin and guilt of the head. "We all existed in that one man. . . . Although the specific form by which each of us was to live was not yet created and assigned, our nature was already present in the seed from which we were to spring."[40] Augustine went beyond the notion of a corrupted seed to suggest that sin also pertains to sexual procreation. Augustine also claimed that infants contract hereditary sin from Adam. Unless their guilt and concupiscence are removed by Holy Spirit regeneration and baptism, infants will endure a just damnation.

Luther judges that as a result of Adam's Fall the human race became totally corrupted, inclined toward evil, guilty before God, and exposed to divine wrath. Luther's explication of original sin (*Erbsunde*) is bleak. The sinner is *curvatus in se* (bent in on himself), habitually seeking selfish ends. He is filled with avarice, lust, anger, hatred, and a host of other vices. Having forsaken God, the sinner's nature is wholly corrupted. "All our faculties are leprous, indeed, dull and utterly dead."[41] Moreover, the sinner exists in a condition of spiritual servitude; apart from grace one is unable to do anything good spiritually. In relation to God, the will is hopelessly bound in its sinful orientation. Thus, "he that will maintain that man's free-will is able to do or work anything in spiritual cases be they ever so small, denies Christ."[42] Yet Luther admitted that in secular matters the will is free to perform what he called deeds of "external" or "civil righteousness."

Luther concludes that the Fall totally destroyed the *imago Dei,* defined as righteousness and wisdom. The human person's dominion over the animals represents but a "relic" of the lost image. In fact, Luther maintains that the sinner exists in the image of the Devil. The natural endowments of intellect, will, and emotions (not constitutive of the *imago*) remain severely corrupted in the sinner. Luther, the traducianist, followed Augustine in postulating that guilt, depravity, and condemnation were transmitted to the human race by procreation. "The human seed, this mass from which I was formed, is totally corrupt with faults and sins. The material itself is faulty."[43]

Calvin similarly affirms that Adam's sin brought upon his posterity guilt, a depraved nature, and liability to punishment. "All of us, who have descended from impure seed, are born infected with the contagion of sin."[44] Thus all persons participate in original sin, which Calvin defines as "depravity and corruption of our nature, diffused into all parts of the soul, which first makes us liable to God's wrath, then also brings forth in us those works which Scripture calls 'works of the flesh.'"[45] For Calvin this depravity is total in that sin corrupts every part of the person. "The whole man is overwhelmed—as by a deluge—from head to foot, so that no part is immune from sin."[46] In particular, Calvin affirms that the will is so vitiated by sin that, although free in everyday matters, it is not able to respond positively to God. The sinner's will is not compelled by any external force but is driven by a contrary internal compulsion, namely, by the promptings of his fallen nature. As for the *imago,* Calvin argues that the sinner's natural endowments (intelligence, will, and emotions) are corrupted by sin. His spiritual endowments (faith, love of God, holiness), however, are altogether lost. How does Calvin interpret the relation between the sin of Adam and that of the race? He appears to approximate the representative position; God ordained that the fate of Adam—the legal head of humanity—should be the fate of each member. "The contagion does not take its origin from the substance of the flesh or soul, but because it had been so ordained by God that the first man should at one and the same time have and lose, both for himself and for his descendants, the gifts that God had bestowed upon him."[47] Calvin maintains that infants experience the baneful consequences of original sin, which effects nevertheless are uniquely their own.[48] Elect infants are regenerated by a secret work of the Holy Spirit.

The Reformed Confessions likewise speak to the issue of original sin. The Belgic Confession, article XV states:

> We believe that through the disobedience of Adam original sin is extended to all mankind; which is a corruption of the whole nature and a hereditary disease, . . . and which produces in man all sorts of sin, being in him as a root thereof, and therefore is so vile and abominable in the sight of God that it is sufficient to condemn all mankind.

A similar view is affirmed by the French Confession of Faith (art. XI), the Heidelberg Catechism (Lord's Day 3, Q. & A. 7), the Second Helvetic Confession (chap. 8), and the Thirty-Nine Articles of Religion (art. IX). The Westminster Confession of Faith (chap. 6) unites the Augustinian theory of natural headship with the federal notion of Adam's representative headship.

The Westminster Confession (chap. 9) reiterates the Reformed position on the bondage of the will in matters spiritual. "Man, by his fall into a state of sin, hath wholly lost all ability of will to any spiritual good accompanying salvation." Similarly, the French Confession of Faith (art. IX), the Heidelberg Catechism (Q. & A. 8, 9), and the Second Helvetic Confession (chap. 9).

W. G. T. Shedd was a leading advocate of the seminal or natural headship theory for the imputation of Adam's sin. Shedd maintains that God imputed to each of Adam's descendants guilt, depravity, and the punishment of death, for the reason that the race was in Adam in undistributed form. That is, the entire psychico-physical human nature, not yet individualized, existed in Adam and Eve when they perpetrated the first sin. Shedd claims the active verb *hēmarton* in Romans 5:12 denotes the work of the common human nature in Adam rather than the countless deeds of individuals in subsequent history. Because all persons are guilty co-agents with Adam, the following holds: "The individual Adam and Eve were no more guilty of this first act . . . than their descendants are; and their descendants are as guilty as they."[49] Shedd guards against Christ's involvement in sinful Adamic nature by arguing that the Logos assumed only a part of humanity, namely, that flesh and blood derived from Mary.[50]

A. H. Strong, who holds to the same natural headship theory of sin's transmission, advanced a popular view of the spiritual condition of infants. Infants participate in the common guilt and depravity of Adamic sin and so need to be saved by Christ. But as opposed to those who have personally transgressed, infants prior to the age of moral accountability are characterized by "a relative innocence,"[51] i.e., by absence of premeditation, naïveté, and trustfulness. For this reason infants are the objects of divine compassion and receive a special application of the atonement, Strong surmises, at the soul's first view of Christ in heaven.

The covenant theology of Cocceius (d. 1669) gave rise to the federal headship theory of sin's imputation. Espoused by Owen, the Westminster Standards, and the old Princeton School, the federal headship or representative theory is typically set forth by L. Berkhof. Like the seminal theorists, federalists insist that the effects of the Fall to Adam were guilt, depravity, and punishment in the form of spiritual and physical death. Indeed, from Adam "sin flows on as an impure stream to all the generations of men, polluting everyone and everything with which it comes in contact."[52] Berkhof explains the spread of Adam's sin to his posterity not in terms of natural headship, but in terms of his status as head of the race in the covenant of works. Thus when Adam sinned as federal head, God imputed his guilt to all humanity, by virtue of which every person is born with a depraved and sinful soul. Adam's posterity did not directly participate in his sinful act, but through the forensic (i.e., judicial) imputation of guilt based on legal unity, "God adjudges all men to be guilty sinners in Adam."[53] This representative theory for the transmission of sin is usually linked with the creationist position for the soul's origin. The view also judges that infants are afflicted with original sin and need salvation through Christ. Infants born into a Christian family have the promise of salvation by virtue of their status in the covenant of grace. When the parents are not Christians, an infant may be the object of God's secret election.

Other valuable evangelical discussions of the Fall and sin are provided by G. C. Berkouwer,[54] Bernard Ramm,[55] and Millard J. Erickson.[56]

BIBLICAL TEACHING

Which historical explication concerning the Fall and the condition of persons in sin we choose to accept depends on the teachings of inspired Scripture, to which we now turn.

The Pentateuch

If the first great epic drama recorded in Scripture is creation (see chap. 1), the second is the Fall of the human race into sin. It is possible that the Genesis accounts of creation and the Fall originated by what Ramm calls "divinely inspired reconstruction."[57] But whereas Barth considers the account of the Fall to be saga and Adam the paradigm for the moral experience of every person, Ramm focuses on "generic Adam," "generic Fall," and "generic sin."[58] Later biblical attestation of Adam (Rom. 5:14; 1 Cor. 15:22, 45; 1 Tim. 2:13–14), the serpent (2 Cor. 11:3; Rev. 12:9), and the Fall (1 Tim. 2:14) as historical realities suggest that we should view the Genesis 3 narrative both as historically valid and as paradigmatic of the spiritual experience of each person coming into the world. That is, every man and woman replicates Adam's and Eve's experience of sin, alienation from God, and punishment.

The history of humankind begins in a paradisiacal setting in Eden. In the Garden environment God made provision for all the person's physical, social, and spiritual needs. In the center of Eden God placed two trees, the tree of life and the tree of the knowledge of good and evil (Gen. 2:9). The first, the tree of life, played a special role in sustaining human life. Thus after sinning, the first pair was driven from the Garden, since partaking of the fruit of this tree was alien to their fallen condition (cf. Gen. 3:22–24). The tree of the knowledge of good and evil, whose fruit God had forbidden to be eaten (Gen. 2:17), symbolized the full range of ethical knowledge that the partaker would come to experience. That is, by disobediently eating of the fruit of the second tree Adam would come to know good by the loss of it, and evil by personal, painful experience.[59] God's purpose in placing Adam and Eve in the Garden with the prohibition against eating the fruit of the second tree was one of testing. That is, in a condition of innocence where the will and affections were capable of inclining either to good or evil, humans could move to a state of confirmed righteousness only by a process of testing and moral decision making. In the divine plan, Adam and Eve must determine whether they would live righteously under God's liberating authority or whether they would pursue meaning independently of their Creator. Confronted with the second tree and the divine command in respect of it, Adam and Eve faced the fundamental issue of obedience to God, the Lord of life.

The inspired account of the Fall of

the human race occupies but twenty-four verses. "The serpent [who] was more crafty than any of the wild animals the LORD God had made" (Gen. 3:1), should be viewed as a reptile that Satan employed as his mouthpiece. The Genesis 3 record and its interpretation by Jesus (John 8:44) and John (1 John 3:8; Rev. 12:9) indicates that the real tempter was Satan himself. The serpent, in dialogue with Eve (vv. 1–4), first cast doubt on the word God had spoken ("Did God really say?") and then expressly denied that same word ("You will not surely die"). Lack of confidence in God's truth (unbelief) thus constitutes the first step in spiritual defection. Moreover, Satan falsely suggested to Eve that God forbade the eating of the fruit for the selfish reason that he did not want them to be like himself (v. 5). In addition to the promptings of Satan, Eve experienced in the tree itself a threefold temptation (v. 6). She first sensed that the tree was "good for food" (material temptation), then that it was "pleasing to the eye" (aesthetic temptation), and finally that it was "desirable for gaining wisdom" (intellectual temptation). John similarly speaks of the threefold enticement that comes from the world order ruled by Satan: "the lust of the flesh and the lust of the eyes and the pride of life" (1 John 2:16 RSV). Jesus experienced a similar threefold temptation in Matthew 4:1–11.

The Fall consisted of the inner defection of the soul from God outwardly manifested in the act of eating the forbidden fruit: Eve "took some and ate it. She also gave some to her husband . . . and he ate it" (v. 6). A classical interpretation that identifies the eating with sexual intercourse is mistaken, for, among other reasons, Adam and Eve each partook independently. Rather, via an inner attitude of unbelief and self-exaltation—not through any magical potency within the tree—Eve and then Adam willfully disobeyed the clear command of God. We readily add that each subsequent sin in the world replicates that of our first parents. "It begins with the darkening of the understanding, continues with the excitement of the imagination, stimulates desire in the heart, and culminates in an act of the will."[60]

More than two-thirds of Genesis 3 is devoted to explicating the far-ranging results of the spiritual defection of our first parents. Thus Adam and Eve (1) were afflicted with a profound sense of guilt, for the text says (v. 7) that their eyes were opened to their nakedness, even as the serpent had foretold. That is, now they knew evil experientially in the form of shame and a sense of the unworthiness of the flesh. Moreover, the first pair (2) experienced *estrangement,* a broken relationship with God, or spiritual death (vv. 8–10). Thus whereas formerly they had sweet communion with God in the Garden, following their defection Adam and Eve hid themselves from God's presence. So the sinner's habitual experience is one of flight from God, motivated by fear of his holiness and power (v. 10). In addition, (3) they were overcome with *depravity,* or a fallen, sinful heart (vv. 11–13). Adam and Eve's spiritually twisted nature is reflected in the evasive answers they gave to God. Adam blamed the helper God had given him for his misdeed, whereas Eve blamed the serpent. Clearly evident here is the sinful human tendency to transfer personal responsibility for transgressions to another. And finally, (4) Adam and Eve were punished with *physical death* by being banished from the garden lest they should eat of the tree of life and live forever (vv. 22–24). From the cradle, all sinful human beings begin to die.

As a result of the fall of Adam and Eve, God cursed the serpent that Satan indwelt (v. 14). The repulsive form and movement of snakes is a consequence of the divine curse upon these reptiles. The fact that the serpent was cursed "above . . . all the wild animals" concurs with Paul's declaration that God judged the entire animate and inanimate order in consequence of Adam's sin (Rom. 8:20–21). Verse 15 records God's judgment on Satan. "I will put enmity between you and the woman, and between your offspring and hers; he will crush your head, and you will strike his heel." This text predicts the agelong conflict between the people of God and the forces of evil. The head of each side would do spiritual battle with the other. Satan would wound the Messiah, but "he," the principal seed of the woman (Gal. 4:4), would crush the Devil altogether. The church rightly designates this verse the *Protoevangelium* (the first announcement of the Gospel).

As a consequence of sin, God punished the woman with the pain of multiplied conceptions (v. 16). Now women experience suffering in their fundamental role of bearing children. The sentence "Your desire will be for your husband, and he will rule over you," we saw in chapter 3 anticipates the sinful struggle for power between the sexes. The woman sinfully seeks to control the man, and the man responds in kind by exceeding the God-instituted ordering relation (1 Cor. 11:3, 7–8; Eph. 5:22–25; 1 Tim. 2:12–14; Titus 2:5) to dominate selfishly the woman. Genesis 3 continues by relating that God punished the man in his calling as a man. Thus (1) God cursed the ground that man must work (vv. 17–18), so that both man and his environment are on the same fallen basis. Moreover, (2) the strenuous labor to which God consigned him (v. 19) both retards his physical deterioration and serves as a restraint against sin. This sentence God pronounced leads many unsaved to conclude that life is weariness and vanity (Eccl. 1:8; 4:8, 10). Finally, (3) God condemns man to death: "Dust you are and to dust you will return" (v. 19; cf. vv. 22–24). This punishment underscores the repetitive litany in the genealogy of Genesis 5:5, 8, 11, et al.—"and then he died."

Genesis 4–11, which covers more than two thousand years of history, is a highly condensed narrative whose purpose is to highlight humankind's spiritual condition subsequent to the Fall. Adam's immediate family demonstrates the harsh consequences of sin in the human race (Gen. 4:1–16). When Cain's offering was not accepted by the Lord and his heart was filled with jealousy and hatred toward his brother, Cain brutally beat Abel to death. Man against God thus became man against his fellowman. When confronted by God, Cain added to the sin of murder the sin of lying. Yahweh pronounced a curse on Cain, and the latter wandered across the earth without finding rest for his sinful soul. From the line of Cain came Lamech, the first polygamist, who not only killed a man that had inflicted a lesser wound on him but also proudly boasted about his excessive revenge (Gen. 4:23).

A new chapter in the progress of moral evil occurred when "the sons of God" (*b^enê-'^elōhîm*) took as their wives "the daughters of men" (Gen. 6:1–3). It is preferable to interpret "the sons of God" as the descendants of godly Seth (cf. Hos. 1:10), who grieved the Lord by polygamously marrying unbelieving women. The intensiveness of moral evil in the antediluvian era is expressed in the words "The LORD saw how great man's wickedness [*ra'*] on the earth had become" (Gen. 6:5), and its extensiveness is expressed in the latter part of the same verse, "and that every inclination [*yēṣer*] of the thoughts of his heart was only evil [*ra'*] all the time" (cf. v. 11). This same verse affirms the inward nature of sin; the noun *yēṣer*, from the verb *yāṣar*, to "create, devise," connotes a plan deliberately fashioned in the mind (cf. Gen. 8:21). Vriezen comments concerning Genesis 6:5, "A more emphatic statement of the wickedness of the human heart is hardly conceivable."[61] These evil intentions inevitably gave way to deeds of violent degradation (vv. 11–12). Since the whole earth had become morally corrupt, God became angry (v. 3) and resolved to destroy the people with the Deluge (vv. 7, 13). Even after the awesome judgment of the Flood, the inspired writer attests the pervasive sinfulness of the human heart: "Every inclination [*yēṣer*] of his heart is evil [*ra'*] from childhood" (8:21).

The experience of Noah following the flood reveals the endemic character of sin. Noah appears as "a righteous man" (Gen. 6:9), with whom God made a gracious covenant (9:8–17). Yet in spite of such character and privilege Noah became drunk and shamefully exposed himself before his son (vv. 20–23). Notwithstanding the Fall and the horrible expressions of sin, Scripture attests that, however blemished, the sinner retains his status as image-bearer of God (9:6). God's command that the penalty of death be exacted for murder is linked to wanton destruction of the *imago Dei*. The account of the building of the tower at Babel dramatizes the vanity of societal existence without God (11:1–9). The desire of the people to crowd together rather than disperse throughout the earth (cf. Gen. 1:28) reflects the sinner's fundamental insecurity. Their plan to build a tall tower so as to "make a name for ourselves" (v. 4) discloses the prideful quest to attain autonomy vis-à-vis God. The fact that the project was abandoned before completion (v. 8), suggests that human aspirations sought apart from God are never fully realized.

Even specially chosen people were not exempt from sin. Abram in Egypt deliberately lied to Pharaoh, telling him that Sarah was his sister, and this led Pharaoh to take her as his wife (Gen. 12:11–20; cf. 20:2–13). The account of the destruction of Sodom and Gomorrah (Gen. 19:1–29) relates that all the male inhabitants of Sodom, both young and old, practiced homosexuality (vv. 4–5). Moreover, Lot, Abraham's nephew offered the Sodomites his two virgin daughters for their sexual pleasure (v. 8). The attempt by evil men to break into homes to molest the occupants (v. 9) attests the violence rampant in Sodom. God's anger toward such raw depravity is seen in the supernatural judgment meted out on the cities of the plain (vv. 24–26).

The subsequent history of God's dealings with the chosen people likewise discloses the horrible faces of human sin. Jealous over their father's special love for Joseph, the brothers plotted to kill the lad (Gen. 37:18–20), threw him into a cistern (v. 24), sold their brother to Midianite merchants (v. 28), and then lied to Jacob, telling him that Joseph had been killed by a wild animal (vv. 31–33). Moreover, Moses, the great deliverer of Israel, began his career by killing an Egyptian and burying him in the sand (Exod. 2:12). Moses and Aaron sinned at Kadesh by smiting the rock and so were not allowed to enter the Promised Land (Num. 20:6–13; 27:14). God consigned Israel to forty years of wilderness wandering because of their persistent stubbornness, provocation, and idolatry (Num. 14:20–35). Aaron's comment to Moses sums up the condition of the human heart: "You know how prone these people are to evil" (Exod. 32:22).

The moral laws God gave Israel highlight the complex character of sin. Whereas God condemned the volitional perpetration of crimes such as stealing, lying, and defrauding one's neighbor (Lev. 19:11–16), he also proscribed hidden thoughts or intentions such as bearing a grudge or hating a brother in the heart (vv. 17–18). The same distinction between sins conceived in the mind and sins volitionally committed occurs in the Ten Commandments (Exod. 20:3–17).

When God consigned most of Israel to death in the wilderness, he made an exception in regard to their children: "Your children who do not yet know good from bad—they will enter the land" (Deut. 1:39). We may infer that since they lacked moral discernment and personal responsibility, God judged the children innocent of the rebellion in the wilderness and so did not subject them to the common judgment (cf. Num. 14:29–31).

Poetry and Wisdom

We find an allusion to the Fall in the statement of the Teacher: "God made man upright [yāšār], but men have gone in search of many schemes" (Eccl. 7:29). The Psalter acknowledges the reality of inherited sin with unusual candor: "Even from birth the wicked go astray; from the womb they are wayward and speak lies" (Ps. 58:3). David's admission "Surely I was sinful at birth, sinful from the time my mother conceived me" (51:5) indicates that underlying his adultery with Bathsheba was a sinful nature that he acquired at conception from a sinful father and mother. With good reason one could say that "this is the Old Testament's greatest statement of original sin."[62]

The literature freely acknowledges the darkness of moral depravity. Eliphaz describes the sinner as "vile and corrupt, who drinks up evil like water" (Job 15:16; cf. 25:4). Depravity is universally ingrained in human life. So the psalmist writes, "They are corrupt, and their ways are vile; there is no one who does good. . . . Everyone has turned away, they have together become corrupt; there is no one who does good, not even one" (Ps. 53:1, 3; cf. 14:1, 3; Prov. 20:9). When compared with the righteous God, the sinful person is a "maggot" and a "worm" (Job 25:6). God's response to humans' sinful orientation is "anger," "indignation," and "wrath" (Ps. 90:7, 9, 11; cf. Job 20:23). Human depravity expresses itself in hardness of heart (Ps. 95:8), hatred of God (Ps. 139:21), and slavery to sin (Prov. 5:22). The last text suggests that sin exerts a paralyzing power; it captures and binds those who embrace it. The Teacher, moreover, emphasizes that the sinner finds life futile or "meaningless" (*hebel*; Eccl. 1:14; 2:11, 17; 3:19, et al.). Nothing can bring permanent satisfaction; not philosophy (1:12–18), not sensual pleasure (2:1–3), and not wealth (2:4–9; 5:10–17). To persons alienated from this Creator, life is frustration, anxiety, and enigma. All that sinners can anticipate is death (2:14–15; 7:2) and judgment (12:14). The spiritual condition of sinners, furthermore, is one of objective guilt. For failure to live up to the demands of the law God reckons sinners blameworthy before the bar of divine justice (Ps. 69:5). In addition, the Psalms provide insight into the spiritual and psychological effects of guilt on persons. In Psalm 38 David describes guilt (*'āwôn*) as a crushing burden that he can scarcely bear (v. 4). It produces a range of psychosomatic symptoms (vv. 5–7). Guilt torments the mind (vv. 8–9), destroys the person's zest for life (v. 10), and causes social isolation (v. 11). In a word, guilt produces a thoroughgoing sense of dis-ease (Ps. 32:3–4).

Original sin, in addition, incurs a just penalty. Scripture testifies that in the present time sin brings its own retribution. "The trouble he causes recoils on himself; his violence comes down on his own head" (Ps. 7:16). In a moral world, the sin a person commits inevitably returns to haunt him (cf. Ps. 9:15; Prov. 26:27). God may execute punishment by cutting short the life of a wicked person (Ps. 55:23). So the psalmist confesses, "Like sheep they are destined for the grave, and death will feed on them" (Ps. 49:14; cf. 9:17). But beyond death lies the day of judgment, when "the heavens will expose his guilt" (Job 20:27) and the sinner will face the wrath of an offended God (20:26, 28–29).

The literature represents sin as a complex reality that encompasses both the person's inner life and the wicked acts he commits. In Proverbs 6:16–19 sinful deeds such as lying and brutality arise from ungodly attitudes and intentions, which in turn arise from a corrupt "heart" or nature. Psalm 58:2 teaches that behind specific acts of injustice lies a perversely calculating heart (*lēb*). Cf. Prov. 24:8–9.

The Prophetic Literature

Isaiah 53:6 attests both sin's universality ("We all, like sheep, have gone astray") and sin's individuality ("each of us has turned to his own way"). Sin in the Prophets is both collective ("Ah, sinful nation, a people loaded with guilt," Isa. 1:4) and personal ("I am a man of unclean lips," Isa. 6:5). Jeremiah 17:9 powerfully portrays the depravity of the human heart: "The heart is deceitful [*'āqōb,* crooked] above all things and beyond cure [*'ānuš,* sick]. Who can understand it?" At the personal level depravity manifests itself in sinful pride and arrogance (Isa. 14:11–14; Dan. 5:20), in conceit (Isa. 16:6), in stubbornness (Jer. 5:23; 16:12), in rebellion against God (Isa. 30:9; Ezek. 12:2), in moral uncleanness (Isa. 64:6; Jer. 2:23), and in impulsively wicked behavior (Jer. 2:24–25; cf. 6:7). Sinners are intellectually darkened in their minds (Isa. 42:7) and volitionally paralyzed in their wills (Isa. 61:1). Apart from grace sinners are incapable of altering their dispositions. Thus Jeremiah 13:23 reads: "Can the Ethiopian change his skin or the leopard its spots? Neither can you do good who are accustomed to doing evil." One authority comments, "Here is a classic example of loss of freedom of the will through persistent sinning. Sin becomes natural."[63]

The prophets also powerfully accentuate the social dimensions of sin. Israel's rulers oppressed the foreigner and mistreated the fatherless and widows (Ezek. 22:7). The powerful and wealthy exploited and defrauded their neighbors (Ezek. 22:12; Mic. 3:1–3). The rich lived luxurious and degenerate lives at the expense of the poor (Amos 4:1; 5:11). Judges sold verdicts to the highest bidder (Mic. 3:11), and corrupt priests taught for a price what people wanted to hear (v. 11). The poor, moreover, were deprived of justice in the courts (Amos 5:12). Micah sums up the state of affairs in Israel. "All men lie in wait to shed blood; each hunts his brother with a net. Both hands are skilled in doing evil; the ruler demands gifts, the judge accepts bribes, the powerful dictate what they desire—they all conspire together" (Mic. 7:2–3).

Sin, both individual and corporate, relationally separates persons from God (Isa. 59:2) and incurs the sentence of objective guilt (Isa. 53:6; Jer. 2:22; Ezek. 22:4; Hos. 12:14; 13:12, 16). Guilt emotionally experienced brings loss of peace (Isa. 48:22), misery (Mic. 7:1), and self-hatred (Ezek. 20:43). The fundamental symptom of guilt is inner restlessness: "The wicked are like the tossing sea, which cannot rest, whose waves cast up mire and mud. 'There is no peace,' says my God, 'for the wicked' " (Isa. 57:20–21).

Sin kindles God's jealousy and anger (Jer. 7:20; Hos. 12:14; Nah. 1:2), and this results in inevitable punishment (Jer. 2:19; Ezek. 28:22; Hos. 12:2). Simply put, "the LORD . . . will not leave the guilty unpunished (Nah. 1:3). God's righteous judgment took many forms: drought (Jer. 14:1–6; Amos 4:7), famine (Jer. 14:12–15; Amos 4:6), plagues (Jer. 14:12; Joel 1:4), military defeats (Jer. 5:15–17; Ezek. 5:12), and, finally, dispersion and exile into foreign lands (Isa. 5:13; Jer. 25:8–11).

Old Testament Words for Sin

In large measure the Old Testament explicates its theology of sin by means of several descriptive words. A primary Hebrew word is the verb *ḥāṭā'*, whose root means to "fall short" or "miss the mark." Thus *ḥāṭā'* connotes "to sin" in the sense of missing God's standard (Lev. 5:5, 16; Ps. 51:4; Zeph. 1:17) and, there being no separate word in Hebrew for guilt, the extended meaning of "to bear blame" (Gen. 43:9; 44:32). The cognate noun *ḥēṭ'* connotes (1) sin as failure to measure up to God's standard (Ps. 103:10), (2) guilt (Lev. 20:20), and (3) punishment (Lam. 3:39). Similarly the common feminine noun *ḥaṭṭā't* (used 290 times) signifies (1) sin or disobedience (Exod. 10:17), (2) guilt (Ps. 32:5), and (3) liability to punishment (Lam. 4:6; Zech. 14:19). The noun *'āwôn,* whose root idea is crookedness, likewise bears multiple meanings: (1) perverse behavior or iniquity (Gen. 15:16; Isa. 43:24), (2) guilt (Gen. 44:16; Ps. 32:5), and (3) consequent punishment (Gen. 4:13; Lam. 4:22). The noun *peša'*, the correlate of the verb *pāša'*, to "rebel" or "transgress" (Isa. 1:2; Hos. 8:1), denotes deliberate rebellion or revolt against God's law or covenant. The verb *'ābar,* the root idea of which is motion across, bears the theological meaning of transgressing stipulations laid down by God. Thus Numbers 22:18 reads, "I could not . . . go beyond the command of the LORD my God" and *'ābar* is variously translated "violate," "disobey," "break," etc. (Josh. 7:15; Isa. 24:5; Hos. 8:1).

The noun *reša'*, from the verb *rāša'*, to "act wickedly" (1 Kings 8:47), "incur guilt" (Job 40:8), is commonly translated "wickedness" (Ps. 45:7; Ezek. 3:19). The noun *šeqer* is variously rendered "falsehood,""lie," and "deceit" (Ps. 52:3; Jer. 27:10; Hos. 7:1). The noun *ma'al,* which has the fundamental idea of breach of trust, is translated in the NIV as "unfaithfulness" and "treachery" (Lev. 26:40; 1 Chron. 9:1; Ezek. 18:24). The masculine noun *'āwel* (Deut. 32:4; Job 34:32) and the feminine noun *'awlāh* (Ps. 92:15; Hab. 2:12) derive from the root meaning to "deviate," and so connote "an act or deed that is against what is right."[64] The verbs *šāgāh* (Lev. 4:13; Job 19:4) and *šāgag* (Lev. 5:18; Num. 15:28), to "err," "go astray," denote the committing of unintentional sins that nevertheless require atonement. The verbs *mārad* (Isa. 36:5; Dan. 9:5) and *mārāh* (Num. 27:14; Hos. 13:16) and the noun *m^e^rî* (Deut. 31:27; Ezek. 2:5–8) signify rebellion against God or his commandments. The verb *'āšām* denotes the act of sin that brings guilt and punishment (Ps. 34:21–22; Isa. 24:6; Hos. 5:15). Correspondingly, the nouns *'āšām* (Num. 5:7; Jer. 51:5) and *'ašmāh* (2 Chron. 28:10; Ezra 9:6–7) are commonly translated "sin" and "guilt."

The Synoptic Gospels

Luke the historian attests the reliability of the Genesis account of human origins by identifying Adam (Luke 3:38) as a historical person like Abraham, David, or Jesus. Our Lord, furthermore, acknowledges inherited sin by describing unregenerate persons as intrinsically "evil" (*ponēros,* Matt. 7:11; Luke 11:13) and "sinful" (*hamartōlos,* Luke 24:7). Jesus, moreover, viewed sin comprehensively in terms of (1) persons' underlying disposition, (2) the thoughts or intentions of their hearts, and (3) the resultant acts or deeds. Thus in the first place Jesus employed the analogy of a tree and its fruit (Matt. 7:17–19; 12:33) to teach that the fundamental disposition of persons' hearts directs the course of their lives. "The good man brings good things out of the good stored up in him, and the evil man [*ho ponēros*] brings evil things [*ponēra*] out of the evil stored up in him [*ek tou ponērou thēsaurou*]" (Matt. 12:35; cf. Luke 6:45). Second, Jesus affirmed that the thought or intent that arises from the fallen nature is properly sinful and incurs divine judgment. Thus he who is angry against a brother is guilty of murder (Matt. 5:21–22), and he who lusts after a woman in his heart is guilty of adultery (vv. 27–28). According to Jesus, the inner determination to sin is as culpable as the overt act. Jesus unites the three dimensions of sin in Matthew 15:18–19: "the things that come out of the mouth come from the heart [*kardia*], and these make a man 'unclean.' For out of the heart come evil thoughts [*dialogismoi*], murder, adultery, sexual immorality, theft, false testimony, slander" (cf. Mark 7:20–23).

Matthew 18:1–4 records our Lord's attitude toward children. When the disciples asked who is greatest in the kingdom, Jesus chose a child and commended the child's qualities of teachableness, humility before evidence, and complete trust. Jesus concluded with the words, "your Father in heaven is not willing that any of these little ones should be lost" (v. 14). The phrase "little ones" likely refers to both children and those who become like children in the spirit of their minds. Jesus' saying in Matthew 19:14, "Let the little children come to me, and do not hinder them, for the kingdom of heaven belongs to such as these," suggests that infants become the object of his special saving care.[65]

The Pauline Literature

By juxtaposing Adam with Moses and Jesus Christ in Romans 5:12–19, Paul attests the validity of the Genesis Fall narrative. The apostle, furthermore, certifies the historicity of Adam and Eve and their seduction by the serpent in 2 Corinthians 11:3 and 1 Timothy 2:13–14. Although sin is universal in the human family—"All have sinned [*hēmarton*] and fall short of the glory of God" (Rom. 3:23)—Paul nevertheless views persons as retaining in some significant measure their status as image-bearers of the Creator (1 Cor. 11:7).

In the key theological passage, Romans 5:12–19, the apostle contrasts the effects of the one sin of Adam with the one redemptive act of Jesus Christ. Given the repeated appeal to "one man" and "one trespass" (vv. 12, 15–19), Paul clearly regards the initial disobedience of the first pair as the cause of all the sorrows inflicted on the human race. By using the words "sin" (*hamartia,* vv. 12–13, 21), "transgression" (*parabasis,* v. 14), "trespass" (*paraptōma,* vv. 15–18, 20), and "disobedience" (*parakoē,* v. 19), the apostle views Adam's act as sinful in all respects. In this text Paul argues (1) that Adam's disobedience in Eden involved his posterity in sin. Verse 12 teaches that the whole of the race sinned, not subsequently, but in the first man Adam; the sin of one was the sin of all.[66] Thus Paul writes, "Sin entered the world through one man, and death through sin, and in this way death came to all men, because all sinned." We note in this verse first that the phrase *ep hō* should be interpreted causally in the sense of "for this reason," or "because" (cf. 2 Cor. 5:4).[67] And second, the constative aorist *hēmarton* signifies the particular historical event in which humanity sinned collectively in the primal sin of Adam. Furthermore, verse 19 states, "Through the disobedience of the one man the many were made sinners." The aorist passive of *kathistēmi* ("appoint," "make") may simply mean "became." "Here there is hardly any linguistic or material difference between *katestathēsan* and *egenonto*. The meaning is that 'as the many became sinners through the disobedience of the one man, so the many became righteous through the obedience of the one.' This does not imply that the forensic element is absent."[68] (2) Adam's sin brought upon all persons the curse of physical death. Verse 12, cited above, teaches that universal death is the consequence of universal sin (cf. v. 14). Paul's further statements, "the many died [*apethanon,* aorist tense] by the trespass of the one man" (v. 15) and "by the trespass of the one man, death reigned through that one man" (v. 17) clearly indicate that persons experience death not because of acts of their own, but by virtue of their participation in the sin of Adam. First Corinthians 15:21–22 makes the same point: "death came through a man"; "in Adam all die." Finally (3), Paul teaches that Adam's primal sin resulted in condemnation for all. Thus "the judgment [*krima*] followed one sin and brought condemnation" (*katakrima,* Rom. 5:16), and "the result of one trespass was condemnation (*katakrima*) for all men" (v. 18). *Krima* here signifies the judicial verdict, and *katakrima* the result of it, namely, the execution of condemnation that issues in damnation.[69] "Here the emphasis is on the judicial sentence of God, which on the basis of the act of the head determines the destiny of all."[70] In conclusion, Romans 5:12–21 affirms that Adam's one trespass constitutes all persons guilty sinners, subject to death, and liable to eternal damnation. The ground of God's righteous judgment is the real solidarity of the human family. Consequently when Adam sinned, the entire race sinned and so suffers the awesome consequences of his rebellion.

The section Romans 1:18–3:20 sets forth the moral bankruptcy of humankind in order to establish the sinner's need for Christ. Thus Paul argues that humanity's rejection of the light of the knowledge of God afforded by general revelation results in sin-darkened minds and hearts: "Their thinking became futile and their foolish hearts were darkened" (1:21). Sinful thoughts and imaginations (*dialogismoi*) then give way to sinful behavior, specifically, to false religion and idolatry (v. 23) and to homosexual acts (vv. 26–27). God judges fornication a grievous sin (v. 24), but homosexuality is particularly odious, since it represents a perversion of his purpose for the race as male and female. Having excluded God from their lives, sinners "become filled with every kind of wickedness, evil, greed and depravity. They are full of envy, murder, strife, deceit and malice. They are gossips, slanderers, God-haters, insolent, arrogant and boastful; they invent ways of doing evil; they disobey their parents; they are senseless, faithless, heartless, ruthless" (vv. 29–31). This selective list depicts the depths of moral ruin to which unregenerate humanity has sunk.

In Romans 3:9–20 Paul portrays the entire human race as wholly depraved. In spiritual matters, all sinners are (1) *blind*—"there is no one who understands" (v. 11a), (2) *rebellious*—"all have turned away, they have together become worthless" (v. 12a), (3) *lawless*—"there is no one who does good, not even one" (v. 12b), and (4) *errant*—"no one . . . seeks God" (v. 11b). Human depravity expresses itself in corrupt speech (vv. 13–14) and in perverted deeds (vv. 15–16), with the result that sinners lack peace of mind (v. 17). The experience of humanity under sin thus is one of pervasive depravity—*non posse non peccare.*

Elsewhere Paul locates depravity in the "*sarx*" (Rom. 8:4–5; Gal. 5:16–17, 24), which the NIV often translates as "sinful nature." "*Sarx* is man's unrenewed nature . . . his whole nature ethically viewed as under the dominion of sin."[71] It is that inclination toward sin and self from which specific sins flow (Gal. 5:19–21). Central to depravity is an anti-God bias or an ingrained hostility toward God (Rom. 8:7; Col. 1:21). Depravity, moreover, blinds the mind in relation to spiritual concerns (2 Cor. 4:4; Eph. 4:17–18). First Corinthians 2:14 teaches that depravity results in epistemic inability in the sinner: "The man without the Spirit does not accept [*dechomai*] the things that come from the Spirit of God, for they are foolishness [*mōria*] to him, and he cannot understand them, because they are spiritually discerned." The verb *dechomai* connotes the idea of welcoming (Luke 16:4, 9) and suggests that sinners reject spiritual realities because they appear to be nonsense (*mōria*). Paul, furthermore, represents sinners as volitionally dead in the spiritual realm, or incapable of making any response honoring to God: "You were dead [*nekros*] in your sins and in the uncircumcision of your sinful nature" (Col. 2:13; cf. Eph. 2:1, 5). "Man's sinful condition is lifeless and motionless as far as any Godward activity is concerned."[72] Lacking spiritual power, sinners are enslaved by Satan (2 Tim. 2:26), by the sin principle that rules their lives (Rom. 6:6, 16–20), and by numerous lusts and passions (Titus 3:3). Thus the apostle depicts sinners as helpless bondslaves in the service of sin and Satan. Contaminated by sin in their bodies and spirits (2 Cor. 7:1), sinners morally are assailed by consciences that are "corrupted" (Titus 1:15) and "seared" (1 Tim. 4:2).

By virtue of universal sin and depravity, Paul indicts humanity as guilty and culpable before God. The apostle states that since both Jews and Gentiles have violated God's standards, "the whole world [is] held accountable [*hypodikos*, 'under judgment'] to God" (Rom. 3:19). Elsewhere Paul states, "Cursed [*epikataratos*, "under penalty"] is everyone who does not continue to do everything written in the Book of the Law" (Gal. 3:10). Again, "Scripture has shut up all men under sin" (Gal. 3:22 NASB), which means that all persons languish under the guilt and condemnation that follows from sin. God's response to depravity and guilt is wrath, that righteous displeasure of the Holy One that results in punishment. "The wrath [*orgē*] of God is being revealed from heaven against all the godlessness and wickedness of men who suppress the truth by their wickedness" (Rom. 1:18; cf. Eph. 5:6; 1 Thess. 2:16). The most fearful aspect of retribution is the eschatological wrath that God will mete out against sinners on the last day (Rom. 2:5; 1 Thess. 1:10). The penalty prescribed for sin is death (Rom. 6:23), both physical (Rom. 8:10), spiritual (Eph. 5:14), and eternal (2 Thess. 1:9).

The Johannine Literature

By describing Satan as "the father of lies" and a "murderer from the beginning" (John 8:44; cf. 1 John 3:8), Jesus certifies the historical facticity of the Genesis account of the Fall. When John the Baptist addressed Jesus as "the Lamb of God, who takes away the sin [*hamartia*] of the world!" (John 1:29), he acknowledged that the human family languishes under the burden of a common corruption and guilt. Jesus appears to have taught inherited depravity with the words "Flesh gives birth to flesh" (John 3:6). As Plummer observes, "what is born of sinful human nature is human and sinful."[73] Jesus further taught (John 5:42) that sinful and depraved persons lack the love for God the Law demands (Deut. 6:5). Indeed, sinners emotionally hate Jesus and the Father (John 15:18, 24). The perfect tense of the verb *miseō* in the preceding verses suggests that the animosity is a permanent rather than a fleeting emotion. Depravity, moreover, results in intellectual blindness (Rev. 3:17) and volitional inability (John 6:44) in spiritual matters. When Jesus taught that "everyone who sins is a slave [*doulos*] to sin" (8:34), he meant that the condition of the habitual sinner is one of volitional servitude to the lower nature and malignant powers. John perceives that "the whole world is under the control of the evil one" (1 John 5:19).

The inevitable response of the holy God to moral depravity is fierce anger (*thymos,* Rev. 14:10, 19; 15:1, 7) and wrath (*orgē,* John 3:36; Rev. 16:19; 19:15). Thus by virtue of their unbelief and God's righteous judgment, sinners legally suffer the sentence of condemnation. "Whoever does not believe stands condemned already" (John 3:18). Here and now the penalty of sin is death, both physical (1 John 5:16–17) and spiritual (John 5:24; 1 John 3:14). Hereafter the penalty will be eternal death, or endless exclusion from the presence of God (John 5:29; Rev. 20:13–15).

Other New Testament Literature

James teaches not only that evil desire is the root of particular sins but also that the human heart is fundamentally sinful: "Each one is tempted when, by his own evil desire [*epithymia*], he is dragged away and enticed. Then, after desire has conceived, it gives birth to sin" (1:14–15). "This verse, in fact, so far from being opposed to the doctrine of original sin, substantiates it."[74] Sin and depravity result metaphysically in the separation of the spirit from the body (2:26), morally in licentious conduct (1 Peter 4:3; 2 Peter 2:14; Jude 7) and a guilty conscience (Heb. 9:9, 14; 10:2), emotionally in crippling inner conflicts (1 Peter 2:11) and the gnawing fear of death (Heb. 2:15), relationally in enmity toward God (James 4:4) and others (4:1), and volitionally in hardness of heart (Heb. 3:8, 15) and bondage to sinful passions (2 Peter 2:19). Failure to fulfill the law of God, even at one point, results in guilt (*enochos,* James 2:10), the punishment of which is physical death (Heb. 9:27; 1 Peter 4:6) and spiritual death (James 1:15; 5:20). In spite of human depravity, God views persons as constituted in his image (James 3:9). The perfect form of the verb (*gegonotas*) in the phrase "men, who have been made in God's likeness" underscores persons' continued status as divine image-bearers.

The intricate argument of Hebrews 7:4–10 illumines the issue of how Adam's sin affected the entire human family. Verses 9 and 10 are most relevant for our discussion: "One might even say that Levi, who collects the tenth, paid the tenth through Abraham, because when Melchizedek met Abraham, Levi was still in the body [literally, 'in the loins,' [*osphys*] of his ancestor." F. F. Bruce observes that "an ancestor is regarded in biblical thought as containing within himself all his descendants"[75] If we take verse 10 in its literal sense—"loins" being the source of physical generation (cf. v. 5)—then the notion of racial solidarity and the seminal theory, in particular, is supported.[76]

New Testament Words for Sin

Negatively, the New Testament describes sin as *harmartia,* a missing of the mark or a failure to attain God's standard (Matt. 1:21; Rom. 5:12–13, 20–21; 1 John 1:9); compare *hamartēma,* which focuses on the consequence of such failure or fault (Mark 3:28; Rom. 3:25; 1 Cor. 6:18). The word *anomia,* that connotes departure from God's law, is commonly translated by the NIV as "lawlessness" or "wickedness" (Matt. 23:28; Titus 2:14;

1 John 3:4). The noun *adikia* (Rom. 1:18, 29; 2 Peter 2:15; 1 John 5:17) possesses the root idea of absence of righteousness and is frequently translated "wrongdoing" or "wickedness." *Apeitheia,* which fundamentally signifies lack of faith, is often rendered "unbelief" or "disobedience" (Rom. 11:30, 32; Eph. 2:2; 5:6; Heb. 4:6). The noun *asebeia,* from the verb *sebomai,* to "worship," signifies impiety or irreligion and is translated "godlessness" (Rom. 1:18; 11:26) or "ungodliness" (Titus 2:12). Finally, the nouns *agnoia* (Acts 3:17; 17:30; Eph. 4:18) and *agnoēma* (Heb. 9:7) connote "ignorance" of God's holy requirements.

Positively, *parabasis* constitutes a breach of the law or a violation of a commandment, and so is translated "transgression" (Rom. 4:15; Gal. 3:19) or "violation" (Heb. 2:2). *Paraptōma,* from the verb *parapiptō,* to "fall away" (Heb. 6:6), signifies a fault or offense, and so is commonly rendered by the words "trespass" (Matt. 6:14–15, KJV; Rom. 5:15–18, 20) and "transgression" (Rom. 11:11–12; Eph. 2:1). *parakoē,* from the verb *parakouō* meaning "fail to hear," signifies overt "disobedience" to God (Rom. 5:19; 2 Cor. 10:6; Heb. 2:2). The noun *ponēria,* whose root idea is evil or ill-natured, connotes human character as wicked and depraved (Luke 11:39; 1 Cor. 5:8; Eph. 6:12). The adjective *ponēros* describes persons as morally evil or wicked (Matt. 7:11; 12:35; 2 Thess. 3:2). The noun *epithymia,* from *thymos* meaning "passion," signifies the evil desires and lusts that reside in the heart (Rom. 1:24; Gal. 5:16; James 1:14–15; 1 Peter 2:11; 1 John 2:16–17). The reality of guilt that follows the various sins of omission and commission is indicated by the noun *opheilēma* ("debt" or obligation, Matt. 6:12) and the adjective *enochos* ("guilty" or liable to punishment, Matt. 5:21–22; 1 Cor. 11:27; James 2:10).

SYSTEMATIC FORMULATION

Which elements of the historical views of the human moral condition cohere in a systematic doctrine that makes sense of the extensive evidence available in Scripture and human experience? A systematic discussion must begin with the status of humans before and after the Fall.

Our First Parents in God's Image

Ontologically in the image of the eternal God, the souls of Adam and Eve (after their creation) have an unconditional *everlasting existence.* Others hold that they had only a conditional immortality. Their souls would live forever only if they partook of the fruit of the tree of life. Physically we may agree that the body would live on and on only if they had eaten of the life-giving tree. Conditional immortality applies, however, only to the body. The human spirit had more than a conditional existence. [77] The day Eve and Adam ate the forbidden fruit, they experienced the potential for physical death and its processes began. What was conditional was the morality of their existence and their fellowship with God. Their spirits exist forever, as we argued in the previous chapter.

Our first parents also reflected a likeness to the sovereign God *functionally* in the faithful use of their personal intellectual, emotional, and volitional capacities. Adam and Eve knew, loved, and served God and each other. Their thoughts, desires, and actions were relationally loving but also morally just. In their work they were able effectively to maintain dominion over other creatures on earth. As stewards accountable to God, they were faithful. Adam and Eve were joyful vice-regents in the providential kingdom of God on earth (Gen. 1:26, 28; Ps. 8:6–8; Heb. 2:6–8).

Morally, Adam and Eve were originally righteous like God. Adam and Eve before the Fall were upright in character and used all of their capacities to worship the Creator and serve his purposes in Eden. They were motivated by love for God and each other so that their actions were in accord with God's revealed will. Hence the consequences of their sin affected the well-being of themselves and of God's kingdom on earth. They portrayed God's moral character as revealed subsequently by the incarnate Christ. In essence humankind is not evil, but good. Goodness or righteousness is not something distinct from them that was added to them, but a quality of human existence created in the divine image. Humanness as created is not merely morally neutral nor is it evil; on the contrary, it is good.

Relationally, prior to the Fall Adam and Eve enjoyed unbroken fellowship with their Creator and Sustainer. Apparently it was common for them to consciously encounter their Maker morning and evening (Gen. 3:8). The first pair enjoyed also faithful loving relationships with each other. No evidence of suspicion, envy, jealousy, or hatred occurred before the Fall. Male and female were like God (Gen. 1:27; 5:1–2) in having mutual relations of respect, love, and trust (Gen. 2:18, 20; 1 Cor. 11:11–12). God created Eve out of Adam, differentiating female from male in the unity of mankind. Their marriage relationship as "one flesh" restores the unity. "Mankind" equals male and female. The biblical account of the creation of man, and then of woman from man, provides a basis both for the essential unity of male and female as human and the relational unity of one husband and one wife. "When God created man, he made him in the likeness of God. He created them male and female and blessed them. And when they were created, he called them 'man'" (Gen. 5:1–2).

So the whole original internal and external context of human life was one of *peace (shalom).* Both Old and New Testament terms for peace indicate rest, safety, freedom from care, trustfulness, security, understanding, and ease. The peace that comes from God is not so much the opposite of war as of any disturbance in communal well-being. Hence the original *shalom* covered human well-being in the widest sense of the word.[78] The original human state was not one of evolving from a brute type of existence through the survival of the fittest to a more "human" existence. Humanity's deepest struggles are not those of animals evolving to a higher form of existence, but of unique kinds of beings in God's image suffering from the loss of peace. Adam and Eve lost their loving and trustful relationship with God; their former moral uprightness; and their intellectual, emotional, and volitional integrity.

The Factual Fall

Instead of continuing to trust, love, and enjoy their Creator with their whole beings, at a point in time and space Eve and Adam disbelieved and disobeyed God. Their sinful rebellion occurred at a point in human history as an *actual fact.* The narrative in Genesis 3 is not merely a mythical illustration of how all men and women sin. It records the actual beginning of moral evil among humans. After presenting informative "accounts" of the origins of the earth, vegetation, animals and man, the author presents the origin of moral evil and the consequent natural evils. Although the biblical narrative has some symbolic aspects, the symbols occur in a literal framework. Bernard Ramm calls the events of the Fall "datable historical events," but he joins Barth in denying that they are "actual history."[79] Ramm apparently hesitates here because he does not regard the record complete. But no historical records exhaustively duplicate every detail of an event. Brief reports, we maintain, can nevertheless be accurate. From inspired revelation we can *know* in part.

The *temptations* of our first parents involved temptations much like our own. They gave attention to an inherently wrong possibility, felt its enticement, and desired to do it. Such temptations by themselves are not sin. They sinned when they continuously coveted the forbidden fruit, deliberately decided to eat it (possibly planning to pick it unobtrusively), and finally ate it. Inwardly they sinned, when yielding to the enticements, by questioning the truth of God's word (Gen. 3:1), denying the reality of death for sin, desiring forbidden pleasures, and seeking to know as God knows. Outwardly they sinned when they finally partook of the fruit. Also today men and women are tempted to (1) question God's Word, (2) seek to know evil as well as good experientially, (3) deny the reality of death, and (4) seek divine powers. New Age occult emphases like these are far from new. They are as old as the race. As at the beginning, the ultimate source of these ideas today is the ultimate deceiver, Satan.

Adam's and Eve's first sins *symbolize the fall of all men and women.* Genesis 3 not only describes the literal fall of our first parents but also vividly illustrates how all men and women yield to temptation. Realistically, Adam and Eve stand for all human beings because at the time they constituted the entire human population. (We noted the unity and solidarity of the race in the previous chapter.)

Our reference to our first parents as symbols in no way denies their literal significance. *Symbols* involve three factors: (1) the factually existent symbol itself, (2) something other than itself that it denotes, and (3) a point of similarity between the two. Additional considerations make it highly probable that Genesis 3 contains a real symbolism embodied in actual things. Just as Adam was both the first literal man and symbolic of all humanity, so two literal trees symbolized life and knowledge, and a literal serpent symbolized Satan. If the account of Eve's and Adam's sins was not factual, then at what point in the history of Genesis does the text suddenly begin to speak about actual humans on this actual earth? Our Lord and his disciples who were inspired to write the New Testament took the Fall and surrounding events literally and factually. Hence those who accept Jesus' lordship today interpret Genesis as he did. The biblical account of the Fall explains not only how human sin originated, but also by way of illustration how every person sins. The literal significance need not be denied to support the universal symbolism; neither need the universal symbolism be denied to support the literal significance.

Furthermore, Adam, as the first human being, represents every human being morally and legally. Adam's sin may justly and legally implicate all Adam's human descendants as a consequence of God's solemn promise to him that if he even touched the tree in the middle of the garden he would die (Gen. 3:3). Covenant theologians think this teaches a "covenant of works" specifying the parties to the agreement, the condition, and the results if the condition is not met. The parties to the covenant were God and mankind's first representative (Adam), the covenant was conditioned on obedience, and the penalty for disobedience was death. Although the context does not explicitly call this a "covenant," the text has the elements of a solemn promise or legal agreement made by God made with Adam. In Paul's theology Adam's sin implicated his descendants. Adam has a relationship to the fallen race parallel to Christ's relation to the redeemed (Rom. 5:12–18). Adam's one sin brought condemnation to all generated in the fallen human family (vv. 16, 18); Christ's one sacrifice brings justification to all who have been regenerated in his moral and spiritual family. The theological value of Christ's death for all, furthermore, depends on the literalness of his incarnation in human flesh (1 John 4:1–3; 2 John 9). It follows that in Paul's parallel the theological effect of Adam's sin also depends on the literalness of his one act of sin. Because Adam literally sinned, he can really represent all his descendants. Adam's representation of all humans is not an arbitrary legal fiction, however. His legal representation is justified by the fact that each descendant has an Adamic nature not only as human but also as depraved. As Jesus taught, "Flesh gives birth to flesh" (John 3:6).

Consequences of the Fall for Adam and Eve and All Humans

Inwardly, by falling into the foul whirlpool of temptations, both Adam and Eve developed a strong desire for sin's seductiveness in general, and love for specifics not resisted led to habitual sins. Even if their words and acts appeared externally to adhere to God's revealed will, their motives were not for his glory. So struggle with fleshly loves tainted every aspect of their natures. Their inward hearts became inclined to sin. Inwardly Adam and Eve were now lawbreakers and rebels against the Lawgiver. Their hearts, the very centers of their natures, had become deceitful and desperately wicked. Instead of being loving creatures in reflecting God's likeness, they had become insolent. Their essential inclinations were changed from those of believing and obedient children of God to those of believing and obedient children of the Devil.

Functionally, Adam and Eve's use of their capacities to think, feel, and will became misdirected, misused, and terribly complicated in the fallen world. Eve's distinctive roles in childbirth and in her marriage were no longer to be free from trouble (Gen. 3:16). And Adam's activities also began to entail pain, perspiration, and frustration. The Fall debilitated all their distinctively personal capacities to think, feel, and act with conduct and motivations that please God.

Morally, also as sinners they brought on themselves a verdict of guilty as the efficient causes of their sins (*reatus culpae*). The all-knowing divine Judge found them to blame for abusing the marvelous self-determining capacities he gave them and violating moral principles of a healthful life that flow from his nature. So they received the sentence deserved for the heinousness of their crime. And they lived their remaining time on earth in fear of physical and eternal punishment that justly follows (*reatus poenae*). What Adam and Eve *were* morally was far from what they *ought to have been.* From descriptive accounts of each other as psychologists and sociologists they might not have appeared far out of line with each other's moral discernment. But their originally righteous natures had become prone to sin.

Spiritually, although dependent on the Holy One for their existence, Adam and Eve no longer had unbroken fellowship with God or each other. Having knowingly and deliberately rebelled against God's rule of their lives, enmity arose between Satan and Eve and between the offspring of the Devil (John 8:44) and of the woman (the Messiah and his regenerate followers (Gen. 3:15). Our first parents became alienated from fellowship with the Holy One and strangers to his spiritual blessings. Instead of enjoying communion with their Maker, they found themselves trying to hide.

Ecologically and environmentally,

God banished Adam and Eve from the Garden of Eden and judged their environment. God judged the ground "because of" Adam, who then found his work to require "painful toil" (Gen. 3:17). The ground produced thorns and thistles for Adam and he was to eat of the plants "by the sweat of his brow" (vv. 18–19). As Paul later explained, "the creation was subjected to *frustration,* not by its own choice, but by the will of the one who subjected it, in hope that the creation itself will be liberated from its *bondage to decay* and brought into the glorious freedom of the children of God. We know that the whole creation has been *groaning* as in the pains of childbirth right up to the present time" (Rom. 8:20–23). Natural evils (such as hurricanes, volcanos, floods) in general are a part of the penalty for moral evils. Even so we may not trace a specific occurrence to a specific sin.

Relationally, or socially, the very next generation openly exhibits the outward evidence of inner jealousy and hatred. Cain's murder of his brother Abel typified the family, social, and political problems that follow in human history individually and collectively.

Ontologically, in spite of the loss of communion with God and the impairment of their natures, fallen people remain in God's likeness as living and active personal spirits. Human beings continue to be of great value in themselves. No human should be murdered, because every man and woman remains in God's image metaphysically (Gen. 9:6). And because everyone remains in the image of God, we ought not even curse people (James 3:9). Luther overstates the effect of the Fall when he says, "Man who was little different from the angels is now little more than a brute."[80] Although at times sinners may act like beasts, human beings remain everlasting spirits like God. So the worst criminals deserve our respect for what they are, even when we must legally oppose what they have done. And because humans remain in the *imago Dei,* God is not "totally other." We cannot agree with Kierkegaard, Barth, Bultmann, and their followers, who deny any analogy of being between God and humans, for humans remain in God's likeness. An analogy of being continues between God, who is spirit, and humans, who are physically clothed spirits, even though God's being is noncontingent and ours is contingent.

Not only did Adam and Eve suffer these consequences of sin, but so have all their descendants, whom they represented. All their offspring, for example, have lived in environments far from Edenic. In the present state of restlessness and longing for lost fellowship with God, we may try to find peace in less-demanding gods. We fail to find lasting peace, however, in materialism, hedonism, humanism, mystical unions with nature, science, education, and political action. Such idols leave us alienated from ourselves, from God, and from others and leave us troubled with anxiety. "The wicked are like the tossing sea, which cannot rest, whose waves cast up mire and mud. There is no peace, says my God, for the wicked" (Isa. 57:21). Our depraved hearts are restless, as Augustine well knew, until they find their rest in God. Because of liberal, unitarian, and other views that deny the biblical support and the moral justice of any transmission of either Adamic depravity or Adamic guilt, it is important to explore the meaning and support of these hypotheses.

A Tendency to Insolence Inherited by All

Adam's sins were not entities like books that could be passed on to his children, but Adam and Eve reproduced after their kind, not only ontologically, but also morally. For that reason every one of their Jewish and Gentile descendants actually commits sins (Rom. 1:18–3:20). From the fountainhead of the race everyone has received an inherent propensity to defy God's ways. Adam's first rejection of God not only corrupted his unsullied ability to believe and obey God but also affected the nature of all his offspring. All descendants of Adam have evidently received a perverse nature with impaired abilities to know, love, and serve God. All, when informed of God's righteous demands, tend to become insolent.

As Jesus taught, "flesh gives birth to flesh" (John 3:6). "Flesh" sometimes refers to physical life in itself without moral implications (Phil. 1:22–24), sometimes to the next of kin (Lev. 18:12), and sometimes human ancestry (Rom. 4:1). But in emphasizing the necessity of regeneration to Nicodemus, Jesus Christ indicated that morally perverse parents beget children with inclinations to moral perversity. When used morally, the "flesh" refers to an aversion to God and his righteousness. So Paul exhorts, "Do not . . . indulge the sinful nature" (Gal. 5:13), or "gratify the desires of the sinful nature" (v. 16). "For the sinful nature desires what is contrary to the Spirit, and the Spirit what is contrary to the sinful nature" (v. 17). In moral contexts, then, "flesh" designates the the degenerative tendency of personal agents to use the power of contrary choice in opposition to the will of God. The "flesh" involves a general inclination to think, feel, choose, and act in ways contrary to God's pleasure. It may be illustrated in the life of Zedekiah, when he was a twenty-one-year-old king of Judah. He did not humble himself before Jeremiah the prophet when Jeremiah spoke the Word of the Lord; he rebelled against King Nebuchadnezzar, became stiffnecked, hardened his heart, and would not turn to the Lord, the God of Israel (2 Chron. 36:11–13).

By nature the "heart" of a human is "deceitful above all things and beyond cure" (Jer. 17:9). Just as the evil tree brings forth evil fruit, the aversion of the human heart to God's ways issues in sinful deeds. The general influence of depraved human nature leads self-determining human agents to specific acts of unwillingness to open ourselves to God's wisdom and insensitivity to our neighbors' needs. The specific sins may include thoughts, emotions, attitudes, motives, words, and acts. The "flesh" exhibits itself in "sexual immorality, impurity and debauchery; idolatry and witchcraft; hatred, discord, jealousy, fits of rage, selfish ambition, dissensions, factions and envy; drunkenness, orgies, and the like" (Gal. 5:19–21). In other instances the flesh may produce more "splendid vices," but they are vices nevertheless! These include pride of accomplishment, self-worship, self-aggrandizement, fear, child abuse, employee abuse, prisoner abuse, and abuse of members by cult leaders. Religious people may also defy God's righteousness under the pretense of conformity to it! Pharisaically we may add to biblical standards, pray and tithe to be seen of men, and despise people who do not adhere to our traditions. Whether in sensuality, materialism, intellectualism, emotionalism, voluntarism, scientism, or cultism, defiant cravings dominate the minds and enslave the bodies of the unregenerate (Eph. 2:3) and continue to harass children of God by grace.

"I tell you the truth," Jesus said, "everyone who sins is a slave to sin" (John 8:34). In our fallen condition, Paul explains, we are "controlled by the sinful nature" (Rom. 7:5). Sin has dominion over the unregenerate. Regularly yielding to the flesh, they become dominated by a fleshly mind set (8:5, 7). Because of this inherent inclination of motive as well as thoughts, words, and acts, their hardened, stubborn hearts are unable to obey God's law (8:3) or to please God (v. 8). Everything is tainted in life according to the flesh and nothing is good without qualification (7:18). Like Paul, by nature we have within ourselves the inability to do the good that we desire (vv. 18–20).

The Bible also refers to people dominated by fleshly or evil natures as the "world" (*kosmos*). The term "world" sometimes has no moral connotation in references to the heavens and earth as the dwelling place of humanity and the theater of history. In other contexts "world" refers to the unregenerate people who dwell on the earth. The people of the world are ruled by demonic powers (1 Cor. 2:6; Eph. 2:2) and in irreconcilable conflict with God's rule.[81] Jesus charged the disciples to take the gospel to the whole world (Mark 16:15), clearly referring to all people struggling with fallenness. Again the field is the world (Matt. 13:38) and Christians are to be the light of the world (5:14). Christians are in the world but not of the world system. Believers are to love those who dwell on the earth for Christ but they are not to love "the cravings of sinful man" (1 John 2:16) and the desires of the world that pass away (v. 17). Christians are not to let evil desires dominate or rule them. By the Spirit of grace believers in Christ no longer let their sinful propensity dominate their lives.

Depravity Is Holistic

The fleshly desires of the human heart affect *every human capacity of the whole person*. But a person, not a part of a person, thinks about the possibility of disbelief and disobedience, imagines the emotional pleasures of going his or her own way, and deliberately decides to yield to peer pressure (or other temptations). A person created to know, love, and serve God knows, loves, and serves self, others, or something in creation more. Our sins have corrupted all our personal capacities and relationships. The taint of idolatrous passions affects us holistically. The mind is not exempt, as some rationalists imagine. The conscience is not exempt, as some moralists think. The emotions are not exempt, as some romanticists might wish. And the will is not exempt from the taint of sin, as some activists might hope. It is no mere addition to our essential humanity that is lost in the Fall (as in the traditional Roman Catholic view): our essential nature is corrupted and our essential relationships are broken.

"Holistic depravity" conveys better than "total depravity" the fact that all our abilities and our best achievements are tainted by evil without implying that we are all as bad as we could possibly be. No capacity of our unrenewed nature escapes the taint of our sinful hearts. What the older Reformed writers called a person's "agencies" and their "excellencies," we are calling a person's "capacities" and their "uses" or "functions." The mental capacity remains, but the mind has become unreceptive ("blind") to truth about divine spiritual realities. The desires and emotions no longer find their fulfillment in the Holy Spirit. And the will is predisposed to sinful motivations, choices, and actions. Instead of using our capacities to know, love, and obey our Creator, we prefer to know, love, and serve God's creatures. As sinners we tend to be preoccupied with untrue thoughts, impure desires, and unjust conduct. Having desired forbidden knowledge, illicit love, and irresponsible power, we became inclined toward unwise, unfair, and unloving acts. Hence we fail to enjoy all the excellent by-products that could have been ours from a use of our intellects, emotions, and wills for God's glory. So our best attempts to fulfill the cultural mandate tend to be tainted with unworthy motives. Our best efforts in religion, philosophy, the sciences, the fine arts, personal religion, or social reform fail to please the most High. We either tend to pride of achievement in the development of our skills or in claiming premature finality in our thinking, or we immerse ourselves in an unprincipled hedonism and sensuality. The Romans before the fall of their empire desired only bread and circus; our ultimate concerns may be bread and television.

Sinful acts, on an Augustinian analysis, may not appear to be wicked. On the other hand, "worship and service" may be sinful when the humanistic creatures displace the Creator (Rom. 1:25). If our concerns for our families, business, or nation become more ultimate than our concern for God, we sin. Our acts may appear to others to be splendid. If we do not seek first the kingdom of God, however, they are "splendid vices." As Isaiah said, "All our righteous acts are like filthy rags" (64:6). Jesus observed that the Pharisees, though outwardly fasting, praying, and tithing, were inwardly uncaring.

How does the depravity of our hearts affect the varied aspects of human existence?

Depravity of Heart and Human Emotions

Emotions are not inherently wrong, and our original tendency may not directly affect their expression in relation to ordinary interests and relationships. But because of our deceitful hearts they do not delight supremely in God and his righteousness. Our emotional lives become detrimental when they delight in evil rather than good. In our unregenerate condition we gratify the "cravings of our sinful nature" (Eph. 2:3). Repeatedly we give priority not only to bad thoughts but also to harmful words and deeds. As a habitual tendency becomes compulsive (like an addiction) we discover our inability to change our fleshly cravings. But we ourselves, like Adam and Eve, have begun the habits that become compulsive. As a result, even the good that we still choose, we find ourselves unable to do with consistency and purity of loving motives.

The root of all evil, Augustine concluded from his scripturally informed interpretation of his own experience, is wrongly directed desire, affection, or love. When we divert our highest love from the Creator to the creature, we become idolatrous. By seeking our emotional fulfillment in what cannot last and yet what demands more and more from us, we sin. *Lust (libido)* for creatures (like lust for money) we can lose in this changing, temporal world, is the deepest root of evil. Lust for things leads to *vice*—the corrupting of one's own soul and body. Personal vices then lead to *crime*—injuring others. In contrast, *the deepest root of all good is love for the Creator* (whom we cannot lose since he is eternal). Love for the eternal Lord of all leads to *prudence*—conduct to one's own advantage or edification. Prudence in turn leads to *benevolence*—conduct with a view to a neighbor's advantage or upbuilding.[82]

As persons with deceitful hearts we bring sinful desires with us to any environmental structures. The most radical diagnosis of the human predicament does not trace the roots of our difficulties to our environment, our parents, the other sex, or to the party in power in our nations at the moment. The deepest roots of evil in the contemporary world can be traced to our own inner selves. The tendency "to mess everything up" artistically, economically, nationally, and internationally lies within ourselves. When theological writers speak of "original sin," they generally do not refer to the first sin of humans chronologically, but to the fact that sinful proclivities are as original in each new baby as a tendency to cry. To change the analogy, by "original equipment" for an automobile we mean the water pump, brakes, etc., included with each new model of automobile. Similarly, each new human being since the Fall has an *original tendency* to moral evil (often called original sin [sing.]). This is not to say that anyone is born with *original sins* (pl.). All self-determining personal agents responsibly commit sin*s* when they displease God by doing what is counterproductive to their well-being either knowingly or in inexcusable ignorance.

If the desires of our hearts are persistently evil, they further fix the hereditary *perversity of character* received by nature. (1) By valuing the word of others above the Word of God we break the relationship of mutual trust with God, and this leads to mistrust of one another. (2) By desiring our own way above his rule we become estranged, and by misusing God-given abilities to disregard God's moral directives we rebel against his lordship. (3) Repetition of these sins becomes customary; custom not resisted becomes necessary; and necessity becomes enslaving. Thus the inclination becomes inherent in human nature to habitually disbelieve God's words, alienate one self from God, and use God-given capacities in ways counterproductive to God, others, and creation. Hence fallen people not only commit sins but *are* sinners. Humans since the Fall must realistically be concluded to have *sinful natures*.

Depravity and Reason

Fallen human thinking may be highly developed in many areas of research and skill, but it is unreceptive to God's revealed redemptive plans. Depraved people of themselves stubbornly refuse to repent genuinely of their sins. The resurrected Jesus rebuked even the eleven disciples for their lack of faith and their stubborn refusal to believe those who had seen him after he had risen (Mark 16:14). Paul spoke of those who show contempt for the riches of God's kindness, tolerance, and patience because of "stubbornness" and an "unrepentant heart" (Rom. 2:4–5). "The man without the Spirit does not accept the things that come from the Spirit of God, for they are foolishness to him, and he cannot understand them, because they are spiritually discerned" (1 Cor. 2:14). "The god of this age has blinded the minds of unbelievers, so that they cannot see the light of the gospel" (2 Cor. 4:4). Although the light of the sun shines into their very eyeballs the blind cannot see it! Because they are preoccupied with the visible things, their ability to see the invisible atrophies. Hence human mental efforts in the direction of spiritual experience and religion are plagued by error and resist the clear evidence of truth.

This inability of the intellect (*intellectus*) to receive God's redemptive plans (wisdom, *sapientia*) does not necessarily imply limitations on the rational capacity (*ratio*) to investigate changing, material things (*scientia*). Quite the contrary, sinners prefer to make idols of the scientific method, logic, psychology, sociology, even the biblical languages, and other accomplishments in career or family. Thus, however apparently sagacious, the wise of the world are involved in pride and a curious itch for learning the delights of the flesh. They may become experts in rationalizing inherently wrong conduct. Their sins may be splendid, but they are "splendid vices." What about those in the world (in religions, education, etc.) who seek God? Apparently they are only hypothetical persons. In reality, as Paul concludes, "there is no one who understands, no one who seeks God. All have turned away, they have together become worthless; there is no one who does good, not even one" (Rom. 3:11).

For several years Ludwig Wittgenstein realized that he expended his mental abilities on petty and self-destructive concerns. Although study with Bertrand Russell seemed to provide some respite, he left for seclusion in Norway and often thought of suicide. Wittgenstein explained that he thought "he had no right to live in a world where he constantly felt contempt for other people and irritated them by his nervous temperament." He broke off his friendship with Russell primarily because of his own weaknesses and confessed, "My life is *full* of the most hateful and petty thoughts and acts (this is no exaggeration)." Again, "Perhaps you think it is a waste of time for me to think about myself, but how can I be a logician if I am not yet a man! Before *everything else* I must become pure."[83] This outstanding philosopher acknowledged the fact that his great mental abilities were selfishly enslaved and recognized the need for moral purity to set them free.

Depravity and Free Will

A sinful person's capacity of self-determination is fully free when he has both (1) an uncoerced ability to choose among available alternatives (apart from spiritual things) and (2) an ability to do what he desires. Sinners act freely when they choose and act according to their natures. Since the Fall human natures are both finite and depraved, both dependent on God for their life and disposed to rebellion against God's moral rule. The basic conflict is not between the soul and the body, but between the diverted nature of the sinner and his Sustainer.

Both human ontological and depraved natures are logically prior to our existential choices. Atheistic existentialist Jean-Paul Sartre claims that "there is no human nature, since there is no God to conceive it."[84] So he thought that existence (with unlimited choices) logically precedes essences or natures. The existentialists' alleged unlimited human freedom to define ourselves in any way at all seemed to critics a "dreadful" or "a nauseous freedom." In such a total relativism there are no givens for points of reference. Life by the existentialists' totalistic relativism was like traveling in space without any fixed reference point (nothing like a compass, a uniform law of gravity, or a regular speed of light). Totally free existential decisions preceded any patterns.

A total relativist buys freedom in a vacuum by denial of a human nature. Given the reality of God, that dream of freedom is unrealistic, and given the truth of an inscripturated revelation, it is unbiblical. The Old Testament teaches that the moral nature of the human heart determines the morality of the sacrifices, ceremonies, fasts, and feasts. Christ Jesus teaches that the nature of the tree determines the fruit, denying that the fruit determines the nature of the tree. A free choice is not made by a will abstracted from the whole person acting in a vacuum. Whole persons are free when they make uncoerced moral choices and act in accord with their creaturely potential and fallen natures. Realistically, the great freedoms of God's image-bearers must be viewed within the limits of both our finiteness and our fallenness.

Since God sustains us as humans—not gods, angels, or animals—it is pointless to seriously claim free will to choose to be another kind of being. Our dependence on divine providence sets some limits to our meaningful choices, and our God-given finite abilities set some limits to realizing them. Similarly, our fallenness not only blinds our minds and diverts our desires, but also limits our abilities to perform. So we have some limits to our free choices morally. We have numerous alternatives within the range available to our depraved minds, emotions, and wills. But in regard to a whole range of higher spiritual values, motives, and ends we are blinded to them, disenchanted with them, and in rebellion against them.

When choosing and acting according to our sinful natures (doing what comes naturally) we still have *free choice* among the alternatives available to persons unable to receive spiritual things and *self-determination* within the limits of a world curved in upon ourselves. The choices available to fallen "selves" are limited by their fallen inclinations. The unregenerate are "free" when not coerced by an outside force against their wills, but inwardly they are slaves to sin in general and may become addicted to specific unworthy cravings and acts. Alcoholics, for instance, may be unable to change drinking habits that have become compulsive, but as responsible agents they could have stopped before the habit that led to physical dependency. Humans are not the pawns or mere victims of alcohol or other kinds of substances in their environments. Personal agents are responsible also for their responses to the influences of their peers, subcultures, and cultures. "No matter how powerful the external forces," Bernard Ramm argues, "there is a strip of responsibility in every such psyche that cannot be negotiated away."[85]

Freedom of choice and freedom of ability must be distinguished. Sinners may still have some unsuppressed knowledge of God's law by common grace and general illumination. So they may choose not to covet, bear false witness, or get drunk, but they lack the ability to achieve the chosen objective. Depravity does not mean that sinners never have morally worthy ideals that please God. Rather, it means that they lack the proper motivation (the love of God) and that they cannot sustain that conduct perfectly in the strength of the flesh.

It is always important not to make generalizations about human freedom because of the difference that the Fall made, the difference regeneration makes, and the difference glorification will make. Consider now the range of alternative choices available in each situation, whether or not choices contrary to God's pleasure are possible. (1) *Before the Fall* Adam and Eve had the power of contrary choice to please or displease God in motive and act. (2) *Since the Fall* however, unregenerate humans' alternative choices are within a range in which they all come short of pleasing God. The unsaved do not have the contrary choice of loving and serving him above all else, and if they had they would not have the ability to do it. Their ability to achieve the worthy ends chosen is severely limited by their fleshly natures. (3) *After regeneration* believers in Christ have not only the old fallen nature but also a new spiritual nature, and thus they have both the full range of alternatives pleasing and displeasing to God in contrary choice, and the full range of contrary abilities as they walk either in the flesh or in the Holy Spirit. (4) *In the glorified state,* when they are finally made fully like Christ, believers will have only one nature. Finally, when they are glorified with Christ, believers will be confirmed in righteousness and will be like their Lord in being unable to sin. Then they will freely determine themselves according to their glorified natures. Thus human freedom always involves self-determination according to one's nature, but it does not always involve morally good or evil options. At present for the unregenerate, the options are all evil in some degree within the evil kingdom; in the future for the glorified, the options are all righteous in the righteous kingdom.

Depravity and Religion

Holistic depravity results in a total inability to justify ourselves before the Most High. Our repeated idolatrous uses of our abilities to know, love, and serve God leave us alienated from the source of all meaning and purpose in life. With that break in faith we place ourselves at the center of the universe. Attempting to become autonomous, we make ourselves, our family, or our group our "god." There follows the need for endless material acquisition to defend one's self and one's security against all opponents.

So the holistically depraved persistently suppress the truths of theism in universal revelation and of the gospel in special revelation. Or worse, they do so while hypocritically advertising an adherence to them. Countless suppressions of revealed truth are disclosed in the theological diversity of the new religions and cults, and even in the major divisions of christendom. As commendable as these movements may appear to be, no amount of devotion to humanly devised educational, economic, political, moral, or religious causes can by themselves renew anyone's personal fellowship with a holy God. The fact that people do not love God as they ought does not mean that they are irreligious. What is remarkable is what they will worship and serve! After relativizing the Absolute, they may absolutize any relative loyalty. They may place ultimate value in any created thing—spouse, children, business, political party, animals, and endless idols. Both making God small and exalting created things are obviously evil and apparently worthy icons.

Regenerate leaders with the best of motives (love for God) and chosen ends (the glory of God) may choose fleshly strategies or unjust means for attaining them. Not only corruption in the papacy throughout its history but also corruption in high Protestant echelons, even among groups standing for separation from the unbelieving religious and secular world, disclose the need to be aware of subtle temptations in handling finances, maintaining marital fidelity, and keeping the centralities of the Christian faith central.

Depraved People in Society

Sinners fail not only to love God above all, but also to love others as themselves. Sooner or later these delinquencies lead to isolation and loneliness. So sinners miss the mark socially as well as individually. Having alienated themselves from God, sinners alienate themselves also from relatives, in-laws, neighbors, church members, other citizens of their nation, and others of other countries and races and cultural levels. Young sinners, for example, may need to accept responsibility for their own decisions and no longer blame their parents. Like the prodigal son, they may need to come to their senses and confess, "Father [and mother], I have sinned against heaven and against you" (Luke 15:21). Parents as sinners also may need to confess to their children that they have sinned against them by failing in their calling to love faithfully, to educate morally, and to discipline them wisely.

The effects of self-centeredness and injustice have hurt not only the hungry, the poor, and minorities of all sorts but also divinely established institutions of the family, the nation, and the church. So human history has missed the privileges attendant upon authentic caring for others.[86] Those who have no more ultimate concern than themselves become estranged from others and tend toward the idolatry of narcissistic self-worship. To center our highest values on ourselves is sin. Made for God, the human self finds its security, peace, and hope in God and not in itself. Without that foundation, sin shatters the most fundamental relationships we have.

The deceitfulness of fallen human nature may occasion special relational temptations for people with *economic status or power*. The excitement to turn out bigger and better products in greater quantities can be for the good of the users, but it may entail a waste of the earth's limited resources. It may also entail excessive pollution of the air or nearby water supplies. It may needlessly waste coal or gas. If we allow this to happen, we sin against the Creator, his commands, our greedy selves, our neighbors, our descendants, and the creation of the greatest of all designers, architects, artists. Exploitive abuses pervert, waste, and ultimately destroy God's great creation. Whatever new energy sources we may develop we cannot pursue ideals of affluence, comfort, mobility, and leisure indefinitely. The "basic cause of the energy crisis," Wendell Berry insists, "is not scarcity; it is moral ignorance and weakness of character."[87]

Quite apart from theological premises, Berry argues:

> We don't know *how* to use energy, or what to use it *for*. And we cannot restrain ourselves. Our time is characterized as much by the abuse and waste of human energy as it is by the abuse and waste of fossil fuel energy. Nuclear power, if we are to believe its advocates, is presumably going to be well used by the same mentality that has egregiously devalued and misapplied man- and woman-power. If we had an unlimited supply of wind power, we would use that destructively, too, for the same reasons.[88]

Board members, administrators, and managers of businesses ought to avoid possibilities of sinfully exploiting the talents and energies of employees. Employees also need to consider the possible effects of their sinful nature on the quality of their work.

The outworkings of depravity may also be writ large in a city, state, county, province, nation, or the United Nations by those in *political positions of power*. The "powers" (*dynameis*) of this world are distinguished from angels and demons (Rom. 8:38–39). Their philosophies are based on the "basic principles of this world" rather than on Christ (Col. 2:8). The powers were created by Christ (Col. 1:16) and so are not inherently evil. But the great powers of the world and society, though beyond the control of individuals, may come under the control of demons. If and when human or demonic powers are involved in destroying God's creation, Christians must contend against them. Paul exhorts us to contend against the powers of this dark world (Eph. 6:12). Whether they be intellectual, moral, economic, or political forces destructive of humans, they are powers with which we must reckon.[89]

Leaders with power in any type of government may disregard the equality of all people before the law and defraud poor citizens and tourists of their inalienable rights. The temptation to pretensions of unreal power, wisdom, and virtue are far greater for political leaders than for most of us. The poor in spirit, the humble, and the tax collectors receive the benediction of Scripture, not because they are not also evil, but for the reason that they are generally more willing to admit their sinful condition. Governmental leaders are also sinners and should not forget that theirs should be a rule of just principles and values that respect freedom of conscience. The lust for more and more power has defrauded many people of their right to own property. The right to property implied in the commandment not to steal should be protected even against the state. The security of property leads to the propensity to save and to invest. Wendell Berry proposes "that as many as possible should share in the ownership of the land and thus be bound to it by economic interest, by the investment of love and work, by family loyalty, by memory and tradition."[90]

Individual and corporate ownerships may create a multiplicity of power centers to rival that of the state. Thus they need a self-correcting mechanism—the consciences of the individuals who are accountable finally to the divine Judge. When many hold property, political power cannot as easily become a monopoly. Hence with informed, critically thinking citizens a democratic capitalism has the potential to be self-correcting. It can change things other than by force with many consciences appealing to objective moral standards. Add to this the sense of constant readiness to meet our Judge, the greater value of investments in eternity, the need for regular proportionate giving to those in need, and the impetus for regular accounting of vice and virtue in preparation for the final audit of our individual stewardship. The innate selfishness and corruptibility of every human being calls for a system of checks and balances to transform selfishness and corruptibility of people with power into a modicum of creativity, virtue, efficiency, and decency.[91]

Collectively, a peoples' policies may be unjust in business, in society, or in government. Although it is common to blame the evils of the world on certain economic structures, the problem is not that the structures (whether capitalist, socialist, or communist) are inherently evil. In any form of economic system or government sinners can abuse other sinners and flout their attempted independence from God. Nevertheless some economic systems and governments are better than others because they have more checks and balances against sinful misuses of power and provide greater freedom for worship and service of God. As Reinhold Niebuhr put it, "Man's capacity for justice makes democracy possible; but man's inclination to injustice makes democracy necessary."[92]

When any state usurps divine prerogatives, even those who deny the reality of demons call it demonic. Christian theists ought not give to their nations the same degree of allegiance given to God. Our pledge of allegiance to any other power must always be *under* our pledge of allegiance to a personal, transcendent God. We are subject to rulers and authorities in order "to be ready to do whatever is good" (Titus 3:1).

Total Inability

Although fallen people can do many wonderful things, as a consequence of holistic depravity sinners face a *total inability* to change their moral natures or achieve perfect justice in society. So they cannot justify themselves before God. Every aspect of human existence is so selfishly oriented that the best persons in any type of endeavor come short of the ideal. Always in all situations, none of us in ourselves do or can live up to any moral principles we propagate, let alone live up to God's *law*. We are glad for all the elements of truth in religious and philosophical ethical systems. But the higher our moral standards, the farther short even the most sincere fall.

All the good deeds or karma we can possibly accumulate will never suffice for the evils we have done. In fifty years as a missionary to India holding conversations with Hindus and Buddhists, E. Stanley Jones did not find one who had attained release from the bondage of countless reincarnations or rebirths. No Eastern pantheistic-occult or Western secular humanist programs can enable sinners to achieve their highest *human potential*. No naturalistic self-esteem or self-realization programs can change the basic perversion of our moral natures. Neither can any New Age spirits of alleged ascended spiritual masters or spirit-guides forgive sins against the Most High, reconcile people to the Lord of all, or regenerate their natures. Realistically we must acknowledge our *total inability* to save ourselves from our self-centeredness and creature centeredness by any type of individual or collective human, creaturely effort. As fallen people, we are unable to change our natures and so free ourselves from poorly motivated and poorly directed uses of our abilities. As fallen, we are unable to justify ourselves from our objective moral guilt before God's moral law. As fallen, we are unable to reconcile ourselves to a God of holy love.

A Comprehensive Concept of Sin

Comprehensive notions of sin ought not limit human sin to *discrete* willed acts or deny the reality of the sinful nature. Finney called such a denial of the deep-seated nature of sin an abomination. In agreement with Finney we have sought to avoid the idea of sin as an ontological entity or thing. But a biblically informed view of sin must include its pervasiveness from our hearts to our attitudes, thoughts, words, and deeds. A full-orbed view of humanness morally encompasses at least an insolent heart with its consequences for every human function and relationship.

No more can comprehensive concepts of sin limit it to *intentional* acts. The Old Testament makes explicit provision for anyone who unintentionally does what is forbidden in any of the Lord's commands (Lev. 4:2), whether the high priest (vv. 3–12), the whole Israelite community (vv. 13–21), a leader (vv. 22–26), or a member of the community (vv. 27–35). Once a year the high priest offered sacrifice for "the sins the people had committed in ignorance" (Heb. 9:7). Since the law was available, ignorance of it was inexcusable, and infractions were still morally wrong and detrimental. Offerings are stipulated for unintentional sins of the community or individuals (Num. 15:22–29), but the penalty for defiant sins was much more severe, the offender being cut off from the people (vv. 30–31).

Our culpability for our morally evil acts is greater according to our degrees of knowledge and intention. We are most culpable when knowingly and deliberately we sin against ourselves, God, others, and creation. There may be less culpability when we do the same things in ignorance, but that does not make them good. It follows that there are degrees of guilt. Jesus said, "To whom much is given much will be required." Our obligations depend on our intent relative to the extent of the number and importance of moral principles knowingly violated, and the number and quality of the relationships broken, and the amount of human and natural energies used up counterproductively. Fortunately God is the final Judge of the degrees of knowledge and intentionality. We do well to judge ourselves that we be not judged. In relation to the culpability of others, no one person ought to become the accuser, jury, judge, and executioner.

Comprehensive concepts of sin, furthermore, cannot be limited to overt deeds. We may sin not only by acting wrongly, but also by failing to act. So a concept of sin must be broad enough to include acts of omission as well as commission. "Anyone, then, who knows the good he ought to do and doesn't do it, sins" (James 4:17). Jesus had said, "That servant who knows his master's will and does not get ready or does not do what his master wants will be beaten with many blows. But the one who does not know and does things deserving punishment will be beaten with few blows" (Luke 12:47).

How can we define *sin* (sing.)? Sin, or the sinful nature, refers to the common tendency of human hearts since the Fall to disbelieve God's Word, to become disenchanted with God's presence, and to disobey God's revealed moral principles whether by action or inactivity. In short, when we speak of sin, we generally refer to our rebellious nature or inclination.

How, then, can we define *sins* (pl.)? Sins in thought, word, and deed are self-determined, responsible acts or inattentions of morally accountable people who (1) yield to the selfish, evil desires of their depraved natures; (2) inexcusably misuse their intellectual, emotional, and volitional abilities; (3) disrespect others' inalienable rights by treating them unfairly, inconsiderately, or uncaringly; (4) violate revealed moral principles necessary for meaningful human existence; or (5) otherwise reject God's wise rule of their lives by seeking to live autonomously.

Every Human Sins

Can any truth claim ever be more fully confirmed by overwhelming empirical evidence than the claim that human beings are not morally what they ought to be? All ordinarily born persons who come to an age of moral accountability misuse their abilities, break relationships, and fail to please God by obeying moral principles. Those who have no special revelation sin against the truth about God that can be known in nature and against his moral requirements in their hearts. The Jews, who received the ministry of the Old Testament prophets, sinned also against that additional revelation. So did the people who heard and saw the ministry of Jesus Christ and the Gospels. And those who also had the revelation of the apostles and the rest of the New Testament have failed to live up to it. All Jews and Gentiles are sinners (Rom. 1:18–3:20). All people sin, whether poor or rich, male or female, older or younger, activists or researchers, politicians or scientists, students or professors, seminarians or veteran missionaries. "As it is written: 'There is no one righteous, not even one; there is no one who understands, no one who seeks God' " (3:10).

What about the "innocence" of children and adolescents? Recalling his childhood after he became morally accountable, Augustine wanted to love his Creator, but did not. He could not remember a time when he was innocent. He knew that, like David, he must have been conceived and born in iniquity (Ps. 51:5). He asked God, Suppose I don't love you, is it all that important? More than God he loved leisure play for its own sake, disliked his studies in school, and hated the discipline of parents and teachers. Many destructive delights pulled him away from God. As a student of rhetoric he sought a reputation for eloquence. He would be very careful not by a slip of the tongue to "murder" a word like "human being." If the fury of his feeling succeeded in actually bringing about the murder of his enemy (a human being), he would not give it a second thought. He told many lies to his teachers and parents and stole things he did not need, just for the love of stealing. Augustine loved sports and plays and "itched" to imitate the actors in the spectacles. When he was outplayed in sports, he tried to win games by cheating; yet when he was caught, he would start an argument rather than admit he was wrong. Meanwhile if he caught someone else cheating, he became furious and accused that person in no uncertain terms. Is this the innocence of childhood? Summing up his youth, Augustine confesses, "I sought for pleasure, honor, and truth, not in God, but in his creatures, including myself and others, and so fell into sorrow, confusion, and error."[93]

Why Every Last Person Sins

It is not enough to say with Reinhold Niebuhr that sin is inevitable. That simply moves the problem back a step. Then we must ask, Why is moral evil inevitable? *Why* does every morally accountable person sin?

Surely if by nature we were morally and spiritually good, or even neutral, there would be some people who would not yield to the influences of a poor environment. The most adequate account of the universality of sin traces it to our inheritance of an inner propensity to misuse our abilities by worshiping and serving ourselves more than our Creator. In the words of our Lord, "Flesh gives birth to flesh" (John 3:6). Jesus explained that evil fruit is produced because the tree is evil. He viewed humans as by nature inclined to desire, think, and do evil.

At its headwaters the stream of the human race went astray—in the space-time Fall. Granting the unity of the race and a traducian origin of the soul, each person receives from fallen parents, and they from theirs, back to Adam and Eve, an inherent tendency to sin. That is why every last human being inevitably sins. Everyone sins because everyone has an innate disposition to sin. We are sinners by choice because we are sinners by nature, and we are sinners by nature because we are sinners by choice. We are self-determined, but the nature of the self is inclined to rebel against moral norms. We cannot blame our sin on others or on circumstances. Circumstances provide only the occasion to yield to temptations or resist them. As self-determining agents we freely choose according to our natures. Hence our best activities are acknowledgments of the deceitfulness of our hearts (Jer. 17:9). As one sophomore put it, we are "primordial stinkers." We bring with us to our environments an inherent tendency to mess up everything.

Justice for All, Guilt for All

Because the Scriptures teach that God as the final Judge is just and that God's purposes involve moral laws, it is impossible to eradicate legal terminology from an understanding of sin. The loving and righteous Judge finds human sinners *morally guilty* (Rom.1:18–3:20). On evidence beyond any reasonable doubt God finds us guilty of rebellion against the Source of life and the principles for sustaining meaningful life on earth. Having undermined the bases of life with its values, we receive the deserved sentence, we are *destined to die* (Rom. 6:23). All face the physical death of separation of the spirit from the body (James 2:26). All sinners are spiritually dead or alienated from God's fellowship (Eph. 4:18). And, apart from receiving the atonement of the Messiah, all will continue to be estranged from God eternally (John 3:36).

What are the *grounds* of judgment, guilt, and punishment? Is God's entire judgment system just? Consider the following points:

1. We are accountable for breaking faith with the Creator (who has life in himself), defecting from the values indispensable to meaningful life as God's image-bearers. On these grounds alone all fallen people are indeed objectively guilty, whether or not they have guilt feelings. Before God himself we find ourselves repeatedly guilty of illicit desires, relationships, words, and acts. Guilt feelings that are not rooted in such sinful desires, relationships, and acts may be dismissed by friends and counselors with ease. But real guilt is incurred from idolatrous desires, the

breaking of relationship with God, and defecting from God's kingdom.

2. God's image-bearers are specifically accountable for moral excellence as disclosed in God's moral law. God revealed his changeless moral nature and its norms for life in relation to himself and others in three major formulations: (1) the basic moral requirements implanted in human hearts (Rom. 2:14–15), (2) similar principles disclosed for the commonwealth of Israel (Exod. 20:1–17), and (3) nine of the Ten Commandments repeated in the New Testament for the guidance of believers in churches. Not one of Adam's depraved race has measured up to the moral law in any of its formulations every day of his life. All who have come to an age of responsibility for decisions between right and wrong are accountable for their behavior. All who inexcusably sin are under condemnation (Rom. 1:18–3:20).

3. Another ground of divine judgment is deliberate disbelief of the gospel and rejection of Christ (John 3:36; Heb. 2:2–4). Although all are under the sentence of separation from God for time and eternity and await its execution, not all have the sentence executed. Believers in Christ do not face that punishment, because their substitute suffered it in their place. To reject Christ's atonement is to reject the one basis on which God can remain just and with integrity justify the ungodly (Rom. 3:25). Those who never heard of Christ are not said to be punished on the basis of rejecting him but on the basis of the revelation they did have (Rom. 1–3). The unevangelized are responsible for the moral law they did know and inexcusably failed fully to keep. "Whoever does not believe stands condemned already because he has not believed in the name of God's one and only Son" (John 3:18).

The general principle of judgment is that to whom much is given, of them much is required (Luke 12:48). We have degrees of responsibility according to the amount of truth revealed to us. A just judge gives a person exactly what is deserved. The Judge of all the earth will not punish anyone more than he or she deserved or merited. Although all are guilty in some measure, there are different degrees of premeditated disbelief and disobedience. As there are degrees of light and responsibility, so there are degrees of punishment (Matt. 11:20–24; Heb. 2:2–3).

4. God also judges the entire race for the one sin of Adam (Rom. 5:12, 16, 18). On what basis can we be guilty for the sin of another? Although Paul does not make the basis explicit in Romans 5, he emphasizes elsewhere a realistic solidarity of the race. From the Judeo-Christian point of view, humans are not a mere company of individuals like angels. God apparently created each angel, for angels do not marry or procreate. All humans, in contrast, compose a single race, for God commanded the original parents to be fruitful, increase in number, and fill the earth (Gen. 1:28). Eve is the "mother of all the living" humans (Gen. 3:20). The genealogies trace all humans back to Adam (Gen. 5; 1 Chron. 1:1; Luke 3:38). Paul could say to the Athenians, "From one man [God] made every nation of men, that they should inhabit the whole earth (Acts 17:26).

The oneness of the human race, thoughtful Christians recognize, is supported also by the natural fatherhood of God and brotherhood of all mankind. Even though not morally or spiritually children of God in Christ by the new birth, all men and women have physical life and breath by the providence of our Father who is in heaven. The providential unity of humanity also provides a basis for viewing all the descendants of Adam as organically one with their forefather. Although Paul did not explicitly refer to Adam's natural headship of humankind in Romans 5, he simply assumed a natural headship of Adam in his theological argument. On the same assumption he wrote that "in Adam all die" (1 Cor. 15:21–22).

What about the moral and legal standing of infants who die? Infants born of flesh are flesh (John 3:6; cf. Ps. 51:5; Eph. 2:3); they are included in the universal sentence of the race in Adam (Rom. 5:16, 18) and physically die (v. 12). Nevertheless infants who die do not suffer the eternal penalty, for *that penalty falls only on those who themselves responsibly sin.* Parents who responsibly sinned in the wilderness died there and did not enter the Promised Land. But children who did not yet "know good from bad" were not punished for their parents' sins; they entered the Promised Land (Deut. 1:39). The age of responsibility here indicated was twenty years for inclusion in the census of adult citizens (Num. 14:29–31). Other passages show that children may suffer the natural consequences of their parents' sins until the third and fourth generations (Exod. 20:5; 34:7), but their spiritual relation to God, whether good or bad, was not determined by their parents. "The soul who sins is the one who will die" (Ezek. 18:20). Children are not capable of responsibly committing the sins attributed to those who eternally alienate themselves from God. For reasons like these, minors who die before reaching moral accountability, will not suffer the execution of the penalty of imputed condemnation.

Since infants cannot repent and believe to receive the benefits of Christ's atonement, they must receive them by a special application. Theirs is not a different ground of salvation, but a different mode of application.[94] Punishment in Scripture is always merited and fits the crime. Infants who die, not knowing right from wrong, are not punished eternally for their parents' sins. That principle is operative when parents who sinned in the wilderness would not go in to the Promised Land, but their children who did not know good from bad would go in (Deut. 1:39). Children may suffer temporal consequences of their parents' sins to the third and forth generation, but the eternal welfare of each soul is determined by itself irregardless of whether the parents were wicked or good (Ezek. 18). So, although under the sentence of eternal death by reason of the solidarity of the race, infants who have not themselves responsibly sinned, will not suffer eternally.

Other indications that children will be saved in addition to those from the general principles of divine judgment come from Christ's special concern for them. Jesus said that children exemplified the humility of his kingdom (Matt. 18:2–5). They should not be caused to stumble (vv. 6–9) and should not be looked down on (v. 10). Furthermore, "the Father is not willing any of these little ones should be lost" (vv. 12–14). "Let the little children come to me," Jesus said, "for the kingdom of heaven belongs to such as these" (19:14). Although these passages are not as explicit as we might like, they may justify a special application of the provisions of Christ's atonement to children. Since they have not responsibly committed any sins and have no sins of which to repent, and since they could not consciously believe on Christ to deliver them from their innate inclination to sin, surely Christ will pardon them of their sinful natures and welcome them to his kingdom, whether or not the parents are in the covenant, whether or not they have had the child undergo infant baptism or last rites.

It can be of considerable comfort to grieving parents to assure them that a child's death is a sure sign of his or her election. This doctrine of justification at death for infants who have not become moral agents can be extended to others whose development has not ever attained a state of moral accountability. It cannot be extended, however, to any who have themselves responsibly sinned. That would contradict other express principles of moral judgment.

APOLOGETIC INTERACTION

Should Theology's Starting Point Be Human Need?

Ludwig Feuerbach's theology is an illustration of what happens when one begins theology with anthropology under the assumption that one can know nothing in itself. Emphasizing human experience with Schleiermacher, he concluded that all his alleged knowledge of God is merely an enlargement of ideas about human experience. His "theology" turned out to be nothing but an abstraction and externalization of humanism. His "knowledge of God" turned out to be merely his knowledge of humanity.[95]

Rudolph Bultmann also started with interpretations of humanity's needs. Considering Heidegger's existentialist philosophy the closest to the heart of the New Testament message, he assumed that our selfhood is not the expression of a pregiven nature but rather that it is created in personal choices. Subjectivity became subjectivism when he found it impossible to talk about God's transcendence and his action in history. Lacking any ontological referent for God, statements about God again turned out to refer to humans (except for a contentless "faith"). Bultmann's thought was more anthropology than theology.[96]

Paul Tillich's method of correlation also began with an analysis of the human situation. Tillich sought to give Christian answers to the existential questions stimulated. Human existence, he felt, is filled with anxiety and meaninglessness. It is estrangement. Reconciliation is a matter of anticipation, expectation, and an unfounded faith, but not of reality.[97] He ruled out all but one cognitive statement about God in himself: "The statement that God is being-itself is a nonsymbolic statement."[98] Tillich experienced the healing power of symbols that point to "the ground of being." He considered the Fall to symbolize the human situation universally. Tillich's analysis of human need can contribute in some measure to an understanding of our need, but it fails to acknowledge a personal God to whom we are to be reconciled, the reality of sinful human nature, and objective guilt before God's law. Although Tillich knows one cognitive assertion about God, most of his "theology" turns out to be anthropology.

Reinhold Niebuhr supplies another example of beginning theology with an existentialist analysis of human needs. As a result of the paradox of nature and spirit, he thought, we are anxious about our existence. Anxiety is not sin, but it leads inevitably either to sinful pride or to sensuality. To meet these needs Niebuhr offers faith in Christian myths. He thought cognitive knowledge of God impossible because of an alleged dialectic between eternity and time. With only paradoxical metaphysical knowledge and few criteria for selection among human mythologies, some have wondered why he chose Christian myths over those of the attractive mythologies of the Greeks or Hindus. Niebuhr's most important work begins, "Man has always been his own most vexing problem." After a study of Niebuhr's trenchant analysis of the human predicament in *The Nature and Destiny of Man,* one becomes convinced that if his mythological prescription is all we have, man will continue to be "his own most vexing problem."[99]

Well-meaning theologians who start with descriptions of human needs but have no cognitive revelation find difficulty getting beyond human experience to the living God who thinks, feels, wills, speaks, and relates in holy love. Without a cognitive revelation from God, the finest finite, fallen minds distort the truth of general revelation and know neither God nor themselves in themselves. Having sold the birthrights to truth in order to be relevant at their times, these theologians come short of a biblical diagnosis of human need itself. None of them soundly concluded that our deepest problems involve more than estrangement from ourselves and anxiety about the meaningfulness of our lives, fate, and death. None discovered that humans have real guilt before God's objective, moral law and a depraved nature that explains why all inevitably alienate themselves from their Creator.

We do better to include among our initial hypotheses a biblically disclosed assessment of our deepest need and see if without contradiction it accounts more coherently for the givens of inner and outer human existence. A comprehensive classical doctrine of sin as developed in the Systematic Formulation above proposes a more adequate and viable explanation of our moral experience than contradictory options. Our view makes sense of our goodness, for the *imago Dei* has not been totally destroyed, and of our depravity, for we lack ability to do the good we envision. The doctrines of creation in the *imago Dei* and the factual fall provide the most coherent accounts of humankind's awesome potential for great good or inestimable evil. The explanatory power of a biblical assessment of our moral and spiritual need fits human social experience also, including corruption in high places, oppression of the poor, countless efforts to justify oneself (in philosophies and religions before moral law or karma), and an inner longing not filled by anything in creation.

Convinced of both the truth and relevance of a biblical diagnosis of human fallenness, the doctrine of humanness as fallen provides a beneficial conversational point of contact with people anxious about human destiny. With the nuclear threat to a third of the population on earth, humanistic concerns are understandable! According to the Book of Revelation, however, not all life will be destroyed before Christ returns. Points of contact with non-Christians include more than our humanness as persons, they include also our unfaithfulness to the source of all being, values, and beauty, and our unethical conduct toward God's creation and especially toward his image-bearers.

Are Monistic Diagnoses Coherent or Viable?

The Neoplatonic hypothesis that moral evil is a mere *privation of being*—a lack of being and goodness—or *finiteness,* helped Augustine overcome the Manichaean notion that sin is a distinct material substance, but it did not for long adequately explain his experience. His problems did not stem from a lack of being, but from a perverse use of his own capacities. He struggled with the aversion of his will against God's desires. The hypothesis that sin was a rebellion of the will against its Creator made more sense of Augustine's own experience. He admitted that he had stolen pears, not for the sake of need, but for the sheer delight of getting away with it. Sin as rebellion also best accounted for the crumbling Roman Empire in Augustine's time. It remains the most coherent view of personal and social corruption today. Our deepest problem is not what we lack in ourselves but our failure to use to their full potential the abilities God gave us.

Many Hindu, Buddhist, and New Age monists today think that humans are holographic manifestations of God and that evils stem from a lack of consciousness of our infinite potential. In their imagined reality we are small fields of energy in one all-encompassing field of energy. By considering our spirits metaphysically distinct from God, they feel, we suffer from many illusions. Humans are not individual persons; there is but one world soul. Humanity's deepest problems stem from a lack of knowledge of our own pantheistically conceived inner divinity. Evil is an illusion that can be overcome by visualizing things as divine or imagining that we can evolve beyond moral evil.

Resurgent monistic diagnoses of the human predicament come short in all three criteria of truth. Let us consider the serious flaws that monism suffers:

1. Monistic explanations of evil are *self-contradictory*. If there were but one world soul or divine causal agent, then who is it that suffers the illusion of evil's reality? No other "mortal mind" exists to be deceived into accepting the reality of physical bodies or sin. Paradoxically a New Age ad said, "It is a sin to call a person a sinner!" Furthermore, in a monistic worldview there are no distinct other persons to persuade of pantheism, for all persons (sic) are one.

The monistic hypothesis not only is self-contradictory; it also flatly contradicts biblical teaching. The Scriptures never blur the bifurcation between the being of the eternal Creator and the being of created image-bearers. Any functional, moral, or reflectional likeness to God in contingent beings ought not be confused with continuity with the noncontingent being of God. Although limited, physical, and distinct from God, humans as created were "very good." Since the Fall humans experience a real difference between good and evil, between uprightness and unrighteousness.

Monists who regard contradictions acceptable abort any meaningful thought and communication. If two contradictories may both be true, then we may affirm not only that "all is one" but also that "some beings are not one." Again, we may affirm both that "all evil is unreal," and that "some evil is real." If we may assent to contradictories as true, then all statements are true. In that case "true" has lost all significance, and we may as well hold that all statements are false. All meaning and communication become impossible if we can affirm and deny the same thing at the same time and in the same respect.

2. Monistic explanations of morality and immorality also lack explanatory power. A mere illusion of our distinctness fails to account for our personal self-consciousness and accountable self-determination. No person ever advances beyond the real differences between good and evil. Humans everywhere and always are accountable moral agents. Any hypothesis that regards humans divine fails to explain adequately humanity's pervasive envy, jealousy, bitterness, hatred, covetousness, lust, terrorism, drug abuse, spouse abuse, child abuse, and murders. A far more probable proposal is that humans in every generation have an inherent inclination to destructiveness. The alleged unreality of sin, sickness, and death is also counteracted experientially by the pervasiveness of churches, hospitals, and funeral homes. The Bible's teaching never minimizes the sinfulness of evil, even in the lives of the heros. Realistically Scripture asserts that humans are *not what they ought to be*. The deepest human problem is not ignorance, but insolence.

3. A monistic view of injustice is not only logically inconsistent and factually inadequate, it also *lacks existential viability*. No finite, fallen person can live unhypocritically with belief in his or her own divinity. Devotion to hatha yoga

exercises, or mindless meditations cannot fundamentally change our ontological reality or our moral perversity. Persistence in disciplined self-mortification to produce sensory deprivation or altered states of consciousness may seem to attune adherents to the cosmos, but they are not transcendent enough. They do not provide a just basis on which to reconcile sinners to the Holy One. No imagined paranormal activities or quantum leaps in our spiritual evolution can ever make us ontologically divine or morally as righteous as Christ. We agree with Marilyn Ferguson that human beings need personal and social transformation.[100] But *self*-transformations, however sincere and sustained, are insufficiently radical. Beliefs that monistic visions will save humanity are unfounded. Where such visions have flourished, as in India, they have not approached utopia. "The problem is human perversity, not human perception."[101]

Monistic views are not viable insofar as they think that our unique personalities are unreal appearances and that a belief in their reality is the source of evil. Transpersonal psychologist Ken Wilbur imagines that

> mankind will never, but never, give up this type of murderous aggression, war, oppression, and repression, attachment, and exploitation, until men and women give up that property called personality. Until, that is, they awaken to the transpersonal. Until that time, guilt, murder, property, and personality will always remain synonymous.[102]

In contrast, we have presented evidence that humanity's deepest predicament arises, not from being distinct persons, but from our faithless and unprincipled use of our abilities to think, feel, will, discern, and relate. Each person in God's creation is of inestimable worth. What God wants to take from us is not our ontological uniqueness, but our unjust desires! Holistic depravity means that no repetitious visualizations can ever satisfy justice, change our own natures, or put ourselves right with God. We fallen people need Jesus Christ's satisfaction of justice in our place, the Holy Spirit's regeneration of our inner natures, and the Father's gracious acceptance of us as repentant believers into his fellowship.

Is Human Nature Morally Neutral?

Unitarianism strongly opposed the doctrines of depravity and condemnation (even more than it attacked Trinitarianism).[103] Unitarians alleged that the original nature of human persons was *morally neutral*. Human conduct becomes "sinful" when it becomes antisocial. To act contrary to accepted social customs or mores is wrong. Antisocial conduct, furthermore, could become psychologically unhealthy. Immoral behavior is maladaptive rather than adaptive behavior. It violates relatively useful laws for a modicum of social decorum. From a biblical perspective, however, the adjustment given top priority is adjustment to God. Maladjustment to God and his moral rule is far more devastating than maladjustment to an established society or to its reformers and revolutionaries.

According to secular humanist Corliss Lamont, human nature is neither morally good, nor depraved, but morally neutral. "What the scientific study of human motives shows is that human nature is neither essentially bad nor essentially good, neither essentially selfish nor essentially unselfish, neither essentially warlike nor essentially pacific."[104] Because Lamont finds human nature "essentially flexible and educable," he rejects the "hoary half-truth" that "you can't change human nature." How does he expect to change it? "One of the great aims of Humanism is the transformation and socialization of human motives. This is a sector where human nature can be drastically reconditioned and reshaped."[105] To do so he appeals to an unending debt to the collective culture of mankind and a corresponding obligation to serve the common good. Apparently, the most prominent scientific humanists of each generation define for the rest what the collective culture and the common good requires. Lamont lists their "doctrinal statements" in an appendix that includes "Humanist Manifesto I, 1933," and "Humanist Manifesto II, 1973").

Lamont laments the fact that propaganda and cultural conditioning spur on "selfish, and violent impulses."[106] He does not say where "selfish and violent impulses" come from. The admission of evil impulses seems contradictory to Lamont's theory of essential moral neutrality. The function of the community (school) for this humanist is "to guide and redirect emotional life; to replace antisocial passions, motives, ambitions, and habits by those that are geared to the common good."[107] Humanism's naïve confidence in education to solve humanity's problems arises from its unrealistic optimism about the pliability of the human moral condition. And with no absolute right or wrong, Lamont's humanism replaces good and evil in view of God's revelation with social and antisocial behavior in the eyes of influential humanists. Secular humanism has had a powerful influence on the teachers and administrators of our tax-supported public schools, and some of these leaders of today's youth are now open to pantheistic and occult cosmic humanisms. Even if Christian schools are proposed as an alternative, moral theists ought not abandon public education to naturalistic and pantheistic philosophies of education. In pluralistic societies academic freedom should give equal opportunity to a view of humanity in the moral context of a theistic world-view.

Is Human Nature Essentially Good?

Confucianism claims that by nature human persons are *inherently good.* Mencius taught that human nature is essentially good. Any evil in it results from changes made on it by external influences.[108]

Liberal theology in the first half of the twentieth century also denied an inherited moral depravity, affirming instead humanity's inherent goodness and inevitable progress.

In the liberal tradition theologian L. Harold DeWolf rejects the Augustinian doctrine of hereditary sinfulness and imputed guilt. The liberal theologian does admit that sin came into the world through one man and that sin begets sin, both within the sinning individual and in those he or she influences. Sin is so influential that "all human beings who who have long lived at a responsible level of development are actual sinners."[109] Why do all intrinsically good people inevitably sin? All persons suffer temptations to sin and disabilities in resisting temptations, DeWolf claims, as a result of the sins of past generations.[110] The influence of previous generations has so effectively counteracted our essential goodness that

> we do not find it equally as easy to be true to our duty and to be false to it. To relax moral effort and "let nature take its course" is to drift into indolence, sensuous indulgence, cowardice and selfishness. We do not drift into industry, purity, courage and loyal generosity. Movement toward moral perfection is upstream.[111]

Liberalism's confidence that education and other influences would result in inevitable progress has been shattered by the Nazi holocaust, by repeated wars, and by many acts of terrorism.

But having admitted the universality and inevitability of sin, the liberal doctrine of humanity's inherent goodness can apply only to the time before the Fall. Liberals need a literal, historical fall to account for the radical change in humanity's moral condition. Instead of their earlier naïve faith in inevitable human moral and cultural evolution, liberals now have a pessimistic view, sensing a devolution from humanity's original goodness to its universal corruption. Early historical indications are that it did not take centuries for the Fall to occur.

Edward Wilson's attempt to articulate a socio-biological rationale for the pervasiveness of evil traces moral evil to *our gene pool*. It is our genes that make us what we are. In the light of the evidence above for both the inner spirit and the body, this physical explanation appears to be oversimplified, though it may be helpful as far as it goes. Wilson's prescription for humanity's problems through the gene of altruism also seems insufficient. A biological basis of all social behavior cannot account for the fact that in recorded history the human species has been at war forty-eight percent of the time.[112]

Sigmund Freud's explanation of human fallibility suggests that it can be traced, not to a sinful nature, but to *childhood traumas* that produce conflicts within the self between the drives, impulses, and determinations (the id); the conscience (superego); and the socially acceptable self (the ego). As descriptively accurate as this view of such inner conflicts may be and as helpful for counseling purposes, it fails to explain the source of the universally acknowledged higher values and, particularly for present purposes, the universal and inevitable antagonism to them.[113]

B. F. Skinner attributed human immorality to parental and societal *punishment*. Denying freedom and blaming punishment for creating more evils, he has not accounted for the origin of evil. Many have lived with little punishment during a permissive generation in wonderful environments controlled by many scientific advancements. But sin continues to multiply in its subtlety and extent.[114] The truth in the diagnoses of these writers may help in recognizing and alleviating symptoms, but their diagnoses fail to identify the underlying cause of universal and inevitable sinfulness.

Are Society's Structures the Source of Human Evil?

Karl Marx explained human evil as *economic maladjustment*. In *Das Kapital* he attributed the inevitable injustices of humans to one another to dialectical conflicts between two classes, the bourgeois (the haves) and the proletarians (the have nots). But such a dialectical determinism does not do justice to the evidence above for personal self-determination. The continued power of individual choice may be seen in the dissidents' refusal to conform to the Soviet's "classless society."[115] Alexander Solzhenitsyn and others have demonstrated that moral decisions come from within and are not imposed on us even by a coercive society. Class conflicts contribute to much human evil, and as far as possible ought to be justly avoided. But apart from an intrinsically sinful disposition, class conflicts do not account for all the evils of mankind. A Marxist diagnosis does not explain the evils done by people of the same class to one another, nor does it explain evils that persist in "socialist" efforts toward classless societies.

Liberation theologians also attribute the root of human evil to economic oppression of the poor by unjust *social structures*. Jose Miranda, in *Marx and the Bible,* argues that for Paul, sin has supraindividual dimensions. Sin has characteristics, he claims, not reducible to the sum of individual sins. Miranda quotes Romans 7:17, 20: "As it is, it is no longer I myself who do it [evil], but it is sin living in me." A "supraindividual force," he claims, gains control over whole peoples and becomes incarnated in social structures. The power of sin increases its own power and control over people and "forces" us to act in a certain way even while we try to be conscientious observers of the law and think we are struggling against sin.[116]

Although Miranda apparently considers these coercive forces demonic, he does not appear to attribute them to literal demons. He extends Paul's references to "the law" beyond the laws of Israel to those of all civilizations and attributes evils to the oppression of all social orders, and he understands deliverance from "the present evil age" (Gal. 1:4) to be synonymous with deliverance from "the law" (4:5). Law as the primary structural focus of societies is sin incarnate, the institutional condensation of sin created to control humans. Sin, he thinks, is identical to civilization as specified or codified in its laws.[117] Miranda seems to attribute all human evil to oppressive social orders or to all the laws of civilization.

"Christ has redeemed us from the curse of the law by becoming a curse for us" (Gal. 3:13). As Christ became a curse for us, Miranda explains, "he was incarnated into the incarnation of all the human injustice which has been accumulated in civilization and the law."[118] Marxists believed that dialectics would produce justice in the world. Miranda believes that faith in Christ will produce justice in the world—real justice, not merely imputed justice.[119] Marx, Miranda says, is on the same side as the biblical authors, for he does believe there is hope for our world.[120] Authentic justice is justice for all peoples, for humans, not as abstractions, but as working, struggling persons[121] Early liberal thinking attributed human evil to antisocial behavior; liberationists now attribute evil to acceptance of the social status quo.

As challenging and relevant as Miranda's interpretation of structural sin seems, there are several debatable points: (1) We are not justified in making generalizations about all human laws from Paul's references to Old Testament Jewish laws given by special revelation or even Pharisaic interpretations of them. The Ten Commandments and other biblical laws cannot be regarded as the incarnation of evil. We must distinguish those laws that accurately express principles of God's moral nature from those that do not. Believers in an inscripturated revelation concerning the law of Israel cannot accept generalizations about all laws as sin incarnate and oppressive. Miranda's approach hopefully will increase our sensitivity to unjust social structures, unjust administrators, and enforcement personnel wherever they are found. But Jesus and Paul did not attack all the laws of civilization. They opposed superficial interpretations of revealed principles by inauthentic Pharisees. God's revealed laws are still to be reflected in society to restrain outbreaks of evil among depraved people.

The problems with lawful societies did not stem from laws, for the law Paul spoke about is holy, just, and true (Rom. 7:7, 12). The problems with the law, Paul taught, resulted from the fact that it "was weakened by the sinful nature" (8:3). Miranda's diagnosis fails to pierce to the hearts of those in power in any social structure. His diagnosis is not sufficiently radical. He needs to challenge, not all civilization, but the moral depravity in the hearts of oppressive political leaders. The deepest problems with the law Paul talked about were more personal than structural. Paul himself, in his inner being delighted in the law of God (7:22). But he found another principle in his fallen nature: the "flesh" (v. 18) waging war against that delight. The most important battle Paul fought was between two natures within himself. In the final judgment, God judges, not social structures or legal codes, important as these are, but individuals responsible for formulating, administering, and enforcing just laws and living by them.

The best way to liberate the oppressed is to deliver the dynamite of the gospel to the oppressors to regenerate their hearts to renew their abilities to think, feel, and act justly. Every other legal and moral means toward justice should also be utilized. But no other will be as effective as the power that turned an oppressor named Saul into an evangelist-theologian named Paul. Surely some cultures are to be preferred to others, but in the power centers of every culture oppressive evils may come to dominate. With apologies to Lord Acton (who said that power corrupts and absolute power corrupts absolutely), it is not legal power that corrupts humans, but corrupt human natures that abuse legally given powers. It is not absolute power that corrupts humans, but fallen humans corrupt any situation in which they are unaccountable to others. Because humans are the source of evil, no one is good enough or wise enough, as Plato concluded in his *Republic*, to be given unaccountable, absolute power. Without a doctrine of original sin, Miranda lacks an explanation of the inherent evil of every culture, subculture, and institution.

The failure of all of these views to explain the problem of evil indicates that acts of sin do not originate with the social or structural environments. Sinful acts are not merely conditioned responses to inherited cultural givens or unfortunate social situations. External temptations presented by the great deceiver provided occasions for our original parents to sin, but the act of yielding to the temptations came from within them. They deliberately sinned in a most positive context before the curse. Personal sin is not caused by the environment, nor by the tempter. Moral decisions and actions originate, after all, in the hearts of morally accountable human agents (Prov. 4:23–27; Matt. 12:33–37; Mark 7:14–23). Persons, not situations, are the efficient, culpable causes of moral evil.

Our environment today is far from that before the Fall. The different degrees of difficulties in our environments came about as a result of divine judgment on personal sin. Environmental and structural hypotheses emphasize occasions of evil that we ought to avoid when possible. Not every human being inevitably responds to situational factors (injustice) in unethical ways: unjust and oppressive acts of enemies may be occasions either to lure us toward sinful acts in turn or to return good for evil. Even the characters of unregenerate self-determined spirits are not determined by the circumstances. The unregenerate make their own choices and exercise their own abilities in accord with their own desires. Unless we are forcefully coerced, we are not mere victims of an evil society. Under identical conditions (such as those at the stock exchange on Wall Street) one person may yield to temptation to dishonesty, another may not. Or the same person may yield to the attendant temptations at one time and not at another. Motives also may vary, and those of the fallen and unregenerate may never be for the glory of God. But occasions of sin must not be confused with the efficient or blameworthy personal causes of sin.

Why Do All Humans Sin?

What accounts for the universal and inevitable sin of human beings? We have set forth above a biblical case for receiving from our sinful parents an *inclination to desire and do* what is contrary to the Spirit (Gal. 5:16–17) involving a traducian view of the origin of souls and the solidarity of the human race. Here we seek to point up the adequacy of the biblical view to account for human experience.

The view that humans have endemic sinful tendencies accounts for the *universality of evil* better than the view that blames infinitely variable external influences. It indicates why humans of any cultures invariably (1) desire to be like God, (2) challenge the wisdom of God's revealed truth, (3) rebel against God's rule by moral law, and (4) tend to reject the gracious offer of the gospel concerning Christ's atoning provisions. In all of our mature stages of growth, more blameworthy than any influences of our peers, parents, or teachers in our lives are our own fallen desires, purposes, and distorted interpretations.

Overwhelming evidence that humans bring a sinfully inclined nature to their environments can be found in any cultural context. Sin breaks out and bears its bitter fruit in communist, socialist, and capitalist economies. People bring sinful tendencies with them to all areas of society, not only to the inner cities but also to the suburbs and rural farms and castles. Education is no cure, for the highly educated struggle with sinful inclinations as well as those not formally educated. Immoralities and injustices occur among prominent educators, legislators, law-enforcement personnel, and prison officials.

Thus the Christian doctrine that we are sinfully inclined at the control center of our thoughts, desires, and wills provides the most coherent way to account for humanity's moral experience. Those holding to the hypothesis of an original tendency to sin can understand why people of all levels are, according to one author, chronic, systematic, and hypocritical liars.[122] We can understand why literature portrays the story of human existence as one of a conflict between good and evil and why philosophies and systems of ethics that do not face up to human endemic evil lack realism, relevance, and explanatory power.

The Christian doctrine of depraved tendencies helps us understand why every psyche is to some degree a disordered psyche. We can understand why all of us can use physical, psychological, and spiritual counsel and help. Given a view of inherited fleshly desires, we can understand political and economic unrest and the need for accountability and as many checks and balances as possible in order to achieve as much justice as possible. The doctrine of a universal, inherent tendency to sin accounts also for actual sins by religious people in religious organizations: mainline, evangelical, separatist, and cultic. In all honesty before God, others, and ourselves, we must admit our own sinful tendencies. Until we acknowledge our sinful desires, we cut ourselves off from the possibility of radical forgiveness, regeneration, and reconciliation.

Has Prevenient Grace Removed Inherited Depravity?

Although people are by nature depraved, Wesleyans and Arminians suggest that the Holy Spirit in a universal ministry of grace (based on Christ's universal atonement) removes from all people hereditary corruption and guilt for Adam's sin.[123] As a result of this alleged prevenient grace, our inherent depravity becomes only a hypothetical condition already universally alleviated.

We have been able to find no explicit scriptural basis for this presalvation work of the Holy Spirit enabling all human beings to respond to moral law or the gospel. John 16:8–10 makes it clear that the Spirit convicts the world of guilt for sin because the world remains in unbelief, but that passage does not say that the Holy Spirit changes the fleshly desires and abilities of all fallen people. An appeal to Titus 2:11 also fails to support a doctrine of prevenient grace. It was Christ, not the invisible Holy Spirit, who "appeared" for all (2 Tim. 1:10) and will appear again (Titus 2:13). Whatever Paul teaches in Titus 2:11 does not contradict the condition he described a few verses earlier: "to those who are corrupted and do not believe, nothing is pure. In fact, both their minds and consciences are corrupted. They claim to know God, but by their actions they deny him. They are detestable, disobedient and unfit for doing anything good" (Titus 1:15–16). In Paul's mind the prior advent of Christ for all people had not in fact changed the unbelievers' inability to respond to spiritual things mentally, morally, or volitionally. For that change a special work of the Holy Spirit is needed.

All the passages on the human condition refer to actual depravity of human desires and acts, not simply to a hypothetical condition already removed on the ground of Christ's universal atonement. As born of the flesh, pre-Christians *are* flesh (John 3:6). The fleshly human nature has nothing good in it (Rom. 7:18). Unregenerate human nature is set on its own desires and hostile to God, meriting his displeasure and spiritual separation from God (Rom. 8:5–8). The fleshly person gratifies his own thoughts and desires and follows the ways of the spirit at work in the disobedient (Eph. 2:1–3). The pre-Christians' minds are darkened and their hearts are hardened, separating them from God (Eph. 4:18). By nature people are slaves to the law of sin (John 8:34; Rom. 7:25). (See also Gen. 6:5; Ps. 51:5; Isa. 48:8; 64:6; Jer. 17:9). An overwhelming amount of explicit biblical teaching refers to humans as depraved after Christ completed his work on the cross. These and similar passages cannot be reinterpreted on behalf of a supposition that lacks scriptural support.

Can Sinfully Inclined People Be Responsible?

If the desire and tendency to sin is hereditary, can we be responsible for committing sins? Can people be justly accountable for doing what comes naturally?

May we ask another question? If a God of truth did not call the deceitful heart what it is, would God be intellectually honest? Would God be morally just if he said our selfish inclination was not evil, but good? Would God be genuinely caring if he did not inform us of our terminal moral condition? Our sinful choices, desires, and acts are not coerced from outside ourselves. Freely and habitually we determine our behaviors according to our own natures.

It is contradictory, Emil Brunner thought, to say, "Humans are slaves to sin" and "Every sin is an actual decision."[124] But we have not found it insoluble to say, "God cannot sin, or, in effect, God is a slave to righteousness" and "Every act of God is an actual decision." God is free always to choose according to his nature and always does what is righteous. Freedom does not always involve contrary choice, but it always involves self-determination (see vol. 1, chap. 8). So it is not contradictory to say that the moral nature of moral agents is enslaved to sin and that every self-determination made according to that nature is freely, and so responsibly, sinful (in motivation if not in external act).

In no way can God with integrity call these self-determined acts of disbelief and disobedience "good." If there is to be any justice in history, the divine Judge can never call evil inclinations or the habitual sins that result from them "good."

Can Others Be Justly Condemned for Adam's Sin?

Some who accept an inherited inclination to sin consider it unjust to find all humans guilty for the one sin of Adam. Can the guilt of one person be justly transferred to others? We consider it unfair to be blamed for another's crime or to have the alien guilt of another held against us. Liberals and others rightly find the transference of sins meaningless. Sins are not entities that can be passed along to others. Sins are attitudes and actions of persons. And in ordinary circumstances it is unjust to attribute to anyone the injustices of someone else.

How then can a just God find us guilty and sentence us for Adam's sin? As Ramm says, the Scriptures do not answer this problem explicitly but from them we may gather the elements for an inferred answer.[125] Adam alone was guilty in the sense of being culpable or personally blameworthy for his first sin, Ramm thinks, and Adam's descendants are guilty only as liable for the sin's consequences. Indeed the children suffer from the consequences of an alcoholic parent. Ramm's view is true in what it asserts of consequences, but it fails to account for imputed guilt.

Paul teaches explicitly that God passed judgment on Adam's sin and found all guilty. "The judgment followed one sin and brought condemnation" (Rom. 5:16), "death reigned" (v. 17), and "the result of one trespass was condemnation for all men" (v. 18). *Condemnation* is a judicial term for judging a person guilty and deserving of punishment. Although sins as such cannot be transferred, these verses teach the transfer of the legal guilt of one person to others he represents. How can that be just?

One can voluntarily accept another's moral standing with its consequences. Paul voluntarily asked for a slave's obligations to be put on his account. He told Philemon to receive a runaway slave as himself, and, he added, "if he has done you any wrong or owes you anything, charge it to me" (Philem. 17–18). Paul asked that the slave's indebtedness be put to his account, or imputed to him.

Two other imputations in Scripture may help to understand the principles at work. First, although our sins as such are not literally laid on Christ, he voluntarily assumed human sinners' guilt and as their substitute suffered the penalty for their sins (Isa. 53:6; 2 Cor. 5:14, 21; 1 Peter 2:24; 3:18). A second imputation occurs when Christ's perfectly righteous standing before God's law and its rewards is put into the accounts of those who accept it by faith (Rom. 4:3, 6, 9, 24). In this case imputation involves the gracious transfer of righteousness of one person (a sinless substitute) to the legal standing of those who believe and are reborn into God's family.

The third scriptural imputation is the most problematic. It is the imputation of Adam's guilt and penalty to all human beings apparently without their choice. "The judgment followed one sin and brought condemnation" (Rom. 5:16), and "the result of one trespass was condemnation for all men" (v. 18). Every human being does come under the sentence passed on the father of all, for all will receive from him a sinfully inclined nature that must be called what it is. The fact of imputed guilt is simply affirmed in Scripture. To deny that fact is to deny the authority of the inspired Word. However, what is recorded is authoritative for good reasons. We ought to do our best to discover what those reasons may be.

How can God justly find all people guilty for the sin of the first man? Some

Augustinians have argued that a just basis of imputing alien guilt is based on a legal relationship of all to Adam. Inferring a covenant with Adam for all his descendants in Genesis 3, Adam knowingly and legally acted for all humanity. Hence covenant theologians refer to the federal headship of Adam. They illustrate forensic headship by pointing out that the legal head of a country acts for its citizens. When the legal President or Prime Minister acts ceremonially and officially, he or she acts for all that country's citizens. If the leader legally implicates the people in war, all are at war and suffer the consequences. If it is an unjust war, the citizens are collectively implicated. Whatever validity there may be to theories of collective guilt should make more understandable covenant theology's concept of the covenant of works and collective guilt for the sin of Adam.

A second Augustinian school of thought finds the justification of the collective sentencing of the race in Adam on the basis of Adam's natural headship of a unified race. A hint of how we could have sinned in Adam may be indicated by the statement that Levi, before he was conceived, paid tithes in the body of his forefather Abraham as the latter paid tithes to Melchizedek (Heb. 7:4–10). This reflects the realism with which the solidarity of the chosen people in Old Testament times was understood. Assuming the solidarity of the human race, the guilt of Adam is not entirely "alien" to us. Adam's guilt and penalty was that of the entire "kind" generically. On this realistic unity of all in Adam's natural headship, the forensic headship is no mere legal fiction. We can well hold both the natural and the legal headship of Adam, since the two concepts are not mutually exclusive and some evidence can be found for both.

God must call our moral condition and consequent status what they are. The closest thing to an explanation of Paul's meaning comes in Romans 5:12. Through the one person sin and death came to all because all have sinned. Commenting on this passage, Alford found that death passed on all because of both original and actual sin. We all sinned "in the *seed,* as planted in the nature by the sin of our forefather; and in the *fruit,* as developed by each conscious responsible individual in his own practice"[126]

Part of the difficulty here is understanding the point of the parallel Paul draws between the condemnation for the one act of Adam and the justification by the one act of Christ. The attribution of guilt, to be just, must be merited, but the attribution of righteousness in justification must be unmerited. Retaining this distinction, the point of the parallel may be this: all born of Adam are condemned and all born again by faith in Christ are justified. Or in another way of explaining the parallel between Adam and Christ: in Adam the sentence of condemnation passed upon the whole human race, but it is effectually executed only upon those who responsibly sin; in Christ the verdict of justification is provided for the whole race, but is effectual only for those who trust him and are born again. This last formulation is especially important, for although all are justly under the sentence of their natural and legal head, none will suffer the execution of the penalty who have not themselves responsibly sinned. Hence responsible sinful choice and action of a person must have taken place before that person suffers the penalty of eternal death. None will suffer eternally for being born in Adam's fallen race alone.

RELEVANCE FOR LIFE AND MINISTRY

Check Up on Your Ultimate Concern

What is your ultimate concern? What do you value most of all? Is your highest value pleasing God in the way his Word makes clear? Or is it getting your own fleshly way, achieving success, and receiving praise? Our *raison d'etre* is not self-aggrandizement. Neither should our highest goal be living for others. Allocentricity, good and important as it may be, if not done for the glory of God is idolatrous service of the creature more than the Creator. We must not substitute the second greatest commandment for the first. Nor should we give the last six commandments priority over the first four. The Christian has not been redeemed to serve things. Neither is our supreme good centered in the things we can accumulate. Tacentricity, (to coin another word from the Greek *ta* for "things") can be deceptively appealing when many of these things can be greatly used for the glory of God. How subtle is the temptation to make automobiles or houses of greater value than they serve under Christ's *sapiential* rule.

The ultimate concern in our world of values should be the triune God and the values of God's kingdom. The ultimate concerns and excitements of theists should be theocentric. If your life is under the lordship of Christ, your values will also be kyriocentric. Since his lordship comes to expression in the written revelation, Christians ought also be revelation-centered, not worshiping the Bible but following its informative teaching. In terms of the revealed content Christians ought to be doctrinally centered, as was their Lord. The doctrinal framework supplies the skeleton for the flesh of morality.

Never Call Evil Good

In reality all Christians must face up to an ultimate difference between good and evil. Moral reality is not monistic but dualistic. What we are is not what we ought to be. A radical difference exists between satanic injustice and divine justice as revealed by Christ and the Scriptures.

If our loyalties are with the kingdom of God, we will detest the kingdom of Satan, which subtly seeks its destruction. We live in the midst of a moral and spiritual war undertaken by Satan against Christ. By natural birth we find ourselves loyal slaves of the evil forces in the cosmos. To enter the kingdom of God we must be born again. Then believers face a lifelong spiritual exercise program to build up their moral and spiritual immune systems to resist the forces that attack their well-being as individuals, families, churches, and nations.

"Woe to those who call evil good and good evil, who put darkness for light and light for darkness, who put bitter for sweet, and sweet for bitter (Isa. 5:20). One of the factors leading to the Charles Manson murders was his belief in monism. Since all was one, he reasoned, there was no ultimate difference between helping Sharon Tate and murdering her. From a monistic perspective all actions are relative, and nothing is either right or wrong. From a biblical perspective God is absolutely just, and Satan, who fights against God's righteous kingdom, is inherently evil.

Insofar as we bear the image of God we have loyalties to our holy Creator; insofar as we are depraved we value the deceptions of the great destroyer. Naturally inclined toward selfishness and the self-destructive, we need divine revelation to revise our thinking and we need divine illumination to enable us to receive and obey its instruction.

Candidly, we must call moral evil "sin." The biblically informed avoid euphemisms for sins such as lying, lust, or covetousness. Excusing themselves for such sins, people often say, "That was only human." We should be honest and say, "That was only sinful." Sin is not part of the essence of humanness. People were fully human without sin before the Fall; Christ was fully human on earth without sin; and believers will be fully human in glory without sin. Sins express, not the essence of humanity, but fallen peoples' fleshly desires, designs, and actions.

We ought not call the purchase of slaves, for example, "merely human." Uses of our freedom that deprive others of theirs are "sin." Charles Hodge, for example, as a leading Presbyterian theologian at Princeton Seminary in the years prior to the American Civil War, at first saw no sin in the institution of slavery as he narrowly defined it, and at one time he bought a slave. But his theoretical support of an abstract idea of slavery must be judged against his outspoken and increasingly intense disapproval of American slavery (from 1836 to 1849). Hodge became a strong spokesman for the abolition of slavery.[127]

Recently black theologians have questioned whether Christians are in effect calling racist attitudes and practices human or sinful. And Latin American liberation theologians have recently called on Christians to consider to what extent the evils of endemic unemployment, hunger, and disease are the result of sin. Have we failed to discern the evil of others' landlessness when a handful possess most of the land? By condoning capitalist, socialist, and communist abuses of power in neocolonialism, international cartels, and dictatorial governments are we in effect calling evil good? Have we a need to develop our moral discernment as Charles Hodge did his?

Respect and Love Sinners

The *imago Dei* ontologically remains undestroyed in all persons, however dominated they may be by the works of the flesh. However overtly depraved, all humans in their being remain constitutionally image-bearers. All of them remain persons, and none ought to be treated like things (such as pornographic commodities). All are potentially recoverable, as far as we know. If Paul "the chief of sinners" could become Paul the apostle, then we must not give up hope for our relatives and neighbors, nor for leaders of cults or gangs. It is not a waste of time to relate wisely and lovingly to sinners.

Following the example of Jesus, Christians ought to makes friends of sinners while separating themselves from the sinful practices of pre-Christian people. Jesus was the friend of tax collectors and sinners (Matt. 11:19) while remaining morally and spiritually separate from sinners. Believers in whom the moral and spiritual image of God is being renewed remain in the world, but Christ wants his followers to be set free from enslavement to sin by the truth he taught and exhibited. The Lord prayed, not that the Father take us out of the world, but that he would protect us from the evil one (John 17:15). We are here to exhibit God's *agape* love for the unrighteous. We must not let "moral" termites quietly eat away the foundation of our relationships with God, relatives, friends, employees, employers, church members, and other fellow citizens by the abuse of God-given abilities.

Feel Toward Sin What God Feels

To deal effectively with morally counterproductive behaviors we need to feel toward them as God does. With the help of descriptive anthropological, psychological, sociological, and historical analyses we may understand better than those before us the multiplicity of factors predisposing people to sin. But we cannot thereby rationalize away its atrociousness. Descriptive understanding of antecedents provides background for caring relationships but does not change the need for moral discernment of sin's infamy. The Creator knows better than all the rest of us together how understandable sin is in a fallen world. But God hates the insolence that destroys his creative, providential, and redemptive work. "There are six things the LORD hates, seven that are detestable to him: haughty eyes, a lying tongue, hands that shed innocent blood, a heart that devises wicked schemes, feet that are quick to rush into evil, a false witness who pours out lies and a man who stirs up dissension among brothers" (Prov. 6:16–19). Such sins shatter the peace of God's creation and of persons God so highly values. Sin is to the spirit what cancer is to the body. "To fear the LORD is to hate evil; I hate pride and arrogance, evil behavior and perverse speech" (8:13).

Of the Lord's anointed it was said, "You love righteousness and hate wickedness; therefore God, your God, has set you above your companions by anointing you with the oil of joy" (Ps. 45:7). To follow the moral paradigm of Christ is to hate wickedness (Heb. 1:9). "Let those who love the LORD hate evil" (Ps. 97:10). Business success, movies, and television make self-destructive sin so appealing that we may need to step back in order to evaluate and despise broken promises, greed, envy, covetousness, theft, jealousy, short tempers, anger, murder, covetousness, theft, lust, and harmful sexual conduct. Let us say with the psalmist, "I will set before my eyes no vile thing. The deeds of faithless men I hate, they will not cling to me" (Ps. 101:3) and "I gain understanding from your precepts; therefore I hate every wrong path" (Ps. 119:104). Until sin is the stench in our nostrils that it is in God's, we will not grasp the seriousness with which he takes it. Hatred of sin is necessary if one is to have the determination to overcome it.

Fight Temptation

We must be clear that temptation is not sin. Jesus was tempted as we are, but without sin. But we ought not use the distinction between temptation and sin to rationalize repeated entertainment of temptation. We sin when we lack fidelity to what is right and pleases our Creator. A temporal advantage may seduce us away from pleasing our eternal Creator. A desire to go beyond the bounds of temperance may entice us into gluttony or covetousness.

Sin should be distinguished also from appreciation of the beauty of God's creation in its highest forms. We may admire the beauty of nature, the great works of art, the build or figure of a person of the other sex. This, however, must not become a rationalization for a prurient interest in pornography. Aesthetic admiration is one thing, lust is another. What is morally wrong is to lust for a person who has belonged, belongs, or will belong to another. One who has given himself or herself in a lifelong commitment to a spouse and lusts for another violates the covenant in the marriage commitment with that person and loses integrity before God as well as humans. Analogously, we may appreciate the valuable acquisitions of others so long as we do not covet for ourselves what belongs to them.

Because of the consequences of sin for time and eternity Jesus taught in the strongest figurative language that Christians should take action to correct or avoid the sources of their own temptations: "And if your hand or your foot causes you to sin, cut it off and throw it away from you; it is better for you to enter life maimed or lame than with two hands or two feet to be thrown into the eternal fire. And if your eye causes you to sin, pluck it out and throw it from you" (Matt. 18:8–9 RSV). "Because of the temptation to immorality, each man should have his own wife and each woman her own husband. . . . Do not refuse one another . . . lest Satan tempt you through lack of self-control" (1 Cor. 7:2, 5, RSV). Young church members and leaders like Timothy should make every effort to "treat younger men like brothers, older women like mothers, and younger women like sisters, in all purity" (1 Tim. 5:1–2, RSV).

With media advertisements tempting us to spend our money for what rusts, gets worn out, and perishes, good stewards must develop Holy Spirit–enabled self-control of their finances. We should learn to be content with food and clothing, for "people who want to get rich fall into temptation and a trap and into many foolish and harmful desires that plunge men into ruin and destruction. For the love of money is a root of all kinds of evil. Some people, eager for money, have wandered from the faith and pierced themselves with many griefs" (1 Tim. 6:9–10).

Such are the subtleties of temptation that we can so defend our individual rights as to make society defenseless against unprincipled individuals. When every neighbor becomes a potential adversary in court, we have lost ordinary selflessness. Christians ought to fight the temptation to go to court. The backlog of litigation threatens the right to a speedy trial and discriminates against the poor, who cannot afford prolonged legal battles. Citizenship not only protects rights, but also demands that we put the good of others ahead of our advantage.

One way to fight temptation is by keeping eternity's values in view. Follow the example of Moses, who "chose to be mistreated along with the people of God rather than to enjoy the pleasures of sin for a short time" (Heb. 11:25). We also do well to quote relevant Scripture as did the Lord Jesus Christ. He effectively fought the tempter by quoting God's authoritative Word (Matt. 4:1–10). We should avoid tempting others. "Temptations to sin are sure to come," Jesus said, "but woe to him by whom they come!" Insofar as it is within our control, we ought not tempt others. "It would be better for [the person who causes another to sin] to be thrown into the sea with a millstone tied around his neck than for him to cause one of these little ones to sin" (Luke 17:1–2, RSV). Hence Christians do everything in their power not to tempt others to gossip, lie, cheat on examinations, steal, or fail to keep their word.

In a time when you are tempted, turn to Old Testament examples intended to keep us from "setting our hearts on evil things" as they did—idolatry, sexual immorality, testing the Lord, and grumbling. "These things happened to them as examples and were written down as warnings for us. . . . So, if you think you are standing firm be careful that you don't fall!" (1 Cor. 10:6–12). In countertemptation warfare wield the sword of God's Word as Jesus did (Matt. 4:4–10). Memorize and quote Paul's encouragement to the Corinthians: "No temptation has seized you except what is common to man. And God is faithful; he will not let you be tempted beyond what you can bear. But when you are tempted, he will also provide a way out so that you can stand up under it" (1 Cor. 10:6–13).

Entertain Realistic Expectations of Yourself and Others

In our youth, particularly, we may expect more of *ourselves* than is possible for us to accomplish in a fallen world. Political individualism or self-government, even with a return to nature's surroundings, will not result in utopia. Nature remains under a curse, and sinners in themselves are not capable of faithfully practicing austere self-denial of the fleshly nature throughout life. And if any could for a time continuously overcome their fleshly inclinations, that would not be redemptive for sins already committed. A less severe type of self-government provides a commendable ideal. To the best of our ability we may wisely guide our conduct toward worthy ends.[128] But even with our best efforts, the bent of our sinful nature means that we will come short of the ideal of self-control and wise self-management in every aspect of life.

In a fallen world we must overcome perfectionist expectations of *spiritual leaders*. B. B. Warfield has traced the tragic results of several perfectionistic movements among Christians—those of the so-called higher life, Keswick, and victorious life.[129] The ideal, as Jesus taught, is to be perfect as God is perfect (Matt. 5:48), and Christians should aim for nothing short of moral perfection. It is beneficial to strive for a grade of 100 on a theology paper, but the perfect paper has yet to be written. Similarly, in morality we strive for total Christlikeness, but the reality is that none of us can achieve that in this life. Until we do, we ought not to expect its accomplishment in others. Pelagians reason that if perfection is commanded it must be possible. But Augustinians know that human nature has been so corrupted by the Fall that the ideal of perfection cannot be attained in this life.[130]

Human depravity necessitates some form of government and also keeps any type of *government* from perfection. A well-constructed union, James Madison believed, would have the advantage of controlling the violence of faction. As long as reason continues fallible and people are at liberty to exercise it, different opinions will be formed. As long as the connection subsists between reason and self-love, opinions and passions will have a reciprocal influence. The effects are seen in the unequal faculties for acquiring property. So the latent causes of faction and the propensity of mankind to fall into mutual animosities are thus sown in the nature of humanity. Neither an individual nor a group can be the judge and the parties of their own causes. Not even an enlightened diplomat can adjust these clashing interests. Since political power cannot remove the causes of faction, "relief is only to be sought in the means of controlling its effects. Relief from the effects of depravity is at best what the American government was explicitly formed to provide."[131]

Realistic expectations must also be held in relationships of the sexes and *family* life. A naïve optimism is not possible for one acquainted with the subtleties of fallenness among men and women. We must keep our critical faculties about us as we hear the fantasies about "love" in popular music and novels. Similarly the biblically informed should have realistic expectations for parent-child relationships. Here also we tend to give our own interests greater importance than they deserve. Selfish desires and inclinations have serious consequences in families. Since all are fallen, we will not expect to be perfect spouses, parents, or children.

Realism ought also to characterize our expectations for *religious organizations*. We will not find a perfect church, mission station, denomination, interdenominational organization, or small-group Bible study. Critical discernment and accountability are as imperative in religions as elsewhere, because (1) not all supernatural persons and experiences are of God; (2) Satan masquerades as an angel of light (2 Cor. 11:1–4, 15); (3) temptation presents evil in its most favorable light, even as a good; (4) worship is not always of God; (5) humanitarian service is not always for building God's kingdom; (6) prayer meetings are not always directed to the triune God; (7) biblical quotations are not always used as God intended them;

(8) Bible studies may be twisted to one's own destruction (2 Peter 3:16); (9) prophets and apostles may be deceived or false; (10) fine-appearing people may falsely claim to be Messiahs, and dedicated founders of religious groups may not be of God; (11) the best of fallen human beings in this life come short of God's standards; (12) spiritual disciplines and devotional methods may be directed toward idols as well as the true God; and (13) God's social institutions (families, nations, and churches) can be used for evil purposes as well as good.

Remind All of Their Moral Accountability

As self-determining agents humans are responsible for their choices and actions. We tend, however, to blame others or situations for our sins. In self-pity we may develop an ethic of irresponsibility. We say something like this: "Blame it on God, the government, heredity, the environment, parents, economic changes, peer pressures, or being unloved and unwanted; but don't blame it on me, the very center around which the whole universe revolves!" However, self-analysis and self-pity may lead to self-hate and finally the obsession to be rid of the self. That is one of the appeals of the Eastern and New Age religions. From a Christian perspective, however, the self is not absorbed; it is renewed (Eph. 4:24; Col. 3:10).

It is often alleged, "You can't teach morality." On the contrary, if you can teach and exemplify immorality, you can teach and exemplify morality, though because of sinful inclinations it will be more difficult. The old rules on safe sex make more sense than ever. That person is chaste who limits sexual contact to his or her lifelong partner. The sexual revolution promised unlimited fun but overlooked the disastrous consequences that have followed. Survivors from the front lines of the revolution return leaving a trail of broken marriages, increased teenage prostitution, hard-core pornography, child abuse, and epidemic diseases like AIDS.

The Ten Commandments represent the basic elements necessary for the most minimal well-being of any society. Advocates of chastity on moral and religious grounds do so for very positive, not negative reasons. The Judeo-Christian revelations place a very high value on healthy sexuality, emphasizing the deep joys and lasting fulfillment found in intimacy with faithfulness. When Scripture advocates exclusive, committed, and lifelong monogamous relationships, it does so, not from a sense of Victorian prudery, but because God knew that the sort of freedom and loving abandon necessary to true sexual enjoyment are by-products of faithful relationships, and not of extracurricular sexual activity. Attempts to be value-free or value-neutral in sex education imply that values are so relative as to be meaningless. A society that has no shared values one day will discover that it is not a society at all.

Radically Diagnose the Human Plight

Superficial diagnoses of the human predicament result in superficial resolutions. The body is essential to full humanness but is not the blameworthy cause of evil, and so the punishment of the body in asceticism is not sufficiently radical. "Radical" proposals for educational advancement, economic fairness, psychological adjustment to the environment, and self-improvement, valuable as they may be, are not sufficiently radical. They are cover-ups of our deepest moral and spiritual disease.

The most profound human predicament is rooted in the inner person. The fallen human heart has a basic tendency to turn away from God's ways. Until the inner self is born anew all the education, culture, and environmental improvements, like aspirin, may remove symptoms, but they do not address our most radical need. Until a provision is made for reconciliation to the transcendent, personal God, all other spiritual disciplines will serve only like band-aids. We are glad for them, but unless there is a healing process underneath the surface, we have only covered up our problem. Until sinners are divinely acquitted of their objective guilt, redeemed, and reconciled the efforts of counselors, educators, and ministers may remove certain guilt feelings, but they will fail to address the deepest need. Humans universally are depraved, alienated, and condemned. Only those with the gospel of Christ have the resources to address these radical needs.

Even evangelicals need to rediscover the poignant truth of human lostness. Jesus was clear on his major purpose for coming into the world. "For the Son of Man came to seek and to save what was lost" (Luke 19:10). Many of Christ's alleged followers are unclear about their primary *raison d'etre* because pastors and teachers have neglected the unpopular doctrine that sinners are lost. Although evangelicals deny being universalists, many appear to be universalists by their neglect of teaching on the tragic nature of sin and its awesome results. If we imagine that lost sinners are already in the kingdom of God, we are deceived. Jesus said to Nicodemus, a member of the Jewish ruling council: "I tell you the truth, no one can see the kingdom of God unless he is born again" (John 3:3). Since church members hear so little about the plight of unbelievers, it is not surprising that in general they seem to lack motivation for evangelism. Jude said, "Snatch others from the fire and save them" (v. 23).

In what ways can we bring the doctrine of lostness back into the life of the church? It may help to recall what we were before our conversions. Remembering our depravity, guilt, and alienation, we can marvel at our redemption, forgiveness, and reconciliation. We do not suggest preaching and teaching lostness alone. Always preach and teach divine grace for lost humans. Presenting a combination of need and the grace to meet it overcomes the abuses of communicating either without the other. "Consider therefore the kindness and sternness of God: sternness to those who fell, but kindness to you" (Rom. 11:22).[132]

Deliver the Divine Indictment to the Lost

Acutely aware of the divine indictment of all human beings even in high places (Rom. 1:18–3:20), we, like the prophets and apostles, must deliver to every human the divine summons (Jer. 15:19; Ezek. 18:30, 32). As Paul told the distinguished Aeropagus court at Athens, the university center of the ancient world: "[God] . . . now commands all people everywhere to repent" (Acts 17:30). Some people may be highly sensitive to their sins, but others may need to be reminded that they are not all what they should be.

What approaches may be used to help people deeply realize their sinfulness? With traditional Lutheran and Reformed preachers, declare the standards of the moral *law*. Like Christ we may give prominence to the summation of the first four commandments. Love God with your whole being. Ask anyone who is hesitant to confess his sinfulness: "Have you always loved God with all your abilities?" Then ask a question based on Jesus' summation of the last six commandments: "Have you always loved your neighbor as yourself?" If necessary point up some everyday failings of your listeners. In addition you can suggest that their need may be indicated psychologically by guilt feelings, a lack of a healthy self-image, and failures in close relationships.

With the Old Testament Prophets we may underline the subtleties of hypocrisy spiritually, relationally, and vocationally. The wisdom of Proverbs may help point up lacks in personal character, functions, and relationships. Or the Spirit may use a study of James to convict a person of the sins of the tongue that like a fire produce a whole world of evil and point out the failure of our deeds to measure up to our words. From James we may expose favoritism, quarrelsomeness, spiritual unfaithfulness, pride, slander, boasting, oppression, and wandering from the truth. Like James, Jesus and existentialists particularly expose hypocrisy.

Helmut Thielicke helps people realize their sinfulness by presenting existential analyses of *gospel stories*. Many people today are able to identify with the Samaritan woman at the well, the prodigal son, and Zaccheus. And we can learn from Jesus' approach to them.

Some have realized their lostness when face to face with the converging eschatological *signs of the end of the age* and the return of Christ. Others may need an existential shock treatment from accounts of near-death experiences of their peers and of the deaths of some. Indeed, they may begin to realize that though "crime does not pay," sin does. The wages of sin is *death* (Rom. 6:23)—physical, spiritual, and eternal. Along with subjects neglected in recent preaching and teaching add that of *judgment* to come (Heb. 9:27).

Most tellingly we may see our sinfulness, not by comparisons with what the majority may be doing, but with the sterling life of Jesus Christ. To show people their sin, Ramm (following Barth) recommends preaching *Christ as the ideal human.*[133] Surely the Savior is the exemplar of righteousness par excellence. In his upright presence we sense how far short we come from the divine righteousness. Christ fulfilled the law and the prophets, loved his heavenly Father and his neighbors, taught the importance of readiness in view of the signs of his return, and disclosed people's everyday, psychological, and existential shortcomings. Hence in referring to Christ as the paradigm of humanness, we incorporate elements of the other approaches. Jesus himself used the other ways to remind people of their moral and spiritual need. Upon occasion he exposed failures to fulfill the law. He also warned of the signs of the end of the age, no doubt evoking fear in some people. In talking with individuals, Jesus used psychology wisely, identifying with others' interests and needs. He also presented parables with vital existential significance. By portraying the sterling character of the Messiah, we help people realize that they are not all that they ought to be, and that they need to repent.

REVIEW QUESTIONS

To Help Relate and Apply Each Section in This Chapter

1. *Briefly state the classical problem* this chapter addresses and indicate reasons why genuine inquiry into it is important for your worldview and your existence personally and socially.

2. *Objectively summarize the influential answers* given to this problem in history as hypotheses to be tested. Be able to compare and contrast their real similarities and differences (not merely verbal similarities or differences).

3. *Highlight the primary biblical evidence* on which to decide among views—evidence found in the relevant

teachings of the major divisions of Scripture—and decide for yourself which historical hypothesis (or synthesis of historical views) provides the most consistent and adequate account of the primary biblical data.

4. *Formulate in your own words your doctrinal conviction* in a logically consistent and adequate way, organizing your conclusions in ways you can explain clearly, support biblically, and communicate effectively to your spouse, children, friends, Bible class, or congregation.

5. *Defend your view* as you would to adherents of the alternative views, showing that the other views are logically less consistent and factually faced with more difficulties than your view in accounting for the givens, not only of special revelation but also of human experience in general.

6. *Explore the differences the viability of your conviction can make in your life*. Then test your understanding of the viability of your view by asking, "Can I live by it authentically (unhypocritically) in relation to God and to others in my family, church, vocation, neighborhood, city, nation, and world?"

MINISTRY PROJECTS

To Help Communicate This Doctrine in Christian Service

1. *Memorize one major verse or passage* that in its context teaches the heart of this doctrine and may serve as a text from which to preach, teach, or lead small-group studies on the topic. The memorized passages from each chapter will build a body of content useful also for meditation and reference in informal discussions.

2. *Formulate the major idea of the doctrine in one sentence* based on the passage memorized. This idea should be useful as the major thesis of either a lesson for a class (junior high to adult) or a message for a church service.

3. *State the specific purpose or goal of your doctrinal lesson or message*. Your purpose should be more than informative. It should show why Christians need to accept this truth and live by it (unhypocritically). For teaching purposes, list indicators that would show to what extent class members have grasped the truth presented.

4. *Outline your message or lesson in complete sentences*. Indicate how you would support the truth of the doctrine's central ideas and its relevance to life and service. Incorporate elements from this chapter's historical, biblical, systematic, apologetic, and practical sections selected according to the value they have for your audience.

5. *List applications of the doctrine* for communicating the difference this conviction makes in life (for sermons, lessons, small-group Bible studies, or family devotional Bible studies). Applications should make clear what the doctrine is, why one needs to know it, and how it will make differences in thinking. Then show how the difference in thought will lead to differences in values, priorities, attitudes, speech, and personal action. Consider also the doctrine's possible significance for family, church, neighborhood, city, regional, and national actions.

6. *Start a file and begin collecting illustrations* of this doctrine's central idea, the points in your outline, and your application.

7. *Write out your own doctrinal statement on this subject in one paragraph* (in half a page or less). To work toward a comprehensive doctrinal statement, collect your formulations based on a study of each chapter of *Integrative Theology*. As your own statement of Christian doctrine grows, you will find it personally strengthening and useful when you are called on for your beliefs in general and when you apply for

service with churches, mission boards, and other Christian organizations. Any who seek ordination to Christian ministry will need a comprehensive doctrinal statement that covers the broad scope of theology.

PART TWO

CHRIST'S ATONING PROVISIONS

CHAPTER 5

GOD'S ETERNAL SON INCARNATED

God's Eternal Son Incarnated

THE PROBLEM: HOW COULD THE ETERNAL WORD OF THE DIVINE SPIRIT (JOHN 1:1) BECOME A TEMPORAL CHILD OF HUMAN FLESH (JOHN 1:14)?

The name of Jesus has become a household word in our day. In popular magazines, billboards, and bumper stickers the life and teachings of the carpenter of Nazareth have become the subject of ordinary conversation. Should we follow popular thought and view the One about whom history is divided merely as a noble prophet, teacher, or moralist? Or, as Christendom traditionally has affirmed, is the Jesus attested in history the divine Spirit himself manifested in a human life? If he is the second person of the Trinity (cf. vol. 1, chap. 7), in what sense did the Son of God empty himself in becoming a man (Phil. 2:7)?

Christian faith, by definition, centers on the person of Jesus Christ. The Anglican theologian W. H. Griffith Thomas appropriately entitled one of his books *Christianity Is Christ*. Emil Brunner similarly stated that "the Christian religion is summed up in the revelation of God in Jesus Christ."[1] Moreover, according to orthodox Christianity, the heart of Christology is the coming of the Logos into time and space by birth through Mary. The focus of Christian confession, then, is the Christmas event—the fact that the transcendent God has visited and redeemed his people in Jesus of Nazareth.

Given the centrality of Christ in the Christian scheme of things, it is not surprising that Jesus Christ is profoundly related to other doctrines of the faith. We established in volume 1, chapter 7, that within the essential unity of the Godhead the Logos exists eternally as the second divine person begotten of the Father. In volume 2, chapter 4, we confirmed that the human race is justly condemned and, without divine intervention, will perish eternally. Furthermore, how we answer the question in this chapter will influence our understanding of the reality of Jesus Christ (chap. 6), the significance of his death on the cross (chap. 7), and the meaning of his resurrection (chap. 8).

A number of issues surround the study of the person of Jesus Christ. Methodologically, does Christian reflection begin with Jesus as God and move to think about him as man? Or does it begin with Jesus as man and consider what it means to call him God?

Expressed in other terms, is Christology more responsibly done "from above" or "from below"? Classical theology has generally taken the former approach (the metaphysical), whereas modern critical thought has pursued the latter approach (the ethical). Furthermore, does Christ's person inform his work as most orthodox Christians have insisted, or does the work he performed explicate his person? Some theologians such as G. C. Berkouwer suggest that Christ's person and work ultimately are inseparable. Moreover, was Jesus of Nazareth conscious of being the Messiah? For what purposes did Jesus live and die? Why was Jesus Christ a stumbling block to Jews and foolishness to Greeks? (1 Cor. 1:23). An additional issue to be faced is the historic Christian claim that Jesus was supernaturally conceived of the virgin Mary. Was the virgin birth necessary for the incarnation of the God-man and for the begetting of a man free from sin? Or could Christ be the Savior of the world independently of his virginal conception? Is it possible for a person to be saved without assenting to the miracle of the virgin birth? Furthermore, was Mary herself sinless? If not, was Jesus without sin? Could Mary be said to be the "mother of God"?

The present chapter explores the meaning of Christ's preexistence, and the humiliation of his incarnation and birth of Mary.

ALTERNATIVE INTERPRETATIONS IN THE CHURCH

Kenotic Theologians

A number of theologians in Germany and later in England developed so-called kenosis theories of the incarnation. The term *kenosis* comes from the Greek text of Philippians 2:7, which refers to the fact that the One eternally in the form of God (or equal with God) emptied himself to become a man. These theologians attempted to do justice both to the claims for the second person of the eternal Trinity and to the growing interest in the human figure of Jesus portrayed in the Gospels. The kenotic theories thus sought to mediate between theological orthodoxy and liberalism. In general, "kenoticism interprets the incarnation as the transformation of God into man, or the exchange of divinity for humanity."[2]

Here we mention two major types of kenotic Christology. The first, championed by Thomasius and Delitzsch in Germany and by Gore and Fairbairn in England, was the less radical of the two. Thomasius distinguished between God's relative attributes (omnipotence, omnipresence, omniscience) and his immanent attributes (holiness, power, truth, love). In an act of self-limitation, the eternal second person of the Trinity was said to have divested himself of the relative attributes when he assumed the limitations of space and time. Having given up the divine form of existence for a creaturely form of existence, Jesus acquired a genuinely human consciousness and passed through all the stages of normal human development. Thomasius insisted that if the Son of God had retained the so-called relative attributes, he could not have lived a truly human existence. At his exaltation to heaven, Christ reassumed the relative attributes that he had temporarily set aside. Delitzsch similarly maintains that the Logos gave up the relative attributes without surrendering the identity of his divine being.

> The incarnate Logos is not in possession of the eternal *doxa*, for he looks back longingly after it (John 17:5). He is not omniscient, for he knows not . . . the day and the hour of the end (Mark 13:32). He is not almighty, for the power over all things is given to him . . . after his resurrection (Matt. 28:18). He is not

omnipresent, for he ascended up, that he might fill all things (Eph. 4:10).[3]

The second group of kenotic theories, advanced by Gess, Godet, Clarke, and Mackintosh, took the kenosis doctrine to its logical extreme. They interpreted Philippians 2:7 in the sense that at the incarnation the Logos gave up *all* the divine attributes, laid aside his deity, and so was transmuted into a man. Gess insisted that when the Son became a man, not only did he lay aside all the divine perfections but, initially at least, he had no consciousness of his Logos-nature, no longer experienced the mutual indwelling of the Father and the Spirit, and ceased to govern the universe. At the incarnation the Trinity of God was profoundly altered. When Christ later returned to the Father in heaven, he regained the divine life he possessed prior to his incarnation. Godet upholds a similar incarnation by divestiture. He insists that in John 1:14 ("The Word became flesh") the verb "became" signifies a profound alteration in the subject's mode of being, and the predicate "flesh" connotes complete human nature. Thus the incarnation means not "two natures or two opposite modes of being coexisting in the same subject, but a single subject passing from one mode of being to another."[4] In his essential being, the Logos depotentiated himself into the form of a man, although his personal subject or ego remained the same. Following the ascension, the Son regained his original divine state. All these kenotic theologians upheld Christ's preexistence and deity, and most subscribed to his virgin birth.

Progressive or Gradual Incarnationists

I. A. Dorner, together with a few other European theologians, sought to do justice to critical opinion about Jesus by propounding the theory of progressive incarnation. According to this proposal, "the incarnation is not indeed to be conceived as finished from the beginning, but as gradually developing."[5] Progressive incarnationists rejected the notion that the Logos assumed human nature and a human mode of existence at the moment of Jesus' conception or birth. Rather, Dorner explicates the incarnation developmentally as a moral union of the Logos and the humanity of Jesus. That is, by a gradual moral process that respects Jesus' human development, the Logos became more fully joined to the representative head of humanity. At the beginning of his life, Jesus was not the God-man. But as Jesus yielded himself to the Father in submission and prayer, the Logos progressively penetrated his humanity. The theory postulates that as a result of Jesus' self-surrender to the Father, the separate divine and human egos gradually united into perfect God-manhood. As expressed by Dorner: "The incarnation is not to be conceived as finished at one moment, but as continuing, even as growing, since God as Logos constantly grasps and appropriates each of the new facets that are formed out of the true human unfolding, just as conversely the growing actual receptivity of the humanity joins consciously and willingly with ever new facets of the Logos."[6] The divine and human natures united indissolubly at Jesus' resurrection and ascension to heaven.

Whereas the orthodox view of the incarnation postulates the humiliation of the divine Son of God, the present view upholds the gradual deification of the human Jesus. Moreover, whereas according to the traditional view the incarnation occurred at the beginning of the process, Dorner located the incarnation at the end of Jesus' life. Orthodox authorities charged the progressive incarnationists with following the Nestorian error, in that they posited a nonessential union between the divine and human *hypostases*. Although Dorner upheld Jesus' virgin birth, he severely compromised Christ's deity and preexistence.

Liberal Theologians

The liberal view of Jesus was shaped by at least three assumptions: (1) A growing antipathy to the supernatural and miracles. These theologians viewed the incarnation of a heavenly being as a primitive "myth" unacceptable to the modern scientific mind. (2) The supplanting of ontological concerns by ethical interests. Kant's polemic against knowledge of God in himself in the *Critique of Pure Reason* paralyzed discussion of Christ's preexistence and incarnation. For Kant, the old notion of the Son coming down from heaven is best understood as the embodiment of the eternal ideal in a human life. (3) Emphasis on the divine immanence rather than transcendence. From a pantheistic or panentheistic perspective, liberal scholars focused on the presence of God in the man Jesus, who by word and example functioned as the revealer of God.

Ritschl, following Kant, eliminated metaphysics from theology. Christology, in particular, concerns itself not with ontology, but with value-judgments made in respect of the historical Jesus. Thus Ritschl abandoned theoretical questions about the Logos and the two natures in favor of practical judgments of value, namely, the function Jesus performed in establishing the kingdom. Hence Ritschl maintains, "The origin of the person of Christ—how his person attained the form in which it presents itself to our ethical and religious apprehension—is not a subject for theological inquiry, because the problem transcends all inquiry."[7] Ritschl judges that the notion of Christ's preexistence, in addition to being an illegitimate ontological question, is a semideistical concept that would compromise Jesus' identification with human beings. Preexistence, as reinterpreted by Ritschl, denotes Christ's election as founder of the kingdom of God in the world. Moreover, the incarnation for Ritschl signifies that Jesus was the bearer of an ethico-religious ideal. Ritschl is uncertain whether the incarnation, so defined, occurred once-for-all in Jesus or whether it has been replicated in other noteworthy religious figures.

Adolf Harnack insists that the doctrines of Christ's preexistence and incarnation represent the intrusion of Greek religious philosophy into the sphere of Christianity. Harnack identifies the Greek Logos doctrine as the entry-point for what he calls the acute Hellenization of the faith. That is, early Christian authorities, particularly the apologists, identified Christ with the preexistent Logos who allegedly came down from heaven, united with a man, and performed supernatural works. "The identification of the Logos with Christ was the determining factor in the fusion of Greek philosophy with the apostolic inheritance."[8] This process of Hellenization tragically perverted the simple ethical message of Jesus into "a philosophy of religion." Harnack insisted that we must get behind the Christ of the creeds to Jesus the ethical prophet, who preached the fatherhood of God, the brotherhood of man, and the infinite value of the human soul.

Henry P. Van Dusen maintains that God is incarnate, or immanent, in the experience of every person. He grants, however, that a distinctive incarnation occurred in Jesus Christ in the sense that God uniquely indwelt the soul of the Nazarene. For Van Dusen, the incarnation means that Jesus is "a genuine human person who shared, as freely as is possible for a truly human life, the Vision and Purity and Purpose of God."[9] Van Dusen cautions that the incarnation represents not a total, but only a maximal, indwelling of God in Jesus. "It is mistaken to claim that in Jesus, the whole being of God was present, that God's purpose was fully expressed through him."[10]

The volume entitled *The Myth of God Incarnate,* edited by John Hick,[11] summarizes the contemporary liberal attitude toward the incarnation. Hick and his colleagues insist that the doctrines of Christ's preexistence and incarnation represent ancient myths, where myth is an event, not literally true, that evokes a particular religious meaning in its hearers. How did the so-called myths of preexistence and incarnation make their way into Christian theology? The essayists respond that the early Christians lived in a world where preexistent beings and divine visitations to earth were commonplace. Thus it was natural that believers should have used supernatural, i.e., mythical, categories to represent the significance of Jesus. Since "the present [scientific] climate is alien to the whole Christian position as traditionally conceived,"[12] modern believers must abandon the incarnation as a metaphysical reality, yet retain it as a religious claim. The traditional incarnation language and imagery, the essayists insist, express the truth of God's self-giving love to the world. For modern people who no longer believe in divine visitations, the incarnation means, "I see God in Jesus." Hick interprets the incarnation in adoptionist categories: "Jesus was a 'man approved by God' for a special role within the divine purpose, and the later conception of him as God incarnate, the second Person of the Holy Trinity living in a human life, is a mythological or poetic way of expressing his significance for us."[13]

Most liberal theologians reject Christ's virgin birth for the following reasons: (1) The doctrine is said to be derived from prescientific pagan mythology. Thus Frances Young insists that the virgin birth "as a literal statement of Jesus' origins . . . is virtually inconceivable in the light of modern knowledge of genetics and reproduction."[14] (2) The doctrine is irrelevant to the adoptionist view of Jesus. Russell Aldwinckle reinterprets the virgin birth as a sign pointing to "the new creative and saving activity which now begins in this man Jesus."[15] (3) The virgin birth is said to be inimical to Jesus' full humanity and solidarity with persons. And (4) The virgin birth is viewed as not essential to the church's message of salvation. Some liberals retain the traditional language of virgin birth, while reinterpreting its meaning, e.g., "God is the source of his life," or "Jesus' reality is due to the initiative of God."

Existentialist and Neoorthodox Authorities

This tradition sharply criticizes the liberal caricature of Jesus as a mere man adopted by God. Authorities identify the enfleshment of the transcendent God in the form of a man as a mystery beyond the grasp of human reason. Theologians aligned with the movement minimize the historical aspects of the incarnation while emphasizing the existential. The focus of the incarnation is said to be the meeting of divine and human subjects.

Søren Kierkegaard viewed the incarnation and virgin birth as the absolutely unique event by which the Wholly Other entered time. "The historical assertion is that the Deity, the Eternal, came into being at a definite moment in time as an individual man."[16] By virtue of his assumed infinite qualitative distinction between God and man and eternity and time, Kierkegaard regards the incarnation as offensive to conceptual thought—indeed, as "the absolute paradox." The fact that the Eternal became temporal, that the Absolute became relative, that Being-in-Itself became history is for Kierkegaard an intellectual scandal. "The absurd is—that the eternal truth has come into being in time, that God has come into being, has been born, has grown up, and so forth, precisely like any other individual human being."[17] This rational uncertainty represents a significant gain for Kierkegaard, since he insists that only in the face of so great a paradox can a person truly and passionately "believe."

Guided by Kierkegaard's dialectic between heaven and earth, Brunner denies the existence of any connecting links between the Christ-event and history. The meaning of history, according to Brunner, is ambiguous. Thus, "we are bound to oppose the view that the Christian faith springs out of historical observation, out of the historical picture of Jesus of Nazareth."[18] Brunner here distinguishes between "Christ *after* the flesh" and "Christ *in* the flesh." The former, the Christ known by the historian, because it deals with the realm of relativity, is carnal knowledge. The latter, the Christ known in the divine-human encounter, is properly spiritual knowledge. Brunner thus insists that the incarnation, an event in the primal history (*Urgeschichte*), connotes the encounter between the divine "I" and the human "thou" in which God addresses the person with the divine claim and elicits a decision of faith. Thus defined existentially, incarnation is synonymous with personal revelation. Revelation "is the coming of God in the Word, which is a personal advent, the Incarnation of the Word."[19] Brunner concedes that Christ did assume our humanity. The real focus of the incarnation, however, is not historical, but existential or suprahistorical; it resides in the personal meeting between divine and human subjects.

In view of the foregoing, Brunner regards the historical claim of the virgin birth as "useless speculation." Indeed, "The majestic wonder of the Incarnation of the Son of God is not made greater but smaller by the biological theory of the procreation through one sex alone."[20] Brunner believes that the dogma of the virgin birth is untenable for several reasons: (1) It is lacking in the *kerygma* of the early church. (2) The Matthew 1 and Luke 1 narratives on which the doctrine is based are said to be historically unreliable. (3) The parents of Jesus, who alone knew the facts, gave no report on the subject. (4) The virgin birth affords no security against Christological heresy, for Adoptionists, Arians, and Socinians all accepted it. (5) The doctrine is closely linked with the Docetic heresy and Greek asceticism. And (6) the dogma was derived from the mistaken Septuagint translation of Isaiah 7:14.

Barth started with Kierkegaard's assumption that God is totally other than man. Consequently only God could speak about God. All revelation is Christomonistic, or located in Christ alone. Reacting sharply against the immanentalism of liberal theology, Barth develops a Christology from above. Thus he speaks of "the miracle of Jesus Christ's existence, this descent of God from above downwards."[21] Furthermore, Barth approaches the incarnation from the perspective of the two states, which he views dialectically rather than successively and to which he adapts the two natures. Barth finds in the parable of the Prodigal Son a paradigm of Christ's humiliation and exaltation. The journey of the son into a far country speaks of Christ's condescension and solidarity with sinful humanity. "It is He who descends so deep down to men in order to lift them up so high. It is He who goes into the far country in order that man may return home."[22] Barth argues dialectically that the incarnation is precisely a veiling; Christ conceals himself by the manner in which he reveals himself. That Christ was manifest in folly and weakness—i.e., incognito—rather than in power and glory, places persons before an unavoidable decision. Barth insists that the flesh Christ assumed was not neutral human nature, but Adamic nature, i.e., humanity in the state of disobedience, sin, and enmity against God. Although Christ did not commit particular sins, he nevertheless became a man with a sinful nature like each one of us. Thus Barth writes of Christ: "If He really entered into solidarity with us—and that is just what He did do—it meant necessarily that He took upon Himself, in likeness to us, the 'flesh of sin' (Rom. 8:3)."[23] The other side of Christ's humiliation is his exaltation, which corresponds to the return of the son to the father's home. Here Barth argues that in this movement God raised up humanity into himself. The statement "The Word became *flesh*" (John 1:14) means that Christ became not a man, but humanity as a whole. Thus when Christ returned to heaven in the flesh, he incorporated humankind into the life of God. "In Jesus Christ it is not merely one man, but the *humanum* of all men, which is posited and exalted as such to unity with God."[24]

Barth staunchly defended the virgin birth of Christ. The miracle of Christ's virgin birth for Barth possesses noetic rather than ontic significance. Whereas God could have brought about the incarnation in another way, the virgin birth serves as a "sign" of the fact that *God* has bridged the abyss between eternity and time. The phrase in the Apostles' Creed concerning Jesus' conception—"conceived of the Holy Ghost"—signifies that Christ's existence is due to God's special decision and initiative. The phrase "born of the virgin Mary" connotes that Jesus Christ is the real son of a real woman.

Process Theologians

Followers of Whitehead reject as crassly prescientific the claim that the second person of the triune Godhead literally assumed human flesh. Modern minds must reject "as incredible and impossible the Greek idea of a god who comes down to earth and walks about as a human being."[25] The process worldview renders impossible the idea of an intrusion from outside the natural order. Instead, the incarnation must be interpreted solely in terms of the cosmic world process. The neoclassical vision of the incarnation is rooted in its special understanding of the Logos. Not an eternally divine person, the Logos is identified as the impersonal and timeless principle of order and purpose in the universe, or as the instrument of novelty and the lure for feeling. The Logos, Whiteheadians argue, is immanent in the world *nexus,* luring all entities toward optimal creative transformation. In the Whiteheadian scheme, broadly speaking, the incarnation represents the immanence of the Logos in the man Jesus.

John B. Cobb, Jr., argues that the substantialist model of the incarnation must give way to an experiential relation in which societies of past experiences or events merge in creative synthesis. The incarnation, Cobb insists, describes the indwelling of the Logos, or the power of creative transformation, in the historical Jesus. To be sure, the Logos is incarnate and operative in all persons and religious traditions. But the indwelling of the Logos in Jesus was so complete that it shaped his very being. "In Jesus there is a distinctive incarnation because his very selfhood was constituted by the Logos."[26] In other words, for Cobb, "Christ" designates the incarnate Logos, that is, the power of creative transformation operative in the world.

Professor Pittenger argues that a God

who is so remote and unrelated that he can intrude into nature only from without represents a deistical concept. The catastrophic view of the incarnation disrupts the regular workings of nature and so must be rejected. Consistent with the evolutionary vision, Pittenger claims that God continually incarnates himself in nature and history, thereby energizing the cosmic process. Yet the God who is immanent in the world process is eminently operative in the man Jesus—the latter becoming through this indwelling the special personal agent through whom God acts. "At every point in the existence of Jesus, the divine activity is operative—in teaching, preaching, healing, comforting, acting, dying, rising again. . . . He is indeed the personalized instrument for the Self-Expressive Activity of God."[27]

J. A. T. Robinson claims that as "a genuine product of the evolutionary process,"[28] the man Jesus was divinely raised up to represent the race before God. The notion that God become man should not be regarded as a "bolt from the blue" or a "Christ comet," by which a celestial visitor lands on earth, stays for a while, and then takes off after completing his mission. The old mythological concept of the God-man must be replaced by the functional notion of "God-in-man."[29] Thus Robinson concludes that Jesus "is not a divine or semi-divine being who comes from the other side. He is a human figure raised up from among his brothers to be the instrument of God's decisive work."[30] Jesus is distinctive (not unique or final) in that he emerged from the historical process to serve as the exemplary instrument of God's self-expression.

Process thinkers likewise disavow the virgin birth as mythological and thus meaningless to modern minds. The carpenter of Nazareth was the humanly conceived son of Joseph and Mary. Pittenger speaks for the tradition: "The stories told in the first two chapters of Matthew and Luke are apologetic, or christological, in content, and they cannot be taken as historical narratives. Insistence on a biological virgin birth has been a mistake."[31]

Modern Roman Catholic Authorities

The so-called "progressive" Roman Catholic theologians uniformly approach Christology "from below" (i.e., beginning with Jesus' authentic manhood) and seek to reinterpret traditional Christological language in terms of Christian experience. The classical doctrines of Christ's preexistence, virgin birth, and incarnation are viewed nonhistorically as "poetic imagery" (Hellwig) or as "mythological discourse" (Carmody). Such Roman Catholic authorities, moreover, shift the focus of concern from Christmas to Good Friday and Easter, i.e., not on who Christ was in the beginning, but what he did at the end. In sum, recent critical Catholic scholarship claims that the old ontological way of representing Jesus must be replaced with functional and personalist perspectives. One recent study, for example, gives the following definition of the incarnation: "God chose to take one man's capacity or orientation and so fill it that that man uniquely 'incarnated' God's Word."[32]

Piet Schoonenberg insists that God was initially an undifferentiated being, and thus there was no transcendent, preexistent person called the Son of God. But at a specific moment in time, the second person of the Godhead came into being in the human figure of Jesus (likewise the third person in the Holy Spirit). Thus God changes, indeed, he *becomes* triune through his salvific self-communication. This means, for Schoonenberg, that Jesus is the *natural* Son of God, a single, undivided human being (i.e., the two-natures dogma does not hold). The incarnation, on this showing, means God's whole presence and working in the man Jesus. The focus of Christology is not an alleged Word from eternity who became flesh. Rather, it is "the self-identification of God's being with the human person of Jesus."[33] Schoonenberg calls this pattern, which he judges to be less mythical and more human, "a christology of God's presence" or "a christological humanism."[34]

Hans Küng works a Christology from below by beginning with the life and deeds of the man Jesus and then inquiring about his relation to God. According to Küng, the doctrines of the Son's preexistence, conception by the Spirit, and assumption of human flesh are Hellenistic myths chosen to set forth the meaning of Jesus for faith. The result of this development is that the historical Jesus of Nazareth was overshadowed by the mythical Son of God. But such language, Küng insists, is incomprehensible today and should be avoided in the church's proclamation. "We can no longer accept the mythical ideas of that age about a being descended from God, existing before time and beyond this world in a heavenly state."[35] This mythical "descending" Christology must be replaced by an historical "ascending" Christology, which views Jesus as a man gradually elevated to the status of revealer of God.

Küng observes that the ancient world was replete with myths depicting the miraculous birth of heroes and gods. He holds that the early church utilized the virgin-birth mythology to highlight Jesus' functional role as Son of God and Messiah. But since a supernatural conception adds nothing to Jesus' role as a human spokesman for God, "No one can be obliged to believe in the biological fact of a virginal conception or birth."[36] Raymond Brown, a Catholic biblical scholar, adds that the virgin birth stories are of questionable historicity and extraneous to the Christian message. McBrien identifies the dogma of the virgin birth as an unhistorical "*theologoumenon,*" that is, "a theological belief that is read back into the historical life of Jesus in order to make a point of faith."[37] According to the Notre Dame theologian, the early church fabricated the virginal conception doctrine to communicate the truth that Jesus was one with God from the moment of his conception.

A brief summary of Catholic opinion regarding Mary follows. From the fourth century onward many Catholic authorities expanded the virginal-conception doctrine to affirm the doctrine of Mary's perpetual virginity. Thus it was held that Mary was a virgin not only *before* birth but also *in* birth (Jesus did not pass through the birth canal) and *after* birth (Mary had no marital relations with Joseph and hence no natural children). The name of Augustine[38] could be mentioned in this regard. The generally accepted view was that Mary was miraculously conceived and lived a sinless life. The Council of Ephesus (431) promulgated the dogma of Mary's divine motherhood. Against the Nestorians, Mary was given the title "Mother of God." But throughout the patristic era and beyond, Mariology remained subservient to Christology.

In the medieval era, however, when theology became increasingly divorced from Scripture, Mary herself gradually became a channel for saving grace. Thus many Catholic authorities viewed Mary as mediatrix between Christ and humankind. This conviction possessed the status of a thesis (a pious belief) rather than a dogma (a binding doctrine). According to Bernard of Clairvaux, persons need "a mediator with that Mediator, and there is no one more efficacious than Mary."[39] Bonaventure, Duns Scotus and others, envisaged Mary as co-redemptrix of the human race. A cult of Mary arose in which prayers were made and worship offered to the "Mother of the Redeemer" and the "Queen of heaven." Many Roman authorities upheld Mary's immaculate conception, a dignity that was said to be commensurate with Christ's choice of Mary to be his mother. Other authorities such as Thomas Aquinas rejected the notion of Mary's immaculate conception as inconsistent with the doctrine of universal sin.

By the nineteenth century Mariology had acquired a separate theological status. In 1854 Pope Pius IX, in the bull *Ineffabilis Deus,* promulgated as a dogma of the faith the Immaculate Conception of Mary. As the "God-Bearer" Mary was declared to be free from the stain of original sin from the moment of her conception. In the mystery of sin, however, Mary endured sin's consequences in the form of sickness and death. In 1950 Pope Pius XII certified longstanding legends by promulgating the bull *Munificentissmus Deus,* which dogmatized the Heavenly Assumption of Mary. Instead of succumbing to death, Mary allegedly was translated bodily to heaven and was seated at the right hand of Christ to mediate the prayers of the faithful.

The Second Vatican Council and much contemporary Catholic theology posits Mariology squarely within ecclesiology. That is, while retaining devotion to Mary as advocate and mediatrix, recent Catholic thought subordinates Mary to Christ in the scheme of redemption by relating her to the church. Thus "Mary is, by means of her faith and obedience to the Word of God, a model of the Church and is its preeminent member."[40] Many recent Catholic scholars find little biblical justification for Mary's perpetual virginity, that is her virginity *in partu* (in birth) and *post partu* (after birth). The same scholars deny that belief in the dogmas of the Immaculate Conception and Heavenly Assumption are necessary for good standing in the church.

Many Fathers, Reformers, and Evangelicals

Ignatius, the bishop of Antioch, speaks for the subapostolic age when, against the docetists, he upholds the objective reality of the incarnation. The Son of God or Word, who was with the Father from eternity, became a man in the line of David and thereby revealed the Father. "There is one God, who has manifested Himself by Jesus Christ His Son, who is the eternal Word."[41] The miracle of the virgin birth attested the union of Deity with human nature. Thus typically, Ignatius claims that Christ "was begotten by the Father before all ages, but was afterwards born of the Virgin Mary without any intercourse with man."[42] The confessional type of language used by Ignatius indicates that belief in Christ's preexistence, incarnation, and virgin birth was widely held early in the second century.

The Apologists consistently identified Christ as the enfleshment of the eternal Logos who, by becoming man, revealed and interpreted the Father. Thus Justin Martyr affirmed that the personal Word "preexisted and submitted to be born a man of like passions with us, having a body, according to the Father's will."[43] The disseminated Word illumines the minds of all persons, whereas the incarnate Word saves all who believe. "The Word . . . became man for our sakes, that becoming a partner for our sufferings, he might also bring us healing."[44] Justin expounds the virgin birth doctrine by relating Mary to Eve. As Eve, the virgin believed and obeyed the serpent and thus became the mother of sin, so Mary, also a virgin, believed and obeyed the angel and thus became the mother of the sin-Bearer.[45]

In his important essay *On the Incarnation of the Word,* Athanasius argues that the race languished in a state of moral corruption, death, and impending judgment. The curse and ruin that afflicted sinners' corporeal existence could be undone only as the Word, the image of the Father, assumed the body of our humiliation. "Man would not have been freed from sin and damnation if the Logos had not taken upon himself our natural, human flesh. Neither could man have become Godlike if the Word which became flesh had not come from the Father—if he had not been his own true Word."[46] Thus, having been conceived of a virgin, the Savior made his abode in a body like ours, capable of death. Opposing the notion of a mere functional immanence of the Logos in Jesus, Athanasius insisted that "he became man and did not just come into man."[47] In this state of humiliation, the Word initially performed the work of revelation. By many signs he showed himself to be the Ruler and King of the universe. Then he performed the work of reconciliation by offering his body as a sacrifice for sinful souls. Athanasius believed that the incarnation would not have occurred had the race not fallen into sin. But since humankind did lie under the curse, "He was made man that we might be made God."[48]

Augustine viewed the Word as the preexistent second person of the Trinity who became man in the carpenter of Nazareth. The coeternal Word of God "took on human nature, and thereby became the one Jesus Christ, Mediator between God and man, equal to the Father in his divinity, less than the Father according to the flesh, that is, as man."[49] Following Irenaeus and Athanasius, Augustine insisted that because the human race languished under sin and condemnation, "a mediator was required, that is to say, a reconciler, who by offering a unique sacrifice . . . should allay that wrath."[50] Thus through a miraculous conception wrought by the Holy Spirit, the only Son of God clothed himself with sinless human nature. Said Augustine, "I believe that Christ was born of a virgin because I have read it in the Gospel."[51]

As for the church's early creedal affirmations, the Apostles' Creed, which originated from a second-century Roman baptismal confession, describes Jesus Christ as "conceived by the Holy Spirit, born of the virgin Mary." Plainly, early candidates for Christian baptism were required to assent to the validity of our Lord's virgin birth. Since only essential tenets of the faith were included in the Apostles' Creed, the importance of the virgin birth to the early church is established. The Nicene Creed of 325 and its revision of 381 attest Christ's incarnation and virgin birth: "Who for us men and because of our salvation came down from heaven, and was incarnate by the Holy Spirit and the Virgin Mary." Furthermore, the Chalcedonian Definition of 451 attests Christ's incarnation and virgin birth, and the so-called Athanasian Creed certifies the incarnation (art. 29) as a belief necessary for salvation.

Anselm, in his classic essay, *Cur Deus Homo,* observed that Adamic disobedience disturbed God's design for the universe. God's justice was such that either the debt must be paid or divine punishment must fall. But to punish all persons everlastingly would defeat God's purpose of creation. The only viable alternative was that the debt of sin must be paid and many humans saved. Anselm notes that human persons could not make the needed satisfaction by virtue of their sinful and impotent condition. Only God himself could make amends. But since sinners owe the debt, the satisfaction must be offered by a man. Thus, concludes Anselm, "it is necessary that the same being should be perfect God and perfect man, in order to make this atonement."[52] In the divine plan the eternal Son of God was conceived by the virgin

Mary, was born a man free of Adam's guilt, and surrendered his life as the perfect offering for sin.

Calvin's approach to the incarnation followed that of the Fathers. Since our iniquities estranged us from the righteous God, a mediator was needed who was capable of bridging the gulf between God and sinners. "The situation would surely have been hopeless had the very majesty of God not descended to us, since it was not in our power to ascend to him."[53] The mediator must be God, for only God could conquer sin, defeat death, and make us children of the Most High. On the other hand, the mediator must also be human, for only thus could human flesh be presented as satisfaction to God's righteous judgment. Consequently, "God's natural Son fashioned for himself a body from our body, flesh from our flesh, bones from our bones, that he might be one with us."[54] Calvin attributes Christ's sinlessness (necessary for a perfect sacrifice), not to the absence of a human father, but to a miraculous conception wrought by the Holy Spirit. To the question whether the incarnation would have occurred if Adam had not sinned, Calvin responds negatively and insists that Adam's sin and Christ's coming to earth were united in God's eternal decree. Calvin notes that Scripture closely links Christ's humiliation with the shedding of his blood for the remission of sins.

B. B. Warfield insists that Christ the Son, eternally abiding with the Father, took into his divine personality a human nature and so came into the world for the purpose of saving sinners. The Messiah is "a divine being who has entered the world on a mission of mercy to sinful man."[55] Scripture represents Christ's humiliation as a miraculous event: a supernatural Christ begotten via a supernatural birth effects a supernatural salvation. In Warfield's opinion, Christ's virginal conception by the Holy Spirit is an essential element of biblical faith: "The supernatural birth of Jesus . . . is the expression of Christianity's supernaturalism, the safeguard of its doctrine of incarnation, and the condition of its doctrine of redemption."[56]

Machen claims that one's attitude toward the virgin birth turns on one's view of Jesus Christ. If Jesus is understood to be the incarnate Son of God and Savior, then the New Testament teaching concerning his supernatural conception makes eminently good sense. "Only one Jesus is presented in the Word of God; and that Jesus did not come into the world by ordinary generation, but was conceived in the womb of the virgin by the Holy Ghost."[57]

Additional helpful studies on the incarnation and virgin birth are provided by James Orr,[58] and Millard J. Erickson.[59]

THE BIBLICAL TEACHING

To determine which historical proposal or integration of elements best fit the data, we turn to the primary teachings of Scripture on the subject of Christ's incarnation and birth.

Pentateuch

Immediately following Adam and Eve's disobedience in Eden, God pronounced a series of judgments against the parties that participated in the first sin. In the theologically pregnant Genesis 3:15 text God responded to the serpent, as follows: "I will put enmity between you and the woman, and between your offspring and hers; he will crush your head, and you will strike his heel." Since "seed" (*zera'*) in Scripture designates both posterity collectively and a single offspring, the focus of the text is twofold. The first of these is the hostility that would persist throughout history between the unbelieving followers of Satan and the believing offspring of the woman. Ultimately, however, this divine pronouncement anticipates the struggle between the two personal representatives of the rival parties, namely, Christ ("he," *hû'*) and Satan ("you"). Eve's principal seed, though wounded by Satan, would in the end vanquish the leader of the kingdom of darkness. The point of interest in this Protoevangelium (i.e., first announcement of the Gospel) is that the future Messiah, who would destroy Satan, is described as the "offspring" of *Eve*. The identification of the triumphant Messiah as the *zera'* of the woman remained enigmatic until the New Testament explication of Christ's supernatural conception without male agency (Matt. 1:23; Gal. 4:4). "Not until the virgin birth would the full implication of the promise be understood."[60]

During Israel's wilderness wanderings God ordered Moses to strike a rock at Horeb. When the leader of Israel did as the Lord had commanded, water flowed from the rock, providing refreshment for all (Exod. 17:5–7). The apostle Paul explicates the meaning of this remarkable event in 1 Corinthians 10:4, when he writes that the people of Israel all "drank the same spiritual drink; for they drank from the spiritual rock that accompanied them, and that rock was Christ." "Rock" (*ṣûr*) is a common name for God in the Old Testament (Deut. 32:4, 15; Ps. 18:2, 31; etc.). Thus the meaning of this Exodus text is that the Christ who eternally preexisted his birth in Bethlehem was present with Israel in their wilderness journey as the providential provider of their needs. Juxtaposing Exodus 17:5–7 and 1 Corinthians 10:4, what emerges is an "explicit reference to Christ as preexistent, and his being the source of the people's blessings at all times."[61]

Prophetic Literature

Volume 1, chapter 7 shows that texts such as Psalms 2:7; 45:6–7; and 110:1 attest the real existence of the Messiah prior to his birth at Bethlehem during the reign of Caesar Augustus. The prophet Isaiah likewise confirms Messiah's preexistence with the phrase "Everlasting Father" (*'ᵃbî-'ad*) (Isa. 9:6), which literally describes Messiah as the "father [i.e., possessor] of the ages." Micah makes the same point, when he describes the royal Messiah as one "whose origins are from of old, from ancient times" (*mîmê 'ôlām,* Mic. 5:2). These two texts, Unger argues, convey "the strongest assertion of infinite duration of which the Hebrew language is capable."[62] Many scholars believe that the incident involving God's miraculous preservation of the three devout Hebrews in the Book of Daniel may also attest Christ's preexistence. When king Nebuchadnezzar looked into the blazing furnace, he saw a fourth person who looked "like a son of the gods" (Dan. 3:25). With many Christian interpreters both ancient and modern, we suggest that in this text "more likely we have to do with a preincarnate manifestation of the Son of God."[63]

Isaiah undoubtedly anticipates the kingly Messiah's incarnation with the words, "to us a child [*yeled*] is born, to us son is given" (Isa. 9:6). The seventh chapter of the same prophecy prophetically speaks of the instrumentality of the incarnation, namely, the virgin birth. By way of background to Isaiah 7:14, Syria (Aram) and Israel waged war against Judah, striking fear into the heart of corrupt king Ahaz. In the hour of national calamity, the Lord directed Isaiah to urge Ahaz to be calm and trust in God. The Lord, moreover, invited Ahaz to ask for a sign of divine protection in the present crisis. Wicked Ahaz, however, had already determined not to accept God's provision but to secure military assistance from Assyria (cf. 2 Kings 16:7–8). The prophet thus declared that since Ahaz had turned his back on this particular sign of divine assistance, God would give a greater sign (*'ôt*) to the entire house of David ("you," pl., v. 14). This greater sign, set in the context of God's covenant with David (2 Sam. 7:12–16), would guarantee the perpetuity of the threatened line of David through the promised child. The substance of the new sign forms one of the great prophecies of Scripture: "The virgin will be with child and will give birth to a son, and will call him Immanuel" (Isa. 7:14). This exceptional sign proclaimed the miraculous birth of the Messiah by a virgin. ("While the king calls in an army, God looks to the birth of a child."[64])

The woman who would give birth to the Messiah is described as "the virgin" (*hā'almāh*), and is so rendered by the AV, RV, and NIV. The vast scholarly discussion surrounding the meaning of *'almāh* is best summed up in the article on the word in *Theological Wordbook of the Old Testament,* the heart of which follows: "It seems reasonable to consider that the feminine form of this word is not a technical word for a virgin but represents a young woman, one of whose characteristics is virginity." The article continues: "There is no instance where it can be proved that *'almāh* designates a young woman who is not a virgin."[65] The fact that the Holy Spirit guided Matthew (Matt. 1:23) to employ *parthenos,* the Greek word for a virgin, to translate *'almāh,* clinches the argument that Isaiah predicted the Messiah's incarnation by means of a virginal conception. Orr offers this summation of the import of Isaiah 7:14. "The vision of the prophet sweeps far beyond present events . . . and he beholds in this Son that should be born, this child that should be given . . . the security for the fulfillment of the promise to David, and the hope for the future of the world."[66]

The Synoptic Gospels

The New Testament offers explicit testimony to Christ's eternal preexistence. Jesus states in Matthew 11:27: "All things have been committed [*paredothē*] to me by my Father. No one knows [*epiginōskei*] the Son except the Father, and no one knows [*epiginōskei*] the Father except the Son and those to whom the Son chooses to reveal him." In the midst of his earthly ministry Jesus claimed a profound knowledge of his Father in heaven. Such knowledge and ability to reveal the Father fully could not have been acquired during his lifetime but is best explained on the hypothesis of the eternal communion of the Father and the Son within the life of the triune Godhead. Moreover, as Plummer notes, the aorist tense of *paradidōmi* ("committed") "points back to a moment in eternity, and implies the preexistence of the Messiah."[67]

The birth narratives of Matthew and Luke attest the incarnation of our Lord. Matthew observes that, in fulfillment of the promise of Isaiah 7:14, the infant son born to Mary would be named " 'Immanuel'—which means, 'God with us' " (Matt. 1:23). In Luke's narrative, the angel Gabriel informed Mary that her newborn child would be none other than "the Son of the Most High," the royal Messiah of David (1:32–33). Luke further relates that the Holy Spirit informed the devout Jew Simeon that he would not die before he had seen the Messiah. When Simeon found the infant Jesus in the temple and cradled him in his arms, he thanked God for the privilege of beholding the Lord's salvation incarnate in the child Jesus (Luke 2:25–32). Simeon's song of praise indicates that God's purpose relative to the incarnation was to provide deliverance and salvation (vv. 30–32). Later Luke related Christ's coming into the world to the reality of human sin: "The Son of Man came to seek and to save what was lost" (Luke 19:10; cf. Matt. 20:28; Mark 2:17).

The same birth narratives explicitly attest the reality of our Lord's virgin birth. The patent differences between the two accounts can be explained partly by the thesis that Matthew recounts the birth of Jesus from the perspective of Joseph, whereas Luke formulated his narrative from the angle of Mary's experience. In Matthew's account (Matt. 1:18–25), attention focuses on Joseph who was informed by an angel of the Lord that Mary, his fiancé who was yet a virgin, would bear a child without male agency: "what is conceived [*to gennēthen*] in her is from the Holy Spirit" (1:20). Matthew makes clear that Joseph had no marital relations with Mary "until" (*heōs*) she bore the child (1:25; cf. v. 18). Thus the Roman Catholic postulate of Mary's perpetual virginity is without biblical foundation. Matthew presents the episode as a direct fulfillment of the prophecy of Isaiah 7:14—namely, that a virgin would bear a son whose name would be Immanuel. Finally, Joseph took Mary into his home and legitimized the marriage (short of sexual relations) in obedience to the heavenly command.

In the second account (Luke 1:26–38) Luke, the physician and historian, relates that the angel Gabriel announced to Mary, a humble "virgin" (v. 27, *parthenos*) who delighted in the Lord, that she would be the mother of Israel's Messiah. The Greek word *parthenos,* according to Marshall, "means a young, unmarried girl, and carries the implication of virginity."[68] This is clear from Mary's astonished response to the angel: "How shall this be, seeing I know not a man?" (v. 34, AV). To this the angel responded: "The Holy Spirit will come upon [*epeleusetai*] you, and the power of the Most High will overshadow [*episkiasei*] you. So the holy one to be born [*to gennōmenon*] will be called the Son of God" (v. 35). While not informing Mary precisely how the conception would occur, the heavenly messenger declared that she would conceive miraculously through the special energy of the Holy Spirit.

Contrary to the charges of skeptical critics, the Matthean and Lukan birth narratives agree on a number of significant points: (1) Joseph and Mary were engaged to be married (Matt. 1:18; Luke 1:27). (2) In the betrothed state Mary was a virgin (Matt. 1:23; Luke 1:27, 34). (3) The child was conceived by the Holy Spirit without male agency (Matt. 1:18; Luke 1:35). (4) The name of the son born to Mary was "Jesus," which means, "the Lord is salvation" (Matt. 1:21, 25; Luke 1:31). (5) The child would be the promised messianic Redeemer (Matt. 1:21; Luke 1:32). (6) Jesus would be a uniquely divine person (Matt. 1:23; Luke 1:32, 35). (7) Jesus was born in the town of Bethlehem (Matt. 2:1; Luke 2:4). And (8) Mary and Joseph had a normal married life and begat other children (Matt. 1:25; Luke 2:7–*prōtotokas*, "firstborn"). Indeed, specific mention of Jesus' brothers (James, Joseph, Simon, and Judas) and sisters (Matt. 13:55–56; Mark 6:3; cf. Acts 1:14; Gal. 1:19) contravenes the theory of Mary's perpetual virginity. "It is natural to suppose that the brothers and sisters of Jesus were children of Joseph and Mary."[69]

The fact that both Matthew's and Luke's genealogies of Jesus include Joseph does not disprove the doctrine of our Lord's virginal conception. On the contrary, the round-about manner in which they mention Joseph confirms his role as Jesus' legal rather than natural father. Thus Matthew 1:16 refers to "Joseph, the husband of Mary, of whom was born Jesus, who is called Christ." Similarly Luke 3:23 states that "Jesus . . . was the son, so it was thought, of Joseph."[70] References in the Gospels to Joseph as Jesus' father (Luke 2:27; 33, 41, 48; 4:22; cf. John 1:45; 6:42) merely uphold the importance in Jewish culture of adopted fatherhood.

The Pauline Literature

In order to demonstrate the unrivaled supremacy of Christ, Paul describes the Lord as "the firstborn [*prōtotokos*] over all creation" (Col. 1:15). The text offers no support for the Arian view that *prōtotokos* depicts Christ as the most eminent created being. Rather, according to Lightfoot, the term connotes two main ideas: (1) Christ's priority to creation as eternally preexistent, and (2) Christ's sovereignty over all creation as its Creator and Ruler.[71] The apostle's main point in Colossians 1:15–17 is that as the eternally preexistent One ("He is before all things," v. 17), Christ exercises lordship over the entire universe. In other words, Jesus Christ is "sovereign Lord over all creation by virtue of primogeniture."[72]

When Paul speaks of Christ as God's "Son, who was descended from David according to the flesh" (Rom. 1:3, RSV), he clearly contemplates the Lord's eternal preexistence and incarnation. When Paul adds, "designated Son of God . . . according to the Spirit of holiness by his resurrection from the dead" (v. 4, RSV), he gives a rounded presentation of Christ's three stages of preexistence, humiliation, and exaltation. The apostle's reference in Romans 8:3 to God "sending [*pempsas*] his own Son in the likeness of sinful man to be a sin offering" tersely depicts the enfleshment of Christ and the inauguration of his earthly mission. Bengel observes that the aorist participle *pempsas* "denotes a sort of separation, as it were, or estrangement of the Son from the Father, that He might be the Mediator."[73] A further text, "But when the time had fully come, God sent [*exapesteilen*] his Son, born of a woman, born under the law, to redeem those under law" (Gal. 4:4–5), once again describes Christ's preexistence, incarnation, and saving mission.[74]

The primitive hymn preserved in 1 Timothy 3:16 explicates the heart of the Christian "mystery," namely, the person and history of Jesus Christ. The six rhythmic lines summarize the career of our Lord from his incarnation to his resurrection and ascension. The first line of the hymnodic piece, *hos ephanerōthē en sarki,* clearly affirms Christ's bodily manifestation on earth. The New Testament frequently employs the verb *phaneroō* to describe the incarnation (Rom. 3:21; 2 Tim. 1:10; cf. Heb. 9:26; 1 Peter 1:20; 1 John 1:2). The passive form of the verb here implies the existence of Christ prior to his appearance in the space-time continuum. The phrase *en sarki* denotes that Christ appeared on earth as a real man, a fact attested elsewhere in Paul (Rom. 8:3; Eph. 2:15; Col. 1:22) and in other New Testament writings (John 1:14; Heb. 5:7).

In the context of a discourse on Christian giving, Paul recalled the extraordinary liberality of Christ and interjected a succinct statement on the incarnation: "You know the grace of our Lord Jesus Christ, that though he was rich, yet for your sakes he became poor, so that you through his poverty might become rich" (2 Cor. 8:9). The pregnant phrase *plousios ōn* clearly signifies the Son's preexistence clothed with the glory of the Godhead (1 Cor. 2:8; 2 Thess. 2:14). The words *di hymas eptōcheusen* (note the ingressive aorist of *ptōcheuō*, to be "reduced to poverty") affirm our Lord's transition to the state of humiliation at the incarnation. Christ entered this abject condition when he laid aside the wealth of heaven's glory, assumed our lowly condition, and died a cruel death. The concluding clause of the verse plainly links Christ's incarnation with the atonement; for Paul Christ's person and work constitute an indissoluble whole.

The crowning jewel of incarnational texts is Philippians 2:6–11, an early Christian hymn in praise of Christ that Paul appropriated when writing to the church at Philippi. Just as the previously discussed ethical exhortation to sacrificial giving led Paul to reflect on Christ's voluntary impoverishment (2 Cor. 8:9), so here the apostle's enjoinder to Christian humility prompted the recollection of Christ's incomparable self-renunciation for us. In this text Paul contemplates three states or stages in the existence of the church's Lord: (1) his preexistent condition (v. 6), (2) his incarnation and death, or humiliation, (vv. 7–8), and (3) his triumphant resurrection, or exaltation, to the heavenly realm (vv. 9–11). The opening phrase of the hymn, *hos en morphē theou hyparchōn* ("though he was in the form of God," v. 6a, RSV), speaks of Christ's participation in the divine essence prior to his historical manifestation. One authority translates *hyparchōn* as "being essentially" and adds, "It is said of this divine mode of existence that Christ existed in it in the past. . . . It refers to his preexistence prior to the Incarnation."[75] The hymn continues by declaring that the preexistent Lord "did not consider equality with God [*to einai isa theō*] something to be grasped" (v. 6b). That is, the eternal Christ chose not to regard existence-in-a-manner-of-equality-with-God a treasure to be greedily hoarded. Instead, he voluntarily stripped himself (*ekenōsen*) of his prerogatives as the divine Son (his God-equal position) by "taking the very nature of a servant" (*morphē doulou*, v. 7)—namely, by assuming the form and exhibiting the condition of a common slave. The text indicates that while renouncing participation in the heavenly glory, Christ retained the divine form or *morphē*. "Paul does not teach that our Lord was once God but had become instead man; he teaches that though he was God, he had become also man."[76] The hymn unfolds further the dynamic of the enfleshment of the heavenly Lord: he was "made in human likeness" (*homoiōma*, v. 7b). Christ became in every respect a man like us, sin excepted. The relation is said to be one of "likeness," for in regard to his intrinsic being he was both God *and* man. Lest the reader be misled by the preceding "likeness" relation in a docetic direction, the hymn immediately adds that as to outward appearance (*schēma*) Jesus was, indeed, an authentic man. The One who from eternity possessed the essence and glory of God, and who in an act of supreme self-renunciation assumed the existence of a lowly servant was in truth an authentic man among men.

In opposition to proto-Gnostic teachers who held that the divine emanations and energies were distributed among numerous aeons, Paul insists in Colossians 1:19 that "God was pleased to have all his fullness [*pan to plērōma*] dwell [*katoikēsai*] in him" (i.e., Christ). The "fullness" likely denotes the totality of the divine being and attributes.[77] Far from being parceled out among many intermediaries, the total reality of God made its abode in Jesus of Nazareth. The verb *katoikēsai* may be an ingressive aorist signifying to "take up a permanent abode." In the related text, Colossians 2:9, Paul states that "in Christ all the fullness [*pan to plērōma*] of the Deity lives [*katoikei*] in bodily form [*sōmatikōs*]." The adverb *sōmatikōs* refers to Christ's human body and underscores the fact that at the incarnation the divine essence took upon himself our human nature.

Paul repeatedly affirms that Christ came into the world for the explicit purpose of making amends for sin. "Christ Jesus came into the world to save sinners" (1 Tim. 1:15). The apostle speaks, in addition, of "the appearing [*epiphaneia*] of our Savior, Christ Jesus, who has destroyed death and has brought life and immortality to light through the gospel" (2 Tim. 1:10). Other texts such as Romans 8:3 and Galatians 4:4–5 plainly teach that the chief motivating factor for the incarnation was the salvation of doomed sinners.

The New Testament reader is mildly surprised to find no explicit discussion of the virgin birth outside Matthew's and Luke's gospels. *Prima facie* one might have expected Paul, theologian *extraordinarius,* to have expounded this important theme. The fact, however, that Luke failed to mention the virgin birth in Acts indicates that the argument from silence carries little weight. Given Luke's close relationship with Paul in the ministry of the early church, it is highly probable that the latter knew about the virgin birth, but because of the circumstantial nature of his writings chose not to expound the theme directly. One might also argue with Barth and others that since the virgin birth was not disputed by the early church, Paul felt no need to develop the theme in his letters that primarily dealt with pressing practical problems. Many interpreters have noted that the manner in which Paul discusses the coming of God's Son (e.g., Rom. 8:3; Gal. 4:4) differs from the language customarily used to describe a natural birth. Thus it seems fair to conclude with the judgment of Machen: "The virgin birth is not explicitly mentioned in the Epistles, but is does seem to be implied in the profoundest way in the entire view which Paul holds of the Lord Jesus Christ."[78]

The Johannine Literature

John's gospel is unique in that its opening verses describe the Logos in his supratemporal existence with the Father. The first statement, "In the beginning was the Word" (*En archē ēn ho logos*), signifies that before time or anything else came to be, the Word absolutely *was* (cf. 1 John 1:1). As Westcott observes, "The imperfect tense suggests in this relation . . . the notion of absolute, supratemporal existence."[79] Not only does John affirm the Word's eternal preexistence (cf. 1 John 2:13–14) but also his eternal communion with God: the Word "was with God in the beginning" (*houtos ēn en archē pros ton theon,* v. 2). When nothing but God had being, the Word enjoyed an intimate "I-Thou" relation with the Father (cf. 1 John 1:2). Clearly the first three verses of John's Gospel refute the notion that Christ first became personal either at creation or in the incarnation.

John 8 also explicitly affirms Jesus' timeless preexistence. During a ceremony of the Festival of Tabernacles, four great candelabra were lit to commemorate the pillar of fire that guided Israel through the wilderness. In the midst of the solemn ceremony, Jesus proclaimed to the gathered throng, "I am the light of the world" (John 8:12). Jesus proceeded to assert both that he had a prior existence with the Father in heaven (v. 23) and that Abraham, Israel's revered patriarch, rejoiced to see his day (v. 56). Jesus concluded his dialogue with the Jews with the startling statement: " '. . .before Abraham was born, I am!' " (*egō eimi,* v. 58). By appropriating this self-designation of Yahweh (cf. Exod. 3:14; Isa. 41:4), Jesus boldly claimed that he was the timelessly eternal God.

The Apocalypse presents further evidence of Christ's eternal preexistence. The Savior represented himself to the church at Laodicea as "the beginning [*hē archē*] of God's creation" (Rev. 3:14, RSV), namely, as the originator and sovereign of the cosmos. Christ, moreover, described himself to John with the words "I am [*egō eimi*] the first and the last" (Rev. 1:17; cf. 2:8). In the final chapter of the prophecy, where Christ consummates the course of history, he bears the character of the timeless Sovereign: "I am the Alpha and the Omega, the First and the Last, the Beginning and the End" (Rev. 22:13).

John 1:14, the most complete Johannine statement concerning the incarnation, may be considered from four perspectives. (1) The *subject* of the incarnation is "the Word" (*ho logos*), that is, the divine Logos who existed in communion with the Father from eternity (cf. John 1:1–2). (2) The *substance* of the incarnation: the Word "became flesh" (*sarx egeneto*). The noun *sarx* here connotes human nature without moral disparagement (cf. John 1:13; 3:6; 8:15). John states, not that the Word ceased to be what he was before (i.e., God), but that the Logos assumed our nature and our human mode of existence (sin excepted). "He took the whole nature of man, including its frailty; all that nature in which He could grow, learn, struggle, be tempted, suffer, and die."[80] (3) The *scene* of the incarnation: "and lived [*eskēnōsen*] for a while among us." The verb is the ingressive aorist of *skēnoō,* which means to take up a temporary dwelling place. Just as the divine Presence made its abode in the tabernacle (2 Sam. 7:6), so John claims that God dwelt among us for a season in the man Jesus. And finally, (4) the *substantiation* of the incarnation: "We have seen his glory, the glory of the One and Only [Son], who came from the Father, full of grace and truth" (John 1:14). John and others observed the glory of the majestic God shining through Jesus' human flesh. Thus eyewitnesses testified that the eternal God had indeed become a man in Jesus of Nazareth. John additionally states that Jesus Christ embodies the fullest revelation of the invisible God: "No one has ever seen God, but God the One and Only [Son], who is at the Father's side, has made him known" (*exēgēsato,* 1:18). The aorist middle of *exēgeomai* indicates that Jesus has uniquely "expounded" or "interpreted" the reality of God to finite persons. Christ uniquely reveals the Father to men and women (John 14:8–9).

Opposing the Docetic heresy, which denied that Christ came in genuine human flesh, John affirms in his first letter: "The life appeared [*ephanerōthē*]; we have seen it and testify to it, and we proclaim to you the eternal life, which was with the Father and has appeared to us" (1 John 1:2). Referring here to "the life" rather than to "the Word," John attests the same historical event of the incarnation that he expounded in John 1:14. John adds, "Every spirit that acknowledges that Jesus Christ has come in the flesh [*en sarki*] is from God, but every spirit that does not acknowledge Jesus is not from God" (1 John 4:2–3). John's specification that Jesus came "in flesh" rather than "into flesh" rules out the hypothesis that the Christ descended upon the man Jesus at his baptism. According to John, those who fail to acknowledge that Jesus Christ has come in human flesh (*en sarki*) embody the spirit of the antichrist (2 John 7).

Jesus also spoke of the glory (*doxa*) he shared with the Father from eternity past (John 17:5). Furthermore, Jesus describes himself as one whom God sent into the world on a mission of saving mercy (John 4:34; 5:24, 36). The Lord affirms his eternal preexistence and incarnation by representing himself as the Son of Man who came down from heaven (John 3:13, 31). He is the true bread that descended from the heavenly realm to impart spiritual life to all who will receive him (John 6:32–33, 38, 41,

51). John possessed the unshakeable conviction that Jesus Christ is God's gift of life to the world (John 3:16). He was not a man raised up to represent God, but the divine Son who had come from the Father's presence (John 16:27–28).

John concurs with Paul that the express purpose of the incarnation is the salvation of sinners: "We have seen and testify that the Father has sent his Son to be the Savior of the world" (1 John 4:14; cf. vv. 9–10). Equally directly, John states that Christ "appeared so that he might take away our sins" (1 John 3:5) and "to destroy the devil's work" (1 John 3:8). In a profound sense, Jesus was born and lived that he might die (John 12:27).

Although John does not explicitly mention the virgin birth, it is likely that "the beloved disciple" had some knowledge of Jesus' unique entry into the world. John 8 offers hints that support this hypothesis. At the Festival of Tabernacles the Pharisees raised questions about Jesus' paternity (v. 19) and suggested that he was illegitimately born (v. 41), perhaps of mixed Jewish-Gentile blood (v. 48). Jesus' consistent response throughout this dialogue with the Jews was that his paternity lay with God (vv. 19, 27–28, 38, 49). Indeed, Jesus insisted that the One whom the Pharisees claimed to be their God was none other than his Father (v. 54).

Other New Testament Writings

The opening verses of Hebrews describe the incarnation as the consummation of all God's previous revelations in history: "In these last days he [i.e., God] has spoken [*elalēsen*] to us by his Son" (Heb. 1:2). Christ came forth from heaven and lived as a man to be the final and definitive disclosure of God (cf. Heb. 3:1, which denotes Jesus as "the apostle"). Peter attests Christ's eternal sonship and incarnation with similar imagery: "He was chosen before the creation of the world, but was revealed [*phanerōthentos*] in these last times for your sake" (1 Peter 1:20). The verb is the aorist passive participle of *phaneroō*, to "make plain," or to "manifest," and denotes the historic revelation of God in Christ at Bethlehem. The writer of Hebrews did not doubt, however, that Christ eternally preexisted his manifestation as a man (Heb. 1:10; 7:3; 13:8).

In constructing his case for the superiority of Christ's priesthood, Hebrews teaches that Christ became a man and lived a truly human life, participating in all humanity's experiences, sin excepted (Heb. 4:15). To this end, in Hebrews 2 the author makes several statements about the *nature* of Christ's humiliation. (1) At the incarnation God "made [him] a little lower than the angels" (v. 9). We understand the word "lower" (*brachy*) in the sense of degree rather than of duration, in keeping with the text of Psalm 8:5. The expression may be a Hebraism meaning simply "became man." (2) Christ "shared in their humanity," i.e., he fully participated in our "flesh and blood" (v. 14). In order to attain true solidarity with those he came to save, Christ voluntarily became a human as we are. (3) Christ entered the stream of "Abraham's descendants" (v. 16). The Christ who came to save mortals, not angels, became a member of a particular people, the family of Abraham (Matt. 1:1). Finally, (4) At the incarnation, Christ "had to be made like his brothers in every way" (v. 17). To redeem people, it was necessary (note the verb *opheilō*, expressing obligation) that Christ should become all that we are, and that he should share our pain, sorrows, and trials.

From this discussion of the nature of the incarnation, the author passes to a consideration of the *purpose* for which God became man. His exposition here is even more extensive. (1) Christ left heaven and became a man "so that by the grace of God he might taste death for everyone" (v. 9). The overarching purpose of the incarnation was the concrete fact that Christ should die for sinners (cf. Heb. 9:26). (2) Christ entered time and space in order "to bring many sons to glory" (v. 10). As the pathfinder of salvation, Christ descended to earth that he might direct many believers upward to heaven. (3) Christ became man so that both he and they might be "of the same family" (v. 11). The incarnation opened the door to a new relationship between God and persons. Through faith aliens and enemies now become privileged members of his household. (4) Christ entered the world and died so that "he might destroy him who holds the power of death—that is, the devil" (v. 14). Paradoxically, the death of Christ destroyed Satan and the grip of death the evil one holds over the human race. The Puritan writer John Owen developed this motif in his classic essay *The Death of Death in the Death of Christ.* (5) Christ lived and died to "free those who all their lives were held in slavery by their fear of death" (v. 15). Christ means liberation from the prince of terrors, the fear of death and nothingness. Lastly, (6) Christ became man "that he might make atonement for the sins of the people" (v. 17). Here again, the express purpose of the incarnation is stated to be the propitiatory sacrifice Christ offered on the cross.

SYSTEMATIC FORMULATION

In accord with the redemptive plan (vol. 1, chap. 8), the Father sent his unique Son into the world to do for the lost what they could not do for themselves. In understanding the incarnation what elements of the alternative views may be integrated in a coherent doctrine accounting for all the lines of relevant scriptural data? Consider first the incarnation's visible indicator.

The Sign of Jesus' Virgin Birth

Beyond any reasonable doubt in the first century in Bethlehem a woman named Mary conceived and gave birth to an actual baby named Jesus. Bultmann's view that we can know almost nothing about the historical Jesus has been discredited. The continued discovery of early evidence renders less and less probable the hypothesis that the story of Jesus' birth was a later church invention. The evidence does not support a naïve belief in everything handed down by tradition, but a historical realism.[81] The Gospel accounts are written by contemporaries who investigated what happened (Luke 1:1–4). Those who considered Jesus a literal baby included not only Mary, but also his foster father Joseph, the shepherds, the angels, the Magi, and King Herod. Other evidence for the historicity of Jesus remains to this day—the change in the day of worship from Saturday to Sunday, the change in the calendar, the writing of the New Testament, and the origin of the Christian church. To these critical considerations for the historical Jesus we may add the theological case that Matthew 1 and Luke 1 are part of the informational revelation supernaturally inspired by the all-knowing God (volume 1, pages 115–16; 146–64, supports an informational revelation and supernatural inspiration of the Bible as a whole, including Matthew 1 and Luke 1). The interpretive issues of the birth narratives being minimal, the Bible clearly teaches the fact of Jesus' actual birth.

Mary's conception of Jesus was a biological miracle. Matthew's record indicates that her conception of Jesus was not the result of ordinary sexual intercourse. Mary's pregnancy was extraordinary, according to Matthew, for at least three reasons: (1) She conceived prior to union with Joseph (Matt. 1:18). (2) Joseph, being "a righteous man," acted as an honorable fiancé would under the circumstances. He "did not want to expose her to public disgrace . . . [and] had in mind to divorce her quietly (v. 19). (3) After he had considered divorce, an angel of the Lord appeared to him in a dream and said, "Joseph son of David, do not be afraid to take Mary home as your wife, because what is conceived in her is from the Holy Spirit" (v. 20).

Doctor Luke's investigative report confirms the miraculous conception of Jesus for similar reasons. After the angel Gabriel's announcement of Jesus' coming birth to Mary, she exclaimed, "How will this be, since I am a virgin?" (Luke 1:34). Luke records the angel's explanation: "The Holy Spirit will come upon you, and the power of the Most High will overshadow you. . . . For nothing is impossible with God" (vv. 35, 37). Explicitly both Matthew and Luke deny any role of a man in Mary's conception of Jesus, and both attribute her pregnancy to an extraordinary creative act of the Holy Spirit. The virgin conception and birth of Jesus was indeed a "mighty act" of God, a "wonder," and a "sign."

Why is the rest of the New Testament silent about the virgin birth? Some find allusions to the virgin birth in Matthew 1:16; Luke 3:23; John 1:13; and Galatians 4:4. These passages are marvelously consistent with the fact once it is granted on more explicit evidence, but they are not the best texts for establishing the fact. The silence of the gospels of Mark and John does not contradict the teaching of Matthew and Luke but presupposes them. Mark makes no reference even to Jesus' childhood but begins with Jesus' baptism, and so reference to the birth is not part of his purpose. John's later emphasis on the incarnation could assume the explicit teaching on the conception and birth of Matthew and Luke. It seems clear that the major reason for a lack of other references in the recorded messages in Acts is that this information was not part of the apostles' initial message (*kerygma*) for unbelievers. As J. V. L. Casserley concluded, "The New Testament evidence is not as strong in the case of the virgin birth as it is in that of the resurrection. There is, however, no evidence at all for any other alternative."[82] If we are to judge importance by the number of verses on a topic, then we should note that there is more specific material about the virgin birth than about the creation of mankind in the divine image or the Lord's Supper. Clearly the number of verses on a subject does not determine its importance.

No serious textual difficulties with the extensive passages in Matthew and Luke are found. Matthew's and Luke's accounts of the virgin birth are unquestionably genuine parts of their respective gospels. And "the gospels containing these narratives are genuine documents of the Apostolic Age. The texts of these narratives have come down to us in their integrity."[83] More affirmatively, as J. Gresham Machen said, "it is perfectly clear that the New Testament teaches the virgin birth of Christ; about that there can be no manner of doubt. There is no serious question as to the *interpretation* of the Bible at this point. . . . The only question is whether in making that representation the Bible is true or false."[84] An initial skepticism of such a miracle may be expected. We ought not invent miracles where evidence for them is lacking. It is healthy to ask for explicit biblical evidence. But an initial skepticism is not a good reason for ignoring or denying a conclusive case from two extensive passages.

Although a virgin conception is an impossibility for reductive naturalists and pantheists (except as myth), for theists it is genuinely *possible*. Creation's regular laws do not form a closed system (as we found in studies of creation and providence). The Creator and Sustainer of the ordinary processes can, for purposes of recovering his lost people, work in extraordinary ways. God worked miraculously to deliver his people from Egyptian oppressors. A virgin conception and birth may sound like a mere myth to people who assume the absolute uniformity of nature and who think nature is God. But the Lord of nature is not bound by nature. The sustainer of nature can choose to act unusually through it or independently of its usual processes.

The virgin birth is *not an isolated miracle* but one of a series of mighty acts for redeeming God's people. The series of redemptive acts are the specific messianic predictions of the Old Testament made hundreds of years in advance, and specifically, the prediction of his supernatural birth as a "sign" (Isa. 7:14). Supernaturally Jesus healed the blind, the lame, and the lepers. Supernaturally he raised the dead and calmed the storms. Supernaturally he was transfigured before his disciples. Supernaturally he was raised from the dead, and supernaturally he ascended into heaven. As Ramm has said, "The virgin birth is part of a complex of doctrines (rooted in events) where each doctrine supports the rationale of the other."[85] Since the Messiah's ministry concluded with a miraculous resurrection and ascension, it is appropriate that he entered the world miraculously.

The Significance of Jesus' Virgin Birth

Christ's virgin birth provides a case study in the impossibility of totally separating the historical events from their theological meanings. The sign of the virgin conception (Isa. 7:14) signifies the once-for-all supernatural incarnation of God's eternal Word or Son. We need not decide whether the writers of the Gospels were either historians or theologians. They were both historians and theologians. Their accounts of miracles in general were not only "mighty acts" of God and "wonders" but also "signs" pointing to spiritual truths. So the uniqueness of Jesus' birth was a "sign" that he was not only a human son but also the long-awaited God-sent Messiah on a special mission. Consider several aspects of the significance of Jesus' virgin conception.

1. Jesus' virgin conception and birth signify the *moral miracle* of his *unique holiness*. The angels' announcement of the Spirit's overshadowing added, "So the holy one to be born will be called the Son of God" (Luke 1:35). From conception Jesus was set apart from sinners for the redemption of sinners. It is true, as Ramm suggests, that people who are not sinless may be called holy. But the designation can also refer to God who is sinless, and the context bears out the divine holiness involving sinlessness. Any naturally born person since the Fall has sins (1 John 1:8–10) because a bad tree (heart) brings forth bad fruit (Matt. 12:33–35). But Jesus challenged anyone to prove him guilty of sin (John 8:46). John, who may have known him best, could write, "You know that he appeared so that he might take away our sins. And in him is no sin" (1 John 3:5). A person born of a fallen woman, although tempted for many years as we are, never yielded to the enticements! At the beginning of his human existence Jesus' supernatural conception draws attention to his supernatural sinlessness.

The fact that Jesus had no fallen human father does not mean that he lacked humanity. There is no reason to deny that Mary was fully human or that her child was fully human. To imply that the Holy Spirit could not supernaturally supply the male contribution to the conception of the child is unjustifiable, since the Spirit was involved in the creation of human life in the beginning. Because he is Spirit no physical process is appropriately imagined in the Holy Spirit's "overshadowing" of Mary. The chaste biblical narrative differs greatly from pagan myths of "gods" having intercourse with women.

2. Jesus Christ's virgin conception also serves as a sign of his *deity*. "So the holy one to be born will be called *the Son of God*" (Luke 1:35, italics mine). He would also be called "Immanuel—which means God with us" (Matt. 1:23). An ordinarily born person did not have a previous existence, let alone exist as a member of the Godhead. Had Jesus been born in the usual way, he might have symbolically represented some aspects of God's nature, but he would not have actually been the eternal second Person of the Trinity. The sign of his supernatural birth indicates the supernaturalness of his Person.

3. Jesus Christ's virgin birth draws attention to the eternal Son's *incarnation*. The assertion that the invisible God became flesh cannot be entirely verified by the senses—God cannot be seen. The supernatural aspects of the conception and birth signify Jesus' extraordinary eternal existence; the natural aspects point to his actual involvement with humans in literal flesh and blood. The gestation, birth, and growth processes are *indicii* that here was no mere mythical figure but a literal person in an actual human body. The possibility of full humanness without sin is indicated by Adam and Eve before the Fall and by believers' future glorified state.

4. Jesus' virgin birth from his beginning points up his *redemptive mission*. The angel said, "She will give birth to a son, and you are to give him the name Jesus, because he will save his people from their sins" (Matt. 1:21). Had Jesus been ordinarily born, he would have been a sinful member of the fallen race and represented by its first head, Adam, in whom he would be judged guilty of sin (Rom. 5:16, 18). Jesus came, however, to save the people whom God called out of the world, and he did so by becoming their head. Jesus' supernatural birth indicates that he is not one more member of the depraved, condemned, and alienated Adamic race, but the head of a new order composed of those who have become new creatures by God's grace.

5. The fact of the virgin birth also *confirms the reliability of the prophetic word*. "All this took place to fulfill what the Lord had said through the prophet: 'The virgin will be with child and will give birth to a son' " (Matt. 1:22–23; cf. Isa. 7:14). One's belief in Christ's virgin birth is a test case of one's conviction that "nothing is impossible with God" (Luke 1:37) and of one's belief in God's promises of the supernatural. Faith in the coming birth of a son in elderly Abraham's case involved "being fully persuaded that God had power to do what he had promised" (Rom. 4:21). Similarly Mary became fully persuaded of the prophetic word issued before Jesus' birth that the messianic servant would be born of her though she was a virgin. After the marvelous fulfillment, Christians should not be less fully persuaded that God demonstrated his power to do what he had promised!

The Importance of Jesus' Virgin Birth

Because of its rich significance, the teaching of Christ's virgin birth is *indispensable* to a biblically based Christology and soteriology. Although we can imagine other ways by which God could supernaturally have kept Jesus sinless, in historical actuality the sign of the virgin birth is nonnegotiable. Furthermore, as a highly significant part of divine revelation the story of the virgin birth is inspired and profitable. As such it needs to be taught faithfully to each generation.

Although the doctrine of the virgin birth of Christ is necessary for understanding the implications of salvation, it is *optional evangelistically*. The truth of Jesus' birth of a virgin need not be highlighted in the initial gospel message to unbelievers. No passage of Scripture says explicitly that if you believe in Jesus' virgin birth you will receive eternal life. Each doctrine revealed in Scripture is important and profitable for its respective purposes, but not all are equally important for an initial evangelistic purpose. We need not explain every doctrine in presenting the gospel to the lost.

What, then, does the New Testament affirm that sinners must believe to be saved? This will be discussed and documented further under the subject of the verbal call. Briefly, explicit passages assert that to be saved people must believe, in fulfillment of the (Old Testament) Scriptures, that: (1) Jesus is the Christ, the Messiah, (2) he died for our sins and was buried, and (3) he rose again from the grave (1 Cor. 15:3–4). Although the Scriptures mention those doctrines many times, not one verse asserts that those who believe in the virgin birth will be saved. In all of his conversations with sinners, Jesus did not ask them to accept this doctrine in order to receive eternal life. In all the recorded evangelistic messages of the apostles in Acts, none call for belief in the virgin birth for justification. None of the epistles, furthermore, include the doctrine in summations of the heart of the gospel. Hence we conclude that we need not include teaching on the virgin birth in our initial evangelistic presentations.

Furthermore, to make acceptance of Christ's virgin birth a condition of salvation is to hinder little children from coming into the kingdom of heaven. By way of illustration, at a minister's meeting in Denver in the 1960s a noted preacher declared vehemently that no one could be saved who did not believe that Christ was born of a virgin! He went on to label any seminary that did not teach that truth "liberal." Later in the message the pastor told of his own conversion at the age of six. When he sat down in a pew just ahead of us, a colleague leaned over to ask him, "At the age of six did you know what a virgin was?"

Although one who has not heard of Jesus' virgin birth need not believe it to be saved, it would seem improbable that an adult who has received Jesus as Lord and has become aware of the explicitness of the biblical support and its theological importance would persist in denying its truth. Before the New Testament was available there were no doubt Christians who had not heard of the virgin birth. This fact, however, provides no excuse for rejecting the biblical evidence for the virgin birth. A Christian does not knowingly and deliberately reject an explicit biblical teaching without accountability to divine judgment.

Mary, the Mother of Jesus

No biblical or other evidence gives us reason to believe that Mary was immaculately conceived or miraculously born. Hence we may conclude that she, like all other persons, had a fallen father and mother and from them received a sinful human nature. The biblical teaching indicates that the moral miracle at his conception by the Holy Spirit freed Jesus, not her, from a sinful nature. The child, not Mary, is "the holy one" (Luke 1:35).

Mary, nevertheless, was "highly favored" by God (Luke 1:28) and "found favor with God" (v. 30). She was "blessed" (v. 42) to be chosen from among all the women of the world to be the mother through whom God's eternal Word would become flesh. As the one highly favored to be the mother of the long-awaited Messiah, she was not a bestower of divine grace but the recipient of divine grace. A recipient of grace receives favors that are undeserved. She did not merit the privilege of giving birth to the Messiah; rather, she was chosen among women by sheer grace. Elizabeth too felt favored that the mother of her Lord should come to visit her (v. 43). Elizabeth clearly thought of Mary as a human woman, not a divine mediatrix. As a woman Mary was the mother of the Messiah to whom these godly women looked in faith for salvation. Hence Mary may be honored as the most favored woman in history but not worshiped as sinless or divine. For the real humanity of her Son, it was essential that Mary be fully human. If she were in some sense divine, that would not in any way enhance his deity. But she was indispensable to his being truly human. Since Mary was only human, we ought not worship her.

No Scripture calls Mary "the mother of God." God, being eternal and self-existent (see 1:198–200), can have no mother. Similarly God's eternal Word can have no mother, for he was with God and was God (John 1:1). Mary was the mother of Jesus' humanness, begotten supernaturally from the Holy Spirit. Because Jesus was the long-awaited Messiah, Elizabeth was able to speak honorifically of Mary as "the mother of my Lord" (Luke 1:43). Warfield explains, "Clearly she intends to express by the designation the height of at least Messianic glory; but it does not seem obvious that her thought went beyond the delegated glory of the divine representative."[86] Mary rejoiced in her privilege (vv. 46–47), but she also recognized her "humble state" as God's servant (v. 48).

Although the Scriptures emphasize Mary's virginity until Jesus' birth, scriptural support cannot be found for the Roman Catholic tradition of her perpetual virginity. We have good reason to believe that after the birth of Jesus Joseph and Mary lived together as man and wife and had a family. Jesus' "brothers" are mentioned several times (Matt. 12:46–50 and parallels). Four brothers are named (James, Joseph, Judas, and Simon), and his sisters (plural) are also indicated (Mark 6:3). A document, "History of Joseph the Carpenter," written in Egypt in the fourth century to glorify Joseph and foster his cult, alleges that Joseph was a widower with children at the time of his engagement to Mary, a girl of twelve.[87] The reliable scriptural accounts could easily have mentioned this fact if it were true, so it seems improbable. At any rate, even if Joseph had been a widower with some children by a previous marriage, he and Mary apparently had other children of their own.

In Protestant churches and homes Mary can appropriately be honored—not only on Mother's Day but also on other occasions. Her favor and blessedness among women need not be ignored because of Roman Catholic tendencies to exalt her to a mediatrix. "When the time had fully come, God sent his Son, born of a woman, born under law, to redeem those under law, that we might receive the full rights of sons" (Gal. 4:4). As we exalt the Redeemer, we ought not forget that in the Father's timing the Messiah was "born of woman," and that he was born of this woman, Mary. "After all," Paul Jewett has observed, "if their [Roman Catholic] theology of the Virgin is too high, maybe ours is too low—if indeed we have any theology of Mary at all."[88] An effective Protestant corrective to an unbiblical Roman theology of Mary is not lack of thought about her. The antidote is a biblically founded theology of Mary!

Negatively, a biblically informed Protestant theology of Mary will not allow attention to be taken away from the centrality of Jesus as the incarnate Son of God, the Savior, and the one Mediator. In patristic tradition from Ignatius to Aquinas, "The virgin birth of Jesus gradually became separated from Christology and became attached to Mariology."[89] Because of the popularity of pagan sources the church leaders felt a necessity to Christianize the "Lady," the "Queen," and the "Mother."[90] Faced with similar pressures from some radical feminists today who virtually worship Mary as a goddess, contemporary Protestants need to resist paganizing the faith.

Affirmatively, a Protestant theology of Mary incorporates several points: (1) It regards her as a primary example of the God-given dignity of women. (2) She provides a prime exhibit of a pure, thoughtful, believing, and spiritually vital daughter of Abraham. Her marvelous song of praise reflects Spirit-illumined receptivity to God's Word and a personal relationship with the living Lord of all (Luke 1:46–55). (3) She exemplifies God's strategy of using human agents and women in particular in the accomplishment of his holy and loving purposes. (4) She also exhibits human willingness to accept God's Word and do God's bidding at great personal risk. (5) Mary was betrothed, indicating the importance of a family and home in which to bring up Jesus. (6) With a devout engaged couple, God worked a miracle, signifying the sanctity of conception and birth in the security of the marriage commitment. Synthesizing all of these factors, a Protestant theology of Mary emphasizes God's great esteem for a devout woman in bringing to pass the greatest event in history—the incarnation of God's eternal Word.

Joseph, the Foster Father of Jesus

To complete the family picture we need also to formulate a brief theology of Joseph. Mary was "pledged to be married to Joseph, but before they came together, she was found to be with child through the Holy Spirit" (Matt. 1:18). Even though there were no sexual relations during a Jewish betrothal period, the betrothal could be broken only by divorce. Upon hearing of Mary's pregnancy, Joseph was distressed. He was a righteous man, but he was also considerate and did not want to expose Mary to public disgrace; therefore he sought to divorce her quietly (v. 19). Joseph received the message from the angel of the Lord explaining that the baby was conceived by the Holy Spirit and that he should name him Jesus, because he would save his people from their sins (vv. 20–21). Joseph did what the Lord had commanded and took Mary home as his wife. He had no union with her until she gave birth to a son (vv. 24–25). The family went from Nazareth to Bethlehem to register in his hometown for the census of Quirinius (governor of Syria) because Joseph belonged to the line of David (Luke 2:1–2). Jesus had the right to the throne of David through his legal father, Joseph. When the shepherds came to Bethlehem to see the newborn baby, they found Joseph with Mary and Jesus (v. 16). Luke's genealogy, emphasizing the line of Mary, the blood relative, notes that at the beginning of Jesus' ministry when he was thirty years of age, "he was *the son, so it was thought, of Joseph*" (Luke 3:23, italics mine).

Although he was not the natural father of Jesus, Joseph served as his foster father. Joseph and Mary together served as faithful spiritual parents. Both Joseph and Mary took Jesus to Jerusalem and consecrated him to the Lord (vv. 22–24). When Simeon blessed them and spoke of Jesus' coming greatness (vv. 28–32), the child's "father and mother marveled at what was said about him" (v. 33). Joseph and Mary did everything at his dedication that was required by the Law of the Lord (v. 39). The genealogy in Matthew shows that Jesus was the legal son of Joseph and so was in the line of descent from David and Abraham (Matt. 1:1, 16). When an angel warned Joseph in a dream to flee to Egypt to avoid Herod's attempt to kill the Jewish Messiah, Joseph, sensitive to the Lord's leading, obeyed and moved to Egypt (2:13–14). Again at the leading of the Lord he moved the family back to Israel. For the safety of the child he was led not to settle in Judea but went to Galilee and settled in Nazareth (vv. 19–23). At the Lord's direction Joseph moved the family three times.

Every year Joseph took the whole family to Jerusalem for the Feast of the Passover (Luke 2:41). When at twelve years of age after the Feast Jesus did not leave Jerusalem with his parents, they returned to find him in dialogue with the teachers at the temple. Joseph and Mary had been anxious about him, and when they saw him in the temple, they were astonished at his knowledge (vv. 45–48). After Jesus' baptism he taught in the synagogues, and when he read from the scroll of Isaiah and spoke of its fulfillment in Nazareth, people were amazed at his wisdom and miraculous powers. Understandably they asked, "Isn't this the carpenter's son? . . . Where did this man get all these things?" (Matt. 13:55–56). From these brief indications, the carpenter-father exhibited a sensitivity to the Lord's leading and a faithfulness in worship that contributed to Jesus' early development physically and spiritually. Theologically, Joseph furnishes for all fathers, and especially foster fathers, a worthy example of spiritual faithfulness and unquestioning obedience to the Lord's leading. Together, Joseph and Mary exemplify the values of raising children in a home characterized by spiritual fidelity.

In sum, although the fact that Christ was born of the virgin Mary need not be included in every tract for the lost, our biblical and systematic research has shown that his birth was indeed a mighty act of the Holy Spirit, a wonder, and a sign bearing great theological significance. The actuality of the virginal conception dramatically signifies Christ's sinlessness, deity, incarnation, and mission to save the lost. The fact also exhibits the reliability of one of the most astounding predictions in the prophetic Word. The favoring of Mary to bear and nurture the Messiah displays God's esteem of women and one of their crucial roles in the coming of the divine kingdom on earth. In addition, the account reflects Joseph's character as spiritually perceptive, just, and considerate. Partly as a result of the providential spiritual influence of both Joseph and Mary, Jesus "grew and became strong; he was filled with wisdom, and the grace of God was upon him" (Luke 2:40). The fact that "Jesus grew in wisdom and stature and in favor with God and men" (v. 52) cannot be entirely unrelated to his parents' loving care and spiritual example.

Challenges to Understanding the Incarnation

We turn attention now from the "sign" of the supernatural birth of a baby boy to the even more dramatic event it primarily signified—the incarnation of the second person of the Trinity! The term "incarnation" can be traced to the Latin version of John 1:14 and has been commonly used since the fourth century. In the narrow sense "incarnation" refers to the initial event in which the eternal Word "became flesh," the beginning of his first advent to earth. In a broader sense "incarnation" may refer to the entire experience of human life into which he entered, including the facts of his resurrection and his ascension with his human nature to heaven. In this chapter we generally use the term in its narrower sense, the beginning of his life on earth. The rest of Jesus' life will be in view in the three chapters that follow.

Understanding how God could become a human has presented a great challenge, as pointed up by the number of alternative views. How did a member of the invisible Godhead become visible? How could the eternal even enter time let alone experience time? Could the eternal Son of God be born a human infant? Could the omniscient One grow in knowledge and wisdom? Answers to questions like these are complex because they involve many factors, such as one's grasp of the relevant implications of trinitarianism, the eternal God's relation to all temporal events, whether the accounts of a divine being in history can be interpreted literally or must be taken figuratively, and the compatibility of the divine archetype with a human image-bearer.

At first the case seems strong for a figurative interpretation of the incarnation. It seems impossible for the infinite to become literally finite, the omnipotent to become a weak baby, the omniscient to grow in knowledge as a child, and the omnipresent to walk from one town to another. Immersed in a naturalistic scientific mentality, we are suspicious of the paranormal and of any claims to be in touch with it. Even those who believe in a tri-personal God often restrict the members of the Trinity to their regular activities through nature and take figuratively or mythically some aspects of what the Bible reports that God in fact did. Furthermore the story of God's becoming man through a virgin may seem reminiscent of Hindu and Greek mythology. It sounds like the appearance of springtime, the rising again of life in nature, or a handsome prince coming from above to rescue a sleeping princess.

The Cognitive Significance of the Incarnation

Christmas is first of all a story about God the Father and secondly a story about Jesus. God has not left us to our fallenness and deserved judgment. God mercifully withholds deserved punishment and graciously gives the world's greatest gift. The heavenly Father sent us his unique eternal Son. "Thanks be to God for his indescribable gift!" (2 Cor. 9:15).

The eternal person of the Son took on himself a real human nature. Christ's primary purpose in coming to earth to visit us was to save the lost. The redemptive action seems so important that some relationalists and functionalists have lost sight of the One who accomplished it. The crucial point, they maintain, is what Jesus did, not who he was (in his metaphysical or ontological being). They seem to overlook the fact that the value of Jesus' dynamic work depends on who he *was*. The question Jesus asked must still be answered: "Who do people say the Son of Man is?" Surely he would have been unsatisfied with the reply, "An unknown 'X'."

Essential to the concept of the incarnation is the Father's sending of his precious Son. This implies Jesus' preexistence as the eternal second person of the Trinity (see I:272–75). Although everything is made *by* God, and all humans are made *in* God's image, only Jesus of Nazareth is eternally begotten *of* God. So the coming of the eternal Word into the literal world of Mary in the literal flesh of a baby exhibits God's actual loving presence with us in spite of our sin. "For what the law was powerless to do in that it was weakened by the sinful nature, God did by sending his own Son in the likeness of sinful man, to be a sin offering" (Rom. 8:3; cf. Gal. 4:4). As Wolfhart Pannenberg said, "Jesus was always one with God, not just after a certain date in his life. . . . Were it otherwise, Jesus would not be in person the one revelation of the eternal God."[91] At the beginning of his life Jesus descended from his preexistent trinitarian state and at the end of his advent to earth the glorified One ascended back to the Father.

Although in thought we can distinguish the eternal Son from the man Jesus, "the eternity of the Sonship and the earthly human mode of Jesus' existence are parts of a single, concrete existence."[92] Jesus is the Christ in human flesh. Christology involves the conjunction of the two. And it involves the order of movement from God to man. Christology cannot be adequately done from "below." It must coherently account for the evidence both for his humanness below and for his divinity from "above."

Prophetic Anticipation of the Incarnation

The preparatory movement for the incarnation began centuries before with the Old Testament messianic predictions. The eternal antecedents (in Logos Christologies) must not obscure the historical antecedents in the prophetic writings. The incarnation is the eschatological fulfillment of specific predictions and varied allusions to the effect that God would send the Messiah through the line of Eve, Abraham, and David. The incarnation is also a fulfillment of a Jewish philosophy of history. Thinkers who do not have the Old Testament hope for the last days can easily consider the descent and ascent of Christ a myth from a fantasy world, and a rift may be imagined between the eternal Christ and the historical Jesus. Apart from Israel's messianic hope, the birth and ascension of Jesus become merely illustrations of the significance of life in general. From within the context of Old Testament eschatological promises, however, the announcement that the Son of God became man in Jesus of Nazareth becomes a dramatic fulfillment. Divine promise and fulfillment permeates biblical history coherently with a view of revelation in both information and act.

The damaged divine image in mankind after the Fall still included an obscure consciousness of his original happy condition and an earnest desire to regain it. This was insufficient of itself, however, to effect the great end of his being—fellowship with his Creator. Why did God not send his Son immediately after the Fall? Apparently there needed to be a cultivation of a state in which at least some people would be receptive to him. Gentiles were driven to see their need by the law written on their hearts, and the Jews by Moses' law. By the law the sinner became aware of sin, desired freedom from it and felt the need for redemption. After the earlier illustrations of judgment and grace, God called Abraham to be the father of the people through whom his Son would appear at the appointed time. He strengthened their faith by visible signs of his gracious appearance in many wonderful works. And he sent messages in varied ways by his prophets one after another. "Frequent new revelation kept the expectation alive and rendered it continually more and more definite. "And thus," Hengstenberg argued, "the doctrine of a coming Redeemer, even when partially misunderstood, became the soul and centre of all theocratic expectations."[93]

Summarizing the messianic predictions discussed in the Scripture section, a descendant of Eve would defeat Satan (Gen. 3:15). Then one in the line of

Abraham would bring blessing to the whole earth (Gen. 12:3; 18:18; 22:18). As a son of David, furthermore, he would rule on David's throne forever (2 Sam. 7:12–16; Isa. 9:6–7; 11:1; Jer. 23:5–6). And he would be born in Bethlehem (Mic. 5:2). He would be called Immanuel and would be born of a virgin (Isa. 7:14). The Septuagint Greek translation, compiled during the second and third centuries B.C., used the Greek word for virgin (*parthenos*) to translate the Hebrew *ʿalmāh*, as do the Dead Sea Scrolls, and some of the rabbis from before the time of Christ.[94]

What of those who with Schleiermacher and others find in the Old Testament only indistinct longings and feelings of the need for redemption? Hengstenberg argues that the Lord Jesus Christ and his apostles, although they referred to the Old Testament in different ways (direct quotations, allusions, and similar principles and events), believed the Old Testament Scriptures to contain genuine predictions. Although even after the resurrection the minds of the disciples on the road to Emmaus were kept from recognizing Jesus, he said to them, " 'How foolish you are, and how slow of heart to believe all that the prophets have spoken! Did not the Christ have to suffer these things and then enter his glory?' And beginning with Moses and all the Prophets, he explained to them what was said in all the Scriptures concerning himself" (Luke 24:25–27).

Earlier Jesus had pointed out how people diligently study the Scriptures that testify about him, yet refuse to come to him to have life (John 5:39–40). "If you believed Moses," Jesus said, "you would believe me, for *he wrote about me*" (v. 46, italics mine). Jesus added, "But since you do not believe what he wrote, how are you going to believe what I say?" (v. 47). When Jesus was about to be arrested, he said, "It is written: 'And he was numbered with the transgressors' [Isa. 53:12]; and I tell you that this *must* be fulfilled in me. Yes, what is written about me is reaching its fulfillment" (Luke 22:37, italics mine). "But the Scripture *must* be fulfilled" (Mark 14:49, italics mine). To appreciate the extent of the Old Testament materials, see Hengstenberg's 699-page exposition and defense of Old Testament messianic predictions in his classic *Christology of the Old Testament*.[95] The righteous, devout, and Spirit-illumined Simeon, who waited for the consolation of Israel before his death, saw the infant Messiah in the temple, took him in his arms, and exclaimed, "My eyes have seen your salvation . . . a light for revelation to the Gentiles and for glory to your people Israel" (Luke 2:25–32). Anna also "gave thanks to God and spoke about the child to all who were looking forward to the redemption of Jerusalem" (v. 38).

Was Jesus Conscious of His Incarnation?

Did Jesus believe himself to be the Messiah? Some naturalists deny that he was conscious of his incarnate nature and messianic mission. Some allege that the idea developed in his mind gradually, and some think he used the suggestion as a literary device to gain acceptance for his views. But Jews, Muslims, and others who deny that Jesus ever claimed to be essentially one with the Father, lack a coherent interpretation of the evidence to be laid out in the following paragraphs.

Jesus used unique *messianic titles* for himself. He spoke of himself as "the Christ," "the Lord," "the Son of God," "the Son of Man," and "the Savior." The detailed significance of these self-designations as developed by Geerhardus Vos in *The Self-Disclosure of Jesus* supports his unique identification of himself with his heavenly Father.[96]

Jesus of Nazareth referred to his uniquely divine origin and nature. As "the Son of Man" he claimed that he alone had "[come] from heaven" (John 3:13) and that God "gave his one and only Son" (v. 16). As God's Son he was begotten (of the same nature as the Father), not a creation out of nothing. Jesus said to the Samaritan woman at the well, "If you knew the gift of God and who it is that asks you for a drink, you would have asked him and he would have given you living water" (4:10). She said, "I know that Messiah is coming. When he comes, he will explain everything to us." Then Jesus confessed, "I who speak to you am he" (4:25–26). The Jews tried to kill him because "he was even calling God his own Father, and making himself equal with God" (5:18). Again the Jews understood the import of Jesus' claims for himself and grumbled among themselves saying, "Is this not Jesus, the son of Joseph, whose father and mother we know? How can he say, 'I came down from heaven'?" (6:42). But Jesus continued to say, "I am the living bread that came down from heaven" (vv. 50–51, 58). "The living Father sent me" (v. 57). "What if you see the Son of Man ascend to where he was before!" (v. 62). When the Jews said they knew where he was from, Jesus replied, "I am not here on my own, but he who sent me is true. You do not know him, but I know him because I am from him and he sent me" (7:28–29). The Father "sent me" (8:16, 18). "You are from below; I am from above. You are of this world; I am not of this world" (v. 23). "I came from God" (v. 42).

The Jesus of history spoke of his *preexistence as God.* Jesus said, "Before Abraham was born, I am!" (v. 58). What his first-century hearers understood him to mean became evident quickly. They sought to stone him for blasphemy, "because you," they said, "a mere man, claim to be God" (10:33). From these relatively few passages from the Gospels it becomes evident that Jesus was conscious of being uniquely incarnate and not of this world (not born of the flesh—John 3:6), but virgin-born. His conscious understanding of himself is not what developed in time; only progressively did he choose to disclose his divine nature and mission.

Jesus taught his disciples about his unique *messianic mission.* He said, "The Father judges no one, but has entrusted all judgment to the Son, that all may honor the Son just as they honor the Father. He who does not honor the Son does not honor the Father who sent him" (John 5:22–23). "I seek not to please myself but him who sent me" (v. 30). "I have testimony weightier than that of John. For the very work that the Father has given me to finish, and which I am doing, testifies that the Father has sent me" (v. 36). "I have come down from heaven not to do my will but to do the will of him who sent me" (6:38). Confidently he sets his teaching above that of all others when he says, "But I tell you" (Matt. 5:22, cf. 26, 28). He came to be more than a great prophetic teacher and a sterling example of what he taught: he said he had come into the world "to seek and to save what was lost" (Luke 19:10) by giving his life "as a ransom for many" (Mark 10:45). Early in his ministry he anticipated his death for the lost (Matt. 9:15; Mark 2:20; Luke 5:35). After Peter's recognition of Jesus' messiahship, "Jesus began to explain to his disciples that he must go to Jerusalem and suffer many things . . . and that he must be killed and on the third day be raised to life" (Matt. 16:21). On two other recorded occasions Jesus prepared them for his betrayal and death (Matt. 17:22–23; 20:17–19). Christ envisioned not only the event but also its meaning: "For even the Son of Man did not come to be served, but to serve, and to give his life as a ransom for many" (Mark 10:45). He gave his life not simply as an example of altruism, but as the price of purchasing our freedom from sin. Jesus anticipated not only the fact of the atonement but also a "theory" of its meaning.

In sum, throughout his ministry Jesus applied messianic titles to himself, spoke of his divine origin, taught his divine nature and preexistence with God, and explained his messianic mission. We cannot with intellectual integrity redate and rewrite all these converging lines of evidence to fit a naturalistic denial of Jesus' messianic consciousness. The most adequate account of the historical evidence is that Jesus did indeed exhibit a consciousness of both his divine origin and his messianic mission.

The Incarnate Son's Self-Limitations

To report that God's eternal Son became human is for Paul to say that he "made himself nothing" (Phil. 2:7). Theologians seem to find it easier to discover what the emptying (*kenōsis*) does not mean than what it did mean for the One equal with God to make himseelf "nothing." A spectrum of proposals deserve consideration.

1. In becoming a mere human and a servant, the Son of God gave up *all* of his divine attributes (Godet, Clarke, Mackintosh). But had Christ given up his divine attributes, he would have had no continuing identity and would have been a mere human. The eternal Son left his position in glory, but did not abandon his essential equality with God (v. 6). The reductive hypothesis that he became merely human does not account for the evidence that he remained essentially one with the Father. Our view of the *kenōsis* must account for the indications that he continued to be equal with the Father and "was God" (John 1:1) with all the divine attributes that make up that essence.

2. The eternal Son gave up *some* of his divine attributes—that is, the relative—while retaining the essential (Thomasius, Delitzsch). Or he gave up the natural while keeping the personal, moral, and spiritual (A. B. Bruce and D. G. Dawe). Although this understanding seems to lessen some of the problems initially, it fails to account for Jesus' continued identity as the eternal Son of God. The hypothesis fails to grasp the fact that all of the divine "attributes" are essential qualities, not accidents. By definition, attributes constitute the essence of anything. Without any attributes a thing can no longer be what it is. As essential qualities, God's attributes are not accidents that may come and go. Other evidence indicates that Christ remained the Son of God, so he must have retained all the attributes essential to his sameness of nature with God the Father. His sonship would no longer be what it was if he gave up even some of his divine characteristics.

3. In becoming a man, some suggest, the Son of God covered his divine characteristics so that to others they were completely veiled. Although he appeared as a man, his divine nature was *incognito* (Kierkegaard, Barth, and Brunner). Clearly there is a measure of truth in the statement that unillumined Israelites, having a single glimpse of Jesus walking down the street, would not be likely to exclaim, "There goes God incarnate!" But people who over a period of time heard Jesus teach, came to know his spotless character, and saw his miraculous signs were responsible for concluding that Jesus was what he claimed to be. Peter by divine enablement finally overcame his natural, fleshly resistance to Jesus' authority and affirmed, "You are the Christ, the Son of the living God" (Matt. 16:16).

At other appropriate times the veil of Jesus Christ's human nature was lifted and people saw the progressive revelation of his divine glory. Had Jesus revealed his deity all at once, he would (speaking from the human point of view) have been put to death before completing the training of the Twelve. At Cana, where he gave the sign of turning water to wine, "he revealed his glory, and his disciples put their faith in him" (John 2:11). The death of Lazarus was permitted "so that God's Son [would] be glorified through it" (John 11:4). When Jesus was about to raise Lazarus from the dead he said, "Did I not tell you that if you believed, you would see the glory of God?" (v. 40). Peter, James, and John saw Jesus transfigured and heard the Father say, "This is my Son, whom I love; with him I am well pleased. Listen to him!" (Matt. 17:2–5). So in his high priestly prayer Jesus could say, "I have given them the glory that you gave me" (John 17:22).

Had Jesus' divine nature been totally veiled, he would not have denounced the cities in which most of his miracles had been performed. Those cities will be more accountable in the day of judgment than Tyre and Sidon and Sodom (Matt. 11:20–24). Hence they must have been able to see enough signs of his messianic authority to be justly accountable and judged for their response to them! In view of this evidence, what the Gospels portray is not a totally incognito Christ, but a human disclosing progressively visible indications of his invisible deity.

4. Some have proposed that a merely human Jesus gradually became conscious of his *progressive incarnation* (e.g., I. A. Dorner). To what degree does that hypothesis fit the data? The biblical evidence noted above indicates, not a progressive incarnation, but a progressive revelation by Jesus of his deity and messianic mission. It also shows the disciples' progressive realization of the truth of that increasing revelation.

5. Although the Son did not give up his divine powers in order to experience growth as a human, he gave up *all use* of his divine attributes (Martensen and Gore). All of his miracles on this position were done solely by the power of the Holy Spirit, in much the same way that the prophets and apostles had performed miracles. According to that reasoning, however, the "signs" would have indicated no more than they did for the prophets or apostles. They would not have pointed to his unique divine origin and messianic mission. The view does not fit instances like the transfiguration where his inherent glory was unquestionably revealed.

6. To accentuate Jesus' harmonious relationship to the Father, A. H. Strong emphasized that Jesus relinquished the *independent exercise of his divine attributes*.[97] But his use of his divine powers had always been in harmony with the Father and the Spirit. To say that Jesus gave up a contrary use of his powers seems like reporting that a husband quit beating his wife when in fact he had never beaten her. Jesus could not give up a power of contrary choice in the use of his divine capabilities if he never had acted contrary to the Father and the Spirit. And in a providential sense no human can do anything totally independent of the Father.

7. In addition to giving up his position of equality with the Father in glory (Phil. 2:6), the Son voluntarily gave up *the continuous use* of his divine powers and any *contrary uses of his human capabilities*. Humans can and do use their capabilities in ways contrary to the Father's desires. So when the Messiah adds human capabilities, it makes sense for him to choose not to exercise his human powers contrary to the Father's pleasure. Not only as he came to earth,

but throughout his ministry, he faithfully surrendered to the Father's will and yielded to the Spirit's power. "And being found in appearance as a man, he humbled himself and became obedient to death—even death on a cross!" (Phil. 2:8). Peter exclaimed about "how God anointed Jesus of Nazareth with the Holy Spirit and power, and how he went around doing good and healing all who were under the power of the devil, because God was with him" (Acts 10:38). Hence in agreement with Strong, but in a different way, we underline the harmony of Jesus' acts with the Father's pleasure and the Spirit's enablement.

Much of the time Jesus' unique divinity and messianic mission may not have been dramatically displayed, although it should have been evident in his wisdom, holiness, and love. But it seems probable that when he healed the sick, revealed what was in people, and raised the dead, he considered those appropriate occasions for revealing more of his divine capabilities. Each of these revelations of his divine nature was carried out in harmony with the leading of the Holy Spirit and in fulfillment of the Father's purposes. However, in conjunction with his claims for himself, they signified more than ordinary enablement of a human by the Holy Spirit. Jesus' signs and wonders indicated that he was more than a prophet—that he was God's unique Son. Progressively, then, he revealed his divine nature and messianic mission, and his followers realized progressively that he was exhibiting not merely prophetic but also divine power and authority.

We have not answered all questions and do not claim full comprehension of the incarnation by proposing a view that makes sense of the varied lines of evidence—an intermittent visible use of his divine attributes and a progressive revelation of his deity and mission in harmony with the Father and the Spirit. Exactly how Jesus could choose not to use his omniscience to know the time of his return (Mark 13:32) remains unexplained. We may suggest one possibility that much of the content of his omniscient knowledge (such as the time of his return) was stored in his unconscious, while he grew in wisdom and knowledge as humans do. Although this speculation may remove some unnecessary concern about a way in which the *kenōsis* could be accomplished, many questions remain (e.g., about omniscience having unconscious memories in storage).

However much Scripture reveals of the incarnation, no human mind will be able to fully comprehend it. "Beyond all question, the mystery of godliness is great: He appeared in a body, was vindicated by the Spirit, was seen by angels, was preached among the nations, was believed on in the world, was taken up in glory" (1 Tim. 3:16). We seek to remove only unnecessary roadblocks to understanding and assenting to the incarnation. By affirming this mighty act we highlight its awesomeness and wonder. We simply adopt the interpretive hypothesis that makes the most sense of the converging lines of data. Those include Jesus' continuous sense of identity before and after Bethlehem, his essential deity, his growth as a human in body and spirit, the responsibility of those who heard and saw him to realize who he was, the progressively conclusive "signs," and the disciples' developing realization that he was indeed the eternal *Logos* on a messianic mission in human form.

We conclude, then, that what the eternal Word did *not* give up during his messianic mission was his divine essence and personal identity. What he *did* give up was his heavenly position or glory and the constant use of his divine attributes and consciousness in order to be able to grow in knowledge, obedience, etc. What he *added* was a human nature with a human consciousness that grew and became strong. Our view that Jesus limited the use of his divine attributes, except when appropriate for the accomplishment of his purposes as planned by the Father and led by the Holy Spirit, provides the most probable explanation of the givens with less severe difficulties than those faced by the other hypotheses. On our method we remain open to consider the case for any hypothesis that can account for all the relevant data with greater coherence. More on the human and divine natures of Christ will be found in the next chapter.

No illustrations of the one and only God or his unique acts are perfectly analogous at all points, but Addison Leitch suggested a useful one of the *kenōsis*.[98] When an athletic father plays softball with his young son, he plays on the boy's level. The father will throw at a speed and distance the boy can manage. Dad will hit easy grounders and run just fast enough to make the play interesting for the son. For the purposes of enjoyment and teaching his son to play ball the father gives up, not his more mature abilities, but their unrestrained exercise. Although the father could throw the ball farther and harder, he chooses to suppress his abilities in order to adapt to his son's capacities. Similarly, Jesus' divine powers were not given up but were generally not used or purposefully restricted in their use, so that he could know the human experiences of growth, learning, temptation, suffering, and even death.

By the incarnation we mean, then, that there is a personal divine absolute in history. The transcendent second person of the Trinity actually entered history as a human. At Bethlehem God's eternal Word humbled himself to became incarnate once-for-all, as confirmed by the irrepeatable sign of his virgin birth. Hence relativists need to understand that we have not only an Absolute beyond history, but also an Absolute in history! Humans in history are not left in a sea of relativism without an anchor! God has actually entered history and progressively made himself known in the person and teaching of Christ. God spoke in history as well as in the teaching of his prophetic and apostolic spokespeople. In the inspired Scriptures, then, we have a third absolute. Evangelicals affirm faith in the transcendent God disclosed supernaturally in the Jesus of history and the teaching of Scripture.

Some Purposes of the Incarnation

In several different explicit ways the Scriptures state the varied purposes of the Son's incarnation. We will not here repeat the evidence of Jesus' own consciousness of his own nature and purposes. Consideration of other passages may strengthen the focus on his multifaceted mission. Although we have focused on the beginning of the incarnation in this chapter, the significance of the Messiah's birth can be appreciated only in the light of his entire ministry, atoning death, and triumphant exaltation.

1. The eternal Son became flesh as the great *prophet* to reveal the Father (Heb. 1:2), to make him known (John 1:18), and to manifest the divine being and characteristics in the flesh (1 Tim. 3:16). Jesus came to his own (Jews) on behalf of the truth and through their rejection he came to confirm God's promises, especially those about the inclusion of the Gentiles (Rom. 15:8–9). Jesus came to teach and personally to exhibit God's love for sinners of the whole world as well as of Israel (John 3:16). He came to fulfill the Father's mission by discipling those who would call sinners of every nation to repent, believe the gospel, develop in the church, and then reach others.

2. The eternal Word became flesh

also to become the *priest* to offer himself as the final sacrifice. He came to taste death for everyone (Heb. 2:9), to identify as a brother with the human race, and to make us holy (vv. 11–12). He came to destroy the Devil, who holds the power of death (v. 14), and to free those who all their lives were held in slavery by their fear of death (v. 15). As John put it, "The reason the Son of God appeared was to destroy the devil's work" (1 John 3:8). Christ came "as an atoning sacrifice for our sins (4:10) to satisfy the justice of God (Rom. 3:25–26). In providing for our justification, reconciliation, and redemption he came as the merciful and faithful high priest to make atonement for the sins of the people (Heb. 2:17–18).

3. The eternal second person of the Trinity also came as *king* to rule in a kingdom of inner spiritual vitality and righteousness. Christ came to reveal the grace of God, destroying death and bringing life and immortality to light through the gospel (2 Tim. 1:10). God sent his Son "that we might live through him" (1 John 4:9). So although sinners depend on the heavenly Father as their sustainer, they must be born again to have eternal life and enter Christ's spiritual kingdom (John 3:3–6). God sent his Son to redeem sinners under the law that we might receive the full rights of sons (Gal. 4:4–5). Further development of Jesus' work as prophet, priest, and king will be found in that order in each of the next three chapters.

APOLOGETIC INTERACTION

Why a "Stumbling Block" to Jews?

For many first-century Jews the problems with believing that the Messiah had come from God and that his name was *Yēšua'* (Hebrew) were neither ontological nor moral, for they believed in a living, omnipotent, and holy God. He who created the first Adam could create a second head of the race. But the incarnation contradicted influential Jewish interpretations of Messianic predictions. They had anticipated that the heir of David's throne would be a powerful king anointed by God to deliver Israel from the yoke of the heathen and establish universal peace and endless prosperity from his world capital in Jerusalem. Instead, Jesus was born in the lowliest surroundings and lived in relative obscurity. Although he performed many miracles, he did not perform the "signs" for which the Jews looked. They anticipated "miraculous signs" (1 Cor. 1:22) on a broader social and political scale.

Jews, like Gentiles, wanted the global kingdom of justice, peace, and plenty without first dealing with their iniquities. But Joseph named the baby *Iēsous* (Greek) because he would save his people from their sins (Matt. 1:21). When John the Baptist called them to repentance, the chosen people found it difficult to acknowledge their insolence along with proselyte Gentiles. So for Jews who were seeking a material kingdom but did not feel the need of justification, the Messiah's lowly birth, life, and crucifixion seemed "a stumbling block" (1 Cor. 1:23).

A more careful study of the context of the birth accounts should have prepared Jewish readers for Jesus' humble birth. From Matthew's genealogy (chapter 1) they might have expected the unexpected in God's program for his people. That genealogy lists several women, whose names would not have been required in any legal account. Three of these women were morally of bad repute—Tamar, Rahab, and Bathsheba—and three were foreigners—Rahab, Bathsheba, and Ruth. Knowing how unusually God worked with women as well as men in the past, Jewish readers might have anticipated something extraordinary when they then read, "This is how the birth of

Jesus Christ came about" (Matt. 1:18). Admittedly, however, that fact is much easier to see afterward than it must have been at the time.

In presenting the truth of the incarnation to people with Jewish backgrounds, it is important not to compromise the primary atoning purpose of the incarnation and its provision for Jesus' spiritual kingdom. All of the Old Testament messianic prophecies would be fulfilled, but not all at once. *Yēšua'* read from Isaiah 61:1–2, and said, "Today this scripture is fulfilled in your hearing" (Luke 4:16–21), He stopped with his purpose "to proclaim the year of the Lord's favor." Note the predictions given hundreds of years in advance that were fulfilled in his first coming to restore *shalom* with God. Jesus of Nazareth not only claimed to be the Messiah or Christ (Mark 14:61–62), his claim was also confirmed by many factors beyond his human control. We mention just a few of the predictions he fulfilled: (1) He was born of a woman (Gen. 3:15). (2) He was a descendant of Abraham, who brought blessing to all peoples on earth (Gen. 12:2–3). (3) Jesus also descended from the line of David (2 Sam. 7:12–16; Isa. 9:6–7; 11:1; Jer. 23:5–6; Matt. 1:1–17). (4) He was born in Bethlehem (Micah 5:2). (5) And he was born of a virgin (Isa. 7:14). He preached good news to the poor; bound up the broken-hearted; and proclaimed freedom for the captives, release for the prisoners, and the year of the Lord's favor (Isa. 61:1–2). Although despised and rejected, he was pierced for our transgressions, the punishment that was upon him brought us peace, and by his wounds we are healed (Isa. 53:3–5). These and many other prophecies came to pass in the first century in ways beyond the control of any human to manipulate.

The Messiah's work will be fully completed at his second advent to earth. In his first advent the Messiah came to offer himself as a just basis for the justification, redemption, and reconciliation of all (Jews and Gentiles). In his second advent the mighty Conqueror will return for "the day of vengeance of our God" and to "provide for those who grieve in Zion—to bestow on them a crown of beauty instead of ashes" (Isa. 61:2–4). Then he will establish his universal social and political rule with lasting justice for all. Those who imagine that Jesus failed in his first coming adequately to confirm his claims to be the Messiah miss the tremendous import of numerous signs such as his virgin birth, sinless life, miracles, teaching, ministry to the poor, and resurrection. Jesus did not fail to train his Jewish disciples to preach the Gospel and to plant churches. At the cross the Messiah tore down the great wall between Jews and Gentiles so that both could be united in one spiritual body (Gal. 3:28). People in the Jewish tradition ought not miss the invaluable provisions of the Messiah's atoning death and triumphant resurrection and ascension—personal redemption, justification, and reconciliation. These blessings have powerful social implications as the recipients permeate their respective cultures. Jewish pre-Christians may need to examine again the Messiah's triumphant resurrection, return to heaven, and sending of the Holy Spirit at Pentecost to build the church. They may need to consider afresh Christ's present lordship of believers and his spiritual rule as king of all Jews and Gentiles, not on the basis of race, but of grace. No more coherent account of the first-century phenomena has appeared. And no more viable hope for individual peace or world peace (for Jews and Gentiles) can be found. So many Jews have put their faith in Jesus as their long-awaited Messiah.

Why "Foolishness" to Greeks?

The claim that the eternal Word who was God become a man (John 1:1, 14) was particularly difficult for admirers of Greek culture and its philosophers' worldviews. Paul did not oppose philosophy, but only philosophies opposed to God's revealed wisdom. He disclosed his understanding of Greek philosophy not only in addressing the Stoics and Epicureans at Athens (Acts 17:16–34) but also when he wrote to the Corinthians of the incarnation as "foolishness" to the Greeks (1 Cor. 1:23). Paul could understand the problematic nature of his claims for people who thought the flesh evil and whose God could not move.

Still today there are Greekophiles and those with other philosophies whose version of moral dualism suggests that all spirits are good and that all matter is evil. Hence it becomes morally unthinkable that God should become flesh. The goodness of a spirit would be morally contaminated by inhabiting a human body. For people who believe that matter is our basic problem, presentation of the Messiah's actual incarnation seems to be nonsense and grossly offensive. So before claiming that the eternal Son of God has come in the flesh, we need to point out that the battle between good and evil is not between spirit and matter but between two tendencies of a spirit's thoughts, desires, and volitions. The body is not the basic source of evil, the body is simply the instrument of fallen people's insolence. A divine spirit or a regenerated spirit with good desires and purposes can bring forth good fruit through the body. An understanding of the body as created by God and in itself good may remove one moral roadblock to Christ's assumption of a human body.

The Greeks also upheld a metaphysical dualism in which eternal Being is totally unchanging and inactive and temporal existence is totally changing. On that hypothesis it became impossible for them even to imagine that a truly eternal and immutable person could act or change in any way, and so could not be born, mature, and die. Because of the difficulty of relating their interpretation of the eternal to their interpretation of the temporal, some Greeks denied one or the other. *Heraclitus* denied any changeless reality, considering any changeless being or truth about it as a mere appearance. He maintained that everything is changing, or in flux; nothing is changeless. He said that one cannot step into the same river twice. Greeks influenced by this totalistic relativism might agree that Jesus was a developing human, but they could not consent to his eternal existence in the Godhead.

In contrast, *Parmenides* had said that in spite of kaleidoscopic appearances, nothing changes in reality; all that is, is. "Being doth be." Greeks of this school of thought could agree that the Word *was* (Greek imperfect tense) continuously God (John 1:1), but could not concur that the eternal Word could ever actively change by entering history in human flesh (John 1:14). Meaningfully to present the truth of Christ's incarnation to total relativists or absolute idealists today, Christians must challenge their underlying presupposition concerning reality and appearance. The physical, changing world God created and sustains is real. The body is real. On the presupposition of only one unchanging reality, incarnation will always appear foolish. Adherents need to realize that the ultimate being, though immutable in nature and purpose, has changeless plans for changing events in time. They also need to consider that, as living and active, the God of the Bible can providentially achieve these worthy temporal intentions either conditionally or unconditionally. Then the eternal, second personal subsistence of the Trinity can meaningfully become incarnate in time.

Plato distinguished an eternal, changeless world of universal ideas transcendent to the changing temporal order of particular things. An intermediate Maker *(demiurge)* constructed matter as far as possible after the pattern of these eternal forms or blueprints of things. But the observable world is a faint replica or shadow of the eternal realities. So the ultimate form of the Good could never become mere flesh. Admirers of Plato today need to realize with Augustine that Plato's world of ideas is not above God and they need to identify changeless principles with the Logos. The Word is God (John 1:1). The second person of the Trinity can live and act in time with wisdom, justice, and love, because he *is* wise, just, and loving.

Aristotle held that God, the eternal thinker, is occupied with only the highest objects of contemplation. Hence he thought, not of finite, changing particulars in history, but only of himself! Aristotle's followers might agree with the eternality of the Christ, but could not imagine the eternal Logos even thinking of flesh, let alone becoming flesh. Admirers of Aristotle today need to realize that their Creator not only has an encyclopedic concern for concrete, observable things but is also personally concerned with his creatures because of his self-giving and outgoing love. Until people overcome a deistic notion of God as unknowing and uncaring, the incarnation will remain "foolishness."

Philo, the Jewish philosopher-theologian contemporary with Christ, sought to combine Plato's (Gentile) philosophy with Old Testament (Jewish) theology. Philo stressed that the unchanging God is so transcendent to all human qualities and classifications as to be ineffable. Philo's God sustains the world through intermediate (angelic) powers, the highest of which he called the Logos. According to Philo's view, the Logos was the first created being, but probably impersonal (though at times personalized) and never incarnate. God himself, Philo thought, could never directly contact the world.[99]

To Greeks with such metaphysical and moral presuppositions about God and matter, it seemed nonsensical for a tentmaker to insist that the Son of God had come into time. The most basic absurdity derived from two different views of God. Christians did not start with an impersonal, inactive Principle when they affirmed that he who was God had taken up flesh. Rather, they began with the living God of the Old Testament, the personal, covenant-making God of Abraham, Isaac, and Jacob. Although he is active, Yahweh is immutable in character and purposes. The logical starting point for understanding the incarnation is not the impersonal absolutes (of the Greeks and others today) but the living God of the Bible, the creator of matter. So matter is not inherently evil, removing the moral difficulty. God is also the active creator of man; he made male and female in his image so that ontologically humans, although dependent, are not totally other than God. Having defended the existence of the God of the Bible in apologetics, the claim that the Word became flesh makes sense ontologically and morally. It is not unthinkable that God could adapt himself to the level of his image-bearers for the supreme revelation of the grand plan of redemption.

People continue to find difficulty in grasping the concept of the incarnation because they start with a static Being who is more like that of the Greek thinkers than the living God of Adam and Eve, Abraham and David, and Mary and Jesus. For this basic reason Kierkegaard's and Barth's views of the incarnation and all God's relationships with humans, as J. Oliver Buswell, Jr. pointed out, are beset with numerous unnecessary "paradoxes." Unfortunately these are not merely apparent contradictions, they are alleged to be irresolvable contradictions in the Bible.[100] People today who, like Kierkegaard, find the incarnation an "absurdity" ought to consider whether they are starting with Greek philosophical speculations about God or biblical revelation concerning God's nature and relation to creation.

The problem of the Greeks illustrates the difficulty of defending Christianity piecemeal and the need for the defense of its whole worldview. The specific doctrines of the incarnation and virgin birth make sense in the Judeo-Christian theistic worldview and Trinitarian doctrines. What, then, is the logical starting point for defending a Christian case for the incarnation in a crosscultural context? It is the hypothesis of the God disclosed in the Jesus of history and in the teaching of Scripture.[101] The message of the incarnation is not nonsense, it is the wisdom of God. The wisdom Paul challenges is the wisdom of men like the Greek philosophers who distort the universal revelation. Paul praises the wisdom that comes from God by Spirit-illumined interpretation of special revelation. "The foolishness of God is wiser than man's wisdom, and the weakness of God is stronger than man's strength" (1 Cor. 1:25).

Not a Mere Myth, as Bultmann Claimed

Rudolph Bultmann presupposed a naturalistic worldview with a cosmos closed to any extraordinary activity by a transcendent God. Hence he relativized the absolute in history by interpreting the virgin birth of the incarnate Son of God as an unscientific or unrealistic myth. In the Gospels, however, there is a pervasive testimony to the fact that Jesus was involved with the miraculous. And from the time of the events to their recording there was *insufficient time* for myths to develop.

Furthermore, between the pagan myths and the account of Jesus' virgin birth several *significant differences* stand out. The mythological stories of gods becoming human occur frequently and repeatedly, whereas the virgin birth of Christ occurs only once and once-for-all. The purposes in mythology are immoral, whereas the purpose of the virgin birth is the fulfillment of justice in providing for redemption. The mythological invasions are not historically confirmed, whereas the virgin birth was investigated and recorded by Luke the physician and takes place in a series of many historically confirmed events.

Bultmann's attempt to explain the New Testament concept of incarnation as a redeemer-myth derived from Gnostic sources fails also for *lack of evidence*. Evidence of myths at the time of the New Testament events, not only in the apostolic age but also in pre-Christian times, is lacking. As F. F. Bruce concludes, "Until more positive evidence of the pre-Christian date of this elaborate myth is forthcoming than hypothetical reconstructions from late Mandaean texts can supply, theses like Bultmann's and Schlier's cannot be regarded as having adequate foundation."[102]

Although no specific non-Christian myths may be cited as the source of Jesus' birth narratives, *myths* in general may have *prepared the way for Christ's actual incarnation*. F. F. Bruce explains:

> Quite different is the approach of C. Williams, C. S. Lewis and others, who have maintained that in Christianity the ancient myths have come true, that when God became Man, as Lewis put it, "Myth became fact," so that the aspirations and insights of the human soul which have from ancient times found mythological expression have been given a satisfying

> answer in the historical events of the gospel.[103]

As Clark Pinnock put it, "These ancient tales tell us of mankind's dreams and aspirations; Christmas tells us about God's mighty act to fulfill them all. In Jesus Christ the myths are not so much abrogated as fulfilled."[104]

After a critical examination of mythical interpretations of incarnation, Charles C. Anderson concludes that they are incompatible with the authors' general purpose:

> (1) any attempt to interpret the Bible accurately must begin by taking seriously its self-witness to being the special revelation of God; and (2) in accordance with the divine purpose of special revelation, the Scriptures must be interpreted literally. . . . This is what we should expect if God wished to make himself known to man. He did not conceal that revelation in allegories and myth. To be sure, the communication of divine truth to man had its problems. The necessity of figurative language, metaphor, analogy, etc., could not be avoided. But these devices were used to clarify, not to obscure the message.[105]

First-century eyewitnesses to the life of the Messiah deny a mythological interpretation. "We did not follow cleverly invented stories [myths] when we told you about the power and coming of our Lord Jesus Christ, but we were eyewitnesses of his majesty" (2 Peter 1:16). Paul was equally emphatic. "For the time will come when men will not put up with sound doctrine. Instead, to suit their own desires, they will gather around them a great number of teachers to say what their itching ears want to hear. They will turn their ears away from the truth and turn aside to myths. But you, keep your head in all situations" (2 Tim. 4:3–5). Paul's concern for a sound conceptual base for faith excluded even myths that belonged to his Judeo heritage. "Therefore, rebuke them sharply, so that they will be sound in the faith and will pay no attention to Jewish myths or to the commands of those who reject the truth" (Titus 1:13–14; cf. 1 Tim. 1:4; 4:7).

Were these biblical writers using "myth" in a manner that was relevant to Bultmann and other recent writers? "In each [New Testament] instance it signifies the fiction of a fable as distinct from the genuineness of the truth."[106] Hughes finds the New Testament use "in complete harmony with the classical connotation of the term [Gr. *mythos*], which from the time of Pindar onward always bears the sense of what is fictitious, as opposed to the term *logos,* which indicated what was true and historical."[107] Hence we can understand the view of John in using "Word" as a name for Christ (John 1:1, 14) and Paul's use of it as a synonym for the Gospel. Hughes documents a similar distinction between a true logos and a fictitious *mythos* in Plato, Philo, and Pseudo-Aristeas. And after finding Bultmann, Barth, and Brunner lacking in clarity on this most basic difference, Hughes concludes that their concepts of myth, legend, the poetic, etc., are "incompatible with the classical doctrine of Holy Scripture. The Christ of the Bible is *the Logos,* not *a mythos*; he needs no demythologization at the hands of human scholars."[108]

More Than a Mighty Act of God, as D. M. Baillie Taught

An influential work reflecting the antimetaphysical temper of thought since Kant, Donald M. Baillie, in his book *God Was in Christ,* claims that the New Testament tells us "nothing about who or what Jesus was or did" in himself, but only about the nature of God and God's activity. Whatever Jesus was or did, "it is really God that did it in Jesus."[109] Rather than allegedly "static" terms such as two "natures" in Christ, Baillie prefers "dynamic terms" such as "God acts in Jesus Christ or is revealed in the Christ event." John Knox, similarly limited himself to "dynamic" categories in his *Jesus Lord and Christ*.[110] These writers claim that God's essence was not distinguishable in a theistic worldview prior to the life of Jesus; what Baillie and Knox know of God is reduced to what God *does* in Christ. They know nothing of who God is in himself or who Jesus was in himself. Jesus was merely what he did, or better, Jesus was what God did in him. Although Baillie has no difficulty in affirming the humanity of Jesus, he nowhere affirms his ontological deity. But we emphatically affirm that there is no incarnation unless the one born at Bethlehem was the eternal Son of God.[111]

The mightiness of the mighty act of God at the birth of Jesus depends on the nature of the one born. Long before Chalcedon Jesus asked, "Who do men say that I am?" As a result of what Jesus did they should discern who he was. We must still press that question today. John wrote his gospel in support of the thesis that Jesus is the Christ (the eternal Word of 1:1) so that believers might find spiritual life (John 20:31). The test of counterfeit spirits is their denial that the Christ (the eternal Word) has come in the flesh (1 John 4:1–3). "He who has the Son has life; he who does not have the Son of God does not have life" (1 John 5:12). "Anyone who . . . does not continue in the teaching [this critical doctrine of who Christ is contextually] . . . does not have God." (2 John 9). To support (by giving them hospitality) teachers who can affirm only what Jesus does, and cannot affirm who Jesus is, implicates us in their deceptive work (vv. 10–11). The church did not read changeless metaphysical concepts of the divine being or nature into the Bible, the church read them out of the New Testament. But Baillie has failed to exegete the Christological texts in their cultural context without a modern antimetaphysical bias. So he reduces the message to "dynamic events" among unknown participants.

More Than One of Many Avatars to Hindus and Buddhists

Pantheistic thinkers who regard God as part of the cosmic process claim to believe in the incarnation, not only of Jesus Christ but also of many other "avatars." Avatars are alleged to be human souls of deceased spiritual masters who descend to the earth to carry out a mission. So avatars may be either (1) naturally born, literal humans who in their life on earth realize their own inner divinity or (2) the spirits of dead spiritual masters mythically returning to earth to guide others in a time of crisis. Any person, it is alleged, can become conscious of oneness with God (as Jesus is alleged to have done). However the concept of an avatar or incarnation to help ignorant souls is inherently inconsistent, as an Indian scholar has pointed out: "If there is only one Soul, i.e., God, and the human soul is God, then it does not make any sense for God to get into the bondage of ignorance, forget that he is God and send God [guru or avatar] to enlighten himself [God] from this ignorance, which exists in his own mind!"[112]

Before presenting the incarnation of a personal God's Son to monists, we must, like Paul in addressing the Stoics at Athens, declare the truth about the God they ignorantly worship. In a theistic worldview all things are made by God, but God is not incarnate in everyone or everything. The world is the creation of God's free will and distinct from God ontologically. It is not the automatic emanation of God's being.

How then does the Messiah differ from avatars? (1) Monists worship a man, Jesus, who allegedly became God (or was enlightened) at his baptism (or subsequently); Christians worship God who became man. (2) Avatars allegedly appear repeatedly in countless reincarnations; Jesus Christ came once-for-all. (3) Hindu avatars differ only in degree from other humans; Jesus, although fully human, is also fully divine and differs in kind, from other spiritual leaders. (4) Mythical avatars do not have literal bodies, for the body is considered evil; Jesus lived in a literal body without sin. (5) Returning avatars are not literally born, for a human body would contaminate them with evil;[113] Jesus was literally born of Mary in Bethlehem. According to a Hindu myth of Krishna's birth, for example, "under auspicious skies, transcendental sounds and an overjoyous moon (although not a full moon) a baby was born with four hands, holding a conch shell, club, disk and lotus flower, wearing a jeweled necklace, dressed in yellow silk, wearing a helmet, bracelets, earrings and similar other ornaments all over his body and an abundance of hair on his head."[114] This lavish legend stands in stark contrast to the chaste biblical accounts of Jesus' actual birth to Mary in a literal city, Bethlehem. (6) Hindu and Buddhist "holy men," in contrast to the avatars, are born in an ordinary way and so have sinful natures; Jesus was supernaturally born and sinless. (7) Eastern sages pass on wisdom from the past; Jesus taught wisdom from above. (8) Gurus offer varied kinds of experiences: altered states of consciousness (e.g., Rajneesh's nude marathons and free sex), inner peace and creativity, psychic and occult experiences in the advanced siddhis (e.g., Maharishi Mahesh Yogi's Transcendental Meditation), and ecstatic mystical unions with cosmic consciousness personified as Krishna. In contrast, Jesus calls people to inner regeneration, redemption, and fellowship with the living God, who transcends not only the self but also the entirety of the cosmos.

The difference between an avatar and Jesus Christ became important for me one day at the Christmas season. In a mall in 1980 Santa Claus offered me some candy canes for my children. I accepted them for the fun of it, even though my children were grown. Then Santa Claus requested a donation! I asked, "For what?" After much evasion the contributions turned out to be for the local Hare Krishna temple. I expressed my desire that the costumed Santa should give his time to telling people about the birth of Jesus Christ. "Santa" responded that Krishna is the Christ. As a larger and larger crowd gathered around us, I argued that Christ is unique and Krishna differs from the Messiah in the several ways listed above. In the market places, at the Christmas season and at other times, Christians need to be prepared to set forth the case for Jesus Christ's uniqueness.

More Than an Instance of Universal Incarnation, as Hegel Taught

Theologians, in Hegel's opinion, express in figurative language what philosophers assert literally. So when Christians assert that "God's Son became incarnate," Hegel claims that they mean figuratively that the Absolute is being progressively realized in all of history. He held that the infinite mind (which alone is real) cannot be distinct from, or beyond, the finite and partial. Hegel held to a *kenōsis* of God in all creation and providence. For him art is the embodiment of Absolute Mind in material things. All individual minds are actively developing their potential in increasingly complex forms and are in a sense realizing the Absolute, or God. God is manifested in all the world in the artist's external vision and the mystic's internal vision. And thus Hegel takes the incarnation figuratively for a kind of pantheistic immanence in all human thought.[115]

Absolute idealists like Hegel will not understand the literal, once-for-all incarnation until Christians challenge their basic assumptions concerning the Absolute and its relation to the world. The world is not an emanation of the Absolute, and God is not incarnate in everything. Universal providence is never to be confused with a progressive incarnation. Again, our reason for our hope in the incarnate Christ must be presented as part of the entire Christian belief system involving all our previous doctrines. Through an informational revelation and biblical inspiration we know that the Absolute is a personal God distinct from the cosmos and the minds created in his image. God created the world, not out of his own being, but out of nothing. Although the Lord of all works out his wise, holy, and loving purposes providentially, his being is not continuous with the processes of historical development. In historical reality Jesus of Nazareth uniquely and once-for-all enfleshed the eternal Word. Christ differs in kind (morally and metaphysically as well), not just in degree, from all mere creatures.

More Than a Paradigm of Indwelling

The case is similar in relation to Whiteheadian process theology's figurative interpretation of Christ's incarnation. Dale Moody follows Norman Pittenger in denying that the presence of God in Jesus was different in kind from a panentheistic incarnation (*sic*) of God in creation, the church, and individual Christians. The indwelling of God in the man Jesus differs in degree from God's indwelling in others, Moody says, because it was perfect. Moody revives Pittenger's marital model of unity between husband and wife who become one in will and love. God is the great cosmic Lover who lured Jesus on to do his will in every word and deed. Jesus can be called the incarnation of God because of his free surrender and love in response to the gracious indwelling of God. The condescension of the Logos in becoming human, according to Moody's view, does not feature an emptying of divine glory (a *kēnōsis*), but an emptying of the human will and a divine indwelling (a *skenōsis*). Instead of God's becoming man, a man is united with God! Pittenger, Moody thinks, comes nearest to keeping Christ's humanness and divineness in balance and is alleged to be "Chalcedon in a contemporary setting."[116] But Moody fails to see that having dismissed the ontological referents, he has lost the reality of both Jesus' humanness and his divineness. In losing the ontological categories Moody has lost any substantial connection with the Chalcedonian formulation.

John B. Cobb, Jr., sees the implications of this view more clearly than Dale Moody does. If the deity of Jesus is not different in kind from that of other men, Jesus differs only in degree from Gautama, the Buddha. This is not the result of Cobb's "preoccupation with Buddhism," as Moody argues *ad hominem*. Rather, it is the implication of his indwelling model of the incarnation. In *Christ in a Pluralistic Age,* Cobb does not take the referent of "Christ" to be a permanent entity or concept, but an "image" by which life is ordered and energy directed. What "Christ" names or images is "creative transformation."[117] "To assert that the Logos was incarnate in Jesus in itself, therefore, is true, but insufficient. The Logos is incarnate in all human beings and indeed in all creation." It follows that Jesus is merely "a paradigm case of incarnation" that can be followed by all. Cobb calls Jesus "unique" in degree but not in kind.[118] By way of contrast, the evidence above strongly indicates that Jesus is more than a great teacher and example. He is a divine-human Savior whose once-for-all incarnation confirms the fact that although ontologically human, Jesus is also ontologically divine. Jesus is different in kind both morally (as a sinless human) and metaphysically (as one in essence with the Father).

In view of these varied interpretations of Christ's incarnation it is not enough for communicating the faith to the next generation to receive mere verbal agreement that "Jesus is the Christ." We must ask what interpretation of those words people hold. Do they mean that Jesus is merely the paradigm of the highest yieldedness of a human to God? Do they mean that Jesus was filled with "Christ spirit" as all of us may be (even though in greater degree)? Or do they mean that he is ontologically the eternal Son of God (the second person of the trinity) who became flesh? With an ontological interpretation of Jesus' being, we may also consider him the supreme paradigm of humanness yielded to God the Father in his wise teaching, authentic love, and powerful deeds for the poor and despised. Only an ontological interpretation of his deity as the second person of the Trinity, however, adequately accounts for the scriptural teaching on his essential oneness with God the Father, the uniqueness of the incarnation, and its infinite provisions for the salvation of all human beings.

RELEVANCE FOR LIFE AND MINISTRY

Value Sinful Persons Highly

In the darkest hours of our experience we know that God cares about us. Although transcendent to humans both metaphysically and morally, God has taken the initiative to reach out to us. The incarnation demonstrates in fact that it is no mere myth that God loves sinners in spite of the fact that they are holistically depraved, personally estranged, and deservingly guilty. "This is how God showed his love among us: He sent his one and only Son into the world that we might live through him" (1 John 4:9). God the Son valued lost humans so greatly that he willingly left heaven's glories to seek and to save them! And God the Holy Spirit so prized human rebels that he performed the miracle making possible Jesus' conception by Mary. Abiding with Jesus throughout his life, the Holy Spirit guided and enabled him in the accomplishment of his redemptive mission. The ministries of each person of the Trinity reveals the Triune God's evaluation of sinners as being of inestimable worth.

Not everyone in the ancient world esteemed humans of such great value. Thales thought we were essentially water vapor; others, a combination of fire, air, earth, and water. Some thought the body evil, and others declared it a prison house of the soul. Plotinus despised his parents and wanted to have nothing to do with them. In more recent history the inhumanity of people to one another has led to despair of human worth. During Dietrich Bonhoeffer's imprisonment by the Nazis, he felt personally the enormity of extreme and cruel tortures. So brutal was the punishment Bonhoeffer witnessed in the concentration camps that many prisoners despaired. They asked, "Are humans any more than beasts?" Yes, said Bonhoeffer in *Letters and Papers from Prison*. The martyr could not despise even those who would take his life! "God Himself did not despise humanity," he wrote, "but became man for man's sake." If God did not despise sinful humanity, how could a Christian pastor-teacher?[119]

The eternal Word so valued his fallen image-bearers that he took human form, humbled himself as a human child, became a carpenter's helper, and washed dirty feet. Christ esteemed sinners enough to leave heaven's riches and become poor. Do we his followers prize sinful people enough to leave behind the riches of earth and become poor? Christ gave up being served to serve others. Do we who take his name as Christians seek more to be served than to engage faithfully in servant ministries to sinners? To save the lost the Messiah gave up his life and bore the penalty fallen humans deserved. Even though humanity's functional *imago* is impaired and the relational image lost, Christ did not consider humans mere beasts. To Christ humans are worth living for! Humans are worth dying for!

Not only are fallen humans in general of value to God, persons are of value in particular. You may consider yourself the chief of sinners, but you have worth to God. If you were the only wayward human in the world, we may be assured, Christ would have come into the world for you.

Be Assured That Human History Has Meaning

Although human history does not manifest God's incomparable being, it does realize his awesome plans for his fallen creatures. In God's grand design, linear history has two irrepeatable stupendous climaxes that give meaning to all the rest—the first and second advents of the eternal Word.

At the first advent the one who holds all things together in the entire cosmos (Col. 1:16–17) came to earth as a baby! Many of our contemporaries can find no abiding person or principle to give meaning to their worldview or purpose to their lives. Since Copernicus' discoveries the earth can no longer be considered the physical center of the universe. The sun, as the center of our solar system, seems unanchored in the expanse of endless galaxies. But the cosmos is not a pointless field of diminishing energy destined eventually to burn itself out in the vastness of empty space. And the value of God's image-bearers does not depend on the comparative size or location of their planet. Because he values human lives the transcendent sustainer of the galaxies has come to visit us! The coming to earth of the infinite Sustainer of all matter-energy provides an absolute in nature. So Christians prize not only the personal Absolute transcendent to nature, but also one personal Absolute incarnate on earth! "For God was pleased to have all his fullness dwell in him" (Col. 1:19). The birth of Jesus Christ, then, is more significant than the election of our preferred candidate for president, the meriting of a doctoral degree, or even the discovery of the Salk vaccine to prevent polio. The winning of gold medals at the Olympics, and the victory of one's favorite team in football's superbowl do not compare. And the incarnation stands far above the outstanding productions of actors, musicians, and artists.

The desires of mankind for an ethical hero or a just deliverer have come to realization in Christ. God's Anointed One came into history at the appointed time, at the appointed place, and in the appointed manner. God's eternal Word came into our world as lost mankind's Messiah! God's Son became human flesh on planet earth to exhibit God's nature and teach God's truth. He came to save both Jews and Gentiles from philosophies based only on the principles of this world (Col. 2:8), from blind fate, pointless chance, and unholy spirits. Of all the wonders of history and the world, this is by far the greatest! The incarnation of the Son of the living God is incomparably greater than any of the wonders of the ancient world. God's enfleshment is far more wonderful than the amazing pyramids, Phidias' forty-foot statue of Zeus carved in gold and ivory for the original Olympic games, or the four-hundred-foot-long marble temple of Diana at Ephesus. The greatness of Christ's advent far exceeds that of such natural wonders as Mount Everest, Victoria Falls, or the Grand Canyon. For all the fullness of deity (Col. 1:19) to dwell in a human on earth carries far greater significance than the discovery of wireless communication, atomic power, a computerized information age, or successful round trips to the moon. The Lord of all came to seek and to save us!

In contrast to totalistic relativists for whom history has no center, no purpose, and no abiding meaning, *all history centers in the birth of God's eternal Word.* Oscar Cullmann in *Christ and Time,* seeks to let the Bible speak for itself; so he does not start with a speculative concept of eternity (God totally other than humans), but with God's revelatory actions in history. Cullman feels that God sovereignly works not only in individual encounters but also in a series of happenings. The creative Word, without whom nothing exists, works in every age (*aiōn*), but achieves his redemptive purposes in the fullness of time (*kairos*). Human history may be pictured as an hourglass on its side with all prior happenings leading to the center at Bethlehem, and all events subsequently flowing out from the incarnation.

Cullmann did not do as well in letting the Scriptures speak for themselves on the nature of revelation. God not only acts but also speaks about who he is. In limiting knowledge of Jesus to what he does, Cullmann failed to appreciate the importance of who Jesus was and what he taught. But Cullmann's stress on the mid-point of God's activity in history helpfully focused attention on the once-for-all incarnation.[120] Appropriately, then, Christians mark all events as before Christ's birth (B.C., before Christ) or after Christ's birth (A.D., from the Latin *anno domini,* the year of our Lord). From the time of the focal point of all history (Christ's birth at about 4 or 5 B.C.), then, we live in the "last days" (Heb. 1:2). And we eagerly await the glorious return of our great God and Savior, Jesus Christ (Titus 2:13). The perspective of the Messiah's birth supplies a holistic perspective of all human history.

Rejoice That Your Life Has Significance

The coming of Christ to die for sinners and rise again supplies not only the center of history in general, but also *the crux of our own personal histories!* Although many of our contemporaries think their lives or biographies to be pointless, a personal acceptance of the incarnation of the eternal Lord of the cosmos can provide lasting significance to our own historical experiences. The difference between our lives before and our lives after accepting Jesus as Messiah and Lord can be as great as the difference between Saul the enemy of the faith and Paul its apostle. Acceptance of the Lord of all brings focus to all of the events in our lives both before and after receiving him. Although busy with varied activities, those preparing to minister in Christ's stead consciously center their desires, thoughts, and actions on him. By regular meditation on the incarnation we center our lives on Jesus Christ rather than ourselves or others.

The centrality of the Messiah ought to be reflected in our celebrations. To honor the greatest of all persons ever to live on earth, our celebrations of Christmas should be carefully planned to give the transcendent sustainer of the cosmos, the mid-point of history, and the supreme paradigm of humanness our greatest of honors. Prizing the birth of

God's unique Son above all others, our commemorations of Christmas should reflect the greatest of tributes we can ever give. Our children should realize from our celebrations that the birthday of Jesus is of far greater importance than the birthdays of our spouses, children, or parents. Our jubilation over the greatest event in history should surpass that of our marriage, the births of our children, and the inheritance of a fortune. The indescribable significance of Christ's coming to seek and to save the lost ought never be overshadowed in the commercialism and tinsel of Christmas. Rather, parents should appropriately teach and exhibit the inestimable value of Christ's condescension and self-giving love. And Christian leaders in every church should discerningly plan fitting ways to commemorate God's mercy and love to the undeserving population of our planet. It is understandable that through a liturgical season of six weeks in the East and one of four weeks in the West Christians prepare for Christmas as they prepare for Easter in the Lenten season.[121]

While celebrating Christ's first advent, Christians also anticipate the celebration of his second advent. The fact that Jesus actually came in literal fulfillment of prophecy gives us solid reason for taking literally his promise, "I will come back" (John 14:3). Jesus said that the nations would see "the sign of the Son of Man . . . coming on the clouds of the sky, with power and great glory" (Matt. 24:30). For centuries people of many religions and utopian visions have longed for someone to bring peace to the world. In country after country hopes for new deals and great societies have failed. The utopian hopes of economic determinists and free-market devotees have been shattered in the East and the West by fallen human nature. Similarly unrealistic and destined for disillusionment are visionary utopian hopes by which we assume that we have only consciously to realize our inner divine potential to produce global peace. In contrast, Jesus already came, lived without sin and began his spiritual kingdom on earth. So Christians have well-founded, realistic reasons for anticipating his return as Prince of Peace to rule the world in social and political righteousness. How sad that many in the first century missed the profound point of Jesus' birth, life, death, and resurrection! May those who today call themselves Christian not miss it. And when the Lord Christ comes again, may every reader be watching and working for him!

Believe the Doctrine of the Incarnation

Christians believe in more than theism and moral values. Christians get their name from believing something about Jesus Christ. And what Christians believe about Jesus nontheists and pantheists do not affirm. Christians affirm the eternal Word's incarnation and virgin birth. Christianity focuses on what the eternal Word of God did for all who are not what they ought to be. A *sine qua non* of a Christian statement of faith affirms that the historical Jesus *is* the incarnate Son of God. Christians do not divorce the Jesus of history from the Christ of faith. Rather, they believe that the Jesus of history *is* the Christ. The life-changing story of Christianity centers in who Jesus was as well as what he was able to do for people unable to save themselves. The point of distinctively Christian faith is not that Jesus represents the eternal Christ spirit (or the cosmic spirit of love) as well or even better than other spiritual leaders do or have done. The confession given by Peter and the Jewish and Gentile converts in Acts alone continues among their successors in Christianity today. Christians today, as in the first century, believe that Jesus of Bethlehem, Egypt,

Nazareth, and Calvary, *is* both Lord and Christ (Acts 2:36).

John wrote his gospel "that [we] may believe that Jesus is the Christ, the Son of God, and that by believing [we] may have life in his name" (John 20:31). To receive eternal life one believes in Jesus. But which Jesus? Not the first created angel (Jehovah's Witnesses), not an adept psychic (spiritualists), not a practitioner of divine science (Christian Scientists), not a great avatar (Hindus), not an enlightened one (Buddhism), nor merely "a marvelously good man" (Harry Emerson Fosdick), but the eternal Word (John 1:1) who became flesh and made his dwelling among us (John 1:14, 18). "Here is a trustworthy saying that deserves full acceptance: Christ Jesus came into the world to save sinners" (1 Tim. 1:15). Any Jew or Gentile who believes in the truth of that proposition and "trusts him will never be put to shame" (Rom. 9:33; 10:11). Faithfulness in guarding the truth of the incarnation will keep the most sincerely committed people from devotion to false Christs, who will fail. The Holy Spirit uses the sharp sword of this truth to direct our devotion away from unreal idols to the Christ of reality.

The first Christians determined whether people had the spirit of Christ or the spirit of Antichrist (1 John 4:1–3) by their assent or dissent to the literal meaning of the assertion that God's eternal Word or Son has come "in the flesh." By this doctrine the early church also determined whether candidates for church membership were salvifically related to God. "Anyone who runs ahead and does not continue in the teaching of Christ does not have God; whoever continues in the teaching has both the Father and the Son" (2 John 9). The "teaching of Christ" that John had in mind is clear in his gospel and first epistle. In these contexts, adherence to "the teaching of Christ" does not specify here all that Jesus taught, but the doctrine that John emphasized in his gospel and epistles—that Jesus was the eternal Word who had become flesh (John 1:1, 14; 20:31; 1 John 1:1–3; 4:1–3).

The true story of God's actual incarnation was affirmed from heaven by the Father at Jesus' baptism and transfiguration, claimed throughout his life by Jesus himself, and is subjectively attested by the witness of the Holy Spirit. As a major part of his ministry, the Holy Spirit attests the truth of the good news of Christ's incarnation (1 Cor. 12:3). You "have an anointing from the Holy One, and all of you know the truth. . . . Who is the liar? It is the man who denies that Jesus is the Christ. Such a man is the antichrist—he denies the Father and the Son. No one who denies the Son has the Father; whoever acknowledges the Son has the Father also" (1 John 2:20–23). It is indeed crucial, then, that every member of every Christian home and every Christian church confess that Jesus is the Christ. This is not to say that each must be able to explain the incarnation in technical theological language. Even a child, however, can understand that Jesus, as he said, was "from above," from God, whereas all the rest of us are from beneath, from sinful parents.

Why is belief in the incarnation so important? Athanasius saw clearly that Jesus must be God's eternal Word to be able to provide salvation for all. In *The Incarnation of the Word of God* Athanasius noted that the Father effects the renewal of creation by the same Word who made it in the beginning. The Word became flesh out of the goodness of his Father, for the salvation of humans. The incorporeal and incorruptible Word of God entered our world, stooped to our level in his self-revealing love to keep creation's purpose from coming to naught and to die as a sufficient exchange for all. Jesus' real deity is necessary to the sufficiency of his atonement for all. It is also necessary to renew the debilitated *imago Dei* in mankind so that through it people might once more come to know him. Jesus' real humanity is necessary to put an end to human corruption by his resurrection. For by man death gained its power over men and by the Word made man death has been destroyed and human life raised anew. Christ's body, for him, was not a limitation, but an instrument. In a human body Jesus accomplished two things: he banished death and made us anew.[122]

Belief, as Athanasius knew, does not save us. The faith of sinners for salvation is no more efficacious than its object. No amount of positive thinking about themselves can transform the holistically depraved. People have sincerely trusted a bridge that collapsed. And people have been totally committed to a Rajneesh who has now said, "The joke is over." The incarnate Word alone has the infinite wisdom, power, and righteousness to save all. Belief in the incarnation is necessary to salvation, furthermore, because in a pluralistic world the Holy Spirit's major instrument is truth. The Spirit uses truth about the incarnation to direct our commitments away from humanistic antidotes and pantheistic idols to the one real divine-human person who can save from sin. If the metaphysically real Word of God has not become flesh, Christians have no good news.

Trust the Incarnate Christ

Christians are those who not only believe the doctrine of the incarnation, but also trust the One of whom the doctrine speaks. John wrote his gospel not only that we might believe, but "that by believing [we] may have life in his name" (John 20:31). He proclaimed that the Word of life had appeared, and what John saw and heard he proclaims to us so that we also may have fellowship with other believers, with the Father, and the Son (1 John 1:1–3). The religious experience of the first Christians and of all Christians since has been, not of their own divinity, but of Christ's. The distinctively Christian life involves more than the mere remembrance of him or of imitation of him. Spiritual life involves experience of him through the living, personal Holy Spirit with and in the spirit of the believer. This was Christ's own conception: "Remain in me, and I will remain in you. No branch can bear fruit by itself; it must remain in the vine. Neither can you bear fruit unless you remain in me. I am the vine; you are the branches . . . apart from me you can do nothing" (John 15:4–5). The life-changing spiritual experience of Paul began a personal experience with Jesus Christ. So Paul wrote, "Christ lives in me" (Gal. 2:20) and "To me to live is Christ" (Phil. 1:21).

A person can be a Hindu without trusting Krishna, or a Buddhist without commitment to Gautama, but not a Christian without commitment to Jesus the Messiah. In other world religions one commits oneself to a type of yoga or a noble eightfold path for human achievement, to moral law and spiritual disciplines. A person can be a devout Muslim without devotion to Mohammed. A Muslim does not joyfully sing, "Mohammed, lover of my soul!" The founders of other religions charged people to follow their religious teachings and the practices of human sages and even to follow their examples. But human religious leaders sooner or later reveal their depravity, as did Jim Jones. Christ charged people not only to follow his example, but to believe him, honor him, pray to him, receive his forgiveness of their sins, and abide in him. In following him they did receive his teachings and imitated his life. More than that, however, they believed *on* him as God's Word incarnate. He said, "Trust in God, trust also in me" (John 14:1). If he had not been God in human flesh, their worship would have been idolatrous. Christianity is not merely a religion focusing on the teachings and practices of Christ. Rather, as W. H. Griffith Thomas wrote, *Christianity Is Christ.*[123] A personal relationship to the scripturally revealed Lord Jesus Christ is of the essence of the Christian religion.

Personal communion with Christ leads to love for his heavenly Father. Those who receive the incarnate Son of God find fellowship with the Father. Our "fellowship is with the Father and with his Son, Jesus Christ" (1 John 1:1–3). A spiritual life of communion with Christ and the Father also results in love for others. Those who believe in the divine love expressed in the incarnate Christ do not love only God but also other believers. "And this is his command: to believe in the name of his Son, Jesus Christ, and to love one another as he commanded us. Those who obey his commands live in him, and he in them. And this is how we know that he lives in us: we know it by the Spirit he gave us" (1 John 3:23–24).

The good news of God's gift of his Son still authorizes sinners who will receive him to become children of God (John 1:12) and joint heirs with him of all the riches in glory. "Now if we are children, then we are heirs—heirs of God and co-heirs with Christ, if indeed we share in his sufferings in order that we may also share in his glory" (Rom. 8:17). "If you belong to Christ, then you are Abraham's seed, and heirs according to the promise" (Gal. 3:29). For the Gentiles are heirs together with Israel, members together of one body, and sharers together in the promise in Christ Jesus (Eph. 3:6). To join the people of God one needs, like Mary, to accept God's gracious promises and relate to the Savior of whom they speak.

Have you personally a trustful and loving relationship with the eternal Christ who became flesh?

> Though Christ a thousand times
> In Bethlehem be born,
> If He's not born in thee
> Thy soul is still forlorn.
> —Angelius Silesius

Like Christ, Be in the World but Not of It

The incarnate Word identified with the fallen people of the world in their humanness, but not in their evil. Like our spiritual Master, we are to identify with our human friends in the world, but not to the extent of committing their private sins or public crimes. Jesus said, "They are still in the world" (John 17:11), but he added, "They are not of the world" (v. 14). "My prayer is not that you take them out of the world but that you protect them from the evil one" (v. 15). Among the evils of the world from which Jesus delivers people are materialism, covetousness, hedonism, sensuality, pride, and waste.

Exhortations to separate ourselves from the evils of worldly people may be misconstrued to mean isolation from non-Christians. A Christlike separatism means not waging war as the world does or using worldly weapons (1 Cor. 10:3–5). It means to be poor in the eyes of the world but rich in faith (James 2:5). It means not to crave the things the unbelieving world desires and of which it boasts (1 John 2:15–17). But separation from the world does not mean withdrawal from the world like a celibate monk (1 Cor. 7:9–10). That would not solve all of our problems, for we would take our fallen natures with us into a monastery. Christians involve themselves in the lives of those who most need them. So our Christlikeness can be tested by checking our relationships to others. Jesus did not spend so much time training others for ministry that he had no time for evangelism and service to those in need. Until church leaders not only teach but also exhibit Christlikeness in relating to the world, church people will not gain new converts as Christ commissioned them to do. Again, until leaders challenge church members to use some of their time and energy outside the church with non-Christians, they will have missed much of the relevance of Christ's incarnation.

A spiritual life not only separates from the evils of the world and reaches out to the people of the world, but it also *overcomes* the world's evils. "Who is it that overcomes the world? Only he who believes that Jesus is the Son of God" (1 John 5:5). With spiritual weapons like Christ's "we demolish arguments and every pretension that sets itself up against the knowledge of God" (2 Cor. 10:5). Believers can overcome temptations and addictions because Christ's name is above every other name that can be named in heaven and earth. And believers together can made a difference in the social evils around them.

After discussing separation from the unbelieving world in Anabaptist and community traditions; accommodation to it in the Constantinian, Lutheran, and civil-religion trends; and the transformational model in Augustine, Calvin, and liberation theology, Robert E. Webber integrates elements of truth from each in an incarnational model. He writes:

> My conclusion is that the Incarnation is the center point from which to reflect on the role of the Christian in the world. As a revelation of the Father, Christ was *identified* with the natural and social order, He was separate *from the powers of evil that rule the course of the world, and He began the transformation* that will be completed in His second coming. *This three-sided view of reality points to the relationship that exists between the Christian and the world.*[124]

Like Christ, Give Yourself to Reach the Lost

The Father's sending of the Son into the world is a great motive for evangelistic and missionary service. "As you have sent me into the world, I have sent them into the world" (John 17:18). Our Lord commissions us to go to a lost world, not wait for the world to come to us. The Christian missionary mandate is no mere appendage to theology. The heart of the Christian message contains good news to share with the whole world. The long-awaited Messiah has come! To accept Jesus Christ as the unique and only Son is to accept the need for taking that message to the ends of the earth. Every Christian teacher, pastor, and leader needs to participate in outreach to non-Christians. Outreach is crucial for the essentially Christlike nature of a church. Involvement in missions is not optional, it is required. All church officers should exemplify self-giving love to reach out and touch the unreached with the gospel of God's grace. The church elders should be good witnesses whether or not there is some other committee or group devoting special attention to sending forth laborers into the harvest field.

Although Christians "flesh out" God's purposes personally in the world and in the church, we are not literally extensions of the incarnation. Aware of the uniqueness of Jesus Christ, Christians ought never claim to be extending the incarnation literally. Christ alone and Christ once-for-all is God's unique Son who perfectly fleshed out his purposes in the history. His uniqueness ought never be blurred. We are not kings but ambassadors of the one Mediator. Although we are regenerated, we are at best merely human, and we continue Christ's relationship to the world only in lesser ways. At best, our attempts to identify with humans, separate ourselves from their sins, and transform people individually and collectively are incomplete and tainted.

Nevertheless, "The test of 20th century Christianity," said Sargent Shriver, former President John Kennedy's Director of the Office of Economic Opportunity, "is not how much the poor enter into the life of the church, but how much the church enters into the life of the poor."[125] We need also to care for those of other races. Jesus went out of his way to meet the Samaritan woman at the well and help her believe that he was the Messiah. A black seminary professor, William E. Pannell, observed, "On the one hand, I really do not expect a pagan to act like a Christian toward me. It seems reasonable, on the other hand, to expect those who say they love God to love their brothers. . . . The Christian is practicing a kind of love which is content to relate to people at a comfortable distance. Hence, the presence of the missionary in Sierra Leone, West Africa and the absence of his sponsoring denomination among Afro-Americans."[126]

Like Christ, Humbly Serve Others

Although the eternal Word was spiritually rich beyond description, "yet for your sakes he became poor, so that you through his poverty might become rich" (2 Cor. 8:9). "Your attitude should be the same as that of Christ Jesus: Who . . . made himself nothing, taking the very nature of a servant, being made in human likeness. And being found in appearance as a man, he humbled himself and became obedient to death—even death on a cross!" (Phil. 2:5–8). Like Jesus, we need to exemplify the servant ministry we teach.

"Whoever wants to become great among you must be your servant, and whoever wants to be first must be slave of all. For even the Son of Man did not come to be served, but to serve, and to give his life as a ransom for many" (Mark 10:43–45). Those who understand the basics of Christ's *kenōsis* and incarnation understand that they take marching orders from the master of self-giving service. Jesus exemplified a simple life of self-denial and self-discipline in order to reach the poor in spirit, the poor in health, the poor in friends, and the poor in purse.

Above all, Christians put loyalty to the kingdom of God and his righteousness first. In this changing world, however, our priorities are easily scrambled. Disciples of the Messiah, ask not only what the world can do for you, but ask what you can do for the starving, the ill, the poor, and the lonely of the sinful world. Furthermore, followers of Christ, ask not only what the church can do for you, but what you can do for the church in its ministries to the world around it. Like Christ, Christians minister to those who know they need a physician. "Blessed are the poor in spirit, for theirs is the kingdom of heaven" (Matt. 5:3). As Jesus came in poverty of spirit, so must we.

Christ's incarnation has not yet had its full effect on those who are now born again, let alone on the world. But the incarnation indicates that in spite of the ugliness and pervasiveness of sin, creation is open to its Maker and full of spiritual significance. The incarnation gives us reason to be believing participants in Christ's present spiritual kingdom. And the incarnation gives us reason to hope for the future fulfillment of the rest of the prophets' highest visions.

REVIEW QUESTIONS

To Help Relate and Apply Each Section in This Chapter

1. *Briefly state the classical problem* this chapter addresses and indicate reasons why genuine inquiry into it is important for your worldview and your existence personally and socially.

2. *Objectively summarize the influential answers* given to this problem in history as hypotheses to be tested. Be able to compare and contrast their real similarities and differences (not merely verbal similarities or differences).

3. *Highlight the primary biblical evidence* on which to decide among views—evidence found in the relevant teachings of the major divisions of Scripture—and decide for yourself which historical hypothesis (or synthesis of historical views) provides the most consistent and adequate account of the primary biblical data.

4. *Formulate in your own words your doctrinal conviction* in a logically consistent and adequate way, organizing your conclusions in ways you can explain clearly, support biblically, and communicate effectively to your spouse, children, friends, Bible class, or congregation.

5. *Defend your view* as you would to adherents of the alternative views, showing that the other views are logically less consistent and factually faced with more difficulties than your view in accounting for the givens, not only of special revelation but also of human experience in general.

6. *Explore the differences the viability of your conviction can make in your life*. Then test your understanding of the viability of your view by asking, "Can I live by it authentically (unhypocritically) in relation to God and to others in my family, church, vocation, neighborhood, city, nation, and world?"

MINISTRY PROJECTS

To Help Communicate This Doctrine in Christian Service

1. *Memorize one major verse or passage* that in its context teaches the heart of this doctrine and may serve as a text from which to preach, teach, or lead small-group studies on the topic. The memorized passages from each chapter will build a body of content useful also for meditation and reference in informal discussions.

2. *Formulate the major idea of the doctrine in one sentence* based on the passage memorized. This idea should be useful as the major thesis of either a lesson for a class (junior high to adult) or a message for a church service.

3. *State the specific purpose or goal of your doctrinal lesson or message*. Your purpose should be more than informative. It should show why Christians need to accept this truth and live by it (unhypocritically). For teaching purposes, list indicators that would show to what extent class members have grasped the truth presented.

4. *Outline your message or lesson in complete sentences*. Indicate how you would support the truth of the doctrine's central ideas and its relevance to life and service. Incorporate elements from this chapter's historical, biblical, systematic, apologetic, and practical sections selected according to the value they have for your audience.

5. *List applications of the doctrine* for communicating the difference this conviction makes in life (for sermons, lessons, small-group Bible studies, or family devotional Bible studies). Applications should make clear what the doctrine is, why one needs to know it, and how it will make differences in thinking. Then show how the difference in thought will lead to differences in values, priorities, attitudes, speech, and personal action. Consider also the doc-

trine's possible significance for family, church, neighborhood, city, regional, and national actions.

6. *Start a file and begin collecting illustrations* of this doctrine's central idea, the points in your outline, and your application.

7. *Write out your own doctrinal statement on this subject in one paragraph* (in half a page or less). To work toward a comprehensive doctrinal statement, collect your formulations based on a study of each chapter of *Integrative Theology*. As your own statement of Christian doctrine grows, you will find it personally strengthening and useful when you are called on for your beliefs in general and when you apply for service with churches, mission boards, and other Christian organizations. Any who seek ordination to Christian ministry will need a comprehensive doctrinal statement that covers the broad scope of theology.

CHAPTER 6

THE MESSIAH'S DIVINENESS AND HUMANNESS

The Messiah's Divineness and Humanness

THE PROBLEM: HOW COULD DEITY WITH ALL ITS PERFECTIONS UNITE WITH HUMANITY WITH ALL ITS LIMITATIONS IN A SINGLE INTEGRATED PERSON WHOM WE KNOW AS JESUS CHRIST?

The present chapter continues reflection on the person of Jesus Christ, whom all persons acknowledge to be not only the founder of Christianity but also one of the central figures of human history. Here we focus on how we should understand the person of Jesus Christ, who is said to be the subject of some sixty thousand books written in the past one hundred years alone.

Classical Christian theology traces three stages in the formulation of its understanding of Jesus Christ. The first stage of Christological investigation deals with the Trinitarian problem. As the second person of the eternal Trinity, Christ fully participates in the being and attributes of God. The second stage focuses on the authentic humanity of Jesus Christ. Here most Christians acknowledge that Jesus was a human being as we are (sin excepted). The third and final stage directs attention to the question of how deity and humanity could unite in a single, integrated person. The first stage of the Christological problem was treated in the discussion of the Trinity in volume 1, chapter 7. It was shown that in his intrinsic being and perfections Christ is ontologically God. The transition from the first to the second stages was dealt with in volume 2, chapter 5, where it was demonstrated that the Logos, who existed in eternal communion with the Father, voluntarily entered time and space and became a man in Jesus of Nazareth. The second and third stages in the Christological development—the question of the complete humanity of Jesus Christ and how humanity and deity united in the one person—are investigated in this chapter.

Some within the church have denied the genuineness of Christ's humanity, claiming that he was some sort of heavenly phantom. Others, though they accept the full reality of his human nature, ask how he who was also God could grow emotionally and spiritually and how he could participate in the suffering and death common to our condition. Was Jesus Christ fully tempted as we are? Did he or could he succumb to sin? Could Jesus be fully human if he had no experience of sin?

Other problems surround the issue of the union of deity and humanity in the one person of Jesus Christ. Is the claim that God and man united in a single person logically absurd, as some modern scholars claim? If we emphasize the unity of Jesus Christ, can we at the same time maintain the integrity of his deity and humanity? On the other hand, if we uphold the reality of his two natures, can we posit a union that is entire and complete? If Jesus Christ is an integrated personality, does he possess one will or two? Furthermore, what is the relationship between the divine-human Christ and his fitness to be a sufficient Savior from sin? If Jesus is our example or model, in what respects should believers strive to become like Christ?

Other questions will be addressed in this chapter: Did Jesus Christ in his ministry perform the functions of a prophet? If so, what did his prophetic ministry involve? Furthermore, how important for Christian faith is a body of reliable historical data concerning the life of Jesus of Nazareth? Must the claims and deeds of Jesus be verifiable by the usual criteria of historical research, or does faith rest primarily on certain nonhistorical ideas the church associated with the Christ? Expressed in other terms, which is of greater importance, the Jesus of history or the Christ of faith?

G. C. Berkouwer observes that high points or "crescendos" in the church's reflection on Jesus Christ occurred in four time periods, namely, in the fourth, fifth, nineteenth, and twentieth centuries.[1] Given this fact, our survey of principal interpretations in the church will concentrate largely, but not exclusively, on these great periods of Christological debate.

ALTERNATIVE INTERPRETATIONS IN THE CHURCH

The following four Christological interpretations are the principal ways in which leading figures within the church have sought to explicate the person of Jesus Christ. These groups represent the major ways that human minds have related the deity and humanity in the one person, Jesus of Nazareth.

Docetic, Marcionite, Monarchian, and Bultmannian Reductions of Christ's Humanity

Docetism, which denied the reality of Christ's humanity, was one of the earliest and simplest Christian heresies. Widespread from the end of the first century into the latter half of the second, Docetism was refuted by the apostle John (John 1:14; 1 John 2:22; 4:2–3; 2 John 7), by Ignatius, and by Justin Martyr. Whereas Ebionism was influenced by Judaism, Docetism was shaped by Greek thought. Centuries earlier Plato had postulated a hierarchy of reality from the heavenly Ideas or Forms, that were completely real, to the physical world, which possesses only relative reality. Aristotle contributed in some measure to this outlook by his thesis that God, the Unmoved Mover, is beyond suffering and change. Further influenced by incipient Gnosticism, the early outlook known as Docetism (from *dokeō*, to "seem," "appear"), postulated a rigorous metaphysical and moral dualism between God and matter, or between God and the world. Thus the docetists asserted that the good God cannot be joined to evil flesh. The upshot of this assumption was that Christ's manhood was regarded as only a mirage or a phantasm of some kind but not truly real. Christ's birth of Mary, his sufferings, and his death were mere illusions.[2] The apocryphal Gospel of Peter testifies to the illusory nature of his flesh when it says that the Savior on the cross "kept silence, as feeling no pain" (4:11). The docetists found it impossible to postulate that the divine Christ was properly united to the body of Jesus' flesh. Their solution to the Christological problem was to deny the reality of our Lord's proper humanity. Although the docetic tendency has been less powerful than the opposite denial of Christ's full deity, some medieval theologians, Anabaptists, and conservative Christians so stressed Christ's deity as to lose sight of his authentic humanity.

Marcion's view of Christ was broadly docetic. He believed that Christ came forth as a revelation of the Redeemer God of the New Testament, and thus he had nothing to do with the material world that was the creation of the vengeful demiurge or creator. According to Marcion, Christ was not born of a woman. Rather, he descended directly from heaven as a phantom and appeared suddenly in an illusory body in the Capernaum synagogue in A.D. 29. Since Christ's flesh was a mirage, the events of his daily life, his miraculous works, death at the instigation of the demiurge, and resurrection from the grave were all illusory. Tertullian summed up Marcion's position as follows: "His Christ . . . was not what he appeared to be, and feigned himself to be what he was not—incarnate without being flesh, human without being man, and likewise a divine Christ without being God!"[3]

Monarchianism in its two forms also compromised the true humanity of Jesus Christ. Patripassianism, which claimed that the Father himself was born of the virgin and died on the cross, acknowledged that Christ was fully God. The Savior, however, only appeared to be a man. Sabellianism, which claimed that the three "persons" are merely three names for the three different manifestations of the one God, likewise forfeited the distinction of persons within the Godhead and so postulated a Christ who was a man in external appearance only.

The Bultmannian school, reacting against the certitude with which the liberal *Lives of Jesus* reconstructed the history of the Nazarene, so stressed the kerygmatic Christ that it seriously neglected the Jesus of history. Since the Gospels were viewed as the free creations of the Evangelists, Bultmann claimed that our knowledge of the personality, the words, and the deeds of Jesus is minimal. All we know about the founder of Christianity is the "thatness" of Jesus Christ, his passion, and what the early church (reflecting on its own needs) believed him to be. For Bultmann this is no loss, since the gospel is concerned not with knowledge of the historical Jesus but with a person's encounter with the apostolic kerygma through which one discovers authentic existence. Given Bultmann's disinterest in Jesus as a historical personage, his writings reflect a docetic tendency. "I do indeed think that we can now know almost nothing concerning the life and personality of Jesus, since the early Christian sources show no interest in either, are moreover fragmentary and often legendary; and other sources about Jesus do not exist."[4] Schubert Ogden takes the final step that Bultmann was reluctant to take, namely, to demythologize the "thatness" or the event of Jesus Christ. Thus, according to Ogden, nothing in the Gospels is historical; everything is mythical. This means that the Jesus of history is completely irrelevant to the attainment of self-realization. A person moves from inauthentic to authentic existence solely by his own personal decision.[5]

Ebionite, Adoptionist and Liberal Reductions of Christ's Deity

Ebionism, which Hippolytus and Tertullian linked with one Ebion,[6] the alleged founder of the sect, but which other authorities claim derived from the Hebrew word for "poor" (*'ebyôn*), arose from a Judaizing form of Christianity similar to that which assailed the churches in Galatia in Paul's day. The Ebionites struggled with the problem of how to reconcile strict Jewish monotheism with devotion to Jesus of Nazareth. The heretical Christian sect "solved" the Christological problem by upholding Jesus' humanity but denying his essential deity. Jesus, they insisted, was a genuine man naturally born to Joseph and Mary. By virtue of his strict observance of the law, the Holy Spirit came upon Jesus at his baptism and constituted him the Son of God and Messiah. The Spirit empowered Jesus to serve as a prophet and teacher of the law. At the crucifixion, the Holy Spirit departed Jesus' life, thereby forfeiting his messianic dignity.[7] The Nazarenes were a branch of Ebionites who accepted the reality of Jesus' miraculous virgin birth. Ebionism, which was the earliest humanitarian heresy, represents the *apotheōsis* of a man. It anticipated the adoptionist and Arian views of Christ and was a factor in the rise of Islam.

The Adoptionism championed by Theodotus of Byzantium and Paul of Samosata, concerned to preserve the unity and indivisibility of the Godhead, denied that in Jesus Christ deity personally had united with humanity. Although their formulations were similar, Greek adoptionism and the Jewish oriented Ebionism were not historically related. Paul of Samosata, bishop of Antioch, insisted that the man Jesus, born of a virgin, was indwelt by the Logos of God at his baptism and was thereby equipped with power (*dynamis*) for the exercise of his messianic ministry, hence the name "Dynamic Monarchianism." The bishop claimed that the Logos, the attribute of reason or wisdom in God, had indwelt Moses and the prophets. Yet this impersonal Logos indwelt and energized Jesus more fully than any other man. Through this special presence of the Logos, God adopted Jesus as his Son (Mark 1:11; cf. Ps. 2:7). For Paul of Samosata, the bond between the human Jesus and the indwelling Logos was moral only, being a unity of will and purpose. As a reward for his obedience, Jesus was exalted to heaven at the end of his life to a state of perfect fellowship with God. Paul of Samosata's denial of the proper union of God and man in Jesus Christ was condemned by the Synod of Antioch in 268.

Arius, presbyter of Alexandria (d. 336), maintained with the Monarchians the uniqueness and indivisibility of the one God. As the one absolute Monad, Arius insisted that God's essence cannot be communicated to another. Thus God created the Logos or Christ a finite spirit, albeit the first and highest of all created beings. Plainly not *alēthinos theos,* the Logos was a demigod or subordinate deity. Through the instrumentality of the virgin birth Christ took upon himself a human body. The incarnate Christ therefore was not ontologically God, neither was he fully man, for in assuming flesh the Logos replaced the human soul (*nous*) in Jesus Christ. Although the depreciation of Jesus Christ's deity was more prominent, Arius actually viewed the Savior as half God and half man. The church formally condemned the Arian formulation as unbiblical at the councils of Nicea (325) and Constantinople (381).

The Socinians in the Reformation era believed that Christ was a human prophet of God distinguished from other men in several important respects: (1) Jesus was supernaturally begotten of a virgin; (2) his life was free of sin; (3) he was baptized by the Spirit and endowed with special wisdom and power; (4) he was caught up into heaven and given special revelations from God; and (5) he exercised a ministry as prophet (teaching the divine will), priest (interceding for the saints), and king (protecting and ruling over the church). Thus Jesus was not God, but a man of extraordinary wisdom and power.[8] The rationalistic Socinians dismissed the doctrine of the two natures in Christ as logically absurd. Socinianism later gave way to Unitarianism and exercised a profound impact on nineteenth-century skepticism regarding the divine-human Christ.

Liberal theologians, guided by an antisupernaturalist bias and an antipathy to claims that transcend bare reason, pursued a Christology "from below" and upheld a Jesus who was an inspired human teacher of morality. The English deists, who rejected all divine interventions in history, repudiated the doctrine of the two natures in Christ. Although professing reverence for Jesus, they viewed the Nazarene as the prophet of an ethical religion, contrary to the Pharisees, who commended a ritualistic religion. According to John Locke, Jesus was the Son of God, not ontologically, but by reason of his moral superiority to other men. Thomas Woolston, on the other hand, had doubts whether Jesus was even a good man.[9] H. S. Reimarus, the German deist who launched the quest for the historical Jesus, actively opposed Jesus' divinity and viewed him instead as a Galilean teacher of natural religion. Reimarus claimed that Jesus became involved in politics, failed to win the masses to his messianic vision, and died a defeated man. Jesus' followers fabricated the stories of his resurrection and future return to establish a messianic kingdom.

F. D. E. Schleiermacher stands in the vanguard of the nineteenth-century assault on the two-natures doctrine. Since the essence of religion for Schleiermacher was feeling, he judged the classical Christological formulae that expound the two natures of Christ to be invalid. Employing the categories of German idealism, Schleiermacher directed attention away from the ontological dimension to the ethical. Christ was special because of his unique God-consciousness; i.e., because his inner awareness of God controlled every aspect of his life. Furthermore, due to the strength of Christ's God-consciousness, Schleiermacher could speak of a special indwelling of God in him: "To ascribe to Christ an absolutely powerful God-consciousness, and to attribute to Him an existence of God in Him are exactly the same thing."[10] By virtue of the undisturbed character of his God-consciousness, Christ was absolutely sinless. In view of the foregoing development, Schleiermacher viewed Christ as an absolutely religious man—the ideal man who functioned as revealer of God.

In his rationalistic life of Jesus, the Heidelberg theologian H. E. G. Paulus explained away all the miracle accounts traditionally used to substantiate Christ's deity. Thus Jesus did not walk on the surface of the Sea of Galilee; he strolled along the edge of the shore. Likewise, Jesus never multiplied bread and fish to feed the multitude; rather, when Jesus and the disciples shared their lunch with the poor, onlookers became convicted and did the same. Jesus' so-called healing miracles were performed by means of native medicinal agents. Paulus believed that Jesus was the noblest teacher of humanity that history has ever seen. "The truly miraculous thing about Jesus is himself, the purity and serene holiness of his character, which is genuinely human."[11]

D. F. Strauss, in his influential book *Das Leben Jesu* (1835–36), carried the mythical interpretation of the Gospels to an extreme. The only events of Jesus' life that Strauss judged historical were his baptism by John, preaching in Galilee, rejection at Nazareth, and trial and crucifixion. Everything else Strauss regarded as mythical. Nevertheless, the myths and legends created by the community enshrine the absolute truth that the infinite Spirit has united not with a particular individual but with the entire human race. Thus the message of Christianity is the Hegelian notion that by the union of the Infinite with the finite, humanity suffers, dies, rises from the grave, and lives forever. Jesus, according to Strauss, was a human teacher of morality and a social reformer. His distinctiveness resides in the fact that he grasped most clearly the idea of this union of the Infinite with humanity.

Ernst Renan wrote his *Vie de Jesus* (1863), not from the perspective of Hegelianism but under the impulse of Romanticism. Predisposed against the miraculous, Renan represented Jesus as a man from Galilee, a gentle teacher whom John the Baptist transformed into a religious revolutionary. Quickened by an apocalyptic vision, Jesus assumed the role of Messiah and strove to foster a moral revolution in the then-known world. So great were the achievements of this messianic reformer that his followers called him "God" and fabricated numerous legends to perpetuate his memory. In time Jesus came to cross purposes with the Jewish authorities and, in the course of the struggle, paid the ultimate price. Renan's Jesus, although a religious genius, never rose above the level of a man endowed with a highly developed God-consciousness.

Albert Schweitzer, whose book *The Quest of the Historical Jesus* (1906) propounded a "thoroughgoing eschatology," shifted the focus from the ethical to the eschatological or from the prophetic to the apocalyptic. Jesus, according to Schweitzer, lived in an era aglow with messianic fervor. At his baptism Jesus understood himself to be the heavenly Son of Man who was commissioned to usher in the eschatological kingdom. Jesus sent out the Twelve, expecting that before they returned from their tour of Israel the world would end. When this did not happen, Jesus decided to challenge the political powers and thereby force God to bring in the kingdom. Jesus later was betrayed by Judas and was put to death on the cross, being crushed by the very historical forces he sought to orchestrate. Although Jesus died disillusioned and discredited, his "spirit" lives on to inspire posterity. In Schweitzer's famous words, Jesus

> lays hold of the wheel of the world to set it moving on that last revolution which is to bring all ordinary history to a close. It refuses to turn, and he throws Himself upon it. Then it does turn; and crushes him. . . . The wheel rolls onward, and the mangled body of the one immeasurably great Man, who was strong enough to think of himself as the spiritual ruler of mankind and to bend history to his purpose, is hanging upon it still. That is his victory and his reign.[12]

Schweitzer judges that as a man who mistakenly believed himself to be the Messiah, Jesus must be viewed from our perspective as mentally unbalanced. Least of all was he ontologically God.

Post-Bultmannian Christology reexamined the historical parameters of the life of Jesus. Pursuing a Christology from below, many post-Bultmannian theologians viewed Jesus as a Spirit-filled man. According to Jeremias, Jesus was a human prophet in whom the Spirit, quenched by the sins of Israel, returned with power. Jeremias concluded from a study of the prologue to John's gospel that Jesus as Logos was the man in whom God was uniquely present and through whom God decisively spoke. "As bearer of the spirit, Jesus is not only one man among the ranks of the prophets, but God's last and final messenger. His proclamation is an eschatological event. . . . God is speaking his final word."[13]

Apollinarian, Nestorian, and Eutychian Formulations of the Union

Before considering specific attempts to relate deity and humanity within the one person of Jesus Christ, we summarize two historical tendencies in Christology that were quite different from each other. The first, the Alexandrian school, focused on the metaphysical side of theology. It was concerned to preserve the deity of Christ and so focused on the unity of the Word and Jesus' humanity. Guided by John 1:14, the Alexandrian tradition formulated a *Logos-sarx* (Word-flesh) Christology. A weakness of this approach, however, was that Jesus' humanity was overshadowed by or even absorbed into his deity. The Cappadocian theologians Gregory of Nazianzus (d. 390), Gregory of Nyssa (d. 394), and Cyril of Alexandria (d. 444) reflect the Alexandrian emphasis. Objecting to Nestorianism, Cyril so emphasized the unity of Christ's person that Cyril was (unjustifiably) claimed by the later Monophysite party.[14] Apollinarianism and Eutychianism were extreme expressions of the Alexandrian emphasis.

The Antiochene school emphasized not only the grammatico-historical interpretation of Scripture but also the historical implications of theology. Thus theologians in the tradition focused primarily on the genuine humanity of Jesus and secondarily on his deity, while seeking to preserve the distinctive properties of the two natures. The Antiochenes appealed to Philippians 2:6–8 and so produced a *Logos-anthrōpos* (Word–human being) Christology. The deficiency of this approach was that the essential union of the two natures was minimized. Theodore of Mopsuestia (d. 428) and Theodoret (d. 457), among others, furthered the Antiochene emphasis. The former wrote concerning Christ: "He did not take a body only, but the whole man, composed of a body and of an immortal and rational soul."[15] Taken to its extreme, the Antiochene emphasis resulted in Nestorianism.

Apollinarius (d. 390), bishop of Laodicea and friend of Athanasius, believed with the latter against Arius that in order to save sinners Christ must be both divine and human. Thus his approach to the Christological problem in *Demonstration of the Divine Incarnation* (376) stressed the unity of the person of Jesus Christ. From the perspective of a Platonic trichotomy, Apollinarius maintained that the person is body (*sōma*), sensitive soul (*psychē*), and rational soul (*nous* or *pneuma*). Reflecting on the dynamics of the incarnation, he reasoned that if Christ had a rational human soul he would not be God-incarnate but merely God *in* a man or an inspired man. Moreover, if Christ had a human will, he would be mutable and thus liable to sin. Therefore Apollinarius concluded that at the incarnation the Logos replaced the rational soul (*nous* or *pneuma*) in the man Jesus. That is, the Logos took on human nature (a body and a sensitive soul), but not human personality (a rational soul) in becoming the divine-human being, Jesus Christ. For Apollinarius, the divine Logos was clearly the living center in Jesus Christ. Thus he referred to the Savior as "God-incarnate" and the "flesh-bearing God."

Orthodox theologians commended Apollinarius for upholding the unity of Christ's person without sacrificing his deity. On the other hand, they criticized his proposal by insisting that Christ's human nature would be defective without a sensitive soul (i.e., intellect and will). Moreover, opponents reasoned that if the Logos did not take on human nature in its entirety, he could not be the perfect Redeemer: "What Christ did not assume, Christ could not heal." Many authorities perceived that, although upholding the unity of Christ's person, Apollinarius depreciated the integrity of his humanity. Thus the church repudiated the views of Apollinarius at the Council of Constantinople (381) and burned his theological writings.

Nestorius (d. 451), patriarch of Constantinople, was a leading representative of the Antiochene school of theology. Nestorius objected to the mixing of Christ's two natures and the resultant depreciation of Christ's true humanity as proposed by Apollinarius and Eutyches. He stressed the fact that we must keep separate the two natures of Christ and the two sets of properties associated with those natures. Thus Nestorius insisted that only a created man (not the uncreated God) could be born, grow, suffer, and die. On the other hand, only the uncreated God (not a created man) could be eternal, omnipotent, and omnipresent. These considerations led Nestorius to conclude that at the moment of conception the divine Logos joined with a complete person in the womb of Mary. Accordingly, Jesus Christ consisted of two natures, each with its own set of personal properties bound together by a moral union to form one *prosōpon* or the appearance of one being. The important issue for Nestorius appears to have been that, lest the properties of the two natures be confused, deity and humanity must have come together in a moral and voluntary connection (*synapheia*), rather than in a vital, personal (i.e., essential) union. Nestorius' famous claim was, "I hold the natures apart, but unite the worship." Nestorius likened the union of human and divine in Jesus Christ to the union of a husband and a wife, who become "one flesh" while remaining two distinct persons. In the light of this development, Nestorius refused to speak of Mary as the "God-bearer" (*theotokos*), preferring to give her the title the "Christ-bearer" (*Christotokos*). Because Nestorius upheld the reality of Christ's two natures, but seemingly compromised the integrity of the union of these natures, his views were condemned at the Council of Ephesus (431), and Nestorius was banished to exile in Egypt. Some modern scholarship judges that formulations of Nestorius are less heterodox than traditionally thought.[16]

Reacting against the Nestorian position, Eutyches (d. 454), a presbyter at Constantinople, carried the Alexandrian emphasis to an extreme. Seeking to uphold Christ's deity and the unity of his person, Eutyches claimed that our Lord's humanity merged into his deity and in the process was lost. The outcome, according to Eutyches, was a single person with one divine nature. Others in the tradition maintained that the resultant nature was a *tertium quid*, albeit a nature more divine than human. When Flavian, archbishop of Constantinople, asked Eutyches whether Christ possessed two natures, the latter responded: "I admit that our Lord was of two natures before the union, but after the union one nature." Contrary to Nestorius, Eutyches believed that it was God who was born of Mary, who suffered, and who died on the cross. Thus the docetic element in Eutyches' Christology is evident. Eutyches was tried at the Synod of Constantinople in 448 and excommunicated for his alleged heretical views. A council hastily convened at Ephesus in 449 (the "Robber Synod") and presided over by Dioscorus pronounced Eutyches orthodox. His teachings were repudiated shortly after that (451) by the ecumenical Council of Chalcedon.

In the years following Chalcedon, groups in Syria, Egypt, and Palestine who persisted in the error of Eutyches were called Monophysites. Since they believed that person (*hypostasis*) and nature are inseparable, the Monophysites upheld the one person of Christ with a single composite nature. Also called Theopaschites, their common liturgical formula was, "God has been crucified for us." The Monophysites were condemned at the Second Council of Constantinople (553), but Monophysitism persists in the Coptic, Jacobite, and Armenian churches. The Monothelite controversy, which erupted in the middle of the seventh century, represents the final phase of the ancient debate about Christ's two natures. Led by Sergius of Constantinople, the Monothelites claimed that will is an attribute of the person rather than of a nature. Thus although most Monothelites posited two natures in Christ, they allowed only one divine-human will in the Savior. Some within the church saw in Monothelitism a repudiation of Chalcedon and a return to Monophysitism. Thus the Third Council of Constantinople (681), undoubtedly falsely, asserted that there are two wills in Jesus Christ and that the human will is subordinate to the divine.

Lutheran theology followed the Alexandrian emphasis in upholding the *communicatio idiomatum,* or mutual interpenetration of Christ's natures in the personal union. Determined to avoid the Nestorian error, Luther claimed the full participation of Christ's divine nature in his human nature and vice versa. "Because divinity and humanity are one person in Christ, Scripture . . . ascribes also to divinity everything that happens to humanity, and vice versa. And so it is in reality."[17] Thus Luther maintained that God the Son nursed at Mary's breast, lay in the cradle, suffered, was crucified, and died.[18] On the other hand, Mary's son ascended into heaven, now sits at the right hand of God, and will return to judge the world. Taking the argument a step further, Luther claimed that the properties of Christ's divine nature penetrated his human nature. Thus with respect to his humanity Christ is properly omniscient, omnipotent, and omnipresent. "The Word of God is not separated from the flesh. Where God is, there the flesh of Christ is. But God is everywhere; therefore Christ is everywhere."[19] Given the claim that Christ's body is ubiquitous, Luther understood the Savior to be truly and substantially present "in, with, and under" the bread and the wine at the Lord's Supper. A number of authorities judge that Luther and his followers tended toward Eutychianism and so violated the spirit of Chalcedon, which insisted that Christ's two natures united "without mixture."[20] Orthodox authorities posit the complete deity and complete humanity of Jesus Christ and insist that the two natures united in a single, sinless person. Most, with the exception of some Alexandrians and Lutherans, maintain that in the union Christ's two natures did not commingle, but retained their own peculiar properties.

Most Fathers, Reformed Theologians, and Evangelicals

Early church fathers such as Ignatius and Justin opposed Gnostic and docetic denials of Christ's authentic humanity. While upholding the Lord's full divinity, Ignatius claimed that Jesus was born of Mary, was baptized by John, lived a holy life, truly suffered and died, and rose in a body from the grave. Ignatius testifies to the union of Christ's two natures in the one person as the divinely ordained vehicle of salvation. "Being impassible, he was in a passible body; being immortal, he was in a mortal body; being life, he became subject to corruption, that he might free our souls from death and corruption."[21] Irenaeus in the West likewise affirmed in biblical and nontechnical language the divine-human character of the one person, Jesus Christ. God united with man in order to recapitulate humanity, i.e., to reverse the effects of sin and restore humanity to its God-intended goal. Linking Christology with soteriology, Irenaeus stressed that the efficacy of Christ's redemptive work depends on the complete integrity of his two natures as true God and true man. "If the enemies of man had not been overcome by man, they could not have been truly overcome; furthermore, if our salvation is not from God, we cannot be sure that we are saved. And if man has not been united with God, it would not be possible for him to share in immortality."[22] Tertullian, whose formulation of Christ anticipated the Chalcedonian definition, upheld the reality of the divine and human natures of Christ, while preserving the integrity of their union in the single personal subject. Thus Godhead and manhood united in the one person, Jesus Christ, without the natures being confused or their properties altered. Wrote Tertullian: "We see plainly the twofold state, which is not confounded, but is conjoined in one person—Jesus, God and man."[23]

Augustine blended emphases from both the Alexandrian and Antiochene schools to produce a balanced Christology that was Chalcedonian decades before Chalcedon. According to Augustine, the divine Person united with a complete human nature (a rational body and soul) to constitute the one person of the God-man. Noteworthy is the emphasis Augustine placed on the personal unity of the God-man: "Christ, therefore, is one; the Word, soul and flesh, one Christ; the Son of God and Son of man, one Christ; Son of God always, Son of man in time, yet one Christ in regard to unity of person."[24] Augustine's favorite illustration for the union of the Godhead with man is the union of the soul with the body in the human person. Augustine continues by saying that the Word was not altered by the assumption of humanity. The Word "did so assume a body from the Virgin and manifest Himself with mortal senses, as neither to destroy His own immortality, nor to change His eternity, nor to diminish His power, nor to relinquish the government of the world, nor to withdraw from the bosom of the Father."[25] Furthermore, in the union Christ's humanity was entire, lacking nothing. "No part was wanting in that human nature which he put on, save that it was a nature wholly free from every taint of sin."[26] Augustine notes that Christ took food, rested his body, experienced all the emotions of humanity, and finally died. Thus in the union of God with man, neither deity nor humanity was altered, but each retained its distinctive properties.[27]

The principal creeds of the church enshrine the orthodox view of Christ. The Apostles' Creed upholds the deity of Christ when it confesses faith in "Jesus Christ, His [i.e., God's] only Son, our Lord." The Creed also attests the humanity of Christ by referring to his conception and birth of the virgin Mary, his suffering and death under Pontius Pilate, and his bodily resurrection and ascension to heaven. By reciting the Apostles' Creed, Christians assented to the fact that Jesus Christ was truly God and truly man in one person. The Creed of Nicea (325), formulated to refute the teachings of Arius, and its enlargement in the Constantinopolitan Creed (381), which refutes Apollinarianism, expounds Christ's deity in nonbiblical language. Christ was begotten eternally from the being of the Father and thus is "of the same essence as the Father [*homoousion tō patri*]." Christ, moreover, is truly human, for the Creed adds, "who for us men and because of our salvation came down from heaven, and was incarnate by the Holy Spirit and the Virgin Mary and became human [*enanthrōpēsanta*]." The Creed then confesses Christ's crucifixion, burial, resurrection, and ascension to heaven.

The first Council of Ephesus (431) condemned the teachings of Nestorius, asserted that the one person Jesus

Christ is "true God of true God," and from an Alexandrian perspective designated Mary the Mother of God (*theotokos*). At the Council of Chalcedon (451), more than five hundred bishops dealt with the relation of humanity and deity in Jesus Christ and produced a statement that refuted not only Arianism and Apollinarianism but particularly Nestorianism and Eutychianism. The Chalcedonian Definition, which strikes a balance between the Alexandrian and Antiochene emphases, is commonly regarded the definitive Christological statement. Chalcedon initially reaffirmed the Nicene tradition by upholding Christ's authentic deity and authentic humanity. Then it proceeded to assert the proper union of the two natures in the one person. Accordingly, deity and humanity came together "to form one person (*prosōpon*) and subsistence (*hypostasis*), not as parted or separated into two persons, but one and the same Son and Only-begotten God the Word, Lord Jesus Christ." Finally, Chalcedon confessed the distinctiveness of the two natures in the union. Thus it refers to Christ as "recognized in two natures, without confusion, without change, without division, without separation; the distinction of natures in no way annulled by the union, but rather the characteristics of each nature being preserved."[28]

The last third of the so-called Athanasian Creed, a document formulated in the West in the fifth century, sets forth what one must believe concerning Jesus Christ in order to be saved. This third ecumenical creed upholds the union of deity and humanity in the one person of Jesus Christ, in which both natures retain their unique characteristics. The most important statements concerning the person of Christ follow:

> (30) The right faith is that we believe and confess that our Lord Jesus Christ, the Son of God, is God and man. (31) God of the substance of the Father, begotten before the worlds; and man of the substance of His mother, born in the world. (32) Perfect God and perfect man, of a reasonable soul and human flesh subsisting. (34) Who, although He is God and man, yet He is not two, but one Christ. (35) One, not by conversion of the Godhead into flesh, but by taking the manhood into God. (36) One altogether, not by confusion of substance, but by unity of person. (37) For as the reasonable soul and flesh is one man, so God and man is one Christ.

In the context of the Monophysite controversy, Leontius of Byzantium (d. 543) strove to preserve the integrity of Christ's two natures within the one person by means of the term *enhypostatos*. By this term he meant that Christ's authentic humanity had no subsistence in itself but came to subsist only in union with the Logos from the moment of the incarnation. John of Damascus refined this conceptuality in his classic work *The Orthodox Faith* (Bk. III.1–3). Every nature, John argued, must have a *hypostasis*, or center of personality. Christ's humanity realized personal existence in and through the Logos, for Scripture teaches that the Logos, as the governing principle, assumed human nature, not vice versa.

Calvin's Christology, adhering to the pattern of Chalcedonian orthodoxy, begins with the axiom "It was of the greatest importance for us that he who was to be our Mediator be both true God and true man."[29] For Calvin, everything depends on the true divinity of Christ; only God can conquer sin and restore peace to the soul. Moreover, the punishment due us must be born by a man; hence Jesus Christ must be truly man, with a human body and soul. "God's natural Son fashioned for himself a body from our body, flesh from our flesh, bones from our bones, that he might be one with us."[30] As true man, Christ is distinguished from the common lot by a humanity that is "without fault and corruption."[31] Calvin views the two-natures doctrine not as a mere theoretical construct, but as a necessary feature of God's plan of salvation: "Since neither as God alone could he feel death, nor as man alone could he overcome it, he coupled human nature with divine that to atone for sin he might submit the weakness of the one to death; and that, wrestling with death by the power of the other nature, he might win victory for us."[32] Calvin, however, is careful to insist on the unity of the two natures in the Redeemer. Against Nestorius, there can be no separation of Godhead from manhood: "Both natures are so closely bound up together that Jesus Christ is one Person only."[33] Moreover, against Eutyches, there can be no mingling or fusion of the two natures. "We affirm his divinity so joined and united with his humanity that each retains its distinctive nature unimpaired, and yet these two natures constitute one Christ."[34] Here Calvin distanced himself from the Lutheran *communicatio idiomatum,* which he perceived compromised the integrity of Christ's two natures and thus vitiated the efficacy of his saving work. Calvin does acknowledge, given the unity of the two natures in the one person, that with Scripture we may speak of the human nature as if it partook of the divine attributes, and vice versa (e.g., John 3:13; 1 Cor. 2:8). Finally, Calvin modestly posits what later came to be known as the *extra Calvinisticum;* namely, that during the incarnation the Word was also beyond or outside of (*extra*) Jesus' human nature. Whereas Luther held that the Logos was wholly contained in Jesus' body, Calvin maintained that although the Logos was "completely" present in the historical Jesus, he nevertheless was not confined to his body but filled the world with his immeasurable essence.[35]

The Reformed confessions follow Chalcedon and Calvin in affirming that deity and humanity are permanently united in the one person of Jesus Christ. Although related to one another in a dynamic union, the two natures retain their own distinct characteristics. Hence the properties of Christ's deity are not transferred to the humanity nor are the properties of his humanity transferred to his deity. The Reformed position is set forth in the Belgic Confession (1561), articles 10, 18, 19; in The Second Helvetic Confession (1566), chapter XI; in the Thirty-Nine Articles of the Church of England (1563), article II; and in the Westminster Confession of Faith (1646), chapter VIII.2.

A. H. Strong upholds the full reality and integrity of Christ's divinity and humanity. The latter, consisting of a body and a rational soul, was subject to all the laws of growth and development, yet was free from hereditary depravity and actual sin. Following several earlier authorities, Strong insists that Christ's human nature had no personality apart from its union with the divine nature. That is, "the Logos did not take into union with himself an already developed human person, such as James, Peter, or John, but human nature before it had become personal or was capable of receiving a name. It reached its personality only in union with his own divine nature."[36] Strong thus proposes not *un*personality (*anhypostasia*), but *in*personality (*enhypostasia*). Christ's human nature realized its personality only *in* union with the divine. At Jesus' conception the two natures vitally united to form one person with a single consciousness and will. Jesus' "consciousness and will . . . is always theanthropic—an activity of the one personality which unites in itself the human and the divine."[37] Strong concurs with the orthodox conviction that Christ must unite deity and humanity in one person to be a proper Mediator. "Because Christ is man, he can make atonement for man and can sympathize with man. Because Christ is God, his atonement has infinite value, and the union which he effects with God is complete."[38]

Additional helpful studies on the person of Christ include works by G. C. Berkouwer,[39] John F. Walvoord,[40] and Millard J. Erickson.[41]

THE BIBLICAL TEACHING

To determine which view of the person of Christ is valid, we now investigate the primary biblical teaching on the subject. Volume 1, chapter 7 showed that Scripture identifies Jesus Christ as God. The present chapter examines other evidence for Jesus' deity, evaluates the data for Jesus' humanity, and investigates the problem of the union of deity and humanity in the one person, Jesus Christ.

Synoptic Gospels

The most cursory reading of the Gospels indicates that Jesus of Nazareth was a genuine man. Matthew and Luke testify that Jesus did not descend from heaven full-grown, but was physically born of a young virgin in a manger in the town of Bethlehem (Matt. 1:20–25; Luke 2:6–12). The records suggest that apart from his supernatural conception (see chap. 5), Jesus' prenatal existence, birth, and childhood were indistinguishable from that of any other man. Matthew's genealogy, which traces Jesus's descent from Abraham through the royal line of Israel, establishes the Nazarene as the legal heir to the throne of Israel (Matt. 1:1–17). Luke's genealogy, in reverse order, traces Jesus' physical ancestry through David and Abraham back to Adam, the first man.

As required by the Jewish law, Jesus was circumcised on the eighth day and was consecrated to the Lord in the temple (Luke 2:21–22). Luke reports that prior to the age of twelve, Jesus experienced a perfect physical and moral development (1:80; 2:40). Luke adds that during his youth "Jesus grew in wisdom and stature, and in favor with God and men" (2:52). Thus Jesus "was completely subject to the ordinary laws of physical and intellectual development, except that in his case there was nothing of the influence of sin or shortcoming."[42] The Gospels suggest that Jesus assisted his father at the carpenter's bench (Matt. 13:55) and that after Joseph's death he continued to support his mother and family by working at his trade (Mark 6:3). At about age thirty (Luke 3:23) Jesus was baptized by John in the Jordan River (Matt. 3:13–16; Luke 3:21–22). But whereas others came to the water confessing their sins (Matt. 3:6), Jesus had no need for repentance—hence John's initial reluctance to baptize him (Matt. 3:14–15). Following the baptism, the Spirit led Jesus into the desert to be tempted by the Devil (Matt. 4:1–10; Luke 4:2–13). As a man, Jesus genuinely experienced the power of Satan's offer (1) to change stones to bread, or to satisfy his physical needs; (2) to cast himself to the ground from the pinnacle of the temple, or to seek proof of God's faithfulness; and (3) to receive the kingdoms of the world by worshiping Satan, or to attain kingdom rule without first suffering. Tempted in like manner as Eve in the garden (Gen. 3:6) and like each one of us in the course of life (1 John 2:16), Jesus responded to Satan's enticements by quoting Scripture (Matt. 4:4, 7, 10). In these temptations and others that followed, Jesus chose to obey his Father and thus continued in a perfectly upright and sinless state.

The Synoptic Gospels also relate that Jesus experienced all the normal human instincts and emotions. Physically he felt the pangs of hunger (Matt. 4:2; 21:18), of thirst (Matt. 25:35), and of physical weariness (Matt. 8:24). Spiritually Jesus, like other devout persons, sensed a deep dependence on the Father and so spent many hours in prayer (Matt. 14:23; 26:36–44; Mark 1:35–38; Luke 11:1–4). Emotionally Jesus experienced anger, albeit not a self-centered wrath, but a righteous and controlled indignation against injustice (Mark 3:5). Moreover, Jesus responded to human suffering with deep compassion (the verb *splanchnizomai,* Matt. 9:36; 14:14; 15:32). As Jesus viewed Jerusalem from the Mount of Olives, he recalled the unbelief of its inhabitants, and with profound emotion he wept over the city (Luke 19:41). A few days later in the city Jesus felt great pity for the Jews who spurned God's love and who refused to repent (Matt. 23:37).

The fact that on occasion Jesus' knowledge was limited confirms his authentic humanity. In Mark 5:30–33 Jesus did not know who had touched his clothing, and in Mark 9:21 (because he chose to be ignorant of the answer) Jesus asked the father of a boy convulsed by an evil spirit, "How long has he been like this?" In the Olivet Discourse Jesus himself acknowledged that he did not know the time of his return to earth: "No one knows about that day or hour, not even the angels in heaven, nor the Son, but only the Father" (Mark 13:32; cf. Matt. 24:36, where the reading "nor the Son," omitted in some manuscripts, has sufficient textual support to be retained). We observe that this self-chosen ignorance is not error, for the Gospels represent Jesus as entirely without fault or sin (Matt. 27:4; Luke 1:35; 23:41). Other texts in the Gospels (see below) indicate that on other occasions Jesus drew upon his divine power of omniscience.

The passion narratives vividly display Jesus' manhood. Matthew 26:37 relates that in Gethsemane Jesus "began to be sorrowful [present passive of *lypeō,* to 'be sad'] and troubled" [present infinitive of *adēmoneō*, to "be distressed"]. The following verse confirms that in the garden Jesus experienced intense anxiety and distress: "My soul is overwhelmed with sorrow to the point of death" (cf. Isa. 53:3). Luke adds that so great was his agony, that sweat fell from his body as drops of blood (Luke 22:44). Like any normal person, Jesus longed to avoid the impending crisis. Yet, desiring to be obedient to the Father, he prayed, "Not my will, but yours be done" (Luke 22:42). Nailed to the cross with spikes, Jesus suffered excruciating pain. But even greater than the physical agony was the spiritual pain that occurred when the Father placed on the Son the sins of the world and for a moment broke fellowship with his Beloved. This divine forsaking prompted Jesus' anguished cry of dereliction: "My God, my God, why have you forsaken me?" (Matt. 27:46). Moments later "Jesus called out with a loud voice, 'Father, into your hands I commit my spirit.' When he had said this, he breathed his last" (Luke 23:46; cf. Matt. 27:50). Thus the animating spirit left Jesus' physical body, and he died. Out of love for the Nazarene, Joseph of Arimathea took Jesus' dead body, prepared it for burial, and placed it in a tomb. Surely the Gospel accounts of Jesus' life and death reflect a powerful realism. Having participated in the experiences common to humanity, Jesus was fully a man. Yet he was so perfectly; his manhood was uncorrupted by the dark forces of sin.

On the other hand, the Gospels portray Jesus as manifestly more than a man. This is seen, first, in terms of the divine *qualities* he possessed. During his ministry Jesus frequently displayed suprahuman knowledge or omniscience. Thus he perceived the unspoken thoughts of the Pharisees and the teachers of the law (Luke 5:21–22; 6:7–8). He knew that the crowd believed he had cast out the demon by the power of Beelzebub (Luke 11:17). Also he penetrated the minds of the disciples as they reasoned within themselves who would be the greatest (Luke 9:46–47). And finally Jesus knew that Judas would betray him (Matt. 26:21–25) and that Peter would disown him three times (Matt. 26:31–35).

During his ministry Jesus also displayed the quality of superhuman power, or omnipotence. By his spoken word Jesus stilled the stormy sea, whose ragings threatened to capsize the boat in which he and his disciples were sailing (Matt. 8:23–27). The awesome forces of nature submitted to his will. Jesus' power is also seen in his multiplying five barley loaves and two fish into sufficient food to feed five thousand people, with a dozen baskets of food left over (Matt. 14:15–21; Mark 6:35–44). The same supernatural power is seen in the feeding of four thousand people (Matt. 15:32–38; Mark 8:1–9). The Gospels relate numerous instances of Jesus' power over sickness and disease. The Nazarene healed persons of their paralysis (Matt. 9:5–7), of spinal deformity (Luke 13:10–13), of leprosy (Matt. 8:2–3), of life-threatening hemorrhage (Mark 5:25–29), of fevers (1:29–31), and of blindness (Matt. 9:27–30; 20:30–34). Jesus' power was especially evident in his frequent exorcisms of demons and evil spirits from possessed persons (Matt. 9:32; 12:22; Mark 1:32–34; 5:1–20; 7:25–30). Jesus' power was supremely displayed in acts of restoring the dead to life. By means of a simple touch Jesus caused the deceased son of the widow of Nain to rise up in his bier (Luke 7:12–17), and by his spoken word he brought back from the dead the daughter of Jairus (Mark 5:35–42).

Various suprahuman *deeds* confirmed his divinity, particularly the work of forgiving sins. Jesus remitted the sins of the paralytic lowered through the roof of his home in Capernaum (Mark 2:1–12; Luke 5:17–26). The scribes and Pharisees correctly assessed the significance of this work: "Who can forgive sins but God alone?" (Mark 2:7; Luke 5:21). Later Jesus forgave the sins of a prostitute while dining at the home of a Pharisee (Luke 7:47–50). Said the astonished guests, "Who is this who even forgives sins?" (v. 7:49). Furthermore, the Gospels relate that Jesus exercises the prerogative of judging the world. In Scripture judgment is the work of God alone (Ps. 62:12; Jer. 9:24). Yet Jesus affirms that at the end of the age *he* will execute judgment. In his explanation of the parable of the weeds, Jesus teaches that at the close of the age the Son of Man will consign the sons of the kingdom to eternal bliss and the sons of the evil one to eternal punishment (Matt. 13:41–43). Jesus' story of the sheep and the goats indicates that in the eschaton he will gather the nations before him and reward the righteous with eternal life and punish the unrighteous with eternal judgment (Matt. 25:31–46).

Jesus' identity is further unfolded by the extraordinary *claims* he made for himself. First, he claimed authority over the sacred law of Israel (Matt. 5:21–22, 27–28, 31–34, 38–39). By means of the retort "but I tell you," Jesus claimed the right to reinterpret the moral law of God. Furthermore, Jesus claimed authority over the God-ordained Sabbath (Exod. 20:8–11) when he revealed its true function in the new economy of grace (Matt. 12:8). Jesus likewise claimed authority over the covenant God established with Israel (Exod. 19:3–24:18), for he spoke of the new covenant that he would inaugurate through his shed blood (Matt. 26:28). Moreover, Jesus claimed authority over the kingdom of God itself, when he promised to delegate to Peter authority for the building of the primitive church (16:19). Indeed, Jesus made an extraordinary claim, appropriate to Deity alone: "All authority [*pasa exou-*

sia] in heaven and on earth has been given to me" (Matt. 28:18). On this basis Jesus demanded the absolute loyalty of his followers. They were to choose him over all other loyalties (10:27–38), find in him spiritual refreshment and rest (11:28), follow him in obedient discipleship (4:19), and render worship to him alone (14:31–33; 28:9–10).

In terms of Jesus' *self-consciousness*, the evidence is formidable that he understood himself to be the Son of God and Messiah. After Peter's confession of Jesus' deity at Caesarea Philippi (Matt. 16:16), Jesus informed Peter that his new understanding was given by God himself, and he warned the disciples not to tell others that he was the Christ (vv. 17, 20). Later, before the Sanhedrin, Caiaphas charged Jesus to tell if he was the Christ, the Son of God. Jesus' response according to Matthew (26:64) was, "Yes, it is as you say" (*su eipas*), whereas according to Mark (14:62) it was, "I am" (*egō eimi*). Earlier in his ministry, Jesus exercised reserve about his identity. But when his hour had come, the man Jesus acknowledged before the highest Jewish authority that he was the Son of God and Messiah.

In Judaism a prophet (*nābî'*) was a chosen servant who received a message from God and communicated it to the people. The prophet warned of judgment, called people to repentance, announced salvation, and predicted future events. Deuteronomy 18:15 and Isaiah 61:1 present Old Testament intimations of the prophetic ministry of the Messiah. The Gospels indicate that Jesus' contemporaries viewed him as a prophet (*prophētēs*, Matt. 16:14; 21:11, 46; Luke 7:16; cf. John 4:19; 6:14), and the Lord himself was conscious of his prophetic mission (Luke 4:24; 13:33). Jesus exercised a prophetic ministry chiefly by the words he spoke from the Father (Matt. 17:5). With authority Jesus taught what he had received from above by means of profound sayings, parables, proverbs, and discourses. Infallible predictions of future events were an important component of Jesus' teaching ministry (Matt. 10:26; 24:2–31; Luke 19:41–44). Moreover, substantiating Jesus' prophetic utterances was the powerful example of his prophetic life. Through his deeds of compassion, healing, and judgment Jesus effectively revealed the Father (cf. John 1:18; 17:6).

Primitive Christianity/Acts

A plain reading of Acts confirms that the early Christian preachers upheld Jesus' authentic humanity. In the first Christian sermon Peter acknowledged that Jesus was a descendant of David (Acts 2:30), a man from the town of Nazareth accredited by God (2:22), and one whom the Jewish leaders cruelly killed by impaling him on a tree (4:10; 5:30).

The apostles, however, attributed to the human Jesus *perfections* befitting God alone. Perceiving in Jesus the fulfillment of the Isaiah 53:11 servant passage, the early Christian missionaries represented him as completely righteous and holy (Acts 3:14; 4:27; 7:52). While choosing a replacement for Judas Iscariot, the apostles acknowledged Jesus' omniscience, with the prayer, "Lord, you know everyone's heart" (1:24). Moreover, through the authority and power of the risen Jesus the apostles performed many miraculous signs and wonders (4:30). In Jesus' name they healed a crippled beggar (3:6; 4:10), cast an evil spirit out of a woman who was a diviner (16:18), and brought Eutychus back to life (20:9–10). Evil spirits openly acknowledged the power and authority of the risen Jesus (19:15). Jesus performed these supernatural works in his state of humiliation when he was energized by the Spirit and directed by the Father (10:38).

The apostles also ascribe to Jesus suprahuman *works*. Peter describes Jesus as "the author [*archēgos*] of life" (Acts 3:15). Applied to the Nazarene four times in the New Testament (cf. Acts 5:31; Heb. 2:10; 12:2), *archēgos* denotes that Jesus is the source of life—naturally in relation to all persons and spiritually in relation to those who believe.[43] Moreover, the apostles attribute to Jesus the cosmic work of judgment. God appointed Jesus judge of the human race (Acts 10:42). Paul's statement in Acts 17:31 that God "has set a day when he will judge the world with justice by the man he has appointed" emphasizes that the divine judge will return as *man* (cf. Dan. 7:13–14) to execute his work. Paul envisages the union between Jesus' deity and his humanity as complete and unbroken. Finally, Jesus performs the supernatural work of Savior. Sins may be forgiven only on the basis of the atoning work of the divine Redeemer (Acts 2:38; 5:31; 10:43; 13:38).

Furthermore, the apostles attribute to Jesus a number of divine *prerogatives*. First, Jesus' words possess intrinsic authority (Acts 20:35). Second, devout persons invoked Jesus' name in prayer and worship (7:59–60; 9:14, 21; 22:16). In this regard, Stephen's opening words, "Lord Jesus, receive my spirit" (7:59), recall Jesus' final prayer to the Father while on the cross (Luke 23:46). Similarly, Stephen's last words on earth, "Lord, do not hold this sin against them" (Acts 7:60), approximate Jesus' first prayer to the Father on the cross (Luke 23:34). Stephen clearly understood that he was calling on the name of a divine person. Third, Acts 15:26 applies to Paul and Barnabas what could have been said of all the early missionaries: they were "men who . . . risked their lives for the name of our Lord Jesus Christ."

Acts acknowledges the proper unity of the two natures in the one person, Jesus Christ, when it predicates human characteristics to the person viewed from the divine side and vice versa. Humanity and deity are so united in the God-man that Peter could say that "the author of life" was brutalized and killed (Acts 3:15). Similarly, Paul claimed that the divine Lord bought the church with his own blood (20:28). William Neil translates the last part of verse 28 like this: "the church of God which he obtained with the blood of his Own One."[44] On the other hand, Stephen ascribed divine qualities to the God-man viewed from his human side, when he relates that in a vision he saw the man Jesus enthroned in glory at God's right hand (7:55).

Pauline Literature

Paul intimates in 2 Corinthians 5:16 (cf. 1 Cor. 2:8) that prior to his conversion he readily accepted Jesus as a human prophet but stumbled over his identity as the Son of God. As a Christian Paul acknowledged Christ's humanity as the principal seed of Abraham (Gal. 3:16) and as a descendant of King David (2 Tim. 2:8) whose birth (not conception) of Mary was quite ordinary in human experience (Gal. 4:4).[45] In his discussion of Adam and Christ as the respective heads of the old and the new humanities (Rom. 5:12–21), the apostle three times identifies Jesus Christ as an authentic man (vv. 15, 17, 19). Neither his life nor his death was a phantasm, for Paul attests that Jesus was killed by the Jews who earlier had maltreated the prophets (1 Thess. 2:15). Yet as one "who had no sin" (2 Cor. 5:21), Jesus was the paradigm of humanity as God intended it to be—the one pure man uncorrupted by the slightest moral stain.

The apostle establishes Jesus Christ's deity by ascribing to him several divine *qualities*. Christ's omnipotence is displayed in the mighty power whereby he brings all things in the universe under his control (Phil. 3:21). His immensity is affirmed as Paul writes of "the fullness of him who fills everything in every way" (Eph. 1:23). Phillips renders the latter verse as follows: "The church is his body, and in that body lives fully the One who fills the whole universe." The Christ who fills the entire universe with his Spirit Being (Eph. 4:10) is ubiquitous: Christ's presence pervades everything; there is no place in the cosmos where he is not present and available. In the words of William Barclay, "To Paul the ascension of Jesus meant not a Christ-deserted, but a Christ-filled world."[46] Paul also ascribes to Christ an incomparable *agapē* love. By referring to the "breadth and length and height and depth" of Christ's love (Eph. 3:18–19, RSV), and by claiming that it "surpasses knowledge," Paul infers that the love that flows from Christ's heart infinitely exceeds the love of even the most compassionate human being.

That Christ differs in kind, not merely in degree, from us mortals is evidenced by the *works* ascribed to him. The apostle represents Christ as the cosmic agent of creation: "For by him all things were created: things in heaven and on earth, visible and invisible, whether thrones or powers or rulers or authorities; all things were created by him" (Col. 1:16). In the following verse Paul identifies Christ as the cosmic agent of preservation. "In him all things hold together" (v. 17). The verb *synistēmi* in the latter verse means to "stand together," to "hold together," to "cohere."[47] Without the power of Christ at every moment causing the elements to cohere, the cosmos would disintegrate into a chaos. Furthermore, Paul depicts Christ as the cosmic agent of providence. In 1 Corinthians 10:1–10 the apostle describes Christ's spiritual presence with Israel during their wilderness wanderings providentially supplying all their physical and spiritual needs and even chastening when rebuke was needed to bring the wayward people back to God. Moreover, Paul represents Christ as the cosmic agent of redemption. In the Old Testament God is the One who saves from sin (Isa. 43:3, 11; Jer. 14:8; Hos. 13:4). Yet Paul affirms that under the new covenant it is Christ who delivers from sin. Thus Christ has redeemed believers from the domain of sin and Satan (Eph. 1:7), propitiated God's wrath toward us (Rom. 3:25), reconciled us to God (5:11), purified us from the defilement of sin (Titus 2:14), and destroyed death and opened the gate to heavenly immortality (2 Tim. 1:10). For those who refuse to accept God's offer of grace, Christ is the appointed cosmic agent of judgment. As "judge [of] the living and the dead" (2 Tim. 4:1), Christ will expose the hidden motives of each person's heart (1 Cor. 4:5) and mete out rewards and punishments in accordance with each one's works (2 Cor. 5:10).

Paul juxtaposes the divine and human natures of Christ in several important texts. Romans 9:5 speaks of "the human ancestry of Christ, who is God over all, forever praised!" Without question, Christ is a man descended from the distinguished Hebrew patriarchs (cf. 2 Tim. 2:8). Yet simultaneously and without compromising his authentic humanity, Christ is truly God.[48] Romans 1:3–4 makes the same theological affirmation. On one hand, Jesus Christ "as to his human nature [*kata sarka*] was a descendant of David." Since *sarx* here signifies human nature in its entirety, Paul envisages Jesus Christ as properly a man. The apostle then adds, "who through the Spirit of holiness [*kata pneuma hagiosynēs*] was declared with power to be the Son of God by his resurrection from the dead: Jesus Christ our Lord." Several exegetical comments need to be made in respect of this latter clause. (1) The expression "the Spirit of holiness" is a Hebrew idiom for the Holy Spirit. (2) The aorist passive participle of *horizō,* consistent with its meaning elsewhere in the New Testament (Luke 22:22; Acts 2:23; 10:42; et al.), means to "appoint" or "ordain." And (3) the phrase *en dynamei* ("with power") qualifies *huiou theou* ("Son of God") rather than *horisthentos* ("appointed"). Paul thus affirms that, although Christ was the Son of God in his state of humiliation, by Spirit-energized resurrection from the grave, he was appointed in his state of exaltation Son of God with *power.*[49] The bottom line is that although fully human, Jesus Christ is also in every respect fully God. Paul's discussion in 1 Corinthians 15 of Christ as the second Adam who leads the saints in victorious resurrection from the grave, registers the same point. As death came through the one man Adam, so the resurrection comes through the one man Jesus Christ (v. 21). Yet Christ is distinguished from Adam in that the latter "was of the dust of the earth," whereas the former is "the man from heaven" (vv. 47–49). Paul's identification of Jesus Christ as "the man from heaven" suggests, not that he possessed a body of air (so the Manichaeans), but that although truly human he was simultaneously the divine Son of God (v. 28)—one integrated person simultaneously both man and God.

Paul's grand hymn extolling the humiliation of Christ (Phil. 2:6–11) clearly attests the two natures in the one person of the God-man. Since the passage was exegeted in chapter 5, we need only draw out a few key points that pertain to the discussion at hand. Paul's opening affirmation about Christ Jesus is that *en morphē* he subsists as God (v. 6). Since *morphē* is "the form proper to a being in its objective reality,"[50] Paul claims that prior to the incarnation Christ shared the very being and attributes of God; i.e., he was ontologically God. This is confirmed by the following statement that Christ subsisted in a state of "equality with God" (*to einai isa theō*), which in chapter 5 we defined as existence-in-a-manner-of-equality-with-God. Out of love for humanity and obedience to the Father, Christ laid aside the outward manifestations of his God-equal-existence, which act is explained by three participial phrases. The first, "taking the very nature of a servant" (*morphēn doulou labōn,* v. 7a), indicates that while retaining the *morphē* of God, Christ took to himself the *morphē* (i.e., the nature and characteristics) of a lowly servant. The second phrase, "being made in human likeness" (*en homoiōmati anthrōpōn genomenos,* v. 7b), explains that in the incarnate state he was similar to us but not identical, for he was both God and sinless man. Paul's point here is the same as that made in Romans 8:3: "sending his own Son in the likeness [*homoiōma*] of sinful man."[51] The third phrase, "being found in appearance as a man" (*schēmati heuretheis hōs anthrōpos,* v. 8), suggests that to the most critical human observer Christ deported himself as the man he truly was. The Greek word *schēma* bears the nuance of the "actual form or stature perceptible to the senses."[52] Implicit is the idea that Christ's outward bearing fully corresponded to his inner reality. Thus in the portion of the hymn considered, Paul teaches that at the incarnation the eternal Son of God added to himself what he did not previously possess, namely, a complete but sinless humanity. Without explaining the actual "how" of this reality Paul states that the one person Jesus Christ is both God and man.

First Timothy 2:5 reads as follows: "For there is one God and one mediator between God and men, the man Christ Jesus." Concerning this verse we note the following: (1) Paul suggests that

Jesus Christ is one person with an integrated psychology. (2) Given the emphasis in the context on Christ's representation of man, the apostle stresses the humanity of the Mediator. In addition, docetic tendencies may have prompted Paul to focus on Christ the man. And (3), this text teaches that the union of deity and humanity in Christ is permanent. The divine Son who even now intercedes for the saints is also fully man.

As we saw in the previous section, the unity of deity and humanity in Jesus Christ is so complete that divine characteristics are attributed to the person viewed from the human side (1 Cor. 15:47). More frequently, human characteristics are predicated of the person viewed from the divine side of his being (1 Cor. 2:8; 2 Cor. 13:4; Gal. 2:20).

Johannine Literature

For a writer who devoted much attention to Christ's deity, John was careful to uphold the reality and integrity of the Lord's humanity. Thus John the Baptist (John 1:30), the people of Jerusalem (7:25, 27), the Pharisees (9:16, 24), and the Jews (10:33) regarded Jesus as an authentic man. Pilate exclaimed to the mob who sought Jesus' life, "Here is the man!" (*idou ho anthrōpos,* 19:5)—by which the Roman governor may have meant: "Here he is, poor fellow!"[53] John identifies Jesus' lineage as of the tribe of Judah and the family of David (Rev. 5:5; 22:16). Moreover, Jesus represented himself as "a man" (John 8:40) with a real body (2:19, 21). Yet Jesus' manhood was as God intended humanity to be—perfectly sinless and integrated. The Nazarene flawlessly obeyed the commands of his heavenly Father (8:29; 15:10) and was conscious of not the slightest guilt (8:46; cf. 1 John 3:5).

Emotionally Jesus experienced joy (*chara,* John 15:11; 17:13), anger (the verb *embrimaomai,* 11:33a, 38), and inner distress (the verb *tarassō,* 11:33; 12:27; 13:21). When Lazarus, the brother of Mary, died of an illness, John relates that "Jesus wept" (11:35). Physically, the carpenter of Nazareth thirsted (4:7; 19:28), became hungry (4:8), and experienced fatigue (4:6). Severely weakened from severe beatings and impalement on the cross, Jesus died as any person dies: "He bowed his head and gave up his spirit" (19:30). When a Roman soldier thrust a spear into Jesus' side, water and blood flowed out of the wound (19:34), confirming that he had already expired. Moreover, Joseph of Arimathea and Nicodemus carefully prepared Jesus' body for burial and placed it in a new tomb (19:38–42).

In the light of such facts, John sternly warned against docetic and incipient gnostic denials of Jesus' authentic manhood. He said, "Every spirit that acknowledges that Jesus Christ has come in the flesh is from God, but every spirit that does not acknowledge Jesus is not from God. This is the spirit of the antichrist, which . . . is already in the world" (1 John 4:2–3; cf. 2:22; 2 John 7). Significantly, John wrote that Christ came "in the flesh" (*en sarki*), not that the Christ or an emanation entered "into the flesh," in the sense of descending upon the man Jesus as a temporary enablement. The perfect tense of the verb *erchomai* ("has come") in 1 John 4:2 emphasizes that at the incarnation flesh was permanently incorporated into the person of Jesus Christ.

But that Jesus was more than a man is evident from the divine *qualities* ascribed to him. Jesus affirmed his eternality in John 8:58: "Before Abraham was born, I am [*egō eimi*]." Hear the testimony of John, the disciple who knew Jesus intimately: "We proclaim to you the eternal life, which was with the Father" (1 John 1:2; cf. 5:20). In addition, Jesus declared his self-existence in John 14:6: "I am . . . the life" (*egō eimi . . . hē zōē*). Whereas ordinary mortals affirm, "I have life," Jesus unequivocally states that he *is* the inexhaustible source of physical, moral, and spiritual life. John agrees with Jesus' self-understanding when he declares, "For as the Father has life in himself, so he has granted the Son to have life in himself" (John 5:26). John's words "In him was life" (1:4; cf. 1 John 1:2) connote that Jesus uniquely participates in the self-existent life of the Godhead. John, furthermore, represents Jesus as "the Almighty," or the One endowed with limitless power (Rev. 1:8). One of the prominent qualities ascribed to Jesus in the Fourth Gospel is omniscience. Thus Jesus instinctively knew Nathanael's inner character (John 1:47–48), the history of the Samaritan woman (4:16–18), which of the disciples would betray him (6:64; 13:11), and the treacherous events of his last days on earth (18:4). From their life with Jesus, the disciples concluded that he was all-knowing: "We can see that you know all things" (16:30; cf. 21:17). Texts such as John 3:34 and 5:19, 30 suggest that in his state of humiliation the Lord drew on his supernatural powers only when directed by the Father and energized by the Spirit. Moreover, Jesus Christ is consummately loving (13:34; 1 John 3:16), righteous (1 John 2:1), just (John 5:30), and faithful or reliable (Rev. 3:14; 19:11).

Jesus is also more than a man by the divine *works* attributed to him, the first of which is the work of creation. John 1:3 affirms of Christ: "Through him [*di' autou*] all things were made; without him nothing was made that has been made." John believed that all things in the universe (save God himself) were created through the agency of the Word, who later became flesh (cf. Rev. 3:14). Moreover, in chapter 2 we saw that Christ is the cosmic agent of providence; he opens the seven seals to the scroll and sets in motion the awesome series of events that will consummate the present age (Rev. 5:1–8:1). Also ascribed to Jesus is the divine work of remitting sins universally (John 1:29). Through his work as the Lamb who was slain, Jesus gives eternal life to all who believe (4:14; 5:40; 17:2; 20:31). Jesus understood himself to be the bread of life which, when taken in faith, guarantees the receiver spiritual life without end (6:25–59). Ascribed to Jesus is the divine work of raising the dead on the last day (5:25; 6:39; 11:25), of which his miracle of restoring Lazarus to life (11:38–44) was an anticipatory sign (v. 47). A final divine work that Jesus will perform is that of judging the world. "The Father judges no one, but has entrusted all judgment to the Son" (5:22; cf. v. 27). In John 5:17 Jesus coordinates his working with that of the Father, which implies that he is a person ontologically equal to the Father.

Jesus also made *claims* that are appropriate to God alone. In claiming to be one with the Father (John 10:30), Jesus implied that ontologically he was God (v. 33). Because of the perfect union that exists between the Father and the Son, Jesus could say, "All that belongs to the Father is mine" (16:15). Jesus' prediction that he would rise from the grave (2:19–21) was grounded in his assertion to possess complete authority (*exousia*) over his own life (10:17–18). In relation to others Jesus claimed to be the ultimate object of a person's faith (14:1) and obedience (v. 15; 1 John 5:3). The carpenter from Nazareth, moreover, repeatedly claimed to satisfy the deepest spiritual and emotional needs of humanity (John 4:14; 7:37–38; 8:12; 14:27). He claimed to be the way to God (14:6): to see him is to see God (12:45; 14:9), to know him is to know God (8:19; 14:7), and to honor him is to honor God (5:23).

John makes several explicit statements concerning the union of deity and humanity in Jesus Christ, the most important of which is John 1:14: "The Word became flesh and made his dwelling among us." The verb "became" (*egeneto*) is an ingressive aorist, indicating entrance into a state or condition.[54] The Word, who eternally was in fellowship with the Father (John 1:1–2), entered the world and took to himself "flesh." *Sarx* here connotes complete human nature, with emphasis on its weakness and frailty.[55] John thus states, not that the Word was transmuted into a man, but that while remaining what he previously was (i.e., God), the Word assumed all the characteristics of flawless humanity in a perfect union with a single personal center. According to Westcott, the thrust of John 1:14 "lies in the recognition of the unity of the Lord's Person, before and after the incarnation. His personality is divine. But at the same time we must affirm that his humanity is real and complete."[56] In John 1:18 the apostle emphasizes that the assumption of human nature did not nullify his deity, for so the man Jesus is denoted *monogenēs theos,* "God the only Son" (RSV).

Jesus' postresurrection appearance to Thomas and the other disciples in John 20:24–30 confirms that the one person Jesus Christ is both God and man. Jesus' humanity is evidenced by the fact that the disciples witnessed the nail marks and the spear wound in Jesus' body. His deity is attested (1) by the fact that Jesus supernaturally appeared in the midst of the disciples who had assembled behind locked doors; (2) by the forthright confession of the heretofore doubting Thomas: "My Lord and my God!"[57] and (3) by the fact that Jesus did not correct Thomas but acknowledged the validity of his confession (v. 29).

In 1 John 1:1–2 the apostle also upholds the unity of deity and humanity in the single integrated person. John testifies that Jesus appeared in a human body whose reality the disciples grasped with the three higher senses of hearing ("which we have heard"), sight ("which we have seen with our eyes, which we have looked at," aorist middle of *theaomai,* connoting careful and continuous contemplation),[58] and touch ("and our hands have touched"). On the other hand, John attests Jesus' deity by ascribing to him eternal preexistence—he who appeared "was from the beginning" (v. 1) and "the eternal life . . . was with the Father" (v. 2).

The fact that deity and humanity united in the one person, Jesus Christ, is no theoretical concern, but a datum absolutely necessary for salvation. Thus John affirms, "If anyone acknowledges [*hos ean homologēsē*] that Jesus is the Son of God, God lives in him and he in God" (1 John 4:15). Grammatically this verse is a third-class conditional sentence, whereby the statement in the apodosis becomes a reality when the condition given in the protasis is met. Thus confession that Jesus is the incarnate Son of God is the necessary condition for participating in the life of God. John makes the same point in 1 John 5:5: "Who is it that overcomes the world? Only he who believes that Jesus is the Son of God."

Other New Testament Literature

Hebrews devotes more attention to Christ's humanity than any other New Testament letter. The writer upholds Christ's patient endurance of suffering as an encouragement to Jewish Christians who were being persecuted for their faith in Christ, and he focuses on the death of our Lord as that which qualifies him to be an effectual high priest forever. Thus the descendant from the line of Judah (Heb. 7:14) entered the world in a genuine human body (10:5). He shared our "flesh and blood" (2:14), which is a Hebraism for his full participation in our humanity (cf. Matt. 16:17; Gal. 1:16). The aorist active indicative of the verb *metechō* to "share" or "participate in") "points to the historical event of the incarnation when the Son of God assumed this same human nature and thus himself became truly man and accordingly truly one with mankind."[59] As a man, the Son of God was fully tempted as we are (Heb. 4:15) and experienced all the trials and sorrows common to our lot (2:18; 1 Peter 4:1). Hebrews 5:7 vividly describes Christ's emotional anguish as he faced the prospect of drinking the cup of the world's sins: "During the days of Jesus' life on earth, he offered up prayers and petitions with loud cries and tears to the one who could save him from death." The following verse—"Although he was a son, he learned obedience from what he suffered" (v. 8)—suggests that Jesus Christ, even like the son of a human father, had to learn what it means to obey God in the midst of painful trials.[60] Hebrews 2:17 affirms that in order to liberate sinners from bondage to Satan and death Christ "had to be made like his brothers in every way" (3:17). That is, in complete identification with us, Christ entered into the full range of our human experiences. Yet so that he might function as a perfect high priest, Christ's humanity was without moral taint or stain. Although sorely tempted, Jesus never gave in to sin. Thus Hebrews 7:26 describes Jesus as "holy, blameless, pure, set apart from sinners," and 1 Peter 1:19 represents him as "a lamb without blemish or defect." Hebrews 4:15; 9:14; and 1 Peter 2:22 likewise uphold the sinlessness of Jesus.

Three texts describe Jesus as having been made "perfect." Hebrews 2:10 reads: "It was fitting that God, for whom and through whom everything exists, should make the author of their salvation perfect [*teleiōsai*] through suffering." Similarly, Hebrews 5:9 reads, "Once made perfect [*teleiōtheis*], he became the source of eternal salvation for all who obey him." Hebrews 7:28 employs the perfect passive participle form, *teteleiōmenon*. The verb *teleioō* used in each text means to "complete," "finish," or "perfect."[61] In these three verses it bears the specific sense, to "complete a process."[62] Thus the perfection ascribed to Jesus is not a moral perfection but a soteriological one. Through the process of suffering without sinning, of bringing the perfect sacrifice on the cross, and of being raised above all infirmity, Christ discharged his redemptive work to perfection. In short, the perfection discussed in Hebrews signifies God's "making Jesus, through his sufferings, perfectly qualified to be the Savior of His people."[63]

But the one whose humanity is so vividly described is also the eternal God. First, the writer attributes to the Son the cosmic work of creation. Thus he speaks of God's "Son . . . through whom he made the universe" (*di hou kai epoiēsen tous aiōnas,* Heb. 1:2). The words *hoi aiōnes* signify "the whole created universe of space and time."[64] Hebrews 1:10 takes a creation text directed to Yahweh (Ps. 102:25) and applies it to the Son. The writer envisages Jesus Christ as the builder of the universe in all its immensity (Heb. 3:3–4). Second, Hebrews assigns to the Son the cosmic work of preservation. So the Son is engaged in "sustaining [*pherōn*] all things by his powerful word" (1:3). The present active participle, *pherōn,* connotes Christ's task of upholding and directing the vast universe. Noteworthy is Hebrews' ascription of immutability to the church's Lord: "Jesus Christ is the same yesterday and today and forever" (13:8; cf. 1:12).

Names and Titles of Jesus in the New Testament

Jesus' identity is made clear by names and titles attributed to him in the New Testament. In volume 1, chapter 7 we showed that New Testament writers specifically addressed Jesus as "God" (John 1:1, 18; 20:28; Rom. 9:5; Titus 2:13; 3:4; Heb. 1:8; 2 Peter 1:1; 1 John 5:20). In addition, the New Testament ascribes to Jesus the name and title of "Lord" nearly two hundred and fifty times. Prior to the resurrection, Lord was a common title of respect (Matt. 8:2; Luke 6:46). But following his resurrection and ascension to heaven, the title was conferred on Jesus, especially in the Gentile wing of the church, to designate him the absolute sovereign of the universe (Acts 2:36; 10:36; Rom. 10:9; 1 Cor. 8:6; 2 Cor. 4:5; Phil. 2:11). Thus the apostles applied to Jesus Old Testament citations originally addressed to *Yahweh* (Matt. 3:3; Acts 2:20–21) and to *'ᵃdōnay* (Matt. 22:43–45). As *kyrios* Jesus exercises the functions of deity; i.e., he creates (1 Cor. 8:6), saves sinners (Rom. 10:9, 13), and judges the world (Rom. 2:16; 2 Thess. 1:7–8). In terms of his self-understanding, Jesus applied the title "Lord" to himself (Mark 12:36–37). Paul ascribed to Jesus the title "Lord of glory," which Scripture elsewhere applies to God the Father (Acts 7:2; 1 Cor. 2:8; cf. Ps. 24:8–10; Eph. 1:17).

The New Testament represents Jesus as the "Son of God." The angel Gabriel so designated Jesus (Luke 1:35), as did Satan (Matt. 4:3, 6; note the first-class condition, which assumes that the condition in the protasis, "If you are the Son of God . . . ," is true), Peter under divine illumination (Matt. 16:16), John (1 John 3:8; 5:5, 12, 20), and most frequently the apostle Paul (Rom. 1:4; 8:3; Gal. 2:20; 4:4). Moreover, at the baptism (Mark 1:11) and the transfiguration (Mark 9:7) God the Father certified Jesus to be his Son. Some fifty times Jesus called God his "Father," whereas on several occasions he used Son as a self-designation (Matt. 11:25–27; Mark 13:32). The Jews understood that Jesus made for himself the claim of divine sonship (John 19:7). Thus it is clear that "the synoptic Gospels present a Messiah who was fully conscious of his special relationship to God as Son."[65] The fact that the Old Testament represents Israel as God's son (Exod. 4:22; Hos. 11:1) suggests that Jesus as Son perfectly executes the messianic vocation of the chosen people. But Jesus exercises his messianic calling as the One who ontologically is the eternal Son of the Father. The Son is one with the Father in will (John 4:34; 6:38), in working (14:10), and in very being (10:30). In summary, "the title [Son] also implies a unity of being and nature with the Father, uniqueness of origin and preexistence."[66] The representation of Jesus as "the one and only Son" (*monogenēs huios,* John 1:14; 3:16, 18; 1 John 4:9) upholds the uniqueness of Jesus' sonship: the son of Mary and the Son of God is in a class by himself.[67]

The apostles ascribe to Jesus the name "Holy One" (1 John 2:20; cf. Acts 3:14), or "Holy One of God" (John 6:69). We saw in volume 1, chapter 6 that "Holy One" or "the Holy One of Israel" is a common Old Testament designation for Yahweh, especially in Isaiah. Moreover, Jesus designates himself "the First and the Last" (Rev. 1:17; 2:8) and "the Alpha and the Omega, the First and the Last, the Beginning and the End" (Rev. 22:13)—titles the Old Testament attributes to God alone (Isa. 44:6; 48:12). The title "Word of God," an important Johannine designation of Jesus (John 1:1–4, 14; 1 John 1:1; Rev. 19:13; cf. 1 Peter 1:23), chiefly designates God in his self-expressive activity. The Old Testament refers to the word by which

God creates (Ps. 33:6), reveals himself (Ps. 119:9, 105, 130), sustains the created order (Pss. 147:15–18; 148:8), and effects his will in history (Isa. 55:11). John informs us that the Word or Logos who performs these cosmic functions is the preexistent God (John 1:1–2), who in an act of extreme abasement assumed our humanity (1:14).

An important Christological title is "Messiah" (*messias,* a transliteration of the Hebrew *māšîaḥ*) or "Christ" (*christos,* from the verb *chriō,* to "anoint"). Paul uses *christos* in his letters almost exclusively as a proper name. The title "Christ" was frequently ascribed to Jesus by others (John 1:41; 4:29; 20:31; Acts 2:36; 8:5; Rom. 9:5). Jesus accepted the title three times in the Gospels (Matt. 16:16–17; Mark 14:61–62; John 4:25–26), and this confirms that he understood himself to be the personal fulfillment of Old Testament messianic prophecies. More directly, Jesus applied Isaiah 61:1–2 to himself in the synagogue at Nazareth (Luke 4:18–19; note the aorist form of the verb *chriō*), thus acknowledging his role as the Lord's anointed servant. Whereas contemporary Israel anticipated a triumphant messianic deliverer, Jesus interpreted his role spiritually rather than politically (1 Cor. 15:25). Thus the purpose of his earthly ministry was to inaugurate the rule or reign of God in the hearts of all who would believe and only later to establish a visible, earthly kingdom in power (1 Cor. 15:24–25). Since Israel expected the Messiah to be a king in the line of David (2 Sam. 7:16; Luke 1:32), "Son of David" was a common messianic title applied to Jesus (Matt. 20:30–31; 21:9, 15; cf. Rev. 5:5; 22:16). Yet in Jesus' own mind, the human son of David was simultaneously divine (Matt. 22:42–45).

The title "Son of Man," which occurs some eighty times on the lips of Jesus in the Gospels, derives from the vision of Daniel 7:13–14. The Son of Man, who receives from the Ancient of Days a universal and eternal kingdom, is best understood as both an individual and the ideal representative of the people of God (cf. Heb. 2:6–9). In postbiblical Judaism the Son of Man was a supernatural Messiah who would come at the end of the age and rule in the kingdom of God. Contrary to Jewish expectation, Jesus used the title Son of Man in the context of his humiliation, suffering, and death on the cross (Matt. 12:40; Mark 8:31; John 6:53; 8:28). Yet Jesus also used the title in the context of his future exaltation, world rule, judgment, and second coming to earth (Matt. 16:27; 19:28; 25:31; Mark 14:61–62; John 5:27; 13:31–32; Acts 7:56—the only reference outside the Gospels). In sum, by employing the Son of Man imagery, "Jesus thought of himself in terms of a heavenly Messiah fulfilling on earth a ministry on man's behalf which would culminate in scenes of final glory."[68] The reality of Christ's divine and human natures is implicit in the title.

Paul's equivalent of the Son of Man title is "the last Adam" (1 Cor. 15:45) and "the man from heaven" (1 Cor. 15:47–49). Jesus as the perfect man is the representative of humanity (cf. Rom. 5:15, 17–19) who by his death and resurrection leads the redeemed race to the heavenly world whence he came.

SYSTEMATIC FORMULATION

Attempts to develop Christologies exclusively "from above" (revelation) or exclusively "from below" (historical evidence) are deficient in that they eliminate some of the relevant information (either from below or from above). In contrast, a verificational approach critically considers hypotheses from any source and accepts the hypothesis that accounts for the lines of relevant evidence both from above (revealed meanings) and below (observable evidence). In accord with the extensive biblical data in the previous section, we find most coherent the hypothesis that Christ Jesus was one person with both divine and human natures. Here we develop that view systematically and exhibit its coherence, including its consistency, adequacy, and viability. We begin by exhibiting the view's adequacy to account for the data from below—the observable Jesus in history.

A Person in History

The Son of God not only entered into the world in literal human flesh but also lived for about thirty-three years on earth. His historical existence was significant throughout his mature life and ministry. The above views of Bultmann and Ogden question whether we can know anything historically about Jesus as we try to reconstruct the past by a critical use of ancient records. In *Ancient Evidence for the Life of Jesus,* Gary Habermas, in addition to examining the accurate Gospel accounts, assesses numerous extrabiblical sources from secular historians (Tacitus), government officials (Pliny the Younger), religious records of Jews (Josephus, the Talmud), other Gentile sources (Lucian, Mara Bar-Serapion), Gnostic writings, and others. The seventeen non-Christian sources from within 125 years of Jesus' death are far more than for any other person from ancient times. They indicate that Jesus was a flesh-and-blood person, the brother of James, who lived in Palestine. He was known as a virtuous person who taught the need for conversion, the importance of faith and obedience, the brotherhood of believers, the need for abandoning other gods and worshiping himself, and the idea that his death was the means of life for many. He performed miracles and made prophecies that were later fulfilled. So he had many disciples from both Jews and Gentiles. Some believed he was the Messiah and some worshiped him as God. Because he led Jews astray by teaching apostasy, he would die. He was put to death by Pontius Pilate, who had him crucified during the reign of Emperor Tiberius on the eve of the Passover. After his death his teachings broke out again and witnesses claimed to have seen Jesus alive three days after his death. In addition to all this are the early creeds and other noncanonical Christian sources. Recent archaeological discoveries, furthermore, also support the historicity of Jesus' life, and the same basic view of Jesus as the New Testament does.[69]

At the same time, according to Ronald Nash, attempts to derive the life of Christ and early Christianity from Greek philosophical sources, pagan mystery religions, and Gnosticism have failed to find adequate support. In *Christianity and the Hellenistic World* Nash finds those hypotheses to depend more on naturalistic presuppositions than adequate evidence. The hypotheses of derivation from Greek philosophy, mystery religions, or Gnosticism explain everything but how there came to be a Christian church and how writers could draw from these sources and produce a mythical hero with the uniqueness of Jesus. Nash asks, "Was early Christianity a syncretistic faith? Did it borrow any of its essential beliefs and practices either from Hellenistic philosophy or religion or from Gnosticism?" And after extensive research, Nash answers, "The evidence requires that this question be answered in the negative."[70]

John Stott concludes his work *The Authentic Jesus* by saying,

> Instead of seeking to edit the New Testament witness to Christ, we should feel what Paul called a "godly jealousy" for his glory, and should have an unshakeable resolve to give him the honor which is due his name. In order to do this, we shall

have to renounce the folly of fabricating "a Jesus other than the Jesus we [the apostles] preached" (2 Cor. 11:1–4) and instead hold fast to the authentic Jesus, who is the Jesus of the apostolic witness.[71]

A Fully Human Person

Jesus' humanness is evident in many different ways. Historically, he lived during a certain historical epoch in a distinctive milieux. Physically, he was limited to a relatively small space (in a certain geographical area in which he needed to walk or ride an animal from place to place). Biologically, Jesus hungered and ate, grew tired, slept, suffered pain, eventually died, and was buried. Filially, he obeyed Mary and Joseph (Luke 2:51). Intellectually he grew in knowledge and wisdom (2:40, 52). He could express amazement at the faith of the centurion (7:9) and the unbelief of the men of Nazareth (Mark 6:6), and he did not know the time of his return. Religiously, he regularly attended public worship (Luke 4:16) and, at least in one instance, paid the temple tax (Matt. 17:24–27).

Spiritually, Jesus did not neglect private prayer. He prayed alone very early in the morning (Mark 1:35). He also prayed after ministering to the five thousand (6:46), and he sometimes prayed all night (Luke 6:12). His praying shows that he had a deep sense of felt need. Socially, he attended weddings (John 2:1–11) and banquets with sinners (Matt. 9:10–11) and he especially loved specific people such as Mary, Martha, and Lazarus (John 11:3, 5). Politically, he urged citizens to pay taxes to the state (Matt. 22:21). Psychologically and emotionally, he experienced joy (John 15:11), sorrow (11:35), and anxiety (in Gethsemane).

A Tempted Person

One of the clearest indications of Jesus' full humanity is his genuine struggle with temptations. Jesus experienced severe temptations from Satan to use his divine powers in ways contrary to the Father's redemptive purpose. Starving after forty days of fasting, Jesus could have used his divine power to turn stones into bread (Matt. 4:3). By drawing on those divine powers he could have thrown himself from the highest point of the temple and so, by escaping injury, demonstrate the Father's care (vv. 5–6). By changing his loyalty from pleasing the Father to pleasing Satan, he could have avoided the crucifixion and, insofar as Satan is to be trusted, possessed all the kingdoms of this world (vv. 8–9). Then the devil left him until another "opportune time" (Luke 4:13). No doubt Jesus was also tempted by others around him throughout his ministry. Indeed, he was tempted in every way, just as we are (Heb. 4:15).

Since Jesus was tempted in every way as we are, he must have been tempted sexually as an adolescent and also as a man in the prime of his sexual potency. God created persons male and female, and so sexual desires as such are not themselves sinful or a sign of fallen human nature. As a man, Jesus could have respected and admired women without desiring them for himself. Temptation would occur in enticements to satisfy his sexual desires in a way displeasing to the Father, that is, contrary to his or others' best interests. Undoubtedly, displeasing sexual proposals came to Jesus' attention, were considered, and had a certain allure, as all temptations do. But regularly Jesus willed not to consent to the enticements. Temptation is not sin; entertaining it in the mind and yielding to it in action is sin. And Jesus did not entertain sinful suggestions in his heart or yield to them in action. He neither lusted nor committed adultery. He did not covet what belonged to others nor steal. He did not get angry without cause, nor did he commit murder. He worshiped God only and did not take his Father's name in vain. He loved the Father with his whole being and his neighbors as himself.

Facing betrayal and agonizing death in Gethsemane, Jesus pled, "Father, if you are willing, take this cup from me" (Luke 22:42). So severe was the struggle that he was in "anguish" and prayed more earnestly, "and his sweat was like drops of blood falling to the ground" (v. 44). Although he had no sinful tendencies within himself, no doubt the appeal of sinful options presented themselves to him with even greater force because of his moral purity. As fully human, he felt the full psychological, moral, and spiritual force of severe temptations.

A Just Person (From Human Observation)

It is one thing to be lured by a tempter and another to yield and sin. Although tempted as we are, Jesus was "without sin" (Heb. 4:15). That witness came from varied sources. He himself could say, "Can any of you prove me guilty of sin?" (John 8:46). Alerting his disciples to his approaching departure, he said, "The prince of this world is coming. He has no hold on me" (14:30). When his enemies could not sustain their accusations, Pilate concluded, "As for me, I find no basis for a charge against him" (19:6). His closest disciples, who traveled with him for three years, support his sinlessness. John could say, "In him is no sin" (1 John 3:5). Peter called him "the Holy and Righteous One" (Acts 3:14) and "a lamb without blemish or defect" (1 Peter 1:19). Peter also declared, "He committed no sin, and no deceit was found in his mouth" (2:22) and later stated that Christ died for sins, "the righteous for the unrighteous" (3:18). The writer of Hebrews said that he "was tempted in every way, just as we are—yet was without sin" (Heb. 4:15), and as a high priest he was "holy, blameless, pure, set apart from sinners" (Heb. 7:26). Paul wrote that he "had no sin" (2 Cor. 5:21). So when Paul teaches that God sent his Son "in the likeness of sinful man" (Rom. 8:3), he speaks of the need for Christ to identify with fallen humans to save them but not to partake in their sin.

For the fully human Jesus to be tempted as we are, however, some argue that it was necessary that he have a sinful or fleshly nature. Reinhold Niebuhr and Karl Barth hold that since Jesus was tempted in all points as we are, he must have had a sinful nature like our fallen nature.[72] That Jesus had a morally defective nature is not a necessary inference from the fact that he was tempted as we were. Our problem is not one of mere sins, but a sinful nature, leading John Knox to ask, "Could one have shared in that existence and not participated in that wrongness?"[73] Several considerations make the hypothesis of Jesus' sinful nature implausible.

1. Jesus must have been tempted inwardly, but that is not to say that the temptations originated in the nature of the Holy One. He had the same types of temptations, but that is not to say that they had the same source. What, then, can we infer from his being tempted as we are? It means that he experienced all the same basic types of temptations we do. Jesus became flesh in the physical sense (John 1:14), and he was, according to his human nature, a descendant of David (Rom. 1:3). Therefore he could be tempted in all ways as we are physically.

2. Given a scriptural concept of the flesh in a moral sense, a fallen nature

involves far more than temptations. If Jesus had been fleshly in nature as fallen people are, he would have been "controlled by the sinful nature" (Rom. 7:5). Jesus would have been unable to do good, for nothing good lives in the sinful nature (7:18). If he had had a sinful nature like ours, he could not have obeyed God's law (8:3). And he would have been dominated by a mind-set contrary to the will of the Spirit (v. 5). The mind of Jesus would then have been hostile to God and would not have submitted to God's law, nor could it have done so (v. 7). Had Jesus had a sinful nature as we do, he could not have pleased God (v. 8), and he would have desired what is contrary to the Spirit (Gal. 5:13). Had Jesus been born of sinful flesh, he would have had to be born again to enter the kingdom of God (John 3:3–7). But from conception and birth Jesus was Lord! He did not need to be born again, for his virgin conception involved more than a biological miracle. It involved a moral miracle. As a result of the Holy Spirit's overshadowing Mary, "the holy one" to be born of her would be the Son of God (Luke 1:35, see previous chapter). Had he been a sinner, he would have had to die for his own sins and could not have been the sacrifice for others' sins.

3. It does not require a fleshly—that is, sinful—nature for one to be fully human. Adam's and Eve's natures were fully human and not fleshly before the Fall. And they were subject to temptations as fallen people are. In heaven believing people will be fully human without sin. So Jesus' sinlessness in nature is not logically incompatible with full humanity. We often include sin in the essence of humanity by saying, "What I did was only human!" More accurately we should say, "What I did was only sinful!" Jesus did what was human but not what was sinful. His righteous acts came from a righteous, not a depraved, heart.

4. To atone for sin Jesus came in the *likeness* of sinful man (Rom. 8:3), but he did not come as a sinful man. The term *likeness* involves sufficient similarity to humanness that Jesus could die for sinners as a sin-offering, but it indicates a limit. Paul did not say what Barth interprets him to say, that it was essential for Jesus to have existed as "man who is a sinner" or "in sin-controlled flesh."[74] Barth tends to overlook the term *likeness* in interpreting this verse. He also fails to understand that at the cross the guilt and penalty of our sins were imputed to Christ. Our sins were not transferred to the crucified Messiah. We need to keep in mind the sinless life that made his death for others possible. Jesus' likeness to us was not as an initiator of sin, but as one who could be tempted. "He was passively exposed to sin," Käsemann concludes, "but in distinction from us he did not actively open himself to it. What is decisive for such a perspective is not the susceptibility to sin, but the reality of the sin-offering which was made for us and represents us."[75] It is one thing to say in a metaphoric sense that life is *like* a vapor and another to say that life is a vapor. So it is one thing for Paul to write in Romans 8, after explaining what was involved in the sinful nature in chapters 6–8, that God sent his own Son in the *likeness* of sin-controlled flesh, and quite another to say that he sent his own Son *in* sin-controlled flesh! Jesus did not bring sin with him to his environment, all kinds of temptations came from around him, but he was not a tempter of himself or others.

The hypothesis that Jesus had a sinful nature fails to fit the Scripture's explicit teaching (above and following) that he was totally without spot, blemish, or sin. An alleged inference from his being tempted as we are does not merit greater probability than that explicit evidence. A sinful Jesus of history cannot be divorced from a sinless Christ of faith. Christology rests on both history and theology. In *Luke: Historian and Theologian,* I. Howard Marshall has presented a conclusive case that no necessary conflict rages between history and faith. Rather, "Christian faith is dependent upon historically verifiable events. This was the view taken by Luke, and we have attempted to show in adopting this view he was not taking up an individual point of view but that he was in agreement with the early church generally."[76]

A Fully Righteous Person (From the Father's Perspective)

In addition to the events attested by historical observers, however, we have the invisible meanings of the facts that God gave by special revelation. We look now at what even first-century eyewitnesses could know of Jesus Christ only by revelation from above. This content came through credentialed spokespeople: the inspired prophetic and apostolic writers of Scripture.

The ultimate standard of goodness is what pleases the Father. God the Father looks not only on the outward appearance but also on the heart. So Jesus said, "I seek not to please myself but him who sent me" (John 5:30). Jesus evidently succeeded in pleasing the Father, for both at Jesus' baptism and at his transfiguration God the Father said, "With him I am well pleased" (Matt. 3:17; 17:5). Jesus did not transgress divine law nor deviate from whatever it means to be ethically human. All that he thought, said, and did was motivated by love, energized by the Holy Spirit and was pleasing to the heavenly Father. Hence Jesus not only did not sin, he was not inwardly sinful.

Because he was sinless in the sight of God and man, the Son of God had authority on earth to forgive sins (Matt. 9:6). To the paralytic who was healed Jesus said, "Son, your sins are forgiven" (Mark 2:5). The teachers of the law, thinking this blasphemy, properly asked, "Who can forgive sin but God alone?" (2:6–7). Because he was sinless Jesus did not need to die for his own sins but could offer himself for the sins of others. "No miracle of Christ equals the miracle of his sinless life. To be holy in all thought and feeling, never to fail in duty to others, never to transgress the law of perfect love to God or man, never to exceed or to come short—this is a condition outstripping the power of imagination and almost of belief. Here is a casement opening on a Diviner world."[77]

A Fully Divine Person

In the previous chapter we proposed that although the eternal Word gave up the constant use of his divine attributes, he progressively revealed his divine nature through increasingly specific teaching attested by more and more conclusive miraculous "signs." We need here to consider further whether the view of his full deity can adequately fit the scriptural givens.

Non-Trinitarians often allege that Jesus himself never said, "I am God." Jews and Muslims especially may make a major case out of the fact that he did not explicitly say, "I am God." But in his historical context (including theism and the extensive evidence given for Trinitarianism) he could not be expected to make that claim. For Jesus to say "I am God" would mean far more than it does for monists like Shirley MacLaine, who in her television mini-series, "Out on a Limb," stood on the beach and repeated with increasing conviction, "I am God." She meant that inwardly her soul was made up of the same pervasive energy as is everything else. Her "divinity" transcends herself but not the cosmos. Jesus' God is a personal Spirit distinct from the entirety of the cosmos. In a theistic and Trinitarian perspective, for Jesus to say "I am God" would mean that he imagined himself to be either the heavenly Father or the entirety of the triune Godhead. Taking Jesus' frame of reference into account, the most that Jesus could meaningfully claim was that he was one with the Father. The questions we can reasonably ask of Jesus in context are "Did Jesus ever claim to be one with the Father not only relationally in mind and purpose, but also in essence and being?" and, "Did Jesus claim divine prerogatives and do divine works?

What did Jesus actually *claim* for himself? When he said to Satan, the tempter, "Do not put the Lord your God to the test" (Matt. 4:7), Jesus applied Deuteronomy 6:16 to himself as God. Jesus claimed to preexist with the Father. When he was asked if he was greater than Abraham, he responded, "Before Abraham was born, I am!" (John 8:58). In prayer Jesus spoke of the glory he had had with the Father "before the world began" (17:5). Jesus claimed to be more than one with the Father in mind and purpose; he claimed oneness of power. For a person is as secure in his hand, he alleged, as in the Father's hand (John 10:28–29). So when he said, "I and the Father are one" (10:30), he meant they were one in the attribute of omnipotence. The Jews understood that he was claiming to be God (v. 33); this is why they sought to stone him for blasphemy. He claimed his uniqueness among humans as "the one whom the Father set apart as his very own and sent into the world" (v. 36). Distinctively Jesus alleged, "The Father is in me, and I in the Father" (v. 38). Again the Jews understood him to imply that he was divine and again they tried to stone him for blasphemy. Jesus even claimed to be omnipresent: "And surely I am with you always, to the very end of the age" (Matt. 28:20). In statements like these Jesus claimed that as a distinct person he preexisted with the Father eternally, was one in essence (or attribute) with the Father, and was uniquely sent by the Father into the world. Although Jesus was a person with truly human characteristics, he also taught that he was different from every other human being as ontologically one with the Father.

Furthermore Jesus claimed *divine prerogatives*. He claimed that he is the source of the necessities in an eternal life-support system including spiritual water, food, and light. He said that he was the giver of living water: "Whoever drinks the water I give him will never thirst" (John 4:14, cf. v. 10). He also alleged, "I am the bread of life" (6:48) and "The bread of God is he who comes down from heaven and gives life to the world" (v. 33). The Jews understood that by saying this he claimed for himself a supernatural origin (v. 42). Furthermore, he declared, "I am the light of the world" (8:12). Again, he said, "I tell you the truth, if anyone keeps my word, he will never see death" (John 8:51). At Bethany, where Lazarus lay buried, he said, "I am the resurrection and the life. He who believes in me will live, even though he dies" (11:25; cf. 5:21). Furthermore he encouraged and accepted the worship of the apostles before his death (14:1), and after his resurrection (Matt. 28:17) Jesus exhibited his conviction that he was God. He said, "I am in the Father and the Father is in me" (John 14:11). To Thomas who questioned where Jesus was going after his death, Jesus made this astounding statement: "I am the way and the truth and the life. No one comes to the Father except through me. If you really knew me, you would know my Father as well" (vv. 6–7). Although God alone can forgive sins, Jesus forgave sins (Mark 2:9–10). Jesus also declared that "the Son of Man is

Lord even of the Sabbath" (Mark 2:27). Jesus had the audacity to demand that people should love him more than their own fathers, mothers, brothers, sisters, sons, or daughters (Luke 12:53; 14:26–27). As a matter of fact he made it clear that the Father had given to him "all authority in heaven and on earth" (Matt. 28:18).

Did Jesus at any time *deny* his deity? He disclaimed being the Father, but he never denied being the Father's eternal Word who came from heaven on a mission to save lost human beings. For the purpose of saving the lost he spoke of his functional subordination to the Father and his dependence on the Father. Specifically he said, "The Father is greater than I" (John 14:28). Jesus was sent by the Father into the world to perform a task that he completed in dependence on the Father. Jesus fulfilled his distinct functions in harmony with the work of the heavenly Father and the Holy Spirit. Jesus did not view himself as a human who was deified at his baptism or transfiguration. Repeatedly he spoke of himself as the eternal Son of God or Son of Man who alone had come from above. He alone knew the Father as the Father knew him (John 10:15). When Jesus responded to the rich young ruler, "Why do you call me good? No one is good—except God alone" (Luke 18:19), he hardly denied what he had said of himself so many other times. Rather, he drew attention to who he really was and why he could ask the rich to leave all and follow him (v. 22). None of his references to himself in the state of humiliation deny his claims that he was uniquely and essentially one with the Father from before his conception and birth on earth.

By accepting the fact that Jesus was essentially God in human flesh as he claimed, we can account for much related first-century data or phenomena. The hypothesis of his divine sonship accounts for his *incomparable teaching*. As Jesus taught in the temple courts, "the Jews were amazed and asked, 'How did this man get such learning without having studied?' " (John 7:15). When the temple guards were asked why they did not arrest him, they explained, "No one ever spoke the way this man does" (v. 46). When he had finished his Sermon on the Mount, "the crowds were amazed at his teaching, because he taught as one who had authority, and not as their teachers of the law" (Matt. 7:28–29). The response to Jesus' unparalleled and authoritative teaching and the countless changed lives confirm his astounding claims.

If Jesus is what he claimed to be, we can coherently account also for his *sterling character*. No ordinary fallen person could challenge an audience of friends and enemies as Jesus did, "Can any of you prove me guilty of sin?" (John 8:46). After Jesus was condemned to death as a criminal, Judas, seized with remorse, returned the thirty silver coins to the chief priests and elders and cried, "I have sinned, for I have betrayed innocent blood" (Matt. 27:3–4). Pilate, the judge at Jesus' trial, having found that Jesus had committed no crime, washed his hands in front of the bloodthirsty crowd. " 'I am innocent of this man's blood,' he said. 'It is your responsibility!' " (Matt. 27:24). The thief crucified to the right of Jesus said, "We are punished justly, for we are getting what our deeds deserve. But this man has done nothing wrong" (Luke 23:41). Jesus' closest friends with him in all kinds of circumstances for three years also confirmed the righteousness of his character. Peter likened Jesus to a sacrificial lamb "without blemish or defect" (1 Peter 1:19). John wrote, "in him is no sin" (1 John 3:5).

Granting that Jesus was what he claimed to be, we can explain his *supernatural works*. Jesus healed invalids (John 5:1–15), gave sight to the blind

(9:1–12), cured lepers (Matt. 8:1–4), raised the dead (John 11:38–44), and controlled a furious storm that had nearly sunk the disciples' boat. The disciples woke him saying, " 'Teacher, don't you care if we drown?' He got up, rebuked the wind and said to the waves, 'Quiet! Be still!' Then the wind died down and it was completely calm" (Mark 4:37–39). The terrified followers asked each other, "Who is this? Even the wind and the waves obey him!" (v. 41).

If Jesus was what he claimed to be, furthermore, we can explain his *dying grace*. During his betrayal, his unjust trial, threats of death, and the agony of crucifixion, Jesus exhibited *agapē* love—the self-giving love of God. While in agony on the cross, he prayed for his executioners, "Father, forgive them for they do not know what they are doing" (Luke 23:34). The thief on his right said, "Jesus, remember me when you come into your kingdom" (v. 42). The centurion guarding Jesus exclaimed, " 'Surely he was the Son of God!' " (Matt. 27:54).

If Jesus indeed was what he claimed to be, we can account for his empty tomb and *triumphant resurrection*. Although buried in a cave sealed with a huge rock and guarded by armed soldiers, "up from the grave he arose in a mighty triumph o'er his foes!" The risen Christ left the tomb empty and appeared to several individuals and groups including over five hundred people at once (1 Cor. 15:1–8). Indeed, Jesus "through the Spirit of holiness was declared with power to be the Son of God by his resurrection from the dead: Jesus Christ our Lord" (Rom. 1:4).

What hypothesis provides the most coherent and viable account of Jesus' claims? Was he a good man, a liar, a lunatic, or Lord of all? Good men who made anything like the claims Jesus made for himself would no longer be considered good. Unable to substantiate such claims, they would be judged to be either intentional liars or irresponsible lunatics. Of all persons, Jesus was no liar! He lived and died to stand up for the truth. And Jesus, was no raving lunatic! His teaching and conduct reflected sanity and control in the midst of even the most excruciating circumstances. Purposefully and consistently he revealed who he was, and he supported his claims with a sinless character, incomparable teaching, supernatural works for others, and supremely with his own resurrection from the dead. Since the hypotheses of a good person, a liar, or a lunatic are improbable in the light of the evidence, we need a more adequate hypothesis. Finding that the narrative of the Gospels is a coherent account of these first-century phenomena, we propose that Jesus was in fact all that he claimed to be—one in essence, power, and prerogative with the Father in heaven.

Christ's claims for himself cannot successfully be dismissed as mere projections of the church without a referent. If a group of untrained writers like the disciples could make up the fabulous character who has influenced history more than any other person, they would merit an international literary award. The import of Jesus' claims is recognized not only by friends but also by enemies. There is no mistaking the witness of the apostles who knew him best. One of his closest associates, Peter, concluded that he is "the Son of the living God" (Matt. 16:16) and wrote to "those who through the righteousness of our God and Savior Jesus Christ have received a faith as precious as ours" (2 Peter 1:1). Thomas, after making stubborn attempts to think of him otherwise, exclaimed, "My Lord and my God!" (John 20:28). Jehovah's Witnesses and others should note that the definite article (*hē*) precedes the word God (*theos*), on the Witnesses' own grammatical principle referring to the Jehovah God. And in referring to Jesus as Lord and God, Thomas was not using expletives! The account of Thomas' faith supplies the climactic evidence for believing "that Jesus is the Christ" (John 20:31). Paul speaks of Jesus as "God over all, forever praised" (Rom. 9:5). And Paul anticipates the "glorious appearing of our great God and Savior, Jesus Christ" (Titus 2:13). John thought of Jesus as the eternal Word (*Logos*) of God who became flesh (John 1:1, 14) and as "Jesus Christ, the Righteous One" (1 John 2:1). Rather than recant these convictions born of their direct experience with Christ, these apostles would rather die. They proved their convictions when they became martyrs for their belief. Their faith in Jesus' deity did not contradict God's oneness (in essence) because they recognized not only Jesus' personal distinction from the Father but also his essential oneness with the Father.

If Jesus is who he claimed to be, we can account also for the witness of even the *unholy spirits*. At Capernaum a "channeler" possessed by an evil spirit cried out, "What do you want with us, Jesus of Nazareth? Have you come to destroy us? I know who you are—the Holy One of God!" (Mark 1:23–24). The title indicates Jesus' unique origin more than his messianic mission. Similarly in Tyre and Sidon, when evil spirits saw him, "they fell down before him and cried out, 'You are the Son of God' " (3:11). By recognizing Jesus as the Son of God, demons acknowledged that he was not made like other kinds of beings, but was eternally begotten of the same nature as the Father. The Gerasene man possessed by many demons fell in front of Jesus and shouted at the top of his voice, "What do you want with me, Jesus, Son of the Most High God?" (5:7).

The deity of Jesus, then, is not a late development taught only by the church long after his life was over. It is a doctrine claimed by the Messiah himself. And that claim is confirmed by his sterling character, astounding works, unparalleled teaching, self-giving spirit even in death, and supremely his predicted death-defeating resurrection. With all of these converging indications of his actual incarnation, it is most implausible that a group of untrained writers, editors, and redactors could have invented *The Greatest Story Ever Told* about the greatest person ever to live on earth.

Observe that the Jewish writers of the New Testament do not regard the confession of the deity of Christ as a challenge to monotheism. Functionally Christ strengthened monotheism by always and everywhere championing the glory, teaching, and honor of the Father. Christ's forgiveness of sins and acceptance of worship does not displace these roles for the Father; it contributes to them. Hence adoration of Christ is the direct opposite of all blasphemy. And belief in the Father, the Son, and the Holy Spirit is completely antipolytheistic.

Note also that any denial of the ontological deity of Christ undermines an ontological Trinitarianism. A soundly biblical doctrine either of Jesus Christ incarnate or of the Father, Son, and Holy Spirit inescapably involves ontology or metaphysics. If Jesus is *not* the second person of the Trinity, then a God of undifferentiated sameness has historically revealed himself in different disguises (as Father, Son, and Spirit) to be something that he really is not in himself. It seems very pious to say that we mere humans cannot know God in himself. But to repeat that after God has revealed who he is in himself through the incarnate Christ's person and teaching is to distrust God's supreme personal revelation to mankind.

The One Person Is Both Divine and Human

It is meaningful to think successively, as we have, about the humanity and then about the deity of Christ, but in thinking about the one person concretely it is important always to relate the divine and human natures to each other. The Word came into the world as Jesus in the flesh, and so the babe of Bethlehem is eternal. We seek to understand the relationship of the divineness to the humanness in the one person in respect to each of our basic categories.

Metaphysically, in accord with our critical realism (I:36–37), we have evidence above for asserting that the one concrete person in reality possessed two natures from his conception and birth. The second person of the Trinity condescended to partake in or share our humanity (Heb. 2:14). Elizabeth called the Holy Spirit-fathered infant conceived by Mary while still in his mother's womb "my Lord" (Luke 1:43). The human nature of Christ differs from all other human natures, negatively, by not having a different human personality of its own (*anhypostasia*) and positively, by subsisting *in* the divine personality (*enhypostasia*). Jesus Christ has two natures, but is not two persons. The one person who came from God the Father added to himself a human nature. This understanding preserves the continuity in the incarnation of the divine Logos. The Logos has come in the flesh (1 John 4:1–3). Since Jesus of Nazareth had both human and divine natures, it is futile to seek a reductively human Jesus of history unassociated with the eternal Son of God. The Christ of Christian faith is both human and divine.

Involved in the personal (hypostatic) union are the *two distinct natures*. The two sets of attributes are neither mixed nor confounded. No attribute of the one nature is transferred to the other. Neither is a third hybrid produced. What unites the two natures is that both may be predicated of the one actual person. The two natures exist not merely in a functional harmony, nor are they in a nonmetaphysical way merely communicated to each other. The divine nature is not simply the indwelling Holy Spirit as is the case in all Christians. Nor did the human nature lose anything by its assumption into the person of God's Son. In the God-man we find a complex of two distinct natures, but not a confusion of the two sets of attributes.

The *union* between the divine and human, however, was "personal," but not in name only as nominalists allege. The union of the human and divine natures involved a relation between the Son and the Father, but it was not a merely relational union like the oneness of mind among friends. The union was not merely an accidental union of two entities bound together. Providence was involved, but it was not merely a providential unity similar to the way in which all things hold together (Col. 1:17). Neither is it merely a legal union by the adoption of a human into a divine status at his baptism or some other occasion. The most coherent proposal suggests a personal union of the divine and human natures in one *hypostasia*. Both natures are predicated of the one person. Some of his attributes are divine and some of them are human. Hence we speak of the *hypostatic or personal union* of the two distinct natures. Whatever may be affirmed of either nature may be affirmed of the one person. The one person may be called God or the one person may be called human, not in mere figurative or functional senses, but in a cognitive sense that is true in reality. Whatever happens to the human nature happens to the Son of God, and whatever the Son of God did on earth, he did in and through the human nature.

The actual metaphysical union remains even when in the *kenosis* the eternal Word chose not always to take advantage of his divine attributes (e.g., omnipresence) in order to exist and grow as a child who walked from place to place. At the beginning of the incarnation Jesus' potential humanness was not developed, but it grew as he grew in stature. As the human child grew, however, his personality was realized only in union with the divine nature.[78] Since he did not ordinarily use the latent divine powers, his appearance generally was that of a rather typical human person.

With the Reformed, we stress the distinctness of the natures ontologically; with the Lutherans, we also underline their functional harmony in the acts and relationships of the one person. "Luther . . . does not regard the communication of the divine attributes to the human nature as 'inflexibly physical,' but as 'dynamic.'"[79] How does this general position work out in the life of the God-man?

Intellectually, the fully divine Logos had his divine mind and a fully human rational and intellectual capacity made like God's. The divine consciousness much of the time was sublimated in accord with the progressive revelation of his divine nature. Therefore most of the time the one consciousness was that of the human nature. The divine capability of omniscience was not ordinarily drawn upon, but the human mental capabilities were used in a manner consistent with the divine. When any human mind thinks truth, it thinks thoughts that conform to God's revealed thoughts about reality. So when the growing child Jesus consciously considered truth, he thought in a manner compatible with his divine nature also. Thus he grew in wisdom and in favor with both God and man (Luke 2:40, 52).

Emotionally, as fully divine the one person had the emotional capabilities of God, and as fully human he had the capabilities of the affections of a human made in God's image. Because he humbled himself, the divine affective capacities were not ordinarily utilized. When the human emotions delighted in holiness and were provoked by evil, they were not totally other than God's emotions; they pleased the Father. When the growing child or man emotionally responded to repentant sinners or self-righteous hypocrites, his affective states as such were in harmony with the affective states of the divine nature.

Volitionally, the second person of the Trinity had a divine will and added the volitional capacity of a human divine image-bearer. In the *kenosis* the divine will was not ordinarily utilized, but the human self-determinations of Christ were taken in accord with the revealed will of the Father. So when the growing boy or man chose to respond negatively to temptations or to a need with humble service, his will acted in harmony with the divine will. When he said, "Not my will, but yours be done" (Luke 22:42), he chose to follow the Father's redemptive plan rather than escape the suffering. In no instance did he exercise his divine or human volitional powers independently of the Father's pleasure. The one God-man carried out his Father's wise desires unhypocritically.

Morally, it follows that the human and divine natures are distinguishable but united in the one person. In his condescension God's Son ordinarily chose not to draw on his divine moral strengths, but when in the human nature Jesus judged tempting thoughts to be evil and rejected them, his ethical discernment and action turned out to be in accord with that of the divine nature. So as the growing boy acted with moral accountability and responsibility, he persistently resisted temptation and fled from it. We can understand why the accounts of his life reported that "the grace of God was upon him" (Luke

2:40). Throughout Jesus' life his excellent use of his capabilities morally exhibited an authentic harmony with his divine nature in its absolute holiness.

Relationally, the eternal Son of God gave up the direct fellowship with the Father and Holy Spirit he had enjoyed in heaven. As a spiritually growing human, he spoke and acted as a human in harmony with the heavenly Father and the Holy Spirit. He loved not only the Father and Holy Spirit but also the lost people he came to save. Personally Jesus loved tax collectors and sinners, Jews and Samaritans, prostitutes and physicians, fishermen and teachers, his mother and brothers, the blind and the deaf, children and adults, the hungry and the well-fed, the introverts and the extroverts.

The acts of the one incarnate person always exhibited his human qualities and on appropriate occasions progressively revealed his divine qualities. When the human Jesus performed miracles, both natures functioned concursively and harmoniously. When he died, his human nature suffered and his body began to decay and decompose (Acts 13:35–37). But when he rose again in his glorious body, he reversed the irreversible processes of decomposition and decay. Since his conception, the one person has the two distinct natures forever. The risen and glorified God-man not only lived on earth but ascended to heaven and is now seated with the Father in glory with power over all. God has exalted humanity, not only by creating mankind in his image, but also by uniting the second Adam to the person of the eternal Son.

A Test Case of One's View of the Divine and Human in Christ

Since Jesus Christ committed no sin, the question, "Could Jesus Christ sin?" is purely hypothetical. Usually it is not worth the time to speculate about such "iffy" questions. However, in this case the discussion profits by helping people think through the issues related to Christ's two natures in one person. The discussion also brings out some implications of different interpretations of free will and the importance of taking into account as many lines of evidence as possible in one's method of theological decision making. Consider several lines of argument, all of which need to be taken together for systematic purposes before drawing a final conclusion.

If Jesus could not sin, *how could he experience genuine temptation?* The major premise of arguments that the Son of God could have sinned is that the possibility of sin is necessary to genuine temptation. Must it be possible for one to yield to temptation to be tempted? Must one be able to yield in order to feel the allure of sin? To consider it? The reality of Jesus' temptations to seek peace by occult powers rather than by suffering love should not be minimized (Matt. 4:1–11; 16:21–23; 26:36–41). At the thought of his crucifixion Jesus was "troubled" (John 12:27) and "distressed" (Luke 12:50). Jesus' obedience was not automatic but "learned" (Heb. 5:8). He could genuinely struggle with temptations because being tempted is radically different from falling into temptation. Being "dragged away" by evil desires (James 1:13) is sin. Being tempted to displease the heavenly Father while living in the world is not sin. In order to understand how Jesus could be tempted although he was unable to sin we must grasp the radical difference between temptation and sin. Because a godly person does not commit certain wrong acts, it need not mean that the appeal is not felt. Because an army cannot be conquered, can it not be attacked? Because an army is repeatedly victorious, the victories are not therefore cheap or easy. Christ's victory over temptation was not attained without overcoming suffering and anguish (Luke 22:41–44). People of high character may be attracted by wrong courses of action and have to keep a strong hold on themselves. And in doing so they know that they are making real choices. Yet being true to themselves, they cannot yield. The resistance of temptation may be torture to a person of integrity, whereas the unfaithful yield easily. A truly human Jesus was attracted by wrong courses of action and had to struggle with temptations. Yet being one person faithful to his own divine nature, he did not, and, in the final analysis, could not yield.

Why then did Jesus not yield to his numerous temptations? Did he always resist temptation because of the presence and power of the Holy Spirit? Surely he was indwelt by the Spirit and empowered by the Spirit as are all his followers. But does that constitute the whole answer in view of all the lines of relevant evidence? Is it enough to say that he could have sinned like mere humans, but by the enablement of the Holy Spirit he did not? Did he have both the ability to sin in his human nature and the ability not to sin in his divine nature? Did he never use his divine powers? This hypothesis abstracts the human nature from the divine nature. But in the concreteness of the hypostatic union one nature cannot be divorced from the other. Struggling against the Satanic inducements was not just a Spirit-filled man, but the Spirit-filled God-man. Since Jesus Christ's divine nature was inseparable from his human nature, and since God cannot sin, it becomes impossible that the God-man could actually have sinned.

If Jesus was not able to sin, *how,* it may be asked, *could he be free*? Different concepts of freedom result in different answers to the question. We have found that a power of contrary choice against the Father's will is not of the essence of freedom. There remain many alternatives that are in accord with God's moral principles. God cannot deny himself, and we will not have the power of contrary choice in heaven. In these contexts the essence of freedom is the power of self-determination. Self-determination is always present whether choice contrary to God is possible or not. After struggling, Jesus always resisted temptation because he freely determined to think and do in accord with his sinless human nature and his sinless divine nature. If the human nature could be abstracted from the divine, then like Adam he could have sinned. But the two natures are inseparable in the one Spirit-led person. And even though ordinarily he chose not to rely on his own divine abilities, in the fiercest moments of temptations he could have and may have resorted to his divine powers. Because he was holy in heart, his outward self-determinations were always without sin. What Jesus said and did expressed who he was inside. Jesus was not merely what he did; what he did expressed who he was. Because he was God's Son, in the final analysis, he could not sin.

Did not the *kenosis* make sin for Jesus a "*possibility*?" There is a logical possibility of sin only if we abstract his human nature from the divine nature. Even the *kenosis,* however, does not erase Jesus' divine nature. It meant a limited use of his divine capabilities and a use of his human powers in harmony with the Father's desires. With the limited use of the divine powers, had there been a time when the human nature would have yielded to sin, the divine nature would have prevented this. Given the personal union of the two natures, the one nature cannot be abstracted from the other. So long as Jesus' divine nature was present, his yielding to temptation was not possible actually or empirically. God cannot even tempt people to sin and certainly cannot sin (James 1:13). Hence neither can the God-man.

Consider another relevant perspective, the view from the standpoint of *the Father's eternal plans*. Was not the outcome of the incarnation known from before the foundation of the world? Would not that prior knowledge alone justify the permission of sin? In the Father's omniscience he permitted sin and decreed the plan of salvation based on his "set purpose" (Acts 2:23) to allow wicked men to nail Jesus to the cross to die, the just for the unjust. As it was "impossible for death to keep its hold on him" (2:24), so it had been impossible for the Tempter to provoke him to sin. Decretively it was impossible that Jesus of Nazareth could have sinned and the entire eternal plan of salvation be scrapped.

The most probable conclusion is that although Jesus really struggled with temptation, in any actual sense he could not have sinned. That makes the most sense in terms of the distinction between temptation and sin, and in terms of freedom as self-determination, the enablement of the Holy Spirit, the inseparableness of the human from the divine nature, and the eternal plan of redemption.

APOLOGETIC INTERACTION

Not Contradictories but Subcontraries

According to Søren Kierkegaard, in asserting the deity and humanity of Jesus Christ we attempt the impossible. He assumed "an absolute difference between God and man."[80] Because Kierkegaard thought he was talking about two infinitely different things in every quality, the merging of incommensurables such as time and eternity seemed like merging ice and fire. On his understanding of God and of humanity, no resolution of the paradox of the incarnation was possible. "That God has existed in human form has been born, grown up, and so forth, is surely the paradox *sensu strictissimo*, the absolute paradox."[81] As the supreme offense to human reason, Kierkegaard thought, the incarnation is no mere apparent contradiction. It is an irresolvable paradox or contradiction that can be accepted only by a noncognitive "faith." Although it was objectively uncertain, he could embrace it with a passionate subjectivity and so apparently with a psychological certitude in spite of its absurdity.

Although the present writers do not presume to have full comprehension of the incarnation, we do not find it contradictory. Nevertheless, with all of our explanations there remains much that is not fully understood. How could Jesus voluntarily lay aside the exercise of his divine attributes? How could the divine and human factors interrelate? How could Jesus struggle so intensely with temptation? And there are many other unanswered questions. Much concerning the incarnation remains incomprehensible or mysterious. But a biblically based Christology need not involve one in denying in one paragraph what has been affirmed in another. Whatever may be the case as two actualities existentially relate to each other, a "contradiction" is a logical relationship between two propositions, one of which asserts what the other denies at the same time and in the same respect.

Contradictory propositions in Christology especially, Kierkegaard mistakenly thinks, constitute the Gospel's offense to reason. We may agree with Kierkegaard's desire to stress the uniqueness, the greatness, and the incomprehensibility of the incarnation of the Son of God, but we need not agree with him when he says that the Bible's teaching about the incarnate Christ is logical nonsense. As J. Loewenberg said, "By deft selection and emphasis isolated themes culled from any source may be made to assume contradictory shapes."[82] The Gospel is not foolishness; it is the wisdom of God. The declaration that people are sinners incapable of saving themselves and stand in need of redemption by the incarnate Messiah is offensive but not self-contradictory. It fits the realities of human moral experience all too well. It seems to be absurd, not because it is, but because our fallen intellects are intimately related to our fallen wills and emotions. Our stubborn pride will not admit our inability to justify ourselves, and it will not admit our fleshly desires to go on in the pleasures of the world.

Kierkegaard's unnecessary logical difficulties with the incarnation begin with his *extreme view of God's transcendence*. He assumed an infinite qualitative distinction between the eternal God and temporal humans. Reacting to Hegelian immanence, Kierkegaard tended to remove God from contact with matter and humans, much like the gods of the Greek philosophers. But the God of biblical revelation is not a stranger to time or to people's thought forms. The God of Abraham, Isaac, and Jacob personally relates to the ongoing states of affairs in the world. The living God, though distinct from the world, is active in it. Christ can remain holy as man, since sin is not part of the essence of humanness. By starting with an exaggerated view of divine transcendence, Kierkegaard, like the Greek philosophers whose influence he sought to avoid, manufactured unnecessary contradictions for himself.

Unnecessary logical difficulties with the incarnation also result from Kierkegaard's failure to develop in this connection the implications of God's creation of humanity *in his image*. God, who is personal, made mankind personal in his likeness. Being like God in intellect, we can receive revelation from God and think his thoughts (in part) after him. Like God emotionally, we can respond affectively (in measure) as God feels toward sin. Like God volitionally, we can share God's eternal purposes and determine to help plant his church. Like God morally, we sense an obligation to integrity an authenticity with ethical principles. And like God relationally, as whole thinking, feeling, and willing persons we can fellowship with God as well as others. With J. Oliver Buswell, Jr., we find that "since man is created in the image of God, there is no inconsistency in the concept that God has become man without ceasing to be God."[83]

Kierkegaard's logical problems with Christology also resulted from a view of Christ's *kenosis* that allowed for no real continuity between the divine Son and the Jesus of history. Neither the Father nor the Spirit became flesh, but as the Son of God assumed or added the human nature, he did not lose his divine nature. The eternal Son did not become less divine or give up his divine attributes. As God he did not experience a beginning, a growth, or a death, but in his human nature he experienced growth, temptation, suffering, and death as we do. The incarnate Jesus did not exercise his divine or human attributes except in accord with the Father's redemptive purpose. Contradictions occur only when at the same time the same thing is affirmed and denied in the same respect. Before and after the *kenosis* language about the second person of the Trinity has in view a difference of time and respect. Hence we do not contradict ourselves in what we affirm of God eternally and what we affirm of the eternal Logos in human flesh. Complexity, yes; contradiction, no.

The Jewish philosopher Spinoza likens the doctrine of the incarnation to saying that a circle had become a square, thereby losing all continuity and ceasing to be a circle.[84] A contemporary philosopher of religion, John Hick, uses the same illustration of the incarnation.[85] In response, we suggest that as a circle encompasses a square the two figures together form a more complex geometrical design. The whole complex pattern has two natures with both the attributes of the circle and the attributes of the square. We need not contradict ourselves in reference to the complex design if we affirm that some of the attributes of the complex design are those of a circle and some those of a square. The holistic unity of the design is not thereby divided. The two "natures" need not be confused. The circle remains a circle; the square within it remains a square. The one, "circle-square design" has two distinct natures. We can speak without contradicting ourselves of their essential differences as subcontraries. As such both are true of the complex design. And when such a noncontradictory interpretation of good writers is possible, responsible interpreters ought not jump to the conclusion that they have written logical nonsense.

Reinhold Niebuhr also thought that doctrines affirming the divinity and the humanity of Jesus verge on contradiction in that they ascribe both conditioned and unconditioned qualities to him. Niebuhr thought it possible for a historical person symbolically to point beyond himself to an unconditioned eternity, but considered it impossible for any person to be historical and unconditioned at the same time.[86] Again the importance of one's view of the *kenosis* is seen. The eternal Son of God remained the unconditioned second person of the Trinity, but he freely chose to limit his freedom from space and time in order to experience life in a given space, time, and culture. In speaking about the kenotic Son of God in time, then, we speak of deity in a different respect than in references to either the Father or the Son in glory.

Development of Augustine's illustration may help at this point. The assertion that Jesus is both God and man is analogous to the assertion that one person is both mind (soul, or spirit) and body. Two different sets of attributes are ascribed to a person, but neither set is denied. For a contradiction to be involved, the bodily attributes would have to be both affirmed and denied or the mental attributes would have to be both affirmed and denied. The result of affirming that a person is both soul and body is complexity, not contradiction. Analogously we may affirm that the one person, Jesus, has both the divine attributes (generally unused in his ministry on earth) and the human attributes.

Although J. I. Packer allows for "antinomies" among the "facts" related to the God-man, he maintains that all the givens exist together in the same world. Packer tries to keep his irresolvable "antinomies" from becoming a basis for justifying contradictions in theological statements.[87] However, "antimony" is generally used of two opposing conclusions, each beginning from plausible premises and issuing from valid steps of inference. Kant finds four major antinomies, and Nagarjuna, a Buddhist philosopher, lists fourteen. To the extent that Packer divorces his assertions from the data on which they are based, his statements lack fitness to the givens that he thinks remain in conflict. Statements are true to the extent that they conform to the data presented to us and also conform to the revealed mind of God about what is the case. Neither in God's mind nor in divine revelation as God gave it do irresolvable antinomies remain. If in the minds of those who interpret the faithful words of Scripture antinomies appear, they ought to be attributed to the interpreter, not to the most reliable source of religious truth in the world.

"Evidence" of a famous antinomy in physics has repeatedly been alleged to justify irreconcilable antimony in religious thought. Both the wave and particle models of electron activity are alleged to have equal empirical support. Hence some wags refer to "wavicles!" But Alfred Lande, "Mr. Quantum Physics" for many years in the physics department of Ohio State University, explains, "The real fact is, the electron does not change into a wave. It simply behaves in a wavelike manner under some circumstances, while at other times it behaves as a particle. But all the time, it remains its real self—a particle."[88] The unitary wave theory of Schrodinger fails to fit the evidence, Lande reports, but "strangely enough many theorists in their idle hours still pay lip service to the archaic idea that particles and waves of matter are pictures on an equal level. Particles are the real constituents of matter, and waves are mere appearances produced by the statistical cooperation of many particles."[89] So Lande no longer needs the duality or "double talk" hypothesis. Given a coherent explanation, he writes, "Do not contrast a snake as thing with its occasional wavy shape in order to defend the duality of snake substance."[90]

Those who charge that Christology is contradictory seldom stop to define a contradiction or to distinguish it from a subcontrary relationship of assertions. For example, christological teaching would be contradictory if it asserted that "all Jesus' attributes are divine" and that "some of Jesus' attributes are not divine." Both the affirmation and the denial of the universal truth claim that all his attributes are divine could not be true. In contrast, in a subcontrary relationship neither the affirmation nor the denial is universal, hence both may be true. For example, "Some members of the class are rapid readers" and "Some members of the class are not rapid readers." Again, "Some of the attributes of a person are physical" and "Some of the attributes of a person are nonphysical." Similarly, "Some attributes of the person of Jesus Christ are divine and some are human." Neither the divine set of attributes nor the human set of attributes is said to be all that he has, and so neither affirmation is necessarily false.

Unless we keep in mind that some attributes are human and some are divine (and not being used), we may have logical muddles rather than mysteries. We may not fully comprehend how the divine and the human attributes exist together, but that is not sufficient ground for attributing logical nonsense to the focal point of God's century-spanning redemptive program! We freely acknowledge our lack of full comprehension. But in asserting that both divine and human attributes apply to the one person, we do not violate the logical law of noncontradiction. We do not assert and deny the Son's possession of either the divine or the human sets of characteristics. We acknowledge complexity and lack of full comprehension, but not contradiction or antinomy.

Admittedly also, at first hearing, the doctrine of Christ's two natures may appear to be a *paradox, a seeming contradiction.* Apparent contradictions serve as literary devices to attract further thought. If we define the key terms with some precision and think with care, apparent contradictions in Scripture are resolvable. For example, when Jesus said one must lose one's life to find it, his paradox stimulated thought. We lose our lives in one respect (as dominated by the old sinful nature) and find them in another respect (a new freedom under enablement of the Holy Spirit). The paradoxes of Scripture are not like Buddhist "koans" (contradictions or nonsense) intended to discount use of the intellect in religion. Initially the claim that Jesus was both God and man may seem contradictory. But by remembering that the Creator is not totally other and that God made humans in his image, the eternal Word could add a human nature. The two natures can be predicated of the person of Christ logically in a subcontrary relationship. With these considerations, although we do not fully understand the God-man, we can meaningfully integrate the Scriptural teaching on Christology without imputing to it absolute absurdity. With G. K. Chesterton we pursue extraordinary truths and avoid the flippancy and light sophistry of paradox. Chesterton said, "I know of nothing so contemptible as a mere paradox; a mere ingenious defense of the indefensible."[91]

Christology Both Ontological and Functional

What about the hypothesis that early church leaders under the influence of Greek philosophy escalated biblical poetry (in Christological hymns) from a metaphorical Son of God to a metaphysical Son of God? The New Testament scholar A. M. Hunter, in *Jesus, Lord and Savior,* seeks to communicate the revealed truth about Jesus in less technical terms. He explicitly tried to avoid metaphysical concepts and speak only in moral and personal categories.[92] But this led him to theories of a progressive incarnation or progressive deification that have even greater difficulties fitting the documented givens. Hunter rejects "two natures" but accepts "two personal movements."[93] Is it more meaningful for moderns to say, "The more Christ laid down his life, the more he gained his divine soul"?[94] Having dismissed all ontology, what can Hunter mean by "soul" as distinct from physical life? Hunter's chapter on the person of Christ concludes: "Christian faith is the decision to commit your whole soul and future to the confidence that Christ is not an illusion but the reality of God."[95] How can Hunter dismiss metaphysics in one paragraph and make assertions about "reality" in the next? In a subsequent discussion of Christian paradoxes he said, "Even if we reject the implied physiological miracle [of the virgin conception], we are yet left with a metaphysical one—the coming of the divine Son of God into human life, born of a human mother."[96] Hunter, who started out to avoid metaphysics, has not succeeded, because in referring to the incarnation of Jesus Christ the Bible refers to divine and human realities metaphysically.

Leonard Hodgson similarly attempts to avoid ontological elements in discussing the person of Christ as such. "There is no person 'behind' the word; word is the event by which the person 'happens.'"[97] Flagrantly misinterpreting the facts, he alleges that "Jesus advanced no direct messianic claims on his behalf"[98] and "it is not at all clear in *what* sense Jesus spoke of the Son of Man, if at all."[99] Since Hodgson thinks a christological interpretation cannot be "based on what Jesus may have said or thought about himself"[100] he turns from the content of the Savior's words to his acts, particularly his "verbal acts."[101] What is the most characteristic and significant aspect of Jesus' person? "That he spoke a liberating, truthful, and salvific word."[102] But who "he" is, Hodgson does not know. The phenomenon of speaking, Hodgson thinks, is the important thing, not the content asserted. The "language of Jesus *is* the event of the incarnation."[103] In order to present a less abstract view of Christ, Hodgson repudiates the conjoining of the properties of two natures in one person. In place of the "one person" he substitutes "one speaking" and substitutes *homologia* for *homoousia*.[104] Instead of a conjoining of properties he has "the concurrence" of Jesus' speaking with God's speaking. But Moses and the other prophets spoke by a concursive divine-human operation, and for Hodgson Christ differs not in kind but only in degree: he affirms that in Christ "the homologous relation between the word of God and the word of man finds its completion."[105] The co-presence of God in a merely human person's acts does not account for the passages on the eternal Word's being God and equal with God. If Hodgson had been among the disciples when Jesus asked, "Whom do men say that I am?" he would have said Jesus was another prophet or the greatest of prophets, but not the eternal Son of God.

Michael Goulder also rejects a Christology of substance and replaces it with a Christology of agency. One immediately asks, Agency of what or whom? Goulder confesses, "My faith is not in the unity of substance, but in the unity of activity of God and Jesus; *homopraxis,* if a Greek word is wanted, rather than *homoousia.*"[106] God and a human called Christ acted together in actual practice on this hypothesis, but Jesus was not actually the eternal Word who became flesh. The category of "agency" does not stand on its own, however, unless it becomes a substantive. It is always the agency of someone, a being. But if we have no ontological soul or spirit to act responsibly, we have no morally accountable spiritual agent. To Jesus' question, "Whom do men say that I am?" Goulder apparently would respond, "We do not presume to know who you really are, but your acts appear to be Godlike acts." Goulder's Jesus differs only in degree from the prophets, but Jesus is uniquely the Christ, as Peter said, the son of the living God.

In response to attempts of many like Hunter, Hodgson, and Goulder, who unsuccessfully seek to formulate a Christology without metaphysics, we offer several considerations. What antimetaphysical writers affirm concerning Christ's acts, praxis, functions, and relationships may be true. We differ with what they deny or ignore of Christ's being, for their proposals lack explanatory power to account for all the biblical evidence of who Jesus is. The Chalcedonian formulation of one person with two natures provides the more coherent account of the biblical teaching about both who Jesus was and what he did. By acknowledging the ontological import of numerous scriptural passages we are not endorsing the metaphysical views of particular Greek philosophers. Nothing comparable to the doctrine of the one person with divine and human natures can be found in Plato, Aristotle, or other Greek philosophers. But through them God providentially prepared some basic categories of thought, including some about metaphysics. They were used by the Spirit in the inspired teaching of the New Testament to convey who the triune God is and who Jesus Christ is. When opposing the errors of Greek philosophy, some biblical scholars overlook the values God gave Greek thought-forms and language in the New Testament.

Even Hebrew, which is sometimes thought so radically different from Greek, has in common with it a concern for substantives as well as verbs—for who is speaking or acting as well as the speaking and the acting. The rejection of an ontological Christology often involves a rejection of the Old Testament's explicit teaching that God is to be viewed ontologically. In Judaism from Moses onward God was the independently existent One (Exod. 3:14). In contrast, false gods did not actually exist and so could not speak or act, for there is no spirit or breath in their mouth (Pss. 115:4–7; 135:15–17). As Paul later said, the idols were nothing (1 Cor. 8:4). Only the God who *is* knows, loves, acts, makes covenants, remains faithful to his promised plans, and pursues his people in history. No primitive stage existed with a simple functional pursuit without an ontological personal Subject or holy Agent as referent. Denials of any ontological knowledge of God reflects a suppression not only of the Old Testament but also of universal revelation. "The heavens declare the glory of God; the skies proclaim the work of his hands" (Ps. 19:1). In what God made, all people "clearly see" his "eternal power and divine nature" (Rom. 1:20).

Jesus Christ himself had deep concern for ontological truth. He asked, "Who do people say the Son of Man *is*?" (Matt. 16:13). Again he pressed the issue, " 'But what about you?' he asked, 'Who do you say I am?' " (v. 15). When Nicodemus considered him simply a rabbi, a teacher come from God (John 3:2), Jesus was not satisfied. The climax of Jesus' conversation with Nicodemus emphasizes that Jesus can uniquely speak of heavenly things because "no one has ever gone into heaven except the one who came from heaven—the Son of Man" (vv. 12–13). No alleged progression from reductively poetic or functional language to ontological language occurs in Scripture or in the church. The biblical progression is from the ontological existence of the "Son" or "Word" with God to his ontological or real existence in human flesh. This great event can be expressed literally, and even when figures of speech are used, they convey by way of illustration the greatness of their literal, univocal point.

Jesus' conversation with the Samaritan woman at the well moves quickly from his functional request for a drink, to "If you knew . . . who it is that asks you for a drink, you would have asked him and he would have given you living water" (John 4:10). Not satisfied to be called a prophet (v. 19), Jesus taught the ontological basis of true worship: "God is spirit, and his worshipers must worship in spirit and in truth" (v. 24). The woman mentioned the coming Messiah, and Jesus said, "I who speak to you am he" (v. 26). To follow Jesus' example in teaching Christology, we must emphasize not only what his teachings, works, and example were but also *who* spoke, engaged in praxis, and provided the paradigm of moral and spiritual excellence for all people of all times and cultures. The normative value of his example and the infinite value of his atonement depend on the uniqueness of his inner being.

Had Jesus claimed merely a functional unity of thought and purpose with the Father the Jews would not have charged blasphemy. Nor would they have sought to stone him if he claimed divine sonship merely as a legal inheritance. Because he claimed an ontological oneness with God, he seemed to commit blasphemy. Jesus claimed an identity of divine actions (John 5:21). What was true of the Father was true of the Son, not only in the giving of life (John 5) but also in the holding of believers in his hand (John 10). Jesus himself taught that what we are in our hearts determines what we say and do. His being or character takes priority in his thought even over his deeds. " 'I tell you the truth,' Jesus answered, 'before Abraham was born, I am!' " (John 8:58; cf. 13:19).

It is anachronistic to attribute to the New Testament writers the antimetaphysical spirit of post-Kantian philosophy and theology. As in the first century Christians must continue to live in Christ Jesus as Lord. "See to it that no one takes you captive through hollow and deceptive philosophy, which depends on human tradition and the basic principles of this world rather than on Christ. For in Christ all the fullness of the Deity lives in bodily form, and you have been given fullness in Christ, who is the head over every power and authority" (Col. 2:6–10). Still today people in Third-World countries believe in real spirits (divine, demonic, angelic, and human). If we are to interpret the Scriptures in their first-century historical and cultural contexts, we cannot impose on them a discredited logical postivist notion of "literal" meaning limited to presently observable sense data. That is one of the mistakes of the contributors to *The Myth of God Incarnate*.[106] Paul's metaphysical assertions concerning Christ are well documented in the section above entitled "The Biblical Teaching." The one who humbled himself as a human and servant enjoyed a status equal with God's, for he was "in very nature God" (Phil. 2:6). No radical difference appears between the ontological concern of Jesus and that of Paul. When confronted on the road to Damascus, Paul was not satisfied with a phenomenal experience. He asked, "Who are you, Lord?" (Acts 9:5). On that occasion Paul did not receive a full answer. Later he gave the answer in no uncertain ontological terms. In Paul's thought it is because Christ is the image of the invisible God, the firstborn over all creation and before all things (ontologically) that he serves functionally as the creator, sustainer of all, and head of the church, and the world's reconciler and peace maker (Col. 1:15–20). The relational and functional values of Paul's exhortations depend for their worth on logically prior metaphysical realities. Actions are no substitute for character and being, they flow from the heart. So we need not choose against ontological categories to emphasize functional values. Rather, we utilize both ontological and functional categories as do the Scriptures. The pragmatic values of Jesus' functions on behalf of mankind depend on the nature of the one who acts.

The Augustinian and Chalcedonian doctrine of Christ's person as really divine and human rests ultimately on the claim to be a comprehensive (but not exhaustive) analysis of the biblical teaching. That has been evident in the biblical section above. "Chalcedon did not adopt philosophy; it took some basic philosophical words and forged a theology based on Scripture. Its logic is a systematization of the logic inherent in Scripture, not a philosophical corruption of primitive texts."[107] For that reason, although the Chalcedonian formulation may be popularized for mass consumption, its ontological import must not be lost. Its biblical foundation is so highly probable as to be beyond reasonable doubt. "Ontological christology is part of the biblical revelation which cannot and must not be compromised in the name of historical and/or cultural relativism."[108]

Not Orthodox Because Politically Victorious

According to Don Cupitt's contribution to *The Myth of God Incarnate*, "What we have been taught to call 'orthodoxy' was in fact merely the form of Christianity which happened to triumph over the others."[109] Apparently, in Cupitt's view of providence God does not influence developments in doctrine in the history of church councils. One view just "happened to triumph over the others" apparently for less than adequate reasons or worthy motives. Cupitt's evaluation commits the genetic fallacy in reasoning by dismissing the objective validity of an idea because of the circumstances of its origin. Pressures from persons in political authority at some of the church councils do not account for the classical acceptance of a doctrine among people of all levels of different cultures and periods of history. Because at one point the party in political power favored an idea does not make it either true or false. Similarly, the political leaders' opposition to certain doctrines in history did not determine the truth or falsity of those doctrines. Might does not make right. Neither does might at any given time make reliable tenets with classical appeal at all times and cultures.

As the above research has indicated, the classical doctrine of one person with two natures has appealed to students of the evidence in different cultures and periods of history because it proposes the most coherent account of the strands of relevant biblical and historical evidence. Reasoning like Don Cupitt's commits the genetic fallacy of thinking that certain factors culturally surrounding the origin of an idea determine its validity. To determine the objective validity of the Chalcedonian formulation, Cupitt needs to consider the consistency and adequacy of the view and evaluate its viability with those guidelines. Cupitt adds, "In retrospect the Christ of the Eastern Church looks all too like the Hellenistic king," and "the Christ of the Western Church looks like one who died to seal the authority of the patriarchal family as a model for the organization of church and state."[110] A comprehensive concept of Christ includes worthy elements of fidelity to the family and of kingship. To the degree that a view without contradiction integrates with all the relevant data, it has probability of being true, however lowly the cultural conditions and motives of the origin of the idea. To the degree that the hypothesis does not meet these criteria it lacks probability of being true, however exalted the motives in the hearts of the conveners of the church councils or contemporary scholars. The appeal of orthodox Christology classically may be appreciated when it is realized that some other views have not received the same kind of classical recognition in East and West and among Roman Catholics and Protestants. The hypotheses of Mary's sinlessness and ascension to heaven, for example, have not had the same overwhelming degree of coherence with the relevant evidence.

Jesus Is Not a Dead Spiritual Master

According to *The Aquarian Gospel of Jesus the Christ,* during his unrecorded childhood years Jesus traveled to India and studied under Hindu holy men and himself became a Hindu spiritual master. Allegedly he also traveled to Persia, Assyria, Greece, and Egypt, learning and speaking. He then returned to the Near East where he was baptized by John the Harbinger. In Egypt, supposedly, Jesus received his mystic name and number and passed seven tests of brotherhood, received the seventh and highest degree, and was crowned "The Christ" in the Great Lodge of the heavens and earth.[111]

As a boy, transcriber Levi H. Dowling (1844–1911) received a vision that he would "build a white city," and the publishers say that it was a book—*The Aquarian Gospel.* From "Visel the holy one" Dowling received a "commission" to read a message in the Akashic records for men of the New Age, the Piscean Age. "Take up your pen and write."[112] Of all the vibrations allegedly left by every person in the universe in the Akashic records, Levi became attuned to the "tones and rhythms of Jesus of Nazareth, Enoch and Melchizedec." Exercising his developed mediumistic ability between 2 and 6 A.M., he "transcribed" messages "true to the letter" received from the Universal Mind; these messages have been called by some Orientals the Akashic records.[113]

Had Jesus received years of instruction and practice in Hindu-Buddhist religion of the first century, abundant evidence of these perspectives should appear in the biblical records of his teaching. But Jesus' teaching and life, interpreted by sound principles of hermeneutics, does not disclose the assumptions of Hindu-Buddhist pantheism or occultism. Jesus' general outlook reflected the theistic worldview of

Judaism based on the Old Testament, not a pantheistic and occult worldview. His belief system did not include a pantheistic interpretation of the Father-motherhood of God and a spiritual brotherhood of all humans. Although Jesus emphasized that by creation all are naturally dependent on the heavenly Father for their existence, apart from God they are morally and spiritually not children of God but children of the Devil, the Great Deceiver (John 8:44). Because people are born of the flesh, Jesus insisted that fallen humans must be born again. By that he did not mean born in many reincarnations, but once, inwardly by the Holy Spirit (John 3:1–8).

Jesus did not teach a form of monism when he said, "The kingdom of God is within you" (Luke 17:21). With these words he referred to the way in which the kingdom comes (v. 20). Christ's rule comes to individuals by the Holy Spirit, and as he had said to Nicodemus, "The wind blows wherever it pleases. You hear its sound, but you cannot tell where it comes from or where it is going. So it is with everyone born of the Spirit" (John 3:8). And as individuals are regenerated by the Spirit, the kingdom of God is among them (plural) or in their midst. Jesus did not teach Eastern distinctives such as the divinity and infinite potential of humans, repeated reincarnations or rebirths of the soul, vegetarianism, or celibacy. The Jesus of historically attested biblical sources advocated no occult ways to manipulate the Father's will to our advantage. Quite the contrary, he repudiated occult practices as demonic. The "signs" he performed were done in public, in broad daylight; they were not occult manipulations in the dark. They were visible or verifiable signs, wonders, and mighty acts. And many times Jesus Christ demonstrated his authority over demonic powers. In contrast to mere meditation or magical manipulation of vibrations, Jesus taught his disciples to offer praise and requests to a personal God.

It is naïve indeed to accept intuited messages as from spirits (even spirits who call themselves Jesus) without subjecting them to critical testing. Some messages may be naturalistically explained as projected contents of a channeler's own unconscious mind. Even if intuited messages are not from the unconscious and actually come from spirits, not all spirits are necessarily knowledgeable or trustworthy. According to the Holy Scriptures demonic deceivers as well as angelic spirits exist. Sudden intuitions may be either true or deceptive. Hence the Bible wisely urges discernment in spiritual disclosures: "Dear friends, do not believe every spirit, but test the spirits to see whether they are from God" (1 John 4:1). What is the test? "This is how you can recognize the Spirit of God: Every spirit that acknowledges that Jesus Christ has come in the flesh is from God, but every spirit that does not acknowledge Jesus is not from God" (vv. 2–3). A crucial test of reliable and unreliable spirits is their allegiance to the incarnation of the eternal Son of the living God.

The *Aquarian Gospel,* unfortunately, fails this test. It denies that Jesus of Galilee is the eternal Christ. It says that Jesus is a pattern of the Christ spirit and that "Christ is not a man. The Christ is universal Love, and Love is King."[114] It says that the Christ does not refer to any particular person but only to a spirit of love and brotherhood with which anyone can be "christed." Other spiritists have claimed to channel messages from Jesus, but they regularly affirm pantheistic and occult views of Jesus as a human who attained mediumship or spiritual mastery. They flatly deny the explicit biblical doctrines of Christ as the eternal Word who became flesh.

Representatives of eastern and occult spirituality often allege that Christians need not give up their faith to accept a monistic belief system involving occult manipulations of spiritual forces. However, anyone who regards Jesus as one of many men who became spiritual adepts flatly denies the central doctrine of biblical revelation—the unique cosmic lordship of Jesus who was God and became flesh. Candidly Eva Dowling in the introduction to her husband's book acknowledges that an orthodox belief "is wholly at variance with the teachings of Jesus himself and of his apostles."[115] But the many lines of biblical evidence above point up their error. According to "the Aquarian [ascended] Masters in council" in typical theosophical language, Jesus was a remarkable child, qualified to be an avatar, and lived as a pattern for the sons of men to show the possibilities of man. Jesus is alleged to have said, "What I have done all men can do, and what I am all men shall be."[116] Never do occultists affirm that Jesus is the Christ. Instead, they deny that central affirmation of New Testament Christians. The spiritists' Jesus is a human who learned from the wisdom of the sages like other avatars. Jesus is little different from many others in whom the Christ spirit (of Father-Mother Love) is said to manifest itself again and again at the beginning of every age.[117]

No one can loyally follow two spiritual masters (Matt. 6:24), even though both are called "Jesus." On one hand, if we devote ourselves to a human who became divine as all others are allegedly able to do, we reject the lordship of the biblically revealed eternal person of the Trinity who became human once-for-all. On the other hand, to worship and serve the unique scriptural Lord Jesus Christ is to reject a merely human Jesus who spiritually evolved to consciousness of an impersonal cosmic spirit of love. The lines of spiritual warfare are being sharply drawn between the kingdom of spirituality as an evolutionary development humanly achieved and as a gift of perfect righteousness by sheer divine grace. Not all are teaching the same thing. Christians teach that God can remain just and accept sinners only by faith in the incarnate Christ and his atoning work. Many non-Christians in other world religions think that without the uniquely incarnate Christ they can evolve morally into higher kinds of beings. Jesus did not teach moral and spiritual evolution, but rather he taught that we reproduce after our kind morally, "Flesh gives birth to flesh" (John 3:6). Fallen humans can enter the kingdom of God only by the gift of new life from the Spirit of grace.[118]

RELEVANCE FOR LIFE AND MINISTRY

Liturgical and sermonic language generally needs to be more poetic and affective than theological language does. But to avoid hypocrisy "there needs to be at least consistency, if not an identity, between the belief expressed in worship and the belief expressed in the form of reflective theology."[119] The psalmists sang of the great actualities of creation and ordinary providence, as well, and the extraordinary deliverance of the Exodus that happened in history. Is it not insincere "worship" to repeat creeds and sing hymns if in our critical thought we cannot affirm the truths expressed? The revealed truth about Christ not only provides for worship in spirit and in truth, but also helps avoid the disillusionment that follows devotion to imperfect spiritual masters.

One young woman, after coming out of a series of several cults said she had been "spiritually promiscuous!" She finally accepted the biblically revealed Christ, and a sound Christology now enables her in spirit and truth to worship the Messiah who is God, speaks for God, and saves sinners. Christians praise the Lord Jesus Christ and sing and testify about him because of who he is. And because of his divine-human nature Christians follow him as Lord of all.

Bow to Jesus as Your Spiritual Master

We do not need to attempt the impossible task of working our way to the Father in heaven, because Christ has brought God to us (Rom. 10:6–10). Christians prize Christ above all other humans because *"God was pleased to have all his fullness dwell in him"* (Col. 1:19). No more complete resources for spirituality can be discovered in any natural or supernatural powers. In Christ are all the attributes and powers of the Almighty. So Christians value the one Mediator far above all political, educational, athletic, and entertainment greats. Christ rises in stature far above Billy Graham, any pope of Rome, any founder of any other religion, and any spirits of former spiritual masters who would channel messages to the world today. The founders of world religions were ordinarily born humans with fleshly natures who gained some insights from universal revelation. At best any truth they have is partial; the fullness is found in Jesus Christ. But none made such claims for themselves as did Jesus, and none confirmed them with years of sinlessness, such remarkable teaching, astounding works, death for the sins of the world, and a triumphant resurrection. Indeed the ascended Jesus is "both Lord and Christ" (Acts 2:36).

> No mortal can with Him compare
> Among the sons of men,
> Fairer is He than all the fair
> That fill the heavenly train.
>
> S. Stennett

We esteem Jesus above all because we "have been given fullness in Christ, who is the head over every power and authority" (Col. 2:10). Having spiritual completeness in Christ, Christians do not turn from him to mere nature religions, religions of mere law, or religions of endless occult phenomena. Christ abides in the hearts of believers that they may be "rooted and established in love, may have power together with all the saints, to grasp how wide and long and high and deep is the love of Christ, and to know this love that surpasses knowledge—that you may be filled to the measure of all the fullness of God" (Eph. 3:14–19). Although we are not incarnations of God as Jesus was, we can have an abiding personal relationship with him, drawing on a love and power far beyond our own, the greatest love and power in the cosmos.

We honor Christ above all because our love for the Lord of all unites us spiritually to others who similarly love him. Those from all around the earth who bow before Jesus as Lord of all—whatever their racial, political, economic, educational or cultural differences—constitute a great family in heaven and on earth (Eph. 3:14–17). Christians bow before Jesus as Lord of all other good and evil powers in the cosmos. Jesus is Lord of the nations, Lord of our churches, Lord of our families, and Lord of our vocations.

Having begun the Christian life by faith in Christ, "continue to live in him, rooted and built up in him, strengthened in the faith as you were taught, and overflowing with thankfulness" (Col. 2:6). Paul exhorts that, as a Christian, you need to "see to it that no one takes you captive through hollow and deceptive philosophy, which depends on human tradition and the basic principles of this world rather than on Christ" (v. 8). Refrain from judging people by rites, vegetarianism, drink, festivals, New Moon celebrations, sabbath observances, and worship of angels and other spiritual masters (vv. 11–18). Since we died with Christ to the basic principles of nature worship, why should we submit to its rules and regulations? Why resort to practices that have an appearance of wisdom, false humility, and harsh treatment of the body "but lack any value in restraining sensual indulgence?" (vv. 20–23).

Honor the Lord of all in every aspect of your life. In devotion to Christ, "set your hearts on things above, where Christ is seated at the right hand of God" (Col. 3:1). Let your dominant mind-set be on things above, not on earthly things. Distance yourself from the works of the flesh, and clothe yourselves with Christlike qualities (Col. 3:1–14). Let Christ's peace rule in your heart, let the word of Christ dwell in you richly as you teach and admonish one another, and as you sing (vv. 15–16). "And whatever you do, whether in word or deed, do it all in the name of the Lord Jesus, giving thanks to God the Father through him" (v. 17). Glorify Christ in all your relationships—with your spouse (vv. 18–19), your parents, your children (vv. 20–21), your employer, and your employees (vv. 22–4:1). Pray for all who proclaim the mystery of Christ (4:2–4). "Be wise in the way you act toward outsiders; make the most of every opportunity. Let your conversation be always full of grace seasoned with salt, so that you may know how to answer everyone" (vv. 5–6).

Confidently Approach the Most High

We interrupt this program to bring you a special news bulletin! The transcendent Father sent his only Son to live as one of us! The uniqueness of the God-man makes him the one Mediator between God and man (1 Tim. 2:5). To what other founder of any world religion or cult shall we go? All were humans who became "enlightened" by some experience. At most they were fallen sinners who came to be lauded by those who follow their examples. No others are eternally God and became incarnate. The exaltation of Christ alone as Mediator should free us from false messiahs. Our hope spiritually is not in education, a *gnosis* (knowledge or enlightenment), an organization, a spiritual discipline, or a world peace program. The one Mediator is not Eastern culture or Western technology, but a Person. A realization of this truth, as narrow as it may sound, wonderfully liberates believers from oppressions in organization-bound, human-leader-bound, and culture-bound exclusivisms.

Because he is fully human, *Jesus is a sympathetic mediator.* "For we do not have a high priest who is unable to sympathize with our weaknesses, but we have one who has been tempted in every way, just as we are—yet was without sin" (Heb. 4:15). Although the adherents of other religions regard God as an impersonal Absolute, Force, Energy, or a personification ("mother") of nature or the cosmos, Christians alone recognize that a member of the divine Trinity has lived on earth and faced exactly the kinds of frustrations and temptations that we face with close relatives, neighbors, and business associates.

Because of the marvel that Christ was tempted as we are and suffers along with us, Helmut Thielicke explained, "we have a brother in the profoundest danger in life. There is no longer any lonely point in this life. . . . We are not alone in our temptation. He suffers it with us down to the lowest depths which Satan has conceived."[120] And because of the marvel that Jesus was tempted as we are but without sin, "we are certain of his love from all eternity. Christ not only marches on our right hand against death and the devil, but he upholds us from his height, because he is the Lord. The knowledge that we are sheltered by his power gives us that peace which the world cannot give or take away from us."[121]

"Let us then approach the throne of grace with confidence, so that we may receive mercy and find grace to help us in our time of need" (Heb. 4:16, italics ours). Those who by faith identify with Christ need not approach God through countless intermediaries or dead "spiritual masters" in the next life (as Theosophists and others do). Christians need not wait for countless rebirths in order to evolve morally and spiritually to the level at which they can approach the ultimate Reality directly (as Hindus, Buddhists, and others do). In our approach to God we are not limited to having a high priest enter the Holy of Holies once a year as our representative (as in Judaism). We need not convey our heartfelt concerns to human priests or to Jesus' mother, Mary. Those whose trust is in the God-man can enter the Holy of Holies itself and pray to the heavenly Father directly in Christ's name with the Holy Spirit's enablement. At the Father's request we exalt the name of Jesus Christ above every name in heaven and on earth. In that great name we pray and because of that great name the Father hears and answers.

Seek no additional mediator. No religious leader or any hierarchy of living or dead spiritual masters ought to come between young Christians and their heavenly Father. Many insufficiently taught Christians need to hear this warning. They may be easily convinced by well-meaning but false teachers that they can continue to relate to God only through certain organizations or programs. Two interrelated features of the multiplying cults, according to Anthony Hoekema, are "the devaluation of Christ" and "the group as the exclusive community of the saved."[122] Wherever evangelistic fruit appears, faithful ministers in this shrinking pluralistic world need to help young converts devote themselves not only "to the fellowship, to the breaking of bread and to prayer," but also "to the apostles teaching" (Acts 2:42). Without a well-founded doctrine of who Christ is, untaught Christians can easily be persuaded that they need some additional ways to be acceptable to God.

Because of his deity, we may worship the Son as we do the Father. Since Jesus is truly God, we can trust him as we trust the Father (John 14:1). We may adore and value Jesus as we do God the Father. The object of our distinctively Christian worship and obedience is the one person with divine and human natures. Christians offer their highest allegiance to their great High Priest, the once-for-all Sacrifice, the resurrected and ascended Head of the church. We pray to the triumphant Lord with two natures who continues to serve as our Mediator, Advocate, and faithful High Priest. He fellowships with us and liberates us from the kingdom of evil here and now. It is he who will receive the worship of his people when he returns from heaven in glory and power.

Heed and Teach the Teachings of the Greatest Prophet

Moses predicted that after Israel would suffer years of false prophets and astrologers, God would raise up another prophet like him and put words in his mouth (Deut. 18:15–19). Like Moses, Jesus mediated a new and greater covenant. When the long-awaited Prophet greater than Moses came, Peter said, "You must listen to everything he tells you" (Acts 3:22). As the author of Hebrews put it, "In the past God spoke to our forefathers through the prophets . . . , but in these last days he has spoken to us by his Son" (Heb. 1:1).

As chief spokesman for God the Father, Jesus "came from the Father, full of grace and truth" (John 1:14). He "who comes from above . . . testifies to what he has seen and heard" (3:31–32). Again, "the one whom God has sent speaks the words of God" (v. 34). No other prophet had ever seen God, but "the One and Only, who is at the Father's side, has made him known" (1:18). The Word who was with God in the beginning (1:1–2) revealed information important to his hearers to understand the past, evaluate the present, and realistically anticipate the future. Because of the Son's unique eternal relationship with the Father, he cannot be considered one of many merely human prophets who received his message from the Father by special revelation. He declared that "the kingdom of heaven is near" (Matt. 4:17) and that salvation is received by faith in him (John 6:45–47; 8:24).

Jesus proclaimed the requirements of the law and their fulfillment in himself (Matt. 5:17–18). But his new message focused on the long-awaited new covenant, his coming to give his life as a complete atonement, and thus the gospel of grace (John 1:17). Conscious of his own uniquely predicted prophetic ministry, Jesus unrolled the scroll of Isaiah and read from it (Isa. 61:1–2), "The Spirit of the Lord is on me, because he has anointed me to preach good news to the poor. He has sent me to proclaim freedom for the prisoners and recovery of sight for the blind, to release the oppressed, to proclaim the year of the Lord's favor" (Luke 4:18–19). When he told the Samaritan woman the number of her husbands, she said, "Sir, . . .I can see that you are a prophet" (John 4:19). Jesus' prophetic ministry was confirmed by many signs recorded in the Gospels. After he fed the five thousand, the people said, "Surely this is the Prophet who is to come into the world" (John 6:14; see also 7:40). On Palm Sunday, as Jesus rode on a donkey into Jerusalem, the people inquired who he was. "The crowds answered, 'This is Jesus, the prophet from Nazareth in Galilee' " (Matt. 21:11). In his hometown the amazed people asked, "Where did this man get this wisdom and these miraculous powers?" (Matt. 13:54). Knowing his carpenter-father, mother, brothers, and sisters, the people took offense at him. "But Jesus said to them, 'Only in his hometown and in his own house is a prophet without honor' " (v. 57). On another occasion some Pharisees warned him that Herod would kill him if he remained in Jerusalem. Purposefully Jesus determined to complete his ministry there and replied, "Surely no prophet can die outside Jerusalem" (Luke 13:33).[123]

Christians value Christ's teaching above that of others because he did not invent ideas out of his own human heart, but communicated the truths the transcendent Father gave him. Jesus communicated God's changeless truths in the culturally influenced human languages of Aramaic and Greek. Jesus explained, "For I did not speak of my own accord, but the Father who sent me commanded me what to say and how to say it" (John 12:49). In the upper room he reminded his disciples, "These words you hear are not my own; they belong to the Father who sent me" (14:24). Through his teaching Jesus Christ could say to the Father, "I have revealed you" (17:6). "For I gave them the words you gave me" (v. 8). "I have given them your word" (v. 14). "I have made you known to them [the world], and will continue to make you known in order that the love you have for me may be in them and that I myself may be in them" (v. 26).

Unfortunately many people who have been influenced by recent philosophy, anthropology, psychology, and sociology seem to regard a total conceptual relativism more highly than Jesus Christ's prophetic teaching as nonnegotiable truth. One can appreciate the frailty and fallibility of the relative words of fallen and finite humans in general without exalting a totalistic relativism to the only absolute. By holding that no universal and necessary truths can be expressed in human language and that absolute truth resides only in the mind of the transcendent God, a mind that is allegedly totally different from human minds, they make Jesus' teachings (as well as their own, even about God) time-bound and relative. Previously we tried to show that the Lord taught that his own teachings in temporal languages conveyed changeless truths (1:111–12). His teachings in human words originated with God the Father, were true (coherent and viable), were authoritative for all, and give eternal life. Jesus' classical teaching was not time-bound but of relevance to every culture and subculture and of normative value not only for his day but also for all times. "Heaven and earth will pass away," Jesus said, "but my words will never pass away" (Matt. 24:35). Hence the presupposition that no changeless truth can be expressed in human language ought to be dismissed by those who call Jesus Christ their Lord.

No more reliable guidance can be found in the world's religions or philosophies than the teaching of the greatest of all prophets. Those who know and love God today, as in the first century, believe and obey all that the Messiah taught. "Why do you call me 'Lord, Lord' and do not do what I say?" (Luke 6:46). Do you love God the Father? Do you love his eternal Word? No more clear test can be found than your obedience to the Word made flesh. "If you obey my commandments you will remain in my love, just as I have obeyed my Father's commands and remain in his love. I have told you this so that my joy may be in you and that your joy may be complete" (John 15:10–11). Although no one perfectly lives up to all the teachings of Christ, a substantial difference becomes evident between the lives of those whose deepest desire and dominant purpose is to follow Christ at any cost and those whose deepest desire and dominant purpose is selfish pleasures or acquisition of earthly goods.

Ways to Be Like the Supreme Paradigm of Humanness

In the midst of rapid developments in knowledge, immorality, violent crime, terrorism, and corruption in high places, people do well to identify with the best possible paradigm of a just and loving life. Through all the changes in history and culture, Christ remains in every age and context the paragon of human excellence. Neither the phantasms of sorcerers nor examples of other religious leaders come near possessing the beauty of his lifestyle. Mahatma Ghandi, Mother Theresa, Billy Graham, and others have done nobly in many respects but Jesus Christ remains the supreme standard of authentic humanness for those who bear the divine image. None in fields of literature, the media, or ethics can compare with Jesus Christ. And Jesus said, "A student is not above his teacher, but everyone who is fully trained will be like his teacher" (Luke 6:40).

Although we need not be like Christ in every detail, in what ways ought Christians seek by God's grace to be like our incarnate Savior? Jesus' disciples not only believe all that he taught but also become like him in exemplifying (1) God's unchanging character in the midst of change, (2) life according to universally revealed moral principles, and (3) life according to specially revealed redemptive purposes true for all who have sinned in any cultures. We can grow in Christlikeness intellectually, morally, emotionally, volitionally, and relationally.

Intellectually, we can grow in our mental ability to receive his teaching about his own character in relation to his heavenly Father's moral qualities and think his thoughts after him. Jesus' teachings about the human heart provide rich content for meaningful contemplation and application. So do his teachings about moral law and justice in the Old Testament Scriptures, which he knew and applied so well. Our mentalities may become more like his also as we grow in understanding the Gospel of mercy and grace. The Gospel was anticipated in the Old Testament and developed in the New Testament, which Christ endorsed in advance in principle. Christ's life exhibits, as will the lives of his followers, understanding of the Gospel's satisfaction of uncompromising justice, deliverance from the powers of evil on any level, and the transforming dynamic of reconciling love.

Morally, we can mature in qualities of character like the Messiah's, although we can never in this life attain perfection. When we struggle with temptation, we will follow Jesus' example of resisting its most attractive and powerful enticements. We can seek to please the Father in all that we think, say, and do and thus keep a *clear conscience* (1 Peter 3:16). As Paul, who followed Christ, said, "I strive always to keep my conscience clear before God and man" (Acts 24:16). For another thing, we ought to develop *endurance* in tribulation from the world. "Let us fix our eyes on Jesus, the author and perfecter of our faith, who for the joy set before him endured the cross, scorning its shame, and sat down at the right hand of the throne of God. Consider him who endured such opposition from sinful men, so that you will not grow weary and lose heart" (Heb. 12:2–3; cf. 2 Thess. 3:5; 1 Tim. 1:16; 1 Peter 2:23). Jesus was not masochistic, but he did not try to escape the inestimable sufferings from evil persons—sufferings he endured to provide our salvation. In the declared spiritual war of the evil against the good, we too may need to endure discrimination from sinners in our workplace (1 Peter 2:18–20). "To this [suffering] you were called, because Christ suffered for you, leaving you an example, that you should follow in his steps" (v. 21).

Emotionally, by grace we can endeavor to grow in appropriate affective expressions in relation to God, others, and ourselves. Following the example of Jesus, we will rejoice with those who rejoice and weep with those who weep. We will take pleasure in what is good and express wrath at the powers that would destroy the Father's purposes of common and special grace. Strengthened by our Savior's example, however, we will not let our emotions get out of control.

Volitionally, we will decide among courses of action in ways that would merit his approval. As busy as we may be, we will accept invitations to weddings, banquets, breakfasts, and visit with the ill and bereaved. Christ has set a consistent example of obedience to his Father's will (Heb. 5:7–9). Like him, we will pray, "Not my will, but yours be done on earth as it is in heaven" (Luke 22:42; Matt. 6:10). Such a prayer expresses the conviction that the Father's wisdom is greater and better than ours.

Relationally, we ought to live each day, as Jesus did, in communion with the heavenly Father and the Holy Spirit. By the Father's guidance and the Spirit's enablement those who are Christlike will cross barriers of racial, gender, and social prejudice to reflect the justice and love Jesus exhibited with the Samaritan woman at the well. Disciplined followers of Christ can exhibit the respect, consideration, and love he showed toward people such as Mary and Martha of Bethany, Mary the Magdalene, tax collectors, and fishermen.

Similarly in self-giving love we who call Christ Lord will cross age barriers by enjoying children as Jesus did. Like Christ, we will cross barriers of hatred to show love for our enemies. And, like Jesus, we may even lay down our lives for them (John 15:13).

Jesus' lifestyle was exemplary, Michael Griffiths shows, in the ways he related to his family as a child and as an adult. As a child he grew in favor with God and human persons. During those silent years without any spectacular miracles or ministries, he pleased the Father by living as a human being with his parents, his brothers, and his sisters in Nazareth. Apparently he grew in ability to help in the family carpentry business, and his parables show familiarity also with agriculture. We do not know when Joseph died, but when he did, leaving Jesus as the eldest son, Jesus accepted responsibility to care for his mother. Moreover, the Lord's miracles and parables exhibited his appreciation for family affections, such as he displayed in the healings of the daughter of the Syro-Phoenician woman and the daughter of Jairus, the resurrection of Mary and Martha's brother Lazarus, and the parable of the prodigal son. After the example of Jesus, who recognized the divine authorization of marriage and the family from the account of the creation (Matt. 19:1–15), his disciples highly valued their own parents, brothers and sisters, spouses and children, but always under God's rule in these relationships.

Jesus was a diligent worker and chose many working-class people as his disciples. His teachings exhibit several examples of his appreciation for the responsibilities of owners and stewards. Jesus also honored the Sabbath as a day of rest. He was also concerned that his followers get needed rest: "Because so many people were coming and going that they did not even have a chance to eat," he said to his disciples, "Come with me by yourselves to a quiet place and get some rest" (Mark 6:31). Industrious as he was, he did not endorse the overreactions of even Christian workaholics.

If time and space permitted, it would be well worth pursuing Jesus' model of enjoying nature as God's creation, of developing spiritual disciplines, of participating in the political world, and of living a simple lifestyle. Much profit would be gained from considering his working methods in teaching and training people for establishing churches. Jesus used different methods in teaching, natural approaches in personal evangelism, and varied strategies in missions to found a community that changed history.[124]

Ways Not to Be Like Christ

In saying that we should follow Christ's example, we do not mean that unregenerate people in the strength of the flesh can imitate him and so gain salvation. We do not suggest imitation of Christ as a way to self-justification. Efforts to be like Christ are no substitute for justification by belief in his atonement. Rather, in gratitude for justification and regeneration and in the spirit of biblical teaching, we want to become increasingly like him morally and spiritually. We do not suggest play-acting or pretending to be what we are not. If anything is clear in the life of Jesus it is his opposition to hypocrisy and his insistence that life change starts from the heart. Any attempt to be like Christ, therefore, must begin with proper motivation, that is, not for selfish advantage, but for glorifying our spiritual Master. We must be like him in the inner person before we can exhibit his characteristics in our outer behavior. And as millions of Christians follow his paradigm from the heart, the outward results are not all identical. We follow in his steps, not by going to the near East, but by resisting our temptations as he did his by the power of the Holy Spirit and the teaching of the Scriptures. He does not live our lives for us, but he has shown us how to face the basic moral and spiritual challenges in life. How likeness to him works out creatively in our different personalities, family, neighborhood, and cultural situations may vary greatly.

In several ways we need not seek conformity to the image of Jesus Christ. Men need not follow him in appearance with long hair and beards. Women and men need not wear robes and sandals because he did. We need not generally walk to where we want to go, or limit our transportation to donkeys and small boats. We need not shake the dust off our feet if people do not receive our message. We need not wash one another's feet. In many cultures with paved roads and sidewalks, other forms of humble servanthood may be more appropriate, such as washing another's car or polishing another's shoes. We need not always raise our hands in benediction (Luke 24:50). We need not take the Lord's Supper in a reclining position or be baptized in the Jordan River. Radical discipleship does not require that all have as simple a lifestyle as Jesus, who was single and had no family for which to provide. In general, we need not duplicate the nonuniversal cultural specifics of his situation. Some Christians may attempt to replicate such factors, but they ought not make such aspects of his life normative for others nor feel that by doing so themselves they are more holy than others.[125]

When devoted to following the example of Christ we need to avoid making him over into our image. He was not an antiestablishment revolutionary armed with weapons, nor was he an unthinking vassal of the establishment in a grey flannel suit. Jesus was a great teacher but no mere academician. He was a crusader for certain well-chosen and timely causes, but not a blind activist. Jesus was a healer and miracle worker, but he did not make miracles ends in themselves. He taught us to pray by an example—the "Lord's prayer"—but we need not always quote its words. We do not follow his teaching on prayer if we repeat memorized words meaninglessly.

Metaphysically, we can never be divine as Christ was. We should avoid encouragements by pantheistic and occult leaders to visualize ourselves to have infinite divine potential. Jesus never blurred the distinction between the Creator and the creature, or between himself as from above and all others who were from below. Ontologically Jesus is God's one and only Son. Our spiritual problem is not our finite distinctness but our moral rebellion. Hence all appropriate attempts that we make to be like Jesus Christ ought to avoid the blasphemy of claiming to be God, in the God-class, or having an infinite potential. The fullness of Christ may dwell in us, but we ought never confuse ourselves with his power. Our being is not continuous with his divine Being.

How, then, is it possible in any measure to become like the God-man? We are not advocating a hypocritical show of Christlikeness out of selfish motives in the strength of the flesh. Attempts of non-Christians to mimic Christ's outward behavior, though understandable, cannot approach his inner authenticity. The *kenotic* Christ modeled the primary motivation of faithful love and walked in the enduement of the Holy Spirit. So believers in Christ cannot expect to grow in Christlikeness in the flesh. Only as motivated above all by faithful love and as enabled by the Holy Spirit can we make significant and lasting progress in becoming genuinely like our Lord.

REVIEW QUESTIONS

To Help Relate and Apply Each Section in This Chapter

1. *Briefly state the classical problem* this chapter addresses and indicate reasons why genuine inquiry into it is important for your worldview and your existence personally and socially.

2. *Objectively summarize the influential answers* given to this problem in history as hypotheses to be tested. Be able to compare and contrast their real similarities and differences (not merely verbal similarities or differences).

3. *Highlight the primary biblical evidence* on which to decide among views—evidence found in the relevant teachings of the major divisions of Scripture—and decide for yourself which historical hypothesis (or synthesis of historical views) provides the most consistent and adequate account of the primary biblical data.

4. *Formulate in your own words your doctrinal conviction* in a logically consistent and adequate way, organizing your conclusions in ways you can explain clearly, support biblically, and communicate effectively to your spouse, children, friends, Bible class, or congregation.

5. *Defend your view* as you would to adherents of the alternative views, showing that the other views are logically less consistent and factually faced with more difficulties than your view in accounting for the givens, not only of special revelation but also of human experience in general.

6. *Explore the differences the viability of your conviction can make in your life*. Then test your understanding of the viability of your view by asking, "Can I live by it authentically (unhypocritically) in relation to God and to others in my family, church, vocation, neighborhood, city, nation, and world?"

MINISTRY PROJECTS

To Help Communicate This Doctrine in Christian Service

1. *Memorize one major verse or passage* that in its context teaches the heart of this doctrine and may serve as a text from which to preach, teach, or lead small-group studies on the topic. The memorized passages from each chapter will build a body of content useful also for meditation and reference in informal discussions.

2. *Formulate the major idea of the doctrine in one sentence* based on the passage memorized. This idea should be useful as the major thesis of either a lesson for a class (junior high to adult) or a message for a church service.

3. *State the specific purpose or goal of your doctrinal lesson or message.* Your purpose should be more than informative. It should show why Christians need to accept this truth and live by it (unhypocritically). For teaching purposes, list indicators that would show to what extent class members have grasped the truth presented.

4. *Outline your message or lesson in complete sentences.* Indicate how you would support the truth of the doctrine's central ideas and its relevance to life and service. Incorporate elements from this chapter's historical, biblical, systematic, apologetic, and practical sections selected according to the value they have for your audience.

5. *List applications of the doctrine* for communicating the difference this conviction makes in life (for sermons, lessons, small-group Bible studies, or family devotional Bible studies). Applications should make clear what the doctrine is, why one needs to know it, and how it will make differences in thinking. Then show how the difference in thought will lead to differences in values, priorities, attitudes, speech, and personal action. Consider also the doc-

trine's possible significance for family, church, neighborhood, city, regional, and national actions.

6. *Start a file and begin collecting illustrations* of this doctrine's central idea, the points in your outline, and your application.

7. *Write out your own doctrinal statement on this subject in one paragraph* (in half a page or less). To work toward a comprehensive doctrinal statement, collect your formulations based on a study of each chapter of *Integrative Theology*. As your own statement of Christian doctrine grows, you will find it personally strengthening and useful when you are called on for your beliefs in general and when you apply for service with churches, mission boards, and other Christian organizations. Any who seek ordination to Christian ministry will need a comprehensive doctrinal statement that covers the broad scope of theology.

CHAPTER 7

CHRIST'S ONCE-FOR-ALL ATONING PROVISIONS

Christ's Once-for-All Atoning Provisions

THE PROBLEM: WHAT DID JESUS CHRIST'S DEATH ON THE CROSS OF CALVARY ACHIEVE FOR SINFUL AND CONDEMNED MEN AND WOMEN?

The major religions of the world focus primarily on the life and teachings of their founder or leader. While by no means neglecting Jesus' instruction, Christianity uniquely assigns chief importance to his sufferings and death as interpreted by the Scriptures. The focal importance to Paul of Christ's passion is evident in his figurative statement to the church at Corinth: "I resolved to know nothing while I was with you except Jesus Christ and him crucified" (1 Cor. 2:2; cf. 1:18; Gal. 6:14). A growing number of contemporary liberal and mediating theologians focus attention on Christ's earthly life while minimizing the significance of his suffering and death on the cross.[1]

In this chapter we investigate the question of why biblical people view the cross of Christ as the center where many lines of Christian conviction converge. How does Calvary illumine the character of God, such as his love, holiness, faithfulness, righteousness, and abhorrence of evil (vol. 1, chap. 6)? How does the cross relate to human persons after Eden in a condition of sin and alienation against God (vol. 2, chap. 4)? Moreover, how is the cross linked with the person of Jesus Christ (chaps. 5–6)? Did the second person of the Godhead, who abandoned heaven to become a man, do for us spiritually what we sinners could not do for ourselves? How is the cross related to the Christian doctrine of salvation? What has the cross on which Christ died 1,900 years ago to do with our salvation today? Furthermore, why is the cross the major symbol of the Christian church? How does Calvary relate to the *ekklēsia* or the worldwide family of God (vol. 3, chaps. 5–6)? Finally, how does the death Christ suffered during his first advent relate to his second advent (vol. 3, chaps. 7–9)? Biblical eschatology deals with the future God has planned for the people of God who glory in the cross of Christ. Given the profound relatedness of the cross to other Christian doctrines, Warfield's comment is appropriate: "Not only is the doctrine of the sacrificial death of Christ embodied in Christianity an essential element of the system, but in a very real sense it constitutes Christianity."[2]

In the present chapter we enquire into several vital but debated issues associated with the death Christ died. In the context of universal sinfulness, how can alienated men and women be restored to fellowship with a holy God? Millennia ago Job posed the question, "How can a mortal be righteous before God?" (Job 9:2). Later the apostle Paul inquired how God could be perfectly just and yet justify the ungodly (Rom. 3:25–26). To answer these questions we must address the meaning and significance of the death Christ died. What does the cross Jesus bore nearly two thousand years ago accomplish for people today? Did a once-for-all transaction occur at the cross, or does it simply evoke a personal relationship to Christ? Did the cross accomplish something objectively, or is its impact only subjective? If the former, how could one person bear the guilt and penalty of all the people who have ever lived? Moreover, what is the meaning and significance of the biblical metaphors traditionally used to describe the work of Christ, such as passover sacrifice, ransom, redemption, propitiation, victor, and reconciliation?

Furthermore, is it valid to affirm that Christ functioned as a great high priest on our behalf? If so, what does the symbolism of priesthood connote in relation to our Lord? We need also to interact with the widely debated question in Christendom: For whom did Christ die? Did the Father send his Son into the world to die for all persons or only for the elect? Might there be a viable alternative to these two popular interpretations? Finally, does Scripture teach that between his death and resurrection Christ descended to the nether regions of the earth to preach to human spirits allegedly imprisoned there? How valid is the statement in the Apostles' Creed "He descended to hell"? The issues addressed in this chapter on the cross of Christ may seem complex and difficult. But as Emil Brunner has said, with some overstatement, "He who understands the cross aright . . . understands the Bible, he understands Jesus Christ."[3]

ALTERNATIVE INTERPRETATIONS IN THE CHURCH

The crucial question of what the death of Jesus Christ accomplished for persons alienated from the life of God has been variously explicated in the church. For purpose of evaluation by scriptural evidence, we will now survey the varied historical proposals for understanding the cross.

The Classic or Ransom View

Many patristic authorities to the time of Anselm and a few contemporary theologians interpret the atonement as a cosmic victory over sin, death, and Satan. This classic, dramatic, or ransom theory, which depicts God triumphing over hostile forces that enslave persons, was the dominant view in the church for a thousand years. The interpretation found considerable favor with early Christians surrounded by oppressive satanic activity in the pagan world. The theory focuses not on Christ's bearing the sinner's penalty or propitiating God's wrath but on the Savior's delivering humankind from enslaving powers. The theory assumes at least two forms: (1) Following Mark 10:45, some interpreters viewed Christ's death as a ransom paid to the Devil. The world, they argued, had fallen under Satan's dominion by virtue of sin. At the cross God delivered Christ over to Satan in exchange for the souls of those he held captive. But Satan could not hold Christ, thus the Son of God rose powerfully from the grave. (2) Guided by Colossians 2:15, other authorities claimed that God did battle with Satan, triumphed over death and the Devil once-for-all, and rescued those held captive by the powers of darkness.

Irenaeus interpreted Christ's death as a victory over sin, death, and the Devil. Through Edenic transgression, humanity fell under the dominion of Satan. By recapitulating in himself all the experiences of humankind and by rising from the dead, Christ conquered Satan, thereby freeing believing sinners from his power and giving them eternal life. Wrote Irenaeus: "Reasonably redeeming us with his blood, Christ gave himself as a ransom for those who had been led into captivity."[4]

Origen maintained that by reason of sin humanity was bound in the clutches of Satan. In exchange for the freedom of souls held under his sway, Satan demanded the blood of Christ. When God gave Christ to the Devil as a ransom (*lytron*), Satan released the imprisoned souls. Origen continues by stating that Satan was deceived in the transaction on two counts: (1) Christ's humanity hid his deity so that when Satan swallowed the bait of Christ's flesh he was caught on the hook of his deity; and (2) Satan discovered that he could not hold Christ in hell and on the third day the Savior rose powerfully from the grave. Origen summarizes as follows: "The evil one reigned over us until the soul of Jesus had been given to him as a ransom—to him who deceived himself, thinking that he could be master over Jesus, not realizing that he did not suffer the agony which he applied to hold him down."[5]

John of Damascus used the same imagery, except that he identified the enemy that was snared as death rather than Satan. "Death approaches and eagerly swallowing the bait of the body is transfixed by the hook of the divinity. And so having tasted that innocent and life-giving body, itself is destroyed, vomiting up all those whom it had previously swallowed."[6]

Gustaf Aulén claims that the sometimes crude metaphors of the Fathers convey the important truth that God in Christ triumphed over sin, death, and the Devil. In a great cosmic drama that issued in his death, Christ fought against and overcame malignant spiritual powers. As a result of that victory captive persons were freed and gained the hope of eternal life. The central theme of the classic view "is the idea of the Atonement as a divine conflict and victory; Christ—*Christus victor*—fights against and triumphs over the evil powers of the world, the 'tyrants' under which mankind is in bondage and suffering, and in him God reconciles the world to himself."[7] Aulén claims that the *Christus victor* motif, much neglected in modern theology, faithfully reflects the teachings of Scripture and of Luther. Aulén cites the prediction of warfare between Christ and Satan in Genesis 3:15, the Lord's exorcism of demons in the Gospels, and texts such as Colossians 2:15, Hebrews 2:14, and 1 John 3:8. Clearly Aulén's *Christus victor* motif emphasizes Christ's kingly rather than priestly office.

The Moral Influence Theory

This subjective view of the atonement focuses on the change of attitude Christ's death produces in sinners. Proponents claim that there were no obstacles in God that needed to be overcome in order to restore sinners to fellowship with their Creator. From the divine side no satisfaction of justice and no placation of wrath was required. The only barrier to salvation lies in estranged persons themselves, i.e., in their sinful pride and stubborn wills. This theory maintains that the love of God displayed on the cross overwhelms sinners' hostility and persuades them to repent and be reconciled to God. First advanced as a theory by Peter Abelard in the medieval era, the moral influence theory finds many adherents among modern liberal theologians.

Proceeding from a view of sin as contempt of God, Abelard claimed that Christ's death provides a compelling demonstration of God's suffering with his creatures. The spectacle of Christ impaled on the cross causes people to recognize their selfishness, melts their stony hearts, and moves them to be reconciled to God. The sufferings of the innocent Christ on the cross stir sinners to love the One who so manifestly loves them. At bottom, then, people are saved by the compelling power of God's self-giving love. "Christ died for us in order to show how great was his love to mankind and to prove that love is the essence of Christianity."[8] Abelard believed that the cross exerts the most powerful moral influence in human history.

The Socinians modified Abelard's views with themes from Renaissance humanism. Their conception of the atonement was rooted (1) in a Pelagian understanding of the essential goodness of human nature, (2) in a humanistic vision of God that allowed for no wrath against sin, and (3) in an adoptionist view of Jesus as human prophet chosen by God to be his Son. The Socinians claimed that in his life and death Jesus modeled the moral life that God expects humans to live. The enduring example of Jesus' obedience unto death inspires persons to pursue self-reformation. Said Socinus, "Christ takes away sins because by heavenly promises He attracts and is strong to move all men to penitence, whereby sins are destroyed. . . . He draws all who have not lost hope to leave their sins and zealously to embrace righteousness and holiness."[9] As sinners repent and strive to live morally, they experience God's forgiveness. Socinus believed that Christ's death was but a preliminary stage to the crucial event of his exaltation to heaven. Undertaking in the heavenly world the office of priest, Christ there offered the true sacrifice, which is his representation of believers before the Father.

Horace Bushnell, the father of American liberalism, believed that the cross displayed God suffering in love with his creatures. "It is not that the suffering appeases God, but that it expresses God—displays, in open history, the unconquerable love of God's heart."[10] Subjectively the death of Christ releases a moral power in the world that softens hardened hearts and leads sinners to repentance. Primarily Christ's death "was designed to have a renovating power in character."[11] Seeking to retain some link with orthodoxy, Bushnell suggested that concepts such as divine anger, sacrifice, blood, and expiation ("the altar form") convey the "sentiments, states, and moral effects in the worshippers, which . . . they were unable to conceive or speak of themselves."[12] Although retaining the traditional language, Bushnell viewed the atonement as the power of love that evokes repentance and transforms character.

L. H. DeWolf also subscribes to the moral view of the atonement. He claims that at the cross sinners, (1) negatively, discover the vileness of their sin vividly represented and, (2) positively, learn that God lovingly suffers with them in their alienation. Thus as men and women contemplate the cross on which God acted in Christ, "they are moved to place their hope in the Father, repent with faith, and aspire to serve him in obedient love."[13]

The Satisfaction or Juridicial Theory

This theory of the atonement, also called the Latin view, first arose in the patristic West and achieved full expression in the Middle Ages. In suggesting that the death of Christ chiefly satisfies the wounded honor of God, medieval theologians were influenced by the concept of a feudal overlord whose dignity was injured by his serfs. While reflecting a keen awareness of sin and the solidarity of the race, this theory focused largely on God's injured honor and paid less attention to the penal and substitutionary nature of Christ's death. Unlike the focus of the previous two theories, that of the juridicial theory is primarily Godward.

In his essay *Cur Deus Homo* (*Why God [Became] Man*), Anselm claims that sin is the failure to render God his due, namely, entire subjection and obedience. When a person disobeys God and sins, he offends God's honor and violates the divinely ordained order of the universe. God's nature is such that he requires either satisfaction or punishment for sin. But since God willed that sufficient persons should be saved to replace the number of fallen angels (a judgment borrowed from Augustine), satisfaction for sins must be made. In addition, the medieval mind held that the recompense must be proportional to the dignity of the offended party, in this case God. Consequently, finite persons cannot make an infinite satisfaction for the offense committed against the Lord of the universe. In any case sinners have nothing to offer God, for they already owe God everything. "Sinful man cannot at all accomplish this justification, because a sinner cannot justify a sinner."[14] Thus adequate satisfaction must come from one who is divine, that is, from God himself. On the other hand, satisfaction must be paid by one who genuinely represents humanity. Thus satisfaction must be made by one who is both God and man. "If only God can make this satisfaction and only a man ought to make it: it is necessary that a God-man make it."[15] Wherefore God was born of a virgin, and the sinless Jesus Christ voluntarily suffered and died, thereby accruing more merit than needed to pay the debt humanity owed. God accepted the surplus of Christ's passion, credited it to the account of the sinful race, and thus is disposed to restore to fellowship all who trust in Christ's saving provision.

How does Anselm's satisfaction theory differ from the view of many Reformed and Evangelical theologians? First, Anselm made the idea of satisfaction virtually the whole of his theory. And second, he "saw *satisfaction* for our sins as the offering of compensation or damages for dishonor done." Packer continues this point, saying that "the Reformers saw it as the undergoing of vicarious punishment (*poena*) to meet the claims on us of God's holy law and wrath (i.e., his punitive justice)."[16]

Several later medieval theologians modified Anselm's theory of satisfaction rendered to God's injured honor. Hugh of St. Victor combined Anselm's juridicial theory with the classic view of ransom from the dominion of Satan. Accordingly Christ rendered satisfaction to God for the dishonor sinners caused him. Now aligned with persons, God is disposed to free sinners from Satan's domination. Alexander of Hales and Bonaventura generally followed the Anselmic scheme, though both appeared reluctant to posit the absolute necessity of Christ's death as Anselm had done. The English Reformer John Wycliffe also followed the main lines of the Anselmic satisfaction motif.

The Governmental or Rectoral Theory

Hugo Grotius, the Remonstrant jurist and theologian, first expounded the governmental theory of the atonement. Grotius envisaged God as world Ruler who preserves moral government. His key scriptural text was Isaiah 42:21: "The Lord was pleased, for his righteousness' sake, to magnify his law and make it glorious" (RSV). Grotius sought to forge a middle ground between the Socinians and the Calvinist Reformers.

Against the Socinians he argued that God exacts punishment for sin, albeit not out of retribution but for the maintenance of the moral order of the universe. And against the Reformers he insisted that Christ did not bear the full penalty of human sin, nor did he propitiate God's wrath.

Objectively, Grotius maintained that the death of Christ was a real offering made to God, an offering that displays the divine justice. Although divine love modified the demands of strict justice so that God need not exact the full penalty for sin, the offering of Christ did render God favorable so that he could pardon sins and restore sinners to fellowship. God could have relaxed his law altogether and not punished Christ, but such a course would not have achieved the maximal deterrence for future sins. Here the subjective component of the atonement comes into view. For Grotius the punishment inflicted on Christ is exemplary in that it communicates God's hatred of sin and strikes fear into the hearts of persons so that they will forsake evil and seek personal reformation. Grotius argues, "God, who has supreme power as to all things not unjust in themselves, and who is liable to no law, willed to use the torments and death of Christ for the setting up of a weighty example against the immense faults of us all."[17] For Grotius, the main emphasis of the atonement is subjective: Christ's death motivates sinners to repent of their sins and reform their lives.

The older Arminians followed the viewpoint of Grotius. John Miley, a Methodist theologian, rejected the penal satisfaction theory advanced by the Protestant Reformers. Said he, "The Wesleyan soteriology . . . excludes the satisfaction theory, and requires the governmental as the only theory consistent with itself."[18] Arguing that sin and guilt could not be imputed to the sinless Son of God, Miley concludes that Christ did not bear the punishment due to our sin. "The sufferings of Christ are not, and cannot be, an atonement by penal substitution."[19] Advancing the governmental theory, Miley claims that Christ's sufferings are atoning in the sense that they uphold law and serve the interests of moral government. God exacted a penalty for human sin in the form of the death of Christ. But Christ's death fulfills justice not as a substitute of penalty, but insofar as it serves a rectoral end. The sufferings of Christ avail in that they maintain the honor of the divine Ruler, manifest the ugliness of sin, foreshadow the punishment of the unrepentant, and restrain sin by striking fear in the hearts of persons. Miley concludes, "The chief rectoral value of penalty, simply as an element of law, is through the moral ideas which it conveys, and the response which it thus finds in the moral reason."[20]

J. Kenneth Grider, a Nazarene theologian, likewise upholds the governmental view of the atonement:

> According to this theory, Christ did not pay the penalty for our sins; instead, he suffered for us. Scripture never says that Christ was punished for us, or paid the penalty, as Calvinists teach. . . . His death was of such a nature that a holy God could accept it as a *substitute* for penalty. Its merits as a substitute could provide a moral basis for forgiveness without compromising either God's holiness or the integrity of moral government.[21]

Arminian theologians consistently uphold a universal atonement: Christ died for the purpose of providing salvation for the entire world. Thus Arminius succinctly affirmed: "Christ died for all men and for every individual."[22] Desiring that none should perish in their sins, God bestows prevenient grace universally and extends salvation to all through worldwide gospel proclamation. Arminians such as Miley aver that an unconditional atonement makes universal salvation theoretically possible. But since many persons fail to respond to the gospel in faith, not all actually are saved. The Arminians press their position by asking how persons could be held guilty for refusing to believe what was not intended for them. Miley reasons that the broader the intent of the atonement, the greater the good that accrues. He suggests that a universal atonement optimally fosters the maintenance of moral government. He concludes, "The atonement, as a provision of infinite love for a common race in a common ruin of sin, with its unrestricted overture of grace and requirement of saving faith in Christ, is, and must be, an atonement for all."[23]

Neoorthodox Reconciliation Theory

Opposing liberalism's subjective understanding of the atonement, Karl Barth affirms that the death of Christ objectively reconciles the world to God. Seeking to be like God, humankind is godless, guilty, and condemned to death. To make amends, the divine Son descended into a strange land to experience rejection. In depicting the atonement Barth freely uses the language of substitution.[24] Yet Barth's view of the atonement diverges significantly from the orthodox representation. He denies that Christ by suffering propitiated the wrath of the offended God. Rather, by his incarnation and death Christ, our Representative, united human nature (*humanum*) to his divine nature. Said Barth of Christ's earthly experience: "He takes human being into unity with His own."[25] Thus at Calvary, in solidarity with Christ, humankind suffered and died. Barth rejects the notion that Christ bore the penalty of sin in our place. On the cross the wrath and the punishment of God fell both on him *and* on us. "In His person, with Him, judgment, death and end have come to us ourselves once and for all."[26] Furthermore, united with Christ in his resurrection, humanity participates in the Lord's victory over death and the Devil. Concerning the final end of humanity, Barth affirms, "Our exaltation took place in Him."[27] Barth insisted that God pardons sinners not by means of a penal satisfaction, but simply on the basis of his determination to forgive—which act of forgiveness satisfies the requirements of his righteousness. "His forgiveness makes good our repudiation and failure and thus overcomes the hurt that we do to God, and the disturbance of the relationship between Himself and us, and the disturbance of the general relationship between the Creator and the creation."[28]

The presupposition of this act of justification and reconciliation is the eternal covenant that God made with the human race. In volume 1, chapter 8, Barth postulated that God eternally elected himself in Jesus Christ for suffering and death. In this respect the cross signifies the rejection of the Son of God. In addition, God eternally predestined sinful humanity in Jesus Christ for salvation. In this latter respect the cross signifies the election of humankind in the Son. Ontically, Barth maintains that the death of Christ achieved a cosmic victory; the entire world has been won back to the Father. "In the death of Christ both the destroying and the renewing have taken place for all men. . . . Unbelief has become an objective, real and ontological impossibility and faith an objective, real and ontological necessity for all men and for every man."[29] But noetically, Barth acknowledges that not all persons are aware of their redeemed status. The Spirit's task, he argues, is to awaken this realization of reconciliation in the hearts of every human being. Although Barth removes the event of reconciliation from history to so-called meta-history, his position is that Christ not only died for all but that in the triumph of grace Christ will bring all persons savingly to himself. Barth's position regarding the intent of the atonement is clear: through the death of Christ God willed to save all persons.

Hendrikus Berkhof, a contemporary Dutch theologian, broadly follows Barth's line of reasoning. Berkhof interprets the human dilemma as estrangement and guilt due to sin (where guilt is a relational, not a forensic concept). Christ's death should not be interpreted in terms of the old concepts of vicarious penalty or propitiation of the divine wrath, which Berkhof holds to be alien to the the modern mindset. Rather, the terms that best describe the atonement are "representation" and "reconciliation." That is, by representing a sinful race before God, Christ identified with sinners and restores them to fellowship with their Creator. Berkhof insists that Christ effected this representation not by the cross only, but through the totality of his earthly life. Berkhof summarizes his position as follows: "Representation signifies that in him the relationship is restored, that is, that which *from our side* obstructed the relationship simply does not count anymore in the light of his perfect love and obedience" (italics mine).[30] Berkhof concedes that the exact connection between the cross and reconciliation is not clear. "The NT asserts the 'that,' but has no answer to the 'why' and the 'how.' That is God's secret."[31]

Some modern theologians replace concepts of substitutionary sacrifice and penal satisfaction with the idea of representation and vicarious identification. Thus Vincent Taylor writes, "No offer of penal suffering as a substitute for his own will meet his need, but a submission presented by his representative before God becomes the foundation of a new hope."[32]

Many Fathers, Reformers, and Evangelicals

The apostolic fathers advanced no single theory of the atonement, but articulated a number of biblical motifs. Clement of Rome described the work of Christ, using the language of substitution. "Because of the love which he felt for us, Jesus Christ our Lord gave his blood for us by the will of God, his body for our bodies, and his soul for our souls."[33] Ignatius expressed the idea of our Lord's vicarious atonement: "All these sufferings, assuredly, he underwent for our sake, that we might be saved."[34] According to the *Epistle to Diognetus*, Christ's substitutionary death justifies the wicked, and his righteousness covers sins:

> God gave up his own Son as a ransom for us—the holy one for the unjust, the innocent for the guilty, the righteous one for the unrighteous, the incorruptible for the corruptible, the immortal for the mortal. For what else could cover our sins except his righteousness? . . . O sweet exchange! O unfathomable work of God! The sinfulness of many is hidden in the Righteous One, while the righteousness of the One justifies the many that are sinners.[35]

In the East Cyril of Jerusalem describes the cross in terms of penal substitution, although he grounds the sentence of death in God's veracity rather than in his justice:

> We were enemies of God through sin, and God had decreed the death of the sinner. One of two things, therefore, was necessary, either that God, in his truth, should destroy all men, or that in his loving-kindness, he should remit the sentence. But see the wisdom of God; he preserved the truth of his sentence and the exercise of his loving-kindness. Christ took our sins "in his body upon the tree; that we, having died to sin," by his death "might live to justice."[36]

Athanasius taught that in order to solve the problem posed by human sin and condemnation God sent the divine Word into the world. In his body the Son bore the penalty and paid the debt that sinners owed to God. Thus Christ offered "the sacrifice on behalf of all, surrendering his own temple [body] to death in place of all, to settle man's account with death and free him from the primal transgression."[37] For Athanasius Christ's death was a penal satisfaction of the divine sentence of death. By virtue of Christ's cross and resurrection, death is annulled and believers are raised to immortality.

In the West Augustine synthesized previous insights into a comprehensive view of the atonement. Original sin brought humanity under the divine sentence of condemnation and death. In love Jesus Christ yielded to the snare of the Devil and endured the punishment that sinners justly deserved. Wrote Augustine: "Christ bore for our sakes sin in the sense of death as brought on human nature by sin. This is what hung on the tree. . . . Thus was death condemned that its reign might cease, and accursed that it might be destroyed."[38] In making this sacrifice to satisfy the divine justice, Christ functioned as both priest and oblation, as both offerer and offering.[39] Christ's death achieved several significant benefits, the first of which is placation of the divine wrath. "When the Father was angry with us, he looked upon the death of his Son for us and was propitiated towards us."[40] Christ's penal sacrifice, furthermore, delivers saints from satanic bondage, cleanses sins, reconciles to the Father, and offers the church an example of humility, patience in suffering, and faith in God.[41]

Luther taught that Christ in his life and death bore the sin, guilt, and punishment of a condemned race. On the cross the Savior endured the divine wrath against transgressions and the sentence of death the law justly demanded. As a result of his propitiatory sacrifice, Christ frees trusting souls from the curse of the law; reconciles God and sinners; imparts perfect righteousness; and conquers sin, death, and the Devil. Luther sums up his position thus: "Putting on your sinful person, he [Christ] bore your sin, death, and curse. He became a sacrifice and a curse for you, in order thus to set you free from the curse of the law."[42] Although one important outcome of the cross is the destruction of sin and Satan, Aulén is not correct in asserting that Luther primarily represents Christ's work in terms of the classical theory of triumph over Satanic powers.[43]

Calvin held that for sinners to be freed from sin's curse, a fitting sacrifice must be offered. Thus the "big idea" of Calvin's discussion of the cross is the notion of vicarious sacrifice. First, Christ is our sin-bearer. Through his life and especially his death, the Savior bore our guilt, the wrath of God, and the penalty due us. "The Son of God, utterly clean of all fault, nevertheless took upon himself the shame and reproach of our iniquities."[44] Second, Christ is the believer's righteousness. God reckoned Christ's suffering to the elect as perfect moral rectitude: "We are made righteous in him . . . because we are judged in relation to Christ's righteousness."[45] Calvin elaborates the "big idea" of vicarious sacrifice by means of three key theological concepts, the first of which is *propitiation.* This depicts the work of Christ in its Godward aspect. By his substitutionary sacrifice Christ satisfied the demands of a just God and appeased the divine wrath for all who believe. So Calvin asserts, "God, to whom we were hateful because of sin, was appeased by the death of his Son to become favorable to us."[46] Calvin's second term is *redemption,* which represents the manward focus of the cross. By his sacrificial death Christ liberates elect believers from sin, guilt, and the penalty of death.[47] Calvin's third word is *reconciliation,* which represents both the Godward and the manward sides of Christ's work. Formerly hostile to sinners by reason of their unrighteousness, God for Christ's sake is now reconciled to repentant sinners. "Christ had to become a sacrifice by dying that he might reconcile his Father to us."[48] On the other hand, the cross impacts man and so reconciles sinners to God. Thus "God appointed Christ as a means of reconciling us to himself."[49] Calvin claims that Christ performs his mediatorial work by executing the three offices of prophet, king, and priest.[50] As Prophet Christ proclaimed the grace of God and assists the church in its proclamation of the gospel. As King he rules over, guides, and protects the church. And (most relevant to this chapter) as Priest he expiated sins by his sacrifice and eternally intercedes before the Father on behalf of his people.

B. B. Warfield asserts that by the complete obedience of his life Christ fulfilled the demands of the law that Adam failed to keep and that by bearing the penalty of our sin through his sacrificial death he satisfied the justice of God. "Our Lord's redeeming work is at its core a true and perfect sacrifice offered to God, of intrinsic value ample for the expiation of our guilt; and at the same time is a true and perfect righteousness offered to God in fulfillment of the demands of his law."[51] By means of his vicarious sacrifice Christ propitiated the wrath of God, secured forgiveness of sins, delivered his people from Satanic bondage, reconciled God to sinners and sinners to God, and liberated us from the burden of the law as a way of life.

Concerning the intent or purpose of the atonement, most patristic authorities held that Christ died for the sins of the world. Athanasius maintained that in the divine scheme of things "death there had to be, and death for all, so that the due of all might be paid."[52] Cyril of Jerusalem affirmed that "Jesus truly suffered for all men."[53] While not speaking clearly on the issue, Augustine seemed to suggest that Christ died for the world, although the cross is effectual only for those who believe.[54] As for John Calvin, several recent scholars believe that although Calvin held to double predestination he also taught a doctrine of unlimited atonement.[55] In his *Institutes* Calvin wrote, "It is certain that the Lord offers us mercy and the pledge of his grace both in his Sacred Word and in his sacraments. But it is understood only by those who take Word and sacraments with sure faith, just as Christ is offered and held forth by the Father to all unto salvation, yet not all acknowledge and receive him."[56] In his later commentaries Calvin more clearly postulates an unlimited atonement. With regard to Galatians 5:12 Calvin affirms: "God commends to us the salvation of all men without exception, even as Christ suffered for the sins of the whole world."[57]

Other moderate Calvinists point out that Christ's saving provision includes many racial benefits, such as the common blessings of life, the restraint of evil, an objective provision sufficient for all, the removal of every obstacle on God's side for the forgiveness of sins, and the future resurrection of the dead.[58] On the other hand, they seek to do justice to texts that indicate a special purpose for those persons given to Christ out of the world. They point out that 1 Timothy 4:10 indicates a twofold purpose in the cross, namely, general benefits for all people and saving benefits for elect believers. In a sermon entitled, "General and Yet Particular," C. H. Spurgeon maintains that Christ's death fulfilled a twofold purpose: "There is a general influence for good flowing from the mediatorial sacrifice of

Christ, and yet its special design and definite object is the giving of eternal life to as many as the Father gave him."[59] The observation of Charles M. Horne is instructive: "God's salvation is one. As applied to non-Christians, it includes their preservation in this life and the enjoyment of certain blessings which come to man by common grace. As applied to believers, however, this salvation extends into eternity. This view would seem to be the best one, because it gives the power force to the word *especially* [1 Tim. 4:10]."[60] In a similar vein Robert P. Lightner claims that Christ's saving provision reaches every member of Adam's race. Yet its redemptive benefits are applied only to those who believe, i.e., to the elect.[61] Donald G. Bloesch arrives at a similar conclusion in language colored by the thought of Barth.[62]

Scholastic Calvinism, however, narrowed the intent of the atonement and claimed that Christ died solely for the purpose of saving the elect, the exact number of whom are actually brought to salvation. Thus proponents argue that the design of the cross was not merely to provide salvation but to *secure* the salvation of those persons the Father gave to the Son. Christ allegedly died for all who were related to him, just as Adam sinned for all who were related to him. For high Calvinism the question "For whom did Christ die?" follows from God's logically prior elective decree. Since antecedent to his decree to create humanity God purposed to save some persons and to condemn others, the high Calvinist claims that Christ died solely for those predestined to life.

In the Westminster Confession the divine decree assigning people to life or death (chap. III) precedes discussion of the work of Christ (chap. VIII). It is clear that its doctrine of election controls its doctrine of the atonement (XI.4). The Confession concludes that Christ died to obtain redemption for the elect only: "The Lord Jesus . . . purchased not only reconciliation, but an everlasting inheritance in the kingdom of heaven, for all those whom the Father hath given unto him" (VIII.5; cf. VIII.8). The Canons of Dort likewise treat the doctrine of election (I.1–18) prior to the person and work of Christ (II.1–9). God willed that the efficacy of the cross should extend only to the elect. "It was the will of God that Christ by the blood of the cross . . . should effectually redeem out of every people, tribe, nation, and language, all those, and those only, who were from eternity chosen to salvation and given to Him by the Father." (II.8).

John Owen judges that none of God's intentions or purposes fail to eventuate. If Christ died for all and not all are saved, then Christ died ineffectively, which cannot be. If God loves all and not all are saved, then God loves ineffectually, which also cannot be. Thus Christ did not die for all, and God does not love all people. Says Owen: "We deny that all mankind are the object of that love of God which moved him to send his Son to die."[63] God's love is reflected in his will to save the elect, the heirs of the covenant of grace, for whose sins Christ made satisfaction on the cross. Owen concludes that if the death of Christ accomplishes all that the Father intended, "then died he only for those that are in the event sanctified, purged, redeemed, justified, freed from wrath and death, quickened, saved, etc.; but that all are not thus sanctified, freed, etc., is most apparent: and, therefore they cannot be said to be the proper object of the death of Christ."[64]

Other Calvinist authorities who uphold a limited atonement include Jonathan Edwards, Francis Turrettin, Charles Hodge, A. A. Hodge, W. G. T. Shedd, L. Berkhof, Loraine Boettner, John Murray, and R. B. Kuiper. In each of these theologians the intent of the atonement is governed by the logically prior doctrine of election. Roger Nicole prefers the concept of "definite atonement" or "particular redemption." Christ died for the specific purpose of redeeming those whom the Father had given him.[65]

Offended by what he judged to be the harsh double predestinarianism of scholastic Calvinism, Amyraut in the seventeenth century propounded the theory of hypothetical universalism. According to this view, the covenant of grace included a universal, conditional covenant and a particular, unconditional covenant. Against scholastic Calvinism, Amyraut insisted that God willed the salvation of all persons on the condition that they believe. That is, the Father appointed Christ to suffer for the sins of the entire world. God, however, foresaw that no sinners would respond in faith, hence he implemented the particular or unconditional covenant. Here, against the Arminians, who denied that God brings the redeemed to faith, Amyraut argued that since none are able to come to God on their own, God effectively creates saving faith in the elect and reprobates others. Amyraut thus upheld an ideal universalism supplemented by a real particularism. His scheme could be represented as follows: "Christ died for all persons sufficiently, but for the elect efficiently." Amyraut's position was championed by later scholars such as Cameron of the Saumar Academy, Richard Baxter, John Bunyon, Samuel Hopkins, and Heinrich Heppe.

The "Descent of Christ Into Hell"

Based on such Scriptures as Psalm 16:10; Matthew 12:40; 27:52–53; Ephesians 4:9; 1 Peter 3:18–20; and 4:6, many church authorities affirm that between his death and resurrection Christ descended to the nether regions to preach the gospel to deceased persons. According to Eastern fathers such as Clement of Alexandria, Origen, Cyril of Alexandria, and John of Damascus, Christ in hell proclaimed the gospel to evangelize unbelieving dead. Clement, for example, averred that Christ preached to Jews who strove to live according to the law and to Gentiles who sought to live according to philosophy.[66] Western fathers such as Tertullian and Augustine held that Christ descended to the lower regions to unite faithful patriarchs and prophets to himself. Mention of Christ's descent to hell appeared in a late fourth-century recension of the Apostles' Creed and in the Athanasian Creed (no. 38). Medieval theologians followed Thomas Aquinas, who held that Christ's soul went to hades to bestow the fruits of his passion upon Old Testament believers, who had been excluded from glory by virtue of original sin.[67] Roman Catholics believe that as a result of the descent into hades the souls of those who died in faith were united to God and were raised to heaven at Christ's ascension. Lutherans generally hold that by descending to hell Christ completed his triumph over Satan and passed judgment on the unsaved held there. Calvin, on the other hand, understood the descent to hell as a figurative description of Christ's penal sufferings on the cross. What could be more hellish, he asked, than for the spotless Son of God to bear the torments of sin and to be forsaken by the Father?[68] Most Reformed and evangelical authorities have followed Calvin in interpreting the *descensus ad inferna* in a figurative sense.[69]

The theory of vicarious sacrifice, supplemented by such motifs as moral example, ransom, and triumph over Satan, has also been capably expounded by A. A. Hodge,[70] W. G. T. Shedd,[71] and H. D. McDonald.[72]

BIBLICAL TEACHING

Which interpretations of the significance of Christ's death we accept will be determined by considering the various strands of the relevant biblical teaching on the subject, for Scripture is the primary source of Christian thought and commitment.

The Pentateuch

Shortly after the Fall, God said to Satan who was in the guise of a serpent, "You will strike his heel" (Gen. 3:15). This prediction indicates that the Messiah's redemptive victory would be achieved at the cost of suffering. Early in the patriarchal history sacrifices were made to deal with sins against God. According to Genesis 4:3–4, Cain brought an offering (*minḥāh*) to the Lord from his crops, whereas Abel brought an offering (*minḥāh*) from the firstlings of the flock. Although each brought offerings from his own occupation, Cain's was made in unbelief, whereas Abel's was made in sincere trust and commitment (Heb. 11:4). As a result Abel's sacrifice effectually atoned for sins that are hateful to a holy God.

The first explicit mention of an altar occurs after the Flood when Noah sacrificed burnt offerings to God for deliverance from the deluge (Gen. 8:20). Later Abraham (12:8; 13:18), Isaac (26:25), and Jacob (33:20; 35:7) established altars for sacrifice to the Lord. "How clearly the patriarchs understood the meaning of their sacrifices one cannot say, but that they had a concept of vicarious atonement seems quite clear (Job 1:5)."[73] Abraham's near slaying of his son Isaac as a burnt offering (*'ōlāh*) in the region of Moriah (Gen. 22:1–18) prefigures the substitutionary death of the Messiah two millennia later. Isaac ascended the mountain, bearing the wood on which the sacrifice would be laid (cf. John 19:17). When Isaac inquired about the lamb for the burnt offering, Abraham responded, "God himself will provide the lamb for the burnt offering, my son" (v. 8). As Abraham was about to slay his son on the altar, the angel of the Lord showed him a ram caught in a thicket. Abraham then "took the ram and sacrificed it as a burnt offering instead of his son" (v. 13). The phrase "instead of his son [*taḥat bᵉnô*]" clearly affirms the substitutionary nature of the animal sacrifice.

The key to Israel's sacrificial system was the Passover (*pesaḥ*) in Egypt (Exod. 12:1–30). God commanded each Hebrew household to slay an unblemished yearling lamb or goat at twilight and to apply the blood of the victim to the doorframe of their houses. For the Israelites who obeyed God's instructions the sprinkled blood secured exemption from the divine judgment. But in the case of the unbelieving Egyptians, who were not sheltered by the blood, the Lord struck dead all their firstborn men and animals (vv. 29–30). The Passover ritual clearly was sacrificial in nature, for verse 27 designates it as a "Passover sacrifice" (*zebaḥ-pesaḥ*). This atoning sacrifice resulted in Israel's deliverance from the land of bondage (Exod. 14). Concerning the Passover sacrifice the following may be said: "The blood has atoning power and points to the blood of the Lamb that will take away the sin of the world (John 1:29, 36)."[74]

The Levitical sacrificial system plainly sets forth the concept of penal substitution and atonement. In the burnt offering (*'ōlāh*, Lev. 1:3–17; Judg. 13:16; 1 Sam. 7:9–10), the fellowship or peace offering (*šᵉlāmîm*, Lev. 3:1–17; 7:11–21; 2 Sam. 6:18), the sin offering (*ḥattā't*, Lev. 4:1–35; Num. 6:14–16; 2 Chron. 29:23–24), and the guilt offering (*'āšām*, Lev. 5:14–6:7; Num. 6:12; 1 Sam. 6:3–4), a sacrificial procedure was followed that generally involved the following elements: (1) An unblemished animal, connoting the idea of moral perfection, was presented at the door of the sanctuary by the offerer.

(2) The offerer placed his hands on the animal's head, signifying identification with the victim and the transfer of the penalty of sin to the substitute. (3) The animal was slain by the offerer (in later times by the priest), signifying that death is the just punishment for sin. (4) The priest sprinkled the blood of the victim on the altar and around the base of it, the blood representing the life of the victim (Lev. 17:11). And (5) the offering, in part or in whole, was burned on the altar of burnt offering, its fragrance ascending to God as a pleasing aroma. Repeatedly Scripture indicates that the purpose of these sacrifices was "to make atonement" for the offerer (e.g., Lev. 1:4; 4:20; 5:13; Num. 5:8; 8:12; 15:25). The Hebrew verb *kāpar,* commonly translated in the Piel, "make atonement," fundamentally means to "cover" or to "hide," and in a sacrificial context means to propitiate God's wrath, expiate sins, and restore fellowship between God and sinners.[75] The grain offering (*minḥāh,* Lev. 2:1–16; Num. 5:15, 18; Judg. 13:19) was a bloodless offering comprised of meal, oil, and incense. Part of the grain offering was burned on the altar, and part was given to the priests for food. "The idea of atonement is not specifically present in *minḥāh,* although that of propitiation certainly is."[76] With many scholars we judge that the offerings cited above anticipate the vicarious sacrifice of Christ. "The laws in Leviticus remind us then of Christ's death and what he has done for us. . . . The worshiper might well feel very much deprived when he had paid for a choice lamb to be sacrificed. But it reminded him that the animal was a ransom, a substitute payment instead of his own life."[77]

The annual Day of Atonement (*yôm hakkippurîm,* Lev. 23:27; 25:9) was the most important cultic celebration in the Old Testament. In preparation for the solemn event the high priest sacrificed a young bull as a sin-offering and a ram for a burnt-offering to atone for his sins and for those of the priesthood (Lev. 16:11–14). He sprinkled the blood of the bull on the front of the golden lid of the ark or the "atonement cover" (AV, "mercy seat"; *kappōret,* meaning "covering" or "expiation"; cf. Exod. 25:17). Then the high priest sacrificed the first male goat brought by the people as a sin-offering and sprinkled its blood on and in front of the "atonement cover" in the Holy of Holies, thereby expiating the uncleanness of the people (Lev. 16:15–19) and making atonement (*kippurîm*; cf. Exod. 29:36; 30:10; Num. 5:8). This act of blood shedding, according to Leviticus 17:11, represents God's ordained way of securing atonement. The high priest then laid his hands on the head of the second goat (the "scapegoat," AV, NIV) and confessed all the sins of the community, thus symbolically transferring guilt from the people to the victim. The second goat became a sin-bearer, as it irretrievably carried the sins and iniquities of the people into the wilderness. The scapegoat signifies an important result of atonement, namely, the expiation of sins.

Whereas in Judaism the prophet represented God to the people, the priest represented the people before God. The Hebrew priest offered sacrifices to Yahweh to atone for sins (Exod. 18:12), officiated in the sanctuary (Deut. 18:5), and interceded for the people (Joel 2:17). Genesis 14:18–20 refers to Melchizedek, "king of Salem" and "priest of God Most High," who performed sacerdotal functions before the Lord. The Book of Hebrews identifies this God-fearing Canaanite priest-king as a type of the eternal priesthood of Christ.

Poetical Books

Israel's hymnbook contains several vivid prefigurations of the sufferings of

Christ. The most descriptive occurs in Psalm 22. Although this song immediately refers to David's own trials, the poet's vision transcends the present moment to embrace the passion of the coming Messiah. Thus the Savior's God-forsakenness and cry of desolation are anticipated in verse 1 (cf. Matt. 27:46; Mark 15:34). The words "My God, my God, why have you forsaken me?" imply penal substitution. Indeed, they express "the punitive separation Christ accepted in our place, 'having become a curse for us' (Gal. 3:13)."[78] Furthermore, verses 7–8 depict the mocking insults that were hurled against Christ at Calvary (cf. Matt. 27: 39, 44; Luke 23:35); verses 14–15, the excruciating physical suffering he experienced; verse 16, the piercing of his hands and feet (cf. Luke 24:39–40); and verse 18, the dividing of his garments (cf. Luke 23:34; John 19:23). Additional anticipations of the Savior's passion occur in Psalms 34:20, 69:4, 9, 21; 109:25.

Psalm 40:6–8 (quoted in Heb. 10:5–7) indicates that although the animal sacrifices provided a certain benefit, they would be superseded by the coming Messiah who would do God's will and fulfill the law. "His will with regard to sacrifice would be fulfilled when a person, in the full freedom of personal moral choice and qualified so to act, would devote himself and his human life to doing God's will by offering his own body."[79] The psalmist, moreover, was aware of the fact that "God" his "Savior" (Ps. 65:5) had atoned for the sins of the faithful. "When we were overwhelmed by sins, you atoned for our transgressions" (Ps. 65:3; cf. 78:38). David uses the piel of *kāpar*, possibly referring to the propitiation effected by the blood sacrifices on the Day of Atonement. Psalm 49:7–9 acknowledges that a mere human is incapable of redeeming himself or another from the power of death. No mortal can provide a ransom (*kōper*) powerful enough to deliver from the grave. Yet in faith the psalmist confesses that "God will redeem [the Qal of *pādāh*] my life from the grave (v. 15)." His point is that God himself pays the ransom price and redeems the trusting soul from the grip of sin, death, and Satan. Ransom (*kōper*) elsewhere in the Old Testament denotes money paid to redeem the life of a person (Exod. 21:30), to free a murderer (Num. 35:31), and to purchase the freedom of a relative (Lev. 25:50–52).

The Psalms explicate God's redeeming work by means of the verb *pādāh,* to "rescue, deliver, ransom" (Pss. 31:5; 44:26; 69:18). The psalmist affirms of the Lord: "He himself will redeem Israel from all their sins" (Ps. 130:8; cf. 34:22). The noun *pᵉdût* connotes the redemption that God effects through the atoning sacrifices. Thus "he provided redemption [*pᵉdût*] for his people" (Ps. 111:9; cf. 130:7). Finally, God's redeeming activity is conveyed by means of the verb *gā'al,* to "redeem, avenge, do the part of a kinsman." God redeemed by delivering Israel from slavery in Egypt (Pss. 74:2; 77:15; cf. Exod. 6:6; 15:13) and by rescuing persons from the consequences of sin (Pss. 103:4; 107:2). Thus the Lord is known as Israel's "Redeemer" (*gô'ēl;* Job 19:25; Ps. 78:35).

Looking backward to the account of Melchizedek in Genesis and forward to the Messiah's advent, David identified Christ as a radically new kind of priest: "The Lord has sworn and will not change his mind: 'You are a priest forever in the order of Melchizedek' " (Ps. 110:4). David took notice of Melchizedek, a unique, non-Aaronic priest superior to the Jewish ministrant, neither the commencement nor the termination of whose office Scripture records. It remained for the writer of Hebrews to develop the full Christological implications of Melchizedek's royal priesthood.

Prophetic Literature

The Old Testament prophets richly portray the passion of the future "servant" and "branch." Isaiah writes that when confronted with terrible physical and emotional sufferings the Messiah neither resisted nor shrank back (Isa. 50:5). The prophet Zechariah acted out a parable to dramatize the final rejection of the Good Shepherd for a mere thirty pieces of silver (Zech. 11:12–13; cf. Matt. 27:3–10). Isaiah predicted Messiah's maltreatment by the people and his patient endurance of sufferings (Isa. 53:6–7). Messiah's disfigured appearance and marred form reflect the abuse and pain he endured (52:14). Isaiah adds that the Messiah "was numbered with the transgressors," anticipating Christ's crucifixion among common criminals (53:12; cf. Luke 22:37; 23:33). At Calvary, the Messiah was judged like a criminal, and his life was cut off by a violent death (Isa. 53:8). Bewildered and guilt-stricken, the people would gaze upon the one they had pierced (Zech. 12:10; cf. John 19:34, 37). Fittingly Isaiah describes the Messiah as "despised and rejected by men, a man of sorrows, and familiar with suffering" (Isa. 53:3). Finally, after the shepherd had been smitten, the sheep (his disciples) would flee and be scattered (Zech. 13:7; cf. Matt. 26:31, 56).

Eight centuries before Christ, Isaiah foresaw Yahweh's servant bearing the burden of sin that estranged us from God. "Servant" (*'ebed*) in Scripture is used of (1) great men of God (Isa. 20:3; 37:35; 44:2), (2) the covenant people Israel (Isa. 41:8–9; 42:19; 49:3), and (3) thc divine Messiah. That *'ebed* cannot be limited to contemporary human personalities but is a designation of the Christ is clear from several considerations: (1) The servant is given a mission to Israel (Isa. 49:5–6; 52:5–6); (2) the accomplishments of the servant are yet future to Israel (Isa. 42:4; 49:6; 53:11); (3) the works the servant performs are suprahuman (Isa. 42:6–7; 53:11–12); and (4) the New Testament specifically identifies the servant as Jesus Christ (Matt. 12:17–21; Acts 8:32–35).[80]

The focus of the fourth servant song (Isa. 52:13–53:12) is Messiah's substitutionary sacrifice for sins. The prophet writes, "Surely he took up our infirmities and carried our sorrows" (53:4; cf. Matt. 8:17). The verb *nāśā'* ("lift up" or "bear") and *sābal* ("carry" or "transport"), together with the juxtaposition of "he" and "our," clearly communicate the idea of substitution. Isaiah reiterates the "big idea" of substitution throughout chapter 53 of his prophecy. Thus in verse 6, "the LORD has laid on him [hiphil of *pāga'*, 'cause to fall on' or 'assail'] the iniquity ['āwôn] of us all." Likewise, in verse 11, "he will bear [*sābal*] their iniquities [*'ᵃwônîm*]," and verse 12, "he bore [*nāśā'*] the sin [*ḥēṭ'*] of many." Verse 5 affirms the vicarious nature of Christ's suffering: "He was pierced for our transgressions, he was crushed for our iniquities." Similarly, verse 8: "For the transgression of my people he was stricken." Verse 10 represents Christ's death as a "guilt-offering" (*'āšām*). "By calling it a guilt offering, the suffering of the Servant of the Lord is placed in the category of substitutionary satisfaction."[81] Verse 5 indicates the outcome of the Messiah's substitutionary sacrifice: "The punishment that brought us peace was upon him." The divine judgment he bore provided sinners peace with God and salvation (cf. Eph. 2:14–15; Col. 1:20). The only coherent conclusion that can be drawn from Isaiah 53:4–12 is the following: "The coming servant, Messiah, lifts up and takes upon himself man's sickness and bears the weight of his worrisome sorrows. Nothing could more graphically portray the vicarious sacrificial work of Christ who bore the penalty for man's sin so that man may receive God's righteousness and stand justified before him."[82] In addition, Daniel 9:24 provides a comprehensive description of the work of "the Anointed One." Some 490 years after the decree to rebuild Jerusalem the Messiah would appear "to finish transgression, to put an end to sin, to atone for wickedness [*lᵉkappēr ʿāwôn*], to bring in everlasting righteousness."

The prophets elaborate Messiah's atoning work via the imagery of ransom and redemption. The verb *pādāh* alone (Mic. 6:4; Zech. 10:8) or in combination with *gā'al* (Jer. 31:11; Hos. 13:14), signifies the act of delivering or rescuing through the payment of a price.[83] The verb *gā'al,* meaning to "redeem" or "recover from bondage," places the emphasis on the release obtained (Isa. 44:22–23; 63:9; Lam. 3:58; Mic. 4:10). Thus the Lord is "the Redeemer" of Israel (*gô'ēl*; Isa. 41:14; 49:7; 60:16), and the people of God are "the redeemed" (*gᵉ'ûlîm*; Isa. 35:9; 62:12). An important work of the Messiah, then, is to liberate many who are bound by the power of sin and Satan. His task is "to free captives from prison and to release from the dungeon those who sit in darkness" (Isa. 42:7; cf. 61:1). An important concomitant of redemption is expiation—the removal of the guilt and stain of sin. Thus Yahweh declares, "I . . . am he who blots out your transgressions, for my own sake, and remembers your sins no more" (Isa. 43:25). Jeremiah 33:8; Zechariah 3:9; 13:1 also describe God's work of cleansing from sin.

Messiah's priestly work of vicarious sacrifice is represented in the fourth servant song (Isa. 52:13–53:12), discussed above. Moreover, the prophet Zechariah describes the postexilic coronation of the high priest Joshua, son of Jehozadak. Ultimately royal and priestly functions will be united in one called "the Branch," or Messiah. So Yahweh says: "It is he who will build the temple of the LORD, and he will be clothed with majesty and will sit and rule on his throne. And he will be a priest on his throne" (Zech. 6:13).

The Old Testament makes only minimal reference to the intent of Messiah's death. Isaiah 53:4–6 seems to indicate that the Messiah bore the penalty for the sin of the Jewish people. First-century Jews believed that Christ suffered for his own sins, but Isaiah states that he was afflicted for the nation. Isaiah further indicates that although Messiah bore the sin of many, his death was effectual for some—i.e., for the believing remnant of Israel. Thus Messiah bore "the punishment that brought us peace" (v. 5). The statement of verse 11—"My righteous servant will justify many"—refers to the multitude of people who in faith appropriate Messiah's atoning work. Hebrews 9:28 captures the sense: "Christ was sacrificed once to take away the sins of many people." Micah 4:2 seems to suggest that the Messiah's work would be effectual for those who believe.

Synoptic Gospels

Matthew and Luke record the angelic announcements to Mary and Joseph that the name of Mary's child would be Jesus (*Iēsous*), a transliteration of the Hebrew name Joshua (*yᵉhôšûaʿ*), who saved Israel from her enemies and which means "Yahweh is salvation" (Matt. 1:21; Luke 1:31). Matthew explicitly states that the purpose of Jesus' coming was to "save his people from their sins" (v. 21). The crucial event of Jesus' baptism by John in the Jordan (Matt. 3:13–17; Mark 1:9–11; Luke 3:21–22) signifies (1) the divine commission to public ministry (cf. Matt. 21:23–27), (2) Jesus' dedication to his vocation of suffering and death, and (3) his identification with those he came to save. The phenomena accompanying Jesus' baptism are significant. The descent of the Spirit in the form of a dove connotes Jesus' endowment with divine power for the fulfillment of his messianic ministry. And the heavenly voice (Matt. 3:17), which is a conflation of Psalm 2:7 and Isaiah 42:1, suggests that the divine Son would perform his messianic work in fulfillment of the Isaianic prophecies concerning the servant of the Lord.

Jesus spoke about his death in Mark 10:45 (cf. Matt. 20:28): "The Son of Man did not come to be served, but to serve, and to give his life as a ransom [*lytron*] for many [*anti pollōn*]." This saying points to Jesus' vicarious suffering and death: (1) because the Lord applies to himself Isaiah's description of the suffering servant (especially Isa. 53:10–12) and (2) because *anti* with the genitive case is a preposition of substitution signifying "instead of" or "in the place of."[84] The noun *lytron,* "price of release" or "ransom price," was widely used in classical Greek to denote the payment made to free a slave or a prisoner. The metaphor connotes that Jesus' death possesses an atoning dimension in that it wipes out guilt, and it has a liberating dimension in that it sets spiritual captives free from sin and the Devil. Jesus' saying makes no mention of the one to whom payment is made. The metaphor simply conveys the truth that it cost God dearly to free sinners from spiritual enslavement.

That Jesus' death involved substitutionary atonement is clear from his institution of the Lord's Supper. The reading of Luke 22:19, retained in the ASV, NASB, and NIV, indicates that Jesus took bread, broke it, and said: "This is my body given for you [*hyper hymōn*]." After that (v. 21) the Lord took the cup of wine, gave thanks, and said, "This cup is the new covenant in my blood, which is poured out for you [*hyper hymōn*]." Mark's account (Mark 14:24) reads, "which is poured out for many [*hyper pollōn*]." Compare Matthew's account (Matt. 26:28), which uses the phrase *peri pollōn—peri* being equivalent in meaning to *hyper.*[85] The preposition *hyper* in these texts means "in behalf of" or "in place of" and so connotes substitution: Jesus gave his flesh and blood (i.e., his life) on behalf of sinners.[86] Furthermore, Jesus' sayings imply that his death supplanted the old Mosaic covenant sacrifices (Exod. 24:6–8) and inaugurated the new covenant promised by the prophet Jeremiah (Jer. 31:31–33). In the old covenant Moses made burnt and fellowship offerings to the Lord and sprinkled the blood of animals on the altar, thereby temporarily propitiating God's anger and expiating sins. Jesus suggests that his death rendered an atonement for sins that was perfect and permanent.

Jesus' death served not only as a ransom (*lytron*) but also as redemption (*lytrōsis*), the latter word meaning "deliverance" or "release." Thus in Luke 1:68 (cf. 2:38) Zechariah acknowledges that through Mary's child the Lord "has come and has redeemed his people." The deliverance Zechariah anticipated through the Christ includes Israel's liberation from political bondage (v. 71) as well as release from the guilt and power of sin (vv. 77–79). The word "redemption" (*lytrōsis*) in Zechariah's prophecy is equivalent to the word "salvation" (*sōtēria*, "deliverance") in verses 69, 71, 77. That Christ delivers from the bondage of sin and death is clear from the incident in the synagogue at Nazareth, where Jesus read from the servant passage of Isaiah 61:1–2. In fulfillment of this prophecy, Jesus indicated that the Lord had sent him "to proclaim freedom [*aphesis*] for the prisoners" and "to release the oppressed" (Luke 4:18). Whereas *aphesis* sometimes means "forgiveness of sins"

(Matt. 26:28), here in Luke it means "release from captivity."[87] Jesus' priestly ministry of self-oblation is discussed above under the categories of vicarious sacrifice, ransom, and redemption.

The death of Christ also exerted a moral and spiritual influence on people who viewed it. According to Luke 23:39–43, having heard Jesus petition the Father to forgive those who had crucified him (v. 34), and having observed the firm faith of the Innocent One, a criminal who hung on the cross believed that Jesus could save him. Similarly, a Roman soldier who observed Jesus' confidence in God in the face of a humiliating death became convinced that the Nazarene's claims were true; he confessed, "Surely this man was the Son of God!" (Mark 15:39).

The totality of Jesus' life as well as his death should be viewed as a sacrifice to God. In his complete obedience to the will of the Father (John 14:31; Heb. 10:7–9) and in his entire fulfillment of the law and its demands (Matt. 5:17; Gal. 4:4), Jesus "fulfilled all righteousness" (Matt. 3:15).

Concerning the intent of Christ's death, Jesus invited all persons burdened with Jewish legalism to come to him for spiritual refreshment (Matt. 11:28). On the other hand, an angel of the Lord announced to Joseph that Mary would give birth to a son named Jesus, who would "save his people from their sins" (1:21). The *laos* referred to clearly is the new Israel, the people who would believe in Christ. Mark 10:45 is relevant to the present discussion: "The Son of Man did not come to be served, but to serve, and to give his life as a ransom for many [*anti pollōn*]." Most commentators recognize that this saying reflects the thought of Isaiah 53:11–12, which we saw refers to the believing remnant in Israel. Furthermore, in the Qumran literature "the many" commonly describes the elect within the community. Thus "many" in Mark 10:45 likely refers to the saved who have been bought from slavery by Christ's blood. "The 'many' are the redeemed community who have experienced the remission of sins in and through Jesus' sacrifice and so are enabled to participate in the salvation provided under the new covenant. . . . He freely yields his life in order that God's will to save his people may be effected."[88]

Pauline Literature

Paul frequently represents Christ's death as a substitutionary sacrifice for sins. He insists that the message transmitted to him by the earliest Christians was a matter "of first importance." The heart of this early Christian confession is that "Christ died for [*hyper*] our sins" (1 Cor. 15:3). Elsewhere Paul writes of God's "sending his own Son in the likeness of sinful man to be a sin offering" (*peri hamartias,* Rom. 8:3). Furthermore, Paul establishes a direct relationship between Christ's death and the Old Testament Passover sacrifice: "Christ, our Passover lamb [*pascha*], has been sacrificed" (1 Cor. 5:7). This reference to the Jewish Passover indicates that the blood of Christ shed on the cross propitiates the divine wrath, delivers from the guilt of sin, and secures exemption from divine judgment. Contemplating the suffering servant of Isaiah 53, Paul wrote, "God made him who had no sin to be sin for [*hyper*] us" (2 Cor. 5:21). As our substitute, Christ suffered God's wrath against sin that we might receive God's righteousness. "God placed our sins on the sinless Jesus and as our substitute in our place God punished him with death."[89] In a similar vein Paul writes, "Christ redeemed us from the curse of the law, by becoming a curse for [*hyper*] us" (Gal. 3:13). Here the curse (*katara*) is the sentence of death that hung over all persons as law-breakers. In addition, the apostle succinctly states that Christ "gave himself for [*hyper*] our sins" (Gal. 1:4; cf. Rom. 5:6, 8; 8:32; Gal. 2:20; Eph. 5:2; Titus 2:14). Once again *hyper* with the genitive connotes both representation ("on behalf of") and substitution ("in place of").

To describe the results of Christ's death Paul uses the figure of a ransom payment. In what may be an echo of Jesus' words in Mark 10:45, Paul refers to "the man Christ Jesus, who gave himself as a ransom [*antilytron*] for all men" (1 Tim. 2:5–6). The compound word *antilytron,* which literally means "substitute-ransom," denotes "what is given in exchange for another as the price of his redemption."[90] Paul's words "You were bought at a price" (1 Cor. 6:20; 7:23; cf. Acts 20:28), affirm that Christ on Calvary paid the price that sets believers free. The question, To whom was the price paid? goes beyond the main point Paul wished to make. The apostle proceeds to speak of the liberation from sin and Satan that is obtained by the costly sacrifice of Christ: "In him we have redemption [*apolytrōsis*] through his blood" (Eph. 1:7; cf. Rom. 3:24; Col. 1:14). "In the Pauline writings it [*apolytrōsis*] figures largely to designate the deliverance from sin and its penalty brought about by the propitiatory death of Christ."[91] This deliverance wrought by Christ is affirmed by the verbs *lytroomai* ("redeem," "liberate") in Titus 2:14, by *exagorazō* ("buy out of the market place," "redeem" from slavery) in Galatians 3:13; 4:5, by *rhyomai* ("rescue," "deliver") and by *methistēmi* ("remove from one place to another") in Colossians 1:13, and by *exaireō* ("rescue," "deliver") in Galatians 1:4. Elsewhere Paul teaches that Christ's death liberates from servile bondage to sin (Rom. 6:6–7, 14, 20, 22) and death (8:2).

Another significant outcome of Christ's death is reconciliation of God and sinners. The verb *katallassō* means to "effect a change," to "reconcile," and was used in classical Greek in the sense of "restoring the original understanding between people after hostility or displeasure."[92] Theologically reconciliation connotes that the relationship of enmity between God and sinners is changed to one of friendship. Paul writes in Romans 5:10 that before being reconciled to God by the death of his Son, "we were God's enemies." Does the enmity that prevents reconciliation reside on God's side or ours? The answer appears to be that it lies on both. Cranfield makes the following comment: "The enmity which is removed in the act of reconciliation is both sinful man's hostility to God (Rom. 1:30; 8:7) and also God's hostility to sinful man (this aspect is particularly clear in 11:28), though the removal of God's hostility is not to be thought of as involving a change of purpose in God."[93] With enmity on both sides abolished and the separation breached, Paul can write, "We . . . rejoice in God through our Lord Jesus Christ, through whom we have now received reconciliation" (*katallagē,* Rom. 5:11). In 2 Corinthians 5:18–21 Paul teaches that it is God who initiates reconciliation (*katallagē*). Through Christ God eliminated the chasm between himself and wayward sinners and established a communion that formerly was absent. As seen above, the event of reconciliation presupposes the removal of God's enmity vis-à-vis sinners through Christ's propitiatory sacrifice.

Moreover, reconciliation involves the nonimputation of sins or justification, for Paul in v. 21 speaks of the reconciled sinner's attaining the "righteousness [*dikaiosynē*] of God," namely, that state of being righteous in relation to the law. In Ephesians 2:12–16 Paul elaborates on the idea of reconciliation; through the work of Christ, Gentiles, "who once were far away," are united to the covenant people (vv. 12–15). With the partition between Jew and Gentile broken down, God is creating a new humanity in Christ. In addition, through Christ God is uniting both Jew and Gentile to himself: "His purpose was . . . in this one body to reconcile both of them to God through the cross" (vv. 15–16). Paul's verb in verse 16 is *apokatallassō,* which means to "turn from hostility to friendship, to reconcile."[94] The apostle mentions without elaboration reconciliation on a cosmic scale in Ephesians 1:10 and Colossians 1:20. Although not teaching universal salvation, these texts suggest that the discord and fragmentation characteristic of the fallen universe ultimately will give way to harmony and unity as Christ sovereignly rules over the created order.

Paul perceives that the life and death of Christ achieved a mighty victory over malignant spiritual powers. Thus through his public ministry and passion Christ has "destroyed death" (2 Tim. 1:10)—the aorist participle of *katargeō* indicating that through Christ death has been rendered inoperative or annulled. Elsewhere Paul asserts that by his death and resurrection Christ gained the victory (*nikos*) over the mortal adversaries—law, sin, and death (1 Cor. 15:55–57). Employing vivid images from the ancient world, Paul describes the victory Christ gained at the cross over hostile spiritual forces: "Having disarmed the powers and authorities, he made a public spectacle of them, triumphing over them by the cross" (Col. 2:15). The first verb, the aorist middle of *apekdyomai,* signifies that at the cross Christ stripped, as one puts off a garment, the evil powers that assailed him. The imagery is that of a deposed monarch stripped of the robes of his office. "The use of the double compound is probably to stress that it is a complete putting off and putting away, which makes a falling back into the former manner of life impossible."[95] The last verb, the aorist of *thriambeuō,* connotes that at the cross Christ roundly conquered these powers, leading them in a triumphal procession, much as a victorious general would lead his captives in a public display through the streets of the city. Thus through his life and death Christ disarmed and despoiled all hostile powers that threaten the citizens of the kingdom.

Paul also views the death of Christ as a powerful example of Christian conduct. Since the cross is the supreme demonstration of divine love (Rom. 5:8), Paul summons the Ephesian Christians to imitate Christ's love by living a compassionate life (Eph. 5:1–2). Moreover, Paul enjoins the Philippians to adopt an attitude of humility and unselfish concern for others. This mindset is achieved as the believer follows the example of Christ, who, in the supreme act of self-renunciation, divested himself of the divine glory, assumed our lowly humanity, and went obediently to the cross (Phil. 2:3–8).[96] Moreover, reflection on the fact that Christ suffered and died on their behalf will compel (*synechō,* "press together," "constrain") Christians to live the rest of their lives for the good of others (2 Cor. 5:14–15). Clearly, then, one outcome of Christ's death is the stimulus to moral action it affords Christians. Yet in every instance where Christ's death is presented as an example to be followed, the fundamental truth of his death as a substitutionary sacrifice for sin is also present.

An important Pauline text on the atonement, Romans 3:21–26, deserves special consideration. The central idea of this passage is how God justifies or declares righteous both Jews and Gentiles. The apostle begins by considering the *manifestation* of justification (vv. 21–23). "But now a righteousness from God [*dikaiosynē theou*] . . . has been made known" (v. 21). The righteousness that Paul contemplates (thirty-five times in Romans and twenty-four times elsewhere) is the legal status of right-standing with God. Cranfield observes that *dikaiosynē* signifies "a status of righteousness before God, which is God's gift."[97] This righteousness is (1) conferred independently of law-keeping (v. 21a), (2) attested to by the Old Testament (v. 21b), and (3) appropriated by faith in Jesus Christ (v. 22).

Second, Paul considers the *means* of justification by faith (vv. 24–25), which is given in two word-pictures. The first is the imagery of redemption: both Jews and Gentiles "are justified freely by his grace through the redemption [*apolytrōsis*] that came by Christ Jesus" (v. 24). The noun *apolytrōsis* speaks of the liberation or emancipation that occurs through payment of an appropriate price.[98] The second word-picture is that of propitiation: "God presented him as a sacrifice of atonement [*hilastērion*], through faith in his blood" (v. 25). The meaning of *hilastērion* in this verse has been widely debated. Authorities such as Dodd, Von Rad, Richardson, and the RSV interpret *hilastērion* subjectively and translate it "expiation"—that is, as the cleansing of sin. Others such as F. F. Bruce, guided by the LXX where *kappōret* is frequently rendered by *hilastērion,* translates the word as "mercy seat," the golden cover of the ark where atonement was made. Still other authorities translate *hilastērion* as "propitiatory sacrifice" and interpret it as the self-oblation of Christ that placates the divine wrath and purges sin from the conscience.[99] The third interpretation satisfies the greatest amount of data with the least number of difficulties. Thus (1) in the Greek world *hilastērion* meant to placate the anger of an offended person or god; (2) the LXX has the verb *exhilaskomai* in several places (Zech. 7:2; 8:22; Mal. 1:9) in the sense of appeasing God; (3) in the Old Testament the verb is never used with sin as its object; (4) the *hilas-* word group often occurs in the context of the divine wrath (Rom. 3:5; 5:9); and (5) in the LXX when *hilastērion* connotes mercy seat it always has the article. In summary, when Paul describes the work of Christ he utilizes the language of the law court ("justified"), the slave market ("redemption"), and the temple ("propitiatory sacrifice").[100]

Finally, Paul refers to the *rationale* of justification (3:26): God "did it . . . so as to be just and the one who justifies the man who has faith in Jesus." By giving Jesus as a vicarious sacrifice, God was able (1) to remain true to his holy nature, which cannot overlook sin; (2) to uphold his law, which stipulates that sin be punished by death; and (3) mercifully to acquit sinners, who were deserving of death.

The preceding discussion of Christ's death as a substitutionary offering and Passover sacrifice that ransoms, redeems, and reconciles sinners to God clearly attests his completed priestly work as victim.

Concerning the intent of Christ's death, Paul indicates a twofold purpose in the cross, when he writes of "the living God, who is the Savior of all men, and especially [*malista*] of those who believe" (1 Tim. 4:10). Arguing from the universal to the particular (cf. Gal. 6:10; Phil. 4:22), the apostle indicates that the atonement conveys general benefits to all persons in the present and special benefits to believers both in the present and in the future (cf. "the present life and the life to come" [1 Tim. 4:8]). God is the Savior of all persons here and now in the sense that he preserves them in existence, provides them with the blessings of common grace, delays the execution of his judgment, removes every obstacle from his side to the pardon of repentant sinners, and provides salvation for those who die in infancy. He is the Savior of believers in the specifically redemptive sense that he ransoms, redeems, and reconciles such persons to himself.

Given this twofold purpose in the atonement, Paul sometimes refers to the universal dimension of the cross. Thus he writes of "the man Christ Jesus, who gave himself as a ransom for all men [*hyper pantōn*]" (1 Tim. 2:6). That this phrase refers to all persons and not merely to the elect is clear from verse 2, where the *hyper pantōn* includes kings and rulers. Paul's statement in verse 4 that God "wants [*thelei*] all men to be saved and to come to a knowledge of the truth," signifies God's will of desire that may be sinfully violated. On the other hand, Paul may have written these words with an eye to Gnostic teaching that viewed enlightenment or salvation as the privilege of a spiritual elite. Paul's statement "For the grace of God has appeared, bringing salvation to all men" (Titus 2:11, NASB), may support the universal dimension of the atonement, though the phrase "all men" may signify "all classes of people," given the discussion of men and women, slaves and free in the preceding context (cf. Acts 2:17; 9:35).

On the other hand, the apostle clearly affirms a special, salvific intention in the cross. Urging husbands to love their wives, Paul states that "Christ loved the church and gave himself up for her" (Eph. 5:25). Just as a man may love other people generally but his wife supremely, so Christ loves humankind with one degree of affection and his people with a still deeper measure of love. In the same category is 2 Corinthians 5:14–15. The "all" for whom Christ died are all believers who, in becoming Christians, died to their old nature and became united with Christ.

Johannine Literature

By means of several pregnant metaphors the fourth gospel presents Jesus' death as a substitutionary sacrifice for sins. Thus John the Baptist said of Jesus, "Look, the Lamb of God, who takes away the sin of the world!" (John 1:29; cf. v. 36). "Lamb" (*amnos*) signifies the animal used as a sacrificial offering and likely recollects the lamb of Isaiah 53:7 as well as the Paschal lamb, for the Passover feast was near at hand when the Baptist spoke these words (John 2:13). In the Apocalypse Christ is represented as a Lamb (*arnion*) twenty-seven times (Rev. 6:16; 7:10; 12:11; 13:8; et al.). There the Lamb takes his place on the throne of God, executes the eschatological judgment, and is worshiped. Nevertheless, he is the Lamb that was slain (5:6, 9, 12; 13:8). By representing Christ as *arnion,* Revelation indicates that the victorious Lord is also the Christ crucified for sins. "The judge of all the earth is he who died for us, and even as sovereign Lord he still bears the marks of his passion."[101] Furthermore, Jesus describes himself as "the bread of God" (John 6:33) or the "bread of life" (vv. 35, 48). In the context of his speaking about the manna given to Israel in the desert (vv. 31, 49), Jesus indicates that he is the spiritual food that sustains eternal life. Jesus' words "This bread is my flesh which I will give for [*hyper*] the life of the world" (v. 51), connote that the eternal life offered to the Jews would be secured by the sacrifice of himself. Jesus also described his work in terms of the metaphor of the shepherd: "The good shepherd lays down his life for [*hyper*] the sheep" (John 10:11; cf. v. 15). Of his own accord and in full obedience to the Father, Jesus surrendered his life on behalf of others. On the cross Jesus gave demonstration to the truth of John 15:13: "Greater love has no one than this, that one lay down his life for [*hyper*] his friends."

Caiaphas uttered prophetic truth to the Sanhedrin when he said, "You do not realize that it is better for you that one man die for [*hyper*] the people than that the whole nation perish" (John 11:50). Caiaphas viewed Jesus' death as a matter of political expediency, but John interpreted this unwitting prophecy in terms of Jesus' vicarious death for both Jews and Gentiles (vv. 51–52). John further explicates the theological significance of Christ's death by affirming that he is "the propitiation for our sins" (*hilasmos peri tōn hamartiōn hēmōn* [1 John 2:2; 4:10, NASB]). *Hilasmos,* like *hilastērion* discussed above, connotes "propitiatory sacrifice" and indicates that Christ's death appeased God's anger toward sin and changed his attitude vis-à-vis sinners from displeasure to favor. Thus, "By the *advocacy* of Christ (*paraklētos*) God is *propitiated (hilasmos)* and we are *reconciled to him (katallagē)*."[102]

In addition to writing of the vicarious sacrifice that propitiates God and effects reconciliation, John cites other implications of Christ's death. Christ's blood functions as the ransom price that purchased sinners for God (Rev. 5:9). Moreover, his sacrificial death frees believers from bondage to sin (John 8:36; Rev. 1:5). Through his work on the cross Christ overcame Satan's tyranny and destroyed his evil work (John 12:31; 1 John 3:8; Rev. 12:11). In addition, the blood of Jesus purifies lives from the defilements of sin (1 John 1:7; Rev. 7:14). And finally, John saw in Jesus' life and death the ultimate pattern of self-sacrificing love (John 15:12; 1 John 3:16).

John 3:16 affirms that God's love for sinners moved him to give his Son as a free gift to the world. At one level God's love embraces all humanity. John twice designated Jesus "the Savior of the world" (John 4:42; 1 John 4:14). The Samaritans expressed the hope, later confirmed by John, that the Messiah would be given not for the Jews alone but for the benefit of the entire world. It is important to note that " 'Savior' covers all aspects of Christ's work for men, and 'world' the totality of mankind."[103] John's statement in 1 John 2:2 (NASB) about Jesus being "the propitiation for our sins; and not for ours only, but also for those of the whole world," should be understood with the preceding texts. "The propitiation that has availed to wipe out their [i.e., the believers'] sins is sufficient to do the same for all. Jesus is 'the general Savior of mankind' as well as the particular Savior of each believer."[104] Concerning the Baptist's saying in John 1:29, "Look, the Lamb of God, who takes away the sin of the world!" the word *kosmos* does not necessarily denote every person on earth (1:10; 6:33; 12:19; 17:14; 1 John 5:19). The text indicates that the Lamb will expiate the sins of persons without regard to nationality or race.

The specifically redemptive dimension of Christ's death is evident in John 10, where Jesus states that he lays down his life for "the sheep" (*ta probata,* vv. 11, 15). The sheep are those given to Jesus by the Father (v. 29); they recognize Jesus' voice and follow him (v. 27), and to them the Son gives eternal life (v. 28). "In John *probaton* denotes Christ's elect people, 'his own.' "[105] Jesus died to bring these to God. Moreover, in his high priestly prayer Jesus prays not for the world but for those the Father has given him out of the world (17:6, 9). Elsewhere in Scripture Jesus or the Holy Spirit intercedes especially for believers (Rom. 8:26–27, 34; Heb. 7:25; 1 John 2:1). Hebrews clearly teaches that Christ's self-oblation and intercession represent the two principal components of his high priestly ministry. For those for whom Christ redemptively died he intercedes. Thus specifically Christ exercises his priestly ministry on behalf of believers. John confirms this conclusion in 1 John 3:5: "You know that he appeared so that he might take away our sins;" here *tas hamartias* plainly refers to the sins of believers.

Other New Testament Literature

The central section of Hebrews develops the work of Christ under the rubric of high priest. Hebrews 4:14–5:10 and 7:1–28 argue the superiority of Christ's *priesthood* to that of the Levitical order. Thus God appointed Aaron high priest over Israel to offer gifts and sacrifices for sins (5:1–4). Aaron's priesthood, however, was not perfect, for he first had to offer sacrifices for his own sins and he had to repeat the sacrifices year after year. Consequently by an irrevocable oath God appointed his own sinless Son (Heb. 4:15; 7:26) to be high priest of a radically new sacerdotal order typified by Melchizedek, the godly priest-king of Salem (5:5–10). This "king of righteousness" and "king of peace" exercised a priesthood that was superior to that of the Aaronic order (7:1–10) for several reasons: (1) Abraham, the ancestor of Levi, paid tithes to Melchizedek; (2) Melchizedek blessed the patriarch Abraham; and (3) Melchizedek "lives on" (NASB), whereas the Levitical priests all succumbed to death.

Hebrews proceeds to argue that Jesus' singular self-*sacrifice* was superior to the repeated offerings of the Jewish priests. The sacrifices offered by the Aaronic high priest on the Day of Atonement, effecting only ceremonial cleansing, failed to purge the inner life of the worshipers: "It is impossible for the blood of bulls and goats to take away sins" (10:4; cf. 9:9). The Day of Atonement ritual was not meaningless but served as a "shadow" (8:5) or type of the perfect sacrifice of Christ. Faithful to the will of God, Jesus our "great high priest" (4:14) surrendered his life and shed his blood once-for-all as the truly efficacious sacrifice (10:5–10, 12; 7:27; 9:26, 28). The writer thus adds, "We have been made holy through the sacrifice of the body of Jesus Christ once for all" (Heb. 10:10).

Guided by the suffering-Servant imagery of Isaiah 53, Peter likewise upheld Christ's substitutionary sacrifice: "He himself bore our sins in his body on the tree" (1 Peter 2:24), and "Christ died for sins once for all, the righteous for the unrighteous" (*dikaios hyper adikōn,* 1 Peter 3:18). The perfect sacrifice of the body of Christ on Calvary purges sins (Heb. 1:3; 9:26, 28), expiates the guilt of sin (*eis to hilaskesthai tas hamartias,* 2:17), obtains divine forgiveness (9:22; 10:18), and restores sinners to fellowship with God (1 Peter 3:18). Hebrews adds that Christ's sacrifice on the cross destroyed death and the Devil (2:14) and liberates sinners from the grip of sin and Satan (2:15; 9:15; cf. 1 Peter 1:18). The second aspect of Christ's high-priestly work emphasized by Hebrews, his ministry of intercession, will be examined in chapter 8.

Although the primary emphasis of Hebrews and the Petrine letters is on the propitiatory and expiatory worth of Christ's death, both uphold the exemplary value of Christ's death for the believer. Peter reminds persecuted Christians, "Christ suffered for you, leaving you an example, that you should follow in his steps" (1 Peter 2:21; cf. 4:1–2). And the writer of Hebrews urged his readers: "Let us fix our eyes on Jesus, . . . who for the joy set before him endured the cross, scorning its shame, and sat down at the right hand of the throne of God" (Heb. 12:2).

Concerning the design of the atonement, Peter writes of false prophets and teachers who "secretly introduce destructive heresies, even denying the sovereign Lord [*despotēs*] who bought them" (2 Peter 2:1). As we have seen, in its figurative use *agorazō* means to purchase or ransom from the slave market of sin (1 Cor. 6:20; 7:23; Rev. 5:9). The probable interpretation of this text is that Peter judges the prophets on the basis of their own Christian profession, and so describes them as those who have been "bought" by Christ.[106] Second Peter 2:2 suggests that these have denied their Master and Lord by blatant immorality—Peter's word is *aselgeia* (cf. 1 Peter 4:3; 2 Peter 2:7, 18; Jude 4), which means "repeated habitual acts of lasciviousness."[107] The way Peter describes the false teachers (vv. 12, 17, 19) and the fact that tney faced certain judgment (vv. 1, 3, 12) suggests that, although professing Christians, they were unregenerate. "These false teachers professed the name of Christ. . . . They made it known that Jesus had bought them, but they eventually rejected Christ and left the Christian communitiyy.[108] Thus Peter does not suggest that Christ's ransom work applies to all people.

The writer of Hebrews affirms that the end or purpose of Christ's incarnation and passion was that "by the grace of God he might taste death for everyone" (*hyper pantos,* Heb. 2:9). When expressing an advantage that accrues to a person, *hyper* usually means "for the benefit of."[109] Thus the writer affirms that in the broadest, nonredemptive sense Christ's humiliation and death avails for every person.

The "Descent of Christ Into Hell"

Some interpret Psalm 16:10—"you will not abandon me [*nepeš*] to the grave [*šᵉʾôl*], nor will you let your Holy One see corruption [*šāḥat*]"—as the conviction that God would rescue Jesus' soul from hell, to which it had descended between his death and resurrection. But as we saw in chapter 11, *nepeš* frequently means the entire person. Moreover, the word *šᵉʾôl* commonly denotes the grave (Gen. 37:35; 1 Sam. 2:6; Pss. 6:5; 30:3, et al.).[110] Thus the immediate focus of the text is that God would deliver David's life from the peril of death. But prophetically (cf. Acts 2:31) it means that God would deliver the Messiah from death at the resurrection, and that his body would not decompose in the grave (note the Hebrew parallelism between the two lines of the verse).

Others cite Matthew 12:40 as proof of Christ's descent to hell between his death and resurrection: "For as Jonah was three days and three nights in the belly of a huge fish, so the Son of Man will be three days and three nights in the heart of the earth." The figurative phrase "in the heart of the earth" (*en tē kardia tēs gēs*) was prompted by the language of the Jonah story (Jonah 2:2–3). It is highly probable that " 'the heart of the earth' is not *hades,* but the grave."[111] Thus this text affirms only that Jesus to the Hebrew mind was in the grave three days and three nights.

Matthew 27:52–53 is more perplexing. The most satisfactory interpretation appears to be that the earthquake that followed Christ's death and broke open the tombs reminded Matthew of the eschatological judgment that would occur at the resurrection of the dead. From such a perspective, following Jesus' resurrection the saints rose from the grave and entered the holy city to be reunited with believers who had gone before. "The point being made is clear: with Christ the general resurrection has begun; the power of death is now vanquished."[112] The liberation of deceased saints from the netherworld as a result of the preaching of Christ appears not to be taught by this text.

Paul's main point in Ephesians 4:8–10 is that at his ascension Christ gave spiritual gifts to his church. The "captives" Christ led in his train at his exaltation are the hostile powers he defeated at the cross (cf. Col. 2:15). After mentioning Christ's ascent Paul cites the Savior's descent in order to make the point that Christ is Lord over heaven and earth and thus is competent to give gifts to believers. The phrase "descended to the lower, earthly regions" (*eis ta katōtera merē tēs gēs*, v. 9) involves an appositive genitive and should read: "descended to the lower regions, that is, the earth."[113] Thus Paul reflects awareness of the *katabasis-anabasis* (incarnation-exaltation) motif commonplace in the early church.

On balance 1 Peter 3:18–20 does not support a mission of Christ in hades. "The spirits in prison" (v. 19) are neither Old Testament saints nor fallen angels but unbelievers now deceased (cf. 1 Peter 4:6). The message Christ preached was neither the victory of his resurrection, nor final condemnation, but an appeal for repentance. And Christ preached not between his death and resurrection but during the time of Noah. The sense of the passage is as follows: Christ, in the realm of the Spirit, preached repentance through Noah while God patiently waited during the building of the ark. Christ preached to human spirits, who in the intermediate state are now in prison (hell) because of disobedience and godlessness. This interpretation fits the purpose of the context (1 Peter 3:13–22), which encourages the suffering minority, like Noah, to bear courageous witness to a hostile, unbelieving world (especially 3:15–16; cf. 2:12).[114]

Others appeal to 1 Peter 4:6 as support for the *descensus ad inferna*. The context focuses on the inevitable persecution that Christians scattered throughout the Roman Empire had to face. Mention of the preaching of the gospel to the *nekroi* is best understood as proclamation to those who had heard the message, who believed, and who subsequently died. Opponents of Christianity objected that the faith of these believers availed for naught, since they died just as unbelievers do. Peter responds to this challenge by affirming that from a human point of view (*kata anthrōpous*) the deceased believers appear to have been judged in the body for their sins, but from the divine point of view (*kata theon*) they live eternally in the Spirit.

Our study of the preceding texts leads to the conclusion that an alleged descent by Christ into hell to preach the gospel either to the unsaved or to Old Testament saints rests on slender evidence and ought not be pressed as certain dogma.

SYSTEMATIC FORMULATION

The previous gathering of the biblical data has exhibited the substantial unity in a diversity of teaching genre on atonement throughout the centuries and in varied cultures in the progress of special revelation. We now attempt to formulate a systematic and normative statement for the present by incorporating biblically supported elements from the historical views and by seeking to avoid their weaknesses.

Humanity's Radical Need

Understanding of Christ's atonement as the basic prescription for human need requires a grasp of the *radical diagnosis* of the human predicament. If diagnoses of the human plight are environmental, the prescriptions for their improvement will start with changing structures in the surrounding society. Many diagnoses trace the human predicament to "fallout" from technology, economic or political structures (capitalist, socialist, or communist), religious institutions, or psychological conditioning by them. But we have found that humans personally are responsible agents. God's creative image-bearers can respond in different ways to the same situation. Environments occasion moral conduct but do not determine humanity's moral nature.

The deepest issues of life are from within, since *all humans are inherently disposed to evil.* In all cultural contexts the most deeply rooted issues are whether our inner attitudes and behavior are just and loving before God and neighbor. In any situation the most profound issues have to do with a self-determining person's moral integrity and spiritual faithfulness to the purposes of the God of Scripture. While all religions find something wrong between humankind and a "higher power," not all grasp the seriousness of each person's plight before the transcendent, righteous God of Scripture, who judges without respect of a persons's economic, social, or political status.

Our innate moral plight is real. It is no illusion that we have corrupted our own natures, exploited the limited resources of nature, alienated ourselves from different races, and abused every type of economic structure. In all of this and more we have been unfaithful to our Creator and Sustainer, his incarnate Son, and his written Word. The One responsible for the moral order of the universe operates according to nonnegotiable principles of justice. By his moral principles the best of us come far short of being all that we ought to be.

People who forget about the reality of our plight may ask, "Could not a loving God simply forget about our sin?" Since God is both knowledgeable and responsible, God cannot deny the reality of humanity's perversity with its tragic consequences. The absolutely just and honest One cannot tamper with the actual evidence. We humans have more than guilt feelings, we have *real guilt* before God. Repeatedly in offending others we have offended the Most High. We have violated the justice and spurned the love of the source and support of all values. We have rejected their disclosure in our hearts and in the Scriptures. Beyond that, we have despised his incarnate Son. God's integrity does not permit him to call our moral evil "good."

Our endemic moral affliction is *humanly incurable*. We cannot transform our own natures. In our insolent rebellion we are unable to (1) provide a basis on which God can forgive us while he remains honest and just, (2) liberate ourselves from our fallen propensities to corrupting ourselves and others, (3) reconcile ourselves to God's fellowship, or (4) restore peace to all the cosmos. Nothing fallen humans can do personally, educationally, socially, economically, politically, or religiously is sufficient to attain perfect righteousness and peace (Rom. 10:1–3).

Will the Father not receive us if we just return like the prodigal son? Interpretations of the parable of the prodigal son should emphasize its primary purpose. In context (along with the parables of the lost sheep and the lost coin) the parable of the lost son primarily teaches rejoicing in heaven over one sinner who repents (see Luke 15:7, 10, 24, 32). It does not teach the grounds on which the heavenly Father can justly accept sinners in his holy presence. Hermeneutically it is unwise to base one's doctrine and hope of salvation on one parable, and it may be disastrous to rest one's eternal destiny on a parable given for a different purpose. A much sounder approach considers the numerous, extensive didactic passages on depravity (and the fact that no holistically depraved people do in fact on their own return to God) and on the necessity of the atoning work of Christ. God himself cannot welcome sinners back in a way that leaves them under condemnation, in bondage to evil, and estranged from his fellowship. The Creator's original purposes, glory, name, honor, justice, and love must be vindicated. The faithfulness of God's written Word concerning sin's consequences must be upheld: "The soul who sins is the one who will die" (Ezek. 18:4, 20; Rom. 6:23). The parable of the prodigal son illustrates the point that when any sinner repents and trusts the Savior, the Father celebrates in heaven and elder sons should rejoice on earth! It does not teach the basis on which the Father can remain just and justify the ungodly.

The basic human plight, apart from God's grace, is terminal. By violating the principles that make meaningful life possible for God's image-bearers, we have forfeited the right to life. Receiving what we deserve, all fallen people equally receive the sentence of death (Rom. 6:23)—physical, spiritual, and eternal. In sheer mercy, however, the divine Judge has freely chosen to postpone deserved punishment. It is "because of the LORD's great love we are not consumed" (Lam. 3:22).

The Just and Loving Divine Initiative

By sheer grace the heavenly Father took the initiative in unfathomable love to send his unique Son (John 6:39), and in love the Son became human to pay the just penalty for the lost (Luke 19:10). God's just and loving initiative on behalf of sinners has been illustrated by the story of two classmates who graduated from law school. One used his knowledge of law to get around it and became a noted criminal. The other used his mastery of law to support it as an attorney and later as a judge. One day the two classmates met in court. Because of their earlier acquaintance the judge was tempted to pronounce the lightest sentence possible. Instead, he decreed that his guilty former classmate must pay the highest possible fine for the offense he had committed. To the further amazement of the court, the judge stepped down from behind the bench, embraced his law-school friend, and paid the criminal's fine in full. In a far greater way than this, the Judge of the world, whose moral law was constantly violated, found us guilty and pronounced the just sentence of death. Then, leaving heaven, the Son became a man, lived without sin, and paid in full the inestimable penalty for our sins. To demonstrate how he remains just while justifying the ungodly who believe, the Father sent the Son as a sacrifice of atonement (Rom. 3:25–26). The Judge who found us guilty came in the person of his own Son to atone for our sins.

What motivated such a marvelous satisfaction of justice? The *primary motives* of the atonement were to satisfy justice and to redeem undeserving sinners in self-giving (*agapē*) *love*. Because God is just and loving, all of his providential and covenant activities are just and loving. But in the supreme manifestation of divine justice and love, "God so loved the world that he gave his one and only Son" (John 3:16). God the Father does not love us because Christ died for us, but Christ died for us because God the Father loved us (Rom. 5:6–8; 1 John 4:9–10). Out of self-giving love the Son came into history by the power of the Holy Spirit and died, satisfying justice for our sins according to the Father's eternal purpose (2 Cor. 5:14–15; Eph. 3:11).

The cross fulfilled the loving purpose the three divine persons had designed in their *eternal covenant* with its immutable promises justly to save sinners. God revealed that eternal covenant of just love in different ways to different people: to Eve, Noah, Abraham, Moses, David, Isaiah, and others prior to Christ's incarnation and death. Without the giving of a life (the shedding of blood) for a forfeited life, amnesty is not just (Heb. 9:22). The Old Testament versions of the covenant as revealed to Moses required the offering of animal sacrifices and ceremonies. Even though

God's repentant people offered sacrifices with faith in the messianic promises available at their point in the progress of revelation, we have the Mediator of a new (outworking of the eternal) covenant (v. 15). After Christ's crucifixion believers do not need repeated animal sacrifices, for our sins are remembered no more (10:17–18). Indeed the news concerning Christ's death signifies a better covenant based on better promises (8:6). "The 'covenants of the promise' (Eph. 2:12) are God's guarantees that he will provide salvation in spite of man's inability to keep his side of the agreement."[115]

Christ Died Willingly

From the beginning Jesus anticipated the sacrifice of his life for sinful people. In his death he was not a helpless victim of a political upheaval or a mere miscarriage of justice in the courts. He chose to give up the glory of heaven (Phil. 2:6–8) and come into the world as the Lamb of God (John 1:29). He identified himself with human "flesh and blood" (Heb. 2:14), human conditions (v. 17), and human sufferings (v. 10). After Peter confessed the deity of Jesus (Mark 8:29), Jesus spoke plainly and repeatedly of his coming suffering, death, and resurrection (vv. 31–32; 9:31; 10:32–34). He would "give his life a ransom for many" (Mark 10:45). Jesus determined also the time of his death. Earlier he had avoided enemies to prevent death from happening prematurely. Later he hastened events so that his self-sacrifice occurred on the day the paschal lamb was offered. Christ, not Judas, was Lord. To Pilate he said, "You would have no power over me if it were not given to you from above" (John 19:11). On the cross Jesus remained Lord of hatred, praying for the forgiveness of his tormentors. Jesus chose the place, time, and manner of his death. Even in the giving of his life, Jesus was not a victim, but the victor.

Because Jesus purposefully gave up his life, his death cannot be blamed ultimately on either Jews or Gentiles. Proximately, however, both Jews and Gentiles as depraved sinners evoked his death. It was not just Jews who cried out, "Crucify him!" Both Gentiles and Jews opposed Jesus. So Peter and John prayed, "Indeed Herod and Pontius Pilate met together with the Gentiles and the people of Israel in this city to conspire against your holy servant Jesus, whom you anointed" (Acts 4:27).

The Messiah Died Physically and Spiritually

Questioning people sometimes ask, if God died, how did the world survive without him for three days? The Messiah's death did not mean his annihilation. "Death" designates, not annihilation, but separation. Separations occurred in at least two senses. First, Jesus *died physically* as his spirit was separated from his body. "The body without the spirit is dead" (James 2:26). Jesus' body was buried and his "unclothed" spirit or soul waited for the resurrection of his body. Before giving up his spirit, Jesus suffered one of the most agonizing forms of physical death.

Second, the Son *died spiritually* by being separated from the Father's fellowship. Relationally the Father and Son had enjoyed unbroken fellowship from before creation. But as Jesus bore the guilt and penalty of the world's sin, he suffered far more than physical pain. Suffering the anguish of alienation and estrangement from the Father, he cried, "My God, My God, why have you forsaken me?" (Matt. 27:46). Under the wrath of God upon all our sins he was crushed like grapes in the winepress. He experienced the hell we should have experienced. Although from the biblical evidence it is not probable that he literally descended into hell, Jesus experienced the hell of God-forsakenness and divine wrath for the sins of the world.

Jesus Could Die for Others Because He Was Sinless

Neither the life nor the death of Jesus can be understood apart from each other. The early Eastern theologians and recent relational thinkers associate the redemptive activity of our Lord with the totality of the incarnation, treating the cross as one element within it. The Western theologians increasingly emphasized the cross, almost dissociating the death of Jesus from his life. The death and the life of Christ are inseparably related. If Jesus had not actively and fully obeyed the Father's will and lived a holy life, he would have had to die for his own sins. His perfect keeping of God's law (active obedience) throughout his life enabled him to offer the perfect sacrifice (in passive obedience) on the cross.

In a sense the entirety of Jesus' life was lived for us. "Through the whole of Christ's life there ran an element of infinite humiliation, especially in his death. Every act, therefore, was in one aspect an item of vicarious suffering, and in another aspect, an item of vicarious obedience to the will of his Father."[116] From the beginning the pattern of the cross was evident in the presence of his willingness to have himself "made nothing" (*kenosis*, Phil. 2:7). And the full significance of dying to temptations reaches its consummate height at Calvary. Attempts of some thinkers to give priority to the incarnation rather than to the atonement do not account as coherently for the evidence. James Denney explained, "It is the atonement which explains the incarnation: the incarnation takes place in order that the sin of the world may be put away by the offering of the body of Jesus Christ."[117]

Christ Died in Our Place as a Sacrifice

Early in written revelation God taught sinners the need for a substitutionary *sacrifice*. "For the life of a creature is in the blood, . . . it is the blood that makes atonement for one's life" (Lev. 17:11). As the the high priest offered the blood of a healthy lamb on the altar, one life was given in place of another life. These animal sacrifices were temporary object lessons typologically illustrating the coming work of the Messiah. At the annual celebration of the Passover the Judge and Savior were the same person. Salvation was by substitution of a firstborn lamb, and the lamb's blood had to be sprinkled, indicating a personal appropriation of the divine provision. Similarly, on the annual Day of Atonement, the high priest offered two goats. One was sacrificed, and the blood sprinkled in the usual way. On the living goat's head the priest was to lay both his hands and confess over it all the wickedness and rebellion of the Israelites. It would carry all their sins to a solitary place in the desert (Lev. 16:21–22).

The sacrifices were both *representative* and also *substitutionary*. "*A representative* is one who acts on behalf of another, in such a way as to involve the other in his action. A '*substitute*' is one who acts in place of another in such a way as to render the other's action unnecessary."[118] The Christ serves as our legal representative as a result of the eternal covenant of grace or plan of salvation. The implications of Christ's representation are considered below in the "Relevance for Life and Ministry" section. If an instructor has a substitute taking the classes for her, she does not teach those classes. Since the biblical evidence indicates that Christ as the sinners' substitute received the sinners' guilt and penalty, believers do not experience them. The penalty for an infraction cannot justly be demanded twice.

As Isaiah foresaw, the suffering servant "took up our infirmities and carried our sorrows, . . . was pierced for our transgressions, crushed for our iniquities; the punishment that brought us peace was upon him, and by his wounds we are healed. We all, like sheep, have gone astray, each of us has turned to his own way; and the LORD has laid on him the iniquity of us all" (Isa. 53:4–6). Emphatically the servant's suffering is "punishment for the sins of others."[119] "It is clear from the Old Testament usage," John R. W. Stott concludes, "that to 'bear sin' means neither to sympathize with sinners, nor to identify with their pain, nor to express their penitence, nor to be persecuted on account of human sinfulness (as others have argued), nor even to suffer the consequences of sin in personal and social terms, but specifically to endure its penal consequences, to undergo its penalty."[120]

The New Testament frequently shows how Jesus fulfilled the teaching of Isaiah 53. In numerous other ways the New Testament brings out the fact that vicariously Christ accepted our guilt and suffered our penalty. Explicit passages make clear that "one died for all" (2 Cor. 5:14; Heb. 9:28; 1 Peter 2:24). The preposition "instead of" (*anti*) "always has the idea of equivalence, substitution or exchange present; it *never* has the more general meaning 'on behalf of, for the sake of' (see Matt. 20:28; Mark 10:45)."[121] Christ did more than represent our guilt and penalty, he received them. Hence believers need not live under a sense of legal guilt or experience sin's deserved penalty.

The preposition "for" or "over" (*hyper*) "*may* and often *does* include the stricter idea 'instead of' and if the context warrants, we may so understand it."[122] The substitutionary significance of *hyper* is clear in the context of Galatians 3:10–13. At a class in New York City, Greek scholar A. T. Robertson found the message of the cross in three prepositions: (1) All who rely on observing the law are *under* (*hypo*) a curse (Gal. 3:10). Robertson likened that to being under Damocles' sword hanging by a thread. (2) Jesus became a curse *for* (*hyper*) us (v. 13). As the sword of divine judgment dropped, Jesus interposed his body "over" or "in place of" ours, and the sword fell on him instead of on sinners. (3) So Jesus redeemed believers *from* (*ek*) the curse of the law (v. 13). He died that believers might live "out from in under" the law that can only condemn because of the weakness of our natures.[123]

Additional *illustrations* of substitution may help. During the civil war substitutes volunteered to fight in the place of those drafted for service. In the National Football League a substitute plays in place of another team member. In January 1975 a judge in Cleveland, Ohio, sentenced a young lady to three days in jail for possession of an unregistered gun. According to the Associated Press report, her boyfriend accepted the sentence for her because, he said, "a jail is not a good place for a lady." According to the judge, such substitutionary bearing of punishment was "unusual but legal." The young lady did not go to jail.[124] At Auschwitz, in June 1941, because a prisoner had escaped, a Nazi officer sentenced ten men to death by starvation. When Polish Sergeant Gajowniczek heard his name, he screamed that he wanted to see his wife and children. Then suddenly Father Kolbe stepped forward and offered to take the place of the man with a family. Annually Frank Gajowniczek places a wreath at Auschwitz where the Franciscan monk died in his place.[125]

Several *questions* about Christ's substitutionary sacrifice may arise. Did Jesus suffer exactly the same kind of punishment all sinners must have suffered? If different in kind, was his penalty equal in amount? If less in amount, did he suffer an equivalent punishment? Did he suffer the torment of the finally lost? In what sense was his punishment eternal? Some have scoffed, "How could a week-end of suffering atone for the sins of the entire human population?"

Questions like these may assume quantitative similarities based on analogies to *fair commercial transactions.* In a commercial setting satisfaction of justice requires payment of the same thing or something of equivalent value quantitatively. Clearly Christ did not suffer on the cross as long as humans have sinned. Neither did he suffer separate blows for each of the billions of humans' sins. His ransom cannot be measured quantitatively. But if a commercial analogy is demanded, we remind people of the infinite value of the God-man's sacrifice of himself. The unlimited significance of the Messiah's death is not worthy to be compared with the finite number of sins committed by finite persons.

The more frequent biblical analogy features a *just judicial transaction* in a criminal court. A convicted criminal usually satisfies the law in a way very different from that of the offense. So although Christ's penalty was quantitatively different from the offenses (in length of time), it entailed the same kind of anguish (separation from the Father). Christ's self-sacrifice satisfied the Administrator of Justice for several reasons. His death (1) had infinite value, (2) met all the demands of divine justice or moral law, (3) propitiated God's righteous indignation, (4) released believing slaves from moral evil, (5) reinforced divine honor, and (6) glorified the divine name by providing for the reconciliation of mankind to himself.

The concept of *substitution is essential* to all of the biblical analogies—passover sacrifice, ransom, redemption, propitiation, victory over Satan, and reconciliation. In each aspect of what Christ did, sinners united to him by faith cannot do for themselves. The divine substitute fully provided for sinners' liberation, forgiveness, and reconciliation. "So substitution is not 'a theory of the atonement.' Nor is it even an additional image to take its place as an option alongside the others. It is rather the essence of each image and the heart of the atonement itself."[126]

Jesus' substitutionary sacrifice completed the work of atonement "once for all" (Heb. 9:12, 25–28). What could be justly done for the salvation of sinners has been done in that unique and irrepeatable historical event. The crucifixion fulfilled all that was planned in and promised in the eternal covenant. The benefits of the cross are also everlasting. "By one sacrifice he has made perfect forever those who are being made holy" (10:10–14). As result of the completeness of that unique and irrepeatable event in history "there is no longer any sacrifice for sin" (10:18). No alleged merits from self-flagellation, penance, purgatory, fasting, praying, giving to the poor, inner-city service, preaching, teaching, evangelizing, parenting, or defending of country can add to Christ's complete provisions.

Having fulfilled the goals of the eternal covenant, the cross *completed the objective transaction* between two parties (the Father and the Son). "It is finished," Jesus declared (John 19:30). As covenanted, the crucified Messiah, so to speak, "signed in blood" his last will and testament, assuring an incorruptible, objective inheritance for its recipients. So a theology of the cross cannot limit itself to relational categories. To do justice to the cross, we need, in addition to a relational theology, a transactional theology. A transactional theology gives a better account of the objective content of covenants and promises conveyed by sentences and the historical completion of the atonement's provisions. What objective "provisions" were signed and sealed in the transaction at the cross?

Christ's Sacrifice Provides Forgiveness of Legal Guilt

In the first century Jesus Christ on the cross took upon himself our *moral guilt*. When the Bible speaks popularly of Christ "bearing sins," it refers to "sins," not as entities, but as standing for the sinners' moral guilt (by divine judgment).[127] When Jesus was "made sin," he willingly accepted our sentence of guilt. As Christ became a sacrificial lamb in our place, he assumed judicial liability for the fallenness of the human race. He willingly said, in effect, "Put the sinners' moral obligations to my account." In discussing sin in chapter 4 we considered the imputation of the legal consequences of Adam's sin to the race (Rom. 5:16, 18). The Scriptures also teach the imputation of the guilt of insolent humans to Christ on the cross (Isa. 53:6; 2 Cor. 5:14, 21; 1 Peter 2:24; 3:18).

On the cross Christ also experienced the *penalty* of our sin. He died in the place of sinners, so that they need not die. To reject substitution is to say that sinners can never be right with God. To put it bluntly, if Christ is not our vicarious sacrifice, we are still under condemnation. If our guilt was not transferred to him and he did not bear our penalty, we are destined to endless alienation from God and enslavement to our own fallen natures.

Because Christ's exchange for sinners is so complete, we can also say that in Christ *we died* to sin (Rom. 6:2). This carries over his legal representation of sinners from Romans 5. The legal significance is supported also by the fact that he died to sin's guilt (certainly not its power over him), and his once-for-all death (6:10) provides for our justification by faith from our sins' legal consequences (5:9). By faith "we were one with Christ in his obedience unto death, as we were one with Adam in his disobedience. Christ's death to sin belongs to us, and is as much ours as if we had borne the penalty."[128] So believers crucified with Christ now have the righteousness that comes from God, the righteousness of the obedient Christ, put to their account (2 Cor. 5:21). Justified by faith in the crucified Christ, believers face no condemnation (Rom. 8:1). But the Messiah's atonement provides more than forgiveness of legal guilt.

Christ's Sacrifice Provides Freedom From Enslaving Addictions

Because those in Christ legally died and were freed from sin, "we should no longer be slaves to sin" (Rom. 6:6–7). Christ paid a great *ransom* to free sinners also from the power of the slave markets of evil. It cost Christ his precious blood to set us free (1 Peter 1:18–19). Bought at such a precious price, the liberated no longer belong to themselves (1 Cor. 6:19–20). "With [his] blood [Christ] purchased men for God from every tribe and language and people and nation" (Rev. 5:9). His ransom was not a commercial transaction with the value paid to Satan; rather, it satisfied divine justice. Christ died to restore the divine image, renewing our abilities to know, love, and serve the transcendent God in creation.

Christ's death paid the inestimable price to free us from the dominion of temptations that come from the flesh, the world, and the Devil. Free from what specifically? Christ's *redemption* provides freedom from morally evil thoughts, attitudes, words, and behavior. Jesus did what the law could not do because of the weakness of our sinful natures—set us free from "the law of sin and death" (Rom. 8:1–4). He paid the awesome price that believers in any culture anywhere in the world would not be enslaved by inner desires of the old fleshly nature such as hypocrisy, covetousness, greed, sexual immorality, drunkenness, witchcraft, chauvinism, and racism. Christ also sacrificed himself that believers should no longer be dominated by pressures from external influences of "the present evil age" (Gal. 1:4), such as unjust business, political, or ecclesiastical pressures. We are freed by Christ, who stood against the world to take a stand against temptations from the powers of the world around us. "So if the Son sets you free, you will be free indeed" (John 8:36).

For what does Christ provide freedom from sin's power? He died that the liberated might build a loving, forgiving community. The Savior "loved the church and gave himself up for her to make her holy, cleansing her . . . and to present her to himself as a radiant church, without stain or wrinkle or any other blemish, but holy and blameless" (Eph. 5:26–27). Christ gave himself "to redeem us from all wickedness and to purify for himself a people that are his very own, eager to do what is good" (Titus 2:14). Those whom Christ rescued from the dominion of darkness are brought into the kingdom of the Son he loves (Col. 1:13) to help establish the rule of holy love on earth. Those legally Christ's are experientially no longer bad trees bringing forth bad fruit but good trees bringing forth good fruit (Matt. 7:17; 12:33–35).

Christ's Sacrifice Provides Victory Over Unholy Spirits

At the cross Christ won a dramatic victory over Satan, the demonic hosts, and their human dupes. The battle analogy for the cross fits the broader context of warfare between the two kingdoms. Conflict between God and Satan began on earth at the Fall and continues (Gen. 3:15). Satan attacked and tempted Christ from his birth to the cross. But what seemed like a victory for Satan turned out to be a triumph over him who holds the power of death (Heb. 2:14–15). Christ "gave himself for our sins to rescue us from the present evil age" (Gal. 1:4). On the cross Christ not only "disarmed the powers and authorities," but "made a public spectacle of them, triumphing over them" (Col. 2:13–15). Instead of meeting evil power with evil power, Christ overcame the powers of evil with good. In holy love Christ transformed history's greatest miscarriage of justice into its final fulfillment of justice. The decisive victory was confirmed by Christ's resurrection from the dead. Mopping-up operations continue until the Second Coming. Meanwhile in encounters with evil powers Christians can overcome Satan by the blood of the Lamb and the word of their testimony (Rev. 12:11).[129] Christ's first-century triumph over the forces of evil provides the base for believers to conquer them today.

Christ's Sacrifice Provides Propitiation and Reconciliation

The cross provides the just ground on which the Father's wrath can be pacified and fellowship restored. Sinners are separated from Christ, excluded from citizenship in Israel, and foreigners to the covenants of promise, without hope and without God in the world (Eph. 2:12). We deserved God's righteous indignation and divine wrath. "Why not wrath? What other possible attitude can God take toward evil and sin but righteous wrath?"[130] What else can a just and loving God do with sinners who, contrary to every benefit of grace, persistently delight in pride, injustice and hatred, but display his wrath (or as Scaer suggests, "give them hell")?[131]

Divine wrath must not be identified with petty jealousy, arbitrary vengeance, or other types of selfish vindictiveness. God's wrath is the reaction of his holy love against sin. Such righteous indignation is not the opposite of love; it is a part or aspect of faithful love.

> God's wrath is an integral constituent of his love. The wrath of God is the active manifestation of God's essential incapacity to be morally indifferent and let sin alone. It denotes the attitude of God in his holy love toward wilful sin. God's wrath is God's grace. It is his grace smitten with dreadful sorrow. It is his love in agony.[132]

Again, "In the total biblical portrayal, the wrath of God is not so much an emotion or an angry frame of mind as it is the settled opposition of his holiness to evil."[133]

How did Christ's death change the relationship between God and sinners? The cross provided for *propitiation* of God's wrath and reconciliation to God's fellowship. Propitiation is "the gracious provision made by God himself, whereby the effects of His righteous anger against sin may be averted and the sinner may receive the blessings of his paternal love without infringement of his holiness and moral government."[134] Because of the propitiatory provision of Christ's death, God can look upon believers without displeasure and believers can be reconciled to God. "God presented him [Christ] as a sacrifice of atonement [or propitiation] through faith in his blood" (Rom. 3:25).

Since God's wrath has been turned away, we can enjoy *reconciliation to God*. Christ not only removed wrath, but reconciled all things in heaven and earth, making peace through his blood shed on the cross (Col. 1:19). We who formerly feared God's wrath now rejoice in the Father's presence (Rom. 5:11). God does not impute our sins to us (2 Cor. 5:19); to believers he imputes Christ's righteousness (v. 21). "Once you were alienated from God and were enemies in your minds because of your evil behavior. But now he has reconciled you by Christ's physical body through death to present you holy in his sight, without blemish and free from accusation" (Col. 1:21–22). The reconciled ought not keep this good news to themselves! God committed to them the ministry of reconciliation (2 Cor. 5:18). So as Christ's ambassadors we implore sinners to be reconciled to God (v. 19–20).

Attempts to place the gospel emphasis on spiritual life of fellowship with God by sidestepping Christ's atonement have not sufficiently faced the varied consequences of sin, including continued alienation. It took the blood of Christ to unite Samaritans and Gentiles with Jews in the church. The way to spiritual life (fellowship with God) for sinners is through death. Through crucifixion with Christ to the old fleshly order of life, we receive the new order of life in love. Unless a grain of wheat falls into the ground and dies, it will not produce the fruit of spiritual life—fellowship with God.

Christ's Sacrifice Provides Reconciliation of Persons to One Another

Christ died also that believing sinners may enjoy also *reconciliation to each other*. Christ's sacrifice provides for a new community, a fellowship of sinners at peace with God and so at peace with one another. Because of the cross Samaritans and Gentiles could be united with Jews in Christ's body, the church. Having put to death their hostility, he made Jew and Gentile one, destroying the dividing wall by abolishing the law and giving both access to the Father by the Spirit (Eph. 2:14–18). At one time we were "uncircumcised, . . . separate from Christ, excluded from citizenship in Israel and foreigners to the covenants of promise, without hope and without God in the world" (vv. 11–12). "But now in Christ Jesus you who once were far away have been brought near through the blood of Christ." So he is "our peace" (v. 14). "Christ loved the church and gave himself up for her" (5:25). Commitment to life under the cross—not race nor economic status—reconciles sinners to one another. People living under the cross should not be expected to meet extraneous requirements for membership in a church.

Because they are forgiven by grace, church members seek to be graciously forgiving. Because they are liberated from the reign of sin (Rom. 6:12), God's people rejoice in making peace with others who have been reconciled to God through faith in Christ. The crucified Christ provides the one foundation on which to build a church (1 Cor. 3:10–15) because he bought the church of God "with his own blood" (Acts 20:28). Christian homes, churches, and organizations enjoy reconciliation and peace to the extent that they are just and loving communities. Families and churches respect members' dignity and rights, and lovingly families and churches go beyond justice in acts of mercy and love.

Christ's Sacrifice Provides for Future Cosmic Peace

Clearly believers do not now enjoy imperishable resurrection bodies, nor has nature been delivered from its thorns and thistles. Some of the provisions of the cross, such as counteracting the physical effects of sin with perfect bodies, await Christ's return. At the resurrection nature also will be "liberated from its bondage to decay" (Rom. 8:21, 23). Then Christ's atoning work will remove all the remaining consequences of sin on the race and the earth.

When the crucified and risen Christ returns, his mission of pacification will overcome Satan and his demonic powers. Our Lord will reconcile not only all things on earth but also "all things . . . in heaven" (Col. 1:20). In context that cannot mean, unfortunately, that every last individual will be in personal fellowship with God. The cosmic pacification Paul has in mind includes the reconciliation of believers and the disarming of unrepentant enemies of the cross (2:15). Having become impotent, the evil forces must submit to Christ's cosmic victory so that his peaceful purposes will be fully achieved.[135]

Atonement: A Multi-faceted Diamond

The above aspects of Christ's death are all encompassed in an integrative view of Christ's atonement. By the general term *atonement,* we refer primarily to the voluntary substitutionary sacrificial death of the divine-human Messiah to provide the just basis by which God could remain holy and restore peace by counteracting all the legal, experiential, relational, and cosmic effects of sin. Through faith in Christ's once-for-all substitutionary sacrifice, God can (1) acquit believers of their real guilt, (2) free them from domination by inherent tendencies to evil, (3) give them power to overcome evil principalities and powers, (4) reconcile believers to himself, and (5) reconcile them to one another. Future provisions of Christ's death and resurrection include (1) the provision of an incorruptible, resurrection body or the complete restoration of the divine likeness and (2) enjoyment of restored Edenic conditions in the millennium and in the new heavens and earth. The basis of such a rich salvation is not faith, but Christ's completed atonement. Faith is the means by which Christ's atoning provisions are personally received.

Illustrations of the atonement point up its different aspects. Analogies implied in biblical teaching refer to substitutionary sacrifice at an altar, acquittal in court, liberation from a slave market, victory on a battlefield, the embrace of reconciled enemies, the relationships of a new family, and inner peace. Thoughts about Christ's atonement are impoverished if they are limited to one of these models: sacrificial, judicial, experiential, or relational. Sin is not justly atoned for by a mere feeling of at-one-ment with the world or a mystical union with the cosmos. Sin is not sufficiently atoned for by a mere judicial decree of acquittal without personal reconciliation to God or experiential deliverance from bondage to unrighteousness. Neither is sin adequately atoned for by a mere liberation from the slave market of sin (in a battlefield of temptation) without divine forgiveness and reconciliation. An integrative concept of the atonement seeks to incorporate the biblically supported facets that the historical views affirm while avoiding their exclusivistic negations.

Can these figurative teachings be gathered together in one coherent doctrine? According to Leon Morris, that "cannot be done"[136] and according to John Stott it cannot be done "neatly."[137] If Morris and Stott mean that the diversity of biblical evidence cannot be adequately incorporated in any single analogy, we concur. However, the nonfigurative points of the respective illustrations are not contradictory, and the integrative synthesis above, though far from exhaustive, coherently incorporates their legal, experiential, and relational significances. In everyday life, furthermore, we combine all three major categories without confusion. Take the case of a divorced couple. Legally they are not married, experientially they may not keep themselves for each other, and relationally they may be alienated and estranged. Then consider the unusual case of divorcees eventually being remarried. Legally their status again is married, experientially they again remain faithful to each other, and relationally they again are reconciled and living together in peace. We might well call such a reconciliation a dramatic victory!

One's doctrine of atonement surely will have as many facets as one's doctrine of sin. Legally sinners are not God's people; experientially they do not remain faithful to God; and relationally they are estranged from God. When sinners believe in Christ's atoning sacrifice, legally they become God's children, experientially they grow in faithfulness to God, and relationally they enjoy peace with God. We find in the cross a many-splendored expression of God's love. We view the cross in a way that is typical of life's experiences in which these distinguishable categories are often intertwined without contradiction. Not all of life or salvation is fully comprehended in such a formulation, but it can make sense of the varied emphases of Scripture.

An even broader term than "atonement" is *salvation*. Salvation includes the eternal plan, the Old Testament preparation, the Son's incarnation, death, resurrection, ascension, the present ministries of Christ and the Spirit, and future realizations at the second coming and in eternity. For clarity of understanding, when we are not referring to salvation in such a comprehensive way, we use the more concrete terms (such as the atoning sacrifice and its just provision for forgiveness, redemption, victory over unholy powers, reconciliation to God and God's people, justification, and sanctification.

For Whom Were the Atoning Provisions Made?

Christ could die for all people, for, because he was divine, his provisions were of unlimited value. People who subscribe to the deity of Christ do not doubt that the provisions of his atonement were of sufficient value for all. The precious blood of the God-man had unlimited value. Surely the Father planned that the sacrifice suffice for the salvation of every lost person. The primary issue does not concern the sufficiency of the atonement's objective provisions as being sufficient for the justification, redemption, and reconciliation of all. Both Calvinistic and Arminian evangelicals affirm that.

Some may ask, "If the price has been paid for all, how can any people justly be punished for their sins?" The provisions of a last will or testament, although provided by a legal transaction, must be personally received to become of personal benefit. Christ's death does not forgive, redeem, or reconcile all, but makes publicly available to all sufficient provisions of forgiveness, redemption, and reconciliation. Several years after Christ's crucifixion and resurrection John wrote, "Whoever does not believe stands condemned already" (John 3:18), and he "will not see life, for God's wrath remains on him" (v. 36). On the basis of Christ's repeated warnings and other teaching about eternity, the hypothesis of universal salvation does not fit the facts. So a distinction must be made between the atonement's provisions and their application to sinners. The Scriptures could not be more emphatic that the atonement is efficient salvifically only for believers.

Even those who remain in unbelief, however, receive the benefits of common grace on the basis of the cross. Because of Christ's death sinners are not consumed *en masse* by divine wrath. The continued blessings of sunshine and rain universally remain possible because of the redemptive plan and provisions. In divine providence the Father may use Christ's powerful example to stimulate humility, justice, and love. Believers in the atonement make a difference in the world (Matt. 5:13–17). So the outworking of evil is not as great generally as it would be without the cross. God's temporal purposes are not unrelated to Calvary. In discussing the Father's plans for history (vol. 1, chap. 8) we emphasized God's purposes for all human beings and his purposes for his people morally and spiritually by faith. In fulfillment of both those purposes the cross is the basis for God's undeserved temporal favors to all sinners and his redemptive grace to those who believe.

A twofold universal and particular purpose for the cross accounts coherently for three types of related passages. We discuss them as follows:

1. The universal purpose accounts for the passages emphasized by Arminians indicating that Christ died for all, for the world, for whoever will believe (John 3:16–17; Rom. 5:18; 2 Cor. 5:14–15; 1 Tim. 2:4; Heb. 2:9; 2 Peter 2:1; 1 John 2:2; 4:14). Passages like these underline the sufficiency of the atonement for all, the desire (but not purpose) to redeem all who sin, and the indirect blessings of common grace for all.

2. A second purpose with a special intent of the cross for the elect accounts for passages that are highlighted by Calvinists: those that teach that Jesus Christ died for the persons the Father gave to him, the many, or the church (Mark 10:45; John 17:9, 20, 24; Acts 20:28; Eph. 1:4–7; 5:25; 2 Tim. 1:9–10). Passages like these indicate that Christ died with a special end in view for those the Father gave him out of the world: the members of his body, the church.

3. A view including both distinct universal and particular purposes for the cross provides the most probable account of Paul's teaching that the living God "is the Savior of all men, and especially of those who believe" (1 Tim. 4:10). What did Paul mean? In view of Paul's teaching that the unbelieving are under the curse of God's wrath, he cannot here be supporting universalism. Furthermore, in view of Paul's emphasis on the provisions of propitiation, redemption, and reconciliation, he does not here tell Timothy that believers enjoy a higher degree of common grace. As we have seen, "salvation" may be used in two ways, more generally for preservation in this life and more specifically for justification, redemption, and reconciliation. This twofold purpose coherently fits not only Paul's frame of reference and a word study of "salvation" but also the temporal-eternal contrast in the context regarding fitness physically and spiritually (v. 8). Furthermore, the grammatical structure is similar to another of Paul's uses of "especially." Paul exhorts, "As we have opportunity, let us do good to all people, *especially* to those who belong to the family of believers" (Gal. 6:10).[138] Parallel to this in grammatical structure is Paul's teaching that Christ is the Savior of all people, but *especially* of those who believe.

The interpretation of "those who believe" (1 Tim. 4:10) turns on whether sinners in fact are able to believe. Has prevenient grace delivered all sinners from their unwillingness and inability to respond to the gospel? In our study of sin we did not find evidence for a restoration of volitional ability to all. Rather, the hypothesis of prevenient grace enabling all humans to believe is contradicted by the numerous descriptions of sinners' present slavery to sin and blindness to spiritual things. Since sinners are unwilling and unable of themselves to believe, it would not be enough for Jesus to give his life for whoever would believe. None would believe! The "whosoever" passages do not discuss the point at issue—the *ability* of people enslaved to sin to receive Christ, any more than the giving of the Ten Commandments presupposes the ability of people to keep them. The class of all who would believe apart from a special call and enablement of the Spirit of grace is an empty class. So it would be in vain for Christ to provide forgiveness, redemption, and reconciliation "to whom it may concern." Given the present actuality of depravity, none would believe. Rather, Christ died to provide the just basis for (1) the undeserved temporal blessings of common grace and general revelation for all and (2) justification, sanctification, and glorification for God's people, those the Holy Spirit effectually calls out of the world. Some of the issues of election and the lost have been treated in volume 1, chapter 8. For more on the divine initiative in calling and the Holy Spirit's special enabling of the elect to believe, see volume 3, chapter 1.

APOLOGETIC INTERACTION

Must Human Sin Be Punished?

Much has been said recently about rehabilitating sinners who are also criminals, but little has been said about retributive justice. Retributive justice is served when criminals receive the penalties deserved for the injuries they have caused others. Rehabilitation is served when a criminal turns from a life of crime to work for a living and contributes to a peaceful society. The goals of both retribution and rehabilitation are ends sought by Christ's atonement. The cross satisfies justice in bearing our retribution and directly seeks our reconciliation to God and neighbor. The resultant process of sanctification rehabilitates a believer to a productive life in the church and the world.

Can sinners not be rehabilitated without the punishment of their sin? Since retribution at present is the most controversial issue, consider two of Leon Morris' arguments for reconsidering the value of retribution:[139] (1) Governments have no right to punish merely for reformatory and deterrent purposes. Unless a person deserves to the punished, society ought not inflict suffering. The penal system is at fault unless there is just desert. Punishment is just only when deserved. As violators of the law, we pay the penalty because we owe it, and for no other reason. Only when a government has the right to punish is it legitimate to exercise that right for rehabilitative purposes. (2) Punishment must in fact be retributive if it is to be reformatory. If people know that they are being punished unjustly it will not reform them. Of first importance it is necessary that justice be done, that sin be punished. The retributive character of punishment, A. E. Taylor argued, is a doctrine "really indispensable to sound ethics."[140]

Immanuel Kant argued at length for the importance of vindicating justice in society:

> The notion of ill desert and punishableness is necessarily implied in the idea of voluntary transgression; and the idea of punishment excludes that of happiness in all its forms. For though he who inflicts punishment may, it is true, also have a benevolent purpose to produce by the punishment some good effect upon the criminal, yet the punishment must be justified first of all, as pure and simple requital and retribution; that is, as a kind of suffering that is demanded by the law without any reference to its prospective beneficial consequences; so that even if no moral improvement and no personal advantage should subsequently accrue to the criminal, he must acknowledge that justice has been done to him, and that his experience is exactly conformed to his conduct. In every instance of punishment, properly so called, justice is the first thing, and constitutes the essence of it. A benevolent purpose and a happy effect, it is true, may be conjoined with punishment, but the criminal cannot claim this as his due, and he has no right to reckon upon it. All that he deserves is punishment, and this is all that he can expect from the law that he has transgressed.[141]

In addition to the moral imperative of oughtness in itself, for theists God's integrity, God's Word, and God's moral order are at stake. As Warfield said, "Indiscriminate forgiveness of sin would be precisely the subversion of the moral order of the world."[142] If a moral order is operative, in it the consequences of sin ought to fall upon the sinner. In the human experience the consequences of sin do not always appear to fall upon the sinner, but sometimes fall upon others. In that case the sinner ought to make restitution, making good the wrong as far as possible. No one can completely undo a wrong, especially against God. Still the sinner ought to be punished in order to vindicate righteousness. The person sinned against may forgive the sinner, but in this case the one who forgives suffers for the sinner as a substitute. The guilt is not artificially transferred, but the one who forgives bears in his own person the penal consequences of the other's sin.[143]

The moral order of the world is not something distinct from God, or God's justice and love, as so-called governmental theories of the atonement imply. The principles of morality and providence are rooted in the nature of God himself. " 'Satisfaction' is an appropriate word, providing we realize that it is he himself in his inner being who needs to be satisfied, and not something external to himself."[144]

Did Jesus Actually Die?

Some skeptically inclined people may ask, "Did Jesus really die?" Many lines of evidence indicate that he did. Mythical interpretations of the Gospels do not account for their historical reliability. The *cultural factors* surrounding the death fit the historical context in both method and motive. In the Roman and Jewish cultures crucifixion was common. As one of the most cruel methods of execution ever practiced, the Romans reserved it for criminals, slaves and other "nonpersons" convicted of murder, rebellion, or armed robbery. Among the Jews no distinction was made between the curse of hanging and crucifixion (Deut. 21:23). Both the Jews and Romans had motives for putting Christ onto the cross. Jesus frequently challenged the hypocrisy of the Jewish establishment, arguing that unless their righteousness exceeded that of the scribes and Pharisees, they would in no way enter the kingdom of heaven (Matt. 5:20). By speaking of his kingship and kingdom Jesus aroused enemies in the Roman tetrarchy also. Gentiles were as responsible for his death as Jews.

The primary visible *sign* of Jesus' death was his shed blood. The Messiah's shed blood, however, was not of magical value. Its significance stood out, rather, as a "visible sign" of his ultimate sacrifice, the offering up of his life for others. It was the visible indication of the invisible, new covenant. The preciousness of the Messiah's truly human blood came from its union with his divine nature. Jesus' shed blood was of inestimable worth, not because of inherent magical properties, but because it was the blood of the incarnate Logos.

Several converging lines of evidence conclusively support the fact that Jesus died. He "gave up his spirit" (Matt. 27:50) and "breathed his last" (Mark 15:37). Finding Jesus already dead, the soldiers did not break his legs as they did those on his right and left (John 19:31–33). One of the soldiers had pierced his side with a spear, bringing a sudden flow of blood and water (v. 34). Pilate questioned whether Jesus was already dead, summoned the centurion, and learned that it was so (Mark 15:43–45). Then Pilate gave the body to Joseph of Arimathea. Joseph wrapped it in a clean linen cloth and placed it in his own new tomb that he had cut out of rock and then rolled a large stone in front of its entrance (Matt. 27:57–60). The evidence from both his friends and his enemies places the fact of Jesus' death beyond reasonable doubt.

The evidence leads us to affirm that Christ's death occurred in actuality. If a distinction between *Historie* and *Geschichte* is made, he died in both respects! The testimony is not limited to believing followers of Christ. There were the unbelieving soldiers and no doubt others who had cried, "Crucify him!" Jesus' followers were hardly strong believers when he died. They struggled to maintain their faith through the experience of deep sorrow. Only after the appearances of the risen Christ did they interpret these events in faith, that is, in terms of *Geschichte,* or *Heilsgeschichte*. The belief in his death did not precede the observation of the evidence for the fact. And that evidence convinced both friends and enemies.

As an irrepeatable historical event, Jesus' death occurred *once-for-all*. To hold with Roman Catholicism that the sacrifice of Calvary is continued and made effective by its representation in the Eucharistic sacrifice amounts to an implicit denial of the historicity and uniqueness of Christ's person and death.

The once-for-all happening occurred as an *objective* event. The tendency of recent theologians to make the atonement a subjective experience or feeling within Christians does not do justice to its historicity. These things were not done in a corner but in broad daylight and before unbelievers as well as believers.

Christ's death was an *influential* event. In the preface to his book, *Great Sermons on the Death of Christ,* Wilbur Smith contrasts the preeminent place given the death of Christ in the New Testament with the insignificant references to the death of other great figures in history. Smith quotes the description of Napoleon's death and burial as given in an *Encyclopedia Britannica* article and observes, "The death of Napoleon was about the least important episode of his life, whereas it was the great event in the life of Christ."[145]

Christ's death became the *focal point* of history. As described by Albert A. Trevor in his *History of Ancient Civilization,*

> In the later years of Tiberius, probably soon after 30 A.D., occurred in Judea an event unnoticed by Romans, the crucifixion of Jesus. Yet this seemingly insignificant affair was to become the central point of future history, and the despised Galilean was destined to triumph over all the gods and emperors of the Roman world.[146]

Can Sins Justly Be Transferred to a Third Party?

The response to this question begins by challenging its assumption. The query presupposes an inadequate view of who Jesus is. Jesus is not some disinterested third party, but truly God, one with the offended party, and truly human, one with the offenders. We answer this and some other important questions briefly in view of the content in this and the two preceding chapters.

How Could One Death Atone for All?

Again the question fails to take account of who Jesus Christ was and is. He is not just one other finite human, but also the eternal Son of God. The precious blood of Christ is not that of one mere human. The death of the God-man has inestimable value, the value of the offered life of the infinite Son of God. His incarnate life is of unlimited inherent worth and with its sacrifice God the Father was well pleased.

Can Sins Be Transferred?

To restate the question, Is it not unjust to punish one person for another's sins? Sins are not substances that can be passed along from one person to another as in a bucket brigade. The word "sin" in Scripture often refers to its guilt and penalty. Indeed an innocent person considers it unjust to be blamed and punished for another's crime against his will. But no principles of justice are violated if one freely chooses to accept another's blame and take another's punishment so that the guilty person may go free.

Does a Substitutionary Atonement Make Sinners Passive?

Quite the reverse is true. People enslaved to sin cannot redeem themselves. Atonement must be provided for them. When Christ gave his life for sinners, they were spiritually incapacitated. Although active in ways displeasing to Christ, in motives and service pleasing to him they are completely passive. However, the response of sinners to Christ's death is far from passive. The sinners' repentant, believing, and consecrated response to the cross involves active participation in new moral and spiritual life. The affirmative actions involved are considered in relation to sanctification.

Do We Place a Mythological Emphasis on Jesus' blood?

According to the Old Testament, blood was necessary to life (Lev. 17:11, 14), and the shedding of blood meant death. Since death is the just consequence of sinful living, there could be no just remission of sin without the shed blood, if not that of the sinner, that of a substitutionary sacrifice. It is "the blood that makes atonement for one's life" (v. 11). At the Passover God said, "When I see the blood [of a sacrificial lamb on the doorpost], I will pass over you. No destructive plague will touch you when I strike Egypt" (Exod. 12:13). The blood on the entrance to the house indicated that the inhabitants acknowledged their deserved judgment and by faith had offered a substitutionary sacrifice. "The OT, therefore, indicates that atonement for human sin was obtained by the death of an acceptable substitute, rather than by its life."[147]

In New Testament times rebels against moral principles still deserved to die, but Jesus shed his human blood as the sinless Lamb of God in our place. The significance of Jesus' shed blood is not life set free, but "life given up in death."[148] Jesus' shed blood had no magical effects or mythical significance. Although inseparable from his divine nature, his fully human body had fully human life that depended on fully human blood. The shedding of Jesus' blood carried great significance also as confirmation of the fact that the God-man was giving up his life in accord with the Father's covenant. Jesus said, "This is my blood of the covenant, which is poured out for many for the forgiveness of sins" (Matt. 26:28). Like a will, this new covenant had force only after "the death of the one who made it" (Heb. 9:16; 12:24). Since Jesus' life was actually given as the once-for-all sacrifice with all its rich significance, we need attach no mythological value to his blood. The preciousness of Jesus' blood (1 Peter 1:18–19) comes from his personal significance as the Son of God incarnate and from all the covenanted provisions of the atonement that his substitutionary sacrifice secured.

Because you are bought with such a price, "you are not your own" (1 Cor. 6:19–20). "You were bought at a price, do not become slaves of men" (7:23). Ministers are to "be shepherds of the church of God, which he bought with his own blood" (Acts 20:28). Eternally we will sing praise to the Lamb who with his blood "purchased men for God from every tribe and language and people and nation" (Rev. 5:9).

Is the Substitutionary Sacrifice Central to Christian Faith?

William Hordern charges that whereas evangelicalism makes atonement (and one view of it) central to Christianity, neoorthodoxy makes incarnation central and is hesitant to make any doctrine of the atonement final. The ultimate purpose of the incarnation, however, was to provide the atonement for the hopelessly lost. Hence the cross cannot be divorced either from the incarnation or from the core of Christianity.[149]

In ministry as well as thought evangelical Christians should give priority to the fact and meaning of the death of the incarnate Son of God. The experience of holistically depraved people trying to imitate Jesus, or identify with him, or take him as their representative shows that they need Christ's redemption and reconciliation first. The atonement is central to spirituality in the ministry and teaching not only of evangelists but also of pastors and theologians. Christ's substitutionary sacrifice supplies a key to the unity of Scripture, the purpose for the incarnation, the union of justice and love in God's nature, and genuinely Christian personal and social ethics.

Should We Politicize the Cross?

Jürgen Moltmann's theology illustrates how panentheistic and process assumptions can affect views of human sin and Christ's atonement. Hope for humanity's future, Moltmann says, comes from the remembrance of Christ's incarnation and death, for Christ suffers in the world's sufferings. Moltmann's immanent God exists in the living deeds of men.[150] So social action is Christian when the activists perform it as an act of identification with Christ.[151] Moltmann rejected an apathetic God unmoved by the world's suffering, but he fails to realize that biblical theism has a God who is afflicted in all the afflictions of his people (Isa. 63:9). Moltmann so identifies his "God" with suffering that unfortunately his processive God seems insufficiently transcendent, living, and active as a personal spirit to do the mighty acts necessary to correct the human plight.

Since Moltmann's God includes humanity, he includes evil. Moltmann imagines "a rebellion in God himself."[152] Essential to understanding the cross, Moltmann thinks, is his unorthodox version of trinitarianism as "an eschatological process open for men on earth, which stems from the cross of Christ."[153] Moltmann finds it impossible to grasp how Jesus could really be God and at the same time be forsaken by God.[154] Undercutting a distinction between the provisions of the cross and their reception, he writes, "All being and all that annihilates (including Auschwitz) has already been taken up in God and God begins to become 'all in all.' "[155]

Moltmann glibly labels capitalism "sin" and prescribes a democratic socialism for salvation from the circle of poverty.[156] He does not call technocracy, as an institutionalized cause of misery, sinful, but "inhuman." Similarly, Moltmann might have said that society's problem is "inhuman abuses of capitalism" rather than "capitalism." Depraved humans can and do abuse any form of economy or human government. Some forms may be more easily abused than others, however, because of fewer checks and balances on those in authority and power. Moltmann's key to liberation from the vicious circle of force is "democracy."[157] In our judgment, democracies may have many checks and balances to minimize evils of coercion, but democratic governments cannot bring the just and lasting peace that either regeneration or the actual return of the transcendent Christ will bring.

The church of the insulted, poor, and oppressed, Moltmann argues, "must take sides in the concrete social and political conflicts going on about it and in which it is involved, and must be prepared to join and form parties."[158] But the forming of Christian political parties does not follow from biblically sound teaching of the cross. Christians can misuse political power, as history has repeatedly indicated. Christians need to fulfill their responsibilities as citizens, but may not agree on full-blown economic structures or political parties and programs. The atoning provisions of God's grace at Calvary has been enjoyed by people of all different tribes and nations in history. The provisions of the cross transcend any economic or political structure. When it is necessary to take sides socially and politically, Christians ought always to remain loyal above all to the Savior of people from *all* sides.

The example of Jesus' life does not support a politicizing of his death. Jesus lived in a province of the Roman Empire in the midst of a society seething with discontent as a result of injustices. In those circumstances the Messiah opposed violence in general and refused to lead a violent revolution as a Zealot, but he headed a spiritual kingdom for the poor in spirit. What was the nature of the Messiah's good news for the poor, release for the captives, and liberty for the oppressed (Luke 4:18)? He addressed evils endemic in human nature, more than the oppression of the Roman Empire. He discouraged attempts to reestablish Jewish national freedom. He did not teach socialism in a democracy. He treated the deeper root of our problem—our personal relationships to God and one another. He liberated people from the peace-shattering sins of prejudice, pride, greed, barriers of class, wealth, and hypocrisy. Apparently the evil fruit would come forth from evil trees in any economic or political system, and with new hearts God's people would work to overcome evil in any social context. Changed hearts will not change society automatically, but people with renewed abilities to discern evil, feel it deeply, and do the good that they should, will make a difference.

The liberation that in the New Testament parallels the Exodus experience (and the cross) is directly a liberation from personal sin and social evil within the control of redeemed people. Instead of destroying the present social order, Jesus sought to demonstrate a more radical way of love to God and neighbors.[159] Christ liberates the poor, not in the sense of attacking economic structures directly, but by undercutting the world's value system. The *sumum bonum* can be neither material advantage nor a different economic structure.

> While, then, Jesus did not campaign directly for economic revolution, nor set out for his disciples a programme for doing so, he nevertheless preached and lived such values and attitudes that those who take him seriously can neither exploit nor ignore the plight of the exploited. Socio-economic liberation if it was not his direct aim, is the proper concern of those who accept his radical value system.[160]

As Richard J. Mouw says,

> Unless human beings are willing to forsake the futile patterns of pretending to be their own lords, they will be liberated from one form of oppression only to be victimized by other forms. Political and economic restructurings are important elements in the total kingdom picture, but they are not by themselves the total picture.[161]

The basic issue facing Christians, according to Mouw, is, "What kinds of actions, if any, are compatible with commitments of those who are living in grateful response to what God did in the cross of Jesus Christ?" or, "What kinds of actions are proper effects of the cross?"[162] In considering proposed answers in different cultural contexts, Christians need to be encouraged by the assurance that eschatologically the risen Christ will not only restore creation but will also eliminate injustice and bestow both personal and institutional righteousness. Until that great *kairos,* the present age need not be considered merely a holding action. The present opportunities present a challenge to do what is within our power to overcome evil with good. That demands getting our facts straight, critically using a responsible method of decision making, willingness to take responsibility for our actions, and authenticity in living by them. In this approach we do not politicize the cross, but develop the indirect significance of identification with the crucified Christ for our relationships to others in the contexts of varieties of socialist, communist, or capitalist political structures.

Did All Actually Die With Christ in the First Century?

Karl Barth considers Christ's sacrifice more than a provision for a just amnesty, redemption, and reconciliation. Barth proposes that the cross in the first century *actually justified all fallen human beings*. The atoning work of Christ does not present a mere possibility of salvation (Thomasius). Barth insists that "this possibility has to become actuality."[163] "That Jesus Christ died for us does not mean, therefore, that we do not have to die, but that we have died in and with him, that as the people we were we have been done away and destroyed, that we are no longer there and have no more future."[164] When raised by the Father, Jesus was justified as a man and "in him as the Representative of all men all were justified."[165] So in Christ

> all were justified, converted, sanctified and called.[166] In the death of Jesus Christ both the destroying and the renewing *have* taken place for *all* men. . . . Therefore objectively, really, ontologically, there is a necessity of faith for them all. . . . Unbelief has become an impossibility and faith an objective, real and ontological necessity for all men and for every man.[167]

Barth's hypothesis comes short of confirmation by all three of our criteria of truth—noncontradiction, adequacy, and viability:

1. A letter from one who attended Barth's 1961 lectures in Germany indicated that he found the theologian's *inconsistencies* on election "maddening":

> God's grace is irresistible, but man can succeed in resisting it. Christ's redemptive work is all-inclusive and 100% effective, but the possibility of damnation remains (though Barth refuses to decide between particularism and universalism because to do so would be to usurp the divine prerogative of judgment—if forced to choose, Barth candidly admitted he would choose universalism). Not everyone will necessarily be saved, but no one can suffer hell (though one could possibly suffer the "shadows" of hell—whatever that means). Christ will be in hell as well as heaven, and on and on. It is maddening.[168]

Barth correctly insisted that Christ died in the first century to provide more than a mere possibility of salvation. Christ's atonement assured the fulfillment of the redemptive plan, but that plan included not only Christ's just provision for amnesty, but also the Holy Spirit's conviction, calling, and regeneration of unbelievers. Christ's victory at this point guaranteed that the reaching of God's people would be just and would take place subsequently. But after the cross the Holy Spirit had to come to help people go out as witnesses and to help sinners receive the message, repent, and believe. People are justified and sanctified only when they hear the gospel, believe it, and trust Christ. These eventualities were foreknown in the first century but not realized then.

2. Barth's failure to distinguish the objective provisions from their actual subjective reception at the moment of faith also *fails to fit the scriptural data:* (1) Spiritually Christ himself divided humanity into two spiritual classes—the lost and the saved, but Barth has only one class, in which all humans are already justified and sanctified. Unscripturally Barth gives all humans the same spiritual status. "Thus the so-called 'outsiders' are really only 'insiders' who have not yet understood and apprehended themselves as such."[169] (2) Prior to faith, sinners, according to Scripture, are not united to Christ and are not forgiven, redeemed, or reconciled. (3) Barth minimizes the importance for redemption of the Holy Spirit's ministries of calling, regenerating, justifying, sanctifying, and glorifying the foreknown and predestined (Romans 8:28–30). (4) Barth's view of informing people that they are already in God's kingdom has none of the urgency of Christ's ministry. The apostles then

pled with sinners in behalf of Christ to make the decision that appropriates the provisions of the cross and settles one's eternal destiny. (5) The view that all are objectively sanctified fails to fit the facts of human experience. All too obviously, as we know from hearing or reading the daily crime news, all human beings are far from holy. The inhumanity of humans to one another remains a major problem among the peoples of the world, religious and nonreligious. Prior to regeneration people today remain actually in slavery to sin, alienated from God, and under condemnation. Apart from the distinction between the atoning provisions and their application, it seems impossible to make sense of fallen humanness.

3. Barth's view of an actualized universal justification and sanctification is not viable. Barth speaks of more than a legal status: he insists on an actual justification and sanctification. Christians honest with themselves cannot hold that they are actually as holy as God is holy. Socially Christians could not live by that view without hypocrisy in any known church or in a non-Christian business, labor union, or political party. Legally, in the first century Christ did provide a just basis for some universally experienced blessings. On the basis of his atonement divine wrath has not already consumed the whole fallen human race; instead, God bestows the benefits of common grace universally. But it is impossible to live unhypocritically with Barth's claim that all humans are now really renewed or sanctified.

Did Believers Die With Christ in the First Century?

Some people who hold to exchanged-life emphases teach a version of what Barth taught for all humans but limit it to those who are believers in Christ. Victorious-life writers may affirm that all believers actually died with Christ on the cross in the first century. The view places a believer's crucifixion with Christ (Gal. 2:20) at Calvary rather than at the point of the person's faith in the Savior. The argument is that as all humans were realistically in Adam when he sinned, so all believers were realistically in Christ when he died. Charles Solomon argues that being "in Christ" means being in him eternally and so "we were in him *at the cross*."[170] The putting off of the "old nature," it is alleged, "was done by the operation of the Cross, according to Romans 6:6."[171] When was our old nature crucified (Greek aorist tense) with Christ (Romans 6:6)? The context indicates that when we were "baptized into Christ Jesus," we were "baptized into his death" (v. 3). So "you died" (Col. 3:3) when you identified with Christ by faith and exhibited your faith in baptism. Realistically, believers died with Christ when they were converted. Legally, or covenantally, believers were represented by Christ's once-for-all death on the cross. Decretively, of course, believers are foreknown because they were chosen in Christ from before the foundation of the world.

Although all people were "in Adam" genetically and have his nature by birth, people are "in Christ" only when by faith they are born anew and receive a new nature. At the cross our legally received Substitute suffered the guilt and penalty our sins deserved, and the good news is that we did not need to be there! The believers at Rome died with Christ (past tense) at the point of their faith, new birth, and baptism. At their regeneration believers also rose with him and received a renewed nature in his image (and all the present provisions of the cross). Both the definitive divorce from the former way of life dominated by the flesh and the definitive beginning of resurrection to a new way of life dominated by the Holy

Spirit marks the meaning of baptism that beautifully witnesses to these realities in the world. As John Stott explains,

> These verses [Rom. 6:3–5] probably allude to the pictorial symbolism of baptism. When baptisms took place in the open air in some stream, the candidate would go down into the water . . . and as he went down into the water, whether partially or totally, he would seem to be buried and then to rise again. His baptism would dramatize his death, his burial, and his resurrection to a new life.[172]

We actually died and rose with Christ when we inwardly turned from former spiritual masters to Jesus Christ. Then it was that by faith we received the blessings of redemption, forgiveness, and reconciliation for which he died once-for-all. Our union with the eternal Christ does not make the succession of events of our lives in time less real. God's foreknowledge of our sinful condition and our faith at a point in time does not make the temporal event of the cross or of our reception of its benefits less temporal.

Since the provisions of the cross become ours at the crisis of conversion signified by baptism, the realization of these great blessings ought to take place then. Well-instructed believers should not need a subsequent crisis of identity to determine whether their ultimate identification is with Christ and his kingdom or with Satan and his dominion. If these teachings have not been taught, or have been misconstrued, then by the illumination of the Holy Spirit they need later to be realized and internalized. And exchanged-life emphases have helped meet this need. Apart from some realization of the believer's death with Christ, we wonder if the meaning of repentance, faith, and regeneration to a new life was understood inwardly when the person outwardly claimed to believe and was baptized to confess these very commitments publicly.

Is the Meaning of the Cross Merely Subjective?

Some interpreters find no objective provisions for sinners completed in the first century and make salvation depend wholly on one's subjective response to Christ's crucifixion. D. M. Baillie speaks for many when he says, "We are dealing with a realm of personal relationships and nothing else."[173] J. A. T. Robinson also denies any objective transaction between two parties at the cross. He finds getting saved an experience like that of the prodigal son as we "come to ourselves." He says, "It is a coming home, or rather being received home."[174] Paul Van Buren asked what Jesus' death accomplished, saying it was "not an objective ransom, substitution or redemption." By regarding people as sinners forgiven and by proclaiming their forgiveness, "Jesus convinced them that they were released from the burden of their guilt and the consequences of their acts."[175] The cross, Van Buren claims, is

> a discernment situation, i.e, for those who "see." If taken as a cosmological assertion, however, this is "meaningless" in terms of a [positivistic] verifiability theory of meaning. In the form of a confession of faith the statements suggest a situation in which the history of Jesus has been or might be seen in a new way and the speaker's commitment to what he has now "seen."[176]

Surely sinners are illumined to receive the meaning of the cross, and do testify to it. The question is whether their witness is true. Is it consistent with the meaning the Holy Spirit inspired in Scripture? Do the meanings sinners read into or out of the cross hold for God as well? Interpreters of the cross will not lose heart or be disillusioned if their affirmations have objective validity. The faithful words that Jesus is the Messiah and that he died for our sins are reliable because they are true historically and revelationally. Certainly personal relationships are involved in the biblical analogies, but relationships can be based on spoken and written affirmations in objective covenants and promises. The sincerity of the personal commitment to the cross is crucial on the subjective side, but also indispensable is the objective truth of the eternal covenant and the good news of its promises.

Are the psychological benefits more important than Calvary's objective provisions? J. Norman King attempts to address human psychological and existential problems without an objectively real God, guilt, atonement, or justification! Human loneliness, despair, and death, he thinks, can be overcome by an experience of the "infinite mystery at the depth of human existence." King thinks that "the past can be redeemed by including the integration achieved in guilt within a new positive option which ratifies one's orientation to the self-bestowing infinite mystery."[177]

Healthful psychological integration of sinners is important but in itself does not displace the need for the once-for-all historical reality of the cross with all its pathos and revealed meaning. The Scriptures indicate that the subjective distinctive of the new and better covenant is that God puts his laws in believers' minds and writes them on their hearts (Heb. 8:10–11). The previous covenant with its repeated sacrifices did not cleanse once for all; it left people feeling guilty (10:2). Under the new covenant believers have been "made holy . . . once for all" (v. 10); God forgives them and remembers their lawless acts no more (vv. 17–18). Some of the greatest subjective benefits of the cross have been dismissed by denying its once-for-all objective provisions for a clear conscience. We defend the objective provisions of the cross because they are indispensable to its subjective values for God and believers.

RELEVANCE FOR LIFE AND MINISTRY

At an ugly cross the incarnate Word has made known who God really is (John 1:18), and he is far from Aristotle's unmoved and uncaring Mover. The historical cross discloses an invisible personal Spirit who knows, cares, speaks, and acts in the midst of our spiritual blindness and moral decadence. Behind the cross is an invisible God who knows all about history's public and private problems of evil. Behind the cross is a God who understands when people in the midst of the anxieties, meaninglessness, and tragedies of life think he has forsaken them or even died. Behind the cross is a living God who cares about us just as we are. Behind the cross is a God who covenants with his Son to save those who know they need a physician. Behind the cross is a faithful God who keeps his word. Behind the cross is a God who acts on planet earth in human history. Behind history's worst miscarriage of justice is a God who acts mercifully and graciously on behalf of undeserving rebels. Behind the agony of the cross is not a God of cheap grace, but a God whose grace cost him dearly. Behind the death on the cross is a God who remains just while providing for the justification of the insolent. Behind that cross is the God who turned the gross injustice of Jesus' death into a marvelous instrument of justification, redemption, and reconciliation. Behind the cross is the God who on the third day turned the enigma of Good Friday into the triumph of Easter.[178] To grasp the objective meaning of the cross in some measure is to feel poignantly its subjective impact.

Experience the Moral Impact Personally

Jesus gave up his life because of your sins and ours. The final reason for his death was not his betrayal, his first-century enemies, the religious establishment, the political establishment, but ourselves. He went through the anguish of physical and spiritual death because of the sins of all fallen humans of all times. All of us are contributors to his death whenever we disbelieve him, disobey him, deny him, betray him, follow him far off, or subject his name to public disgrace. "Before we can begin to see the cross as something done *for* us (leading us to faith and worship), we have to see it as something done *by* us (leading us to repentance)."[179] At the cross

> God overturned the judgment of the world, and with it exposed as idols its standards of righteousness, wisdom and power. The cross confronts us with the demand to turn away from the present age with its standards and values—which when greatly magnified lead to the "God of this present age"—and instead bring our thinking about God, ourselves and his world into conformity with the cross.[180]

Moved to repudiate our sinful disposition, we turn to God in gratitude. We love God because he first loved us. We want to love in a similar self-giving way (Eph. 5:2). Viewing Jesus' humility and perseverance, we humble ourselves (Phil. 2:3–8), endure opposition from sinful people (Heb. 12:2–3), emotionally suffer for doing good and make no threats or retaliate (1 Peter 2:21–23), and physically suffer in order to do the will of God (4:1–2). Like the thief on the cross at Christ's right, we are moved to receive Jesus as King. The attractive power of the cross moves us to live no longer for ourselves but for him who died for us (2 Cor. 5:14–15). As imitators of Christ we choose to give up ourselves as fragrant offerings and sacrifices to God (Eph. 5:1–2). We acknowledge the element of truth in the moral influence and example hypotheses.

Isaac Watts expressed classically the Spirit-illumined Christian response to the cross.

> When I survey the wondrous cross
> On which the Prince of Glory died
> My richest gain I count but loss,
> And pour contempt on all my pride.
>
> Forbid it Lord, that I should boast
> Save in the death of Christ, my Lord;
> All the vain things that charm me
> most,
> I sacrifice them to His blood.
>
> Were the whole realm of nature mine,
> That were a present far too small;
> Love so amazing, so divine,
> Demands my soul, my life, my all.

Live Under the Sign the Cross

When archaeologists dig up a place of worship in the desert sand and find in it the sign of the cross, they can be virtually certain that it was a Christian church. From the very first the Christian faith was distinguished from the religions that surrounded it by its worship of the crucified Christ. Still today Christians portray their inner faith in Christ outwardly by a cross. If a single symbol of Christian faith is chosen, nothing is more distinctive than the cross. No founder of any of the world's religions died for his followers' justification, redemption, and reconciliation.

Christians hang crosses from necklaces, pin them to lapels, and place them on the steeples of their churches. Symbols of the cross stand primarily, not for what we do for Christ, but what the Savior did *for us*. The spiritual value of displaying the cross derives from the users' *faith* in Christ and his once-for-all sacrifice, with its marvelous provisions. Many make the sign of the cross and meditate at the stations of the cross. Even the sign of the cross becomes valueless, however, if it be regarded as a mere fetish, charm, or amulet. It ought never become a magical symbol. Neither should it become an occasion for mystics to be spiritually absorbed in Christ's sufferings. The significance of the sign of the cross does not point to the mystical sufferings and resignation of Jesus' devout followers. By believing the gospel and trusting Christ we become partners with Christ. We then no longer view ourselves separately as sinners, but as legal partners with Christ: it is now Christ and the believer incorporated. The partnership's assets include all the rich spiritual provisions of Christ. They meet all believing sinners' obligations. Some say, "It does not matter what you believe so long as you have faith, or have faith in Christ." But the Scriptures say that we receive atonement "through faith in his blood" (Rom. 3:25). The Lord's final will (testament) leaves propitiation, redemption, and reconciliation to all who will receive them.

Although other uses of the sign of the cross are optional, Christ did request his followers to give *two visible signs* of their faith in him—baptism and the Lord's Supper. *Baptism* is an initiatory rite expressing several great truths. (1) Baptism signifies one's confession of personal guilt. The baptized believe not only that all have sinned, but they also acknowledge, "I have sinned and deserve to die under the wrath of God." (2) One's baptism also indicates a personal reception of Christ's death as substitutionary. He died, not just for all people in general but for me personally, or in my place. (3) Christian baptism should signify a personal reception of the provisions of forgiveness from my guilt, redemption from the domination of sin in my life, and reconciliation to open fellowship with God and God's people. (4) In other words, baptism signifies that the candidate ceases depending on his or her own sin-tainted works and dies with Christ to fleshly achievements. The once-for-all burial in water pictures one's crucifixion with Christ and death to, or separation from, former evil masters and the dominion of sin in our lives. Rising from the water pictures resurrection to new spiritual life for the Lord of all (Rom. 6:2–3, 10–11). Inwardly by faith and outwardly by the sign of baptism Christians "have been united with him in his death" (v. 5). Having become partners with Christ by faith, his death pays our inescapable penalty. Baptism occurs once-for-all, signifying a decisive alienation to the fleshly loves of our preconversion loyalties. We "[were] crucified with him so that the body of sin might be done away with, that we should no longer be slaves to sin" (v. 6).

Experientially, however, because baptized believers do yield to temptation and sin, they need repeatedly to confess sin, realign their values, and renew fellowship at *the Lord's table*. Partaking of the bread and wine indicate that we thankfully remember his sacrifice in our place, proclaim the propitiatory, redemptive, and reconciling provisions of his sacrifice, and testify to our oneness with those who similarly express their salvation on the basis of Christ's atonement. Believers keep the feast of the Passover, not in boasting of self-justification or in malice, but with sincerity and truth (1 Cor. 5:6–8). The communion table, Protestants insist, is not an altar at which Christ is sacrificed again. God forbid! The great high priest completed the work of atonement and sits at the right hand of God the Father (Heb. 10:11–12). Hence the Reformers removed Roman Catholic references to an altar in their communion services. Instead, God's people meet at a table, the Lord's table. Believers who regularly join others at the Lord's table signify that they continue to live for the purpose for which Christ died.

Rejoice in the Security of Forgiveness (the Cross *for* Us)

A convert to an Eastern religious movement said, "As a Roman Catholic I forever felt guilty. Since my 'enlightenment' I have not felt guilt for three years." It is impossible, however, to live for years without real guilt when we become aware of the holy and loving One's revealed purposes and values. The best of us comes far short of God's righteous standards. Yet, like David, believers can exclaim, "Blessed is he whose transgressions are forgiven, whose sins are covered. Blessed is the man whose sin the LORD does not count against him" (Ps. 32:1–2). *Rejoice!* Although we were unacceptable in our fallen selves the God of the cross accepts believers!

Some of us find it hard to forgive ourselves (as children, parents, and spouses) even though God has forgiven us. What Christianity offers is not a hypocritical denial of guilt, but a candid confession of it in its reality and a just forgiveness based on Christ's atonement. All sinners who believe the gospel and trust Christ have the price of their sin paid in full. Having real guilt (against God), we need the assurance that God forgives. Psychologists as such, helpful as they are, cannot forgive sin against God. Only God can forgive sin and that on the basis of the cross. Having heard the good news and received the propitiation Christ provided, people of faith no longer live under God's wrath for their sin. In the joy of sins forgiven they know that their indictment has been erased and their justification declared.

Become an Agent of Forgiveness

Secure in God's merciful forgiveness and having died to our fleshly desires, we become free to please our Savior. Living daily in the assurance of what Christ did for us, we are free to value his kingdom above all else. So we can enjoy life as *agents of forgiving love.* To live by the forgiveness of God without being forgiving is unthinkable (Matt. 18:23–35). We have become part of a dynamically forgiving movement. Sinners receive forgiveness, not to store it up, but to pour it out like a river of life-giving water. Whether you have something against another (Mark 11:25) or another has something against you (Matt. 5:23), go at once and make peace. Do not let a "bitter root" grow up to cause trouble and defile many (Heb. 12:14–15). Christians ought to forgive as God has forgiven them (Eph. 4:32). Like God, we do not call evil good or deny its reality, but we love evildoers and remember that their sins can be cleansed by Christ's blood. Like our Savior on the cross, we pray, "Father forgive them for they do not know what they are doing" (Luke 23:34). How often must we forgive? As often as we need forgiveness (Matt. 18:21, 22). When Christians living under the cross become agents of forgiving love, our families and churches will become more than communities of the forgiven—they will be forgiving communities.

Conquer Sin's Addictions (the Cross *in* Us)

Christ died to liberate us from sin's control of us. Christians *can* overcome the desires of the old nature. Christians cannot excuse sins by claiming, "That's the way I am." Sinful desires and deeds should no longer dominate our lives. Christ did not come to take away our God-given individualities. All God wants to take from us is our sin. We can embrace and esteem all that we are by creation—our intelligence, conscience, femininity or masculinity, family life, creativity, and need for relationship with others and God. But we divest ourselves of all that we are by the Fall: our moral perversity, the selfishness that spoils our family life, fascination with the ugly and the irrational, our lazy refusal to develop God's gifts, our waste of natural resources, and our antisocial tendencies. Courageously we affirm the worth of all that we are by creation and re-creation; ruthlessly we dismiss all that we have become by the Fall. The cross of Christ teaches us both attitudes. On the one hand, the cross illustrates the value of our created self, since Christ loved us while we were yet sinners. On the other hand, the cross models for us self-sacrifice, the denying of our fallen nature.[181]

Christ paid the ransom to set us free from the power of all varieties of sin. Black (and red) theology reminds us that Christ died to liberate us from racist prejudices and oppressions. Having been bought with such a price, we are not our own—we belong to our Lord. Our weapons are not those of the flesh but those of a Christlike self-giving love. Although we do not politicize the cross, we live a life crucifed to sins of prejudice, as well as other sins. There could as well be yellow and white theologies, for the power of the cross delivers from sinful prejudices in all directions. Christ shed his blood to deliver us from a sinful apathy that lives comfortably with unethical views of racially different people.

Feminist theology justifiably summons Christian men to remember that Christ died to liberate them from the sins of disrespect and exploitation of women, especially the particular women they know. Since chauvinism can work in either direction, Christian women may also need to seek the Redeemer's power to overcome unjust attitudes toward men in general, as well as particular men among their acquaintances.

Theologians from the less materially developed two-thirds of the world ask comparatively wealthy Christians whether we have been set free from covetousness and have become good stewards. Has the ransom Christ paid delivered us from unjust and unloving attitudes toward the poor? Have the followers of the cross who have economic power overcome policies and practices that exploit the poor? Those who live under the cross are not satisfied with its provisions of forgiveness and fellowship with God, important as these are. Believers in the crucified Christ join the Savior, the prophets, and the apostles in proclaiming good news to the poor.

Christ's redemption also brings good news to both young and old. The elderly may disrespect the young, and the young may despise the old. In youth-oriented cultures, especially, the elderly may be disregarded, hurriedly retired, and forgotten. However strong these pressures may be, Christians can find power and grace in the blood of Christ to overcome them.

The atonement that provides forgiveness also provides power for discipleship. Those who believe in the Redeemer's victory over Satan know that some former desires in their lives can pass away. As redemptive deliverance from sin's power progressively makes more differences for more believers it will make a difference in their relationships with others (socially). Let Americans and others who championed slavery repent of the sins of their fathers who championed slavery and instead actively champion black freedom. In any culture disciples of Jesus Christ can begin by exhibiting the power of Christ's atonement to deliver them from their own prejudicial attitudes and acts.

Then unhypocritically they can seek deliverance from the consequences of these sins as expressed in exploitive and oppressive structures. But the weapons of our warfare are not those of the (unjust, fleshly) world. On the contrary, those who know Christ and him crucified demolish strongholds with divine power (2 Cor. 10:4).

Become an Agent of Reconciliation (the Cross *Through* Us)

Do sinful attitudes alienate you from Christians who are younger or older? Of the other sex? Of another race? Of a greater or lesser economic status? Christ gave his life so that as we are reconciled to God we may be reconciled to one another. What unites the body of believers in Christ is not age, sex, skin color, economics, political party, or national loyalties, but repentance for our sins and faith in the Reconciler.

Because God made peace by the cross, those who live under the cross should be powerfully moved to be peacemakers. Peace-making patterned after the cross is quite different from appeasement at any price. The peace that God achieved was not cheap, but costly. To forgive and to ask for forgiveness are both costly exercises. Calvary love was not unprincipled nor unjust. Followers of Christ do not seek peace at the price of justice or morality. Just love requires self-discipline. The object of discipline with our children or our church members is not to humiliate, let alone to alienate, but rather to maintain integrity and to reclaim. The call of disciplinary action is the call to exhibit the tough love of the cross.

People who take the signs of baptism and the Lord's table strive not only for the *ends* of the cross (forgiveness, freedom, and peace), but also to accomplish them by *means* consistent with the cross. For strategies and means consistent with the cross consider the following points.

Never Compromise Justice in the Name of Love

The greatest service of love should not be done with less than moral means. For the great end of saving sinners God's matchless love at the cross went far beyond the demands of justice. As God's gracious plan satisfied moral demands, so must our plans and programs. Our most loving projects for others may go far beyond moral requirements, but they ought never come short of them. The Reverend Jim Jones devoted himself to helping the unreached young, the poor, and the minorities in an inner city. But in spite of his good motives initially, he yielded to unethical means of ministering to human need. Taking his followers to build an ideal society in Guyana, he commanded over nine hundred of them to drink poison and needlessly die. Less dramatically, not less tragically, numerous other people with great potential as pastors and church leaders, seminary students and professors, missionaries and television evangelists, have lost significant opportunities to serve others. Among other reasons, one stands out: often they did not learn the lesson of the cross. If God himself could not do moral evil that good might come, his moral and spiritual children ought not attempt to do so.

More positively, consider Billy Graham whose years of productive evangelistic ministry have been influential for many thousands of people. With all his fame, enabled by the Spirit, Graham maintained accountability to God, God's Son, God's written Word, and God's people. He has maintained his credibility morally and financially. Having been faithful in the seemingly little things, God gave Billy Graham greater and greater opportunities.

Lose Your Life to Find It

To be a follower of Jesus is to go with him all the way to Calvary. It is to be crucified with him. How? Usually not physically, although many martyrs have given their lives to be faithful to God's Word. Many of us may find ourselves some day choosing between faithfulness and physical death. Jesus took up the cross, not to carry it for years, but to die on it for our sin. Those who follow his example do not carry a cross as a burden for a lifetime, but die on it to their old natures. What does it mean to die? Entire books on being crucified with Christ sometimes fail to define the term. Death does not mean annihilation, as we have found, but primarily separation. To die with Christ or take up the cross means decisively to divorce ourselves from the domination of our fleshly desires and habits. To take up the cross is definitely to distance oneself from the peer pressure of worldly conformity and from Satanic deception in doctrine and practice. Some who die with Christ abandon everything, and others remain what they were. To follow Jesus as supreme spiritual master means to demote other loyalties, however good, such as loyalty to education, family, religious status, or employment. To follow Christ is above all to hunger and thirst for righteousness (Matt. 5:6) and to seek first the kingdom of God and his righteousness (6:33). "Whoever wants to save his life will lose it, but whoever loses his life for me and for the gospel will save it" (Mark 8:35). The objective provisions of Christ's cross are received by those who accept its judgment of their selfishness, greed, envy, jealousy, covetousness, and lust. To begin life in Christ's kingdom of light is to make a clean break with Satan's kingdom of darkness.

"The knowledge of the cross brings a conflict of interest between God who has become man and man who wishes to become God."[182] To die with Christ means to have away done with efforts like those of the people at the tower of Babel to rise to God through materialistic acquisitions, political influence, popularity in entertainment, or heroism in sports. To die with Christ is to bear witness to the lordship of Christ before the people of this world in all these fields. It is to experience Christ's suffering love for sinners, the lost, the abandoned, the despised, and the betrayed.

Acceptance of the blood of the covenant in both the Old and New Testaments symbolized not only forgiveness, Leon Morris found, but also consecration.[183] Forgiveness is not the one isolated result of believing in Jesus. By their faith in the crucified Christ God purifies a people for communion with him and service to the world. Only those who are cleansed from sin "may fittingly be termed God's people." The people sprinkled with the blood of the new covenant exhibit "newness of living, for God's people must be *God's* people."[184] The faith that receives forgiveness by sheer grace gratefully serves by love (Gal. 5:6, RSV).

The goal of Christ's followers is not self-absorption but self-giving love, like that of Jesus. Our self-denial is not to become lost in inner devotional or mystical experiences. Having cared for our own needs sufficiently, we can displace selfish ambition with self-sacrifice, comfort with suffering, and lust with service. Christ's priority for his followers is not prosperity, nor dominion, but self-giving service for others. He who would be the greatest in the kingdom of the crucified One would become a servant of all (Mark 10:43). The cross lies at the very heart of the Christian mission to the present world. It is significant in church growth and in crosscultural communication. As John Stott said,

> Jesus first took our flesh and then bore our sin. This was a depth of penetration into our world in order to reach us, in comparison with which our little attempts to reach people seem amateur and shallow. The cross calls us to a much more radical and costly kind of evangelism than most churches have begun to consider, let alone experience. [185]

Develop Values Like Those of the Crucified Christ

Paul had many good reasons to take pride in his fleshly righteousness: "circumcised on the eighth day, of the people of Israel, of the tribe of Benjamin, a Hebrew of Hebrews, in regard to the law a Pharisee; as for zeal, persecuting the church; as for legalistic righteousness, faultless" (Phil. 3:5–6). But having received the righteousness that comes through faith in the crucified Messiah, he considered all that to be loss compared to the surpassing greatness of knowing Christ Jesus his Lord (vv. 7–9). Grateful for the gift of right standing with God, Paul said, "I want to know Christ and the power of his resurrection and the fellowship of sharing in his sufferings, becoming like him in his death" (v. 10).

In the quest for self-esteem, fallen humans need to remember that Christ was crucified by people who were conscientiously moral and religious. Sinners may have some elements of truth about God and morality from universal revelation that serve as points of contact, but, like members of Alcoholics Anonymous, all of us as sinners must look beyond ourselves and admit that divine help is needed if we are to be transformed. "Our self-confidence must be shattered so that amidst the wreckage of our self-esteem we may discover the means by which we may rebuild our understanding of God and ourselves. The cross forces us to a point where we concede our inadequacies and turn instead to God."[186] Even more succinctly, "the cross represents an act of God which is simultaneously annihilating and creative—it destroys our (fleshly) preconceptions of God and in their place allows the living God to make his entrance. The cross places a question mark against all our (fleshly) values"[187] According to our fleshly nature, we expect God to endorse our moral and religious insights, but instead at the cross God shatters them and exposes them for the caricatures that they are.

A theology of the cross humbly sees things as they are in the sight of God's revelation of himself in Christ. "Your attitude should be the same as that of Christ Jesus" (Phil. 2:5). Jesus did not cling to his equality with God, but made himself nothing, becoming a human and a servant who obeyed until death, even death on a cross (vv. 6–8). In humility God's Son faced the realities of human life. He exposed our fleshly origins, named our conduct sin, and exposed us as the slaves we are to it. He left the self-righteous hearts open to the light of truth. But then he died in our place. The incarnate life of the Logos was completed as it was offered up on the cross. Have you found life through death? Strength through weakness? Hope through despair?

By our sufferings for the crucified and risen Christ we do not add any merit to his provisions, but we exhibit our highest loyalty. To large crowds Jesus said, "If anyone comes to me and does not hate his father and mother, his wife and children, his brothers and sisters—yes, even his own life—he cannot be my disciple" (Luke 14:26). In a growing series of confrontations with the Pharisees and attorneys, Jesus castigated them for their fanatic adherence to the letter of the law while denying its heart—justice and love. Then he asked those who continued to follow him against the legalistic establishment whether they would follow when it meant putting his kingdom of justice and love ahead of their usual respect, honor, and love of relatives.

A South African pastor explained that Jesus did not mean literal hatred of close relatives, but that

> while we love them we must realize that love for the Messiah, obedience to the Messiah, comes before and above all. It is to know that a time may come when all other obedience must give way to that obedience, when all other commitments must give way to that ultimate commitment. Nothing, not love of father, mother, wife or children, brother or sister, or even one's own life, must then stand in the way of that obedience.[188]

After alluding to a revealed plan to assassinate him and Bishop Tutu, Allan Boesak added:

> If they kill us, I want you to know: it is not because we have picked up a gun. It is not because we hated them. . . . If they kill us it is not because we have planned revolution. It will be because we have tried to stand up for justice, because we have refused to accept the cheap "reconciliation" which covers up evil, which denies justice, and which compromises the God-given dignity of black people. It will be because we love them so much that we refuse to allow them to continue to be our oppressors.[189]

In that spirit Christians can oppose racism wherever it is found without endorsing either communism's truncated materialistic diagnosis of human need or its economic determinism for a prescription.

Relate to God Boldly Through the Great High Priest

Christ's interrelated and divinely commissioned servant ministries have been viewed as primarily threefold. In the previous chapter on the God-man's life we emphasized his role as the greatest of prophets, but we also mentioned his qualifications as mediator. In this chapter on his death we stress his ministry as the greatest of all high priests. In the next chapter on his resurrection and ascension we will meditate further on his ministry as King, King of kings, and Lord of lords. Thinking about these roles as "ministries" for sinners seems more fitting than the traditional three "offices," though Christ held these official positions by the Father's commission. To avoid making the three aspects of Christ's mission unrelated to each other, Erickson calls them the three "functions" of revealing, reconciling and ruling.[190] Indeed they are all interdependent functions for our sakes and no one would have succeeded without the others. But Berkouwer goes too far in speaking of Christ's "office" (singular).[191] As loving functions for the sake of others, they may be fittingly called ministries, or "servant ministries" as of prophet, priest, and king.

Keeping in mind the interrelationships of Christ's work as prophet, priest, and king, we now consider Christ's distinctive ministry as the greatest of all high priests who offered the sacrifice to end all sacrifices.

1. Jesus Christ ministers as our high priest *in the heavenly sanctuary itself*. Under the old covenant the high priest only once a year on the Day of Atonement entered the temporal replica of the Holy of Holies behind the curtain in the tabernacle to pour the blood of the sacrifice on the mercy seat. The high priest did not have direct access to the immediate presence of God in heaven, and only once a year could enter its earthly symbol. But when Jesus died, "the curtain in the temple was torn in two" (Luke 23:45), portraying the opening of the way directly to God. "For Christ did not enter a man-made sanctuary that was only a copy of the true one; he entered heaven itself, now to appear for us in God's presence" (Heb. 9:24).

2. To the heavenly Father Christ offers his *once-for-all sacrifice for all our sins*. Year after year the Old Testament priests had to offer animal sacrifices which could not make sinners perfect (Heb. 10:1–3). It was impossible for the blood of bulls and goats to take away sins (v. 4). Jesus Christ became not only our priest but also our sacrifice. By the will of God the Father, Jesus Christ sacrificed his body once-for-all (v. 10). The sacrifice need not be repeated year after year "because by one sacrifice he has made perfect forever those who are being made holy" (v. 14). The blood of bulls and goats made recipients ceremonially and outwardly clean (9:13), but "how much more, then, will the blood of Christ, who through the eternal Spirit offered himself unblemished to God, cleanse our consciences from acts that lead to death, so that we may serve the living God!" (v. 14).

3. Our high priest is *empathetic*. He understands our deepest spiritual agony better than any other priest. When we suffer without cause, we may think that we have been forsaken by others and even by God. Sometimes we think no one cares. Like the psalmist, we may question whether God is with us here and now. At times the heavens seem like brass. God appears to take away blessings previously given. But those who cry out to God in suffering echo the death-cry of the Savior. He felt, more deeply than any of us can, the agony of being God-forsaken. So "we do not have a high priest who is unable to sympathize with our weaknesses, but we have one who has been tempted in every way, just as we are—yet was without sin. Let us then approach the throne of grace with confidence, so that we may receive mercy and find grace to help us in our time of need" (Heb. 4:14–16).

4. *In heaven Christ intercedes for us, as imperfect people*. The suffering servant, Isaiah perceived, not only "bore the sin of many" but also "made intercession for the transgressors" (Isa. 53:12). On earth he interceded for the unbelievers who crucified him: "Father, forgive them, for they do not know what they are doing" (Luke 23:34). And he intereceded in special ways for believers (John 17). In heaven Jesus "always lives to intercede for them" (those who come to God through him) (Heb. 7:25). John writes his first epistle so that his readers will not sin. "But if anybody does sin, we have one who speaks to the Father in our defense—Jesus Christ, the Righteous One. He is the atoning sacrifice for our sins, and not only for ours but also for the sins of the whole world" (1 John 2:1–2).

5. *The Messiah's atonement for our sins is complete and permanent*. Like Melchizedek, Jesus is "one who has become a priest not on the basis of a regulation as to his ancestry but on the basis of the power of an indestructible life" (Heb. 7:16). On the word of the Father Jesus is a priest forever (vv. 17, 21). His eternal ministry on behalf of his people assures a better covenant (v. 22). Death prevented other priests from continuing in office, "but because Jesus lives forever, he has a permanent priesthood" (v. 24). "Therefore he is able to save completely those who come to God through him, because he always lives to intercede for them" (v. 25).

6. Christ's atonement makes possible in history *the priesthood of every believer*. On the basis of Christ's atonement all of us can come directly to the Most High for ourselves and others. "Therefore, brothers, since we have confidence to enter the Most Holy Place by the blood of Jesus, by a new and living way opened for us through the curtain, that is, his body, and since we have a great priest over the house of God, let us draw near to God with a sincere heart in full assurance of faith"

(Heb. 10:19–22). Because we have committed sins against the holy God, human priests or good works will never suffice to allow us to approach God himself. From the absolutely holy One we can receive forgiveness on the ground of Christ's completed atonement as often as needed. The priesthood of believers means that none need approach the Almighty through a hierarchy of human priests or a series of alleged Gnostic or theosophical spiritual masters as intermediaries. Only One is our spiritual master (Matt. 23:8–10). And we may approach the supreme Being in heaven itself through Christ directly!

Present the Crucifixion to Children With Care

Truth about the death of Christ is essential for everyone who becomes a Christian, but is not the first doctrine to present to children or adults unacquainted with Christianity. The constructive nurture of our children begins with parental exhibits of fairness for all people and loving and dependable provisions to meet their needs. Against that background we can teach very young children about the Creator and sustainer of all, who is fair to all and wants us to be fair to all. Children also need to learn that people with loving care for them also teach them to avoid physical and moral dangers to their well-being. So caring parents and teachers prepare their children to live in a world where moral evil is very real.

Even the children of the most godly parents are born of the flesh and must learn about the subtleties of temptations, the complexities of their motivations, and their propensity toward sin for its own sake. They will learn about evil in the neighborhood and school, from the cartoons and comics, and through the entertainment and news media. Since they cannot be sheltered from the reality of fallenness, they can learn of the ambiguities and moral culpability of even the heroes of biblical history. From the Scriptures we ought to give them good reasons for rejecting temptations to sin. When children at their different stages come to moral accountability, they may sometimes intentionally hurt others, themselves, and God. They need to know that as much as they desire to please parents and teachers, they will do wrong. When they are old enough to realize their guilt before divine standards, they need more than further nurture in theism and morality. Children old enough to sin knowingly are old enough to hear the gospel of Christ. Loving nurture can show the need for the Messiah, but it cannot displace the necessity for receiving him.

Christians ought to tell their children and grandchildren that God cared enough for them as sinners to send his only Son as a baby. Parents and teachers ought to let children know about the life of Jesus, the supreme revelation of God. "Looking to the Gospels," James Denney observed, "we cannot fail to see that our Lord allowed His disciples every opportunity to become acquainted with Him, and to grow into confidence in Him before He began to teach them about His death."[192] In loving ways parents can help children to prize Jesus Christ, the example of faithful love, righteousness, mercy, and truth. When children understand at their levels of ability that Jesus was not only fair, but also merciful and loving to the undeserving, they are in a better position to understand the significance of his death.

Loving teaching about Christ's death for sinners reveals to young people both the consequence of sin and the cost of redemption from it. At their level of development, children can learn that by faith in the Christ who died and rose they can be forgiven of their guilt before

God's law. They can learn also to trust the crucified one for ability not to commit those sins again. And they can trust Christ for the turning away of God's righteous wrath and for reconciliation to God and others. Children can believe Christ's promises and receive eternal life. But they ought not be coerced or programed into believing by parental or peer pressures. Children need to develop their own convictions and present themselves to God by faith in the Messiah who died for them. Ultimately, their faith must be their own. When children are ready to commit themselves to the Savior, parents should not stand in their way. After their public profession of faith, parents and church leaders need to provide adequate training for their spiritual growth at each stage of their development.[193]

The more one loves, every parent knows, the more one is open to both happiness and sorrow. The more we love our children (and others), the more vulnerable we become to sorrow and disappointment at their hurts and losses. Both the Father and the Son loved greatly, and so throughout Jesus' life of temptation and agonizing death both suffered greatly. Because Father and Son are moved with a feeling of human infirmities, they are afflicted in all the afflictions of parents. Living for Christ is not one glorious television image of "success" with a dazzling flow of words and dollars. Commitment to the suffering servant calls for faithfulness while suffering in this world for his sake. Both parents and children need to view the Christian life with some realism.

Communicate the Message of the Cross Lovingly and Clearly

Any witness to the gospel must be given in love, and certainly love ought to be the primary motivation when working with pre-Christians of any age. Christ lovingly identified with those who were different and demonstrated a solidarity with those who were alien. "While we were still sinners, Christ died for us" (Rom. 5:8). Only in the practical form of love for others in the faith and outside it can Christians bear faithful witness to the One who laid down his life for those he loved. A loving spirit, however, is no substitute for the true story of Christ's death for our sins. As James Denney said,

> To preach the love of God out of relation to the death of Christ, or to preach the love of God in the death of Christ but without being able to relate it to sin, or to preach the forgiveness of sins as the free gift of God's love while the death of Christ has no special significance assigned to it, is not, if the New Testament is the rule and standard of Christianity, to preach the Gospel at all.[194]

Is it not enough lovingly to live for Christ? Some unbelieving spouses may indeed be won without a word by their mate (1 Peter 3:1–2). But no doubt they have heard the gospel from other sources. Generally we need to report the fact of the cross and explain its significance because our lives with their best deeds can be interpreted in many conflicting ways. Sinners must hear that God's Son came into the world and offered his sinless life as a sacrifice for their justification, redemption, and reconciliation. It is not, as Karl Barth claimed, that all are already reconciled to God and need only be informed of this prior fact. That Barthian view robs preaching the gospel of its urgency. For the provisions of the cross to become effective individuals must hear about them and personally receive them. "And how can they believe in the one of whom they have not heard? And how can they hear without someone preaching to them?" (Rom. 10:14). Essential to Christian communication with non-

Christians should be the good news of Christ's atoning provisions!

To preach the cross is not just to tell a story, dramatic and meaningful as stories and myths from different religions may be. To preach the cross is not even to tell this particular story as one among many moving religious stories. To preach the cross is to stand as a sworn "witness" to *this story's truth.* The Gospel, as Paul summed it up, contains assertions tested and found to be true as either historically observed facts or their divinely revealed meanings (1 Cor. 15:1–4). Which *facts* do we report in giving out the gospel? Jesus actually lived, died, was buried, and rose again from the grave. What are the *meanings* of these events included in the communication of the gospel? First, we ought to explain that these events occurred "according to the Scriptures," that is, in fulfillment of true predictions God's prophets made in his written Word. This assumes the plan of a personal God distinct from the world (Heb. 11:6) who has revealed truth to chosen spokesmen and inspired the prophetic writings. Second, proclaimers of the gospel affirm that in fulfillment of those trustworthy writings Jesus is the Christ, that is, the Lord from heaven, the promised Messiah. Third, preachers of the gospel declare that the Messiah died "for our sins." Fourth, they affirm that on the third day, Christ rose again from the dead.

The gospel is not about the human search for God, or human efforts for social justice; the good news reports God's merciful and gracious substitutionary action in Christ to save sinful people. The good news is not what we must do for Christ, but what Christ has done for us! We have shown that belief in the gospel greatly affects the relationships of the reconciled with others socially. But the social effects in human relationships and works are the fruit; the gospel message of the cross as the just basis of reconciliation is the root. Nontechnical passages of Scripture referring to the gospel do not always explicitly distinguish the message from the results of receiving it, but careful preaching and teaching do. Distinctively Christian reconciliation in society results from believing the great news of Christ's substitutionary sacrifice as its just and unifying basis. But the uncompleted responsibilities of creatures (as indicated in the law) ought never be confused with the gospel (the completed work of Christ). Those who want to make the social requirements of the law part of the gospel tragically turn it into bad news. No believers can fully live up to the commandments Christ gave his followers every day of their lives. The law is bad news not only to the unregenerate but also for the regenerate who continue to struggle with the flesh. The gospel is good news that does not focus on what we ought to do for Christ, but what our substitute has done once-for-all for us. Having received the crucified and risen Christ, however, Holy Spirit-enabled Christians do substantially fulfill the law (Rom. 8:3–4).

Give Priority to the Gospel in Your Teaching

The truths of the gospel lead our hearers away from false messiahs and to the One who can save them. By believing the truth of this message and receiving the provisions of the cross people receive eternal life and fellowship with the living God. So the facts and meanings of the gospel ought to take priority in all our oral and written communications with pre-Christians. By Paul's exaggerated statement "I resolved to know nothing while I was with you except Jesus Christ and him crucified" (1 Cor. 2:2), he asserts the central place of the atonement in Christian ministry.

To give priority to any other message

is to become cultic. In a theological context a cult is "a religious movement which claims authorization by Christ and the Bible but neglects or distorts the Gospel, the central message of the Savior and the Scripture."[195] Information about Christ's atonement is essential and central to genuinely Christian ministries. As Bernard Ramm wrote,

> A cult is a religious group which places a secondary need in the position of a primary need. Any group which puts its emphasis on health, or mental hygiene, or some religio-political program is cultic. The chief enemies of man are sin and death (1 Cor. 15), and the divine remedy is Jesus Christ crucified and risen from the dead. This is the first witness of the Bible (2 Tim. 3:15). If the cultists heard the Holy Spirit, they would hear this message. The fact that they do not so speak indicates that they do not hear the voice of the Spirit, which in turn means that they have an improper principle of religious authority.[196]

In the Old Testament the foreshadowing of Christ's atonement is central. In the Gospels the incarnation, sinless life, and death in place of others stand out above all else. The New Testament epistles expound on the significance of the cross as the foundation for all the work of the church with insiders and outsiders. According to Revelation, throughout eternity we will praise the Lamb that was slain. The great confessions and creedal statements of God's people feature the centrality of Christ's atonement. Can any who consider themselves moral and spiritual children of God by receiving Jesus as the Christ focus on a higher priority for both time and eternity?

The church "must learn that external criteria of relevance imposed upon it by society should give way to its inner criterion of relevance and identity—the cross and resurrection of Jesus Christ."[197] Again, it is imperative "that the church bases her understanding of the manner in which power is to be exercised upon a God-given, rather than a secular model."[198] In engaging the forces of evil as Christ did, the church needs to "regain a sense of perspective and a sense of *excitement,* of having something exhilarating to say, as we return to face the world."[199]

REVIEW QUESTIONS

To Help Relate and Apply Each Section in This Chapter

1. *Briefly state the classical problem* this chapter addresses and indicate reasons why genuine inquiry into it is important for your worldview and your existence personally and socially.

2. *Objectively summarize the influential answers* given to this problem in history as hypotheses to be tested. Be able to compare and contrast their real similarities and differences (not merely verbal similarities or differences).

3. *Highlight the primary biblical evidence* on which to decide among views—evidence found in the relevant teachings of the major divisions of Scripture—and decide for yourself which historical hypothesis (or synthesis of historical views) provides the most consistent and adequate account of the primary biblical data.

4. *Formulate in your own words your doctrinal conviction* in a logically consistent and adequate way, organizing your conclusions in ways you can explain clearly, support biblically, and communicate effectively to your spouse, children, friends, Bible class, or congregation.

5. *Defend your view* as you would to adherents of the alternative views, showing that the other views are logically less consistent and factually faced with more difficulties than your view in accounting for the givens, not only of

special revelation but also of human experience in general.

6. *Explore the differences the viability of your conviction can make in your life.* Then test your understanding of the viability of your view by asking, "Can I live by it authentically (unhypocritically) in relation to God and to others in my family, church, vocation, neighborhood, city, nation, and world?"

MINISTRY PROJECTS

To Help Communicate This Doctrine in Christian Service

1. *Memorize one major verse or passage* that in its context teaches the heart of this doctrine and may serve as a text from which to preach, teach, or lead small-group studies on the topic. The memorized passages from each chapter will build a body of content useful also for meditation and reference in informal discussions.

2. *Formulate the major idea of the doctrine in one sentence* based on the passage memorized. This idea should be useful as the major thesis of either a lesson for a class (junior high to adult) or a message for a church service.

3. *State the specific purpose or goal of your doctrinal lesson or message.* Your purpose should be more than informative. It should show why Christians need to accept this truth and live by it (unhypocritically). For teaching purposes, list indicators that would show to what extent class members have grasped the truth presented.

4. *Outline your message or lesson in complete sentences.* Indicate how you would support the truth of the doctrine's central ideas and its relevance to life and service. Incorporate elements from this chapter's historical, biblical, systematic, apologetic, and practical sections selected according to the value they have for your audience.

5. *List applications of the doctrine* for communicating the difference this conviction makes in life (for sermons, lessons, small-group Bible studies, or family devotional Bible studies). Applications should make clear what the doctrine is, why one needs to know it, and how it will make differences in thinking. Then show how the difference in thought will lead to differences in values, priorities, attitudes, speech, and personal action. Consider also the doctrine's possible significance for family, church, neighborhood, city, regional, and national actions.

6. *Start a file and begin collecting illustrations* of this doctrine's central idea, the points in your outline, and your application.

7. *Write out your own doctrinal statement on this subject in one paragraph* (in half a page or less). To work toward a comprehensive doctrinal statement, collect your formulations based on a study of each chapter of *Integrative Theology*. As your own statement of Christian doctrine grows, you will find it personally strengthening and useful when you are called on for your beliefs in general and when you apply for service with churches, mission boards, and other Christian organizations. Any who seek ordination to Christian ministry will need a comprehensive doctrinal statement that covers the broad scope of theology.

CHAPTER 8

CHRIST'S RESURRECTION, ASCENSION, AND PRESENT EXALTATION

Christ's Resurrection, Ascension, and Present Exaltation

THE PROBLEM: HOW SHALL WE UNDERSTAND THE RESURRECTION OF JESUS, HIS ENTRY INTO HEAVEN, HIS SOVEREIGN RULE OVER THE WORLD, AND HIS INTERCESSORY MINISTRY ON BEHALF OF BELIEVERS?

Classically Christianity has been viewed as a religion of resurrection. This is to say that most authorities scattered in different countries and situations understand the Christian faith as profoundly bound up with the Easter event. Even the avant garde Roman Catholic theologian Hans Küng can affirm: "Without Easter there is no Gospel, . . . no faith, no proclamation, no Church, no worship, no mission in Christendom."[1] But the plethora of challenges to the resurrection in the modern world raises the question whether scientifically oriented people can reasonably accept the resurrection of a dead man some two thousand years ago. Modern science, philosophy, and historiography—based on naturalistic assumptions—pose numerous objections to the Christian belief concerning the resurrection of Jesus from the grave. Thus Christian faith and much humanistic scholarship clash head-on relative to this crucial tenet of the faith.

The issue of the resurrection relates in important ways to other Christian doctrines. Many regard Christ's resurrection (variously defined) as the fitting conclusion to his descent to earth (chap. 5) and atoning death on the cross (chap. 7). How we understand the resurrection will influence our comprehension of the application of salvation to believers (vol. 3, chaps. 1–4), the nature of the church (vol. 3, chaps. 5–6), and Christ's rule over the world (vol. 3, chaps. 7–9).

In the present chapter we inquire whether reports of the resurrection of Christ from the dead two thousand years ago are historically factual or merely statements of faith. Did the bodily resurrection of Jesus engender the disciples' faith, or did the rekindling of faith in the disciples' hearts give birth to the resurrection stories? Are the accounts of the resurrection in the Gospels and the Epistles coherent, or are they difficult to resolve and thus of questionable validity? If the resurrection be granted as true, we must inquire whether it involved the literal raising of Jesus' body or only the survival of his soul. Greek philosophy anticipated much modern thought with its view of salvation as the liberation of the soul from the shackles of the body. How compelling are the evidences for the raising of Jesus' body from the tomb? Moreover, is the resurrection an event in ordinary history, like Jesus' death on the cross or the conversion of Saul of Tarsus? Or does the resurrection belong to some suprahistorical realm and therefore elude verification by the ordinary methods of historical investigation?

In addition, if Jesus literally rose from the grave, what can be said about the nature or composition of his resurrection body? How shall we understand the relation between Jesus' earthly body and the body of his resurrection? Of primary importance is the theological significance of Christ's bodily resurrection for the Christian scheme of things. Would Christian life and faith remain viable if Christ had not risen from the dead? C. E. M. Joad, a liberal churchman who became a more orthodox Christian, somewhere said that if he were able to interview any person from the past it would be Jesus of Nazareth. and he would ask Jesus the most important question in the world: "Did you or did you not rise from the dead?"

In this chapter we also investigate whether Jesus' ascension to heaven was an actual event in space and time. How compelling is the evidence for Jesus' elevation to heaven? Moreover, what is the significance of the Son's ascension to the Father for the life of the believer? In addition, we inquire into the meaning and significance of Jesus' exaltation to the right hand of God. How shall we understand this event? Furthermore, what is meant by Christ's ministry of heavenly intercession, and what does this activity accomplish for the individual believer and the church? We discuss also whether the exalted Christ performs the work of king in his stage of exaltation. What does this royal ministry involve? In all these matters we seek to determine the difference faith in the exalted Christ makes for Christian life day by day in the world.

Finally, what light does Christ's resurrection, ascension, and present exaltation shed on the question of the uniqueness of Jesus Christ for salvation? Is the Nazarene the only way to God, or is he but one of several ways, as many modern voices allege?

ALTERNATIVE INTERPRETATIONS IN THE CHURCH

Liberal Denials of the Resurrection

Assuming that at creation God established a religion of nature that was perfect and that no supernatural events disturbed the fixed order of things, deists flatly denied Jesus' resurrection from the grave. Thomas Woolston claimed that the resurrection stories "consist of absurdities, improbabilities and incredibilities."[2] Woolston reiterated Celsus' argument that the resurrection was a deliberate fraud.[3] The disciples either bribed or intoxicated the Roman soldiers, then stole the body from the tomb and pretended that Jesus had risen from the dead. The postresurrection appearances were said to be as reliable as pagan stories of the ghosts of the dead. Peter Annet, in *The Resurrection of Jesus Considered* (1744), also attacked the trustworthiness of the resurrection narratives and claimed that on the cross Jesus did not actually die.

The eighteenth- and nineteenth-century liberal "Lives of Jesus" eliminated all traces of the supernatural from the person of Christ. Writers of the "Lives" offered naturalistic explanations for the Gospel miracles. The most popular interpretation of the resurrection was the swoon theory. According to the Heidelberg theologian H. E. G. Paulus, Jesus fell into a deathlike trance on the cross. But the cool air of the tomb, the aromatic spices, and the earthquake revived him to consciousness. Donning the garments of a gardener (John 20:15), Jesus returned to his disciples and began to teach them. When his strength began to fail, he assembled his followers on the Mount of Olives and blessed them. A cloud moved in to hide Jesus from their sight. Later on the Lord died in obscurity. In his *Life of Jesus* (1864) Schleiermacher likewise argued that Jesus merely lapsed into unconsciousness on the cross and in the cool of the tomb revived and lived for a while among his followers. What came to be known as the resurrection connotes that the believer, animated by Christ's life, achieves perfect union with God. In any case, the essence of true religion is not a dogma, such as the resurrection or ascension; rather, it is the experienced reality of the person's sense of absolute dependence on God. "The right impression of Christ can be, and has been, present in its fullness without a knowledge of these facts."[4]

Others propounded the theft or fraud theory. In *The Goal of Jesus and His Disciples*, published by Lessing in 1778, Reimarus argued that the disciples, discouraged by the failure of Jesus' political mission, conspired to steal his body. After waiting fifty days for the body to decompose, the disciples falsely claimed that Jesus had risen, that he had appeared to them several times, and that he would return in glory to inaugurate his kingdom. O. Holtzmann theorized that Joseph of Arimathea was embarrassed by having a crucified man buried in his family vault. Thus without the knowledge of the disciples, Joseph secretly removed the body of Jesus and buried it in another grave.

Other biographers of Jesus advanced the subjective-vision theory. According to D. F. Strauss, the emotionally distraught disciples hallucinated and "saw" in their minds Jesus risen from the dead. Strauss maintained that the Gospel stories of Jesus' transfiguration, miracles, resurrection, and ascension represent legendary accretions stimulated by "tales" from the Old Testament. By this means Jesus' followers elevated their human teacher into a supernatural Messiah-figure. J. Ernst Renan, in *La Vie de Jesus* (1863), argued that while in a state of profound emotional frenzy Mary Magdalene believed that she saw and heard Jesus in the garden. The poetic Renan wrote of Mary: "O divine hallucination! Her enthusiasm gave to the world a resuscitated God."[5] Like wildfire, Mary's frenzied vision spread to other friends of Jesus. Vision followed upon vision, until all the disciples believed that Jesus was alive. In due course the excitement abated, and the visions ceased to occur.

Theologians such as Fichte, Riggenbach, Keim, and Streeter, unable to affirm Jesus' bodily resurrection, propounded the objective-vision theory. As outlined by Keim, Jesus' spirit survived the death of his body (which slept on in the tomb) and was exalted to the right hand of God. In order to rekindle faith following Calvary, the glorified spirit of Christ appeared to the disciples and communicated with them by a "telegram from heaven." The God-given visions of the exalted Christ were so realistic that the disciples mistook them for a bodily resurrection. Streeter identified the communication as a kind of telepathy and added that the tomb was found empty because an unknown person removed Jesus' body to another place.

Kirsopp Lake, a Harvard theologian, rejects the bodily resurrection of Jesus and suggests that on Easter morning the women visited the wrong grave. When they arrived at an empty tomb, a young man directed their attention to a sealed tomb nearby where Jesus supposedly lay: "He is not here. See the place where they laid him" (Mark 16:6). Frightened and confused, the women fled and told the disciples of the empty tomb, which report encouraged the latter in their belief that they had seen the Lord. Concludes Lake: "The empty tomb is for us doctrinally indefensible, and is historically insufficiently accredited."[6]

Most liberals view Jesus as a human prophet and ethical reformer who labored to advance the kingdom of God. Authorities in the tradition generally rejected the biblical miracles and viewed the Gospel narratives as seriously flawed. Harnack drew a sharp distinction between the "Easter message" of the empty grave and the "Easter faith" that death has been destroyed. Faith must abandon forever the Easter message, for the traditions of the empty tomb and the appearances of Jesus are far from certain historical facts. On the other hand, "the Easter *faith* is the conviction that the crucified one gained a victory over death; that God is just and powerful; that he who is the firstborn among many brethren still lives."[7] Harnack grounds faith, not in historical evidences, such as the alleged empty tomb, nor in human reports, such as Jesus' purported appearances, but in the impression Jesus made on the hearts and minds of the New Testament writers. In fact, Harnack judges that faith has nothing to do with the question of Jesus' bodily resurrection but everything to do with the experienced reality that Jesus is the living Lord. Harnack concludes that the doctrine of Christ's literal resurrection must yield to the existential fact "that death is vanquished, that there is a life eternal."[8] Other liberals, such as Walter Rauschenbusch, W. A. Brown, and Henry Van Dusen focus on the religion of Jesus rather than on dogmas about Jesus. Since most liberals viewed Jesus as a man indwelt by God, traditional doctrines of the bodily resurrection and ascension to heaven were disallowed.

From their philosophical presuppositions, process theologians view the resurrection as the obverse of the incarnation. Whereas the incarnation signifies that God is immanently present in the man Jesus and the world, the resurrection signifies that Jesus is immanently present in God. "It is as meaningful to speak of Jesus raised into God and 'living on' in God as it is to speak of God 'prehended' into and indwelling in—'living' in—Jesus. The first is the supreme instance of resurrection, the second the supreme instance of incarnation."[9]

Process thinkers such as Hartshorne, Hamilton, Griffin, and Mellert assent, not to the objective immortality of Jesus (i.e., his conscious existence beyond death), but to his subjective immortality (i.e., the memory of him in the mind of God). That is, the resurrection is a symbol for the fact that Jesus' thoughts, actions, and experiences have been raised up and incorporated into the reality of God. But Jesus' experiences (as the paradigmatic man) were no different from those of any other human being. "We are indeed, moment by moment, likewise being taken up into the divine nature and 'resurrected' into objective immortality where we become part of the perishable data for future occasions."[10] For process theologians, the resurrection means that the inspiration and genius of a person are "continually being resurrected from the past for the edification of emerging moments of history."[11] Mellert believes that this is particularly true for the great personalities of history, such as Socrates, Buddha, St. Francis, and Jesus. In sum, many process theologians see no conscious life after death and certainly no bodily resurrection of Jesus from the grave.[12]

Neoorthodox Dehistoricizing of the Resurrection

Neoorthodox authorities remove the resurrection of Christ from the realm of verifiable history. Theologians in the tradition claim that the Easter event is not a scientifically demonstrable fact like other events in history, but is a reality to be apprehended solely by faith.

Enlightenment philosopher G. E. Lessing stimulated this emphasis by speaking of "the ugly ditch" that exists between absolute truths and the contingent events of history. Faith rests not on external historical facts, but on the certainty afforded by inner experience. Consequently, Lessing concludes, the New Testament stories of Jesus' resurrection (even if they were reliable) offer no viable basis for the absolute truths of religion. More positively, Kierkegaard accepted the miracle of Christ's resurrection.[13] Yet because of the "infinite qualitative difference" between eternity and time, Kierkegaard insisted that the resurrection cannot be grasped by the historical method. Rather, by a radical leap of faith the believer comes to know the power of Christ's resurrection in his life.

The early, dialectical Barth viewed the resurrection not as an historical event but as a symbol of God's revelatory action. Said Barth of the risen Lord: "Within history, Jesus as the Christ can be understood only as problem or myth."[14] For the early Barth the resurrection was a "nonhistorical" event that bears no essential relationship to historical concerns such as the empty tomb and the personal appearances.

In his *Church Dogmatics* Barth spoke more confidently of the resurrection as an objective event in the space-time world. Thus Christ rose from the dead "in the human sphere and in human time, as an actual event within the world with an objective content."[15] Furthermore, Barth views the resurrection as the verdict of the Father on the Son's obedient representation of the human race on the cross. Whereas on Good Friday the "No" of the Father fell on the Son and sinful humanity, on Easter the "Yes" of the Father fell on the Son and all humanity in him. In other words, the resurrection of Christ signifies that on the cross sinful humanity was irrevocably judged and forgiven. Thus, the resurrection "is the justification of all sinful men, whose death was decided in this event."[16] By such a line of reasoning Barth relates the resurrection to the notion of universal salvation.

Yet Barth adds that because of the presence of "obscurities and irreconcilable contradictions"[17] in the resurrection narratives a coherent account of the Easter event cannot be reconstructed. The mature Barth continued to deny that the resurrection can be validated by modern scientific or historical investigation. Whereas the wars of Caesar and even Jesus' crucifixion can be thought of as historical, the resurrection cannot. Seeking to shelter this extraordinary act of God from historical criticism, Barth judges the resurrection to be the same genre as Genesis 1 and 2—namely, "saga," "legend," and "a 'prehistorical' happening."[18] Said Barth of the Easter accounts: "the stories are couched in the imaginative, poetic style of historical saga, and are therefore marked by the corresponding obscurity. For they are describing an event beyond the reach of historical research or depiction."[19] Barth thinks that the historian, with his critical methods, can neither refute nor confirm the empty tomb and the postresurrection appearances to the disciples.

Furthermore, Barth denies that the ascension was an actual elevation in space observable to the disciples. Not a verifiable event in history, the ascension is "a legend," "a sign of the Easter event," or "a *pointer* to the revelation that occurred in the resurrection of Jesus Christ as the bearer of all power in heaven and earth."[20] The ascension was the last and the most concrete of all the appearances of the Risen Lord.

Emil Brunner identifies the resurrection of Christ as the cornerstone of the Christian faith: "The message of Easter is the Christian message, and the Christian Church is the Church of the Resurrection."[21] Yet like Barth, Brunner refuses to view the resurrection as an event of ordinary history. Following Kierkegaard, who permitted no direct identity between revelation and history, Brunner posits the resurrection as an event of primal history (*Urgeschichte*) that must be differentiated from ordinary history (*Historie*). "It is suprahistory, eschatological history, hence it is no longer historical at all."[22] Brunner judges that the situation would be precarious if faith rested on inconsistencies and legends in the Gospel narratives. Christian faith never arises out of historical data such as the empty tomb or the postresurrection appearances. Rather, for Brunner, faith rests on the proclamation of the apostles who experienced the resurrection as fact. Said Brunner: "In faith we are not concerned with the Jesus of history, as historical science sees Him, but with the Jesus Christ of personal testimony, who is the real Christ."[23] Since the resurrection is an event of primal history, Brunner is reluctant to affirm that Christ rose from the grave on the third day literally and bodily. The language of the bodily resurrection connotes the continuity of Christ's personality and individuality in his supramundane existence.[24] For the same reason, Brunner denies the historical actuality of Christ's bodily ascension to heaven. Spiritually interpreted, the exaltation and ascension signify Christ's "return to the pure transcendence of his prehistorical existence."[25]

For Dietrich Bonhoeffer Christ's glorious resurrection from the dead represents God's "Yes" to Christ and his work, to the believer, and to all that God has made. Faith in the resurrection, however, is not bound up with historical concerns such as the empty tomb. If the resurrection could be verified by history, it would render faith superfluous. Bonhoeffer's bottom line concerning the resurrection is that "we cannot be sure of its historicity."[26] The reality of the resurrection is existentially certified through faith in the apostolic testimony to Christ. Since Bonhoeffer views the entire life of Christ as a stumbling block to reason, he is not surprised that the Lord should depart from this world *incognito*.

Bultmannian Demythologizing of the Resurrection

Whereas neoorthodoxy claimed that the resurrection could not be historically verified, the Bultmannian school more radically viewed bodily resurrection from the dead as an untenable prescientific notion. Bultmann's view of the resurrection was shaped by three principal factors: (1) Form criticism, which examines the oral traditions that undergird the written documents, led Bultmann to conclude that all that can be known about Jesus is that he existed and was crucified under Pontius Pilate. (2) His naturalistic view of history posited a nexus of cause and effect in a closed system. Consequently all alleged miracles, including the resurrection, cannot be accepted as historical events (*Historie*). Bultmann maintains that "an historical fact which involves a resurrection from the dead is utterly inconceivable!"[27] (3) Existentialist philosophy led him to conclude that the New Testament focuses, not on the objective facts of history (such as the bodily resurrection), but on the meaning of the resurrection for personal existence (*Geschichte*).

Thus Bultmann declares that "the resurrection is not an event of past history,"[28] but a Hellenistic cult-myth that found its way into the New Testament. From our modern, scientific perspective we must demythologize the resurrection story, that is, reinterpret it in terms of the possibilities of human existence. For the disciples the resurrection signified the rise of faith in the crucified Lord. As Jesus' followers reflected on his message, his example, and the significance of his death on the cross, they were moved to forsake their old way of life and embrace the new life of victory over sin and death. For Bultmann the resurrection is not an event that happened to Jesus, but one that happened to the disciples. The Marburg theologian thus reduced the Easter *event* to the Easter *faith* of the disciples. Moreover, the risen Christ comes to people today through the call to decision and authentic existence mediated by Christian preaching. This means for Bultmann that Christ is risen in the event of gospel proclamation, which is to say that the eschatological "now" has arrived. Affirms Bultmann: "Christ meets us in the preaching as one crucified and risen. . . . The faith of Easter is just this—faith in the word of preaching."[29] But if Christ's resurrection signifies no more than the rise of faith, where did the notion of a bodily resurrection come from? The early Bultmann suggested that this untenable corporeal view arose from subjective visions prompted by the disciples' intimate relation to Jesus during his lifetime. The later Bultmann appears to have vacillated on this matter. "How the Easter faith arose in the individual disciples has been obscured in the tradition by legend and is not of basic importance."[30]

An influential group of Bultmann's students and followers—such as Ernst Käsemann, Günther Bornkamm, Ernst Fuchs, Hans Conzelmann, Willi Marxen, and James Robinson—have pursued "the new quest for the historical Jesus." Committed to a critical reevaluation of Bultmann, the "new questers" seek to establish continuity between the historical Jesus and the kerygma of the early church. These scholars believe that identity between the earthly Jesus and the exalted Christ must be preserved lest the Easter faith collapse into pure myth. In their studies they ground the Christian message in Jesus' self-understanding or his teaching. Yet given their positivistic view of history and their antipathy to the miraculous, the "new questers" appear no more willing than Bultmann to affirm Jesus' bodily resurrection from the dead.

Günther Bornkamm believes that the Gospels are products of the faith of the Christian community. Consequently what the historian can know is not the Easter event itself but the Easter faith of the disciples. "The event of Christ's resurrection from the dead [is] removed from historical scholarship. History cannot ascertain and establish conclusively the facts about them as it can with other events of the past. The last historical fact available to them is the Easter faith of the first disciples."[31] The significant datum is that the disciples *believed* that Jesus had risen from the dead. What gave rise to their Easter faith was the revelation of Jesus' transcendent selfhood to their hearts and minds. Later the church preserved the faith of the disciples in the form of the Easter stories, including the legends of the empty tomb and the bodily appearances. Bornkamm judges that the resurrection narratives exclude the possibility of an actual corporeal resurrection of Jesus.

Willi Marxen affirms that the basis of Christology is not the post-Easter kerygma but Jesus' ministry and summons to faith. The closest one can get to the resurrection is the event of Simon Peter's faith. But the fact that Jesus calls forth faith from people, even after his death, represents the real miracle. Declares Marxen, "The miracle [of the resurrection] is the birth of faith."[32] That Jesus evokes faith even after his physical death means that the activity of Jesus in the world continues. The early Christians expressed this conviction by means of the saying "Jesus is risen!" Clearly Marxen does not believe that the resurrection was an actual event in space and time. Rather, the resurrection is a vivid pictorial image for the miraculous nature of the faith found in the lives of people even after Jesus' death. The faith Marxen envisages is commitment in response to a call—a faith that would be weakened by appeal to historical evidences. Marxen's thesis that the recorded teachings of Jesus evoke faith in the form of radical commitment does not require the survival of Jesus beyond the grave.

Influenced by logical empiricism's affirmation of the meaninglessness of anything not accessible to the five senses, Paul van Buren draws the sweeping conclusion that theological statements are invalid in a secular age. Whereas the empty tomb can be empirically verified, the claim that the invisible God raised Christ from the dead cannot be so validated. Van Buren maintains that "we would prefer not to speak of the Easter event as a 'fact' at all, not in the ordinary use of the word."[33] The radical postcrucifixion change in the disciples provides a clue to the resurrection. Precisely what happened to the disciples is not open to historical investigation. But on Easter Sunday "a situation of discernment" occurred, which is to say that "the light dawned"[34] upon the hearts of Jesus' fearful followers, providing them with a new perspective on life and death. This liberating power had always been in Jesus; but "on Easter, the freedom of Jesus began to be *contagious*."[35] When the disciples experienced this radical inner transformation, they fabricated the story of Jesus' bodily resurrection from the dead.

Post-Bultmannian Dekerygmatizing of the Resurrection

Scholars to the left of Bultmann complain that the Marburg theologian failed to demythologize consistently and completely. Thus whereas Bultmann believed that everything must be demythologized except the saving event of Jesus Christ, more radical theologians dekerygmatize the faith by claiming that human self-understanding can be achieved without reference to Christ or the gospel. Thus the Swiss theologian Fritz Büri propounds a kind of existential natural theology that has no need of Jesus Christ and his resurrection. The important thing for Büri is that the idea of the Christ is the symbol of love. Similarly, German theologian Herbert Braun argues that the contemporary church must translate the message about Jesus into a more modern metaphor. Accordingly, Braun subsumes the person and work of Jesus under the rubric of human self-understanding. Concerning Jesus' deity and resurrection Braun writes, "In the literal sense in which these terms are used in the New Testament, I cannot accept them."[36]

Schubert Ogden likewise argues that the conditions for authentic existence "can be formulated in complete abstraction from the event of Jesus of Nazareth and all that it specifically imports."[37] Since the view that men and women are in bondage to sin and are powerless to rescue themselves is pure myth, Ogden judges that persons can actualize authentic existence by their own efforts without regard to Christ. "The premise . . . is that man is a genuinely free and responsible being, and therefore his salvation is something that . . . he himself has to decide by his understanding of his existence."[38] Hence the "myth" of Jesus' resurrection possesses no soteriological relevance. So Ogden boldly declares, "If, *per impossibile*, the corpse of a man was actually resuscitated, this would be just as relevant to my salvation as an existing self or person as that the carpenter next door just drove a nail in a two-by-four, or that American technicians have at last been successful in recovering a nose cone that had first been placed in orbit around the earth."[39] Rejecting the traditional distinctions between nature and grace, philosophy and theology, general revelation and special revelation, Ogden claims that what Jesus imparts is available to all people through science and philosophy, particularly existentialist thought. Theology must stress "that God saves man by grace alone in complete freedom from any saving 'work' of the kind traditionally portrayed in the doctrines of the person and work of Christ."[40] Ogden claims that the historic Christian teaching that Christ alone imparts salvation amounts to the heresy of works righteousness denounced by the apostle Paul. For Ogden, then, Jesus Christ and his resurrection from the dead are virtually irrelevant to the human quest for authentic existence.

More recently Ogden emphasizes that Christology must be viable both personally (i.e., existentially) and practically. Thus in *The Point of Christology*[41] Ogden supplements his existential interpretation of Christianity with a new political interpretation that seeks the transformation of the present social order. Whereas Ogden had demythologized and dekerygmatized the faith, he now seeks to "deideologize" Christian belief by interpreting Scripture politically with a view to transforming the basic structures of society.

The Historicism of the Pannenberg School

Pannenberg opposes both the neoorthodox view that relegates the resurrection to the realm of suprahistory and the existentialist view that denies the resurrection any independent reality. Only if the resurrection is a historical fact, Pannenberg argues, does the Christian faith have a stable foundation. In fact, Pannenberg claims that historical research demonstrates to a high degree of probability that God raised Jesus from the dead. "The resurrection of Jesus is an historical event, an event that really happened at that time."[42] Although he holds that the Gospel resurrection narratives are late, legendary, and contradictory, Pannenberg argues that two independent lines of historical evidence confirm the high probability of Jesus' resurrection. The first is the evidence of the empty tomb. Unwilling simply to read off the resurrection from the Gospel accounts, Pannenberg believes that the early Christians satisfied themselves that Jesus' tomb was empty. If the tomb had not been empty, the early church would not have survived as a witnessing community. The second line of evidence focuses on the appearances of the risen Lord to the disciples (1 Cor. 15:1–11). The early date and independent nature of the traditions in the Christian community validate the actual appearances of Jesus to his followers. Pannenberg claims that, rooted in the postexilic Jewish apocalyptic expectation of the end of the world, the resurrection of the dead, and the final judgment, the disciples possessed the language to express Jesus' resurrection from the grave. Pannenberg notes that the term *resurrection* is a metaphor that describes a reality unique to human experience. Jesus' resurrection should be viewed, not as the resuscitation of his former body, but as the emergence of a radically new life in a new body. As for its significance, the resurrection not only confirmed Jesus' claim to divine authority but also served as the principal sign of the irruption of the end of the world in anticipation of the goal of history.

Influenced by the Marxist philosopher Ernst Bloch, Jürgen Moltmann focuses attention on the future and hope. Against Bultmann's existentialism that collapses Christ's resurrection into human self-understanding, Moltmann interprets the resurrection as a unique historical event. "Christianity stands or falls with the reality of the raising of Jesus from the dead by God. In the New Testament there is no faith that does not start a priori with the resurrection of Jesus."[43] Moltmann insists that we cannot talk about the meaning of the resurrection apart from its historical foundation; the resurrection cannot be existentially true and at the same time historically false. Instead of defining the resurrection in terms of the modern positivistic understanding of history, Moltmann requires that we define history in terms of the resurrection. Thus the resurrection of Jesus creates history, where history is the process that presses toward the eschatological goal. "The resurrection is 'a history-making event' in the light of which all other history is illumined, called in question and transformed."[44] More particularly, "The resurrection has set in motion an eschatologically determined process of history, whose goal is the annihilation of death in the victory of the life of the resurrection."[45] Moltmann, however, is vague about the nature of Jesus' resurrection. He judges that the resurrection has no precise analogue to anything in the space-time continuum. "What 'resurrection of the dead' really is and how the rising of Jesus 'actually happened' is something even the New Testament reports of Easter do not claim to know."[46] Both Jesus' resurrection and his appearances to the disciples belong to eschatological history and are subject to future verification. Accordingly, "the resurrection of Christ is without parallel in the history known to us."[47] By claiming that Jesus' resurrection belongs to eschatological history rather than to world history, Moltmann has made concessions to the thought of Barth.

For Moltmann the significance of the resurrection lies in its future-orientation. Thus (1) the resurrection of the crucified is primarily an event of promise. Jesus' resurrection extends to humankind the promise of life, peace, freedom, and truth. The ultimate promise grounded in Easter is, "I am making everything new!" (Rev. 21:5). (2) The resurrection is the ground of hope. Because Jesus rose from the grave, humankind is filled with hope regarding the resurrection of the body, the annihilation of death, and the coming of the genuinely new. And (3) the resurrection represents a call to action. In anticipation of the end-time transformation, the God of the Exodus and the resurrection summons the church to world-wide mission, including the struggle for justice, freedom, and peace.

Most Fathers, Reformers, and Evangelicals

Against docetist denials of Christ's corporeality, the apostolic fathers firmly upheld the Lord's bodily resurrection from the tomb. Thus Ignatius wrote of Christ: "I know and believe that he was in the flesh even after the resurrection."[48] For Ignatius Christ's resurrection was no less a historical event than his birth and death: "I believe steadfastly in the birth, passion and the resurrection, which took place during the procuratorship of Pontius Pilate."[49] The Lord's resurrection is the guarantee of his divine mission and the resurrection of Christian believers in the last day. Pseudo-Barnabas attests both the Lord's bodily resurrection and his ascension: "Jesus rose from the dead, after which he manifested himself and went up to heaven."[50] Similar is the view of Polycarp of Smyrna: "God raised our Lord Jesus Christ from the dead and gave him glory and a throne on his right hand."[51]

The apologists opposed dualistic Greek philosophy that viewed matter as inherently evil and incapable of attaining immortality. In his essay *On the Resurrection,* Justin Martyr states his conviction about Christ in the form of a question: "Why did he rise in the flesh in which he suffered, unless to show the resurrection of the flesh?"[52] To the objection that Jesus' appearances were mere phantasms and not reality, Justin responded that the disciples fully satisfied themselves of Jesus' bodily resurrection by examining his wounds and eating food with him. Irenaeus testified that on the third day Jesus rose from the grave in the flesh and ascended to the Father in heaven.[53] On the basis of Christ's victory, believers also will rise into the presence of God.

Tertullian observed that among his fellow Christians "belief in the resurrection was firmly settled."[54] Tertullian himself upheld the Latin view that the substance of Jesus' resurrection body was identical to the body of his earthly existence. According to Tertullian, Christ's post-Easter appearances confirm that his resurrection body consisted of the same bones, nerves, and veins that constituted his earthly body. However the nature of the resurrection body be defined, Tertullian insisted on the reality of the Easter event: "If the resurrection of the flesh be denied, that prime article of the faith is shaken."[55] Tertullian's perspective on the nature of Christ's resurrection body was shared by Justin Martyr, Methodius, Jerome, Gregory the Great, and most medieval theologians.

Origen in the East likewise confessed the resurrection and ascension of the Savior in a body.[56] Origen judged that Jesus' disciples could not have persevered in the dangerous task of proclaiming Christ if he had not risen from the grave. Yet from his Alexandrian perspective Origen held that the nature of Jesus' resurrection body was somewhere between the phantom view of the Docetists and Gnostics and the material view of Latin theology.[57] Thus at the resurrection Christ's body did not return to its earthly condition, but was transformed into a spiritual form capable of inhabiting the heavens. Accordingly, Origen writes, not of the resurrection of Christ's flesh, but of the resurrection of his body, which was profoundly spiritual. Origen's view on the nature of Christ's resurrection body was shared by Cyril of Jerusalem, Gregory of Nyssa, and John Chrysostom.

Augustine firmly believed that Christ's bodily resurrection, his heavenly ascension, and his session at the right hand of the Father were attested by Old Testament prophecies, by the reports of faithful eyewitnesses, by the courageous preaching of early Christians threatened with martyrdom, and by the miracles wrought by Jesus' followers. As for acceptance of the resurrection, Augustine testified, "The fact is that the whole world now believes that the earthly body of Christ has been taken up to heaven. Learned and unlearned alike no longer doubt the resurrection of his flesh and his ascension into heaven, while there is but a handful of those who continue to be puzzled."[58] Concerning the nature of the resurrection body, Augustine follows Luke 24:39 and the Western tradition; Christ's heavenly body consists of the same flesh and bones as his earthly body. "I believe that the Lord's body is in heaven in the same condition as it was on earth when he ascended into heaven."[59] Although material in substance, the Lord's body is called spiritual because it is energized by the Holy Spirit and because of its freedom of movement from place to place.

Several early Christian creedal statements attest the historical reality of Christ's bodily resurrection, ascension to heaven, and session at the right hand of the Father. The Apostles' Creed testifies concerning Christ: "The third day He rose again from the dead; He ascended into heaven, and sitteth at the right hand of God the Father Almighty." Since Jesus' birth, crucifixion, and burial immediately preceding clearly are historical, so are the parallel statements concerning his resurrection, ascension, and session. Similar convictions are contained in the Nicene Creed and the Athanasian Creed.

Luther accepted the bodily resurrection of Christ on the basis of Old Testament prophecies, reliable eyewitnesses of the event, and the testimony of true apostles. Said Luther, the resurrection "is the chief article of Christian doctrine. No one who claims to be a Christian . . . may deny that."[60] Agreeable with the Western tradition, Luther upheld the resurrection of the flesh that Jesus possessed during his earthly existence. Moreover, Christ's resurrection is profoundly related to human salvation. By rising from the grave, Christ "has destroyed sin and brought righteousness to light, abolished death and restored life, conquered hell and bestowed on us everlasting glory."[61] Luther advanced a unique theory concerning the ubiquity of Christ's resurrected body. Affirming the intercommunication of divine and human attributes (see chap. 6), Luther concluded that both during his earthly sojourn and after his ascension the body of Christ filled heaven and earth. "The right hand of God" to which Christ is said to have ascended is a symbol for the divine power. Thus "Christ's body is everywhere because the right hand of God is everywhere."[62] Later Lutheran theology likewise affirmed that in the state of exaltation the body of Christ was permanently ubiquitous. According to the Formula of Concord, "Now not only as God, but also as man, he . . . is present to all creatures."[63] Quenstedt maintained that the heavenly Christ "is present to all creatures in the universe with a true, real, substantial and efficacious omnipresence."[64]

Calvin firmly upheld the historicity of Jesus' bodily resurrection. "Scorners will treat as a fairy tale what the Evangelists relate as history."[65] Calvin cites numerous evidences that validate the resurrection as a historical event: (1) the armed Roman guard at the tomb, (2) the inability of the Jews to produce the body, (3) the several appearances of the risen Lord to his followers, (4) the fact that the disciples touched his risen body, (5) the witnesses to his ascension to heaven, and (6) Christ's glorious manifestations to Stephen and Paul. Said Calvin: "To discredit so many authentic evidences is not only disbelief but a depraved and even insane obstinacy."[66] Calvin discusses at length the spiritual benefits of Christ's bodily resurrection. Because the Lord rose from the grave (1) sin, death, and the Devil are conquered; (2) perfect righteousness is procured for believers; (3) the power of his resurrection is manifested in us; (4) believers are seated in heavenly glory with Christ; and (5) Christians are assured of bodily resurrection and immortality. While he did not debate the nature of Christ's resurrection body, Calvin does state that the substance of his heavenly body is the same as that of his earthly body. Moreover, the ascension, for Calvin, means that Christ opened for believers the doors of the heavenly kingdom sealed by Adam's sin.

Furthermore, Christ ministers in heaven as our constant advocate and intercessor before the Father. Against the Lutherans, Calvin rejected the ubiquity of the ascended Christ's human nature. Whereas Christ's body was raised up above the heavens, his spiritual presence and power are with believers always. To the question, Is Christ with us now bodily? Calvin responded, "No. There is on one hand the body raised up into heaven; and there is on the other his virtue which is diffused everywhere."[67] Christ's session at the Father's right hand is a metaphor signifying that he now exercises the government committed to him until the day of judgment. "Christ was invested with lordship over heaven and earth, and solemnly entered into possession of the government committed to him."[68]

The Reformed church's Heidelberg Catechism, Lord's Day XVII (Q. 45), asks how Christ's resurrection benefits believers. The answer (A. 45) reads: "First, by his resurrection he has overcome death, so that he might make us share in the righteousness he won for us by his death. Second, by his power we too are already now resurrected to a new life. Third, Christ's resurrection is a guarantee of our glorious resurrection." Lord's Day XVIII focuses on Christ's ascension to heaven. Question 47 deals with the Savior's promised presence with believers. The reply (A. 47) is "In his human nature Christ is not now on earth; but in his divinity, majesty, grace, and Spirit he is not absent from us for a moment." Question 49 inquires about the benefits Christ's ascension brings to believers. The reply (A. 49) reads, "First, he pleads our cause in heaven in the presence of his Father. Second, we have our own flesh in heaven—a guarantee that Christ our head will take us, his members, to himself in heaven. Third, he sends his Spirit to us on earth as a further guarantee."

George Eldon Ladd claims, in regard to the resurrection, that historical evidences and faith must harmoniously interact. Faith is not a blind leap into the dark; neither are historical evidences of such a nature as to demand faith from those with positivistic views of the world. "No amount of evidence can persuade a mind that is closed."[69] Whereas Ladd believes that Jesus' resurrection was an event in history, he holds that resurrection to the heavenly realm cannot be established by strict scientific or historical investigation. Yet Ladd maintains that of all the hypotheses, the supposition of Jesus' bodily resurrection most adequately fits the known facts. Thus Jesus' predictions of his death and resurrection, the phenomenon of the empty tomb, the undisturbed grave clothes, the appearances of the Lord to his followers, the disciples' sudden transformation from desolation and fear to being courageous preachers of the resurrection, the conversion of Saul of Tarsus, and the explosive growth of the Christian church corroborate, for those open to the working of God in history, Jesus' bodily resurrection from the dead. "The bodily resurrection of Christ is the only adequate explanation to account for the resurrection faith and the admitted 'historical facts.'"[70]

As for the nature of Jesus' resurrection body, Ladd concludes that his mortal physical body was transformed into a glorified spiritual body suited for the life of the age to come. Thus it is a body animated by the Spirit of God and endowed with marvelous properties unknown to human experience. For Ladd the theological significance of the resurrection is enormous. If Jesus had not risen from the dead, then his victory over his enemies would be an illusion, his message of the kingdom meaningless, the doctrine of justification a figment of the imagination, the hope of our resurrection a dream, and history would have no meaning, no purpose, and no goal. "If Jesus is not raised, redemptive history ends in the cul-de-sac of a Palestinian grave."[71] Since everything hinges on Jesus' bodily resurrection from the grave, Ladd concludes that "the resurrection may be called the major premise of the early Christian faith."[72]

Other helpful studies on the resurrection include works by W. J. Sparrow-Simpson,[73] M. C. Tenney,[74] and D. P. Fuller.[75]

BIBLICAL TEACHING

Which of the several interpretations with respect to Christ's resurrection and ascension we accept is determined by the teaching of inspired Scripture on the subject. The Bible's evidence must be understood within its own assumptions according to which God is able to perform great signs and wonders at crucial times in regard to his redemptive program (see chap. 2).

Poetry and Wisdom

Luke relates that the risen Christ chided his disciples for failure to understand what was written in the Old Testament about his sufferings and subsequent glorification: "How foolish you are, and how slow of heart to believe all that the prophets have spoken! Did not Christ have to suffer these things and then enter into his glory?" (Luke 24:25–26). Then Jesus added: "This is what is written: The Christ will suffer and rise from the dead on the third day" (24:46). Similarly, Paul cites a piece of early Christian tradition that says Christ "was raised on the third day according to the Scriptures" (1 Cor. 15:4). From the preceding we should expect to find reasonably clear statements concerning Christ's resurrection on the third day and subsequent glorification in the Old Testament. We consider first Psalm 2:7–9: "I will proclaim the decree of the LORD: He said to me, 'You are my Son; today I have become your Father. Ask of me, and I will make the nations your inheritance, the ends of the earth your possession. You will rule them with an iron scepter; you will dash them to pieces like pottery.' " The immediate focus of this text was the enthronement of David's son in Jerusalem as king. Yet Peter affirms that David's saying "You are my Son; today I have become your Father" finds its ultimate fulfillment in Jesus' resurrection from the grave (Acts 13:33). "The New Testament, revealing God's only-begotten Son as co-eternal with the Father, refers the 'today' of Psalm 2:7 to the incarnate Son's resurrection, when, like a king at his crowning, He was 'designated Son of God in power' (Rom. 1:4; cf. Acts 13:33)."[76] Verses 8–9 of Psalm 2 anticipate the world-wide dominion and victorious reign of the enthroned Messiah (Rev. 19:15; cf. 12:5).

Psalm 16:9–11 provides a clear anticipation of Christ's resurrection from the tomb. The immediate focus of the psalm is David's confidence in the hope of eternal life. But guided by the Spirit, Peter (Acts 2:24–28, 31) and Paul (Acts 13:34–37) testify that David in this psalm predicted the resurrection of Christ from the grave. These texts in Acts prove "that David was thinking and speaking of the death and resurrection of Christ, the events which then constituted the source of his own hope."[77] Psalm 118:22–23 likewise anticipates the resurrection of Christ: "The stone the builders rejected has become the capstone; the LORD has done this, and it is marvelous in our eyes." In historical context these verses describe the procession of Israel's king, priests, and people to the temple at the zenith of the nation's power and influence. But Jesus (Mark 12:10–11) and Peter (Acts 4:10–11) confirm that by these words David anticipated the rejection and triumph of "the stone" who is the Messiah.

Psalm 24:7–10 appears to be a prophetic anticipation of Christ's victorious exaltation to heaven: "Lift up your heads, O you gates; be lifted up, you ancient doors, that the King of glory may come in. . . ." Israel sang this psalm as the ark of the Lord, returning from war, approached the gates of the city (cf. 1 Chron. 15:1–16:3). However, "in its later usage it affirmed the victory achieved by Jesus Christ in death and resurrection and anticipated the ultimate and triumphant Advent of the King."[78] The Christian church traditionally has sung these verses on Ascension Day. Psalm 68:18, written in the same historical context as the previous text, anticipates the ascension of Christ, when he would lead captivity captive and share the spoils of his victory (Eph. 4:8).

The Hebrew king exercised a broad range of executive, legislative, judicial, and military powers. In the Pentateuch Jacob's blessing of Judah (Gen. 49:10) points forward to the advent of the royal Messiah who will rule the nations. An oracle of Balaam refers to royal accomplishments early in the monarchy, but this ultimately refers to the future accomplishments of the Messiah (Num. 24:17). Nathan's prediction that David's dynasty would endure forever through his offspring (2 Sam. 7:13–16) anticipates the messianic King who was both the son of David and the Son of God (cf. Luke 1:32–33).

The Psalter clearly reflects expectation of a royal Messiah. Psalm 2, which depicts the reign of the Davidic king, yet envisages the future "Anointed One" (v. 2), messianic "King" (v. 6), and "Son" (v. 12), who will vanquish the nations and rule over the earth. Psalm 45, a marriage song for a Hebrew monarch, prophetically describes the splendor of the messianic King and his righteous reign. Psalm 72, a Davidic psalm that extols the glory of Solomon's reign, likewise looks forward to the just and universal rule of the royal Messiah. Psalm 110:1 was written on the occasion of the enthronement of David as king in Jerusalem. Since the king functions as God's vice-regent, he is invited to take the place of honor: "The Lord says to my Lord: 'Sit at my right hand until I make your enemies a footstool for your feet.'" Yet Jesus (Matt. 22:44), Peter (Acts 2:34), and the letter to the Hebrews (1:13) look to the future and apply this psalm-text to the ascension, heavenly session, and world-rule of the exalted Christ. Psalm 110:4 indicates that the Messiah's throne is also a priestly throne, and as a royal priest Christ lives forever to mediate between the Father and his people (Heb. 5:6, 10; 6:20; 7:11).

After being severely tried by the Devil and falsely charged by his counselors, Job saw with the eye of faith a "witness" (*'ēd*), an "advocate" (*śāhēd*), and an "intercessor" in heaven who pleads his cause before God (Job 16:19–21). "This passionate longing for a heavenly witness on his side strikingly points forward to the Christian thought of 'an advocate with the Father, Jesus Christ the righteous' (1 John 2:1). Here faith is reaching out for a 'God for us.'"[79] We understand this "witness" to be identical with the "Redeemer" (*gô'ēl*) of Job's confession in 19:25: "I know that my Redeemer lives, and that in the end he will stand upon the earth." Transported to the future, Job contemplates the risen Vindicator or Advocate who faithfully pleads his cause in heaven. "No Christian can read vv. 25–27 without finding the passage a mirror of the one who 'always lives to make intercession' (Heb. 7:25), who has 'brought life and immortality to light through the Gospel' (2 Tim. 1:10)."[80]

Prophetic Literature

After describing the Servant's death as a "guilt offering" (Isa. 53:10a) that justifies many persons (v. 11b), Isaiah states that the Servant "will see his offspring and prolong his days" (v. 10b). That is, after contemplating the spiritual seed who were to gain an inheritance through his death, the Messiah will be revived back to life and live eternally. "Life in 'length of days' acquires unique significance because it is life after death, the life of one resurrected (cf. Rev. 1:8). . . . Not only the cross but also the open tomb is clearly shown in this wonderful prophecy."[81] The contrast in verse 11a between the Servant's experience of soul-suffering and his seeing "the light of life" also suggests resurrection. Verse 12, moreover, prefigures the Servant's priestly ministry of intercession: "he bore the sin of many, and made intercession for the transgressors." The hiphil of *pāga'* means to "entreat" or to "intercede" (cf. Jer. 15:11). The text anticipates Jesus' prayer for his crucifiers (Luke 23:34) as well as his postresurrection intercessory ministry.

In the light of New Testament statements that the Old Testament predicted Christ's resurrection after three days (Luke 24:46; 1 Cor. 15:4), Hosea 6:2 takes on fresh significance: "After two days he will revive us; on the third day he will restore us, that we may live in his presence." Although the immediate focus of this text is the restoration of Israel to the land (cf. v. 1), the reference to the third day prompts the Christian reader to contemplate the resurrection of Christ. Faith comprehends that the Messiah's resurrection from the dead provides the only viable ground for the resurrection of the people of God.[82] To describe the victory Christ's resurrection wrought over sin and death, Paul quotes from the saying of the Lord in Hosea 13:14: "I will ransom them from the power of the grave; I will redeem them from death. Where O death, are your plagues? Where, O grave, is your destruction?" Furthermore, in the light of Jesus' explicit saying in Matthew 12:40, we conclude that Jonah's incarceration and deliverance from the belly of a whale (Jonah 1:17–2:10) foreshadowed the death and resurrection of Christ. With this judgment many interpreters concur.[83] Jonah's rescue from "the pit" (Jonah 2:6) recalls David's statement about deliverance from the grave (Ps. 16:10), a statement that was applied by Peter in Acts 2:27 to Christ's resurrection. Moreover, Daniel in a night vision saw "one like a son of man, coming with the clouds of heaven. He approached the Ancient of Days and was led into his presence. He was given authority, glory and sovereign power; all peoples, nations and men of every language worshiped him. His dominion is an everlasting dominion that will never pass away" (7:13–14). This appearance of the heavenly son of man (cf. Matt. 26:64; Mark 14:62) before the divine Father and his appointment as universal Judge was possible only on the basis of his resurrection and ascension to the heavenly world.

Isaiah sketched a magnificent portrait of the supernatural birth, impeccable character, and peaceful reign of the royal Messiah (Isa. 2:1–4; 7:14; 11:1–10; 32:1; 33:17; 42:1–7). Jeremiah likewise beheld the "righteous Branch" and Davidic "King" who "will reign wisely and do what is just and right in the land" (Jer. 23:5–6). Daniel in a vision saw that the "son of man" is King of all the earth. So the latter "was given authority, glory and sovereign power; all peoples, nations and men of every language worshiped him. His dominion is an everlasting dominion that will not pass away" (7:13–14). Ezekiel prophetically contemplated the Messiah serving as a shepherd, prince, and king forever over the restored house of David (34:22–24; 37:24–25). Micah portrayed the Messiah as "one who will be ruler over Israel" (5:2), whereas Zechariah wrote of the coming Davidic prince who would unite in himself the office of ruling king and ministering priest (3:8–9; 6:12–13; 9:9–10).

Synoptic Gospels

Whereas the Gospels were written about one generation after Jesus' death, the traditions concerning his cross and resurrection were transmitted to the evangelists by reliable eyewitnesses. The Gospels indicate that on several occasions Jesus predicted his resurrection from the dead. In Matthew 12:38–40 the teachers of the law and the Pharisees demanded that Jesus provide a miraculous sign that would corroborate his messianic authority. Jesus' response—"none will be given it except the sign of the prophet Jonah" (v. 39; cf. Matt. 16:4)—suggests that confirmation of his messianic authority would be given by his resurrection from the grave as foreshadowed by the Jonah typology. Matthew's statement that the Son of Man would remain in the grave "three days and three nights" (v. 40) does not contradict Jesus' actual stay in the tomb from Friday night to Sunday morning, since Jews reckoned part of a twenty-four hour day as a whole (cf. Matt. 27:63; Mark 8:31, "after three days"; Matt. 16:21; 17:23, "on the third day"). Furthermore, Jesus spoke of his death and resurrection following Peter's confession at Caesarea Philippi (Matt. 16:21; Mark 8:31; Luke 9:22), immediately after his transfiguration (Matt. 17:9; Mark 9:9, where the transfiguration was a direct anticipation of his exaltation and parousia), to the disciples in Galilee (Matt. 17:22–23; Mark 9:31), prior to entering Jerusalem (Matt. 20:19; Mark 10:33–34; Luke 18:32–34), and immediately after the Last Supper (Matt. 26:31–32; Mark 14:27–28). Considered together, these teachings of Jesus indicate that the goal of his life was death and resurrection. Moreover, contrary to popular Jewish expectations of a human Messiah, Jesus recalled Daniel 7:13 and spoke of the session of the Son of Man in the place of highest honor at God's right hand in heaven (Matt. 25:31; 26:64).

After Jesus had been betrayed and arrested, out of fear for their own personal safety "all the disciples deserted him and fled" (Matt. 26:56). The only ones who remained close to Jesus during the last hours were a few women (Mark 15:40–41). We see the reaction of Jesus' friends to his arrest in the experience of a young man who broke free from the grasp of the police and fled naked into the night (Mark 14:51–52). By recording this incident, Mark wished "to emphasize that *all* fled, leaving Jesus alone in the custody of the police. No one remained with Jesus, not even a valiant young man who intended to follow him."[84] Even Peter, who had confidently boasted that he would never disown Jesus (Matt. 26:33–35), later, in the courtyard of Caiaphas vigorously denied three times that he knew Jesus (Matt. 26:69–75; Mark 14:66–72; Luke 22:55–62). Peter's bitter weeping indicates extreme remorse over his lack of fidelity to the Lord.

The Gospels disclose beyond any shadow of doubt that Jesus died on the cross. Jews and Romans scourged, beat, and nailed him to the cross by large nails through his hands and feet. Enduring the excruciating pain of crucifixion for six hours, Jesus remained conscious to the very end. Then he died in agony, with a cry of trust to his heavenly Father. The Roman soldiers did not break Jesus' legs as they did those of the two thieves, because they were convinced that he had already died (John 19:33). Instead, with a spear one of the soldiers pierced Jesus' side, from which flowed blood and water (v. 34). After Joseph's request to obtain the body of Jesus for burial, the centurion reported to Pilate that the Nazarene had died (Mark 15:44–45). Then Joseph and his servants took Jesus' body from the cross, wrapped the corpse tightly with fine linen, placed it in a new tomb, and closed the tomb with a large stone (15:46). Mark relates that "Mary Magdalene and Mary the mother of Joses saw where he was laid" (15:47), thus ruling out the likelihood that the women later went to the wrong tomb. Matthew records an incident that refutes the allegation of the Jews that the disciples stole Jesus' body (Matt. 27:62–66). The chief priests and Pharisees requested of Pilate that a Roman guard be posted at the tomb to insure that the body would not be stolen. "So they went and made the tomb secure by putting a seal on the stone and posting the guard" (v. 66). A later vignette shows the disciples disillusioned and despondent over Jesus' crucifixion. "Their faces downcast" (Luke 24:17), two disciples, walking on the road to Emmaus, admitted, "We had hoped that he was the one who was going to redeem Israel" (v. 21). The disciples regarded Jesus as a conquering Messiah who would free Israel from her enemies (2:38). But when the Lord died a sudden death on the cross, the hopes of his followers died also.

Since the Evangelists describe Jesus' resurrection and subsequent appearances from their unique perspectives, it is not surprising that we have different but harmonious accounts of what actually transpired. We believe that a reasonably accurate synthesis of the Easter events can be made from the Gospel narratives, as follows: Early Easter Sunday morning Mary Magdalene, Mary, and Salome visited the tomb to anoint the body of Jesus with spices. Approaching the place, the women discovered the guards struck unconscious and the stone rolled away from the entrance. Inside the tomb were two angels surrounded with dazzling glory, one of whom said to the women, "Why do you look for the living among the dead? He is not here; he has risen!" (Luke 24:5–6). After this incident was reported to the disciples, Peter and John ran to the tomb. Peter entered the tomb and found it empty and the linen shroud and head cloth neatly wrapped and lying separately (John 20:6–7). Struck by the fact that a thief would not have taken time to unwrap the grave clothes and arrange them neatly, John immediately believed in the Lord's resurrection (John 20:8). Mary Magdalene, thinking that Jesus' body had been stolen, returned to the tomb weeping. Peering inside the tomb, she saw two angels sitting where the body of Jesus had been lying. Suddenly the risen Jesus appeared to Mary, but she did not immediately recognize him. After Jesus tenderly addressed her, Mary recognized the Lord and physically grasped him. Jesus then said to her, "Do not hold on to me [*mē mou haptou*], for I have not yet returned to the Father" (v. 17). *Mē* with the present imperative of *haptomai* signifies that Jesus commanded Mary to cease clinging to his body. Then Jesus told her to report his future ascension to the disciples. Sight and touch persuaded Mary that Jesus had, indeed, risen in a body from the dead (v. 18). Thereafter, when the other Mary and Salome reached the tomb, Jesus disclosed himself to them. They too fell before Jesus and grasped his feet. The Lord ordered them to tell the disciples to meet him in Galilee (Matt. 28:10).

Meanwhile the Roman guard related to the chief priests the extraordinary events that had occurred at the tomb.

The chief priests and elders bribed the guards with a large sum of money to say that the disciples had come by night and stolen Jesus' body (Matt. 28:11–15). In this scene the Roman guards bore testimony to the fact that Jesus had miraculously risen from the grave. Luke 24:34 indicates that the first apostle to encounter the risen Jesus was Simon Peter in the region of Jerusalem (cf. 1 Cor. 15:5). Then Jesus appeared to Cleopas and another disciple on the road to Emmaus, miles from Jerusalem (Luke 24:13–32). Along the way Jesus conversed with the pair, interpreted the Scriptures concerning himself, and shared a meal with them. Then suddenly Jesus disappeared from their sight. When the ten disciples (without Thomas) were gathered behind locked doors discussing these things, Jesus suddenly appeared in their midst and said to them, "Look at my hands and my feet. It is I myself! Touch me and see; a ghost does not have flesh and bones, as you see I have" (Luke 24:39). Then Jesus ate a broiled fish the disciples had given him. The ten related to Thomas this encounter with the risen Lord, but Thomas remained unconvinced that a corpse could return to life. One week later, when the eleven were again gathered behind locked doors, Jesus suddenly appeared in their midst and said to Thomas: "Put your finger here; see my hands. Reach out your hand and put it into my side. Stop doubting and believe!" (John 20:27). Overwhelmed by the sight and touch of Jesus' wounded body, Thomas' skepticism turned to conviction, and he cried out, "My Lord and my God!" (v. 28).

Having gone to Galilee as instructed by the Lord (Matt. 28:10), seven of the disciples were fishing on the lake. Then they saw Jesus on the beach without recognizing him. The risen Lord directed the disciples to a huge catch of fish. This miracle caused John to realize that the stranger was Jesus. On the shore of the lake Jesus took food with the disciples (John 21:1–14). Later Jesus appeared to the eleven on a mountain in Galilee, gave them the Great Commission, and promised to be with them forever (Matt. 28:16–20). Paul's statement that Jesus appeared to more than five hundred of the brothers at one time (1 Cor. 15:6) may refer to the appearance on the mountain, or it may pertain to a different meeting. Back in Jerusalem, Jesus appeared to James the brother of Jesus (v. 7), an encounter that undoubtedly led to James' conversion (cf. John 7:5). At the end of the forty days Jesus instructed his disciples to wait for the enduement of the Holy Spirit that would enable them to witness to him (Luke 24:49; Acts 1:4–8). Then Jesus led his followers to the Mount of Olives and blessed them. Luke the historian writes that "while he was blessing them, he left them and was taken up into heaven" (Luke 24:51; cf. Acts 1:9). Thus from the Mount of Olives, a specific place three-quarters of a mile east of Jerusalem, Jesus physically took leave of his followers and entered the invisible world. Luke adds that two angels, dressed as men in white, assured the disciples that the Lord would return in the same manner that he went up to heaven (Acts 1:11). Thus in this final encounter with his disciples Jesus closely linked his ascension, mission, and parousia. The mission of the glorified Lord must be carried out until he returns from heaven.

With regard to the Synoptic resurrection narratives, the non-evangelical scholar J. A. T. Robinson is impressed by their credibility:

> When we turn to the gospels, their evidence on the empty tomb is in substance unanimous. There are, indeed, differences of detail which at times have been given an exaggerated prominence. . . . None of these, however, is the kind of difference that impugns the authenticity

> of the narrative. Indeed they are all precisely what one would look for in genuine accounts of so confused and confusing a scene. . . . But details of description apart, the basic witness is extraordinarily unanimous. . . . Many in fact will continue to find it easier to believe that the empty tomb produced the disciples' faith than that the disciples' faith produced the empty tomb.[85]

The Gospel writers, particularly Matthew, teach that Jesus was the messianic King. Eastern astrologers, guided to Bethlehem by a star, inquired: "Where is the one who has been born king [*basileus*] of the Jews?" (Matt. 2:2). Prior to his entry into Jerusalem on a donkey Jesus declared that the prophecy of Zechariah 9:9 was about to be fulfilled: "See, your king comes to you, . . . gentle and riding on a donkey" (21:5). Pilate reflected popular convictions when he asked Jesus, "Are you the king of the Jews?" (27:11; cf. Mark 15:2; Luke 23:3). The Lord responded in the affirmative: "Yes, it is as you say [*su legeis*]." As Jesus hung on the cross the Roman soldiers mocked and reviled him: "Hail, king of the Jews!" (v. 29), and the inscription placed over his head read: "THIS IS JESUS, THE KING OF THE JEWS" (v. 37). Jesus himself was conscious of the fact that he was the messianic King (19:28; 22:43–45; 25:31, 34, 40) who would rule over a kingdom. The "kingdom of heaven" (7:21; 13:11) and the "kingdom of God" (Mark 12:34; Luke 17:21) synonymously refer to the redemptive rule of God in Christ that defeats malignant spiritual powers and liberates his people. The Gospels indicate that the kingly rule of the Messiah was realized invisibly and spiritually at his first advent (Matt. 3:2; 12:28–29; Luke 17:21), and will be instituted visibly and materially at his second advent (Matt. 19:28; 25:31, 34, 40; Luke 1:33).

Primitive Christianity/Acts

Luke relates in Acts 1:3 that after his passion Jesus "showed himself to these men and gave many convincing proofs that he was alive." The Greek word for "convincing" (*tekmērion*) in classical Greek meant "strict proof." Thus "Luke intends the events following the appearance of the risen Christ to be treated as infallible evidence."[86] Luke, a careful historian, was convinced that the appearances of the risen Lord to his followers were genuine rather than illusory. In his history Luke records two appearances or revelations of the glorified Lord. The first occurred after Stephen's confession of Christ before the Sanhedrin. "Stephen, full of the Holy Spirit, looked up to heaven and saw the glory of God, and Jesus standing at the right hand of God" (Acts 7:55). That Jesus was standing at the side of the Father attests his ministry of advocacy. "He is standing as advocate to plead Stephen's case before God and to welcome him into God's presence."[87] The second revelation of the ascended Lord was given to Saul, the arch-persecutor of the church, seven years after the Ascension (Acts 9:3–9). Nearing Damascus, Saul was surrounded by a bright light from heaven (the glory of God) that struck him blind for three days. In addition, Saul heard the heavenly Lord speak to him and instruct him what to do. That these were sense phenomena is confirmed by the fact that Saul's companions saw the light and heard the voice (Acts 22:9). "What is beyond question historically is that the fanatical oppressor of the Nazarenes, who left Jerusalem 'breathing threats and murder' (v. 1), entered Damascus mentally shattered and physically blinded and became on his recovery the foremost protagonist of the beliefs he set out to extirpate."[88]

Before ascending to heaven Jesus commanded his followers to wait in

Jerusalem for the descent of the Holy Spirit that would empower them for mission (Acts 1:4–5). As Peter later stated, the Spirit could be given only after Christ had conquered death and ascended to the place of honor at the Father's right hand (2:33). In preparation for that event, Luke depicts the eleven selecting an apostle to replace Judas. The primary qualification of the new apostle was that he must have observed the Lord's life and resurrection (1:21–22a). And the principal task of the newly appointed apostle was that he "must become a witness with us of his resurrection" (v. 22b). Then on the day of Pentecost, as the Father had promised, the Holy Spirit fell on the disciples and empowered them to witness to the risen Christ by their lips and their lives (Acts 2:1–4).

Filled with the Spirit, Peter addressed the crowd of Jews who had gathered in Jerusalem for the festival. The man who had thrice denied his Lord boldly proclaimed that although wicked men had cruelly nailed Christ to a cross, "God raised him from the dead, freeing him from the agony of death, because it was impossible for death to keep its hold on him" (Acts 2:24). Marshall observes that here Peter uses a powerful metaphor: "Death is regarded as being in labor and unable to hold back its child, the Messiah."[89] To substantiate Christ's resurrection Peter quotes from Psalm 16:8–11. In this psalm David wrote about the Messiah not about himself, for after David died, he was buried and suffered corruption. Peter continued the thought by declaring that Christ's resurrection was not merely a revivification but an exaltation to the heavenly realm. To prove this point Peter appealed to Psalm 110:1: "Exalted to the right hand of God, he has received from the Father the promised Holy Spirit" (v. 33). Peter concluded his message by stating, "God has made [*epoiēsen*] this Jesus, whom you crucified, both Lord and Christ" (v. 36). Peter offers no adoptionist Christology; rather, he declares that via Jesus' resurrection and ascension God openly declared him to be the Lord, Christ, Prince, and Savior that he truly was (Luke 2:11).

In his second Jerusalem sermon Peter alluded to Isaiah 52:13 by saying, "The God of Abraham, Isaac and Jacob, the God of our fathers, has glorified his servant Jesus'" (Acts 3:13). Then he declared to the Jews: "You killed the author of life, but God raised him from the dead. We are witnesses of this" (v. 15). Brought before the Sanhedrin for teaching the resurrection of the dead in Jesus (Acts 4:2), Peter boldly stated that the One whom the Jews brutally killed "God raised from the dead" (v. 10). After being imprisoned for speaking in the name of Jesus (5:18), Peter and the apostles continued to proclaim the risen Lord: "The God of our fathers raised Jesus from the dead—whom you had killed by hanging him on a tree. God exalted him to his own right hand as Prince and Savior. . . . We are witnesses of these things" (vv. 30–32). Later, in the first sermon to a Gentile audience Peter declared to the household of Cornelius events that were publicly enacted—namely, that Jesus was anointed by the Spirit, worked miracles, was killed by the Jews, and that "God raised him from the dead on the third day and caused him to be seen" (10:37–40). Peter was convinced that Christ's resurrection was as much a verifiable historical event as his earthly deeds and death. Underscoring the belief that Christ's appearances were not mere visions, Peter added that he was seen "by witnesses whom God had already chosen—by us who ate and drank with him after he rose from the dead" (v. 41).

At Pisidian Antioch, in his first major sermon, Paul proclaimed the resurrection of Christ as the heart of his Gospel: "God raised him from the dead, and for many days he was seen by those who had traveled with him from Galilee to Jerusalem" (Acts 13:30–31). The former Jewish rabbi saw Christ's resurrection foreshadowed in Psalm 2:7; Isaiah 55:3; and Psalm 16:10. On Mars Hill in Athens the apostle also preached the Good News of Jesus and his resurrection (17:30–32). Paul argued that Jesus' resurrection constitutes proof that God will judge the living and the dead with justice (v. 31; cf. Acts 10:42). Later, in his defense before the Sanhedrin, Paul precipitated a controversy between the Pharisees and the Sadducees by upholding Christ's resurrection as the guarantee of the general resurrection of the dead (23:6–10). Moreover, in his defense before Festus and Agrippa, Paul related the story of his encounter with the risen Christ near Damascus (26:12–18), which was precisely what Moses and the prophets said would happen (v. 22). Rebutted by Festus as deluded, Paul responded: "What I am saying is true and reasonable [*sōphrosynē*, rational]' " (v. 25). The apostle then emphasized the empirical nature of his case by appealing to factual evidence known to the king (v. 26).

The above data confirms that Christ's resurrection was not only the cornerstone of the Christian faith but also the heart of the apostolic proclamation. The sermons of the early Evangelists reflect a common pattern: in fulfillment of prophetic Scripture David's greater Son was killed by the Jews, was buried, rose again on the third day, was exalted to the right hand of God in heaven as Lord of all, and will return on the last day to judge the living and the dead.

Pauline Literature

The letters of Paul, written less than twenty years after Jesus' death, represent the earliest New Testament documents. During his visit with Peter and James in Jerusalem (Gal. 1:18), Paul received firsthand reports of the events associated with Jesus' final days on earth. The Epistles indicate that the focus of Paul's message was the death and resurrection of Jesus Christ and his exaltation to the right hand of God. Paul recounts his own encounter with the risen Christ on the Damascus road some three years after the resurrection: "God . . . was pleased to reveal his Son in me so that I might preach him among the Gentiles" (vv. 1:15–16). Paul regarded this manifestation of Christ to him as the last of the Lord's postresurrection appearances (1 Cor. 15:8, "last of all"). Paul, moreover, states that that encounter with the risen Lord was a necessary condition for apostleship: "Am I not an apostle? Have I not seen Jesus our Lord?" (1 Cor. 9:1; cf. Gal. 1:1).

Paul records in his letters the earliest Christian confession of faith: "Jesus is Lord!" (1 Cor. 12:3; cf. John 13:13). Lordship signifies Christ's universal dominion by virtue of his resurrection from the dead. The apostle also writes: "If you confess with your mouth, 'Jesus is Lord,' and believe in your heart that God raised him from the dead, you will be saved" (Rom. 10:9). First Corinthians 15:3–5 reflects an early creed much older than the letter itself. Mention of "receiving," the fourfold use of (*kai*) *hoti,* and the non-Pauline vocabulary suggest that Paul cites an early Christian testimony to the resurrection: "For what I received [*parelabon*] I passed on [*paredōka*] to you as of first importance: that Christ died for our sins according to the Scriptures, that he was buried, that he was raised on the third day according to the Scriptures, and that he appeared to Peter, and then to the Twelve." Paul likely added verses 6–8 especially to establish that Christ's resurrection could be verified by living witnesses and secondarily to validate his own apostleship.[90] In Romans 1:3–4 Paul reproduces an early Christological creed that says of David's most eminent offspring: ". . . who through the Spirit of holiness was declared with power to be the Son of God by his resurrection from the dead: Jesus Christ our Lord." The phrase "with power" modifies the aorist passive verb "was declared" (*horisthentos*) and signifies that Christ's bodily resurrection from the grave publicly certified that he is the divine Son of God. The power that openly displayed Christ as the Son of God is "the Spirit of holiness," or the Holy Spirit, the third person of the Godhead. Paul cites an additional Christological creed in 2 Timothy 2:8: "Remember Jesus Christ, raised from the dead, descended from David." The perfect tense of the verb *egeirō* (to "raise") attests the Lord's ongoing state: Christ was raised from the dead and continues to live. The preceding citations of early Christian conviction confirm that "for Paul the resurrection of Christ was the most prominent Christian truth, containing as it does the guarantee of all other aspects of the work of Christ."[91]

In 1 Corinthians 15, the classic text on the resurrection, Paul expounds the negative consequences of denying the Easter event. If Christ is not risen from the grave, then the following prevail: (1) Christian faith and preaching is worthless: "If Christ has not been raised, our preaching [*kērygma*] is useless [*kenos*] and so is your faith" (v. 14). *Kērygma* connotes the content of the preached message, and *kenos* bears the figurative meaning, "without content, basis, truth or power."[92] (2) The apostles then would be false witnesses: "We are then found to be false witnesses about God, for we have testified about God that he raised Christ from the dead" (v. 15). (3) There would be no forgiveness of sins: "Your faith is futile [*mataios*, empty, aimless]; you are still in your sins" (v. 17). (4) The dead in Jesus have perished, and salvation is an illusion: "Then those also who have fallen asleep in Christ are lost" (v. 18). (5) Christians who now endure hardships in hope of the world to come would be objects of special pity: "If only for this life we have hope in Christ, we are to be pitied more than all men" (v. 19). (6) Life is inexplicable, and hedonism proves to be the only option: "If the dead are not raised, 'Let us eat and drink, for tomorrow we die' " (v. 32).

But the apostle asserts that "Christ has indeed been raised from the dead" (v. 20; cf. 2 Cor. 13:4; 1 Thess. 1:10). Whereupon Paul enumerates in his letters many spiritual benefits that accrue to believers on the basis of the Lord's certain resurrection: (1) Christ's resurrection guarantees the justification of his people: "He was delivered over to death for our sins and was raised to life for our justification" (*dikaiōsis*, Rom. 4:25). On Easter sin was put away and righteousness restored to those who believe. (2) The believer now participates in the new quality of life provided by the risen Christ: "Just as Christ was raised from the dead through the glory of the Father, we too may live a new life" (Rom. 6:4; cf. vv. 5, 8). Elsewhere Paul describes the believer as positionally seated with Christ and sharing his resurrection life: "God raised us up with Christ and seated us with him in the heavenly realms in Christ Jesus" (Eph. 2:6; cf. Col. 3:1). "Here it is a symbolic resurrection from the spiritual 'death' brought about by sin into a new quality of life shared with Christ. It describes a spiritual transformation available to the Christian *now* in this life."[93] (3) Christ's resurrection and ascension to heaven result in the bestowal of spiritual gifts to his church (Eph. 4:7–10). "Christ's enthronement over the universe is the guarantee that nothing needful for the church is lacking."[94] (4) Christians participate in the power of Christ's resurrection for effective service: Paul writes of the Father's "incomparably great power for us who believe. That power is like the working of his mighty strength, which he exerted in Christ when he raised him from the dead and seated him at his right hand in the heavenly realms" (Eph. 1:19–20; cf. Rom. 7:4; Phil. 3:10). (5) Christ's resurrection is the pledge and guarantee of the bodily resurrection of all who belong to him: "By his power God raised the Lord from the dead, and he will raise us also" (1 Cor. 6:14; cf. Rom. 8:11; 1 Cor. 15:21–23; 2 Cor. 4:14; 1 Thess. 4:14). Paul refers to Christ as "the firstfruits of those who have fallen asleep" (1 Cor. 15:20, cf. v. 23) and "the beginning and the firstborn from among the dead" (Col. 1:18). (6) Christ's exaltation to heaven marks a new phase in his kingly rule over the entire universe: "God exalted him to the highest place and gave him the name that is above every name, that at the name of Jesus every knee should bow, in heaven and on earth and under the earth, and every tongue confess that Jesus Christ is Lord" (Phil. 2:9–10; cf. 1 Cor. 15:24–27; Eph. 1:20–22).

Seated at the Father's right hand, Christ exercises a mediatorial ministry on behalf of his people. "For there is one God and one mediator [*mesitēs*] between God and men, the man Christ Jesus" (1 Tim. 2:5). Paul represents the glorified Christ as the sole intermediary between the Father and humans. The apostle stresses the Savior's humanity because it is the human race he represents. Paul specifies Christ's heavenly ministry of intercession in Romans 8:34: he "is at the right hand of God and is also interceding [*entynchanei*] for us." The verb *entynchanō* here bears the figurative sense of "petition," "appeal to," or "entreat."[95] In secular Greek it was used of a person's bringing a petition before a king on behalf of another.[96]

Paul attests the present aspect of Christ's kingship in terms of his rule over the church as "head." So Christ "is the head of the body, the church" (Col. 1:18; cf. Eph. 1:22; 4:15; 5:23; Col. 2:19). The image of "head" (*kephalē*) connotes that Christ sovereignly rules and governs the community of believers who respond with submission.[97] In this regard the apostle writes of believers entering the kingdom of Christ (Eph. 5:5; Col. 1:13). In addition, Paul observes that Christ functions as Lord of all demonic spiritual agencies that enslave persons (Col. 2:10), both in the present age and in the age to come (Eph. 1:21). In consequence of his obedient death and exaltation, Christ possesses complete authority over all creation (Phil. 2:9–11). As for the future aspect of Christ's kingly rule, Paul writes of Christ's work of judgment (2 Tim. 4:1) and the unleashing of punishment on the unbelieving world (2 Thess. 1:7–10). Moreover, at his second advent believers will be ushered "into the eternal kingdom of our Lord and Savior Jesus Christ" (2 Peter 1:11). Then after Christ has vanquished every evil power he will surrender the kingdom to the Father, that the Father may be all in all (1 Cor. 15:24–28).

Comparing the believer's future body to the resurrected body of the Lord, Paul makes a few observations about the nature of the latter. In contrast with the body of flesh Christ possessed during his humiliation, Paul describes the body of the resurrected Lord as a "glorious body" (*sōma tēs doxēs*; Phil. 3:21). Moreover, Paul states that "the last Adam [became] a life-giving spirit" (*eis pneuma zōopoioun*; 1 Cor. 15:45). The apostle means by the latter phrase that the body with which Christ rose from the grave was animated by the Spirit and was thereby fitted for a new mode of existence in the heavenly realm. So Paul refers to that body as a "spiritual body" (*sōma pneumatikon*; v. 44), that is, a body energized not by mortal *psychē* but by immortal *pneuma* with all accompanying glory (cf. 2 Cor. 3:18).

Johannine Literature

The "sign" (*sēmeion*, miracle, pointer, proof) is an important concept in John's gospel. The purpose of the signs Jesus performed was to "prove Jesus' identity as the Christ of God, who brings the fullness of eschatological salvation."[98] Thus John wrote: "Jesus did many other miraculous signs [*sēmeia*] in the presence of his disciples, which are not recorded in this book. But these are written that you may believe that Jesus is the Christ, the Son of God, and that by believing you may have life in his name" (John 20:30–31). Jesus identifies his resurrection from the dead as one of the most important of these signs. When the Jews demanded of him a "miraculous sign" (*sēmeion*) that would prove his divine authority, Jesus responded with the promise: "Destroy this temple, and I will raise it again in three days" (John 2:19; cf. vv. 21–22).

Jesus' statement "I lay down my life that [*hina*] I may take it again" (John 10:17, NASB) suggests that the goal of his life on earth was resurrection from the dead. In order to impart resurrection life to others, Jesus had to die and rise from the grave. Moreover, because Jesus has within himself supernatural resurrection power, he is able to raise the dead on the last day. This is the meaning of Jesus' words at the death of Lazarus: "I am the resurrection and the life. He who believes in me will live, even though he dies" (11:25). Or as the Lord later said to his disciples: "Because I live, you also will live" (14:19).

Jesus taught not only about his resurrection, but also in diverse ways about his ascension or entry into the invisible world. Thus the Lord spoke of leaving this world (John 13:1), of going back to the Father (14:12; 16:10, 28), and of ascending to where he was before (6:62). As the reward for conquering death, the Father exalted the Son by sharing his heavenly throne with him (Rev. 3:21; cf. 22:1). An important theme in the fourth Gospel is Jesus' glorification (John 7:39; 12:16, 23; 13:31–32; 17:5). When teaching about his impending death, Jesus said: "The hour has come for the Son of Man to be glorified" (12:23). Prior to his betrayal by Judas Jesus prayed, "Father, glorify me in your presence with the glory I had with you before the world began" (17:5). Thus Jesus' glorification began at the cross but was not complete until his return to the Father.[99] The aged John on the Isle of Patmos had a majestic vision of the living, exalted, and glorified Lord clothed with a body (Rev. 1:12–18). Endued with power and glory, the heavenly Lord spoke to John saying, "I was dead, and behold I am alive for ever and ever!" (v. 18).

John also underscores the saving benefits of Christ's resurrection, ascension, and heavenly session: (1) Christ's glorification is the precondition for the outpouring of the Holy Spirit, who continues the saving work of the historical Jesus. John observes that during his earthly ministry "the Spirit had not been given, since Jesus had not yet been glorified" (John 7:39). In the final discourse with his disciples, Jesus spoke of the "Counselor" (*paraklētos*) who would be with believers forever as Revealer, Interpreter, and Helper (14:16, 26; 15:26; 16:7). So Jesus said to his followers: "It is for your good that I am going away. Unless I go away, the Counselor will not come to you; but if I go, I will send him to you" (John 16:7). (2) Jesus' exaltation guarantees the believer's ascent to the Father's home. The Lord's resurrection and ascension opened the doors to heaven that had been sealed since Adam's rebellion. Jesus comforted his disciples by saying, "I am going . . . to prepare a place for you. And if I go and prepare a place for you, I will come back and take you to be with me that you also may be where I am" (14:2–3). (3) Since he has risen and ascended to the Father's side, Jesus Christ functions as the believer's advocate and intercessor. In 1 John 2:1 the word *paraklētos* is used of the ascended Lord: "But if anybody does sin, we have one who speaks to the Father in our defense—Jesus Christ, the Righteous One." "Advocate is a term with a legal ring about it, and it often indicates the counsel for the defense. It is the friend at court."[100] And (4) Jesus' exaltation to heaven inaugurates his sovereign rule over people, kings, and nations. Citing Psalm 89:27 ("I will also appoint him my firstborn, the most exalted of the kings of the earth"), Revelation 1:5 describes the glorified Lord as "the firstborn [*prōtotokos*] from the dead, and the ruler of the kings of the earth." The slain Lamb is portrayed as conqueror; so the Lamb stands in the center of the heavenly throne and receives worship (Rev. 5:6; cf. the Lamb standing on Mount Zion, 14:1).

Other New Testament Literature

Peter observes that the flood in Noah's day signifies the water of believer's baptism, which in turn represents Christian salvation: "This water symbolizes baptism that now saves you. . . . It saves you by the resurrection of Jesus Christ, who has gone into heaven and is at God's right hand" (1 Peter 3:21–22). Peter means that salvation comes to us through the resurrection of Jesus Christ, who has ascended to heaven and is seated at the place of honor, with angels, authorities, and powers subject to him. "Not the act [baptism] but the event that lies behind what the act symbolizes is the only meritorious basis for salvation."[101] Compared with the despair associated with his rejection of Christ, Peter declares that the resurrection provides the believer with "living hope" of eternal life and "an inheritance that can never perish, spoil or fade" (1 Peter 1:3–4). Christ's resurrection alone accounts for the dramatic change in Peter's life. Scripture indicates that during Jesus' lifetime his brothers neither understood his mission nor followed him (Mark 3:21; John 7:3–5). Yet after the resurrection James emerged as a leader in the Jerusalem church (Acts 12:17; 15:13; Gal. 1:19; 2:9). In the letter that bears his name, this brother of our Lord identifies himself as "James, a servant of God and of the Lord Jesus Christ" (James 1:1). The appearance of the risen Lord to James likely was the reason for his radical spiritual transformation (1 Cor. 15:7). The same applies to Jude, another brother of Jesus, who identifies himself as "a servant of Jesus Christ and a brother of James" (Jude 1; cf. Acts 1:14; 1 Cor. 9:5).

Hebrews' description of Christ's exaltation is unique. The two principal moments in the Old Testament sacrificial ritual were the slaughter of the victim and the presentation of its blood inside the sanctuary. In arguing the superiority of Christ, the author compares the Jewish ritual to Christ's death on the cross and his appearance in the sanctuary on high. Hence Hebrews affirms much about Christ's death and his entry into the presence of God, but little about his resurrection as such (but see Heb. 13:20). Thus Hebrews 1:3 states, "After he had provided purification for sins, he sat down at the right hand of the Majesty in heaven" (cf. Heb. 10:12; 12:2). The act of sitting (aorist of *kathizō*) signifies that Christ's work of purifying sins is completed. Furthermore, Hebrews describes

Christ's exaltation in terms of the exercise of his high priestly ministry in the heavenly sanctuary. "We do have such a high priest, who sat down at the right hand of the throne of the Majesty in heaven, and who serves in the sanctuary, the true tabernacle set up by the Lord, not by man" (8:1–2). Likewise the letter refers to "the inner sanctuary behind the curtain, where Jesus . . . has entered on our behalf. He has become a high priest forever, in the order of Melchizedek" (6:19–20).

As the believer's great high priest, the Christ who was tempted as we are is fully able "to sympathize with our weaknesses" (Heb. 4:15). In the midst of dangers or temptations, believers are assured that Christ suffers along with them. The letter also says of our high priest, "Because he himself suffered when being tempted, he is able to help [*boēthēsai*] those who are being tempted" (2:18). The heart of Christ's representation of the believer in the heavenly sanctuary is his ministry of intercession. Hebrews 7:25 states, "He is able to save completely those who come to God through him, because he always lives to intercede for them." The focus of *eis to panteles* may be both qualitative (to the uttermost) and temporal (for all time).[102] The verb *entynchanō*, to "intercede," upholds both Christ's presentation and his representation of the believer. Presentation connotes Christ's perpetual presence before the Father in the vigor of his completed sacrifice (cf. Exod. 12:13). So Hebrews 9:24 declares that Christ "entered heaven itself, now to appear for us in God's presence [*to prosōpon tou theou*]." Representation means that Christ mediates the prayers of believers and pleads their cause with the Father.

SYSTEMATIC FORMULATION

The numerous interrelated events of the great Mediator's life and work can be put in perspective in terms of the *two stages* (often called "states") that Paul describes—humiliation (Phil. 2:6–8) and exaltation (vv. 9–11). The stage of Christ's *humiliation* includes the following steps, previously considered: (1) The eternal Word left the glory of heaven, limiting the use of his divine powers; (2) was born as a human of the virgin Mary; (3) lived as a human without sin; (4) died for sinners; and (5) was buried.

From Humiliation to Exaltation

In this chapter we focus on the stage of Christ's *exaltation* with its several steps: (1) Jesus came back to life and abandoned his grave clothes; (2) left his tomb; (3) appeared visibly, audibly, and tangibly to over five hundred disciples on different occasions over a period of 40 days; (4) confirmed his universal authority by uniting Jewish and Gentile believers in the church and inaugurating a new age or dispensation ("these last days" Heb. 1:2); (5) commissioned his disciples to take the good news of his spiritual kingdom to the entire world; (6) ascended to the highest position in all reality, "the right hand of God"; and (7) began his present ministry of intercession for his people.

The teaching of the New Testament does not allow us to isolate the resurrection and ascension from the Father's eternal purpose or the Son's incarnation, life, and death. Christ's exaltation must be considered in connection with his person as the incarnate Logos with both his divine and human natures.

> It is because he who lives and acts in this situation is divine and human *in one Person,* that all he does in our fallen existence has a dark side and a light side, a side of humiliation and a side of exaltation—the one is the obverse of the other, but as the Mediator he has come to overcome our darkness and baseness and

> to build a bridge in and through himself over which we may pass into the light and glory of God.[103]

So Christ's exaltation is considered in connection with the whole of Christ's life as he entered the arena ruled by the forces of evil. Having overcome in the battle with temptation, his eternal purpose can be fulfilled. The New Testament does not present us with isolated events, one after the other, but a connected series of events. So we not only distinguish the two stages of humiliation and exaltation, but we relate them to each other. The crucified One is the one who was raised and ascended; the exalted One is the one who became incarnate and was crucified for our sins.

Resurrection, Not Mere Revivification

What is meant by "resurrection"? It does not mean a temporary revivification like that of Lazarus or Jairus' daughter, who would again face the necessity of dying. In a secondary sense, however, Lazarus is said to have been resurrected (John 11:23–25, 43). Interpreters ought not assume a priori that they know what is meant by the unique "resurrection" of the second Adam. We may need to grow in our understanding of the Bible's teaching, avoiding oversimplification by affirming a doctrine comprehensive of all the elements in the views that find biblical support. Some defenders of a literal, bodily resurrection focus on the similarities to his previous body with little reference to its new powers, while some so emphasize the new spiritual qualities that they lose the physical continuity. From either a literal or spiritual perspective, people ought not to be so quick to defend a doctrine that they fail to define what they seek to guard.

The word "resurrection" derives from the Latin *re* ("again") and *surgere* ("to rise"). The Greek equivalent is *ana* ("up," or "again,") and *stasis* ("stand"), or *egersis* (a "rising" or "raising"). What rises or stands again is what was buried—the outer person, Jesus' body. The derivative meaning of "resurrection" has not essentially changed in general use. To obtain a comprehensive biblical meaning, our *definition* synthesizes the similar and different aspects of the relevant biblical teaching. Hence Christ's resurrection refers to the miraculous once-for-all act that not only united Jesus' buried body with his spirit again but also gave his identifiable body capabilities of transcending the limits of space, time, and natural laws, such as indestructibility and power.

What was raised from the dead was not Jesus' human soul, spirit, or inner person—which in accord with our anthropology survived death—but his human *body*. When the disciples had thought they saw a spirit, Jesus emphatically replied, "Look at my hands and my feet. It is I myself! Touch me and see; a ghost does not have flesh and bones, as you see I have" (Luke 24:39). The data emphasize his corporeal existence, making it impossible to interpret the event as a psychical or ectoplasmic materialization, as alleged in spiritualism. So we speak of the resurrection of Christ's body rather than of his person, against some oversimplified holistic thinking. When Jesus died, his spirit departed from his body; so his body was buried. Hence it was the body that was raised up again. Christ's raised body was visible, audible, and tangible. Specifically the corporeal characteristics are emphasized by the eyewitnesses (at the end of each Gospel) and by Paul's comparison of the corruptible body buried and the incorruptible body raised (1 Cor. 15:35, 42–44). The Scriptures explicitly refer to the resurrection of others' mortal or lowly bodies as a result of Christ's resurrection (Rom. 8:11; Phil. 3:21). Furthermore a bodily resurrection is consistent with our previous study of humanness. A holistic view of a person is oversimplified if it does not account for the difference between the body and the soul or spirit.

Christ's resurrected body manifested significant *differences* from the body that slept in Mary's arms, hungered, wept, and died. Divine power did not merely resuscitate Jesus' corruptible body, which would then experience another death. God's power transformed its nature, so that it became an incorruptible, spiritual, and glorious body (1 Cor. 15:42–44). The body that died was corruptible; his post-Easter body is imperishable. The buried body was dishonorable; the raised body honorable. The crucified body in itself was subject to natural laws; the spiritual body was not limited by them (1 Cor. 15:42–44). The evidence sufficiently emphasizes the glorified qualities as safeguards against any merely physiological or naturalistic explanation.

What did Paul mean by a "spiritual body"? "Spiritual" is an adjective, "body" is a substantive (v. 44). The apostle does not speak of a bodily spirit, but a spiritual body. A spiritual body is a resurrected physical body with greater capacities as an instrument of the spirit. Among its new powers are those of being incorruptible and giving life (v. 45). With the many new powers of his new life Jesus could leave the grave clothes, disappear from the sealed and guarded tomb, triumphantly appear to fearful disciples behind locked doors, and ascend to heaven. Unquestionably Jesus' raised body had remarkable new capacities. His resurrection was the first fruits of those who died (1 Cor. 15:20). Then when the head of the redeemed race comes to earth again, he will raise "those who belong to him" (v. 23). Christ's resurrection is the first of a unique kind (*sui generis*) of mighty acts. And that mighty act, like the cross, took place once-for-all. Christ's resurrection is irrepeatable. Hence "resurrection" in Scripture cannot mean reincarnation in a series of different corruptible human bodies.

Was Jesus' resurrected body the same body in which he died? Although it had significant differences, there were also significant *similarities*. An adequate view must account for both similarities and differences. When resurrected, Jesus' body was verifiable visibly, audibly, and tangibly. He could be recognized, and those who knew him best identified him as the same person. Speaking of his body Jesus said, "Destroy this temple, and I will raise it again in three days" (John 2:19, 21). When the risen Jesus appeared to the disciples, he said, "Look at my hands and my feet. It is I myself." (Luke 24:39). Those who had been with him for three years and were best able to identify him exclaimed, "It is the Lord!" (John 21:7). Christ's body had been temporarily glorified on the Mount of Transfiguration (Matt. 17:13). Christ's resurrection body was the former body transfigured permanently. Notwithstanding all of the new powers and glory, there remains a verifiable continuity of the resurrected body with the body on the cross.

Paul's analogy helps to unite the similarities and differences. The body that was buried is like a seed that is sown in the earth; the body that was raised is like the wheat that grows from the planted seed (1 Cor. 15:35–38). Although the full-grown wheat is very different from the seed, the point is that the buried seed has an *organic continuity* with the wheat. Who could regard a magnificent oak tree as the material reconstruction of the acorn? But there is an organic connection between the two. Without a continuity between the body buried and the body raised, as Godet argued, "we could no longer speak of resurrection. Death would not be vanquished; it would keep its prey. God would simply do something new by its side."[104] Although a long time may elapse between the death of believers and their resurrection, Paul's teaching is that the resurrection of believers will be like Christ's.

How can we hold to a physical resurrection when Paul teaches that "flesh and blood" cannot inherit God's kingdom (1 Cor. 15:50)? The point of Paul's idiom is that by natural power Jesus' untransformed body could not rise again and ascend to be with the Father. "Flesh and blood" is an idiom for unaided and unchanged natural human powers. It was Jesus' transformed and supernaturally endowed body that ascended to the throne of God's kingdom. When Peter made his great confession, "You are the Christ, the Son of the living God," Jesus replied, ". . . this was not revealed to you by man [flesh and blood], but by my Father in heaven" (Matt. 16:16–17).[105] Supernatural illumination enabled Peter to overcome his blindness to the observable supernatural indications and to affirm Christ's deity. Christ performed his miracles in the flesh, but their power and significance were not ultimately of the flesh, but of God.

We conclude that the resurrection body is an observable physical body but supernaturally incorruptible and able to enter heaven. No merely natural power could reverse the irreversible forces of decay and decomposition, transform the body, and cause it to exist at the "right hand" of God. Natural laws were not violated but overruled by their Creator for a redemptive purpose. Christ arose and ascended by a power transcending the natural powers of "flesh and blood." Passive and active aspects may be discerned in his resurrection. Christ gladly yielded to the will of the Father as the mighty act of the Father and the Spirit graciously gave him a more glorious body. The eternal Word himself also participated in raising up again this bodily "temple" as he promised (John 2:19). When he had his incorruptible body, the glorified Christ actively moved through the burial clothing, out of the grave, and appeared to over five hundred people.

Confirmable Signs of Christ's Resurrection

Although no one saw Jesus rise and leave the tomb, evidence of his resurrection overcame the disciples' reticence to believe it. The event occurred in sharp antithesis to what they had expected theologically, and it was in genuine conflict with the framework of the secular world view at the time. To the Jew it was a stumbling block and to the Greek nonsense because the evidence required a Copernican revolution in their theology and cosmology.

The first indication from Scripture that Jesus had risen was *the empty tomb*. The possibility of Christ's resurrection presented itself as the women found the formerly well-sealed and guarded tomb open and empty. A tomb could be empty for many reasons; therefore the empty tomb's evidential value does not stand alone. But in association with other converging lines of evidence—Christ's appearances, the grave clothes, the change in the disciples, the conversion of Saul, the formation of the church, and the writing of the New Testament—it becomes strong.

Another indication that Jesus had risen from the empty grave was the *cadaver wrappings*. Probably Jesus's body was wrapped as Lazarus' body had been—"his hands and feet wrapped with strips of linen, and cloth around his face" (John 11:44). Although Lazarus came out of his grave in response to Jesus' command, others had to take off the grave clothes and let him go (v. 44). In the case of Christ, John looked in and saw the strips of linen lying there, but Peter went into the tomb, bent over, and saw the strips of linen lying there as well as the burial cloth that had been around Jesus' head. "The cloth was folded up by itself, separate from the linen" (John 20:3–7; cf. Luke 24:12). Apparently the glorified body that passed through walls and through locked doors previously had without assistance passed right through the burial clothes. In John's mind the burial clothes excluded Mary's theory that the body had been stolen, for the thieves would not have left the grave clothes as John found them. "Finally the other disciple [John] who had reached the tomb first, also went inside. He saw and believed" (John 20:8).[106]

A third immediately observable indication of Christ's resurrection involved the series of Christ's *appearances* over some forty days. The word "appeared" (1 Cor. 15:5) means "that the risen Lord takes the initiative to make himself known to the disciples. The disciples did not come into Easter Faith by some kind of process of self-recuperation."[107] The disciples did not gullibly believe Christ's resurrection. They tested other hypotheses unsuccessfully. At first they thought he was a gardener, another traveler on the way to Emmaus, or a ghost. These hypotheses did not hold up as the evidence was confirmed by more and more witnesses. On one occasion when the crucified, buried, and risen Jesus suddenly stood among the disciples, "They were startled and frightened, thinking they saw a ghost. He said to them, 'Why are you troubled, and why do doubts arise in your minds? Look at my hands and my feet. It is I myself! Touch me and see; a ghost does not have flesh and bones, as you see I have' " (Luke 24:37–39).

"When he had said this, he showed them his hands and feet. And while they still did not believe it because of joy and amazement, he asked them, 'Do you have anything here to eat?' They gave him a piece of broiled fish, and he took it and ate it in their presence" (Luke 24:40–43). "He was not seen by all the people, but by witnesses whom God had already chosen—by us who ate and drank with him after he rose from the dead" (Acts 10:41). Before he ascended, over five hundred people had seen the risen Christ, most of whom were still living when Paul wrote 1 Corinthians. In effect Paul invites his first-century readers to check his report of the resurrection with the living eyewitnesses.

Thomas would not accept the conclusion of the other disciples who had reported that Christ was alive. He said, "Unless I see the nail marks in his hands and put my finger where the nails were, and put my hand into his side, I will not believe it" (John 20:25). A week later Jesus appeared through the doors that were locked and invited Thomas, "Put your finger here; see my hands. Reach out your hand and put it into my side. Stop doubting and believe" (v. 27). Persuaded by the sight of the resurrected Christ, Thomas said to him, "My Lord and my God (v. 28)!"

Jesus did not rebuke Thomas for wanting critically to examine the evidence for himself. He had warned about counterfeit Christs and false prophets who would do many powerful works in his name. The Lord did not advocate building a house on sand. Faith should be based on conclusive evidence of confirming signs. Jesus knew, however, that he would not be continuously available for others to examine. So Jesus said, "Because you have seen me, you have believed; blessed are those who have not seen and yet have believed" (John 20:29).

The object of our faith—the risen Christ—is no longer visibly available. But strong converging lines of written testimony continue to indicate that, indeed, he rose. Although the *object* of Christian faith can no longer be seen (the ascended Christ), the *evidence* for faith in the risen Messiah can be seen in historically reliable and inspired accounts of the visible signs. It was not the disciples' "faith" that produced the idea of Christ's resurrection. The conclusiveness of the lines of physical evidence produced the disciples' faith in Christ's resurrection. Still today we accept Christ's resurrection because we are convinced by the evidence that it happened in fact and as the Holy Spirit attests that evidence, he overcomes our pride and reluctance. For additional lines of evidence and argument for the resurrection, see the section "Apologetic Interaction" below.

The Revealed Significance of Christ's Resurrection

Although the event was empirically confirmable, its meaning for God and man was cognitively (propositionally) revealed. The apostles were not only eyewitnesses, but specially chosen and gifted spokesmen for God. By the Holy Spirit they recalled and wrote what Jesus had disclosed of the significance of his life, death, and resurrection. Paul, who saw the risen Lord (1 Cor. 15:8), did not make up his gospel message. "I did not receive it [the gospel] from any man, nor was I taught it; rather, I received it by revelation from Jesus Christ" (Gal. 1:12). He could observe the fact that Christ had risen; he received information by revelation that Christ had died "for our justification," etc. According to the inspired scriptural revelation, what was the theological significance of the resurrection?

1. One after another, Christ's appearances exhibited his glorified existence and so *confirmed Jesus' earlier claims for the authority of his person*. The resurrection powerfully declared that he was what he had claimed to be, the One from above (John 8:23), *the Son of God* (Rom. 1:4). The fulfillment of the predicted sign of his resurrection also confirmed his claims to be the *Messiah* (Matt. 12:40; 16:21; 17:9; 20:19; John 2:19, 21). Jesus' claims to authority for himself do not stand alone and are not self-authenticating any more than those of the founders of other religions. Like the claims of God's prophets and apostles, they must be confirmed by the coming to pass of his signs. Facing the supreme test, Jesus predicted the verifiable sign of his resurrection. As Wolfhart Pannenberg has said, "Everything depends upon the connection between Jesus' claim and its confirmation by God."[108]

2. Christ's resurrection *confirms the Father's acceptance of his atoning sacrifice and its provisions*. The resurrection is a sign certifying the satisfaction of the Father in both justice and love. The Father's will prospered in his hand, and both Father and Son are satisfied (Isa. 53:10–11). The Father did not forsake the guilt-bearer on the cross permanently. He restored Jesus not only to physical life but also to his spiritual fellowship! The sign of Christ's resurrection assures people that the long-awaited ground of salvation has been realized.

3. Christ's resurrection *certifies that sinners through faith in Christ can now enjoy the peace of present justification* (Rom. 4:25). Now it becomes clear how sinners can with justice be called righteous. Christ's substitutionary death and triumphant resurrection make possible the just acquittal of sinners. Whether or not believers are Jews, they are justified on the ground of the risen Christ's atoning sacrifice (Acts 3:25–26; 10:46). At the point of faith justification is the legal verdict that forgives sins and imputes Christ's perfect righteousness (Rom. 3:21–26). Hence there is now no

condemnation for those who are in Christ Jesus (8:1). "Therefore, since we have been justified through faith, we have peace with God through our Lord Jesus Christ" (5:1).

4. The Messiah's resurrection *assures believers' eschatological justification.* Christ's unique resurrection stands at the beginning of the era that from the Old Testament Jewish perspective is known as the "last days." It marks the dramatic beginning ("firstfruits") of eschatological events. As such it verifies believers' acceptance before God the Father in Christ, not only in the present but also for the entire *aeon* of the last days, including the day when believers will appear before the judgment seat of Christ (2 Cor. 5:10). Christ's resurrection assures believers that the acquittal now received by faith will be confirmed by God's verdict in their final judgment (Rom. 8:33–34). That assurance is secure because neither the resurrection nor justification derive from any quality or ability of sinners. Both occur solely by God's gracious authority on the basis of Christ's atonement and resurrection.[109]

5. The Scriptures do not as explicitly state that Christ rose *for the redemption and reconciliation of sinners,* but these provisions would not be available had the story of Jesus ended at the cross. Such a termination would have been an unmitigated tragedy. It would have become the supreme evidence that injustice and irrationality have the last word in life on planet earth. But Christ has risen! He has demonstrated his power to provide emancipation from decay, freedom from addictions, restoration of broken fellowships, and communion with God the Father. All the New Testament teaching concerning redemption and reconciliation was written subsequent to, and on the basis of, Christ's resurrection. The water of baptism "now saves you," Peter writes, "—not the removal of dirt from the body, but . . . it saves you by the resurrection of Jesus Christ, who has gone into heaven and is at God's right hand—with angels, authorities and powers in submission to him" (1 Peter 3:21–22).

6. The resurrected Christ *becomes the last Adam, the new head of the race.* The risen Christ began a new order of spiritual, life-giving existence for all who are in solidarity with him by faith. "For as in Adam all die, so in Christ all will be made alive" (1 Cor. 15:22). "The first man Adam became a living being; the last Adam, a life-giving spirit" (v. 45). The old order of being subject to death pertains to all who were born of fallen Adam's race. The new kind of existence is made up of all who are "in" the sinless Christ by faith and it anticipates eternal life, including the resurrection of the body. The invitation to believe is to be given universally, but the new order of being is entered only by those who receive Christ's redemptive kingdom and are delivered from the kingdom of darkness. Paul develops the theological importance of Christ's headship in contrast to Adam's not only in 1 Corinthians 15 but also in Romans 5. Through a generic solidarity with Adam all are condemned to die; but through a believing solidarity with Christ all are graciously given the gift of his righteousness (justification).

7. Christ's resurrection also *signifies that Jesus Christ is Lord of all.* Before he ascended, the risen Lord could triumphantly report, "All authority in heaven and on earth has been given to me" (Matt. 28:18). God the Father has put everything under him (1 Cor. 15:27–28). Jesus was Lord of the discouraged and scattered Jewish disciples, who become apostles, that is, witnesses of the resurrection. He becomes Lord also of all who have believed through their witness. The primitive Christian apostolate did not carry

out the commission of another great rabbi but of the Messiah, the one teacher who was a Savior and rose from his grave. By faith in the one who demonstrated authority over all demonic forces, the early believers turned the first-century world upside down. In Christ there is neither Jew nor Gentile, male nor female (Gal. 3:28). And one day every knee will bow to him as Lord of all. The Lord of all reality will reign "until he has put all his enemies under his feet" (1 Cor. 15:25).

8. Christ's resurrection *assures the resurrection of all.* Paul's belief that "there will be a resurrection of both the righteous and the wicked" (Acts 24:15) is clearly rooted in Christ's resurrection. Jesus had said, "All who are in their graves will hear his [the Son of Man's] voice and come out—those who have done good will rise to live, and those who have done evil will rise to be condemned (John 5:28–29). The one who raised the Lord Jesus from the dead will also raise believers with Jesus and present them in his presence (2 Cor. 4:14). Christ's resurrection was the "firstfruits" of those who have fallen asleep (1 Cor. 15:20). "For as in Adam all die, so in Christ all will be made alive. But each in his own turn: Christ, the firstfruits; then, when he comes, those who belong to him" (vv. 22–23). Another indication of the "resurrection of those who belong to him" is Jesus' reference to "the resurrection of the righteous" (Luke 14:14). As believers, we have reason to anticipate that Christ, "by the power that enables him to bring everything under his control, will transform our lowly bodies so that they will be like his glorious body" (Phil. 3:21). Christ's resurrection demonstrates the error of those who identify the Christian hope exclusively with the immortality of the soul. The whole person is redeemed. But Christ's resurrection does not by any means imply the denial of a continued existence in an intermediate state.[110] His spirit was not annihilated between his death and resurrection; it was committed to his Father's keeping.

9. Christ's resurrection *signifies that he will be the ultimate Judge of all.* Peter testified that he who rose from the dead is "the one whom God appointed as judge of the living and the dead" (Acts 10:42). Paul concluded his message to the Gentiles at Athens with a warning that the day of God's grace has its limits. "[God] has set a day when he will judge the world by the man he has appointed. He has given proof of this to all men by raising him from the dead" (Acts 17:31). Again, Christ's resurrection is a public fact that provides conclusive evidence not only for those with prior knowledge and faith but also for all human beings.

10. Christ's resurrection *assures the Lord's continuing presence in the church.* The church belongs exclusively to the Lord. It is made up of believers who are "in him" forensically, who fellowship with him relationally, and who are made new creatures by him experientially. The resurrected Lord is alive and present in the church (Eph. 1:19–23). However frail and fragile the church may be, where his people are gathered the glorified Christ is in their midst. However weak the church may appear to the world, the Lord is with her in resurrection power. If you are ever tempted to give up on the church, remember the resurrection! The living Lord will build his church. Open yourself to his presence in united worship and remembrance as you partake at his table. Believers in Christ ought not stand outside the church criticizing its acknowledged weaknesses. Believers actively participate in a church to help it become more fully what it can be by the power of the risen Christ.

The Verifiable Sign of Christ's Ascension

Jesus' ascension was God's mighty act concluding the incarnation; it took the crucified and resurrected Messiah from the earth to the Father's glorious presence in heaven. As at Jesus' other postresurrection appearances, he ascended (was raptured) bodily from his disciples, "before their very eyes" (Acts 1:9). His resurrection body, which had passed through closed doors, now passed through the atmosphere. After giving many convincing proofs for the forty days that he was alive (Acts 1:3), Jesus provided a further unforgettable signal that his earthly ministry was completed.

The fact of the Messiah's ascension is supported by predictions before the event and reports afterward.

1. *In anticipation* Jesus gave the disciples good reason to expect his ascension. When he said that he was the bread who came down from heaven (John 6:58), many of the disciples said, "This is a hard teaching. Who can accept it?" (v. 60). Aware that his disciples were grumbling about this, Jesus said to them, "Does this offend you? What if you see the Son of Man ascend to where he was before!" (v. 62). He said that he would return to his Father's house to prepare a place for his disciples (14:2–3), "I am going to the Father" (v. 12), and "I am going away and I am coming back to you (v. 28). To Mary after his resurrection Jesus said, "Do not hold on to me, for I have not yet returned to the Father" (20:17).

2. *In retrospect,* having commissioned the disciples, the risen Christ led them to the vicinity of Bethany, and while he was blessing them "he left them and was taken up into heaven" (Luke 24:51). Again, "he was taken up before their very eyes, and a cloud hid him from their sight. They were looking intently up into the sky as he was going" (Acts 1:9–10). The apostles had witnessed his life from his baptism to "the time when Jesus was taken up from [them]" (1:22). John could report, "No one has ever gone into heaven except the one who came from heaven—the Son of Man" (John 3:13). Paul says Christ was "taken up in glory" (1 Tim. 3:16).

A literal interpretation of the event is also supported in several ways. Like Jesus' other miracles and appearances, his ascension was not limited by the laws of nature. So the necessity of life-support systems for ordinary human space travel does not make the ascension impossible. A literal rapture is impossible only if we forget the incorruptible nature of Jesus' resurrection body. Christ ascended in the powerful, spiritual body that overcame death and corruptibility. He passed through the atmosphere both without a space-suit and without ill effects because his glorified body could not be destroyed by less oxygen, radical changes of temperature, or differences of air pressure.

Does our modern knowledge that the earth is round make a literal interpretation impossible? The fact that "up" at one place on the globe is "down" on the other side of the globe does not change the observations of the disciples. From Jerusalem they saw him go "up" into the sky (Acts 1:9, 11). The primary point is not the location of heaven, but that Jesus left the observable, created world. But we cannot help asking, Where did Jesus go? He went "through the heavens" (Heb. 4:14). That may mean through (1) the earth's atmosphere and (2) the cosmic heavens of the sun and stars to (3) the transcendent abode of God.[111] Jesus "ascended higher than all the heavens" (Eph. 4:10). He returned to the place from which he came; he returned "where he was before" (John 6:62); he returned to the Father (14:12). His prayer was answered as he was glorified in the Father's presence with the glory he had with him before the world began (17:5). "For Christ did not enter a man-made sanctuary that was only a copy of the true one; he entered heaven itself, now to appear for us in God's presence" (Heb. 9:24).

Since the heavens, even the highest heaven, cannot contain God (1 Kings 8:27) and since God is everywhere present in the universe, it is impossible to locate the Father or the Son at a particular place in space and time, such as some nova far out in space. Hence it has become commonplace to say that the ascension involved not a change of place but a change of state. Jesus' transformation to a glorified "state" of existence, however, had already occurred at his resurrection. The ascension in fact involved a change of place—a physical removal from the earth. So Christ's ascension involved both a change of place and a change of position and authority (to "the right hand of God").

We do not take the "right hand of God" literally, for God is a spirit. Since a spirit does not have a flesh-and-bones body, it cannot have a literal right hand. Hence the young Mormon literalist need not have worried. She thought the Father's right hand must be getting very tired because Jesus has been standing on it all these years! The figurative expression "right hand of God" refers to the position of highest authority and power given by the Father over every other power in all of reality.

Is Christ's body now in heaven? The one person, with his human nature inseparable from his divine nature, ascended to the Father. Is his body visible there? Yes, his body is with the Father. But its new spiritual powers may allow it to be invisible as well as visible. Since on earth the resurrected Christ could disappear as he chose, we ought not be surprised that neither Russian cosmonauts nor American astronauts have visibly seen the ascended Lord when traveling in space. With due consideration of modern cosmology, we can imagine no more meaningful sign of the culmination of the Messiah's incarnate ministry on earth and glorious return to the Father in heaven than a visible ascension into the sky (Acts 1:11).

The Revealed Significance of Christ's Ascension

The verifiable and confirmed event of Christ's ascension carries rich *theological significance*. The sign was confirmed by eyewitnesses; we derive its meaning from propositional revelation given through Jesus and the apostles as preserved in the reliable accounts of inspired Scripture. The miraculous event of the ascension is the second mighty act (with the resurrection) drawing attention to Jesus' exaltation and several important theological tenets.

1. The ascension *marked the end of Christ's incarnate appearances and revelations* (until his second coming). A dramatic event was necessary so that the disciples would not be kept in suspense, anticipating more appearances and disclosures. The ascension also kept them from wondering what finally became of their Lord. Furthermore, by ascending, Christ ended his prophetic ministry on earth for this age. He would not appear visibly to people on earth until his second coming in power and glory. Hence alleged visions of Christ during the present age need to be examined critically. Some alleged visions of Christ may be the fabrications of religious con artists, some may be deceptions from evil spirits, and some may be figurative ways of referring to contemporary applications of Christ's biblically recorded teaching. In any case the content of alleged visions must be tested to determine whether

they do or do not contradict biblically revealed truth. With his ascension the Lord Jesus Christ completed his teaching ministry on earth.

Until his second coming he sits at the Father's right hand. "After he had provided purification for sins, he sat down at the right hand of the Majesty in heaven" (Heb. 1:3). This seated position or "session" as theologians have called it indicates the completion of his incarnate work on earth and the assumption of authority as King. Clearly he has chosen not to appear visibly on earth again until his second coming. The Holy Spirit now draws attention to Christ, attests the truth of what he taught, and may act in supernatural ways as he wills. But the Holy Spirit does not now add new content to the divine revelations given through accredited prophetic and apostolic spokespeople in the Scriptures. Through the written Word a follower of Christ can be "thoroughly equipped for every good work" (2 Tim. 3:17). Christ has said what he wants to say, and the heavens remain silent until Christ returns in power and glory.

2. Christ's ascension *reversed his kenosis*. The eternal Word had "humbled himself and became obedient to death—even death on a cross!" (Phil. 2:8). Faithfully he completed all that he could do on earth to provide for salvation. "Therefore God exalted him to the highest place and gave him the name that is above every name, that at the name of Jesus every knee should bow, in heaven and on earth and under the earth, and every tongue confess that Jesus Christ is Lord to the glory of God the Father" (vv. 9–11). What God's Son did not take advantage of in coming to earth as a human he receives and freely uses again; he assumes again the full authority and power and glory that he left and adds a triumphant position. Christ no longer limits the use of all his divine attributes as he did during the state of humiliation. Having accomplished the redemption of sinners, the second person of the Trinity remains the same ontologically, but Christ's exalted position and honor are even greater because of his accomplishments in his incarnation, crucifixion, and resurrection.

3. Christ's ascension *inaugurated his heavenly ministry as King and Lord of the cosmos*. On earth Jesus' authority over evil spirits had previously indicated that the Lord was here, that his kingdom was at hand, and that in the King the kingdom had indeed come. The fact that God exalted Jesus to his right hand, along with his resurrection, further confirmed that he is both Lord and Christ (Acts 2:33–36). The Messiah who died and rose again and is now ascended is indeed all that he claimed to be. The Lord who resides at the Father's right hand presently reigns with power and authority above every created being in heaven and earth.[112] All other powers—angels, authorities, and rulers—must now submit to him (1 Peter 3:22). The conqueror of sin, Satan, and death on earth now rules, not only over all persons and institutionalized powers on earth but also over all heavenly angelic powers and demonic powers.

4. Christ's ascension *clarified the meaning of his present rule on earth*. The ascension pronounced the final *no* to the disciples' hopes of an economic and political messianic kingdom during the present age. Many Jews were looking for military deliverance from foreign oppression and for universal peace. Legalistic interpreters of Old Testament promises of liberation unfortunately overlooked its teaching on the necessary preparations of repentance and forgiveness. But the incarnate Messiah liberated many from demonic oppression and established his present rule. "My kingdom," he said, "is not of this world" (John 18:36). His present au-

thority does not center in an earthly capital. Christians do not have an enduring city now—not Jerusalem, Rome, Mecca, Salt Lake City, Moscow, Washington, or Wheaton. He who came from above rules morally and spiritually at present in the thinking, feeling, willing, and relating of those who receive him as Savior and Lord. Christ's rule over believers can be experienced in whatever economic or political situations they find themselves. He is not satisfied with the status quo in any country, and his followers should not be. But as we work for more justice and mercy, we ought not identify the ascended Christ's kingdom with any present political, economic, educational, or religious institution. Not even institutional churches or denominations can be identified with Christ's kingdom.

5. Christ's ascension also *marked the beginning of his present ministries as head of the church.* Although the kingdom is not the church, Christ who rules the cosmos also rules the church. Christ ministers as head of the church in at least three ways.

a. From heaven the exalted Christ *sends the Holy Spirit to those who believe in him.* Previously "the Spirit had not been given, since Jesus had not yet been glorified" (John 7:39). "Exalted to the right hand of God, he has received from the Father the promised Holy Spirit and has poured out what you now see and hear" (Acts 2:33). On the day of Pentecost Christ sent the Holy Spirit to those who believed in him as the Messiah who is Lord. Ever since then, both Jews and Gentiles receive the Spirit by believing the fact that the Messiah has come and by trusting him. Christ sends the Spirit to endue people of faith with power for witnessing (Acts 2:4), to remain with them, and to lead and guide his people in their various ministries.

b. The exalted Christ *builds the church* as he planned to do (Matt. 16:18). Although now in heaven, Christ remains "head over everything for the church" (Eph. 1:20–23; Col. 1:18). He gave his Spirit to work with believers, not only individually but also collectively. Prior to the ascension the Spirit brought people into God's kingdom through the new birth (John 3:3–8). After the ascension the Spirit's new work introduces (or "baptizes") Jewish and Gentile believers into his body, the church (1 Cor. 12:13). Christ through his Spirit gives members of his body gifts (Eph. 4:7–11). He also nurtures (4:16; 5:24; Col. 2:19) and sets apart the church for service (Eph. 5:26). Although transcendently in heaven, in these and other redemptive ministries Christ fulfills his promise to be immanently present as active with his people. "And surely I am with you always, to the very end of the age" (Matt. 28:20). Believers do not now experience Christ's glorious presence in heaven, but they can never escape his presence in his universal providential activities and his particular redemptive activities in their lives. He is present in the activities Scripture attributes to him personally and in the activities Scripture attributes to the Holy Spirit (who is one in essence with him), whom he has sent to abide with us.

c. The exalted Christ *intercedes for believing members of the church* (Rom. 8:34; 1 Tim. 2:5). At the right hand of the Father Christ now pleads the case of believers who sin (1 John 2:1). We could not have a better attorney to plead our case. He is the advocate with universal authority and power who has been installed at the head of the government of heaven and earth. At the same time the Righteous One knows what it was like to be a sojourner in this world (Heb. 2:14–16). Having offered up himself for our salvation, he ever lives (9:11–28) to make intercession for us. Christ pleads our case in heaven itself, or the heavenly Holy of Holies (6:19–20; 8:1–2). The best indications of what he prays for may be seen in his prayers on earth, and especially those for his disciples and all who would believe through them (John 17). When he knew he would remain in the world no longer (v. 11), he pled with the Father, "Protect them by the power of your name . . . so that they may be one as we are one" (vv. 11, 20–23), "protect them from the evil one" (v. 15). "Sanctify them by the truth; your word is truth" (v. 17). I have made you known "in order that the love you have for me may be in them and that I myself may be in them" (v. 26).

6. The resurrected Christ's exaltation *will culminate in his powerful and glorious visible return* in the clouds of heaven as he ascended (Acts 1:11). When the Victor returns, every eye will see him, even those who pierced him (Rev. 1:7). His presence will again be manifested in his incarnate body, but he will not be the "meek and lowly Jesus" of the typical artist's imagination. He will come as the resurrected, ascended, and glorified Lord with eyes like blazing fire (1:14) and wielding a sharp double-edged sword (v. 16). He will judge those who reject the gospel and "bring salvation to those who are waiting for him" (Heb. 9:28). His spiritual kingdom will break out into the open, and visibly the glorified Messiah will rule the entire earth and cosmos. The kingdom, which has been progressively revealed and developed, will finally be consummated by the Prince of Peace.

(7) Christ's ascension *is the first instance of the rapture of a glorified body* (1 Cor. 15:20). Associated with the resurrection of saints is the rapture of those who will be alive at the time of Christ's return. When he returns, "we who are still alive and are left will be caught up together with them in the clouds to meet the Lord in the air" (1 Thess. 4:16–17). Christ has already demonstrated the possibility of a bodily rapture. That may have been foreshadowed also in the translations of Enoch and Elijah. But we have no indication that they received resurrection bodies for their departures, so Christ remains the first to be resurrected and raptured. The resurrection will occur before dead or living believers will be raptured (4:13–17). Anyone who believes in the ascension of Christ's glorified body should not have insuperable difficulties believing in the possibility of the ascension of others in glorified bodies.

8. Christ's ascension *assures the existence of a resurrected and glorified human body and spirit in the Father's immediate presence*. Leaving the earthly scene, the Lord in his glorified humanness entered the heavenly sanctuary (Heb. 6:20; 9:12, 24). Just as "the right hand of God" is figurative, so is the heavenly "sanctuary." It is another analogy for the immediate presence of the Father. Although it belongs to God to be at the place of ultimate authority, wisdom, love, and power, a human nature went there! And Christ's glorified humanness remains in the Father's immediate presence. Jesus' raptured body need not be always visible, however, for in the glorified body Jesus could appear and disappear at will. The human body and spirit interact with each other in this life and even more effectually in the glorified state. Christ's ascension secures us in the belief that when we will be resurrected and will ascend and be like him, we will be able in our wholeness directly and joyfully to relate not only to our Savior, but to God the Father and God the Holy Spirit. What higher hope could enliven the hearts of humans in this life?

APOLOGETIC INTERACTION

How Important Is the Facticity?

The importance of the factual question is momentous, for the claims of

Christ for himself and the validity of his atonement rest on his resurrection. Is it true that Jesus physically rose from the dead? The issues were clearly drawn in a formal debate at Liberty University in 1985 between atheistic philosopher Antony G. N. Flew and Christian philosopher Gary Habermas. In the debate Flew denied and Habermas affirmed a literal, physical interpretation of the accounts of Christ's resurrection. But both agreed on a literal resurrection's supreme theoretical and practical importance as a distinguishing characteristic of Christianity and not of any other world religion.[113]

If Jesus was not physically raised, the Messiah has not come and Jesus has lost his integrity. If Christ did not rise, belief in his claims for himself or anything he taught is discredited. Jesus admitted as much. After Jesus cleansed the temple, the Jews asked, " 'What miraculous sign can you show us to prove your authority to do all this?' Jesus answered them, 'Destroy this temple [his body], and I will raise it again in three days' " (John 2:18–19). Less figuratively on other occasions he explained that he would be killed "and after three days rise again" (Mark 8:31; 9:31; 10:34). If the most important sign given of his true authority did not occur, we have no reason to believe that he was even a true prophet of God. "If what a prophet proclaims in the name of the LORD does not take place or come true, that is a message the LORD has not spoken. That prophet has spoken presumptuously. Do not be afraid of him" (Deut. 18:22). If Christ did not rise, no one ought to trust him even as a prophet.

If Christ did not rise, furthermore, the gospel deceives. From the beginning the heart of the good news headlined eyewitness testimony to Jesus' resurrection. The conclusion to each Gospel affirmed in detail not only his crucifixion and burial, but also his resurrection. The Christian church began when Peter declared that, as prophesied, it was impossible for death to keep its hold on Jesus Christ, his body did not see decay; "God raised this Jesus to life," and, Peter added, "we are all witnesses of the fact" (Acts 2:24–32). Paul, having received the gospel from the Lord and his apostles, passed on

> as of first importance: that Christ died for our sins according to the Scriptures, that he was buried, that he was raised on the third day according to the Scriptures, and that he appeared to Peter, and then to the Twelve. After that he appeared to more than five hundred of the brothers at the same time, most of whom are still living, though some have fallen asleep. Then he appeared to James, then to all the apostles, and last of all he appeared to me also, as to one abnormally born (1 Cor. 15:3–8).

Those who do not affirm that Christ rose do not preach the gospel that Paul preached.

If Christ has not been physically raised, furthermore, no one has been forgiven, redeemed, or reconciled and the Christian church has lost its *raison d'etre*. Justification, a provision of Christ's atonement, Paul taught, is conditioned upon our inner belief in Christ's resurrection (Rom. 10:9–10; cf. 3:23–25). No amount of passionate commitment to a false message can reconcile us to the God of truth. If Christ has not been raised, neither Paul, Augustine, nor Billy Graham have ever actually been born again. If Christ has not been raised, the primary basis of Christian unity has been swept away. No one ought to continue in the apostle's teaching, the breaking of bread, fellowship, or prayer. If Christ has not been raised, all the alleged theological significance of his humiliation and exaltation have collapsed, and Christians who believe the lie are to be pitied (1 Cor. 15:14–17). Without a basis in reality claims to the existential values of the Messiah's crucifixion, resurrection, and ascension are inauthentic.

So much rests on the reality of the resurrection that it is little wonder that debate swirls around its facticity. The basic questions in the debate concern its possibility, purpose, and actuality.

Could Christ's Resurrection Have Happened?

Would the first-century evening news have reported Christ's resurrection and ascension? Were they observed events at particular times and places? Could TV cameras have filmed Christ coming back to life, going through the solid rock of the still-sealed tomb, and later cooking breakfast for his disciples?

By definition, the atheist understands the miracle of the resurrection and ascension as a logical impossibility. If nature is the highest reality and its laws are invariable, no power can overrule those laws. Since no miracles are possible a priori, alleged testimony like that for the resurrection and ascension are usually ignored, reinterpreted as myth, or humorously dismissed as absurd.

Forty students laughingly dismissed Christ's ascension as a parody on Ascension Day in May 1967. They thought that their knowledge of space travel reduced Christ's ascension to nonsense. On one end of a long cord they fastened several gas-inflated balloons; on the other, a crude effigy of Christ made of tissue paper and cardboard. As high noon approached, the crowd began a hilarious countdown from 100. The volume of the shouting and the air of boisterous jollity heightened until with a mighty shout of "Zero" and "Blastoff" the crowd released the cord holding the the balloons and the effigy. A naïve bystander did not realize what the raucous crowd was mocking until, as the balloons ascended dragging behind them the paper Christ, he heard one of the men quote Scripture: "Men of Galilee, why do you stand looking into heaven? This Jesus, who was taken up from you into heaven, will come in the same way as you saw him go into heaven." Who were these people? The participants in this charade were not communists taunting Christians, and they were not hecklers on drugs. They were students preparing for Christian ministry on the campus of a well-known seminary.[114]

More generally, naturalists ignore the evidence for Christ's resurrection and ascension. According to invariable natural law, dead men stay dead. Naturalists often prejudge the evidence, assuming a priori what is to be proved, that all events can be naturally explained. In this context naturalists also tend to make natural laws more than they are. Scientific laws statistically describe what generally occurs. They neither cause events nor keep any specific event from happening in human history. If nontheists are not to beg the question, then, they ought to examine carefully the indications that Christ rose from his tomb. Historical evidence cannot be erased by the fiat of philosophers. Pannenberg comments, "The weakness of Professor Flew's position in the dispute with Professor Habermas was his a priori assumption of the inconclusive character of the evidence and his reluctance to enter into a serious discussion of the historical detail."[115]

Rudolph Bultmann studied the New Testament thoroughly but reinterprets the resurrection accounts to fit his assumed closed system of natural laws. So he alleges that the resurrection accounts amount to prescientific myths of first-century people expressed in a crude "world picture." To make the reports meaningful to people with a scientific model of the universe, the New Testament scholar dismissed what he thought were the husks of literal meaning and embraced only what he considered their existential significance.

There are others who take the account of the resurrection seriously, albeit mythically, not literally. Was Christ's resurrection a myth? Myths are symbolic expressions of something beyond history—a universal, ever-existent ground of all visible phenomena. The application of the concept of myth to the resurrection meant a leveling down of the particular to the universal and the changing of a special revelation into general revelation. But Christ's resurrection is not parallel to a recurring event like the sprouting of perennials in spring. The Gospels are an expression of the religion divinely initiated by the incarnation, death, and resurrection of one unique person in the flesh, not a general nature religion. The apostles were not interested in proclaiming a general religious truth in the symbolic language of myth, but a specific truth in empirically observed facts. And the risen Lord is not presented as a new cult hero to stand alongside others. As a result of his confirmed resurrection, the apostles held that he alone is Lord. The supernatural uniqueness of Christ's resurrection, Walter Kunneth concludes, forbids any application of the concept of myth and makes impossible any analogical relationship with other myths of religious history.[116]

From the time of Bultmann's writings to the present the scientific models of the world have dramatically changed. Mechanistic models have given way following the discovery of atomic energy. The assured, predictable, closed system of natural law, which Bultmann assumed, has been shaken. Although scientific world pictures come and go, the metaphysical, ethical, and factual questions remain the same. In any century have we to do with a living God who can perform mighty acts like the resurrection and ascension of the Messiah?

A fundamental error of Bultmann was to confuse the scientific world picture of his day with a metaphysical worldview (a closed one). The God of the Bible, whom the heavens cannot contain (1 Kings 8:27), is not limited by our changing world pictures. The power of the transcendent, living, and active God brought Jesus Christ back to life. The resurrection has ineradicable significance in every culture on earth (prescientific or scientific) and at every stage of scientific knowledge of the world. It is tragic to perform open-heart surgery upon the Christian faith in an attempt to substitute for the risen and ascended King of kings one of many naturalistic spiritual masters. Christianity at its heart involves unique mighty acts in the space-time world. The most coherent view of the scriptural evidence affirms that the eternal Logos came, died, was buried, rose again, and ascended in a publicly verifiable, literal human body.

Alan Richardson examined Bultmann's view as a hypothesis to be tested by continually checking with the New Testament documents and other relevant evidence from the period. This verificational method necessarily involves a personal or subjective element but not an absolute subjectivism or historical relativism. One historical interpretation can be shown to be better (more coherent and viable) than another.[117]

> Thus, for example, R. Bultmann's hypothesis that the theology of the New Testament is a mythological conglomeration of Jewish apocalyptic and Hellenistic gnostic ideas which have somehow coagulated round the name of Jesus of Nazareth, about whom little certain historical knowledge can be attained, must be studied to see whether it gives a rational and coherent explanation of the New Testament evidence.[118]

The more adequate hypothesis, Richardson finds, is that Jesus himself was the prime author of the striking reinterpretation of the Old Testament theology found in his own reported teachings and in the New Testament as a whole. Among those teachings Richardson included are the new covenant, the new Israel, the reinterpreted messiahship, and the reign of God.[119] Richardson regards Bultmann's denial of Christ's resurrection as an event in history "a compromise with post-Enlightenment historiography" and "a sign of the disintegration of contemporary Protestantism."[120] Why the early celebrations of Easter, he asks, if nothing extraordinary happened on Easter Day?

Unfortunately Barth also ascribed a reductive naturalism to all history (*Historie*), although historiography need not be limited to antisupernaturalists. Unless Christians challenge the naturalistic presuppositions, it will do little good to join Barth in calling the resurrection a "saga" or interpreted history (*Geschichte*) rather than a "fact." Ramm thinks Barth's case "the best of the options because he has most thoroughly understood the nature of the historical issue."[121] Those who defend the objectivity of the resurrection, Ramm thinks, underplay its unique character, and those who seek to guard its uniqueness shade away its historical factuality.[122] From the beginning we have emphasized both the uniqueness and the factuality of Christ's resurrection. Insofar as the body is uniquely incorruptible, powerful, and glorious, those truths come from propositional revelation; insofar as the body is continuous, visible, audible, and tangible, it was verified publicly by eyewitnesses. We integrate both the continuity and the uniqueness as a visible sign laden with invisible meanings.

If a transcendent personal God who has purposes for our world exists, ordinarily we expect regular natural laws, but there is no reason why God cannot act in extraordinary ways. If God were merely an idea within our own heads, or a formless life-force that we could tap for our purposes, a miracle like the literal resurrection would be impossible. But belief in the living God of the Bible provides the most coherent and viable explanation of why there is anything at all, why it is orderly, why there are persons, and why in conscience and history there is a difference between right and wrong.

> If we are in fact spirits, not Nature's offspring, then there must be some point (probably the brain) at which created spirits even now can produce effects on matter not by manipulation or technics but simply by the wish to do so . . . . every time you move your hand or think a thought. And nature . . . is not destroyed but rather perfected by her servitude"[123]

He who created the body as an instrument of spirit can restore one ravaged by sin and make the body become an even more wonderful instrument (of spirit). The peak Christian experience is not a contentless mystical contemplation from which the environment and the senses are banished but a full realization of God's presence as nature and spirit are finally harmonized. Every state of Christ's resurrection body perfectly expresses his spiritual state and his spiritual state is supremely just and loving, wise and powerful. So Paul's question to Agrippa is appropriate: "Why should any of you consider it incredible that God raises the dead?" (Acts 26:8).

The living Spirit who made humans unique can also actively pursue sinners in history like a hunter, king, or husband. As C. S. Lewis found,

> There comes a moment when the children who have been playing at burglars hush suddenly: was that a *real* footstep in the hall? There comes a moment when people who have been dabbling in religion

> ('man's search for God'!) suddenly draw back. Supposing we really found Him? We never meant it to come to that! Worse still, supposing He had found us? So it is a sort of Rubicon. One goes across; or not. But if one does, there is no manner of security against miracles. One may be in for anything."[124]

With good reason to believe in the reality of the God of the Bible, unquestionably the miracle of Christ's resurrection could happen.

Should Christ's Resurrection Happen?

It would be pointless for God to resurrect Abraham Lincoln for an atomistic appearance to a bartender for no particular reason. But Jesus Christ is not just another person, and his resurrection is no isolated event. Why should Christ have been raised? Is it not enough that Jesus lived and died? No, it is not enough.

Christ's resurrection completes the purposes of the whole century-spanning program of salvation. It powerfully fulfills divine justice and love. It dramatically culminates the Messiah's saving mission. The purpose of Christ's resurrection is not to celebrate the joys of spring but to save the lost. The resurrection exhibits God's concern for the world of fallen people with all the literal blood, sweat, and tears their sins entail. God is not like an executive away on a trip, but more like a loving father willing to go to any length to recover a lost child. In order to reconcile sinners God transcended his usual method of working and performed miracles. By astounding signs and wonders God delivered enslaved Israelites from Egyptian bondage, brought down the walls of Jericho, and established Israel in the Promised Land. When Baal worship threatened to destroy the line of the coming Messiah, God spewed fire from heaven onto Elijah's altar. Christ's resurrection is part of a redemptive program that included numerous miraculous events for important redemptive purposes.

In the fullness of time the Messiah came into the world by the miracle of the virgin birth. Jesus healed the sick, gave sight to the blind, predicted the future, and quieted nature's violent storms. In this context it is not surprising that he should say, "Destroy this temple and in three days I will raise it up again." The resurrection was the grand climax of a series of mighty acts in the life of the incarnate Word of God.

Several important things were accomplished by the crucified Christ's resurrection historically and theologically. As we have documented above, it fulfilled his predictions, demonstrated the truth of his claims, and certified the Father's acceptance of his atoning provisions. It assures believers' justification, redemption, and reconciliation today. And in the world to come it guarantees their own reembodiment and acceptance with the final Judge. Indeed it constitutes God's empirical signature on the bottom line for every aspect of salvation. On the one hand, if Christ's tomb was not emptied, the faith of every Christian has been in vain. All who have trusted him were deceived and remain in their sins. On the other hand, if he came forth from the tomb, such a mighty act of God has tremendous significance for sinners of all time.

Should the resurrection happen? Indeed, it should. But many things that would be great never take place in fact.

Did Christ's Resurrection Happen?

Human knowledge of the conclusion of Christ's unique life is not totally different from the knowing of all past events. We do not learn about ancient history with an intuitive psychological certitude, but a probability based on research of credible ancient documents. The most coherent interpretation, then, has the greatest probability of conveying the truth. Some theologians, such as P. Althaus, think that intuition can open an "immediate, prescientific relationship to past history, across centuries and millennia, which bears within itself unconditional certainty about this past life."[125] But Pannenberg aptly responds, "Intuition always requires confirmation through detailed historical observation. . . . The only method of achieving at least approximate certainty with regard to the events of a past time is historical research."[126]

Insofar as the sign of Christ's resurrection was literal and physical, it can be subjected to historical research; insofar as the sign involved revealed conceptual meanings, it cannot be subjected to testing by the five senses. It is still necessary to verify as far as possible the prophetic or apostolic sources of the revealed meanings and our interpretations of their teachings. Futile is the quest for a reductively historical Jesus, in the sense of a Jesus apart from such supernatural events as the resurrection and ascension with their supernaturally revealed meanings.

Can we integrate the varied accounts of the resurrection coherently? Many think the four Gospels are full of glaring discrepancies and so find harmonies impossible (e.g., E. Brunner, W. Marxen, N. Perrin). Christian scholars were certain that this does not mean the narratives cannot be reconciled, but for a long time no one had brought forth a convincing harmony. Challenged by this problem, John Wenham, in Jerusalem in 1945, set out to determine whether a convincing harmony of the resurrection accounts was possible. After thorough examinations of the sites in and around the city, Wenham was at first impressed with the intractable nature of the discrepancies. On the first Easter morning did five women go to the tomb (Luke), three (Mark), two (Matthew), one (John), or none (Paul)? Did they visit the tomb while it was still dark (John) or when the sun had risen (Mark)? Were the messengers who spoke to them men (Mark one, Luke two) or angels (Matthew one, John two)? Were the messengers inside the tomb (Mark, Luke, and John), or did they start outside the tomb and finish inside (Matthew)? Did Christ appear to a number of women who held his feet without rebuke (Matthew) or to one whom he forbade to touch him (John)? Did Christ appear to the eleven disciples in Galilee (Matthew) or in Jerusalem (Luke)?[127]

Wenham's insatiable curiosity motivated study of the Greek text, extensive further research, and map making. He reported:

> I gradually found many of the pieces of the jigsaw coming together. It now seems to me that these resurrection stories exhibit in a remarkable way the well-known characteristics of accurate and independent reporting, for superficially they show great disharmony, but on close examination the details gradually fall into place.[128]

Although some details remained uncertain, Wenham proposes the following harmony. Of special evidential value were Christ's initial appearances for eight days in Jerusalem where Joseph's well-known garden and empty tomb could be checked by first-century friends and enemies. In the first fifteen days Christ appeared at least seven times quietly teaching individuals and groups about the kingdom of God. After this preparation he met the great gathering in Galilee. To counter their hope for a political kingdom in Jerusalem, he regathered the disciples and recommissioned them as apostles in Galilee, reconstituting the Christian movement. In the atmosphere of Galilee they were weaned afresh from the ideal of a temporal Jewish messianic kingdom until they were ready to be sent back to the city that had crucified their Lord to begin their worldwide witness. In Jerusalem the transformed apostles waited for the coming of the Holy Spirit on the day of Pentecost.[129]

The appearances occurred in a kind of progressive revelation of Christ's exaltation as people were able to receive it. The women who first saw the opened and empty tomb and heard the angels' explanation were ready before the men. Jesus met and spoke first to one of them and then to the others. Then after hearing the women's account and seeing the empty tomb and the grave cloths, the two men walking to Emmaus were joined by Jesus; he explained his mission and gradually revealed facts about the fulfillment of prophecy concerning himself. This prepared them for the commissioning of the official witnesses: Peter, the eleven, Thomas, the five hundred, and finally his own brother James, who would one day lead the Jerusalem church. There remained only the last farewell and the coming of the Holy Spirit before they would courageously preach Christ crucified and risen, turning the world upside down.[130]

> So ends an investigation which we believe has shown that the charge of irreconcilability brought against the resurrection stories has not been substantiated. Rather it has shown that these records exhibit the characteristics of accurate and independent reporting, for superficially they show great disharmony, but on close examination the details gradually fall into place.[131]

Other scholars have set forth harmonizations of the resurrection narratives confirming the possibility of a coherent integration of the Gospel records in the light of recent knowledge.[132]

Differences of detail occur in reporting emergencies today with all the instant communication facilities available for highly trained news investigators and writers. With such a confusing flurry of untraceable, sudden appearances for forty days in the first century, it is amazing that the differences are not greater. "There may even be a virtue in the fact that the evangelists present such diverse accounts, for it shows their independence of each other and suggests that the points on which they do agree are likely to be all the more historically reliable."[133]

On what points do the records agree? The biblical records consistently present the following *data that demand explanation* from the standpoint of any worldview. We here present certain undoubted phenomena of the first century and ask how the reader proposes to account for each and all of them together.

1. *Jesus of Nazareth died and was buried.* We noted the biblical evidence for the fact of his death in the previous chapter. The claim that he was not raised because he did not die does not fit the facts. An expert on executions was not likely mistaken when he found Jesus dead and so did not break his legs to speed death. A Roman soldier pierced him with a sword. Both his loved ones and enemies concluded he had died. Joseph of Arimathea buried him in his own tomb. The tomb was a cave, the entrance to which was closed with a huge boulder. Roman soldiers sealed the tomb and stood guard over it.

According to the theory that Jesus did not really die, he, the one who had no sleep throughout the mistreatment and trial the night before and who was too weak to carry his cross, suddenly revived and became strong enough to break out of the graveclothes and the sealed cave and overpower the armed guards. Then the wounded victim overwhelmingly convinced his disciples that he had triumphantly conquered death! Jesus, in his mere humanness, would not have had the strength for such a performance. And even if he had done so, he would have deceived his followers until they too became party to a pious fraud. Whatever else may be thought of Jesus and his followers, no responsible scholar regards them premeditated deceivers. It is beyond reasonable doubt that Jesus died and his body was buried.

2. After the crucifixion *a resurrection was unexpected.* In spite of Jesus' several attempts to prepare his disciples for his death, they were not prepared for what took place. Having misinterpreted the nature of his present kingship, the disciples were disillusioned and confused. In that condition psychologically they were not capable of inventing a story of his triumphant resurrection and ascension.

3. On Easter Sunday both women and men confirmed that *the tomb was open and empty.* Before dawn an earthquake had occurred, and an angel had come and rolled the boulder back up the hill. If the tomb was not empty, how does one account for the successful emergence of Christianity in Jerusalem where belief in the resurrected Christ could have been disconfirmed by opening his grave?

4. *The grave clothes were undisturbed,* indicating that Jesus left them without unwrapping them. To the observer it was evident that Jesus' body had passed through the grave clothes, leaving them as they had been wrapped.

5. For a period of forty days the living *Jesus appeared* to individuals and to groups of up to five hundred. At first the observers tried to explain the empirical evidence in other ways. But after seeing and hearing Jesus and being invited to touch his wounds, even the most skeptical were convinced that he was alive again. Among the witnesses were those who were best qualified to recognize him—those that had been with him for three years.

6. As a result of their eyewitness experiences with the risen Christ, *the disciples were transformed.* In forty days their despair changed to hope, their disbelief to faith, their fear to courage. In just six or seven weeks from the crucifixion to the day of Pentecost, Peter, who had denied his Lord three times, boldly proclaimed Christ's resurrection a short distance from his grave. Something provoked the belief of doubting Thomas, Jesus' brother James, and Jesus' enemy Saul. If it was not Jesus' resurrection that transformed the disciples, what was it? Certainly not a legend.

7. *A new movement arose* in Jerusalem and quickly advanced throughout the region. It was based on the belief that Jesus was alive. If it were not for the resurrection, Jesus' Jewish followers might have formed a sect of Judaism, but not a distinct religion. There is nothing but the resurrection to distinguish the first Christians from any other Jews of their day. Nor would the disciples have been tenacious enough to keep up their distinctiveness over against the pious Judaism to which they otherwise belonged if it had not been for their unshakeable convictions about Jesus' resurrection. The primitive message did not limit itself to general philosophical statements but concentrated on specific happenings. Distinctively the sect of the Nazarenes reported that Christ rose. Either that belief was rooted in fact, in a serious misapprehension, or in a deliberate lie. It was not a sect with a new philosophy to propagate, nor was there a dominating personality. It was a body of people bearing witness to the alleged resurrection of a historical figure.[134]

Several observable indications of Christ's resurrection have continued to the present day:

8. The *Christian church still exists today.* Apart from this triumph of Christ, the church would not have begun or continued. As one wag put it, other businesses run like the church

would have become extinct long ago! The frailty and fallibility of church leaders has become notorious in literature and the media. Had it not been for its confidence in the One who conquered sin and death, the church would long ago have disappeared.

9. Christians generally practice *Sunday worship*. The change in the day of worship from Saturday to Sunday took place and remains evident today. If not the resurrection, what remarkable first-century event can explain that major transformation of a longstanding Sabbath tradition?

10. The first century produced the written *New Testament*, which remains to this day. If Jesus did not rise, what first-century event did motivate the written preservation of the apostles' teaching? Had Jesus not risen, few would have been interested in apostolic doctrine. Apart from the resurrection, the discouraged group after the crucifixion and burial would not have had the heart or the motivation to write the books of the New Testament.

11. *The Calendar* directs attention to what happened before Christ (B.C.) and after the birth of the Lord (A.D.). If Jesus did not rise, what event in history better accounts for the change in the dating of all events that later occurred?

In sum, if the incarnate Word did not rise, what other life-transforming, history-changing, first-century event does account for all of these eleven phenomena? Deception, mistake, bribery, hallucination, etc., are inadequate explanations. The liberals have decimated each other's proposals until most have abandoned attempts to propose naturalistic explanations. The hypothesis of hallucinations does not account for the number, the variety, and the abrupt cessation of the appearances. The swoon theory does not fit the overwhelmingly probable evidence that Jesus died (see vol. 1, chap. 7). The same kinds of evidence and method of reasoning that conclusively support Jesus' death conclusively support his resurrection from the dead. These lines of evidence empirically confirmed by many witnesses are as significant for pre-Christians as for Christians. God "has set a day when he will judge the world with justice by the man he has appointed. He has given proof of this to *all men* by raising him from the dead" (Acts 17:31).

As a graduate student at Cornell University in a course on philosophy of religion, Gordon Lewis presented a case like this in a paper on Paul's classic religious language at Athens (Acts 17). Professor Irving Singer, a philosophical analyst, responded in the margin of the paper, "This makes the case for a bodily resurrection meaningful." It was encouraging to hear a naturalist admit the cognitive significance of the historical data. As Antony Flew admitted, a naturalistic presupposition that miracles are impossible "should not be the end of the affair. For historians, like everyone else, ought to be ever ready, for sufficient reason, to correct their assumptions about what is probable or improbable, possible or impossible. And this readiness should allow that even the qualification *secular* may, for sufficient reason, have to be abandoned."[135]

Professor Singer then raised a probing question that may be expected from any naturalist. "How do you know that it was *God* who raised him from the dead?" Briefly, an answer to that question reverts to how we know anything about a transcendent being (see vol. 1, chaps. 2–4) and what may be known about God (see vol. 1, chaps. 5–9). We found reason to believe in two supernatural powers—God and the fallen angel Satan. So the question becomes, Was Christ raised from the grave by the power of God or by the power of the devil? The need for discernment between good and evil spirits arises in interpreting any supernatural phenomenon. Whether a miracle is ultimately done by divine or by demonic power is best answered by assessing its purposes. Did it serve the ends of God's righteous kingdom or of Satan's evil kingdom? In the context of its prophetic anticipation and all of its moral and spiritual significance above, behind Christ's resurrection was the power of the Holy One. If doubt remains, many inspired biblical texts explicitly reveal the fact that it was God who raised Jesus from the dead (Acts 2:24, 32; 3:15, 26; 4:10).

What Form Does the Apologetic Take?

In drawing responsible conclusions about Christ's resurrection, we seek to avoid two extremes. We cannot dismiss history as unimportant in favor of a transcendental call to conversion or inner witness of the Spirit, nor can we dismiss the transcendent Spirit's illumination in favor of such history as can be confined within the assumptions of naturalistic presuppositions. On the one hand, attempts to discover the Jesus of naturalistic history have ended in a *cul de sac*. On the other hand, a gospel that cares only for the apostolic proclamation and denies that it either can or should be tested for its historical antecedents is only a thinly veiled gnosticism or docetism. Christian historical apologetic, if it is respectable, welcomes careful scrutiny of its method. Even Helmut Thielicke, who stresses the existential implications of the gospel, has wisely cautioned, "Nothing can be the object of our faith which stands in evident contradiction to the factual. . . . The Easter faith would then be possible only by means of schizophrenia of our human consciousness—which would be unbearable and unallowable."[136]

The verificational method of reasoning used throughout *Integrative Theology* does not imagine that anyone can be totally objective in examining this evidence or come to it with a mind free of all prior conclusions. More realistically the method simply invites readers to carefully consider the consistency and adequacy of hypothetical explanations and accept the most adequate explanation. If God exists as revealed in Christ and Scripture, we have a coherent account of all eleven lines of evidence. Several scholars have utilized variations of the hypothetical method of reasoning. C. F. D. Moule, for example, "attempts simply to display a selection of the phenomena which need to be reckoned with, and to ask, What do you make of these? Can you make sense of them as history without importing precisely the value-judgments to which the original Christians were led? Conversely, can you account for the value judgment without the historical basis?"[137] Open to alternative hypotheses, Moule invites his readers to propose a more coherent account if they can.

Having employed a verificational or critical method, George Ladd concluded,

> The only hypothesis which adequately explains the "historical" facts, including the empty tomb, is that God actually raised the body of Jesus from the realm of mortality in the world of time and space to the invisible world of God, and that Jesus was able to appear to his disciples in different ways on different occasions. Admittedly this is not a "historical" explanation; it involves *theology*—a belief in God. . . . Does such a faith mean a "leap in the dark"? By no means."[138]

Ladd did not seek by a "historical" reasoning from naturalistic assumptions and a blank mind to "prove" the resurrection in some compulsive sense. It was his purpose, he said, to exhibit the historical facts and show that the hypothesis of Christ's bodily resurrection is the most adequate explanation without self-contradiction. That is the meaning of confirmation or "proof" in most factual issues.[139] Although Ladd calls his approach an "inductive method," his starting point is not a totally objective, blank mind but hypotheses to be tested. Hence New Testament scholars who follow Ladd in this are not following an inductive method of reasoning, in spite of advertising "inductive Bible studies." When admittedly starting with hypotheses to be tested, New Testament scholars use a method more like the verificational method of reasoning (reminiscent of Edward John Carnell, Ladd's colleague for many years). New Testament scholars would avoid the naïveté of alleging a blank mind at the beginning of their research if they explicitly adopted a verificational method.[140]

Does Scientism Have All the Answers?

Often it seems that science has all the answers. For reliable knowledge about the weather, illness, and any physical or historical possibilities people do not go to the minister, but to the scientists. The attempt to empty nature of God since the Enlightenment, however, fails to account for Christ's empty tomb and appearances. On either a naturalistic or pantheistic worldview dead people stay dead. Once decomposition and decay have begun, they continue. But on one occasion this natural process did not have the last word. *A power distinct from nature and atomic energy reversed irreversible natural laws of decomposition and overcame death itself!*

Christ's resurrection demonstrated *the Creator's transcendent power over nature's irreversible laws in space and time.* Although occurring in space and time, Christ's resurrection cannot be explained within space and time. Neither naturalistic nor pantheistic hypotheses can adequately account for the fact of Christ's resurrection. It confirms a divine power above or over nature. The resurrection shows that the divine power is not so far removed that God cannot act in extraordinary ways within and upon nature. The deistic hypothesis does not account for the facts of the first century. The most coherent account of the regularities of nature and history and the miracles of the first century is a theistic, biblical worldview.

Does the Problem of Evil Have an Answer?

On occasion it seems that evil gets out of control in history. Then people cry out, "Why does not God do something about it?" God has done something about it! Providentially God prevents and overrules much of the evil. But the crucifixion and resurrection exemplify God's mightiest acts to this point in response to the problem of evil. At Calvary it seemed that evil had triumphed, but evil and death did not have the last word. The resurrection and ascension did! History is not merely the arena of impersonal spatial and temporal forces. Bound up with space and time in historical events are the interactions or intentions of human agents and, above all, those of the divine Agent. Numbers of fallen human agents conspired to take the life of Jesus—Judas, Herod, Pilate, Jews, and Gentiles (Acts 4:27). God permitted their evil but overruled history's worst evil to provide salvation for all! However great a hold moral evil may have in your life, God can transform it. The resurrection has demonstrated God's power to deliver from sin's power and from its tragic consequences. *Christ's resurrection demonstrated God's ability to transform history's worst injustice into its greatest good.*

Christ's incarnation, life, death, and resurrection did not occur in some kind of suprahistory, touching our fallen world only in a tangential manner. The eternal Word came in actual, literal history. The tendency to speak of timeless events or crises in the early Barth and Brunner, and in Bultmann, Dodd, and Reinhold Niebuhr is inadequate. Far from violating or abrogating time, the risen Christ has created a new age or aeon. So the church fulfills its mission of overcoming evil in the overlap of the two times, the present evil aeon that will pass away and the new righteous aeon that has already come in the triumph of Christ. Spiritually, the end time "has telescoped itself into the present and penetrated the Church through the coming of the Spirit."[141] Because of its participation in the new creation, the church can continue to live on earth and in history only through being crucified with Christ to the present evil powers. What does the future hold from the standpoint of the centrality of Christ's incarnation, death, and resurrection in history? We expect ethical crises to the end of time, but Christ's resurrection assures our own final victory over sin and death. In the light of our coming *telos* we ought not give in to the evil of the present age, but overcome it by making responsible decisions along the way.[142]

Is Jesus Christ the Only Reconciler?

Is the crucified and risen Christ the only religious leader to have justly provided for forgiveness, redemption, and reconciliation to God? Few issues are as sensitive as this in a pluralistic world of instant communication.

To avoid an unhealthy exclusivism John Hick proposes a Copernican revolution in Christian theology, a paradigm shift from a Jesus-centered to a God-centered model. He sees the great world religions as different responses to the one divine reality. When Hick calls Jesus the Son of God, he announces that the myth of Jesus is the means by which he came to know God.[143] Many Eastern thinkers also regard all faiths as relative ways to the one transcendent God. Paul F. Knitter rejects a miraculous resurrection and favors the disciples' subjective faith as producing Christ's resurrection, and also takes a theocentric view of Christianity and a nonnormative reinterpretation of the uniqueness of Jesus Christ.[144]

Fully aware of relativism in religion, Ernst Troeltsch argued that historical phenomena are not all the same and that they all have values that call for choices among them. He found Christianity superior to the religions of nature (Hinduism and Buddhism) and of law (Judaism and Islam) because it gives greater value to personal existence. Nature religions, by dissolving humans in the divine essence, forfeit all positive meaning and content in the divine Being. Christianity does not deny the empirical world as actually given and experienced but builds on it, transforms it, and eventually raises it to a new level. The Absolute entered history in Jesus of Nazareth, and only his crucifixion and resurrection make possible this achievement for souls ensnared in depravity and guilt. Jesus Christ represents the only complete break with the limits and conditions of nature (and process) religions. And Jesus Christ provides the only satisfaction of absolute justice for religions of law. People must make a choice between meditation on nonbeing or redemption and reconciliation through faith and growth in grace.[145]

It is important that we neither absolutize relatives nor relativize the incarnate Absolute. But if the Absolute has come into history in the Lord Jesus Christ, we must not relativize his incarnation to the level of other religious leaders. "The only reason for being a Christian," said Stephen Neill, "is the overpowering conviction that the Christian faith is true." And as Alec Vidler said of Christianity, "Either it is true for all men, whether they know it or not; or it is true for no one, not even for those people who are under the illusion that it is true." After citing these statements Elton Trueblood added, "In the long run, the best reason for dedication to the spread of the faith of Christ is the conviction that this faith conforms to reality as does no other alternative of which we are aware."[146]

Although admittedly many who have held to the exclusivity of the truth of the gospel have been arrogant, we seek to respect the right of people in other traditions to differ. Tolerance is often mistaken for agreement with others. It does not take tolerance to be kindly to those who hold similar convictions. Tolerance involves respect and consideration for those committed to contradictory views on issues of importance. Belief in the truth of some religious statements and the realities they designate need not be maintained in an intolerant attitude. Those who believe in the risen Messiah should care about those who reject him and should avoid any unethical attempts to persuade them. Although Paul and the other apostles were convinced of the uniqueness of Christ, they did not resort to coercive programing or deprograming of others. Both non-Christians and Christians in a civilized pluralistic world have the freedom to engage in dialogue and discussion in an effort to persuade one another of the truth of their views.

People must be free to conclude whether or not the Messiah has come and was crucified and raised for all humans of all times and cultures. It cannot be both ways without self-contradiction. The price of rejecting the law of noncontradiction (with Knitter and others) is forfeiture of the possibility of meaningful affirmation about anything at all. If all assertions are equally true, they are all equally false, and we are reduced to meaninglessness or silence. The law of noncontradiction cannot be refuted, since it is the necessary condition of any intelligible communication in the East or West. Illustrating the necessity of choice, Stephen Neill says, "Whom shall we follow—eastern teachers who tell us that the world is evil or illusion? Western teachers who tell us to accept the world, because we can do no other? Jesus, who tells us that the world is God's world, and therefore essentially good and serviceable?"[147] Whom shall we follow? Eastern teachers who tell us that Jesus was one more avatar who did not physically come into the world, literally die for literal sins, or literally rise? Or shall we believe the confirmed signs and revealed significance of the Messiah's life according to inspired Scripture?

When Peter says, "Salvation is found in no one else" (Acts 4:12), he is not pronouncing a narrow-minded a priori prejudice. He is reporting that Christ has uniquely done what others neither have done nor can do. What founder of any other religious movement: (1) claimed to be the unique, once-for-all divine incarnation? (2) lived a fully human life without sin and so was worthy to die in place of sinners? (3) was God so that he could bear the penalty of all human sin? (4) could identify as fully with both God and humans as mediator? (5) died to propitiate the Father's righteous wrath, redeem, and reconcile? (6) predicted his or her resurrection and came back to life in triumph over sin and its death penalty? (7) ascended to the place of highest power over every other power in heaven and earth? and (8) was uniquely in the image of God and so able to recreate sinners in God's image and bring peace to the entire world?

We ought not confuse the issues of the objective validity of an assertion with a subjective agreement with its content, or a personal commitment to its referent in reality. A personal commitment to the Savior does not change the universal validity of the truths of the gospel. In religion we are concerned with both personal and propositional truths. Conceptual truths guide us away from counterfeit Christs to the living Christ who alone has demonstrated power over death. It is not our commitment that saves us, but the one in whom we place our trust. False beliefs do not become true simply by being internalized.

In view of the evidence in volume 1, chapter 7, we affirmed with overwhelming probability and objective validity that Jesus was both truly human and truly divine. Hence he differed from Abraham, Krishna, Buddha, Mohammed, Joseph Smith, and Mary Baker Eddy not merely in degree, but in kind. There have been many other great teachers and fine examples; but there have in fact been no other propitiators, redeemers, and reconcilers. If salvation from our moral predicament were attainable by an immediate, direct mystical experience of God the Father, the Son of God would not have needed to come or die for sinners. But since God himself acted decisively in history in order justly to save sinners, we cannot agree with those who think that by mystical intuition or spiritual disciplines they can by-pass faith in Christ's incarnation, death, and resurrection. Non-Christian mystics may experience oneness with the cosmos and its energy or even become aware of its Creator's existence, but apart from the provisions of Christ they do not enjoy personal fellowship with the Creator, who is not only distinct from the cosmos but also righteous.

The deepest question is not how we can come to God or become aware of God's existence. All religions lead to God—as Judge! Before him eventually every knee will bow. The root question is, How can sinful people come to God as Savior? What non-Christian, non-Evangelical religion provides for a just punishment of sin and acquittal of sinners? Many today are like the Jews in Paul's day. Paul said, "They are zealous for God, but their zeal is not based on knowledge. Since they do not know the righteousness that comes from God and sought to establish their own, they did not submit [themselves] to God's righteousness" (Rom. 10:2–3). Our heart's desire and prayer to God for people trying to build up good *karma* (works) is like Paul's for the Jews—that they may be saved (v. 1). Christians need not strive for perfect *karma* through imagined endless incarnations in order to attain the perfection of heaven because by faith they have received the righteousness that comes from God—Christ's perfect *karma*.

Since Jesus is Lord of all, the highest lordship by its very nature can have no equals. Jesus cannot be added to a god shelf along with 330 million other Eastern Hindu deities or a similar number of Western materialistic idols. Every other lordship is either (1) only derived and dependent on Christ's power, or (2) a presumptuous and enslaving lordship in rebellion against Christ's authority. Christ's right to rule has been authorized by his resurrection and ascension for all people in every culture and in every situation. In the finest of human cultures followers of the Lord Jesus Christ will introduce people not to their previous cultures, but to the Lord over all cultures and world religions—the risen Lord classically revealed in the written Word.

Since God the Father has inaugurated the exalted Christ as Lord of all, Walter Kunneth argues, "where the risen Christ is, there is God. God is where the risen Christ holds sway." He then continues, "God is the God who has raised Christ: he is the God of the resurrection. Thus because of the Easter event, there can be no other [redemptive] knowledge of God than in and through the knowledge of Christ as the Lord."[148]

On the basis of several converging lines of evidence, with Saul, who became Paul, we conclude beyond reasonable doubt that "Christ has indeed been raised from the dead" (1 Cor. 15:20). God the Father did not abandon his one and only Son! God is faithful; God kept his word! Death is not stronger than God's love! Jesus' claims for himself are true! He is the Messiah! His death provides salvation! He is not only Messiah, he is Lord! His spiritual kingdom has come! He will return to extend it! History has a goal! He is head of his church! The church is going somewhere!

RELEVANCE FOR LIFE AND MINISTRY

Faith

On the solid basis of the confirmed evidence and revealed truth, our trust in the crucified, risen, and ascended Lord Jesus Christ will never be futile. Those united to Christ by faith are no longer under legal condemnation; believers are legally justified! Believers are no longer dominated by their own depravity, that of the peers in the world or that of the devil; believers are liberated! Believers are no longer estranged; they are reconciled to God and one another! Believers are no longer spiritually dead; believers have eternal life.

At times however, we yield to temptation, break relationships, and question our legal standing. A certain former student admired his pastor and former Bible college professor greatly. For years the alumnus served as chairman of the board of his hero's large church. Then one Sunday morning he had to do the hardest thing in his life. He had to explain to the church that his hero had resigned, effective immediately. After over two decades of ministry in that pulpit he would not appear again, because he had committed adultery. This alumnus' most important personal relationship with a Christian leader had exploded in his face. He said he nearly lost his faith. He would have, he surmised, if he had not remembered the conclusiveness of the case for Christ's resurrection and so of the objective truth of Christianity. During his disillusionment with a Christian leader, he remembered the fact of Christ's triumph.

In the final analysis, as important as personal relationships may be, a Christian's faith does not rest in frail and fallible human disciplers, but in the risen Christ. When we face criticism, hardship, poverty, disillusionment, or sorrow, we need to remember that God is not dead. The psalmist often cried out because the heavens seemed to be like brass. If ever it appeared that God was not relevant to the human situation, it was at Calvary. Christ himself cried out, "My God, my God, why have you forsaken me?" (Matt. 27:46). But the Father was there transforming history's worst injustice into a triumph of grace! In all our private meditations, family devotions, and public teaching and preaching, church leaders ought to feature far more than is usually done the resurrection and exaltation of the Savior to the right hand of the Father.

When everything collapses around you and your work, remember Christ's death-conquering resurrection and triumphant ascension! These objective facts provide a solid base for faith and the following great subjective blessings.

Peace

The risen Christ approached his fearful and confused disciples in the first century with the words "Peace be with you." (John 20:19, 26). In anticipation of leaving them Jesus earlier said, "Peace I leave with you; *my peace I give you*. . . . Do not let your hearts be troubled and do not be afraid" (John 14:27). Christ has provided for reconciliation and peace within ourselves as well as with God and others. He rose and intercedes for us to give us peace. "The Lord is near. Do not be anxious about anything, but in everything, by prayer and petition, with thanksgiving, present your requests to God. And the peace of God, which transcends all understanding, will guard your hearts and minds in Christ Jesus" (Phil. 4:4–7). After urging meditation on whatever is right, pure, lovely, admirable, excellent, or praiseworthy, Paul adds, "And the God of peace will be with you" (vv. 8–9).

Like Christ and Paul, we could well use "peace" as a greeting or farewell. In good times and bad it can remind us that the triumphant Lord is near. So long as the greeting does not become an empty formality, it can be refreshing and uplifting. Christians have more to say to one another than "Hi," although that may give some recognition of personal worth. So in public services (as Episcopalians do) or in private relationships, we may greet our friends with the words "The peace of the ascended Lord be with you."

"He himself is our peace" (Eph. 2:14). When estranged from themselves and others, Christians need the Messiah's peace. Even when facing prejudicial relationships like those between Jews and Gentiles, we recall that "he himself is our peace." Christ's presence with his disciples restores *shalom*. Recognition of one's personal presence is not entirely a matter of physical immediacy, effective historical influence, or psychological immediacy. We can recognize a personal presence through verbal signs or enacted signs.[149] So by continuing in the apostles' doctrine, fellowship, prayer, and breaking of bread we appreciate our risen Lord's just and loving presence with his people.

And even in the frontlines of battle with unholy spirits the Lord's peace sustains us. The gospel of peace is like well-designed footwear that enables soldiers to walk through the battles of life (Eph. 6:15). The peace of Christ, the conqueror of Satan, is part of the armor that enables us to stand in the front lines against all the devil's schemes. Christ fits our feet with the readiness for defeating the demonic by believing (continuously) the gospel of peace. Appropriation of that peace makes for good footing in warfare against evil powers.[150] Inner tranquility comes not from meditating on meaningless sounds to deny the reality of evil, but by meditating on the God of peace, who brought back from the dead our Lord Jesus (Heb. 13:20).

Purpose

Because of Christ's resurrection, Christians *live teleologically*. With Paul they say, "I want to know Christ and the power of his resurrection and the fellowship of sharing in his sufferings, becoming like him in his death, and so, somehow, to attain to the resurrection from the dead" (Phil. 3:10–11). Believers already share legal status with Christ as crucified and risen (Col. 2:12–13; 3:1). So believers desire also to know experientially what it means to suffer as Christ did for others and by the power that raised Christ from the dead to overcome temptations and testings.

As a result of the resurrection, a Christian has a distinctive goal (a *telos*) in life. As Paul put it, "He died for all, that those who live should no longer live for themselves but for him who died for them and was raised again" (2 Cor. 5:15). Our purpose in life is not to serve ourselves but our risen Lord and others in his name. Just before ascending, Jesus explained how we could serve him: fulfill his global commission by the power of the Holy Spirit. Before ascending he predicted that "repentance and forgiveness of sins will be preached in his name to all nations, beginning at Jerusalem" (Luke 24:47). World Christians live to equip the church for its global mission focused on communicating the gospel. Whatever else Christians do in meeting other needs of people, Christ's last request must be obeyed: "Therefore go and make disciples of all nations, baptizing them in the name of the Father and of the Son and of the Holy Spirit, and teaching them to obey everything I have commanded you. And surely I am be with you always, to the very end of the age" (Matt. 28:19–20).

Power

The ascension must have been a traumatic experience for the disciples. Psychologically Peter and the apostles needed to mature from a position where they expected the incarnate Christ to do things *for* them, to a position where they looked to the ascended Christ to do things *through* them. The ascension occasioned a new relationship to their Lord. No longer could they depend on the physical Jesus in the energy of their sinful natures; now they must live by faith in the no-longer-visible Christ in the strength of the Holy Spirit (Rom. 8:4).

The divine power that raised Christ from the dead raises up those buried with him in baptism to *newness of life* (Rom. 6:4). In dependence on the power of the resurrected and ascended Christ we can overcome satanic powers. Christ's resurrection revealed the Creator's ability to overrule the irreversible forces, not only of nature but also of human nature. From a natural perspective it is impossible to change human nature. The power that raised Christ from the grave and exalted him above all can deliver us from the strongest tendencies to sin and enable us to live in justice and love. Even before the resurrection Jesus gave the Twelve power and authority to drive out all demons, to cure diseases (Luke 9:1), and to overcome all the power of the enemy (10:19). Paul could easily have torn down the problem-plagued believers at Corinth, but the risen Lord gave Paul apostolic authority for building them up rather than pulling them down (2 Cor. 10:8; 13:10).

Christians pray for resurrection power for one another. As Paul prayed for the Ephesians pray that your family and church may be enlightened to know

> his incomparably great power for us who believe. That power is like the working of his mighty strength, which he exerted in Christ when he raised him from the dead and seated him at his right hand in heavenly realms, far above all rule and authority, power and dominion, and every title that can be given, not only in the present age but also in the one to come (Eph. 1:18–21).

Do you need inner strength to cope with the pressures of life? Paul prayed "that out of his glorious riches he may strengthen you with power through his Spirit in your inner being" (Eph. 3:16).

Ability for every good work we attempt is possible because of the risen Christ. "May the God of peace, who through the blood of the eternal covenant brought back from the dead our Lord Jesus, that great Shepherd of the sheep, equip you with every good thing for doing his will, and may he work in us what is pleasing to him, through Jesus Christ, to whom be glory for ever and ever. Amen" (Heb. 13:20–21).

Communion

Fellowship with the living Christ in prayer is a blessing made possible by his exaltation. Our communion with God does not depend on our efforts or eloquence. Our heavenly Advocate expresses what we cannot utter. So, important as periodic introspection may be, we ought not be forever taking our own spiritual temperatures. Our acceptance with God the Father rests, finally, not on our internal or external achievements, but on the exalted Messiah's completed work! He serves as the attorney for believers, pleading our causes before the Father. He has never lost a client and will not lose your case, for the grounds on which he pleads for sinners are the gracious provisions of his atonement and resurrection.

Counting on our Savior's fellowship with the Father, we can commune with God with our whole being and all our capacities. "I will pray with my spirit, but I will also pray with my mind" (1 Cor. 14:15). Aware of your union with Christ by faith and the great truths of Christ's death, resurrection, and ascension for us, we may explicitly appropriate Christ's marvelous provisions as we pray. By faith we can enter into the gracious work of the cross, claiming our personal forgiveness, redemption, and reconciliation. By faith we count ourselves dead to sin but alive to God in the exalted Christ (Rom. 6:11).

Prayer

To help realize the values of being crucified and risen with Christ in your life, develop the practice of "doctrinal praying." Join pastor-author Mark Bubek in this prayer:

> I enter by faith into the mighty work of the crucifixion of my Lord. Thank You that through the blood of Jesus Christ there is not only cleansing from the penalty and guilt of sin but moment-by-moment cleansing, permitting me to fellowship with You. Thank You that the work of the cross brings Satan's work to nothing. Deliberately and by faith, I bring all of the work of my Lord on Calvary directly against Satan's workings in my life. I will accept in my life only what comes by way of the cross of Christ. I chose to die to the old man. I count him to be dead with Christ on the cross. . . .
>
> I enter by faith into the full power and authority of my Lord's resurrection. I desire to walk in the newness of life which is mine through my Lord's resurrection. Lead me ever more into a deep understanding of the power of the resurrection. I bring the mighty truth of my Lord's victory over the grave against all of Satan's workings against Your will and plan for my life. The enemy is defeated in my life because I am united with the Lord Jesus Christ in the victory of his resurrection.
>
> By faith I appropriate and enter today into my union with the Lord Jesus Christ in His ascension. I rejoice that my Lord displayed openly His victory over all principalities and powers as He ascended into glory through the very realm of the prince of the power of the air. I rejoice that He is seated in victory far above all principalities and powers and that I am seated there with Him. Because of my union with my Saviour, I affirm my full authority and position of victory over Satan and all of his kingdom of darkness.
>
> By faith I enter into the benefit and blessedness of my union with Christ in his glorification. It is my joy to choose to obey Him who is my Shepherd. I ask for You to lead me in Your path today. As my great High Priest, I appropriate your high priestly work into my life today. Thank You, Lord Jesus Christ, for interceding for me and being my advocate with the heavenly Father. Thank You for watching over me and leading me, that Satan may gain no advantage over me. Grant me wisdom to discern all of the devil's deceivings and temptations.[151]

Hope

After God's eternal Son had humbled himself to become human and to die on a cross, "God exalted him to the highest place and gave him the name that is above every name, that at the name of

Jesus every knee should bow, in heaven and on earth and under the earth, and every tongue confess that Jesus Christ is Lord to the glory of God the Father" (Phil. 2:9–11).

As enthusiastic as believers in the risen Christ should be, we must warn against the dangers of an unrealistic "resurrection enthusiasm" that forgets the divine order in Christ's life and ours. If humiliation preceded exaltation in Christ's life, how much more must that order be followed in ours. An emphasis on exaltation and victory with Christ that insufficiently emphasizes a prior crucifixion with Christ may lead to unfortunate consequences in several areas. It may result in an unrealistic anthropology, a naïve view of victory in the Christian life, oversimplified advice in counseling, and a triumphalistic missiology and ecclesiology.

Hope for a Christlike style of liberation and peace follows death to selfish pride, covetous greed, and debilitating jealousy. Hope for a Christlike victory over such temptations begins with a Christlike death to them. In his humiliation the Lord of our lives is Lord first of all because he was willing to die to sin's seductions. We must not make the mistake of the first-century Jews who wanted the kingdom of glory without the kingdom of suffering. Our hope of enjoying life abundant begins with our willingness to serve Christ without it. In the present life our hope is never fully realized, so we walk by faith. Hope comes from faith in the exalted Christ.

In his life, death, and resurrection Jesus lived the life of faith and spoke words of faith. At present we too must walk by faith and express words of faith as we talk with others. Our faith in the risen Christ leads to faithfulness in words and works. On the day of Pentecost Peter's thesis confirmed by Christ's recent resurrection and ascension asserted that the crucified Jesus was "both Lord and Christ" (Acts 2:36). Still today, "if you confess with your mouth, 'Jesus is Lord,' and believe in your heart that God raised him from the dead, you will be saved" (Rom. 10:9). Ascension Day services and others may well proclaim that there is no sphere in which those who confess that "Jesus is Lord" are absolved from a faith that obediently works by love.

As we weep at the graves of our loved ones, we need to remember that death cannot separate us from the love of God in Christ Jesus our Lord (Rom. 8:38–39); our spirits continue in eternal fellowship with God. But after death our spirits long to be clothed with bodies. In times of bereavement Christians also remember Christ's resurrection. The hope it evokes is stronger than death. "Christ has indeed been raised from the dead, the firstfruits of those who have fallen asleep. . . . As in Adam all die, so in Christ all will be made alive" (1 Cor. 15:20–22). When we are raised imperishable and immortal, death will be swallowed up in victory (vv. 52–54). "The sting of death is sin, and the power of sin is the law. But thanks be to God! He gives us the victory through our Lord Jesus Christ. Therefore, my dear brothers, stand firm. Let nothing move you. Always give yourselves fully to the work of the Lord, because you know that your labor in the Lord is not in vain" (vv. 56–58). The best of lives end short of their fullest promise and potential. Death, however, does not have the last word! We shall rise! And we will complete what we began here.

Given the reality of Christ's exaltation, we can never face a situation so difficult that there is "no hope." A young Bible school student was called in before the dean for some unacceptable sin. Whatever he was told, the gifted student concluded that for him there was no future. After a lengthy search for him, his body was found in a back room of his old New England church. He had hung himself in the choir robe in which he formerly sang. Pinned to the robe was a note with two words: "No hope." No situation ought to be beyond hope for those who have faith in the forgiveness of Christ's cross and the renewal of Christ's resurrection. The great High Priest and Lord of all ever lives to make intercession for us. However dark the night of your life becomes, remember the resurrection! Remember that Christ lives and can overcome the greatest evils.

"May the God of hope fill you with all joy and peace as you trust in him, so that you may overflow with hope by the power of the Holy Spirit" (Rom. 15:13).

Joy

We rejoice at the achievement of a child, the attaining of a new position, and a victory in sports. How much greater should be our rejoicing at the decisive triumph of Christ and his kingdom over Satan and all his evil powers! Our celebrations of Easter ought to stand out for the greatness of our joy.

Because Christ lives, even though we still struggle with sinful natures and physical weaknesses, we can rejoice. With Peter, "greatly rejoice" and experience an "inexpressible and glorious joy" as you internalize the reality of your new birth and living hope. To early persecuted followers of the risen Christ Peter wrote:

> Grace and peace be yours in abundance. Praise be to the God and Father of our Lord Jesus Christ! In his great mercy he has given us new birth unto a living hope through the resurrection of Jesus Christ from the dead, and into an inheritance that can never perish, spoil or fade—kept in heaven for you, who through faith are shielded by God's power until the coming of the salvation that is ready to be revealed in the last time. In this you *greatly rejoice,* though now for a little while you may have had to suffer grief in all kinds of trials. These have come so that your faith—of greater worth than gold, which perishes even though refined by fire—may be proved genuine and may result in praise, glory and honor when Jesus Christ is revealed. Although you have not seen him, you love him; and even though you do not see him now, you believe in him and are *filled with an inexpressible and glorious joy,* for you are receiving the goal of your faith, the salvation of your souls (1 Peter 1:2–9).

REVIEW QUESTIONS

To Help Relate and Apply Each Section in This Chapter

1. *Briefly state the classical problem* this chapter addresses and indicate reasons why genuine inquiry into it is important for your worldview and your existence personally and socially.

2. *Objectively summarize the influential answers* given to this problem in history as hypotheses to be tested. Be able to compare and contrast their real similarities and differences (not merely verbal similarities or differences).

3. *Highlight the primary biblical evidence* on which to decide among views—evidence found in the relevant teachings of the major divisions of Scripture—and decide for yourself which historical hypothesis (or synthesis of historical views) provides the most consistent and adequate account of the primary biblical data.

4. *Formulate in your own words your doctrinal conviction* in a logically consistent and adequate way, organizing your conclusions in ways you can explain clearly, support biblically, and communicate effectively to your spouse, children, friends, Bible class, or congregation.

5. *Defend your view* as you would to adherents of the alternative views, showing that the other views are logically less consistent and factually faced

with more difficulties than your view in accounting for the givens, not only of special revelation but also of human experience in general.

6. *Explore the differences the viability of your conviction can make in your life*. Then test your understanding of the viability of your view by asking, "Can I live by it authentically (unhypocritically) in relation to God and to others in my family, church, vocation, neighborhood, city, nation, and world?"

MINISTRY PROJECTS

To Help Communicate This Doctrine in Christian Service

1. *Memorize one major verse or passage* that in its context teaches the heart of this doctrine and may serve as a text from which to preach, teach, or lead small-group studies on the topic. The memorized passages from each chapter will build a body of content useful also for meditation and reference in informal discussions.

2. *Formulate the major idea of the doctrine in one sentence* based on the passage memorized. This idea should be useful as the major thesis of either a lesson for a class (junior high to adult) or a message for a church service.

3. *State the specific purpose or goal of your doctrinal lesson or message*. Your purpose should be more than informative. It should show why Christians need to accept this truth and live by it (unhypocritically). For teaching purposes, list indicators that would show to what extent class members have grasped the truth presented.

4. *Outline your message or lesson in complete sentences*. Indicate how you would support the truth of the doctrine's central ideas and its relevance to life and service. Incorporate elements from this chapter's historical, biblical, systematic, apologetic, and practical sections selected according to the value they have for your audience.

5. *List applications of the doctrine* for communicating the difference this conviction makes in life (for sermons, lessons, small-group Bible studies, or family devotional Bible studies). Applications should make clear what the doctrine is, why one needs to know it, and how it will make differences in thinking. Then show how the difference in thought will lead to differences in values, priorities, attitudes, speech, and personal action. Consider also the doctrine's possible significance for family, church, neighborhood, city, regional, and national actions.

6. *Start a file and begin collecting illustrations* of this doctrine's central idea, the points in your outline, and your application.

7. *Write out your own doctrinal statement on this subject in one paragraph* (in half a page or less). To work toward a comprehensive doctrinal statement, collect your formulations based on a study of each chapter of *Integrative Theology*. As your own statement of Christian doctrine grows, you will find it personally strengthening and useful when you are called on for your beliefs in general and when you apply for service with churches, mission boards, and other Christian organizations. Any who seek ordination to Christian ministry will need a comprehensive doctrinal statement that covers the broad scope of theology.

Notes

Chapter 1

[1]Origen, *On First Principles,* III.5.3; cf. ibid., "there were ages [i.e., worlds] before our own, and there will be others after it."

[2]William Newton Clarke, *The Christian Doctrine of God* (Edinburgh: T. & T. Clarke, 1909), 287.

[3]Augustine, *On the Trinity,* III.9.16; cf.: "The hidden seeds of all things . . . are concealed in the corporeal elements of this world." Ibid., III.8.13.

[4]Augustine, *The Literal Meaning of Genesis,* IV.27.44.

[5]Lactantius, *The Divine Institutes,* III.24; cf. Augustine, *City of God,* XVI.9.

[6]Augustus H. Strong, *Systematic Theology* (Valley Forge: Judson, 1907), 392.

[7]James Orr, *God's Image in Man* (London: Hodder & Stoughton, 1905), 95. In the Tyndale commentary on Genesis, Derek Kidner affirms that "God initially shaped man by a process of evolution," having conferred his image not only on Adam, but also on Adam's near human contemporaries "widely distributed over the world." *Genesis, TNTC* (London: Tyndale, 1967), 28–29.

[8]Richard H. Bube, *The Human Quest: A New Look at Science and the Christian Faith* (Waco: Word, 1971), 199.

[9]Bube upholds this model in his article, "Biblical Evolution?" *Journal of the American Scientific Affiliation* 23.4 (Dec. 1971): 140–44. Bube explains, "With all of its admitted difficulties, some form—possibly not understood completely at present—of the General Theory [of evolution] appears to be the best scientific interpretation of the data available from the natural world." "Inerrancy, Revelation and Evolution," *Journal of the American Scientific Affiliation* 24.2 (June 1972): 83.

[10]*A New Catechism: Catholic Faith for Adults* (New York: Herder & Herder, 1967), 264.

[11]Hans Küng, *Does God Exist?* (New York: Doubleday, 1980), 648.

[12]Karl Barth, *CD,* III.1.97.

[13]Ibid., 228–329.

[14]Emil Brunner, *The Christian Doctrine of Creation and Redemption. Dogmatics,* Vol. II, (London: Lutterworth, 1952), 40.

[15]Rudolf Bultmann, *Primitive Christianity* (New York: Meridian, 1956), 18; cf. *Jesus Christ and Mythology* (New York: Scribners, 1958), 69: The only valid meaning of the Genesis account is the "personal confession that I understand myself to be a creature which owes its existence to God."

[16]Irenaeus, *Against Heresies,* V.28.3: "For in as many days as this world was made, in so many thousand years shall it be concluded. . . . For the day of the Lord is as a thousand years; and in six days created things were completed: it is evident, therefore, that they will come to an end at the six thousandth year." Cf. *Epistle of Barnabas,* 15.

[17]Cited by Richard H. Bube, "Creation and Genesis," *Journal of the American Scientific Affiliation* 32.1 (March 1980): 35, and by Robert C. Newman and Herman J. Eckelmann, Jr., *Genesis One and the Origin of the Earth* (Grand Rapids: Baker, 1981), 57.

[18]Wheaton College biologist Pattle P. T. Pun, in his article "Evolution," registers a criticism of the flood-geology school based on current scientific findings, *EDT,* 390.

[19]The *Scofield Reference Bible,* ed. C. I. Scofield (New York: Oxford University Press, 1945), 3,nn.2,4; 4,n.3.

[20]James M. Houston, *I Believe in the Creator* (Grand Rapids: Eerdmans, 1980), 59.

[21]Ronald Youngblood, *How It All Began* (Ventura, Calif.: Regal, 1980), 25.

[22]Nicholas H. Ridderbos, *Is There Any Conflict Between Genesis 1 and Natural Science?* (Grand Rapids: Eerdmans, 1957), 45.

[23]Bernard Ramm, *The Christian View of Science and Scripture* (Grand Rapids: Eerdmans, 1954), 115–16.

[24]Ibid., 116.

[25]Newman and Eckelmann, *Genesis One*, 85–86.

[26]Arthur C. Custance, *Evolution or Creation?* (Grand Rapids: Zondervan, 1976).

[27]Norman L. Geisler and J. Kerby Anderson, *Origin Science: A Proposal for the Creation-Evolution Controversy* (Grand Rapids: Baker, 1987).

[28]Davis A. Young, *Christianity and the Age of the Earth* (Grand Rapids: Zondervan, 1982).

[29]Gleason L. Archer, Jr., maintains: "Genesis 1 was never intended to teach that the sixth creative day, when Adam and Eve were *both* created, lasted a mere twenty-four hours. In view of the long interval between these two, it would seem to border on sheer irrationality to insist that all of Adam's experiences in Genesis 2:15–22 could have been crowded into the last hour or two of a literal twenty-four-hour day." *Encyclopedia of Bible Difficulties* (Grand Rapids: Zondervan, 1982), 60.

[30]Carl F. H. Henry, *God, Revelation and Authority*, 6 vols. (Waco: Word, 1976–83), 6:133.

[31]Kidner, *Genesis*, 56.

[32]As suggested, for example, by Millard J. Erickson, *Christian Theology*, 3 vols. (Grand Rapids: Baker, 1983–85), 1:382.

[33]Walter Brueggemann states that Genesis 2 "is a more intense reflection upon the implications of creation for the destiny of humanity." *Genesis* (Atlanta: John Knox, 1982), 40.

[34]*Eerdmans Concise Bible Handbook*, ed. David and Pat Alexander (Grand Rapids: Eerdmans, 1980), 43. Cf. Pattle P. T. Pun, "Evolution," *EDT*, 392; Youngblood, *How It All Began*, 134.

[35]R. K. Harrison, "Flood," *EDT*, 419.

[36]Henry, *God, Revelation and Authority*, 6:226.

[37]Francis I. Anderson, "Job," *TOTC* (Downers Grove: InterVarsity, 1976), 274.

[38]F. Davidson and R. P. Martin, "Romans," *NBCRev*, 1:144.

[39]Donald Guthrie, *The Pastoral Epistles*, *TNTC* (London: Tyndale, 1957), 77. Cf. H. H. Esser, "Creation," *NIDNTT*, 1:385.

[40]Alfred Plummer, *The Gospel According to St. John* (Grand Rapids: Baker, reprint 1981), 65.

[41]John Gill, *Body of Divinity* (Atlanta, Ga.: Turner Lassiter, reprint 1957), 256.

[42]For extensive argument in defense of usual translations of Genesis 1:1 see Bruce Waltke, *Creation and Chaos: An Exegetical and Theological Study of Biblical Cosmogony* (Portland, Ore.: Western Conservative Baptist Seminary, 1974), 25–32; Edward J. Young, *Studies in Genesis One* (Grand Rapids: Baker, 1964), 1–7.

[43]Thomas E. McComiskey, *bārā'*, *TWOT*, 1: 127.

[44]Ibid.

[45]Ibid.

[46]G. Ch. Aalders, *Genesis* (Grand Rapids: Zondervan, 1981), 53.

[47]C. F. Keil and F. Delitzsch, *Biblical Commentary on the Old Testament* (Grand Rapids: Eerdmans, reprint 1951), *Genesis* 1:46–47.

[48]Henry Alford, *The Greek New Testament*, 4 vols. (Boston: Lee and Shepard, 1872), 4:209.

[49]Ibid.

[50]Keil and Delitzsch, *Genesis*, 46.

[51]Ibid., 49.

[52]Alan A. MacRae, "Principles of Interpreting Genesis 1 and 2," Martin J. Wyngaarden, "Phenomenal Language According to Bernard Ramm," and G. Douglas Young, "The Effects of Poetic and Literary Style on the Interpretation of the Early Chapter of Genesis," *Journal of the Evangelical Theological Society* 2.4 (Fall 1959): 1–16.

[53]Leonard Verduin, *Somewhat Less Than God* (Grand Rapids: Eerdmans, 1970), 20.

[54]Keil and Delitzsch, *The Pentateuch*, 1:45; cf. E. J. Young, *In the Beginning* (Carlisle, Pa.: The Banner of Truth Trust, 1976), 43.

[55]Some discussion of energy in relation to light may be found in F. A. Filby, *Creation Revealed* (Westwood, N.J.: Revell, 1963), 63–71.

[56]Newman and Eckelmann, *Genesis One, 30, 72.*

[57]See Filby, *Creation Revealed*, 72–75.

[58]See Archer, *Encyclopedia of Bible Difficulties*, 59–60.

[59]J. Oliver Buswell, Jr., *A Systematic Theology of the Christian Religion*, 2 vols. (Grand Rapids: Zondervan, 1962), 1:140–41.

[60]Young, *Studies in Genesis One*, 43; cf. Leonard J. Coppes, "*yôm*," *TWOT*, 1:370–71.

[61]Henry M. Morris, ed., *Scientific Creationism* (San Diego: Creation Life, 1974), iv.

[62]Ibid., 21, 215.

[63]Benjamin B. Warfield, *Studies in Theology* (New York: Oxford University Press, 1950), 244; cf. J. Oliver Buswell, Jr., *Systematic Theology* 1:325–43; Robert D. Culver, "Peculiarities and Problems of Chronological Method and Text in the Book of Chronicles" *Journal of the Evangelical Theological Society* 5.2 (Spring 1962): 35–41.

[64]William C. Duke "The American Scientific Affiliation and the Creation Research Society: The Creation-Evolution Issue" (doctoral dissertation, Southwestern Baptist Theological Seminary, Fort Worth, Texas 76122, 1982), 147.

[65]Davis A. Young, *Creation and the Flood* (Grand Rapids: Baker, 1977); Newman and Ecklemann, *Genesis One*.

[66]Richard H. Bube, "Creation (A): How Should Genesis Be Interpreted?" *Journal of the American Scientific Association* (March 1980), 32–37; cf. idem, *The Encounter Between Christianity and Science* (Grand Rapids: Eerdmans, 1968) and *The Human Quest*.

[67]Henry M. Morris, ed., *Scientific Creationism*, 217. See also idem, *The Biblical Basis for Modern Science* (Grand Rapids: Baker, 1984).

[68]Thomas S. Kuhn, *The Structure of Scientific Revolutions*, 2nd ed. (Chicago: University of Chicago Press, 1970).

[69]Gordon Clark, *The Philosophy of Science and Belief in God* (Nutley, N.J.: Presbyterian and Reformed, 1964).

[70]Charles Sanders Pierce. "The Architecture of Theories," *The Monist* 1 (January 1891): 161–76, reprinted in Max H. Fisch, *Classic American Philosophies* (New York: Appleton, Century, Crofts, 1951), 99.

[71]Paul Davies, *God and the New Physics* (New York: Simon and Schuster, 1983), 170.

[72]Robert Jastrow, *God and the Astronomers* (New York: Norton, 1978), 115–16.

[73]Sir Fred Hoyle, "The Universe: Past and Present Reflections," *Engineering and Science* (November 1981), 12.

[74]Ibid., 10.

[75]Ibid., 12.

[76]Ibid.; cf. Richard L. Purtill's argument that it is overwhelmingly more probable that intelligent life was produced by a previously existing mind than by a random process in nature. (*C. S. Lewis' Case for the Christian Faith* [San Francisco: Harper & Row, 1981), 22–27.

[77]Charles B. Thaxton, Walter L. Bradley, and Roger L. Olsen, *The Mystery of Life's Origin: Reassessing Current Theories* (New York: Philosophical Library, 1984), 144.

[78]Ibid., 183.

[79]Ibid.

[80]Ibid., 185.

[81]Ibid.

[82]Ibid., 186.

[83]Harold F. Blum, *Time's Arrow and Evolution* (Princeton: Princeton University Press, 1968), 164.

[84]Robert Jastrow, *Until the Sun Dies* (New York: Norton, 1977), 62–63.

[85]Gordon J. Van Wylen and Richard E. Sonntag, *Fundamentals of Classical Thermodynamics*, 2nd ed. (New York: Wiley, 1978), 243.

[86]Jeremy Rifkin, *Entropy: A New World View* (New York: Bantam, 1980), 46.

[87]Ibid., 231–37.

[88]Ibid., 253.

[89]Ibid., 254.

[90]Concerning the issues of classification see Mortimer J. Adler, "Evolution," in *The Great Ideas: A Synopticon of the Great Books of the Western World* (Chicago: Encyclopedia Britannica, 1952), 1:451–59.

[91]Harold T. Wiebe, "What Can Be Learned from the Evolutionist Who Takes a Hard Look at His Own Theory," *Journal of the American Scientific Affiliation* (December 1966), 116.

[92]G. A. Kerkut, *Implications of Evolution* (New York: Pergamon, 1960), 6–7.

[93]Luther D. Sunderland, *Darwin's Enigma: Fossils and Other Problems* (San Diego: Master Book, 1984).

[94]Charles Darwin, *The Origin of Species* (1859), in *Great Books of the Western World*, ed. Robert M. Hutchins, 49:42.

[95]Ibid.

[96]A. H. Clark, *The New Evolution Zoogenesis* (Williams and Wilkins, 1930); cited by Harold T. Wiebe, "What Can Be Learned From the Evolutionist Who Takes a Hard Look at His Own Theory," *Journal of the American Scientific Affiliation* (December 1966), 116.

[97]Steven M. Stanley, "Evolution of Life: Evidence for a New Pattern" in *The Great Ideas Today 1983* (Chicago: Encyclopedia Britannica, 1983), 8; cf. Stephen Jay Gould, "Darwinism Defined: The Difference Between Fact and Theory." *Discover* 8.2 ((January 1987), 64–69; idem, "The Lesson of the Dinosaurs: Evolution Didn't Inevitably Lead to Us," ibid (March 1987), 51. Gould writes, "We didn't have to evolve at all. Life is a series of complex and unpredictable events, not a straight and narrow path to progress," Gould defends a "punctuated equilibrium." See also "Enigmas of Evolution," *Newsweek* (March 29, 1982), 44–49.

[98]Ibid., 20.

[99]Ibid.

[100]Jastrow, *God and the Astronomers*, 16.

[101]T. A. Goudge, "Henri Bergson," *EP*, 1:292.

[102]Fritjof Capra, *The Tao of Physics* (Boulder, Colo.: Shamballa, 1983), 8.

[103]Ibid., 319–21.

[104]Ibid., 9.

[105]Ibid., 12.

[106]Davies, *God and the New Physics*, vii.

[107]Brunner, *Christian Doctrine of Creation and Redemption*, 8–9.

[108]Ibid., 13.

[109]Ibid., 14.

[110]A. C. Schultz, "Wine and Strong Drink," *ZPEB*, 5:934.

[111]Anderson Spickard and Barbara R. Thompson, *Dying for a Drink* (Waco: Word, 1985), 27.

[112]Ibid., 17.

[113]Ibid., 41.

[114]Ibid., 188–89.

[115]Francis Schaeffer, *Pollution and the Death of Man* (Wheaton: Tyndale, 1970), 49–50.

[116]Rifkin, *Entropy: A New World View*, 234–35.

[117]Alfred A. Glenn, *Taking Your Faith to Work* (Grand Rapids: Baker, 1980), 61–64.

[118]Paul King Jewett, *The Lord's Day: A Theological Guide to the Christian Day of Worship* (Grand Rapids: Eerdmans, 1971).

Chapter 2

[1]Martin Luther, *LW*, 17:125.

[2]Ibid., 45:331.

[3]Huldrich Zwingli, *Commentary on True and False Religion*, ed. S. M. Jackson and C. N. Heller (Durham: Labyrinth, 1981), 272.

[4]Ibid., 273.

[5]John Calvin, *Institutes of the Christian Religion*, I.16.3.

[6]Ibid., I.16.9; cf. ibid., I.16.6; I.17.2; I.18.1.

[7]Ibid., I.18.1.

[8]Ibid., I.18.2.

[9]Jacob Arminius, *The Works of Jacob Arminius*, 3 vols., ed. James Nichols (Auburn and Buffalo: Derby, Miller & Orton, 1853), 1:251.

[10]Ibid.

[11]John Wesley, *The Works of John Wesley*, 14 vols. (Grand Rapids: Zondervan, reprint, n.d.), 6:326; cf. ibid., 6:318.

[12]Charles Finney, *Finney's Systematic Theology* (Minneapolis: Bethany, reprint 1976), 6.

[13]Donald S. Metz, "Providence," *Beacon Dictionary of Theology*, ed. Richard S. Taylor (Kansas City: Beacon Hill, 1983), 428. Cf. Charles W. Carter, ed., *A Contemporary Wesleyan Theology*, 2 vols. (Grand Rapids: Zondervan, 1983), 1:161: God's providence is "based on moral and religious principles in which the action and beliefs of mankind as free moral agents play a vital role. . . . This lays great stress on the fact that God's relationship to the cosmos is one that is based on moral and religious principles. God's providence, His sovereignty and lordship, is exercised in a manner that demonstrates this. This indicates that the teleology of God's providential relationship to His creation is moral and religious."

[14]Thomas Paine, *The Great Works of Thomas Paine* (New York: Bennett & Liberal, n.d.), 151.

[15]Ibid., 29.

[16]Thomas Paine, *Classics of Free Thought*, ed. Paul Blanchard (Buffalo & New York: Prometheus, n.d.), 133.

[17]William Adams Brown, *Christian Theology in Outline* (New York: Scribner, 1911), 219.

[18]Gordon D. Kaufman, *Systematic Theology: A Historicist Perspective* (New York: Scribner, 1968), 258.

[19]Adolf Von Harnack, *What Is Christianity?* (London: Williams & Norgate, 1912), 29. "What happens in space and time is subject to the general laws of motion, and that in this sense, as an interruption of the order of nature, there can be no such thing as miracles." Ibid., 27.

[20]L. Harold DeWolf, *The Case for Theology in Liberal Perspective* (Philadelphia: Westminster, 1959), 94.

[21]Langdon B. Gilkey, "The Concept of Providence in Contemporary Theology," *Journal of Religion* 68.3 (July 1963): 174.

[22]Nicolas Berdyaev, *The Beginning and the End* (Westport, Conn.: Greenwood, 1976), 152.

[23]Ibid., 155.

[24]Rudolf Bultmann, *Essays Philosophical and Theological* (London: SCM, 1955), 76.

[25]Emil Brunner, *The Christian Doctrine of Creation and Redemption: Dogmatics, Vol. II* (London: Lutterworth, 1952), 184.

[26]John Macquarrie, *Principles of Christian Theology* (New York: Scribner, 1977), 250.

[27]Rudolf Bultmann, *Kerygma and Myth* (New York: Harper & Row, 1961), 4.

[28]Heinrich Ott, *God* (Edinburgh: Saint Andrew, 1974), 81.

[29]Rubem Alves, *A Theology of Human Hope* (St. Meinrad, Minnesota: Abbey, 1974), 136.

[30]Albert B. Cleage, Jr., *The Black Messiah* (New York: Sheed and Ward, 1968).

[31]James H. Cone, *A Black Theology of Liberation* (Philadelphia & New York: Lippincott, 1970), 27.

[32]Clement of Alexandria, *Christ the Educator,* II.6.

[33]Clement of Alexandria, *Miscellanies,* IV.12.

[34]Augustine, *The Literal Meaning of Genesis,* VIII.9.17; VIII.24.45.

[35]Augustine, *Eighty-Three Different Questions,* 24; cf. 53.

[36]Augustine, *Enchiridion,* 101.

[37]Carl F. H. Henry, *God, Revelation and Authority,* 6 vols. (Waco: Word, 1976–83), 6:479.

[38]Bernard Ramm, *A Christian View of Science and Scripture* (Grand Rapids: Eerdmans, 1954), 90.

[39]Augustine, *The Christian Combat,* VIII.9.

[40]Augustine, *The Literal Meaning of Genesis,* XI.16.

[41]Augustine, *Sermon on the Mount,* II.3.14.

[42]Henry, *God, Revelation and Authority,* 6:482.

[43]C. S. Lewis, *The Problem of Pain* (New York: Macmillan, 1944).

[44]G. C. Berkouwer, *The Providence of God* (Grand Rapids: Eerdmans, 1952);

[45]Colin Brown, *Miracles and the Critical Mind* (Grand Rapids: Eerdmans, 1984).

[46]G. Ch. Aalders, *Genesis,* 2 vols. (Grand Rapids: Zondervan, 1981), 1:50.

[47]Derek Kidner, *Genesis, TNTC* (London: Tyndale Press, 1967), 207.

[48]W. H. Gispen, *Exodus* (Grand Rapids: Zondervan, 1982), 38.

[49]J. D. Spiceland, "Miracles," *EDT,* 723.

[50]Meredith G. Kline, "Genesis," *NBCRev,* 84.

[51]J. G. McConville, *Ezra, Nehemiah, and Esther* (Philadelphia: Westminster, 1985), 8.

[52]*Eerdmans' Concise Bible Handbook,* ed. David and Pat Alexander (Grand Rapids: Eerdmans, 1980), 103, elegantly expresses the central message of Ruth. God "is the One who orders all the circumstances of daily life, even for the most unimportant people. And so the new-found faith of a Moabite girl, and her sacrificial love for her mother-in-law are woven into the great tapestry of God's plan of salvation. For descended from Ruth is King David, and from the line of David comes the Messiah himself."

[53]McConville, *Ezra, Nehemiah, and Esther,* 173.

[54]See Hugh J. Blair, "Joshua," *NBCRev,* 244, for a discussion of the possible interpretations of the restriction of the sun's light in Joshua 10:12–14.

[55]John Murray, *The Epistle to the Romans,* 2 vols. (Grand Rapids: Eerdmans, 1959–65), 2:108.

[56]Cf. F. F. Bruce, *Romans, TNTC* (London: Tyndale, 1963), 175.

[57]F. F. Bruce, *1 & 2 Thessalonians, WBC* (Waco: Word, 1982), 171–72.

[58]Lewis, *The Problem of Pain,* 115–16.

[59]F. F. Bruce, "The Revelation to John," *NLBC,* 1988.

[60]F. F. Bruce, *The Epistle to the Hebrews* (London: Marshall, Morgan & Scott, 1965), 6.

[61]Charles Hatfield, "Probability and God's Providence," *Journal of the American Scientific Affiliation* 17.1 (March 1965), 18.

[62]Harold S. Kushner, *When Bad Things Happen to Good People* (New York: Avon, 1981), 58.

[63]Oscar Cullmann, *Christ and Time: The Primitive Christian Conception of Time and History* (Philadelphia: Westminster, 1950); see also Carl Henry, "Time," *EDT,* 1,094–96.

[64]William G. Pollard, *Chance and Providence* (New York: Charles Scribner's Sons, 1958), 73–74.

[65]J. I. Packer, *Evangelism and the Sovereignty of God* (Downers Grove: InterVarsity, 1961).

[66]G. Finkenrath, "Secret, Mystery," *NIDNTT,* 3:501–2.

[67]Bornkamm, *"mystērion," TDNT,* 4:824.

[68]Walter L. Leifeld, "Mystery," *ZPEB,* 4:330.

[69]Berkouwer, *Providence of God,* 98.

[70]All four contributors to David and Randall Basinger, eds., *Predestination and Free Will: Four Views of Divine Sovereignty and Human Freedom* (Downers Grove: InterVarsity, 1986), 27–28.

[71]Thomas J. Peters and Robert H. Waterman, Jr., *In Search of Excellence: Lessons from America's Best Run Companies* (New York: Warner, 1983), 238.

[72]Ibid., 85.

[73]Ibid., 73.

[74]Bruce Narramore, *Parenting With Love and Limits* (Grand Rapids: Zondervan, 1979), 38.

[75]Bruce Narramore, *Help! I'm a Parent!* (Grand Rapids: Zondervan, 1972). See also James Dobson, *Dare to Discipline* (Wheaton: Tyndale, 1970); Haim G. Ginott, *Between Parent and Child* (New York: Avon, 1965); idem, *Between Parent and Teen Ager* (New York: Avon, 1969).

[76]Berkouwer, *Providence of God,* 140.

[77]See Gordon Lewis, "Criteria for the Discerning of Spirits," in *Demon Possession,* ed. John Warwick Montgomery (St. Paul: Bethany, 1976), chapter 23. See also Gordon Lewis, "The Bible, the Christian and Spiritualism," *Confronting the Cults* (Phillipsburg, Penn.: Presbyterian and Reformed, 1966), 163–98.

[78]Peters and Waterman, *In Search of Excellence,* 13.

[79]Wilbur F. Tillett, "Providence," *International Standard Bible Encyclopedia* (Grand Rapids: Eerdmans, 1949), 4:484.

[80]Charles Hodge, *Systematic Theology,* 3 vols. (Grand Rapids: Eerdmans, 1946), 1:169.

[81]Gordon R. Lewis, *Judge for Yourself* (Downers Grove: InterVarsity, 1974), 46–60.

[82]Gordon R. Lewis, "Prayer," *ZPEB,* 2:835–44.

[83]Wolfhart Pannenberg, *Anthropology in Theological Perspective* (Philadelphia: Westminster, 1985), 505.

[84]B. A. G. Fuller, "Naturalism," in *Dictionary of Philosophy,* ed. D. Runes (New York: Philosophical Library, 1960).

[85]Carl Sagan, *Cosmos* (New York: Random House, 1980), 4.

[86]Donald M. Mackay, *The Clock Work Image* (Downers Grove: InterVarsity, 1974), 60.

[87]William G. Pollard, *Chance and Providence* (New York: Scribner, 1958), 68.

[88]Ibid., 74.

[89]For a responsible account of what the Bible does teach about the universe in response to Bultmann see R. Laird Harris, "The Bible and Cosmology," *Bulletin of the Evangelical Theological Society* 5.1 (March 1962): 11–16.

[90]Paul Tillich, *The Courage to Be* (New Haven, Conn.: Yale University Press, 1952), 168.

[91]Langdon Gilkey, "The Concept of Providence in Contemporary Theology," *The Journal of Religion* 53.3 (July 1963): 184–85.

[92]Robert A. Morey, *Horoscopes and the Christian* (Minneapolis: Bethany, 1981); see also Gary Jennings, *A Teenager's Realistic Guide to Astrology* (New York: Association, 1971).

[93]H. F. Vos, "Astrology," *EDT,* 93.

[94]Danny Korem and Paul Meier, *The Fakers: Exploding the Myths of the Supernatural* (Grand Rapids: Baker, 1980), 15.

[95]See Mark Bubek, *Overcoming the Adversary* (Chicago: Moody, 1984).

[96]Pollard, *Chance and Providence,* 180.

[97]Ibid., 179.

[98]Donna Platt, "The Key to Weight Control," *Ministry* (March, 1986), 13.

[99]Charles Colson, *Kingdoms in Conflict* (Grand Rapids: Zondervan, 1987), 247–48.

[100]See Mark Satin, *New Age Politics* (New York: Dell, 1979), 24, 47; see also Douglas Groothuis, *Unmasking the New Age* (Downers Grove: InterVarsity, 1986), 111–30.

[101]See Gordon R. Lewis, "How Effective Is Prayer?" in *Decide for Yourself* (Downers Grove: InterVarsity, 1975), 69–73; "Prayer," *ZPEB,* 4:843.

[102]For further applications of God's presence and action in the world see Geoffrey Wainwright, *Doxology: The Praise of God in Worship, Doctrine, and Life* (New York: Oxford University Press, 1980), 79–86.

Chapter 3

[1]This appears to be the focus of Otto Weber's remark when he said, "The issue in the Bible and in the message of the Church is really [i.e., primarily] man." *Foundations of Dogmatics,* 2 vols. (Grand Rapids: Eerdmans, 1981–83), 1:530.

[2]Augustine, *On True Religion,* 12.

[3]Blaise Pascal, *Pensees* (Baltimore: Penguin, 1966), no. 131.

[4]Justin Martyr, *Apology,* 1.28. Cf. ibid., 1.10; *Dialogue With Trypho,* 102, 141.

[5]Athenagoras, *The Resurrection of the Dead,* 12.

[6]Irenaeus, *Against Heresies,* IV.4.3; IV.37.1; V.1.3.

[7]Ibid., V.6.1. Cf. ibid., II.33.5; V.6.1; V.8.1; V.10.1.

[8]Clement of Alexandria, *Miscellanies,* II.19; *The Instructor,* I.12.

[9]Gregory of Nyssa, "On the Making of Man," 9.

[10]Ibid., 15.2. Cf. ibid., 5.2; 16.17.

[11]John of Damascus, *The Orthodox Faith,* II.12.

[12]Gordon H. Clark, *The Biblical Doctrine of Man* (Jefferson, Md.: The Trinity Foundation, 1984), 19.

[13]Ibid., 14–15.

[14]Ibid., 25.

[15]Athenagoras, *The Resurrection of the Dead,* 15. The apologist adds that at death the soul separates from the body, the two to be reunited at the resurrection. Ibid., 16–18.

[16]Origen, *On First Principles,* I.7; II.1–3; II.9.6; III.3–5.

[17]Hilary of Potiers, *On the Trinity,* X.20.

[18]Tertullian, *On the Soul,* 5–9, 27, 36–38. Said Tertullian, "The soul is a seed placed in man and transmitted by him, that from the beginning there was one seed of the soul, as there was one seed of the flesh, for the whole human race." Ibid., 36.1.

[19]Tertullian, *On the Soul,* 15.5.

[20]Peter Lombard, *Book of Sentences,* II.xvi.3.

[21]Bonaventure, "Disputed Questions Concerning Christ's Knowledge," Q. IV.2, in *A Scholastic Miscellany: Anselm to Ockham* (Philadelphia: Westminster, 1956), 394.

[22]Thomas Aquinas, *ST,* 1.93.9.

[23]Ibid., 1.60.5.

[24]Ibid., 1.95.1;1.93.4.

[25]F. J. Corley, "Man," *NCE,* 9:128.

[26]Martin Luther, *LW,* 1:61.

[27]Ibid., 1:62–63.

[28]Philip Melanchthon, *Melanchthon on Christian Doctrine* (Grand Rapids: Baker, reprint 1965), 72.

[29]*Formula of Concord,* "Epitome," Art. I., Affirmative 1.

[30]Cited by Heinrich Schmid, *The Doctrinal Theology of the Evangelical Lutheran Church* (Minneapolis: Augsburg, reprint 1961), 218.

[31]For historical testimonies within the older Lutheran tradition, see Schmid, *Doctrinal Theology,* 166.

[32]See Hugh T. Kerr, ed., *A Compend of Luther's Theology* (Philadelphia: Westminster, 1966), 77–79.

[33]Cited by Schmid, *Doctrinal Theology,* 166–67.

[34]*The Racovian Catechism* (Lexington, Ky.: American Theological Library Association, 1962), 1.2.21.

[35]Gerhard von Rad, *"eikōn," TDNT,* 2:391.

[36]Gerhard von Rad, *Genesis. OTL* (Philadelphia: Westminster, 1961), 60. Cf. von Rad, *"eikōn," TDNT,* 2:392: "Man in his sphere of rule as God's vice-regent is summoned to represent the dominion and majesty of God."

[37]D. J. A. Clines, "The Image of God in Man," *Tyndale Bulletin* 19 (1968): 101. Clines earlier in the article posed the question whether dominion was determinative of the *imago,* or whether it was merely a consequence of it. His conclusion is that "since dominion is so immediate and necessary a consequence of the image, it loses the character of a mere derivative of the image and virtually becomes a constitutive part of the image itself." Ibid., 96.

[38]Leonard Verduin, *Somewhat Less Than God: The Biblical View of Man* (Grand Rapids: Eerdmans, 1970), 27. Cf., "Man is the image-bearer of God and that this image, this God-likeness, evinces itself in dominion-having." Ibid., 49.

[39]Dietrich Bonhoeffer, *Creation and Temptation* (London: SCM, 1966), 37.

[40]Ibid., 39.

[41]Karl Barth, *CD,* III.1.192.

[42]Ibid., 185.

[43]Ibid., 195.

[44]Ibid., III.2.145. Cf. this statement: "Every man belongs to God, and is the object of Christ's redemptive act wrought in history. Every man is destined for the glory of God by

sharing in this redemption, and his whole being consists in the active service of God." *Kirkliche Dogmatik,* III.2.85–86, cited by David Cairns, *The Image of God in Man* (New York: Philosophical Library, 1953), 170, n.2.

[45]Emil Brunner, *The Christian Doctrine of Creation and Redemption: Dogmatics,* Vol. II, (London: Lutterworth, 1952), 69.

[46]Ibid., 56–57.

[47]Ibid., 58.

[48]John Macquarrie, *Principles of Christian Theology* (New York: Scribner, 1977), 76.

[49]Ibid., 231.

[50]John Macquarrie, *An Existentialist Theology* (London: SCM, 1955), 137.

[51]Edmond Jacob, *"psychē,"* *TDNT,* 9:631.

[52]Oscar Cullmann, "Immortality or Resurrection?" *Christianity Today* 2.21 (July 21, 1958), 6.

[53]John A. T. Robinson, *The Body: A Study in Pauline Theology* (Chicago: Regnery, 1952), 16.

[54]Augustine, *Freedom of the Will,* 2.16.

[55]Augustine, *On Christian Doctrine,* 1.22.

[56]In terms of one of his Trinitarian analogies—the triad of memory, understanding, and will—Augustine writes, "I remember that I have memory, understanding, and will; I understand that I understand, and will, and remember; I will that I will, and remember, and understand; and at the same time I remember my whole memory, understanding, and will." *On the Trinity,* 10.11.18; cf. *Letter,* 169. Feelings, love, or desires could be substituted for memory in this quote.

[57]Augustine, *Confessions,* 13.9.10.

[58]Augustine, *Enchiridion,* 11.36. Cf. idem, *On the Trinity,* 15.7.11; idem, *Reply to Faustus the Manichaean,* 24.2.

[59]Augustine, *On the Soul and Its Origin,* 4.3.

[60]John Calvin, *Institutes of the Christian Religion,* I.15.3. Cf. *Commentaries on the Epistles to the Philippians, Colossians, and Thessalonians,* 212, where Calvin states that the image of God, according to Genesis 9:6, is "the rectitude and integrity of the whole soul."

[61]Calvin, *Institutes,* I.15.3.

[62]Ibid. Cf. *Commentaries on the Book of Genesis,* 95.

[63]Calvin, *Institutes,* I.15.4; II.2.12.

[64]Ibid., I.15.4. Cf. *Commentaries on Genesis,* 95.

[65]Cf. *The Westminster Shorter Catechism,* quest. 10, which adds the element of dominion over the lower forms of life: "How did God create man? God created man, male and female, after his own image, in knowledge, righteousness, and holiness, with dominion over the creatures."

[66]John Wolleb, *Compendium Theologiae Christianae,* V.2, in John W. Beardslee, III, *Reformed Dogmatics* (Grand Rapids: Baker, reprint 1977), 56.

[67]Herman Bavinck, *Our Reasonable Faith* (Grand Rapids: Baker, reprint 1977), 213.

[68]L. Berkhof, *Systematic Theology* (Grand Rapids: Eerdmans, 1941), 207.

[69]Ibid., 195.

[70]Augustus H. Strong, *Systematic Theology* (Valley Forge, Penn.: Judson, 1907), 483–88.

[71]*The Scofield Reference Bible,* ed. C. I. Scofield (New York: Oxford University Press, 1945), notes to Genesis 1:26 (p. 5) and 1 Thessalonians 5:23 (p. 1,270).

[72]Calvin, *Institutes,* I.15.5.

[73]Wolleb, *Compendium Theologiae Christianae,* I.5, in Beardslee, *Reformed Dogmatics,* 57.

[74]W. G. T. Shedd, *Dogmatic Theology,* 3 vols. (Grand Rapids: Zondervan, n.d.), 2:7.

[75]Robert L. Dabney, *Lectures in Systematic Theology* (Grand Rapids: Zondervan, reprint 1972), 321.

[76]James Orr, *God's Image in Man* (Grand Rapids: Eerdmans, 1948).

[77]Anthony A. Hoekema, *Created in God's Image* (Grand Rapids: Eerdmans, 1986).

[78]Millard J. Erickson, *Christian Theology,* 3 vols. (Grand Rapids: Baker, 1983–1985), vol. 2.

[79]Derek Kidner, *Genesis, TNTC* (London: Tyndale, 1967), 50.

[80]Clines, "The Image of God in Man," 80; G. Ch. Aalders, *Genesis,* 2 vols. (Grand Rapids: Zondervan, 1981), 1:70.

[81]Cf. John E. Hartley, *"ṣelem,"* *TWOT,* 2:768: "God's image obviously does not consist in man's body which was formed from earthly matter, but in his spiritual, intellectual, moral likeness to God from whom his animating breath came."

[82]Concerning the complex unity that is the person, H. W. Hoehner, "Body, the Biblical View of," *EDT,* 165, comments, "The Scriptural dualism is not the same as Greek dualism, where the soul is the prisoner of the body, but rather the body is the instrument through which the immaterial expresses itself. The

material and the immaterial parts are on a par with each other."

[83]*Lēb* and *kardia* "refer usually to the entire man understood from the point of his governing center, the essential person, rather than the emotional nature as in current English usage." Bruce Milne, *Know the Truth* (Downers Grove: InterVarsity, 1982), 97. Cf. Andrew Bowling, *"lēb," TWOT,* 1:466.

[84]See Bruce K. Waltke, *"nepeš," TWOT,* 2:589; M. E. Osterhaven, "Soul," *EDT,* 1036.

[85]Clark, *The Biblical Doctrine of Man,* 53.

[86]Kidner, *Genesis,* 65.

[87]Robert D. Culver, *"māšal," TWOT,* 1:534. Susan T. Foh, "What Is the Woman's Desire?" *Westminster Theological Journal,* 37 (Spring 1975), offers the following convincing interpretation of the clause in Genesis 3:16 "he will rule over you": "After the Fall, the woman sinfully desires to control her husband. In the ensuing struggle for control, the husband often responds with excessive domination. In this battle between the sexes, the divine pattern (inherent in the creation order) of the husband's loving headship and the wife's faithful submission becomes corrupted and distorted."

[88]C. G. Berkouwer, *Man: The Image of God* (Grand Rapids: Eerdmans, 1962), 71–72.

[89]Michael A. Eaton, *Ecclesiastes, TOTC* (Downers Grove: InterVarsity, 1983), 116.

[90]L. Berkhof, *Systematic Theology,* 194. Berkhof adds, "The Bible, therefore points to two, and only two, constitutional elements in the nature of man, namely, body and spirit or soul." Ibid.

[91]G. Harder, "Soul," *NIDNTT,* 3:683.

[92]J. A. T. Robinson, *The Body: A Study in Pauline Theology* (Chicago: Henry Regnery, 1952).

[93]Joseph Osei-Bonsu, "Does 2 Cor. 5:1–10 Teach the Reception of the Resurrection Body at the Moment of Death?" *Journal for the Study of the New Testament* 28 (Oct. 1986): 89. In this article Osei-Bonsu refutes the thesis of M. J. Harris, *Raised Immortal: Resurrection and Immortality in the New Testament* (Grand Rapids: Eerdmans, 1983), who argues that 2 Corinthians 5:1–10 teaches that the believer is clothed with the resurrection body at the moment of death.

[94]F. F. Bruce, *1 & 2 Thessalonians, WBC* (Waco: Word, 1982), 130. Leon Morris adds, "Paul is not here concerned to give a theoretical analysis of man, but is uttering a fervent prayer that the entire man may be preserved." *1 & 2 Thessalonians, TNTC* (London: Inter-Varsity, 1956), 107.

[95]Fritz Rienecker and Cleon L. Rogers, Jr., *LKGNT,* 375.

[96]Berkouwer, *Man: The Image of God,* 45.

[97]Leon Morris, *1 Corinthians, TNTC* (London: Tyndale, 1958), 151. Cf. H. Schlier, *"kephalē," TDNTAbr,* 429: "The distinction between man and woman is seen here to have an ontological ground, having her life from man and for man." Moreover, on the basis of a computer search of more than 2,300 uses in ancient Greek literature, Wayne Grudem concludes that *kephalē* means not primarily "source" or "origin," but "authority over." See, "Does *kephalē* ("head") Mean 'Source' or 'Authority Over' in Greek Literature? A Survey of 2,336 Examples," in *The Role Relationship of Men and Women,* ed. George W. Knight, III (Chicago: Moody, 1985), 49–80.

[98]G. Delling, *"hypotassō," TDNTAbr,* 1159.

[99]Francis Foulkes, *Ephesians, TNTC* (London: Inter-Varsity, 1963), 155. Donald Guthrie comments on 1 Timothy 2:12–13: "The idea of woman's subjection . . . appears to be inherent in the divine constitution of the human race." *The Pastoral Epistles, TNTC* (London: Tyndale, 1957), 76.

[100]Alfred Plummer, *The Gospel According to St. John* (Grand Rapids: Baker, reprint 1981), 102.

[101]John R. W. Stott, *The Epistles of John, TNTC* (London: Tyndale: 1964), 120.

[102]We noted earlier in this chapter that Gordon Clark explicates the work of the Logos more narrowly in terms of intellectual enablement: "The Logos or rationality of God, who created all things without a single exception, can be seen as having created man with the light of logic as his distinctive human characteristic." *Biblical Doctrine of Man,* 18–19.

[103]Peter H. Davids, *The Epistle of James, NIGTC* (Grand Rapids: Eerdmans, 1982), 133.

[104]F. F. Bruce, *The Epistle to the Hebrews, NLCNT* (London & Edinburgh: Marshall, Morgan & Scott, 1964), 82.

[105]Ibid., 360.

[106]W. L. Reese, "Substance," *Dictionary of Philosophy and Religion: Eastern and Western Thought* (Atlantic Highlands, N.J.: Humanities, 1980), 556.

[107]Colin Brown, "Heart," *NIDNTT,* 2:181–82.

[108]R. Laird Harris, *Man–God's Eternal Creation* (Chicago: Moody, 1971), 12.

[109]Don Cupitt, *The Leap of Reason* (Philadelphia: Westminster, 1976), 112–13.

[110]Gordon R. Lewis, "Paradise," *ZPEB*, 4: 598–99.

[111]Erich Sauer, *King of the Earth* (Grand Rapids: Eerdmans, 1962).

[112]Gordon R. Lewis, "Faith and Reason in the Thought of St. Augustine," Ph.D. dissertation, Syracuse University, 1959. Available from University Microfilms, Ann Arbor, Michigan 48106.

[113]Julius Weinberg, "Abstraction," in *Dictionary of the History of Ideas*, ed. Philip P. Wiener (New York: Scribner, 1968), 1–9.

[114]Gordon R. Lewis, "Francis Schaeffer's Apologetic Method," in *Reflections on Francis Schaeffer*, ed. Ronald Reugsegger, (Grand Rapids: Zondervan, 1986), 69–104.

[115]Orville S. Walters, "Unconscious," in *Baker's Dictionary of Christian Ethics*, ed. Carl F. H. Henry (Grand Rapids: Baker, 1973), 683–84.

[116]Evelyn Underhill, *Mysticism* (Cleveland and New York: World, 1955), 104.

[117]L. I. Granberg and G. E. Farley, "Conscience," *ZPEB*, 1:949.

[118]H. C. Hahn, "Conscience," *NIDNTT*, 1:350.

[119]D. G. Benner, "Emotion," *EDT*, 352.

[120]B. B. Warfield, "The Emotional Life of our Lord" in *The Person and Work of Christ* (Philadelphia: Presbyterian and Reformed, 1950), 122.

[121]Norman Hope, "How to Be Good—And Mad," *Christianity Today* (July 19, 1968), 3–5.

[122]Carl F. H. Henry, *Christian Personal Ethics* (Grand Rapids: Eerdmans, 1957), 499.

[123]C. S. Lewis, *Mere Christianity* (New York: Macmillan, 1952), 90–91.

[124]C. S. Lewis, *Pilgrim's Regress* (Grand Rapids: Eerdmans, 1943), 8; cf. 129.

[125]Harold O. J. Brown, "Romanticism and the Bible," in *Challenges to Inerrancy*, eds. Gordon R. Lewis and Bruce Demarest (Chicago: Moody, 1984), 54.

[126]See Ronald C. Doll, "Motives and Motivation"; Murray J. Harris, "Mixed Motives"; and Stephen S. Smalley, "Singlemindedness," *Baker's Dictionary of Christian Ethics*, 437–38, 427–28, 622–23.

[127]Mary T. Clark, *Augustine, Philosopher of Freedom* (New York: Desclee, 1958), 69.

[128]C. Stephen Evans, *Preserving the Person* (Downers Grove: InterVarsity, 1977), 145; see also George David, *The Eclipse and Recovery of Person* (Bombay: TRACI, 1976).

[129]Jacob Bronowski, *The Identity of Man* (Garden City: Natural History, 1965), 2.

[130]Karl R. Popper and John C. Eccles, *The Self and Its Brain* (New York: Springer, 1977), 11.

[131]Arnold S. Kaufman, "Behaviorism," *EP*, 1:270.

[132]Michael D. Aeschliman, *The Restitution of Man* (Grand Rapids: Eerdmans, 1983), 80. See also Ludger Holscher, *The Reality of the Mind: Augustine's Philosophical Arguments for the Human Soul as a Spiritual Substance* (New York: Routledge & Kegan Paul, 1986).

[133]Richard H. Bube, *The Encounter Between Christianity and Science* (Grand Rapids: Eerdmans, 1968), 80–81.

[134]Evans, *Preserving the Person*, 149.

[135]Ibid., 151–52.

[136]Aeschliman, *Restitution of Man*, 55.

[137]Ibid., 48.

[138]Kaufman, "Behaviorism," 271.

[139]For similar arguments see J. Oliver Buswell, Jr., *A Christian View of Being and Knowing* (Grand Rapids: Zondervan, 1960), 126–60; Bernard Ramm, *Protestant Christian Evidences* (Chicago: Moody, 1954), 58–70; Stuart C. Hackett, *The Resurrection of Theism* (Chicago: Moody, 1957), 220–29.

[140]Popper and Eccles, *The Self and Its Brain*, 355.

[141]Ibid., 378.

[142]Ibid., 374.

[143]G. Stafford Wright, "Man," *NIDNTT*, 2:568.

[144]Berkouwer, *Man: The Image of God*, 23.

[145]Ibid., 35.

[146]Ibid.

[147]Ibid, 196.

[148]Ibid., 203.

[149]Ibid., 205.

[150]Ibid., 235.

[151]Ibid., 259.

[152]Ibid.

[153]Ibid., 264.

[154]Ibid. 269; for other exclusively relational views see Bruce Larson, *The Relational Revolution* (Waco: Word, 1976) and *The Meaning and Mystery of Being Human* (Waco: Word, 1978).

[155]W. Brugh Joy, *Joy's Way* (Los Angeles: J. P. Tarcher, 1979), 32.

[156]Ibid., 163.

[157]Marilyn Ferguson, *The Aquarian Conspiracy* (Los Angeles: Tarcher, 1980), 100.

[158]Ibid., 98–99.

[159]Barth, *CD,* III.2.350.

[160]Ibid., 354.

[161]Ibid., 361.

[162]See also Ray S. Anderson, *On Being Human: Essays in Theological Anthropology* (Grand Rapids: Eerdmans, 1982), 210–11.

[163]Hoekema, *Created in God's Image,* 217.

[164]Arthur Koestler, *The Ghost in the Machine* (London: Hutchinson, 1967), 205–8.

[165]Ibid., 219.

[166]For an informed philosopher's discussion of substance see Albrey Castell, *The Self in Philosophy* (New York: Macmillan, 1965) 50–79.

[167]Stuart Barton Babbage, *Man in Nature and Grace,* (Grand Rapids: Eerdmans, 1957), 17.

[168]Watchman Nee, *The Spiritual Man* (New York: Christian Fellowship, 1986), 1:26.

[169]Ibid., 2:67–127.

[170]William T. Brunner, "A New Theory of Original Sin" *Gordon Review* (1959), 125–37 and William T. Brunner, *Children of the Devil: Fresh Investigation of the Fall of Man and Original Sin* (New York: Philosophical Library, 1966).

[171]Corliss Lamont, *The Philosophy of Humanism* (New York: Frederick Ungar, sixth ed. 1982), 227.

[172]Ibid., 87.

[173]Ibid., 3–8.

[174]John Piper, *Desiring God* (Portland: Multnomah, 1986).

[175]Arthur Dyck, cited by C. Everett Koop, "The Slide to Auschwitz," in Ronald Reagan, *Abortion and the Conscience of the Nation* (New York: Thomas Nelson, 1984), 60.

Chapter 4

[1]Otto Weber, *Foundations of Dogmatics,* 2 vols. (Grand Rapids: Eerdmans, 1981–1983), 1:596.

[2]*The Racovian Catechism,* ed. Thomas Rees (Lexington, Ky.: American Theological Library Association, 1962), 326; sec. V., chap. 10.

[3]Henry Ware, cited by H. Shelton Smith, *Changing Conceptions of Original Sin* (New York: Scribner, 1955), 76.

[4]William Newton Clarke, *An Outline of Christian Theology* (Edinburgh: T. & T. Clark, 1909), 245.

[5]William A. Brown, "The Old Theology and the New," *Harvard Theological Review,* 4 (January 1911): 15.

[6]William A. Brown, *Christian Theology in Outline* (New York: Scribner, 1911), 273–74.

[7]See Jaroslav Pelikan, *The Christian Tradition,* 4 vols. (Chicago: University of Chicago Press, 1971–1984), 4:279.

[8]*The Canons and Decrees of Trent,* Session VI, canon 5.

[9]Ibid., Session V, chap. 4.

[10]Richard P. McBrien, *Catholicism* (Minneapolis: Winston, 1981), 162.

[11]*A New Catechism: Catholic Faith for Adults* (New York: Herder & Herder, 1967), 267.

[12]Piet Schoonenberg, *Man and Sin* (South Bend: University of Notre Dame Press, 1965), 198. Monika K. Hellwig argues from the same perspective: The "focus or orientation of our whole being which we cannot escape is necessarily a sinful one because of the . . . sinfulness of the world as we know it. It is a sinful one because the human community in which we are rooted . . . is out of focus and estranged from its end and purpose in God." *Understanding Catholicism* (New York: Paulist, 1981), 51.

[13]*A Compend of Wesley's Theology,* ed. Robert W. Burtner and Robert E. Childs (Nashville: Abingdon, 1954), 117.

[14]Ibid., 114.

[15]Ibid., 120.

[16]See the *Methodist Articles of Religion,* VIII. Cf. "There is no man that is in a state of mere nature; there is no man, unless he has quenched the Spirit, that is wholly void of the grace of God. No man living is entirely destitute of . . . preventing grace." *Compend of Wesley's Theology,* 148.

[17]H. Orton Wiley, *Christian Theology,* 3 vols. (Kansas City: Beacon Hill, 1952), 2:107.

[18]A. Elwood Sanner, "Total Depravity," *BDT*, 525.

[19]Ibid., 546.

[20]John Miley, *Systematic Theology,* 2 vols. (New York: Eaton and Mains, 1892), 1:521.

[21]*Finney's Systematic Theology,* ed. J. H. Fairchild (Minneapolis: Bethany, reprint 1976), 429.

[22]Ibid., 180.

[23]Karl Barth, *CD,* IV.1.508.

[24]Ibid., III.4.43.

[25]Ibid., III.2.29.

[26]Karl Barth, "No!" in *Natural Theology,* trans. Peter Fraenkel (London: Centenary, 1946), 74 (cf. 20, 22). In this work Barth asserts that the *imago Dei* has been totally obliterated by sin.

[27]Barth, *CD,* I.1.145. Barth's point is that sin is a temporary betrayal of the covenant relation that ultimately will prevail. Thus the person is "the object of divine grace, the partner in the covenant which God has made with him." *CD,* III.2.32.

[28]Emil Brunner, *The Christian Doctrine of Creation and Redemption: Dogmatics, Vol. II* (London: Lutterworth, 1952), 90.

[29]Ibid., 103.

[30]Emil Brunner, *The Scandal of Christianity* (London: SCM, 1951), 56–57.

[31]Ibid., 65.

[32]Reinhold Niebuhr, *The Nature and Destiny of Man,* 2 vols. (New York: Scribner, 1951), 1:186.

[33]Reinhold Niebuhr, *An Interpretation of Christian Ethics* (New York: Meridian, 1956), 86.

[34]Dorothy Sölle, *Political Theology* (Philadelphia: Fortress, 1974), 91. Sölle adds that the notion of original sin "means that man has the capacity for guilt." Ibid., 88.

[35]James H. Cone, "Christian Faith and Political Praxis," in *The Challenge of Liberation Theology,* ed. Brian Mahan and L. Dale Richesin (Maryknoll, N.Y.: Orbis, 1981), 57. Leonardo Boff, a Latin American liberation theologian, comments, "Sin isn't something purely spiritual, something just on the inside. It's exploitation, it's injustice, it's oppression, it's chains on persons in this world, external chains, that destroy them." Leonardo and Clodovis Boff, *Salvation and Liberation* (Maryknoll, N.Y.: Orbis, 1984), 76.

[36]Augustine, *Sermons on the New Testament,* 67.15.

[37]Augustine, *City of God,* XIV.11. Cf. *Against Two Letters of the Pelagians,* I.5; *Letters,* 115.2; *On Rebuke and Grace,* XIII.42.

[38]Augustine, *On the Spirit and the Letter,* 5.

[39]Augustine, *On the Spirit and the Letter,* 48. Cf. ibid., "What was impressed on their hearts when they were created in the image of God has not been wholly blotted out."

[40]Augustine, *City of God,* XIII.14.

[41]Martin Luther, *LW,* 1:66.

[42]Martin Luther, *A Compend of Luther's Theology,* ed. Hugh T. Kerr (Philadelphia: Westminster, 1966), 90. "Godward, or in things which pertain unto salvation or damnation, he has no 'free will,' but is a captive, slave, and servant, either to the will of God, or to the will of Satan." Ibid., 88.

[43]Luther, *LW,* 25:348.

[44]John Calvin, *Institutes of the Christian Religion,* II.1.5.

[45]Ibid., II.1.8.

[46]Ibid., II.1.9.

[47]Ibid., II.1.7. Cf. Calvin, *Commentary on the Gospel According to John,* 1:113: "The corruption of all mankind in the person of Adam alone did not proceed from generation, but from the appointment of God, who has in him deprived us of his gifts."

[48]Calvin, *Institutes,* II.1.8.

[49]W. G. T. Shedd, *Dogmatic Theology,* 3 vols. (Grand Rapids: Zondervan, n.d.), 2:186.

[50]Ibid., 2:188–89.

[51]Augustus H. Strong, *Systematic Theology* (Valley Forge, Penn.: Judson, 1907), 661. Strong theorizes that the reason why Scripture does not speak more explicitly about the salvation of infants may be that some parents might then have killed their children so as to ensure their entry into the kingdom of God. Ibid., 663.

[52]L. Berkhof, *Systematic Theology* (Grand Rapids: Eerdmans, 1941), 221.

[53]Ibid. Berkhof makes the point that guilt is not transmitted seminally but is reckoned forensically to Adam's posterity.

[54]G. C. Berkouwer, *Sin* (Grand Rapids: Eerdmans, 1971).

[55]Bernard Ramm, *Offense to Reason: The Theology of Sin* (San Francisco, 1985).

[56]Millard J. Erickson, *Christian Theology,* 3 vols. (Grand Rapids: Baker, 1983–1985), 2:561–658.

[57]Ramm, *Offense to Reason,* 68. Ramm's thesis that Genesis 1–11 represents "theology by narration"—theology expressed by telling a story—has not been fully substantiated. Moreover, Jesus appears not to have understood Genesis 1–11 in this way. Thus in regard to the first eleven chapters of Genesis, we cannot follow this particular thesis of Ramm with all its theological implications.

[58]Ibid., 71–75.

[59]Herman Bavinck suggests that the second tree was so called because it would demon-

strate whether man would arbitrarily determine what was good and evil, or whether he would allow God to make that determination. *Our Reasonable Faith* (Grand Rapids: Baker, reprint 1977), 218. This explanation seems to deviate from the main thrust of the tree's name—"the tree of the *knowledge* of good and evil."

[60]Bavinck, *Reasonable Faith,* 224.

[61]Th. C. Vriezen, *An Outline of Old Testament Theology* (Wageningen: Veenman, 1960), 210.

[62]Leslie S. McCaw and J. A. Motyer, "The Psalms," *NBCRev,* 483.

[63]Charles L. Feinberg, *Jeremiah: A Commentary* (Grand Rapids: Zondervan, 1982), 110.

[64]G. Herbert Livingston, *"'āwel, 'awlāh,"* *TWOT,* 2:653.

[65]Contrast the statement of R. E. Nixon, "Matthew," *NBCRev,* 840: This text "provides justification for treating children as members of the Christian community."

[66]F. F. Bruce comments, "The whole of mankind is viewed as having originally sinned in Adam." *Romans, TNTC* (London, Tyndale, 1963), 126. Cf. John Murray: "For some reason the one sin of Adam is accounted to be the sin of all." *The Epistle to the Romans,* 2 vols. (Grand Rapids: Eerdmans, 1959–1965), 1:185.

[67]See *BAGD,* 287; Nigel Turner, *Syntax,* vol. 3 of J. H. Moulton, *A Grammar of New Testament Greek* (Edinburgh: T. & T. Clark, 1963), 272; Fritz Rienecker and Cleon L. Rogers, Jr., *LKGNT,* 360.

[68]Albrecht Oepke, *"kathistēmi,"* *TDNT,* 3:445.

[69]See W. Schneider, "Judgment," *NIDNTT,* 3:365. Cf. C. E. B. Cranfield, *The Epistle to the Romans, ICC;* 2 vols. (Edinburgh and London: T. & T. Clark, 1975), 1:287.

[70]Heinrich Oepke, *"katakrima,"* *TDNT,* 3:446.

[71]John Eadie, *Galatians* (Grand Rapids: Baker, reprint 1979), 401. Cf. John Murray, *Romans,* 2:284–85: " 'The flesh' is human nature as corrupted, directed, and controlled by sin."

[72]Francis Foulkes, *Ephesians, TNTC* (London: Inter-Varsity, 1963), 69.

[73]Alfred Plummer, *The Gospel According to St. John* (Grand Rapids: Baker, reprint 1981), 102. Cf. E. Schweitzer, "sarx," *TDNTAbr,* 1006: "In John 3:6 everything human is *sarx. Sarx* is the earthly sphere in which there is no knowledge of God and nothing to save from lostness."

[74]R. V. G. Tasker, *James, TNTC* (London: Tyndale, 1957), 46.

[75]F. F. Bruce, *Epistle to the Hebrews, NLCNT* (London and Edinburgh: Marshall, Morgan & Scott, 1964), 142.

[76]See Heinrich Seesemann, *"osphys,"* *TDNT,* 5:496–97.

[77]Erickson, *Christian Theology,* 613.

[78]H. Beck and C. Brown, "Peace," *NIDNTT,* 2:777.

[79]Ramm, *Offense to Reason,* 82.

[80]Martin Luther, *Commentary on Genesis* excerpts quoted in Kerr, *Compend of Luther's Theology,* 79.

[81]G. W. Bromiley, "World," *ZPEB,* 5:966–67.

[82]Augustine, *On Christian Doctrine,"* III.10.16; Philip Schaff, ed.,*Nicene and Post-Nicene Fathers* (Grand Rapids: Eerdmans, 1956), 2:561.

[83]Norman Malcolm, "Wittgenstein" *EP,* 8:327–28.

[84]Jean Paul Sartre, *Existentialism and Human Emotions* (New York: Philosophical Library, 1957), 15.

[85]Ramm, *Offense to Reason,* 93.

[86]Ibid., 42–43.

[87]Wendell Berry, *The Unsettling of America: Culture and Agriculture* (San Francisco: Sierra Club, 1986), 13.

[88]Ibid.

[89]Erickson, *Christian Theology,* 2:648–52.

[90]Berry, *The Unsettling,* 13.

[91]See Irving Kristol, Paul Johnson, and Michael Novak, "The Moral Basis of Democratic Capitalism" (Washington, D.C.: American Enterprise Institute, n.d.), 16–32.

[92]Reinhold Niebuhr, *The Children of Light and Children of Darkness* (New York: Scribner, 1944), xiii.

[93]Augustine, *Confessions,* Book 1, trans. Shirwood Wirt, (Grand Rapids: Zondervan , 1986), 21.

[94]Strong, *Systematic Theology,* 660–64.

[95]Mark A. Noll, "Feuerbach, Ludwig Andreas," *NDT,* 259.

[96]See J. B. Webster, "Bultmann, Rudolph," *NDT,* 16.

[97]Paul Tillich, *Systematic Theology,* 3 vols. (Chicago: University of Chicago Press, 1951–63), 2:25.

[98]Ibid., 1:238.

[99]See G. Lewis, "Niebuhr's Relativism, Relationalism, Contextualization and Revelation," in *Challenges to Inerrancy: A Theological Response* ed. Lewis and Demarest, (Chicago: Moody, 1984), 145–73.

[100]Marilyn Ferguson, *The Aquarian Conspiracy: Personal and Social Transformation in the 1980s* (Los Angeles: Tarcher, 1980).

[101]Robert J. L. Burroughs, "A Vision for a New Humanity," in *The New Age Rage*, ed. Karen Hoyt (Old Tappan, N.J.: Revell, 1987).

[102]Ken Wilbur, *Up from Eden* (Boulder, Colo.: Shambala, 1981) in Frances S. Adeney, "Transpersonal Psychology: Psychology and Salvation Meet," in *The New Age Rage*, 123.

[103]H. Shelton Smith, *Changing Conceptions of Original Sin* (New York: Scribner, 1955), 76–78.

[104]Corliss Lamont, *The Philosophy of Humanism* (New York: Frederick Ungar, revised and enlarged 1982), 241.

[105]Ibid., 241–42.

[106]Ibid., 242.

[107]Ibid., 247.

[108]Mencius, in Ch'u Chai with Winberg Chai, *The Story of Chinese Philosophy* (New York: Washington Square, 1961), 53–60.

[109]L. Harold DeWolf, *A Theology of the Living Church* (New York: Harper, 1953), 199.

[110]Ibid.

[111]Ibid.

[112]See Edward O. Wilson, *Sociobiology: The New Synthesis* (Cambridge: Harvard University Press, 1975), and Bernard Ramm's discussion in *Offense to Reason*, 23–24.

[113]See *The Major Works of Sigmund Freud, Great Books of the Western World*, ed., Mortimer J. Adler, (Chicago: Encyclopedia Britannica, 1952) vol. 54, and Ramm's discussion *in Offense to Reason*, 19–21.

[114]See B. F. Skinner, *About Behaviorism* (New York: Vintage, 1974) and Ramm's discussion in *Offense to Reason*, 21–23.

[115]Karl Marx, *Capital and Manifesto of the Communist Party, Great Books*, vol. 50.

[116]Jose Miranda, *Marx and the Bible* (Maryknoll, N.Y.: Orbis, 1974), 181.

[117]Ibid., 190.

[118]Ibid., 191.

[119]Ibid., 202.

[120]Ibid., 17.

[121]Ibid., 173.

[122]M. Scott Peck, *The People of the Lie: The Hope for Healing Human Evil* (New York: Simon and Schuster, 1983).

[123]Charles W. Carter, "Hamartiology," in *A Contemporary Wesleyan Theology*, ed. C. W. Carter (Grand Rapids: Zondervan, Francis Asbury, 1983), 267–68; H. Orton Wiley, *Christian Theology* (Kansas City: Beacon Hill, 1952), 352–57.

[124]Emil Brunner, *Man in Revolt* (Philadelphia: Westminster, 1957), 147.

[125]Ramm, *Offense to Reason*, 51.

[126]Henry Alford, *The Greek Testament*, 4 vols. (Boston: Lee and Shepard, 1872), 2:360.

[127]David Murchie, "From Slaveholder to American Abolitionist: Charles Hodge and the Slavery Issue" in *Christian Freedom*, ed. Kenneth W.M. Wozniak and Stanley J. Grenz (New York: University Press of America, 1986), 148.

[128]J. Edmondson, *A Concise System of Self-Government in the Great Affairs of Life and Godliness* (New York: Lane and Scott, 1848).

[129]See B. B.Warfield, *Perfectionism* (Philadelphia: Presbyterian and Reformed, 1958).

[130]See John Passmore, *The Perfectibility of Man* (London: Duckworth, 1970).

[131]"American State Papers," in *Great Books of the Western World*, ed. Robert Maynard Hutchins, 43:49–51.

[132]See Ajith Fernando, "Rediscovering the Doctrine of Lostness," *World Evangelization* 13.49 (Nov.-Dec. 1987): 18–19.

[133]Ramm, *Offense to Reason*, 108.

Chapter 5

[1]Emil Brunner, *The Mediator* (Philadelphia: Westminster, 1947), 212; cf. ibid., 232: "The center and the foundation of the whole Christian faith is Christology, that is faith in Jesus Christ."

[2]George S. Hendry, "Christology," *A Dictionary of Christian Theology*, ed. Alan Richardson (London: SCM, 1969), 60.

[3]Franz Delitzsch, *A System of Biblical Psychology* (Grand Rapids: Baker, reprint 1966), 386.

[4]Frederick L. Godet, *Commentary on the Gospel of John*, 3 vols. (Grand Rapids: Zondervan, reprint, 1969), 1:270.

[5]I. A. Dorner, *A System of Christian Doctrine*, 4 vols. (Edinburgh: T. & T. Clark, 1880–82), 3:340.

[6]Ibid., 3:328.

[7]Albrecht Ritschl, *The Christian Doctrine of Justification and Reconciliation* (Clifton, New Jersey: Reference Book Publishers, 1966), 451.

[8]Adolf Harnack, *What Is Christianity?* (London: Williams & Norgate, 1912), 208.

[9]Henry P. Van Dusen, "The Significance of Jesus Christ," in *Liberal Theology: An Appraisal,* ed. David E. Roberts and Henry P. Van Dusen (New York: Scribner, 1942), 217.

[10]Ibid., 221.

[11]John Hick, ed., *The Myth of God Incarnate* (Philadelphia: Westminster, 1977).

[12]Frances Young, "A Cloud of Witnesses," in *The Myth of God Incarnate,* 32.

[13]Hick, *The Myth of God Incarnate,* ix.

[14]Young, "A Cloud of Witnesses," 47, note 45.

[15]Russell F. Aldwinckle, *More Than a Man* (Grand Rapids: Eerdmans, 1976), 197.

[16]Søren Kierkegaard, *Kierkegaard's Concluding Unscientific Postscript* (Princeton: Princeton University Press, 1941), 512.

[17]Ibid., 188; cf. 187, 528.

[18]Emil Brunner, *The Mediator* (Philadelphia: Westminster, 1947), 158. Brunner's historical relativism led him to conclude that by the ordinary canons of historical research the existence of Jesus is not at all certain. So ibid., 187: "Even the bare fact of the existence of Christ as an historical person is not assured."

[19]Ibid., 286.

[20]Ibid., 325.

[21]Karl Barth, *Dogmatics in Outline* (New York: Philosophical Library, 1949), 96; cf. *CD,* II.2.7.

[22]Karl Barth, *CD,* IV.2.43.

[23]Barth, *CD,* II.1.397. Cf. ibid., IV.1.258: "He took our flesh, that nature of man as he comes from the fall"; ibid., I.2.151–53. Barth's argument is that unless Christ assumed fallen human nature he would not be in solidarity with the race he came to save.

[24]Barth, *CD,* IV.2.49. Cf. *CD,* III.1.54

[25]William N. Pittenger, *The Lure of Divine Love* (New York: Pilgrim, 1979), 11.

[26]John B. Cobb, Jr., *Christ in a Pluralistic Age* (Philadelphia: Westminster, 1975), 139.

[27]William N. Pittenger, "The Incarnation in Process Theology," *Review and Expositor* 71 (1974), 52–53.

[28]J. A. T. Robinson, *The Human Face of God* (London: SCM, 1973), 148.

[29]Ibid., 115.

[30]Ibid., 184.

[31]Pittenger, *The Lure of Divine Love,* 114–15.

[32]John Tully Carmody and Denise Lardner Carmody, *Contemporary Catholic Theology* (New York: Harper & Row, 1985), 45.

[33]Piet Schoonenberg, *The Christ* (New York: Herder & Herder, 1971), 88. He adds that the incarnation "is exclusively a matter of God's presence in this Man, who thereby is God's only-begotten Son." Ibid., 90.

[34]Ibid., 91.

[35]Hans Küng, *On Being a Christian* (Garden City, New York: Doubleday, 1976), 446; cf. idem, *The Incarnation of God* (New York: Crossroad, 1987), 442.

[36]Küng, *On Being a Christian,* 457.

[37]Richard P. McBrien, *Catholicism* (Minneapolis: Winston, 1981), 542.

[38]Augustine, *The Creed,* III.6: "A virgin conceived, a virgin brought forth, and after bringing forth remained a virgin." Cf. *Enchiridion,* X.34; *Sermon,* 192.1.

[39]Cited by McBrien, *Catholicism,* 875.

[40]Ibid., 892. McBrien adds that Mary "is an image, a model, a figure, or a type of the Church and Christian existence." Ibid., 896.

[41]Ignatius, *To the Magnesians,* 8.1.

[42]Ibid., 11.1. Cf. *To the Trallians,* 9: "Jesus Christ the Son of God, who was descended from David, . . . was truly begotten of God and of the Virgin, but not after the same manner."

[43]Justin Martyr, *Dialogue With Trypho,* 48.

[44]Justin Martyr, *Apology,* II.13.

[45]Justin Martyr, *Dialogue With Trypho,* 100. For Justin, the virgin birth is an inviolable datum. Thus he states that "the Word, who is the first-born of God, was produced without sexual union." *Apology,* I.21. Cf. *Dialogue With Trypho,* 84.

[46]Athanasius, *Four Discourses Against the Arians,* II.70.

[47]Ibid., III.30.

[48]Athanasius, *On the Incarnation of the Word,* 54.

[49]Augustine, *Letters,* 137.40.

[50]Augustine, *Enchiridion,* 33. Cf. *Sermon,* 192.1: "He who was God became Man in his effort to make godlike those who were men; without relinquishing what He was, He desired to become what He had made." Cf. *The Creed,* III.6: "The only Son of God . . . , so great a God equal to the Father, was born of the Holy

Spirit and the Virgin Mary that He might heal the proud."

[51]Augustine, *The Christian Combat*, XXII.24.

[52]Anselm, *Cur Deus Homo*, II.7.

[53]John Calvin, *Institutes of the Christian Religion*, II.12.1.

[54]Ibid., II.12.2.

[55]Benjamin B. Warfield, *The Person and Work of Christ* (Philadelphia: Presbyterian & Reformed, 1970), 6–7; cf. ibid, 17: "He came into the world to die."

[56]Benjamin B. Warfield, *Biblical and Theological Studies* (Philadelphia: Presbyterian & Reformed, 1968), 167; cf. ibid., 166: "The Redemptive work of the Son of God depends upon his supernatural birth."

[57]J. Gresham Machen, *The Virgin Birth of Christ* (New York: Harper & Brothers, 1930), 397. The following quotation confirms Machen's insistence that the Virgin Birth is an integral part of the Christian world-and-life view: "If Christ really rose from the dead, if He really was at all the kind of person that He is represented in the New Testament as being, then there is every reason to think that He was conceived by the Holy Ghost and born of the virgin Mary." Ibid., 268.

[58]James Orr, *The Christian View of God and the World as Centering on the Incarnation* (Grand Rapids: Eerdmans, 1948).

[59]Millard J. Erickson, *Christian Theology*, 3 vols. (Grand Rapids: Baker, 1983–1985), 2:661–81, 739–58.

[60]H. L. Ellison and D. F. Payne, "Genesis," *NLBC*, 138.

[61]Norman Hillyer, "1 and 2 Corinthians," *NBCRev*, 1064; cf. Paul W. Marsh, "The First Letter to the Corinthians," *NLBC*, 1440: "Paul's usage goes beyond a mere typological reference—and is a clear statement of the preexistence of Christ."

[62]Merrill F. Unger, *Unger's Commentary on the Old Testament*, 2 vols. (Chicago: Moody, 1981), 2:1863. J. Barton Payne agrees that the two phrases attest Messiah's eternal preexistence: *The Theology of the Older Testament* (Grand Rapids: Zondervan, 1962), 263.

[63]Edward J. Young, "Daniel," *NBCRev*, 692. Cf. idem, *A Commentary on Daniel* (London: Banner of Truth, 1972), 94. Also agreeing with this interpretation is Unger, *Unger's Commentary on the Old Testament*, 2:1624, and Ronald S. Wallace, *The Lord Is King: The Message of Daniel* (Downers Grove: InterVarsity, 1979), 68.

[64]Derek Kidner, "Isaiah," *NBCRev*, 596.

[65]Alan M. MacRae, "*'almāh*," *TWOT*, 2:672. According to Unger, *Commentary on the Old Testament*, 2:1161, *'almāh* "denotes a virgin or young unmarried woman of good repute." So also Kidner, "Isaiah," *NBCRev*, 596.

[66]James Orr, *The Virgin Birth of Christ* (New York: Scribner, 1907), 135. Cf. Unger, *Commentary on the Old Testament*, 2:1162: "The prophet was assuring the nation that though the dynasty of David was being imperiled by foreign powers and debased by rulers such as Ahaz, it would nevertheless not be blotted out, but through the Davidic line the Lord would send a virgin-born Savior, who would save Israel and the nations and establish the promised kingdom over Israel."

[67]Alfred Plummer, *An Exegetical Commentary on the Gospel According to St. Matthew* (Grand Rapids: Baker, reprint 1982), 168.

[68]I. Howard Marshall, *Commentary on Luke*. *NIGCT* (Grand Rapids: Eerdmans, 1983), 64.

[69]R. E. Nixon, "Matthew," *NBCRev*, 818.

[70]The genealogies recorded in Matthew 1:2–16 and Luke 3:23–38 differ in a number of respects. Luke's register is the longer of the two, and it proceeds from Joseph through David and Abraham back to Adam. Matthew's, on the other hand, begins with Abraham and moves through David to Joseph and Jesus. Between David and Jesus the two lists present a different set of names for Shealtiel and Zerubbabel. Of the several hypotheses advanced to account for these differences, the following contains the fewest difficulties. In order to present Jesus as the legitimate Davidic Messiah and heir of the promises given to Abraham (Matt. 1:1), Matthew traces Jesus' legal descent from David to Joseph by citing the person who occupied the throne of David at any given time. Luke, whose primary concern was to uphold Jesus' solidarity with and relevance to all humankind, traces Jesus' natural descent through the Davidic branch to which Joseph belonged back to Adam, the first man. "Luke provides a pedigree of actual descent, while Matthew gives the throne-succession. Matthew's whole attempt was to show, in the face of current calumnies, that the Messiah's genealogy was divinely ordered and legally correct." David Hill, *The Gospel of Matthew*, *NCBC* (Grand Rapids: Eerdmans, 1981), 74. See also I. Howard Marshall, *Commentary on Luke*, 157–61; F. F. Bruce, "Genealogy of Jesus Christ," *NBD*, 410–11.

[71]J. B. Lightfoot, *St. Paul's Epistles to the Colossians and to Philemon* (London: Macmillan, 1890), 144–45.

[72]Ibid., 147.

[73]J. A. Bengel, *Gnomon of the New Testament,* 5 vols. (Edinburgh: T. & T. Clark, 1863), 3:98.

[74]Donald Guthrie, *Galatians. NCBC* (Grand Rapids: Eerdmans, 1981), 113–14, comments as follows: "The form of the verb [*exapesteilen*] . . . implies a sending out from a previous state, and must in the case imply the preexistence of the Son."

[75]G. Braumann, *"morphē," NIDNTT,* 1:706. Augustine, Lightfoot, Vincent, Gifford, Foulkes, and other authorities observe that the participle suggests a time-frame that is both past and present, i.e., "he both was and is God."

[76]Warfield, *The Person and Work of Christ,* 41.

[77]Cf. the NEB translation of *plērōma* in Colossians 1:19: "the complete being of God." J. Schneider, "God," *NIDNTT,* 2:83 defines the term as "the fullness of the being of God and Christ." J. B. Lightfoot, *Colossians and Philemon,* 225, 328, and C. F. D. Moule, *The Epistles of Paul the Apostle to the Colossians and to Philemon* (Cambridge, Cambridge University Press, 1958), 166, interpret *plērōma* as the totality of the divine powers and attributes.

[78]Machen, *Virgin Birth of Christ,* 363.

[79]Brooke Foss Westcott, *The Gospel According to St. John,* 2 vols. in 1 (Grand Rapids: Baker, reprint 1980), 1:4.

[80]Alfred Plummer, *The Gospel According to St. John* (Grand Rapids: Baker, reprint 1981), 71.

[81]See *Integrative Theology* 1:148–54; Craig Blomberg, *The Historical Reliability of the Gospels* (Downers Grove: InterVarsity, 1987), 1–268; R. T. France, *The Evidence for Jesus* (Downers Grove: InterVarsity, 1986); Stephen Neill, *What We Know About Jesus* (Grand Rapids: Eerdmans, 1972); Orr, *Virgin Birth of Christ,* 30–90.

[82]J. V. L. Casserley, "Virgin Birth," in *Handbook of Theology,* ed. Marvin Halverson and Arthur Cohen, (New York: World, 1958), 370.

[83]Orr, *Virgin Birth of Christ,* 227.

[84]Machen, *Virgin Birth of Christ,* 382.

[85]Bernard Ramm, *An Evangelical Christology: Ecumenic and Historic* (Nashville: Nelson, 1985), 70.

[86]B. B. Warfield, *The Lord of Glory* (Grand Rapids: Zondervan, n.d.), 142.

[87]G. F. Hawthorne, "Joseph the Carpenter, History of," *ZPEB,* 3:696.

[88]Paul Jewett, "Can We Learn From Mariology?" *The Christian Century* (August 9, 1967), 1020.

[89]Thomas Boslooper, *The Virgin Birth* (Philadelphia: Westminster, 1962), 50.

[90]Ibid., 80.

[91]Wolfhart Pannenberg, *Jesus—God and Man,* trans. Lewis L. Wilkins and Duane A. Priebe, (Philadelphia: Westminster, 1968), 153.

[92]Ibid., 155.

[93]E. W. Hengstenberg, *Christology of the Old Testament* (Grand Rapids: Kregel, reprint 1970), 8.

[94]See Edward E. Hindson, *Isaiah's Immanuel* (Phillipsburg, N.J.: Presbyterian and Reformed, 1978), esp. 64–80 on "Early Interpretation of Isaiah 7:14." See also J. Skinner, *The Book of Isaiah* (Cambridge University Press, 1900), 1

[95]Hengstenberg, *Christology,* 8.

[96]For a full discussion of this hypotheses and the biblical data see Geerhardus Vos, *The Self-Disclosure of Jesus* (Grand Rapids: Eerdmans, 1954).

[97]A. H. Strong, *Systematic Theology* (Philadelphia: Judson, 1907), 703.

[98]Addison H. Leitch, *Interpreting Basic Theology,* (Great Neck, N.Y.: Channel, 1961), 81–82.

[99]For discussions of the Greek philosophers see Frederick Copleston, *A History of Philosophy: Greece and Rome* (Westminster, Md.: Newman, 1953).

[100]J. Oliver Buswell, Jr., "The Place of Paradox in Our Christian Testimony," *Journal of the American Scientific Affiliation* 17.1 (March 1965): 88–96.

[101]See Gordon R. Lewis, *Testing Christianity's Truth Claims* (Chicago: Moody, 1976), 176–81.

[102]F. F. Bruce, "Myth," *NIDNTT,* 2:646.

[103]Ibid.; compare F. F. Bruce, "Myth and History," in *History, Criticism and Faith,* ed. Colin Brown (Downers Grove: InterVarsity, 1976), 77–100.

[104]Clark Pinnock, "Demythologizing Christmas: Bultmann Had It Backwards," *Christianity Today* (Dec. 11, 1981), 74.

[105]Charles C. Anderson, *The Historical Jesus: A Continuing Quest,* (Grand Rapids: Eerdmans, 1972), 198.

[106]P. E. Hughes, "Myth," *EDT,* 747.

[107]Ibid.

[108]Ibid., 749.

[109]D. M. Baillie, *God Was in Christ* (New York: Scribner, 1948), 66–67.

[110]John Knox, *Jesus, Lord and Christ* (New York: Harper and Brothers, 1958), 225.

[111]Arthur W. Klem, "D. M. Baillie on the Person of Christ," *JETS* 7.2 (Spring 1964): 45–52.

[112]Vishal Mangalwadi, *The World of Gurus* (New Delhi, India: Nivedit Good Books, revised 1987), 251; see also Stephen Neill, *The Supremacy of Jesus* (Downers Grove: Inter-Varsity, 1984).

[113]Swami Bhaktipada, *Christ and Krishna* (Moundsville, W.V.: Bhaktipada Books, 1985), 4.

[114]A. C. Bhaktivedanta Swami Prabhupada, "The Birth of Lord Krishna," *Back to Godhead* (no. 64), 4.

[115]H. B. Acton, "Hegel, Georg Wilhelm Friedrich" *EP,* 3:436, 443.

[116]Dale Moody, *The Word of Truth* (Grand Rapids: Eerdmans, 1981), 424–26.

[117]John B. Cobb, Jr., *Christ in a Pluralistic Age,* 65, 138.

[118]Ibid., 142.

[119]Referred to by Bruce A. Demarest, *Who Is Jesus?* in *The Victor Know and Believe Series,* ed. Bruce L. Shelley (Wheaton: Victor, 1983), 47–48.

[120]Oscar Cullmann, *Christ and Time,* trans. Floyd V. Filson (Philadelphia: Westminster, 1950); 25, 65. See also D. Bruce Lockerbie, *The Cosmic Center: The Supremacy of Christ in a Secular Wasteland* (Portland, Ore.: Multnomah, 1986).

[121]John Tiller, "Advent," in *The New International Dictionary of the Christian Church,* ed. J. D. Douglas (Grand Rapids: Zondervan, 1974), 14.

[122]Athanasius, *The Incarnation of the Word of God* (New York: Macmillan, 1946), 1–45.

[123]W. H. Griffith Thomas, *Christianity Is Christ* (Grand Rapids: Zondervan, n.d.).

[124]Robert E. Webber, *The Secular Saint* (Grand Rapids: Zondervan, 1979), 195.

[125]Cited by William E. Pannell, *My Friend, the Enemy* (Waco: Word, 1968), 33–34.

[126]Pannell, *My Friend,* 120.

Chapter 6

[1]G. C. Berkouwer, *The Person of Christ* (Grand Rapids: Eerdmans, 1954), 14.

[2]So Justin Martyr writes that the Docetists believe that "since he [Christ] was the Son of God, he did not feel what was done and inflicted on him." *Dialogue With Trypho,* 103. Cf. Ignatius, *To the Trallians,* 9–10; *To the Smyrnaeans,* 2; Hippolytus, *Refutations of Heresies,* VIII.1–3; X.12.

[3]Tertullian, *Against Marcion,* III.8.

[4]Rudolf Bultmann, *Jesus and the Word* (New York: Scribner, 1962), 8. Charles C. Anderson, *The Historical Jesus: A Continuing Quest* (Grand Rapids: Eerdmans, 1972), 56, comments: "It is not true that Bultmann denied that Jesus lived, but in his denial of nearly all the history of that life as contained in the Gospels, he has run the risk of doing so in effect."

[5]"The only final condition for sharing in authentic life that the New Testament lays down is a condition that can be formulated in complete abstraction from the event of Jesus of Nazareth and all that it specifically imparts." Schubert Ogden, *Christ Without Myth* (New York: Harper & Row, 1961), 143. For the full discussion of Ogden's elimination of Jesus as necessary for salvation, see ibid., 138–64.

[6]Tertullian, *On the Flesh of Christ,* 14.

[7]Irenaeus, *Against Heresies,* I.26.1-2; V.1.3; Hippolytus, *Refutation of Heresies,* VII.2.2; Tertullian, *On the Flesh of Christ,* 14.

[8]*The Racovian Catechism*, par. 100; cf. *A Dictionary of Christ and the Gospels,* ed. James Hastings (New York: Charles Scribner's Sons, 1906–08), 2:867: "The doctrine of the God-man . . . held a truth for which Socinianism found no expression."

[9]John Orr, *English Deism: Its Roots and Fruits* (Grand Rapids: Eerdmans, 1934), 139–40.

[10]Friedrich D. E. Schleiermacher, *The Christian Faith* (Philadelphia: Fortress, reprint 1928), 387.

[11]Heinrich E. G. Paulus, quoted by Albert Schweitzer in *The Quest of the Historical Jesus* (New York: Macmillan, 1948), 51.

[12]Schweitzer, *Quest of the Historical Jesus,* 370–71.

[13]Joachim Jeremias, *New Testament Theology* (Scribner, 1971), 85; cf. ibid., 84–85: "In Matt. 5:17, Jesus is claiming to be the *eschatological messenger of God,* the promised prophet like Moses (Deut. 18:15, 18), who

brings the final revelation and therefore demands absolute obedience."

[14]See Harold O. J. Brown, *Heresies* (Garden City, N.Y.: Doubleday, 1984), 174–76.

[15]Theodore of Mopsuestia, *Catechetical Homilies,* V.19. Against Apollinarius, Theodore argued that the incarnate Word did not literally *become* flesh: "But when we read that 'he became' (John 1:14), that must not be taken literally, for he was not transmuted into flesh." *On the Incarnation,* 9.

[16]See, for example, Brown, *Heresies,* 172–75, 180, 192.

[17]Martin Luther, *WA,* 26:320; cited in *What Luther Says,* ed. Edward M. Plass (St. Louis: Concordia, 1986), 170.

[18]Martin Luther, *LW,* 45:352, 492–94.

[19]Luther, *LW,* 15:151; cf. ibid., 22:494: "The human nature in Christ shares the glory of all the properties which otherwise pertain to God."

[20]Brown, *Heresies,* 321; H. E. W. Turner, *"Communicatio Idiomatum," Dictionary of Christian Theology* (Philadelphia: Westminster, 1983), 113. For a survey of the *communicatio idiomatum* in post-Reformation Lutheran theology, see Heinrich Schmid, *The Doctrinal Theology of the Evangelical Lutheran Church* (Minneapolis: Augsburg, 1961), 309–47. See also The Formula of Concord, "Epitome," art. VIII and "Solid Declaration," art. VIII.

[21]Ignatius, *Ephesians,* 7; cf. *Trallians,* 10: "God the Word was truly born of the Virgin, having clothed Himself with a body of like passions with our own."

[22]Irenaeus, *Against Heresies,* III.18.7; cf. ibid., III.19.1.

[23]Tertullian, *Against Praxeus,* XXVII.

[24]Augustine, *On the Gospel of John,* 27.4; cf. *Enchiridion,* 35; *Letters,* 137.3; *Selected Sermons,* 7.

[25]Augustine, *Letters,* 137.2; cf. *City of God,* 11.2.

[26]Augustine, *Enchiridion,* 10.34; cf. *Expositions on the Book of Psalms,* 59.2; *City of God,* 13.23. The sinlessness of Jesus Christ is set forth in the following writings: *On Original Sin,* 33; *On Man's Perfection in Righteousness,* 21; *City of God,* 9.17.

[27]Augustine, *On the Trinity,* 1.7.

[28]For an evangelical defense of the Chalcedonian Definition against modern critical objections see Gerald E. Bray, "Can We Dispense With Chalcedon?" *Themelios* 3.2 (Jan. 1978), 2–9.

[29]John Calvin, *Institutes of the Christian Religion,* I.12.1

[30]Ibid., II.12.2.

[31]Ibid., II.13.4.

[32]Ibid., I.12.3.

[33]John Calvin, *CR,* 46:110; cf. *Institutes,* II.14.5: "the Word begotten by the Father before all ages took human nature in a hypostatic union."

[34]Calvin, *Institutes,* II.14.1; cf. ibid.: "He who was the Son of God became the Son of man—not by confusion of substance, but by unity of person."

[35]Ibid., II.13.4; cf. ibid., IV.17.30: "Since the whole Christ is everywhere, our Mediator is ever present with his own people, and in the Supper reveals himself in a special way, yet in such a way that the whole Christ is present, but not in his wholeness."

[36]Augustus H. Strong, *Systematic Theology* (Valley Forge, Pa.: Judson, 1907), 679.

[37]Ibid., 695.

[38]Ibid., 698.

[39]G. C. Berkouwer, *The Person of Christ* (Grand Rapids: Eerdmans, 1954).

[40]John F. Walvoord, *Jesus Christ Our Lord* (Chicago: Moody, 1969).

[41]Millard J. Erickson, *Christian Theology,* 3 vols. (Grand Rapids: Baker, 1983–1985), 2:683–738.

[42]Norval Geldenhuys, *The Gospel of Luke, NICNT* (Grand Rapids: Eerdmans, 1983), 122; cf. Francis J. Hall, *Theological Outlines* (London: SPCK, 1934), 183: "He never grew from moral deficiency to virtue, but was at each stage of his development what He ought to be, exhibiting successively, . . . the highest perfections of a child, of a youth, and of full-grown manhood."

[43]H. Bietenhard, "Beginning," *NIDNTT,* 1:168 comments that the meaning here is "that Jesus brings men to life, and also that Jesus Christ is the author of life." Classical usage supports the meaning, "first cause," or "source" for *archēgos* in Acts 3:15. See H. G. Liddell and R. Scott, *A Greek-English Lexicon* (Oxford: Clarendon, 1940), 252.

[44]William Neil, *The Acts of the Apostles. NCBC* (Grand Rapids: Eerdmans, 1973), 214–15.

[45]F. F. Bruce observes in relation to Galatians 4:4 that "Paul's wording is applicable to anyone of women born." *Commentary on Galatians, NIGTC* (Grand Rapids: Eerdmans, 1982), 195.

[46]William Barclay, *The Letters to the Galatians and Ephesians, The Daily Study Bible* (Philadelphia: Westminster, 1958), 171.

[47]Fritz Rienecker and Cleon J. Rogers, Jr., *LKGNT,* 568; cf. H. Bietenhard, "Beginning," *NIDNTT,* 1:166.

[48]C. E. B. Cranfield, *Romans. ICC,* 2 vols. (London: T. & T. Clark, 1975–79), 2:468–69 insists that the evidence overwhelmingly favors interpreting the latter part of Romans 9:5 in terms of Christ. He prefers the translation " . . . Christ, who is over all, God blessed forever, Amen." See also the discussion in Lewis and Demarest, *Integrative Theology* (Grand Rapids: Zondervan, 1987), 1:265.

[49]So F. F. Bruce, *Romans. TNTC* (London: Tyndale, 1963), 72: "He who during his earthly ministry was the Son of God in weakness and lowliness became by the resurrection the Son of God in power." So also Cranfield, *Romans,* 1:60–64.

[50]J. Behm, *"morphē," TDNTAbr,* 608.

[51]"The *homoiōma* denotes likeness in appearance but distinction in essence . . . . The term *homoiōma* is clearly an attempt to overcome the difficulty of having to say that the Christ in whom human sin is condemned is not himself a sinner . . . Christ is not just a heavenly being with an external human form; he is fully and truly human, but not a sinner." J. Schneider, *"homoiōma," TDNTAbr,* 686. We take issue with Cranfield, who claims that *homoiōma* in Romans 8:3 and Philippians 2:7 extends to Christ's sharing of our sinful nature. Cranfield writes that we "understand Paul's thought to be that the Son of God assumed the selfsame fallen human nature that is ours, but that in this case the fallen human nature was never the whole of him—He never ceased to be the eternal Son of God." *Romans,* 1:381–82.

[52]Schneider, *"schēma," TDNT,* 7:954.

[53]F. F. Bruce, *The Gospel of John* (Grand Rapids: Eerdmans, 1983), 359.

[54]James A. Brooks and Carlton L. Winbery, *Syntax of New Testament Greek* (Washington, D.C.: University Press of America, 1979), 91.

[55]A. C. Thistelton, "Flesh," *NIDNTT,* 1:678–79.

[56]Brooke Foss Westcott, *The Gospel According to St. John,* 2 vols. in 1 (Grand Rapids: Baker, reprint 1980), 1:19.

[57]See Lewis and Demarest, *Integrative Theology,* 1:268 for an exegesis of this text in support of Jesus' deity.

[58]Rienecker and Rogers, *LKGNT,* 784.

[59]Ibid., 670.

[60]Cf. Brooke Foss Westcott, *The Epistle to the Hebrews* (Grand Rapids: Eerdmans, reprint 1974), 128: "The Lord's manhood was (negatively) sinless and (positively) perfect, that is perfect relatively at every stage; and therefore He truly advanced by 'learning' (Luke 2:40, 52), while the powers of His human nature grew step by step in a perfect union with the divine in His one Person."

[61]R. Schippers, "Goal," *NIDNTT,* 2:59.

[62]Gerald F. Hawthorne, "The Letter to the Hebrews," *NLBC,* 1985.

[63]F. F. Bruce, *The Epistle to the Hebrews* (Grand Rapids: Eerdmans, 1964), 43.

[64]Ibid., 4.

[65]Donald Guthrie, *New Testament Theology* (Downers Grove: InterVarsity, 1981), 309–10.

[66]R. S. Wallace, "Christology," *EDT,* 223.

[67]For further insight into Christ's unique sonship see the discussion of the eternal generation of the Son in *Integrative Theology,* 1:275–79.

[68]Guthrie, *New Testament Theology,* 281.

[69]Gary Habermas, *Ancient Evidence for the Life of Jesus* (Nashville: Thomas Nelson, 1984), 87–115, 152–63. See also R. T. France, *The Evidence for Jesus* (Downers Grove: InterVarsity, 1986) and F. F. Bruce, *Jesus and Christian Origins Outside the New Testament* (Grand Rapids: Eerdmans, 1974).

[70]Ronald H. Nash, *Christianity and the Hellenistic World* (Grand Rapids: Zondervan, 1984).

[71]John Stott, *The Authentic Jesus,* (Downers Grove: InterVarsity, 1985), 92.

[72]Reinhold Niebuhr, *The Nature and Destiny of Man,* 2 vols. (New York: Scribner, 1951), 2:73–74; Karl Barth also holds that the flesh Christ assumed was fallen Adamic nature, humanness in a state of sin, but that Christ did not sin, *CD,* IV.2.43.

[73]John Knox, *The Humanity and Divinity of Christ* (Cambridge: Cambridge University Press, 1967), 51.

[74]Karl Barth, *CD,* IV.1.165; idem, *The Epistle to the Romans* (London: Oxford University, 1933), 278–82.

[75]Ernst Käsemann, *Commentary on Romans* (Grand Rapids: Eerdmans, 1980), 217.

[76]I. Howard Marshall, *Luke: Historian and Theologian,* (Grand Rapids: Zondervan, 1970), 52.

[77]Hugh Ross Mackintosh, *The Doctrine of the Person of Christ* (New York: Scribner, 1912), 403.

[78]Strong, *Systematic Theology*, 694.

[79]Francis Peiper, *Christian Dogmatics* (Saint Louis, MO: Concordia, 1951), 239.

[80]Søren Kierkegaard, *Concluding Unscientific Postscript*, trans. David F. Swenson and Walter Lowrie, (Princeton: Princeton University Press, 1941), 195.

[81]Ibid., 194.

[82]J. Loewenberg, ed., *Hegel, Selections* (New York: Scribner, 1929), xii.

[83]J. Oliver Buswell, Jr., "The Place of Paradox in our Christian Testimony," *Journal of the American Scientific Affiliation*, 17.1 (March 1965), 92.

[84]Cited in Henry L. Mansel, *The Limits of Religious Thought* (Boston: Gould and Lincoln, 1860), 319.

[85]John Hick, "Jesus and the World Religions," in *The Myth of God Incarnate*, ed. John Hick (Philadelphia: Westminster, 1977), 178.

[86]Niebuhr, *The Nature and Destiny of Man*, 2:61.

[87]J. I. Packer, *Evangelism and the Sovereignty of God* (Downers Grove: InterVarsity, 1961), 18.

[88]Alfred Lande, lecture: "Why Do Quantum Theorists Ignore Quantum Theory?" Denver University, March 2, 1966, reported in *The Denver Post* (March 3, 1966), 27.

[89]Alfred Lande, *New Foundations of Quantum Mechanics* (Cambridge: Cambridge University Press, 1965), 109–11.

[90]Ibid.

[91]G. K. Chesterton, *Orthodoxy* (Garden City: Doubleday, 1959), 11.

[92]A. M. Hunter, *Jesus, Lord and Savior* (Grand Rapids: Eerdmans, 1976), 115.

[93]Ibid., 117.

[94]Ibid.

[95]Ibid., 118.

[96]Ibid., 167.

[97]Leonard Hodgson, *Jesus, Word and Presence: An Essay in Christology* (Philadelphia: Fortress, 1971), 136.

[98]Ibid., 137.

[99]Ibid., 138.

[100]Ibid.

[101]Ibid.

[102]Ibid., 139.

[103]Ibid., 166.

[104]Ibid., 147.

[105]Ibid., 146.

[106]Michael Goulder, "Jesus, The Man of Universal Destiny," in *The Myth of God Incarnate*, 62.

[107]Bray, "Can We Dispense With Chalcedon?" 9.

[108]Ibid.

[109]Don Cupitt, "The Christ of Christendom," in *The Myth of God Incarnate*, 145.

[110]Ibid.

[111]Levi H. Dowling, *The Aquarian Gospel of Jesus the Christ* (Santa Monica: DeVorss, 1907, reprint 1972), 56-97.

[112]Ibid., 15.

[113]Ibid., 16–17.

[114]Ibid., 13, 265.

[115]Ibid., 13. For an assessment of Hindu gurus in comparison and contrast with Jesus Christ see Vishal Mangalwadi, *The World of the Gurus* (New Delhi: Nivedit Good Books, 1987).

[116]Dowling, *Aquarian Gospel*, 265.

[117]Ibid., 13.

[118]For an evangelical appraisal of recent developments in occultism see Gary North, *Unholy Spirits: Occultism and New Age Humanism* (Fort Worth: Dominion, 1986). For evaluation of another spirit message alleged to be from Jesus, see Gordon R. Lewis, *Confronting the Cults* (Nutley, N.J.: Presbyterian and Reformed, 1966), 175–79, 181–83.

[119]Geoffrey Wainwright, *Doxology: The Praise of God in Worship, Doctrine and Life* (New York: Oxford University Press, 1980), 57.

[120]Helmut Thielicke, *Between God and Satan* (Grand Rapids: Eerdmans, 1958), 75–76.

[121]Ibid., 76.

[122]Anthony Hoekema, *The Four Major Cults* (Grand Rapids: Eerdmans, 1963), 382–85.

[123]On the significance of Christ as prophet see Bruce A. Demarest, *Who Is Jesus?* (Wheaton: Victor, 1983), 70.

[124]See Michael Griffiths, *The Example of Jesus* (Downers Grove: InterVarsity, 1985), 75.

[125]For amplification of each of these aspects of Christ's example see Michael Griffiths, ibid., 136–85.

Chapter 7

[1]On the Protestant side Dale Moody devotes only half a dozen pages to Christ's death in his systematic theology, *The Word of Truth* (Grand Rapids: Eerdmans, 1981). On the Catholic side the Notre Dame theologian Richard P. McBrien devotes fewer than 10 pages out of 1,250 to the cross in *Catholicism,* 2 vols. in 1 (Minneapolis: Winston, 1981).

[2]Benjamin B. Warfield, *The Person and Work of Christ* (Philadelphia: Presbyterian and Reformed, 1970), 425.

[3]Emil Brunner, *The Mediator* (Philadelphia: Westminster, 1947), 436.

[4]Irenaeus, *Against Heresies,* V.1.1; cf. *Proof of the Apostolic Preaching,* 31: "Because death ruled in the body, it was necessary through the body that it should be done away with and man set free from its oppression."

[5]Origen, *Commentary on Matthew,* XVI.8; cf. *Commentary on Romans,* II.13; *Exodus Homily,* VI.9; *Against Celsus,* I.31; VII.17. Gregory of Nyssa proposed a similar view: "In order to secure that the ransom in our behalf might be easily accepted by him who required it, the Deity was hidden under the veil of our nature, that so, as with ravenous fish, the hook of the Deity might be gulped down along with the bait of flesh." *The Great Catechism,* 24.

[6]John of Damascus, *The Orthodox Faith,* III.27; cf. III.1.

[7]Gustaf Aulén, *Christus Victor* (London: SPCK, 1970), 4; cf. 55.

[8]Peter Abelard, *Sentences,* XXIII; cf. "Exposition of the Epistle to the Romans," *LCC,* 10:283–84.

[9]Faustus Socinus, *Praelectiones Theologia,* 591; cited by L. W. Grensted, *A Short History of the Doctrine of the Atonement* (Manchester: Manchester University Press, 1920), 287.

[10]Horace Bushnell, *God in Christ* (New York: AMS, reprint 1972), 216.

[11]Ibid., 192; cf. 212–13.

[12]Ibid., 247–48.

[13]L. Harold DeWolf, *A Theology of the Living Church* (New York: Harper & Row, 1953), 267; cf. idem, *The Case for Theology in Liberal Perspective* (Philadelphia: Westminster, 1959), 77–80.

[14]Anselm, *Cur Deus Homo,* I.23.

[15]Ibid., II.6; cf. II.7,18.

[16]J. I. Packer, "What Did the Cross Achieve?" *Tyndale Bulletin* 25 (1974): 4.

[17]Hugo Grotius, *A Defense of the Catholic Faith Concerning the Satisfaction of Christ Against Faustus Socinus,* trans. F. H. Foster (Andover: Draper, 1889), 100.

[18]John Miley, *Systematic Theology,* 2 vols. (New York: Hunt & Eaton, 1892–1894), 2:168.

[19]Ibid, 2:176; cf. ibid, 2:95: "The vicarious sufferings of Christ are a provisionary substitute for penalty, and not the actual punishment of sin."

[20]Ibid, 2:179. Miley expresses the outcome of the cross in other words in ibid., 2:181: "The cross is the highest revelation of all the truths which embody the best moral forces of the divine government."

[21]J. Kenneth Grider, "Governmental Theory of the Atonement," *BDT,* 240; cf. *A Contemporary Wesleyan Theology,* ed. Charles W. Carter, 2 vols. (Grand Rapids: Zondervan, Francis Asbury, 1983), 1:502–5.

[22]James Arminius, *The Works of James Arminius,* 3 vols. (Auburn and Buffalo: Derby, Miller & Orton, 1853), 1:316. Thomas Watson, the first important systematic theologian of Methodism wrote, "Christ died for all men, so as to make their salvation practicable." *Theological Institutes,* 2 vols. (New York: Lane & Scott, 1851), 2:303.

[23]Miley, *Systematic Theology,* 2:239; cf. H. Orton Wiley, *Christian Theology,* 3 vols. (Kansas City: Beacon Hill, 1952–1953), 2:296: "Arminianism, with its emphasis on moral freedom and prevenient grace, has always held to the universality of the atonement."

[24]Karl Barth, *CD,* II.2.123; IV.1.222, 230–35.

[25]Ibid., IV.2.46.

[26]Ibid., 1.296.

[27]Ibid., 2.294.

[28]Barth, *CD,* IV.1.486. Barth immediately adds, "His forgiveness repels chaos, and closes the gulf, and ensures that the will of God will be done on earth as it is in heaven. What, then, is the guilt of man, in the light of the fact that God encounters him in this way, as the One who pardons his sin?" Ibid.

[29]Barth, *CD,* IV.1.747; cf. *The Faith of the Church* (New York: Meridian Books, 1958), 91: "There no longer exists any object under the curse after what happened at Calvary. By taking over that curse Christ accomplished our acquittal." Cf. also *CD,* II.2.774; IV.1.294; *Dogmatics in Outline* (New York: Philosophical Library, 1949), 119–20.

[30]Hendrikus Berkhof, *Christian Faith,* trans. Sierd Woudstra (Grand Rapids: Eerdmans, 1979), 305. For the full discussion of Berkhof's

position see the section "Death and Reconciliation," ibid., 299–307.

[31]Ibid.

[32]Vincent Taylor, *Jesus and His Sacrifice* (New York: St. Martin's, 1965), 308; cf. ibid., 309: Christ's sacrifice is "the perfect expression of his perfect penitence for the sins of men."

[33]Clement of Rome, *Epistle to the Corinthians,* I.49.5; cf. ibid., I.7.4.

[34]Ignatius, *To the Smyrnaeans,* 2; cf. *To the Trallians,* 2.

[35]*Epistle to Diognetus,* X.2–5.

[36]Cyril of Jerusalem, *Lenten Lectures,* XIII.33; cf. ibid., XIII.18: "Jesus assumed the thorns to remove the condemnation."

[37]Athanasius, *Incarnation of the Word,* XX.2; cf. XX.5; *Discourse Against the Arians,* I.60.

[38]Augustine, *Reply to Faustus the Manichaean,* XIV.3; cf. *On the Trinity,* IV.12–14; *On The Gospel of John,* XLI.6.

[39]Augustine, *City of God,* X.20.

[40]Augustine, *City of God,* XIII.11.15; cf. *Faith, Hope and Love,* 33.

[41]Augustine, *City of God,* XVIII.49; cf. *On the Gospel of John,* XXV.16,18.

[42]Martin Luther, *LW,* 26:288.

[43]Aulén, *Christus Victor,* 101–22.

[44]John Calvin, *Institutes of the Christian Religion,* II.16.6; cf. ibid., II.16.2: "Christ took upon himself and suffered the punishment that . . . threatened all sinners"; cf. ibid., III.4.26.

[45]John Calvin, *Commentary on the Epistles of Paul to the Corinthians,* 2:242.

[46]Calvin, *Institutes,* II.17.3; cf. ibid., II.16.10: "Christ appeased God's wrath and satisfied his just judgment." Cf. ibid., II.17.4; III.4.26; *Commentaries on the Catholic Epistles,* 171–72.

[47]Calvin, *Institutes,* II.16.7; II.17.5; III.4.30.

[48]John Calvin, *Commentaries on the Epistles of Paul to the Philippians, Colossians and Thessalonians,* 159; cf. *Commentaries on the Catholic Epistles,* 240–41.

[49]Calvin, *Institutes,* II.17.2; cf. ibid., III.6.3; III.11.8.

[50]Calvin, *Institutes,* II.15.1–6. For an analysis of Calvin's development of the three offices, which would have a profound influence on later Protestant theology, see John Frederick Jansen, *Calvin's Doctrine of the Work of Christ* (London: James Clarke, 1956).

[51]Benjamin B. Warfield, "Atonement," *Studies in Theology* (New York: Oxford University Press, 1932), 278. Warfield observes that the doctrine of vicarious sacrifice has been upheld by the major branches of the Christian church—e.g., the Greek, Latin, Lutheran, and Reformed.

[52]Athanasius, *On the Incarnation of the Word,* IV.20; cf. *Against the Arians,* I.60: "Suffering in the flesh [the Logos] gave salvation to all."

[53]Cyril of Jerusalem, *Lenten Lectures,* XIII.4.

[54]Augustine, *Enchiridion,* 49; *Homilies on the First Epistle of John,* I.8; cf. *On Nature and Grace, 48.*

[55]R. T. Kendall, *Calvin and English Puritanism to 1649* (Oxford: Oxford University Press, 1979) argues that Calvin taught a universal atonement. Several recent studies maintain that Calvin held a tension between God's purpose for humankind as a whole and his purpose for the elect in particular. That is, Christ's atonement is universal in scope, but God gives saving faith only to the elect. So argue James B. Torrance, "The Incarnation and 'Limited Atonement,' " *Evangelical Quarterly* LV.2 (April 1983): 83–94; Tony Lane, "The Quest for the Historical Calvin," ibid., 95–113; M. Charles Bell, "Calvin and the Extent of the Atonement," ibid., 115–23 ; R. B. Knox, "John Calvin: An Elusive Churchman," *Scottish Journal of Theology,* 34 (1981): 147–56. The following comment from Lane is typical of the above: "Calvin was prepared to recognize *both* God's universal love for all mankind and his desire for all to repent *and* his purpose that some only should be saved. To the feeble human mind these are irreconcilable." 113.

[56]Calvin, *Institutes,* IV.14.7; cf. ibid., II.16.2, 13; II.17.2.

[57]Calvin, *Commentary on Galatians,* 157; cf. his comment on Romans 5:18: "Paul makes grace common to all men . . . because it is offered to all. Although Christ suffered for the sins of the whole world and is offered . . . without distinction to all men, yet not all receive him." *Commentary on Romans,* 211. See also Calvin's comments on Isaiah 53:5; John 3:16; Romans 10:16; Colossians 1:14.

[58]See, for example, Herman Bavinck, *Our Reasonable Faith* (Grand Rapids: Baker, reprint 1977), 361.

[59]C. H. Spurgeon, "General and Yet Particular," *The Metropolitan Tabernacle Pulpit,* 63 vols. (Pasadena, Texas: Pilgrim reprint 1969–1980), 10:233; cf. ibid., 230: "It has pleased

God to put the whole race under the mediatorial sway of Jesus, in order that he might give eternal life to those who were chosen out of the world."

[60]Charles M. Horne, *Salvation* (Chicago: Moody, 1971), 46.

[61]Robert P. Lightner, *The Death Christ Died* (Des Plaines, Ill.: Regular Baptist Press, 1967), 46–47, 55–56. See also by the same author, *Evangelical Theology* (Grand Rapids: Baker, 1986), 209–10. Cf. the comment by Walter A. Elwell, "Atonement, Extent of the," *EDT*, 99: "Paul had no trouble saying that God could be the Savior of all, in one sense, and of those who believe, in another sense (1 Tim. 4:10)."

[62]Donald G. Bloesch, *Essentials of Evangelical Theology*, 2 vols. (New York: Harper & Row, 1978–79), 1:164–68.

[63]John Owen, *The Works of John Owen*, ed. William Goold; 16 vols. (Edinburgh: Banner of Truth Trust, 1965–1968), 10:227.

[64]Ibid., 10:214.

[65]Roger R. Nicole, "The 'Five Points' and God's Sovereignty," in *Our Sovereign God*, ed. James M. Boice (Grand Rapids: Baker, 1977), 31–33; cf. Nicole, "Particular Redemption," in *Our Savior God*, ed. James M. Boice (Grand Rapids: Baker, 1980), 165–78.

[66]Clement of Alexandria, *Miscellanies*, VI.6.

[67]Thomas Aquinas, *ST*, III.1, q. 52, art. 1–8; esp. art. 5.

[68]Calvin, *Institutes*, II.16.10–11.

[69]See *The Heidelberg Catechism*, pt. II, q. 44; L. Berkhof, *Systematic Theology* (Grand Rapids: Eerdmans, 1941), 342–43; G. C. Berkouwer, *The Work of Christ* (Grand Rapids: Eerdmans, 1965), 169–80. But Dale Moody, *Word of Truth*, 387–88, accepts the possibility of a preaching mission of Christ in hades.

[70]A. A. Hodge, *The Atonement* (Grand Rapids: Eerdmans, reprint 1953).

[71]W. G. T. Shedd, *Dogmatic Theology*, 3 vols. (Grand Rapids: Zondervan, n.d.), 2:353–489.

[72]H. Dermot McDonald, *The Atonement of the Death of Christ* (Grand Rapids: Baker, 1985).

[73]Geoffrey W. Bromiley, "Atone; Atonement," *ISBERev*, 1:353.

[74]Hywell R. Jones, "Exodus," *NBCRev*, 117.

[75]R. Laird Harris, *"kāpar,"* *TWOT*, 1:452–53; cf. *BDB*, 820.

[76]G. Lloyd Carr, *"minḥāh,"* *TWOT*, 1:515.

[77]Gordon J. Wenham, *The Book of Leviticus. NICOT* (Grand Rapids: Eerdmans, 1979), 65.

[78]Derek Kidner, *Psalms 1–72. TOTC* (Downers Grove: InterVarsity, 1973), 106.

[79]A. M. Stibbs, "Hebrews," *NBCRev*, 1208.

[80]For convincing discussions that identify the servant of the Lord ultimately with the Messiah, see Walter C. Kaiser, *"'ebed,"* *TWOT*, 2:639–40; Jan Ridderbos, *Isaiah* (Grand Rapids: Zondervan, 1984), 366–73; and J. Barton Payne, *The Theology of the New Testament* (Grand Rapids: Zondervan, 1962), 254–57.

[81]Ridderbos, *Isaiah*, 484.

[82]R. D. Patterson, *"sābal,"* *TWOT*, 2:616.

[83]William B. Coker, *"pādāh,"* *TWOT*, 2:716.

[84]Murray J. Harris, "Prepositions and Theology in the Greek NT," *NIDNTT*, 3:1180; cf. F. Büchsel, *"lytron,"* *TDNT*, 4:342–49; Nigel Turner, *Syntax* (Edinburgh: T. & T. Clark, 1963), 258; vol. III of J. H. Moulton, *A Grammar of New Testament Greek*.

[85]Harris, *NIDNTT*, 3:1174, 1176.

[86]Harris, *NIDNTT*, 3:1196, indicates that *hyper* simultaneously implies both representation and substitution.

[87]H. Vorländer, "Forgiveness," *NIDNTT*, 1:701.

[88]William L. Lane, *Mark. NLCNT* (Grand Rapids: Eerdmans, 1974), 501.

[89]Fritz Rienecker and Cleon L. Rogers, Jr., *LKGNT*, 471.

[90]C. L. W. Grimm and J. H. Thayer, *A Greek-English Lexicon to the New Testament* (New York: American Book, 1889), 50.

[91]C. Brown, *"lytron,"* *NIDNTT*, 3:199; cf. Leslie Mitton, *Ephesians. NCBC* (Grand Rapids: Eerdmans, 1981), 52: "Its main significance is to suggest an entry into a new kind of freedom."

[92]H. Vorländer and C. Brown, "Reconciliation," *NIDNTT*, 3:166.

[93]C. E. B. Cranfield, *The Epistle to the Romans, ICC* 2 vols. (Edinburgh: T. & T. Clark, 1975–1979), 1:267. Millard J. Erickson, *Christian Theology*, 3 vols. (Grand Rapids: Baker, 1983–1985), 2:815, affirms that in reconciliation man turns to God, "but the process of reconciliation is primarily God's turning in favor toward man." Berkhof, *Systematic Theology*, 373, observes that the subjective component of the sinner's reconciliation to God, is secondary to the objective component of God

being propitiated by the vicarious death of Christ.

[94]Rienecker and Rogers, *LKGNT,* 527.

[95]H. Weigelt, "Clothe," *NIDNTT,* 1:315.

[96]"The Christ hymn (vv. 6–11) presents Jesus as the supreme example of the humble, self-sacrificing, self-denying, self-giving service that Paul had just been urging the Philippians to practice in their relations toward one another (vv. 1–4)." Gerald F. Hawthorne, *Philippians, WBC* (Waco: Word, 1983), 79.

[97]Cranfield, *Epistle to the Romans,* 1:202.

[98]Leon Morris, *The Apostolic Preaching of the Cross* (Grand Rapids: Eerdmans, 1965), 12, 18.

[99]For developments of this interpretation see Cranfield, *Romans,* 1:216–17; Morris, *Apostolic Preaching,* 184–202; George Eldon Ladd, *A Theology of the New Testament* (Grand Rapids: Eerdmans, 1974), 429–30; Donald Guthrie, *New Testament Theology* (Downers Grove: InterVarsity, 1981), 467–70; and C. Brown, "Reconciliation," *NIDNTT,* 3:151–60.

[100]F. F. Bruce, *Epistle to the Romans. TNTC* (London: Tyndale, 1963), 107.

[101]J. Gess, "Lamb, Sheep," *NIDNTT,* 2:411.

[102]Alfred Plummer, *The Epistles of St. John* (Grand Rapids: Baker, reprint 1980), 35.

[103]Leon Morris, "2 John," *NBCRev,* 1268. F. F. Bruce comments that "here John ascribes the widest scope to the saving purpose of God." *The Epistles of John* (Grand Rapids: Eerdmans, 1970), 111.

[104]Bruce, *Epistles of John,* 50.

[105]R. Tuente, "Lamb, Sheep," *NIDNTT,* 2:413; cf. H. Preisker and S. Schulz, "Probaton," *TDNT,* 6:689–92.

[106]Berkhof, *Systematic Theology,* 397; cf. George Smeaton, *The Doctrine of the Atonement as Taught by the Apostles* (Edinburgh: T. & T. Clark, 1870), 446–47.

[107]Rienecker and Rogers, *LKGNT,* 774. According to O. Bauernfeind, "*aselgeia,*" *TDNT,* 1:490, the word means "debauchery" or "licentiousness," particularly serious sexual excesses.

[108]Simon J. Kistemaker, *Exposition of the Epistles of Peter and the Epistle of Jude, New Testament Commentary* (Grand Rapids: Baker, 1987), 282.

[109]M. J. Harris, "Appendix," *NIDNTT,* 3:1196; B. F. Westcott, *The Epistle to the Hebrews* (Grand Rapids: Eerdmans, reprint 1974), 47. A. M. Stibbs thus translates *hyper pantos* as "for the benefit of all;" "Hebrews," *NBCRev,* 1197. Cf. Erickson, *Christian Theology,* 2:832, citing H. O. Wiley, who suggests that 2 Peter 2:1 teaches "that there is a distinction between those for whom Christ died and those who are finally saved."

[110]"Originally the word meant just 'the grave' and became specialized for 'hell.'" R. Laird Harris, "*šᵉ'ôl,*" *TWOT,* 2:892. Harris adds, "It may be that *šᵉ'ôl* is just a poetic synonym for *qeber.*" Ibid.

[111]J. A. Alexander, *The Gospel According to Matthew* (Grand Rapids: Baker, reprint 1980), 344.

[112]David Hill, *The Gospel of Matthew. NCBC* (London: Olifants, 1972), 356.

[113]So Turner, *Syntax,* 215; cf. Rienecker and Rogers, *LKGNT,* 531. Francis Foulkes, *Ephesians. TNTC* (London: Inter-Varsity, 1963), 116, adds that the phrase "may mean this earth, so low in comparison with his heavenly home."

[114]See the development by Wayne Grudem, "Christ Preaching Through Noah: 1 Peter 3:19–20 in the Light of Dominant Themes in Jewish Literature," *Trinity Journal,* N.S. 7.2 (Fall 1986); cf. Augustine, *Letter 164,* 15–17.

[115]"Covenant," *Nelson's Illustrated Bible Dictionary,* ed. F. F. Bruce et al. (Nashville: Thomas Nelson, 1986), 260.

[116]A. A. Hodge, *The Atonement,* 254.

[117]James Denney, *The Death of Christ* (London: The Tyndale Press, 1951), 131.

[118]John R. W. Stott, *The Cross of Christ* (Downers Grove: InterVarsity, 1986), 276.

[119]B. Gartner, "Suffer," *NIDNTT,* 3:721.

[120]Stott, *Cross of Christ,* 143.

[121]R. E. Davies, "Christ in Our Place—the Contribution of the Prepositions," *Tyndale Bulletin* 21 (1970): 90.

[122]Ibid.

[123]In the class of J. Oliver Buswell, Jr., as reported in his *Sin and Atonement* (Grand Rapids: Zondervan, 1937), 67.

[124]*The Denver Post* (Jan. 3, 1975), 10.

[125]Patricia Treece, *A Man for Others* (San Francisco: Harper & Row, 1982), vii.

[126]Stott, *Cross of Christ,* 203.

[127]A. A. Hodge, *Atonement,* 170.

[128]George Smeaton, *The Apostles' Doctrine of the Atonement* (Grand Rapids: Zondervan, 1957).

[129]See the historical study by Gustaf Aulen, *Christus Victor* (London: SPCK, 1970).

[130]Samuel J. Mikolaski, "The Atonement and Men Today," *Christianity Today* (March 13, 1961), 3.

[131]David Scaer, *What Do You Think of Jesus?* (St. Louis: Concordia, 1973), 37.

[132]Robert H. Culpepper, *Interpreting the Atonement* (Grand Rapids: Eerdmans, 1966), 133.

[133]W. C. Robinson, "Wrath," *EDT,* 1196.

[134]Roger Nicole, "Propitiation," in *Christian Faith and Modern Theology,* ed. Carl Henry (New York: Channel, 1964), 198.

[135]See Ajith Fernando, *A Universal Homecoming?* (Madras, India: Evangelical Literature Service, 1983), 146.

[136]Morris, *The Cross in the New Testament* (Grand Rapids: Eerdmans, 1965), 400.

[137]Stott, *Cross of Christ,* 202.

[138]See Horne, *Salvation,* 46.

[139]Morris, *Cross in the New Testament,* 385–86.

[140]A. E. Taylor, *The Faith of a Moralist* (London: Macmillan, 1951), 183.

[141]Immanuel Kant, *Praktische Vernuft,* 151, cited by W. G. T. Shedd, *The Doctrine of Endless Punishment* (New York: Scribner, 1886), 122–23.

[142]Warfield, *Person and Work of Christ,* 292.

[143]Buswell, *Sin and Atonement,* 80.

[144]Stott, *Cross of Christ,* 123. For a critical study of a moral government theory in Youth With a Mission (YWAM) see Alan W. Gomes, *Lead Us Not Into Deception: A Biblical Examination of Moral Government Theology,* 3rd ed. (La Mirada, Calif.; Alex Gomes, P.O. Box 1464, 1968).

[145]Wilbur Smith, *Great Sermons on the Death of Christ* (Natick, Mass.: Wilde, 1965), 7.

[146]As quoted in ibid., 8.

[147]R. K. Harrison, "Blood," *ZPEB,* 1:627.

[148]Ibid.

[149]For amplification see William Hordern, "The Essence of Christianity and the Cross of Christ" in Warfield, *Person and Work of Christ,* 1950, 477–530.

[150]Jürgen Moltmann, *The Crucified God* (New York: Harper & Row, 1974), 15.

[151]Ibid., 19.

[152]Ibid., 227.

[153]Ibid., 249.

[154]Ibid., 228.

[155]Ibid., 277.

[156]Ibid., 332.

[157]Ibid., 329–34.

[158]Ibid., 53.

[159]R. T. France, "Liberation in the New Testament," in *The Best in Theology,* ed. J. I. Packer (Carol Stream, Ill.: CTI, n.d.), 189–95.

[160]Ibid., 198.

[161]Richard J. Mouw, *Politics and the Biblical Drama* (Grand Rapids: Eerdmans, 1976), 73.

[162]Ibid., 111.

[163]Barth, *CD,* IV.1.285.

[164]Ibid., 295.

[165]Ibid., 306.

[166]Ibid., 148.

[167]Ibid., 747.

[168]Personal letter from Robert Gundry to Gordon Lewis, March 18, 1961. Used by permission.

[169]Karl Barth, *The Humanity of God* (Richmond: John Knox, 1960), 59.

[170]Charles R. Solomon, *Handbook to Happiness* (Wheaton: Tyndale, 1971).

[171]Charles R. Solomon, *Counseling With the Mind of Christ* (Old Tappan, N.J.: Revell, 1973), 29.

[172]John R. W. Stott, *Men Made New* (Grand Rapids: Baker, 1966), 36.

[173]D. M. Baillie, *God Was in Christ* (New York: Scribner, 1948), 198.

[174] J. A. T. Robinson, *Honest to God* (Philadelphia: Westminster, 1963), 78–83.

[175]Paul Van Buren, *The Secular Meaning of the Gospel* (New York: Macmillan, 1963), 151.

[176]Ibid., 154.

[177]J. Norman King, *The God of Forgiveness and Healing in the Theology of Karl Rahner* (Washington, D.C.: University Press of America, 1982), 90.

[178]On the existential relevance of the cross see Alister E. McGrath, *The Mystery of the Cross* (Grand Rapids: Zondervan, 1988), 79–190.

[179]Stott, *Cross of Christ,* 60.

[180]McGrath, *Mystery of the Cross,* 151.

[181]See Stott, *Cross of Christ,* 282–85.

[182]Moltmann, *The Crucified God,* 71.

[183]Morris, *Apostolic Preaching of the Cross,* 100.

[184]Ibid., 105.

[185]Stott, *Cross of Christ,* 291.

[186]McGrath, *Mystery of the Cross,* 167.

[187]Ibid., 168.

[188]Allan Boesak, *Walking on Thorns* (Grand Rapids: Eerdmans, 1984), 44.

[189]Ibid., 46–47.

[190]Erickson, *Christian Theology,* 2:762–63.

[191]G. C. Berkouwer, *The Work of Christ* (Grand Rapids: Eerdmans, 1965), 63.

[192]Denney, *Death of Christ,* 163.

[193]See the contributions of several authorities to "Building Faith: How a Child Learns to Love God," a supplement to *Christianity Today* (June 13, 1986), 3-I–16-I.

[194]Denney, *Death of Christ,* 157.

[195]Gordon R. Lewis, *Confronting the Cults* (Phillipsburg, N.J.: Presbyterian and Reformed, 1966), 3.

[196]Bernard Ramm, *The Pattern of Authority* (Grand Rapids: Eerdmans, 1957), 35–36.

[197]McGrath, *Mystery of the Cross,* 180.

[198]Ibid., 177.

[199]Ibid., 175.

Chapter 8

[1]Hans Küng, *On Being a Christian* (Garden City, N.Y.: Doubleday, 1976), 381.

[2]Thomas Woolston, *A Sixth Discourse on the Miracles of Our Saviour* (London: 1729), 1; cf. Woolston's *First Discourse on the Miracles of Our Saviour* (London: 1728), 57: the Gospel account of the resurrection "is such a complication of absurdities, incoherences, and contradictions."

[3]For the position of Celsus, see Origen, *Against Celsus,* II:56; cf. Justin Martyr, *Dialogue With Trypho,* 108.

[4]Friedrich Schleiermacher, *The Christian Faith* (Philadelphia: Fortress, reprint 1976), 418.

[5]J. Ernst Renan, *Vie de Jesus* (Paris: Michel L'evy, 1870), 434; cf.: "Mary alone loved enough to dispense with nature, and to have revived the phantom of the perfect Master. . . . The glory, then, of the Resurrection belongs to Mary Magdalene." Renan, *Les Apotres* (Paris: Michel L'evy, 1866), 12–13.

[6]Kirsopp Lake, *The Historical Evidence for the Resurrection of Jesus Christ* (London: Williams & Norgate, 1907), 253.

[7]Adolf Von Harnack, *What is Christianity?* (New York: Williams & Norgate, 1912), 164.

[8]Ibid., 165.

[9]Peter N. Hamilton, "Some Proposals for a Modern Christology," in *Process Philosophy and Christian Thought,* ed. Delwin Brown, Ralph E. James, and Gene Reeves (Indianapolis and New York: Bobbs-Merrill, 1971), 379–80.

[10]Robert B. Mellert, *What Is Process Theology?* (New York: Paulist, 1975), 85.

[11]Ibid., 86.

[12]David R. Griffin, *A Process Christology* (Philadelphia: Westminster, 1973), 12, writes: "Christian faith (as I understand it) is possible apart from belief in Jesus' resurrection in particular and life beyond bodily death in general."

[13]*Søren Kierkegaard's Journals and Papers,* 6 vols. (Bloomington, Indiana: Indiana University Press, 1967–78), 2:252–53.

[14]Karl Barth, *Epistle to the Romans* (London: Oxford University Press, 1933), 222.

[15]Karl Barth, *CD,* IV.1.333; cf. III.2.441–55; IV.1.336.

[16]Barth, *CD,* IV.4.1, 309; cf. ibid., 316: "In virtue of the justification which has come to them in his resurrection, they are no longer what they were but they are already what they are to be. They are no longer the enemies of God but his friends, his children."

[17]Barth, *CD,* IV.1.335; cf. III.2.452.

[18]Barth, *CD,* IV.1.336.

[19]Barth, *CD,* III.2.452.

[20]Karl Barth, *Credo* (New York: Scribner, 1962), 113; cf. *CD,* III.2.453.

[21]Emil Brunner, *The Mediator* (Philadelphia: Westminster, 1947), 563.

[22]Ibid., 583.

[23]Ibid., 159.

[24]Emil Brunner, *The Christian Doctrine of Creation and Redemption: Dogmatics, Vol. II* (London: Lutterworth, 1952), 372.

[25]Ibid., 374.

[26]Dietrich Bonhoeffer, *Christ the Center* (New York: Harper & Row, 1978), 112; cf. *True Patriotism* (London: Collins, 1973), 48: "It is impossible to demonstrate the resurrection by historical method."

[27]Rudolf Bultmann, "New Testament and Mythology," in *Kerygma and Myth,* ed. H. W. Bartsch (New York and Evanston: Harper & Row, 1961), 39; cf. *Theology of the New Testament,* 2 vols. (London: SCM, 1965), 1:295.

[28]Bultmann, "New Testament and Mythology," 42. Since Bultmann believes that the

resuscitation of a dead body from the grave is myth, he undoubtedly believes that the body of Jesus decomposed in the tomb. Ibid., 39.

[29]Ibid., 41; cf. idem, "The Primitive Christian Kerygma and the Historical Jesus, in *The Historical Jesus and the Kerygmatic Christ,* ed. Carl E. Braaten and Ray A. Harrisville (New York and Nashville: Abingdon, 1964), 42: "It is often said . . . that according to my interpretation of the kerygma Jesus has risen in the kerygma. I accept this proposition."

[30]Bultmann, *Theology of the New Testament,* 1:45.

[31]Günther Bornkamm, *Jesus of Nazareth* (New York and Evanston: Harper & Row, 1960), 180.

[32]Willi Marxen, *The Resurrection of Jesus of Nazareth* (Philadelphia: Fortress, 1970), 128.

[33]Paul M. van Buren, *The Secular Meaning of the Gospel* (New York: Macmillan, 1963), 128.

[34]Ibid., 132, 143.

[35]Ibid., 133.

[36]Herbert Braun, *Jesus of Nazareth: The Man and His Time* (Philadelphia: Fortress, 1979), 125.

[37]Schubert Ogden, *Christ Without Myth* (New York: Harper & Brothers, 1961), 143; cf. ibid., 136: "If the fulfillment of our lives as persons is dependent on our individual decisions concerning self-understanding, and so is something for which we ourselves are each responsible, then 'events' like Jesus' . . . physical resurrection, his bodily ascension, and his visible coming again in the clouds of heaven are of no relevance whatever to such fulfillment."

[38]Ibid., 136.

[39]Ibid., 136.

[40]Ibid., 145.

[41]Schubert M. Ogden, *The Point of Christology* (San Francisco: Harper & Row, 1982).

[42]Wolfhart Pannenberg, "Did Jesus Really Rise From the Dead?" *Dialogue* 4 (Spring 1965): 135.

[43]Jürgen Moltmann, *Theology of Hope* (London: SCM, 1967), 165.

[44]Ibid., 180; cf. ibid., 181: The resurrection "is to be called historic because, by pointing the way for future events, it *makes* history in which we can and must live."

[45]Ibid., 163.

[46]Ibid., 197.

[47]Ibid., 180.

[48]Ignatius, *To the Smyrneans,* 3; cf. ibid., 11: The resurrection "was both of the flesh and of the spirit."

[49]Ignatius, *To the Magnesians,* 11.

[50]*Epistle of Barnabas,* XV.9.

[51]Polycarp, *To the Philippians,* II.1.

[52]Justin Martyr, *On the Resurrection of the Flesh,* 9.

[53]Irenaeus, *Against Heresies,* V.31.2; cf. III.19.3; III.23.1.

[54]Tertullian, *On the Flesh of Christ,* 1.

[55]Tertullian, *On the Resurrection of the Flesh,* 2.

[56]Origen, *Dialogue With Heraclides,* 132–40.

[57]Origen, *Against Celsus,* II.62.

[58]Augustine, *City of God,* XXII.5.

[59]Augustine, *Letter 205;* cf. *City of God,* XXII.9; *Faith, Hope and Charity,* 23.

[60]Martin Luther, *LW,* 28:94; cf. ibid.: "Every Christian must believe and confess that Christ has risen from the dead."

[61]Hugh T. Kerr, ed., *A Compend of Luther's Theology* (Philadelphia: Westminster, 1966), 55; cf. Luther, *LW,* 24:346; 25:284.

[62]Luther, *LW,* 37:207; cf. ibid., 63, 69.

[63]Formula of Concord, "Epitome," Art. VIII, Affirmative 11; cf. Article VIII, Negative 11, 13.

[64]J. A. Quenstedt, *Didactico-Polemical Theology,* 2 vols. (Leipzig, 1715), 2:265; cf. *Formula of Concord,* "Epitome," Affirmative, 11: "Therefore now not only as God, but also as man, he . . . is present to all creatures." Cf. also "Epitome," Negative, 11, 13.

[65]John Calvin, *Institutes of the Christian Religion,* III.25.3.

[66]Ibid.

[67]John Calvin, "Calvin: Theological Treatises," *LCC,* 22:101; cf. ibid., 312: "Although withdrawn in respect of bodily presence, he yet fills all things by the virtue of his Spirit."

[68]Calvin, *Institutes,* II.16.15; cf. *LCC,* 22:312.

[69]George E. Ladd, *I Believe in the Resurrection of Jesus* (Grand Rapids: Eerdmans, 1975), 25.

[70]Ibid., 27.

[71]Ibid., 144.

[72]Ibid., 42.

[73]W. J. Sparrow-Simpson, *The Resurrection and the Christian Faith* (Grand Rapids: Zondervan, reprint 1968).

[74]M. C. Tenney, *The Reality of the Resurrection* (New York: Harper & Row, 1963).

[75]Daniel P. Fuller, *Easter Faith and History* (Grand Rapids: Eerdmans, 1965).

[76]Derek Kidner, *Psalms 1–72. TOTC* (London: Inter-Varsity, 1973), 20.

[77]J. Barton Payne, *The Theology of the Older Testament* (Grand Rapids: Zondervan, 1962), 253.

[78]Peter C. Craigie, *Psalms 1–50. WBC* (Waco: Word, 1983), 215.

[79]E. S. P. Heavenor, "Job," *NBCRev,* 431.

[80]Ibid., 432.

[81]J. Ridderbos, *Isaiah* (Grand Rapids: Zondervan, 1984), 484; cf. Leon Morris, *The First Epistle of Paul to the Corinthians. TNTC* (London: Tyndale, 1958), 206: "Isaiah 53:10–12 may fairly be held to prophesy Christ's resurrection."

[82]Cf. Payne, *Theology of the Older Testament,* 276.

[83]F. W. Grosheide, *The First Epistle to the Corinthians. NICNT* (Grand Rapids: Eerdmans, 1983), 350; M. C. Tenney, *The Reality of the Resurrection* (New York: Harper & Row, 1963), 44.

[84]William L. Lane, *The Gospel of Mark. NLCNT* (London: Marshall, Morgan & Scott, 1974), 527–28.

[85]J. A. T. Robinson, "Resurrection in the NT," *The Interpreter's Dictionary of the Bible,* 5 vols. (Nashville: Abingdon, 1962, 1976), 4:46.

[86]G. T. D. Angel, *"Tekmērion," NIDNTT,* 3:571.

[87]I. Howard Marshall, *The Acts of the Apostles. TNTC* (Grand Rapids: Eerdmans, 1980), 149.

[88]William Neil, *The Acts of the Apostles. NCBC* (Grand Rapids: Eerdmans, 1981), 128.

[89]Marshall, *Acts,* 76.

[90]Jerome Murphy-O'Connor, "Tradition and Redaction in 1 Cor. 15:3–7," *Catholic Biblical Quarterly* 43.4 (Oct. 1981): 582–89.

[91]Donald Guthrie, *The Pastoral Epistles. TNTC* (London: Tyndale, 1957), 143.

[92]E. Tiedtke and H. G. Link, "Empty," *NIDNTT,* 1:546.

[93]C. Leslie Mitton, *Ephesians. NCBC* (Grand Rapids: Eerdmans, 1981), 89.

[94]Ralph P. Martin, "Ephesians," *NBCRev,* 1116.

[95]C. E. B. Cranfield, "The Epistle to the Romans." *ICC,* 2 vols. (Edinburgh: T. & T. Clark, 1975–79), 1:423.

[96]Fritz Rienecker and Cleon L. Rogers, Jr., *LKGNT* (Grand Rapids: Zondervan, 1982), 689.

[97]C. Brown, "Head," *NIDNTT,* 2:162.

[98]O Hofius, "Miracle," *NIDNTT,* 2:632.

[99]S. Aalen, "Glory, Honor," *NIDNTT,* 2:48: "The glorification of Jesus is not accomplished merely by his entry into heaven; it becomes a reality by his sufferings, death, resurrection, and finally by the witness of the Spirit."

[100]Leon Morris, "1 John," *NBCRev,* 1262; cf. Rienecker and Rogers, *LKGNT,* 786.

[101]Robert H. Mounce, *A Living Hope: A Commentary on 1 and 2 Peter* (Grand Rapids: Eerdmans, 1982), 58.

[102]So Thomas Hewitt, *The Epistle to the Hebrews, TNTC* (London: Tyndale, 1960), 125: "Christ is able to save completely in time and for eternity." The RSV, Moffatt ("for all time") and NASB ("forever") prefer the temporal meaning, whereas the ASV, Berkeley ("to the uttermost"), NEB ("absolutely"), and NIV ("completely") prefer the qualitative sense.

[103] Thomas F. Torrance, *Space, Time and Resurrection* (Grand Rapids: Eerdmans, 1976), 46–47.

[104]Frederick Godet, *Commentary on Paul's First Epistle to the Corinthians* (Edinburgh: T. & T. Clark, 1893), 404.

[105]"Flesh and blood" stands for "perishable, corrupt, weak, sinful human beings." See note on 1 Corinthians 15:50 in *The NIV Study Bible* explaining "man" in Matthew 16:17.

[106]See J. A. Shep, "Resurrection of Jesus," *ZPEB,* 5:78.

[107]Bernard Ramm, *An Evangelical Christology* (Nashville: Thomas Nelson, 1985), 95.

[108]Wolfhart Pannenberg, *Jesus—God and Man* (Philadelphia: Westminster, 1968), 66.

[109]See Ladd, *I Believe in the Resurrection of Jesus,* 147–48.

[110]Walter Künneth, *The Theology of the Resurrection* (St.Louis: Concordia, 1965), 40.

[111]Wilbur M. Smith, "Heaven," *ZPEB* 3:60–61.

[112]Bruce M. Metzger, "The Meaning of Christ's Ascension" *Christianity Today* (May 27, 1966), 4.

[113]Terry L. Miethe, ed., *Did Jesus Rise from the Dead? The Resurrection Debate* (San Francisco: Harper & Row, 1987), Introduction.

[114]See Editorial, *The Christian Century* (May 24, 1967), 675.

[115]Wolfhart Pannenberg, "Response to the Debate," in *Did Jesus Rise from the Dead? ed. Miethe,* 134.

[116]For further critical discussion of myth see Künneth, *Theology of the Resurrection,* 47–62.

[117]Alan Richardson, "New Testament Theology," in *A Dictionary of Christian Theology,* ed. Alan Richardson (London: SCM, 1969), 229.

[118]Ibid.

[119]Ibid.

[120]Richardson, "Resurrection of Christ," in *Dictionary of Christian Theology,* 290.

[121]Ramm, *An Evangelical Christology,* 97.

[122]Ibid.

[123]C. S. Lewis, *Miracles* (New York: Macmillan, 1948), 114.

[124]Ibid., 180.

[125]P. Althaus, *Fact and Faith in the Kerygma Today* (Philadelphia: Muhlenberg, 1959), 69.

[126]Pannenberg, *Jesus—God and Man,* 99.

[127]John Wenham, *Easter Enigma* (Grand Rapids: Zondervan, Academie, 1984), 11.

[128]Ibid.

[129]Ibid., 123.

[130]Ibid., 124.

[131]Ibid.

[132]Murray J. Harris, *Raised Immortal* (Grand Rapids: Eerdmans, 1983), 69–71.

[133]See C. F. D. Moule, *The Phenomenon of the New Testament* (Naperville, Ill.: Allenson, 1967), 1–20.

[134]Ibid., 81.

[135]Antony Flew, "Negative Statement," in *Did Jesus Rise from the Dead?* ed. Miethe, 6.

[136]Helmut Thielicke, *The Easter Message Today* (London and New York: Thomas Nelson, 1964), 82.

[137]Moule, *Phenomenon of the New Testament,* 81.

[138]Ladd, *I Believe in the Resurrection,* 93.

[139]Ibid., 27.

[140]For a comparison of the methods of reasoning see Gordon R. Lewis, "Schaeffer's Apologetic Method," *Reflections on Francis Schaeffer* (Grand Rapids: Zondervan, 1986), 69–104; and *Testing Christianity's Truth Claims* (Chicago: Moody, 1976).

[141]Kunneth, *Theology of the Resurrection,* 253.

[142]Ibid., 253–54.

[143]John Hick, *God Has Many Names* (London: Macmillan, 1980), 1–5; and *God and the Universe of Faiths* (New York: St. Martin's, 1973).

[144]Paul F. Knitter, *No Other Name?* (Maryknoll, New York: Orbis, 1985), 199–200.

[145]Ideas adapted from Ernst Troeltsch, *The Absoluteness of Christianity and the History of Religions,* trans. David Reid (Richmond: John Knox, 1971), 89–112.

[146]D. Elton Trueblood, *The Validity of the Christian Mission* (New York: Harper & Row, 1972), 56.

[147]Stephen Neill, *The Supremacy of Jesus* (Downers Grove: InterVarsity, 1984), 51.

[148]Künneth, *Theology of the Resurrection,* 136.

[149]See Mark I. Bubeck, *Overcoming the Adversary* (Chicago: Moody, 1984), 82–91.

[150]See Leonard Hodgson, *Jesus—Word and Presence* (Philadelphia: Fortress, 1971), 267.

[151]Bubek, *Overcoming the Adversary,* 98.

GENERAL INDEX

SCRIPTURE INDEX

Genesis

Exodus

Proverbs

Ecclesiastes

Isaiah

Jeremiah

Mark

Luke

Romans

1 Corinthians

Philippians

Colossians

1 Thessalonians

2 Thessalonians

2 John

3 John

Jude

Revelation